LOVE OF WISDOM WITHDRAWN

An Introduction to Christian Philosophy

LOVE OF WISDOM

AN INTRODUCTION
TO CHRISTIAN PHILOSOPHY

by

Ronda Chervin, Ph.D.
Associate Professor of Philosophy
St. John's Seminary

and

Eugene Kevane, Ph.D.
Professor of Philosophy
and Catechetics
Notre Dame Institute

IGNATIUS PRESS   SAN FRANCISCO

Nihil Obstat: Reverend Franklyn M. McAfee
                 Censor Librorum
Imprimatur: + Most Reverend John R. Keating, J.C.D.
                 Bishop of Arlington

Cover by Roxanne Mei Lum

CONTENTS

CONTENTS

PART FOUR
The Renewal of Christian Philosophy

CONTENTS

CONTENTS

PREFACE

Love of Wisdom: An Introduction to Christian Philosophy is designed for courses of study in seminaries, universities, catechetical institutes, and adult education and also for the general reader concerned with understanding the relationship between philosophy and Christian truth.

In our present time of doctrinal confusion, every area of teaching is in need of a return to the roots of truth, consisting in the fruitful intermingling of the philosophical preambles of the Faith with sound theology, and this in the context of the pastoral mission.

In every area of Christian formation there is a need for Christian Philosophy. How can the first article of the Apostles' Creed be understood, for example, unless the faithful have a clear concept of the nature of God? The importance of sound philosophy in the teaching mission of the Church has been stressed in modern times by Pope St. Pius X in his encyclical "The Handing on of Christian Doctrine by Teaching", in the *General Catechetical Directory* (Nos. 108–15), and by Pope John Paul II in *Catechesi tradendae* (No. 71). Such statements, of course, also correspond to the foundational teaching in the area of the relationship between philosophical and theological teaching in the encyclical *Aeterni Patris* and to the teachings of Vatican II (*Optatam totius,* Nos. 14–15).

Love of Wisdom: An Introduction to Christian Philosophy has been written not only to fulfill these pontifical directives but also to overcome a certain barrier to the study of philosophy by Christians, a barrier that has sometimes stood in the way of those most in need of it. We refer to a method of teaching Christian Philosophy in which reason is so far separated from faith that it can appear to be a dry academic exercise with little relevance to the appropriation of the Faith in all its wisdom, which constitutes the primary motive for study on the part of most Christians. While it is the genius of philosophy to present clear ideas, the truth of which can be ascertained by reasoning without faith, we hope in our book to overcome any rationalistic mood by continually showing the reader how reason, faith, spirituality, and catechetical ministry can be related.

Love of Wisdom: An Introduction to Christian Philosophy can be used in a variety of situations, with differing apportioning of the chapters into time sequences ranging from semesters to study evenings according to your needs. Those who wish to teach our book in a sequence of four semesters might want to supplement the text with longer excerpts from primary sources; with a history of philosophy, such as that of Copleston; or especially with guides for the study of philosophical content done in the spirit of the renewal of Christian Philosophy, such as Jacques Maritain's *Introduction to Philosophy,* Etienne Gilson's *Elements of Christian Philosophy,* or any similar works that the teacher may prefer.

This present *Introduction to Christian Philosophy* intends to implement the call of Vatican II for "a more effective coordination of philosophy and theology so that they supplement one another in revealing . . . the mystery of Christ, which affects the whole course of human history" (*Optatam totius,* No. 14). Hence it is not exactly a history of philosophy. It is a study of the content of philosophy, but one laid out on the catechetical framework of salvation history, as St. Augustine advocates in his *First Catechetical Instruction* (3, 5), "From Genesis to the present times of the Church".

Love of Wisdom includes excerpts in a separate section at the end of the book, divided to refer to each part of the main text, to give the reader an acquaintance with some brief texts in the philosopher's own style. This is followed by questions both for greater understanding of the chapter and for drawing out the relevance of the material for spirituality and catechetics.

INTRODUCTION

A Protreptic for the Study of Christian Philosophy

Socrates and Plato frequently exhorted their young students to take up the study and the love of wisdom. Several of Plato's dialogues are models for this kind of thinking and discourse. In Appendix I you will find an excerpt from Socrates' famous defense of the philosophical quest as delivered at his trial in Athens.[1]

Aristotle, fully in the spirit of Socrates and Plato, composed a treatise known in classical times as the *Protrepticus.* Unfortunately, this exhortation to the study and love of philosophy has been lost. However, it is quoted so many times and so copiously across all the classical times that it has been substantially reconstructed in our day. "Philosophical wisdom", Aristotle writes, "is the greatest of all goods and at the same time the most useful." "Why is this?" he asks. "The philosopher, and he alone, lives with his gaze fixed on nature and reality, on the abiding truths and on the imperishable divine.... He ties his life to what is eternal and unchanging, he moors it to first principles, and thus he lives as the master of his own soul."

In explaining this position, Aristotle points out that there are two kinds of knowledge in the human mode of existing: that of the senses, and that of the intellect, with its qualitatively different rational knowledge. It is by this second kind of knowledge that "we achieve everything that is called good". "The acquisition of wisdom", Aristotle concludes in a very practical way for students, "is really much easier than the acquisition of other goods." He proceeds to explain the arguments that show convincingly that this is the truth.

In briefest summary, this is the idea of a protreptic: an exhortation to consider the reasonableness and the humanistic values contained in the study of philosophy and the love of its wisdom. Cicero wrote a dialogue, the *Hortensius,* said to be modeled on Aristotle's work. It is one of Cicero's many treatises in which he brought Greek philosophy to the schools of Rome by expressing it in his chiseled Latin. This particular dialogue also has not survived the vicissitudes of time. But in St. Augustine's time it was in current use in the programs of study.

In Augustine's *Confessions* (3, 4) he recalls his contact as a young man

---

[1] See Excerpts for Introduction, Socrates, p. 385.

nineteen years of age with this protreptic written by Cicero. "In the ordinary course of study," he writes, "I came upon Cicero's exhortation to philosophy, called *Hortensius*. This book changed my affections. It turned my prayers to you, Lord, and caused me to have different purposes and desires. All my vain hopes forthwith became worthless to me, and with incredible ardor of heart I desired undying wisdom. I began to rise up, so that I might return to you."

This episode is a landmark in the life of human culture, in the history of philosophy, and in the life of the Catholic Church, because this contact with Cicero's protreptic was the beginning of the conversion of Augustine, in his adolescent years, to a different path in life than the one on which he had been. After some years of struggle, he emerged victorious, became a Catholic layman, and then a priest, a bishop, and the greatest of the Fathers of the Church. An excerpt in Appendix I provides an indication of the fervor with which Augustine sought truth and the way reason and faith contributed to the answers he found.[2]

Augustine's experience illustrates the importance of the study of sound philosophy for young people. In fact, the *General Catechetical Directory* (no. 88) links the catechesis of adolescents with the official documents of the contemporary Catholic Church by which it has launched the renewal of Christian Philosophy in all Catholic institutions of higher education. This is perhaps the most important and effective single point of exhortation in our day for the study of Christian Philosophy.

There are, however, many other reasons that should persuade us that Christian Philosophy ought to be studied and its wisdom loved. Let us consider a few of the more important ones.

There is the question of the deposit of faith. Christians are exhorted to love and care for this deposit of faith because it is the witness to Jesus in his Lordship. Thus St. Paul exhorts his disciple Timothy to "guard the deposit!" (1 Tim 6:20). What is this deposit? It is the teaching that Jesus gave to his Apostles in his own program of teaching. This deposit is Peter's profession, explained and applied in personal hope and in personal manner of life. It witnesses to Jesus in his divinity and Lordship.

Christian Philosophy assists in guarding this deposit, and indeed in a very fundamental way that cannot be replaced by anything else. The reason for this is the fact that philosophy is the light by which human beings interpret doctrine. Philosophy is the key to hermeneutics (the science of interpretation). Thus Christian Philosophy guards the deposit by maintaining the same meaning today that it had for the Apostles. Christian Philosophy, therefore, provides the natural foundation in right reason for abiding fidelity to Jesus the Divine Teacher from his first coming in humility until his second coming in glory. As the theologians say,

[2] See Excerpts for Introduction, Augustine, pp. 386–88.

"Grace supposes nature." But "nature" is exactly what Christian Philosophy is, in the realm of doctrine.

There is a direct connection between the study of philosophy and the spiritual life. The reason for this is the dependence of the spiritual life of the soul upon the sound and true concept of God. Without this true concept of God, the First Article of the Apostles' Creed cannot be understood correctly. This removes the foundation from the interior and spiritual life. The most fundamental reason for this is the doctrine of creation, which depends on sound philosophy. It is the doctrine of creation that engenders humility of spirit and thus creates the atmosphere in which prayer can take place. A philosophy that does not see intellectually the fact and the doctrine of creation will necessarily induce some kind of schizophrenia into Catholic minds and souls. Thus there are extremely important practical benefits and advantages for each individual person that come from the study of philosophy. But for catechetical teachers it is an absolute imperative, because catechesis depends upon the explanation of the Apostles' Creed, in which the First Article occupies the position of the foundation. It can never be stressed too much that pride is essentially a failure to think correctly about God our Creator and oneself as his creature, whereas humility is seeing him correctly and then considering oneself rightly as a result.

Linked with this importance for the spiritual life is the axiom, which has become commonplace in our day, that "faith has become difficult". Perhaps this is true, perhaps not. It always has been difficult if one's attitude is not correct. In any case, the preambles of faith, such as the objectivity of moral values, the immortality of the soul, etc., have assumed a new degree of importance for each person. If they are not correctly in place, faith does indeed begin to weaken and even becomes snuffed out like a candle. Many Catholics do indeed lose their Catholic faith today because of failure to think correctly in the area of the philosophical preambles of faith. The preambles are by definition philosophical in character.

Linked again with this personal dimension of value and importance in the study of Christian Philosophy is the question of atheism in contemporary life. The rise and spread of philosophical atheism in modern culture are a fact. This fact can be understood in its roots only by philosophical study. When these roots are uncovered, Catholic Christians become able to cope with the contrary influence on religious faith that emanates throughout modern culture from this strange new fact, the presence of philosophical atheism in all aspects of contemporary life and culture.

Consider a particular point in the study of Christian Philosophy that ministers in a practical way to the training and formation of catechists. It is the ability to recognize the different kinds of philosophy. This is as important as the ability to distinguish wholesome foods from poisonous ones. In order to gain this discernment, one must study Christian Philosophy in the context of all human philosophizing, in order to see that it is qualitatively a distinct kind of philosophy in its own right. It is different in quality from other philosophies. It is not the world's philosophy at this or that historical time, however popular such a philosophy might be at its moment. Christian Philosophy is always distinctively itself, never merely relative to history and culture, and always it is the intelligible preamble for handing on the deposit of faith with the same meaning that it had when Jesus taught it to his Apostles.

In the study of philosophy, it is important to adopt the catechetical approach. Is this a new approach? It can be considered new because it is being rediscovered in our time, thanks to the Second Vatican Council. God's plan of salvation history is studied in catechetics, as St. Augustine says, from Genesis to the present times of the Church. Christian Philosophy is studied best in correlation with this plan of God, which is as extensive as human history itself. This is exactly what the Second Vatican Council urges us to do, namely, to study philosophy in correlation with revealed doctrine so that it helps all of us see the mystery of Christ more clearly (see, for example, *Optatam totius,* No. 14).

Many other points illustrating the value, and indeed the necessity, of studying Christian Philosophy could be discussed, especially in these times of doctrinal confusion. But space does not permit. Perhaps all of them can be summarized as follows. The love of wisdom, which philosophy is, in the natural order of human studies leads directly to him who is wisdom and truth incarnate. It was this that St. Justin Martyr discovered at the very beginning of the Christian era, and it is this that denotes the special quality of Christian Philosophy. The adjective "Christian", when used for this human heritage called philosophy, simply means that it is that kind of philosophy that belongs properly to Jesus himself, wisdom incarnate, the Creator of reality and the Redeemer of man. Philosophy is not less philosophy when it is Christian, but more so. This is the point that Pope Leo XIII brought to the attention of the Catholic Church in *Aeterni Patris,* his document that launched the program for the renewal of Christian Philosophy in all institutions of Catholic higher education. Christian Philosophy is philosophy at its best, developed to its fullness, and giving natural reason its most intense power of vision regarding the contours of reality as it really is.

PART ONE

CLASSICAL PHILOSOPHY AND CHRISTIAN PHILOSOPHY

I

PREHISTORIC ORIGINS OF RATIONAL THOUGHT

For centuries since Petrarch and the Renaissance, philosophy has opened its scenario with the Pre-Socratics. The scene shows Thales, Heraclitus, and the rest beginning to raise philosophical questions in those thriving and progressive Greek cities around the basin of the sail-studded blue Aegean. The Pre-Socratics have been portrayed as if they emerged full blown, suddenly and without background, giving birth to the first efforts of pure reason.

Studies made in the past few centuries, in many areas, however, have helped us to realize that the Pre-Socratics did not ask the philosophical questions in all their stark purity. They asked their particular kind of questions in a particular context and out of a particular background.

Therefore, before describing the sort of questions the Pre-Socratics asked and telling what some of their answers were, it will be well to take an excursion into the findings of those studies that have given us a new vision of the nature of mankind's exploration of ultimate questions before the time of the Greeks.

The Thought and Religion of Earliest Mankind

Our knowledge of the origins of philosophy derives from two sources. The first is the variations in thought and religion among contemporary primitives observed by the sciences of ethnology and cultural anthropology. The second is the challenging question of a scientific correlation between the absolute primitives discovered by Westerners in the outreach to mankind since Prince Henry the Navigator and the humans of the absolute beginnings of the sequence of ages in human development identified by archaeology.

To begin, then, with the contemporaries. It is a fact, not a theory, that no irreligious or atheistic tribe or people has ever been discovered in this close scrutiny by Westerners of the ways of life on this planet. Every human tribe and tongue and people and nation follow a religious way of life, with the widest variety of practices, including even human sacrifices.

The net result of the documentation by Westerners in discovering the other ways of life is the fact that the more primitive and externally impoverished the way of life, the more pure and elevated the religious dimension of that life tends to be.

The simplest tribes have *no* procedures for producing food. They live as food-gatherers. These are the absolute primitives who are still to be found living in remote regions of the globe.

Perhaps the most surprising fact about these true primitives is their religion. Under a variety of names and linguistic conventions, which vary from tribe to tribe, it is actually the same religion. Does the unity derive from a common origin? Scientists pose the question, and philosophy too wonders why. What is the hermeneutics, the interpretation of so remarkable a fact, so disconcerting to certain kinds of philosophy? In any case, the fact of this dispersed worldwide unity has been discovered, surprising as it is to the Westerners who have made the discovery.

Even more surprising is the nature of this religion of the food-gathering absolute primitives. When their religious thought and practice are studied, it comes home to Western observers that it is both qualitatively high in its tenets and remarkably interwoven with their daily life. It is indeed human, fully human, in no sense subhuman, for all their lack of economic and social development. These primitives use truly human speech, which sophisticated Westerners can learn and use with them. Grammars and vocabularies of these primitive tongues have been published in great number. Using their language they express judgments about the kinds of things and substances that they encounter and use in daily life. They teach their children which substances are harmful and to be avoided, which are beneficial, and what uses various substances have. Names are given to them all. Social communication takes place by human language. Each family is a teaching entity, handing on to the children a body of knowledge on how to make and use bone needles for weaving and sewing; how to work leather; how to prepare food, clothing, and shelter. These primitives, it must be pointed out again, are fully human. No evidence reflecting some imagined prehuman or subhuman stage has been found in this intensive scientific scrutiny of the human ways of life on earth.

These primitives do not limit their personal concern and the teaching that they hand on to their children to these practices of earthly living. They practice their remarkable religion and also hand it on formatively to their children. In fact, it is the very substance of their way of life and the vehicle of passage for their families from childhood through adolescence to adulthood.

Westerners have found these true primitives deeply religious, with no sign of divorce between their religion and their daily life. It is part of that daily life, indeed, the most important part, which gives meaning to all that they do. When the observers came close to that daily life, seeing it from the inside after gaining the primitives' confidence, they encountered this unique and surprising religion. These far-flung primitives believe in God. They practice prayer. They conceive of the Supreme Being as a Pure Spirit, not a bodily being. He knows all things. He is all-powerful; hence it makes sense to pray to him. They call him their Father. For them he is a person, a spiritual reality, not a natural force or energy in the cosmos. For them God is entirely distinct from the visible cosmos. Even more surprising, these primitives hold and profess a clear concept of creation. They teach their children as a received doctrine that God the Father made this world and is the maker of human beings as a part of the world. These primitives are deeply conscious of the dependence of all creatures upon the Creator, a dependence that characterizes the human creature in a special way.

There is a further surprising fact: the fact, everywhere identified, of the worship of God by sacrifice. Since the primitives are food-gatherers, they take what they find as something provided by their heavenly Father to sustain their lives. It is their custom, with the force of religious law, to sacrifice the first portion of what they gather daily from the bounty of nature to God, their Creator and Provider. Westerners were struck by the fact that the portion sacrificed, with appropriate ejaculatory prayer, is quite small. It dawned upon the observers from the West that this is the original sacrifice of the firstfruits, a symbolic act in the order of religious faith and prayer. It has nothing in common with religious practices found among economically more advanced groups, where food was set aside at tombs in ancestor worship. These primitives do not have such customs. Theirs is the simplest of prayerful sacrifice in recognition of grateful dependence of the human creature upon God in the order of life given and life sustained. For a human being, to live is to exist, and to exist is to live. These primitives do not have schools, even elementary ones, let alone academic higher education with a discipline called philosophy. But they do have a wisdom, and they love it as the very stuff of their way of life. They are not living by animal instinct but in a fully human way, making use of reason both in the practical arts and in thought about the meaning, the purpose, and the guidelines of human living.

The discovery of this religion among the contemporary primitives is a fact of the first order for philosophical inquiry. Hence it may be of interest to cite from the voluminous documentation the work of a pioneer in the discovery of this religion of primitive monotheism. He is Edward Horace Man, a well-educated English civil servant, who in 1858 was appointed colonial administrator of the Andaman Islands. He mastered the native tongue of the aboriginal tribes, publishing an important grammar and vocabulary of the language, and made it his business to understand the native way of thought and life. As a result he was elected to membership in several scientific bodies. His distinguished career culminated with the publication of an early classic in Western man's outreach to the contemporary primitives, *The Aboriginal Inhabitants of the Andaman Islands* (London: The Royal Anthropological Institute, 1885; reprinted 1932). It was received by his peers as "a remarkable work of anthropological research . . . , an exhaustive study conducted with scientific accuracy and systematic care". E. H. Man was one of the pioneers in the discovery by Westerners of the primitive "high gods", identifying among the Andamanese Islanders "a knowledge of, or belief in, a Supreme Being, whom they call *Puluga*. "Of him, they say that he is invisible, was never born and is immortal, and that by him the world and all objects, animate and inanimate, were created, excepting only the powers of evil. He is regarded as omniscient . . . , and is angered by the commission of certain sins" (p. 89).

These aboriginals, furthermore, were discovered by E. H. Man to have had more than merely vague intimations of immortality. They believed that this Supreme Being "is the Judge from whom each soul receives its sentence after death" (p. 90).

> At the resurrection they will be reunited and live permanently on the new earth. . . . All will then remain in the prime of life, sickness and death will be unknown, and there will be no more marrying or giving in marriage. The animals, birds, and fish will also reappear in the new world in their present form. This blissful state will be inaugurated by a great earthquake, occurring by *Puluga's* command. . . . There is no trace to be found of the worship of trees, stones, or other objects, and it is a mistake to suppose that they adore or invoke celestial bodies. . . . No reason is given for the formation of the earth's surface, except that it was according to the will . . . of *Puluga,* the Creator of all (pp. 94–95).

From his knowledge of their resistance to foreigners and of their local history, E. H. Man observes rather drily, "It is extremely improbable that their legends were the result of the teaching of missionaries or others who might be supposed to have landed on their shores in by-gone years" (p. 88).

Religious missionaries form a quite different category of Westerners reaching out to the rest of mankind, the ones symbolized by St. Francis Xavier. Again the documentation is immense. It goes back to the very beginning of modern times. Frequently the missionaries received training in ethnological and anthropological science as a part of their preparation for their challenging call. Here a recent report may stand for this segment of the documentation.

Father E. de Viron spent fifteen years as the missionary parish priest at Ngoma, a village of the Rwanda Republic, a small state carved from what was once the Congo. Rwanda embraces three races, one of which is pygmy, with a total population of three and a half million. At the end of his ministry, this priest drew up a report, which was published in Rome in 1971.

"Among this people", he writes,

> has been handed down from remote times the idea of One Transcendent God. This idea is found also among other African peoples and it places them far above other peoples, even among the great ancient civilizations. . . . This God is called *Immana.* Everything concerning him is found in the traditions, crystalized in the "documents" kept intact in the archives of the memories of generations and generations. This is proved by the names of persons, by the forms of cur-

rent language, and by proverbs and exclamations. . . . Of course faith in God cannot but be accompanied in Rwandese paganism by a whole host of base superstitions.

This missionary priest points out that superficial observers, visitors on safaris, and graduate students on brief field trips see only "the cult of the dead" and "mystical relations with spirits". His long stay, close contact, and especially his familiarity with the indigenous language enabled him to penetrate more deeply and to discern an important empirical fact. "A careful study, and above all personal contact with the witch doctors and their followers, show that the various practices do not wipe out faith and worship of *Immana*. It is seen at once that his name and presence always appear in all the various ceremonies and rites and cast a ray of spirituality over them."

This is simply one short sample chosen at random from a copious supply of similar reports made and published by missionaries. Included in any listing of well-known names representing trained scientists among the missionaries are M. Gusinde, V. Lebzelter, P. Schebesta, and W. Koppers. Such studies culminate in the twelve-volume analytic and synthetic work of Wilhelm Schmidt, *Der Ursprung der Gottesidee* (Münster: 1912–55), on the origin of the idea of God.

As an example of yet another kind of observer, the university professor with his scientific principles, procedures, and studies in the field, one can turn to the published research of the professors A. L. Kroeber, R. B. Dixon, J. H. Leuba, and others in the United States. In particular, they document the discovery of the same Supreme Being worshipped among contemporary primitives isolated in remote areas of California. The classic work of Professor Andrew Lang in Scotland, *The Making of Religion* (1900), should not go unmentioned, for it is a pioneering synthesis of these facts about mankind that Western outreach has gathered. Lang's work represents an early insight into the vast differences in religion among the so-called barbarians. Contemporary primitives possess this monotheistic religion in a state that is more pure and elevated—less mixed with the later rank growth of idolatry, polytheism, magic, and superstition—the more primitive is their way of life. It characterizes the food-gatherers, whereas deviant and degrading practices are observed to set in among the food-producers.

An impressive fact, then, emerges from the observation and research that are part of the Copernican revolution among modern Westerners, that phase of it in which Western man discovers the planet earth comprehensively and goes forth to study the ways of thought and life among the other tribes, tongues, peoples, and cultures. The fact is clear: the more primitive the tribes, the more their religion exhibits a faith in one God, the Father Almighty, Creator of heaven and earth, to whom his human creatures owe worship by prayer and sacrifice in order to express and sustain the moral way of life.

Embedded in the evidence are thought-provoking indicators, certain pointer facts, so to speak, which raise the question of a correlation between the developmental stages of contemporary primitives, as studied by the new post-Copernican science of ethnology, and the developmental stages of mankind in prehistoric time, as studied by the equally post-Copernican sciences of geology and archaeology. For example, the tribes with this religion are located worldwide in remote places of the planet. What is the sufficient reason for such a fact? Are the contemporary primitives, the impoverished food-gatherers of lowest economic development but of highest and purest monotheism, witnesses to the religion of earliest mankind? Do they bear some kind of ethnologically fossilized witness, so to speak, to the original spiritual condition and religious faith of mankind? The question abides. It is one of the supreme hermeneutical challenges of the late twentieth century, and it will call for further consideration.

Human Rationality and the Beginning of Human Thought

The science of archaeology has uncovered both worship by sacrifice and the use of tools at the earliest levels of human remains. This is already a sign of philosophy in action, one may say, for the two fundamentals of philosophy are already present: causal thinking and the concept of creation. Sacrifice is a worldwide and age-old aspect of the phenomenon of man. Sacrifice involves a pattern of thinking that recognizes the dependence of human beings, human existence, upon the Lord and Giver of existence. Human thinking about existence and the offering of sacrifice are closely connected, indeed interwoven. Religion is a practical matter of recognizing the Creator. It is sustained by a particular kind of thinking about existence. Philosophy is involved.

Contemporary primitives practice a variety of sacrifices, all of them social in nature and expressing the corporate life of the tribe or people. Sin offerings have been observed among all such peoples, for they look upon their Supreme Being as prescribing their way of life. The moral law is the law of the heavenly Father. He will judge. He will reward. He will punish. He has his all-seeing eye upon each human being. But, so the primitives profess, this is an optimistic fact, for the heavenly Father intends his human creatures to live forever, indeed in resurrected bodies, as among the Andaman Islanders noted above. This kind of religion is identifiable only in the most primitive ways of life prior to Stone Age patterns. Again, this is scientific indication that it correlates with the archaeologically earliest times of mankind. In any case, contemporary primitives are discovered to have this kind of religious thinking and practice. And they hand it on to their young people in a definite pattern and ritual of tribal teaching. They give their young a full human and moral approach to life as a way prescribed by the heavenly Father.

But it is time to return to archaeology, with its observation that earliest men made and used tools. Human rationality is concretely visible in this set of facts, in a manner quite independent of the question of the earliest religion. To make a tool, one must judge the substance, understanding and naming the kind of thing it is. Causal thinking proceeds. What is it good for? How can I use it to solve this problem? Is there a substance that works better? Human rationality coordinates substances with purposes, and it does so by exercising the power of judgment. This is quite different from the powers of sensory perception, and it draws the line of a specific difference between humans and the lower animals. All the practical crafts, all the empirical sciences and philosophy itself have come forth historically from this exercise of natural reason. From the viewpoint of its focus on the existence of things and its recognition of the source of that existence, furthermore, it is actually more "philosophical" than the highly limited speculation of the Pre-Socratics.

These facts and the direction in which they point have come under heavy fire from an atheistic philosophical hermeneutics as the twentieth century has proceeded. Philosophical atheism has striven mightily to interpret the Copernican revolution in the empirical sciences in favor of a so-called scientific atheism, as if defending as a thesis the idea that the meaning of science is atheism. This philosophical atheism feels a compulsion to sustain as a dogma the idea of a primitive stage of mankind completely devoid of religion. Religion, with its projection of "supernatural beings", could arise only later, after an "evolution", after social classes had arisen, so that it could spin off from their conflicts as an epiphenomenon. An allied philosophical drive has sought to find a prelogical, prerational subhuman stage at the beginning of mankind. Here again the evidence from the contemporary primitives does not fit this particular philosophical desire. They are observed to be fully human in their early type of economic and social development, with no sign of subhumanity. Archaeology supports the same view of earliest mankind. Man appears as a fully rational being from the first identification of him that scientists can make. He uses the first principles of natural reason, without of course reflecting upon them in the way academicians will do much later in human history. He uses a mode of communication, furthermore, that expresses this same rationality in its structure. Thus he is able to pass on to the coming generation what he discovers about the nature, purpose, and practical use of substances so that a social heritage begins to accumulate. The human form of life, while participating in animality, is always a rational form that lives by thinking and teaching rather than by instinct.

The religious thought and practice of the contemporary primitives, this surprising discovery of recent Westerners, is a problem for contemporary atheists. The facts that have been gathered ought not to exist, for they do not fit into the mental categories of the atheistic mind. Sacrifice, for example, is a worldwide phenomenon among the absolute primitives. One tries to explain it as a derivative of magical practices. But magical practices seem to attach to tribes and peoples who are economically more developed, but who somehow do not have the primitive religion. Sacrifice is a puzzle for the atheist, for he does not recognize the doctrine of creation: he simply assumes the existence of things as needing no explanation, much less a recognition of the personal Giver of existence. Then there is the further puzzle of the presence of the doctrine of creation itself among the absolute primitives. How did they arrive at such a concept, which not even Plato and Aristotle could achieve?

Thus the hermeneutical conflict of the twentieth century is born. Pressure mounts upon the atheistic mentality. All such facts must either be explained away or dated at a later time. The atheists have assumed since the beginning of the Copernican revolution that every advance in the empirical sciences bolsters the cause of philosophical atheism. One may say that the rise and spread of atheistic philosophy in the West, in the First World, as men have come to term it, are a function of this hermeneutics of scientific progress. The fact is, however, that philosophy in itself and in all its kinds is something distinct from empirical science in all its branches. In some way that will have to be analyzed later, the atheistic philosophy has been a concomitant of the Copernican revolution in the empirical sciences but not a necessary component of it. For it is not itself an empirical finding. The atheistic movement of modern centuries is a willful hermeneutics or interpretation of the sciences. In the earlier times of the Copernican revolution, the interpretation was convincing to many minds. But this atheistic plausibility was only a temporary illusion. As the progress of the sciences continued and deepened, as its instruments for enhanced observation of the visible cosmos were more and more perfected, the atheistic hermeneutics became more and more untenable.

The natural sciences are gathering facts that point toward a quite different philosophical hermeneutics. They point. They suggest. They raise new questions. They do not philosophize or provide philosophical demonstrations. They are empirical sciences, not philosophy. But their challenge to philosophy is unmistakable. Younger scholars of all three worlds, First, Second, and Third, are increasingly unwilling simply to accept the atheistic hermeneutics and its tendency to impose its interpretation upon the facts of the sciences. Nowhere is this reopening of the dossier and reviewing of the evidence more in order than in the case of the contemporary primitives and the humanity, rationality, and religion of earliest mankind. There is a need, indeed a scientific one, to expose as unscientific every effort to deviate from and distort the evidence by philosophical misinterpretation. This is doubly true, as younger scholars are recognizing, of every effort, born of a strange philosophical will, to suppress the evidence. In 1952, Wilhelm Koppers, professor of ethnology at the University of Vienna, put the philosophical issue graphically in an insight that we shall bear in mind as the present study proceeds, in order to return to the issue after the roots of contemporary atheism have been analyzed. "Twenty years ago", he writes,

it was still possible to publish a pamphlet with the title "How God Was Created"
—by man, it goes without saying. Today, however, the most primitive races
of the earth raise up their voices, as it were, crying in unanimous protest: you are
on a wrong track. . . . The belief in a Father God, handed down by our forebears
from time immemorial, cannot possibly be regarded as a final stage in human
development. He must rather be the starting point, as is shown in our creation
myths: in the beginning there was God the Creator. Is this not also the teaching of
your Bible?

Pantheism: The Ancient and Inveterate Error of Mankind

Whatever the case regarding the religion of earliest mankind, there is no question
that by 4000 B.C., at the dawn of history, mankind as a whole was no longer
practicing that pure and elevated religion to which the contemporary primitives,
as a matter of scientific fact, bear witness. Something appears to have happened
during the long ages of prehistory, something directly significant for philosophy.
Taking a position at about 4000 B.C., one can see a further fact that is a commonplace studied by the science of comparative religion, itself a specialization in
anthropology and ethnology.

This position at 4000 B.C., the time when writing was invented, is the
dividing line between the surprisingly long millennia of prehistory and the
relatively short six thousand years of recorded history.

How long was prehistory? Fifty thousand years? Five hundred thousand?
The length of this time is a hermeneutical battleground. But what difference does
the actual figure make? Some philosophical interpretations desire to extend the
period immensely, into millions of years, for this would seem to minister to the
small changes over long epochs needed by evolutionary philosophy. On the other
hand, some religious interpretations, when motivated by the human glosses of a
biblical chronology, have sought to curtail the length of prehistory. In any case,
the sciences continue refining their methodology with techniques such as radiocar-
bon dating. It has become clear that mankind begins sparsely in the ice ages of the
Quaternary period. It was a long time ago by the mental patterns that prevailed
before the Copernican revolution, yet not one that is indefinitely long, or beyond
human, and fairly accurate, calculation.

Can the very length of prehistory minister to philosophical reflection? It can,
indeed. One must ponder the panorama of mankind at that now relatively recent
date of 4000 B.C.

Human beings, from a sparse scattering, have become numerous. They are
gathered into great pools, so to speak, where favorable conditions have allowed
them to increase and multiply prodigiously. In 4000 B.C. civilizations with cities
and the accompanying literary culture, formalized education, schools, and trade

commerce are flourishing in the great historic centers of China, India, Babylonia, and Egypt. Food production is taken for granted, and mankind has learned how to store and trade the surplus. Nonagricultural ways of life, trades and services of various kinds, can be sustained in the cities.

There is still no sign of an irreligious way of life. Every city centers around its religion, even literally, as the temple towers of the Middle East, for example, the excavated Ziggurat at Ur of the Chaldees, bear witness. But it is a far different religion than the monotheism of the absolute primitives. This is the great fact of facts about mankind. There has been some kind of apostasy, or falling away, from the transcendent Pure Spirit, the heavenly Father, Creator, Sustainer, and moral Judge of mankind. This human condition and situation must be given summary consideration, for it bears upon philosophical anthropology in general and upon the beginning of Greek philosophy among the Pre-Socratics in particular.

The first aspect of the fact is the remarkable sameness of the human condition in 4000 B.C., in each of the four centers of the higher culture, in all the agricultural villages from China to Western Europe, among all the hunting tribes and all the nomadic herdsmen. Everywhere man is religious, indeed, but the object of his worship has changed. For the transcendent Pure Spirit mankind has substituted idols of various kinds, usually related to magical practices connected with successful outcomes in the projects and practices of his earthly life. These idols relate to a pantheistic view of the cosmos. The transcendent Pure Spirit has been reduced to the status of a World Soul. Spirits are thought to inhabit things of the cosmos: totems, sacred groves, amulets, manmade carvings that project and incorporate merely human imagination about spirits and gods. Images reign supreme as objects of worship in this idolatry.

At the invention of writing, leading to the rise of culture and the dawn of recorded history, idolatry prevails everywhere in the areas of civilization. Worship by sacrifice continues universally, but it has been reduced to the appeasement of these manmade gods and cosmic spirits. In fact, it has become a largely perfunctory civic function in the calendar of feast days that mark the life of the ancient city-states.

The long times of prehistory have somehow ministered to this universal outcome of pantheism and idolatry. There is one thing the science of comparative religion clearly demonstrates from the facts it gathers. As the times of mankind proceed across prehistory toward recorded history, this fall into a spiritual darkness becomes ever deeper. Man progresses in economic development and social organization, but his human condition only worsens. He has lost his spirit of prayer to the heavenly Father. The idea of creation is nowhere to be found. And the sense of moral responsibility to the Supreme Being in each human act has dissipated. Pantheism and the idolatrous religiosity that expresses it minister to human willfulness and desires. The falling away from the transcendent Supreme

Being is simultaneously a descent into degrading practices of every imaginable sort. Sex runs riot. One need only study the excavations at Herculaneum, where the vices of ancient Rome have been bared to the modern gaze. Pantheism, the doctrine that God is everything and that everything in the visible cosmos is God, results in the liberation of each self to be his own god. The cultures of antiquity exhibit the documentation in their furnaces of Moloch and their systems of temple prostitution.

Again, one must stress the remarkable unity of this demoralized spiritual condition at the dawn of recorded history. It is a unity at the opposite end of the spectrum from that other unity to which the facts point, the remarkable similarity of monotheistic religion among the absolute primitives, now in 4000 B.C. scattered in remote marginal places of the entire globe and indicated as possible remnants of a once-prevailing and unified original condition of mankind.

Philosophical reflection can only ponder whether this universal condition of apostasy from the transcendent Supreme Being, this universal fall into pantheism and idolatry, reflects some flaw in human nature. Did it take the millennia of prehistory to bring the human condition into a generalized social situation when mankind reaches the time of his great historic cultures? Could this be the reason in the mind of One for whom a thousand years are as one day? A design to allow something about human nature to become socially visible for all men everywhere to recognize? Might it minister to humility of spirit and an openness to redemption from what had become indeed the ancient and inveterate error of mankind?

This is the error of pantheism, with all its attendant religious phenomena. It is an apostasy, a fall from the transcendent Supreme Being and from life in his presence, the life of prayer, recognized dependence, moral fidelity, sorrow for sin, purposes of amendment, gratitude for benefits received, for existence itself, and all such aspects of theistic living. The ancient error of mankind, now inveterate and deeply ingrained everywhere, is a proneness to prefer this world and the things it offers to fidelity to a supreme moral Judge. The apostasy results from a tendency within man somehow not to want that transcendent Supreme Being. There is a wish to avoid his all-seeing eye. Intimately linked with this psychology is the will to take existence for granted, as if it were simply there as a fruit to be plucked, as if it is an eternally given, and given to me as its proprietor. Does this involve philosophy? Whenever existence comes up for consideration, philosophy is involved. The loss of the concept of creation is the opposite side of a coin, the desire to be independent of the Supreme Being and the demands of his moral law.

In any case, it appears that there has been a long decline of mankind into a night of idolatry, a decline that set in early in prehistory and then ripened simultaneously in all the economic and social developments that gradually led to the historic cultures of China, India, Babylon, and Egypt.

Man began his journey at the beginning of human prehistory as a scattering of families. Only a few: archaeology has demonstrated this. The indications are that mankind is a unity because of origin in one human pair. The pointer facts indicate that there was a definite religion, high in thinking and directly related to moral living, that was handed on by a teaching given in those first families. As the times of prehistory proceeded, especially as economic and social development took place, within the families children apparently were not always raised up carefully in the received religion. Merely human thinking, all-too-human thinking, was allowed to intermingle. Thus tribes and peoples could appear with adulterated thinking about God, quite unlike the concept of God found among the authentic and absolute primitives. Mankind continued to be deeply religious, indeed, but believed in the gods rather than in God Almighty, the Creator of heaven and earth. Men across the long ages of prehistory have come to have a rather willful religiosity rather than the definite religion of the primitives, with its prayer, its personalized rites of sacrifice, and its morality linked with the Supreme Being, his judgment, and the afterlife. Religion had fallen to an excessive and even magical concern with control over successful outcomes in this life. Thus the transcendent God has been replaced by pantheism, the idea that the Divine inhabits the natural cosmos, animates its energies, and dwells in manmade representations of gods and demons.

The human condition, then, is universal idolatry at the dawn of history, civilization, and literary culture. The very length of prehistoric time renders this condition intelligible, for time was needed to make the pantheistic error, the darkening of the transcendence of God, both inveterate and universal—universal, that is, apart from the worldwide marginalized remnants of mankind, unified in so puzzling a way by a different kind of religious thought and practice.

Seen in the light of philosophical analysis, this fall from transcendence, this reduction of God to this kind of immanentism within the visible cosmos, has an important consequence for personal living. It represents an evasion of personal guilt, because in pantheism there is no teaching of a set of moral principles or guidelines coming from a personal Being beyond the cosmos. There is no doctrine in pantheism that specifies how men should conduct themselves in each human act in view of the all-seeing eye of the personal transcendent Creator and Judge. This responsibility to God in each human act is evaded in pantheism, which becomes from this point of view a philosophical rationalization of the evasion. Thus the fall from the Supreme Being is in a true and real sense a conversion to the self, which becomes the actual object of the worship. Each person is now free, in one particular way of defining freedom, in the sense of being free to do what he pleases.

The human condition at the end of the prehistoric ages seems therefore to indicate a proneness in human nature to want this kind of liberation. The very universality of the idolatry, the substitution of the self under the myriad masks and guises of the pantheistic religiosity, seems to point to a condition of human nature.

It is clear that if families begin to think this way, the pattern will transfer readily to the children. Thus the error in concept of God will grow in the tribes and villages of prehistory and come to characterize the great historic cultures as indeed an ancient and inveterate error. The cultures will be built upon religiosity, to be sure, but will be quite devoid of the religion that knows the God of the primitives and worships him in prayer and sacrifice. Even the institution of sacrifice itself will suffer from the spiritual decline: it will be interwoven with magical practices and be directed to the numberless gods of polytheism.

The concept of God is the central challenge of human thought and hence of philosophy. Everything in religion depends on the concept of God, and everything in personal and social living depends on religion. All thinking about God turns about the idea of transcendence and the idea of immanence. In the common philosophical heritage, transcendence refers to the way the personal Supreme Being exists as an intelligent reality distinct from the cosmos, above and beyond this visible world. The primitives designate this by their various names for him who is a Pure Spirit, unlike the cosmos, for he transcends the entire order of the senses and nature. Paired with transcendence in thought about God is the concept of immanence. It is difficult for the human mind to achieve this concept accurately in a way compatible with divine transcendence. Thus the human condition promoted that prehistoric fall to a meaning of immanence that denotes the identification of the Divine with the cosmos. This is the ancient error of pantheism.

The challenge of philosophy from the Pre-Socratics across the historic times of the literary cultures will be this matter of rising to a concept of God that denotes the separate Supreme Being, existing above pantheism in all its forms and applications. Philosophy will be the effort of the human mind to understand both transcendence and immanence correctly, as simultaneously valid for God when his mode of existence is rightly understood. What will the Pre-Socratics say? What will Plato and Aristotle say? Plotinus? The Stoics? What they say will be far more intelligible when the long ages of prehistory are pondered and their universal result, that ancient and inveterate error, is considered.

What will Augustine, the founder of Christian Philosophy, say? It is anticipating, of course, but perhaps one may glance ahead to note that he says the transcendent God is closer to each of us than we are to ourselves. Is that a philosophical insight? Indeed it is. But it is thinking that has the support of a daily pattern of personal spiritual life, without which a person proves unable to maintain the realization with any continuity. The mode of God's existence is challenging indeed, so that even the brightest intelligence is reduced to exclaiming "Who is like God?" that rhetorical question that expects the answer "No one is like God!" in the sense that the divine mode of existing is unique.

In summary, then, the ancient error of mankind is pantheism, and it is inveterate because of the very length of prehistory as discovered in the recent Copernican revolution. It has resulted universally because men everywhere take to heart this fallen and unworthy concept of God, this reduction of him to identity with the material cosmos, always with the secret motivation of evading personal guilt. The historic cultures are impregnated with this pantheistic concept of God. With the cultures philosophy comes into view at last, for it will be a product of the complex pattern of literary education that has been developed as the very dynamism of the historic cultures. The Pre-Socratics are now at hand. But they and their doctrines are far different from what they appeared to be in view of the Renaissance five centuries ago, before the Copernican revolution revealed a larger perspective of the past of mankind.

II

THE GREEKS:
PHILOSOPHY AS THE SEVENTH LIBERAL ART

Philosophy originates in the context of the educational systems that sustained the historic cultures of China, India, Egypt, and Babylon. Cultures are complex bodies of social heritage, largely embodied now in written works and into which the oncoming generation is enculturated by formal study in the new social institution of schooling.

The Copernican revolution has affected the science of history in a way no less significant than the way it has revealed the contours of prehistory. Archaeology again was a major factor. For the earliest cities of man, Memphis, Babylon, Ur of the Chaldees, and many others, all contemporaneous with the invention of writing, were found to contain organized libraries with extensive holdings of written records on baked clay tablets. Early in the nineteenth century, because of the deciphering of the Rosetta stone, historians were enabled to read these writings. Entire literatures opened to view. Above all, the historical chronicles kept by the temple priests of each city enabled historians to achieve a new and systematized knowledge of those archaic civilizations, which preceded the Greeks in the first half of the six thousand years of historic time.

These cultures were not philosophical, however, but religious. They were religious in the pattern of the universal pantheistic religiosity and polytheistic idolatry that has been noted. For philosophy, as the term is understood in Western heritage to the present day, one must wait for the arrival of the Greeks upon the stage of universal history in the first millennium before Christ.

Thanks to the flood of new light on the archaic cultures, it is now clear that the Greeks did not spring forth full blown. They had their own cultural heritage, beginning with Homer, and a marked consciousness as a special people because of the richness and practical value of their heritage. But their education and culture had their roots in older civilizations. The Greeks learned from Egypt and Babylon.

The Seven Liberal Arts

Fundamental to the Greek people was its system of education, which they called their *Paideia,* from the root *paid,* meaning "child". It was their systematic process for helping a Greek child become a fully enculturated Greek adult. Westerners have known and admired this process across the centuries as Greek humanism. *Paideia* is an extraordinarily rich word denoting simultaneously "education" and "culture": the process and its outcome both in individual persons and in society as the distinguishing heritage handed on from one generation to the next. Thus the *Paideia* was the very life of the Greek people. Were it deviated from or interrupted, the future of the Greek people would be at stake.

Obviously, therefore, the teachers who sustained this process were fundamentally important professional persons in the Greek way of life. They were called the Sophists, namely, the persons of education, learning, and wisdom. Sophism at that time denoted the cultivation of wisdom, quite the opposite from the meaning of false and deceptive argumentation that it has come to have today.

Were the Sophists teachers of religion? Yes and no. In a perfunctory sense they did indeed enculturate the young into the calendar of religious festivals and the offering of official sacrifices to the various gods in their temples, which constituted the civic life of the Greek city-states. But it was the religion of religiosity, that of the ancient and now doubly inveterate error in its final development as full-fledged secularism. Every vestige of transcendence had disappeared. The Sophists represented an approach in education that confined it to the preparation of youth for success in the political and economic life of the Greek city-states. The Sophists are the classic example of the practical outcome of pantheistic idolatry.

The famed seven liberal arts constitute the lasting achievement of the Sophists. This program of comprehensive literary education, based patriotically on Homer, Pindar, and the other classics of Greek history and literature, was designed to produce the competent and patriotic Greek adult whose mastery of the word of human discourse culminated in the power of political oratory. These tools for enculturating the young have become a part of the central intellectual tradition of the Western world. The question was, and still is, whether these seven arts should culminate in the skills that promise success in the practical affairs of earthly life. Is the nature of wisdom expressed by an educational process that aims simply at practical values? Among the Greeks practical life meant ability to achieve success by means of the spoken word. It meant ability to sway the multitudes in the democracy of the Greek cities, expertise in using rhetorical oratory, in knowing how to win a political following, how to be successful in government, law, medicine, and commercial life. The art of oratory was the key to social and political success. The Sophists organized the Greek liberal arts, therefore, with rhetoric, the science of cultivated human discourse, as the seventh of the seven arts.

The Pre-Socratic Philosophers

The Pre-Socratics, Thales, Empedocles, Heraclitus, and others of the sixth century B.C. whom histories of philosophy list, are credited with launching philosophy on its course. They wondered about the underlying stuff, or elements, of the cosmos. Thinking in incipiently philosophical fashion about the nature of things in the visible cosmos, they accepted the reports of the senses as given. Reality simply and "really" is as humans see it. The reports of the senses are accepted simply as facts. The cosmos is there. It is: it exists in itself the way humans naturally perceive it to be.

The Pre-Socratic philosophers philosophized or wondered about the underlying reality of the cosmos they saw, within the framework of a world picture common to all mankind until the Copernican revolution. They were not alone in accepting this picture of the world. It is common to all the cultures and literatures before the Greeks and Romans, from Egypt, Babylon, and Persia to India and China. The Hebrews were no different, as one can see readily in their literature, which the Western heritage knows as the Bible. The prophet Malachi, for example, sees a future sacrifice that will be offered in every place, from the rising of the sun, as he says, to its setting.

What is this world picture common to all mankind? It has five chief components.

First, the cosmos is geocentric: it centers upon this fixed and stationary earth. The heavens turn about it. Humans do not agonize about their insignificance.

Second, earth is to all appearances flat. Men think the universe has three stories, so to speak: this flat earth is the second story. Below is the netherworld. Above it is that wondrous canopy, the arching and orderly heavens with the moon, the sun, and the display of the stars.

Third, this form of the universe has always been and will always be, even when people believe the myth of the great cycle. People did not dream that the cosmos ever had a different form, or that it might change again. There was no inkling of long eras and epochs of past development. People were not geologically minded.

Fourth, people were not historically minded. History, the corporate memory that makes use of written records, extended back to only about 4000 B.C., when writing was invented, and the clay tablets were inscribed and baked to form the libraries of Babylon. Educated Greeks knew of those older cultures. But hardly any memory existed of times prior to that great invention; there was only the vaguest kind of oral tradition coalescing into some notion of earlier times. No one thought that those times could have been particularly lengthy.

Fifth, from the view of philosophy, there was an absolutely basic characteristic of this world picture. It is the eternity of matter. The material cosmos is simply there, without beginning or end. In other words, existence, that central concern of all philosophizing, is not a question. Matter exists eternally. Obviously this eliminates any thought of a transcendent Divine Creator, any process of creation to analyze and explain, and any reflection on what it might mean to be a creature.

What then of religion? Were the Pre-Socratics irreligious? Definitely not, for they looked upon this visible cosmos as besouled, either animated by a World Spirit or at least by many indwelling spirits. Expressed in different ways and with a variety of emphases, the Pre-Socratics saw the cosmos as something itself divine, the very *locus* of what pantheists call the Divine.

It is clear that the Pre-Socratics philosophize in a particular context. They naively assume all these points, especially the eternity of matter and the divinity of the visible cosmos. They ask only what element matter is made of, whether water or air or fire or perhaps irreducible "atoms", the Greek word for "indivisible particles of matter". They sought the *physis,* or nature, of the visible cosmos. It is true that the Pre-Socratics bequeathed a "physics", a philosophy of science based on the empirical world view of the unaided senses, rather than a philosophy as such. Philosophy is primarily concerned with existence, something quite distinct from the stuff from which bodily things are made.

The question of wisdom, the kind of wisdom young persons should be taught to love, was not raised by the Pre-Socratics. They were teachers fully in the tradition of the Sophists. But they did not question the central drift and tendency of the secularized rhetorical education that was the established system of Greek culture.

Socrates

For this questioning one must turn to Socrates. With him philosophy is actually born. With him educators must decide which art is rightly the seventh, the one in which the educational process culminates, the one that defines the purpose, outcome, and goal of education. Should this seventh art be rhetoric? Or is wisdom something else? What is true wisdom? If it can be defined and it is found to be different from the rhetorical education offered by the Sophists, should the oncoming generation not be taught to love it? Should the *Paideia* not be reformed in terms of love for this true wisdom? Are the values of the Greek heritage sustained adequately by a merely rhetorical education designed to implement secular success and nothing more? Is this all there is to man?

It is clear that such questions, and they are Socrates' questions, challenge the established system of education and culture. It can be dangerous to challenge establishments. That mysterious death sentence, which was imposed upon Socrates as a corrupter of the youth of Athens, thus becomes comprehensible.

The birth of philosophy is indeed dramatic. It deserves a pause to look more closely at the conflict between Socrates and the Sophists, a conflict that has endured not only throughout antiquity but even across the Christian era, and especially in the modern period since the Renaissance to the present day.

Implicit in the approach of the Sophists to education and culture was a concept of man and knowledge together with their own idea of truth. At the heart of their *Paideia* was the cultivation of a person so polished and powerful with the spoken word that he could persuade and convince an audience on any political proposal or question or its contradiction. Both became equally true. Truth becomes what is advantageous. Thus the seven arts, culminating in the science of rhetoric, which gives this power of persuasion, open the way to leadership and success in all walks of civic life. All this is taught in the context of the traditional virtues of the Greeks, with their paradigms in the heroes of earlier times, centering upon the Homeric literature. This is secularism, the reduction of the human mode of being to the affairs of earthly life, assuming that that is all there is to man. It implies something like the pragmatism of William James in early twentieth-century America. James taught that the truth of an idea is its cash value in practical affairs. For the Sophists man has only one kind of knowledge, the perceptions of his senses. Education is the development of cleverness for life in the world of the senses. Their view of human nature was not unlike the idea that man is nothing but a more evolved animal, who therefore exhibits a more advanced cleverness. In philosophical terms, the approach of the Sophists implies materialism and skepticism and assumes that there is no difference from the lower animals in the human mode of being and activity, no difference in kind.

Socrates rose up against this kind of thinking in the established teaching profession. A teacher himself, he became known as the gadfly of Athens, taking advantage of every conversation on the streets and every opportunity for discourse and discussion in the marketplace. Socrates became famous for his method of analytical dialogue. He pursued the Sophists relentlessly, exposing the weaknesses of their thinking before the court of sound reasoning and from the viewpoint of the *Paideia*. His arguments centered upon the failure of the Sophist approach to sustain the true values of Greek humanism. The heritage that Greeks love and that gives them their distinctive character as a people will decline and fall for lack of a solid rational foundation. The Sophists, professional representatives of wisdom, as their name indicates, do not profess true wisdom. True wisdom, Socrates taught, comes from the knowledge of abiding truth, truth that is true throughout every vicissitude of practical affairs, one and the same, and always quite other than its opposite, which can only be falsehood.

Many young people listened willingly to Socrates.

Rhetoric, Socrates taught them, has its place in human affairs and on the program of the seven arts. But it is not the culminating art, as if mere power with the spoken word were the purpose of human culture and the end of man. Education should culminate in the ability to see and judge the truth of the inner word of human thought. This inner word conceives abiding truth about the human values, values such as the nature of justice in itself, of peace in itself, of goodness in itself, of truth in itself, and all similar imponderables that are nevertheless realities. The external word of human discourse, with all the power of rhetorical cultivation, will have as its true object the persuasive expression of the truth about the abiding values of Greek cultural heritage. Thus education will raise up persons of integrity, who will provide civic life with the leadership it needs.

"Know thyself", Socrates admonished. If you really know yourself, you will recognize that human nature has a power of knowing distinct from the sensory apparatus, a second kind of knowledge that reflects a specific difference in man. Man differs in kind from the beasts of field and forest because of the intelligence that gives him his rational powers. Since we are human beings, different in mode, our education must cultivate the specifically human in us, or it will not be a true humanism and the values of the Greek heritage will founder for lack of their abiding rational foundation. To see this great truth about humanity, about the *Paideia*, about education and culture, is wisdom itself. Young people should be taught to love this wisdom. Love for this wisdom of the abiding intelligible truths should be organized as the culminating discipline, the seventh of the seven liberal arts. The word "philosophy" is born to denote the discipline that teaches this wisdom and the love for it.

Controversy and conflict broke out in Athens. Socrates was raising questions that challenged the age-old secularized condition of human culture and the vested interests of the Sophists as the established teachers. Socrates was condemned to death as a menace to the youth of Athens. But he had launched an ongoing discussion of the nature of man and of the question whether the intelligibles exist as knowable truths abiding throughout the changing appearances of the senses and the vicissitudes of earthly life. This question of the nature and purpose of the *Paideia* persists after Socrates throughout classical antiquity, and indeed to the present day. Does "philosophy" exist as the seventh of the seven arts? What is the purpose of human culture? There were indeed some streaks of dawn in the Pre-Socratic wonder about the stuff of the cosmos. But philosophy itself actually begins with Socrates and his dialectical method of pursuing the abiding intelligible truths of human education and culture.

Plato

Plato was Socrates' gifted student who continued his program for the reform of the Greek *Paideia*. The program of rhetorical education is to be replaced by the ideal of philosophical education. The seven arts are to be reorganized. Rhetoric will become a preparatory and preliminary study. Philosophy, understood as the science of wisdom and virtue, will be the seventh of the arts. It will crown the education of youth. There will flow into society a new potential for truly wise and clear-sighted leadership with a healthful effect upon civic affairs. Cultural life will be stabilized on sound foundations by the persons who know and love wisdom because they have been formed in the true humanism of the renewed and reformed *Paideia*.

The famous Dialogues of Plato are studied to this day for their literary beauty as well as their documentation of this vast enterprise for the philosophical reform of Greek education and culture. In them Plato introduces his teacher,

Socrates, in discussion with the best-known Athenian Sophists of the day. Philosophy is visibly at work in his Socratic method of rising above the merely pragmatic to the level of the abiding intelligible truths, upon which the cultural values rest.[1]

Plato is one of the most convincing and lucid exponents of philosophical anthropology, which recognizes two qualitatively distinct kinds of knowledge in man. The second and immeasurably higher kind of knowledge is available to man because of his intelligence. It is the power of knowing and judging results from human rationality. This is the specific difference that separates the human mode of being from that of the brute beasts. Man is obviously an animal, endowed with the sensory apparatus proper to the animal mode; but he is also rational. The *Paideia* must cultivate this specifically human power in its educational program and process in order that the resulting social culture may be authentically human, a true humanism that has handed on its values to the young. Thus it will live in history. Otherwise it will founder.

All of this implies that man has a power to see by an intellectual light, different in kind from the sensory light that activates the bodily senses. In this higher kind of light man sees the intelligible truths, abidingly true, and thus he comes to understand and to love the values that such truths support with new insight and personal dedication.

As you will read in the selected excerpts in Appendix I, Plato taught that these intelligible truths, these ideas conceived by the properly educated and cultivated intelligence, correspond each to an Idea that exists as such in a world of Ideas, which transcends the world of this visible cosmos. In that higher world the Idea of Justice exists as such, and the Idea of Temperance, and so on, up to the Idea of the Good, which is the highest and most noble of the Ideas. Plato's philosophy, taught as a liberation of the human spirit from the prison of the senses, is clearly an effort to rise to a transcendent order of reality, above and beyond sensory experience, existing apart from the cosmos, not subject to the particularity of concrete instances of justice or goodness and the limitations of the material universe. This is the meaning of Plato's metaphor of the cave in his *Republic,* where he describes the prisoners who can see only the shadows on the walls of the cave, shadows produced by the real objects they cannot see. The philosophical *Paideia* is an education that cuts the bonds of man to the changeable world of sense and its flux of mere opinion. As the education proceeds, the prisoners turn toward the intelligible light and its sources, climbing out of the cave to the world above, where they see, by intellectual insight and understanding, the Ideas in themselves. They have come into personal possession of the intelligible truths. They have become lovers of wisdom. And the discipline that accomplishes this immense benefit for young

[1] See Excerpts for Part One, Plato, pp. 389–93.

persons and through them for culture and society is philosophy itself, the seventh of the seven arts. It has guided and animated and given purpose to the entire process of the education of youth. Such young people will be indeed "philosopher-kings", fit to rule the democratic republic of Athens.

Such was Plato's concept of philosophy. The nobility of the project has never ceased to attract Western man. What is frequently missed is the fact that philosophy was born in this Socratic conflict with the Sophists over the nature, purpose, and process of Greek humanism, its *Paideia,* or system of education, and its concept of culture.

What is still more frequently missed are the shortcomings of Plato's philosophical teaching. He had a powerful thirst for wisdom and saw clearly that true wisdom is transcendent knowledge. It goes beyond mere pragmatism, crass materialism, and the selfish skepticism that uses doubt about abiding principles as a false liberation to do what one pleases. But Plato's doctrine remained immersed in pantheism and the eternity of matter. There will be a direct line from his teaching to that of Plotinus in late classical times and to Spinoza and Hegel in Modern Philosophy. For all his noble aspirations, from which he has been known through the centuries as "the divine Plato", his teaching was only a groping toward transcendental reality. He never reached the concept of God as the Father Almighty, Creator of heaven and earth. The contrast between Plato's teaching in Athens, highly cultivated and academically organized, with the religious thinking and practice of the remote and marginalized primitive tribes of Plato's day is a matter for careful philosophical reflection and analysis. Those absolute primitives rediscovered by Western man in the Copernican revolution were pursuing their humble yet qualitatively elevated way of life in Plato's day, totally unknown to the sophisticated world of Greek culture.

Aristotle

Aristotle studied under Plato and then became a teacher in Plato's Academy, the famous school of higher education organized by Plato in the sacred grove of Academe, a suburb of Athens. In due time Aristotle founded his own Peripatetic school, so called from his custom of walking with small groups of advanced students, while teaching in seminar fashion. He always considered himself a Platonist, however, and he was indeed fundamentally at one with Socrates and Plato against the Sophists. He too recognized that second and higher kind of knowledge that specifies man, defining man outright as a rational animal. He was dedicated, accordingly, to the cause of philosophical reform in the *Paideia* and the development of philosophy, the science of wisdom and virtue, as the seventh of the seven arts.[2]

---

[2] See Excerpts for Part One, Aristotle, p. 394.

Aristotle made one major change in Plato's teaching. He rejected the concept of a separate world where the Ideas, the abiding intelligible truths, exist somehow as such. These ideas are indeed real, Aristotle teaches; the Sophists of all types are wrong and a threat to human culture by their failure to recognize them. But these ideas exist here on the planet earth, in the things of sense, as the forms that give them their various ways of being. These forms are known by the intelligence, which understands them, conceives them inwardly, and thus knows them as intelligible truths. The intelligence, Aristotle taught, is a power in human nature that corresponds to an intelligible light. Thus man comes to know the abiding truths, drawn from the forms of things in the cosmos, which ground the ethical values and thus sustain the heritage of human culture.

Aristotle takes his position with Socrates and Plato against the materialism and skepticism of the Sophists. Man knows an order of reality beyond sensory appearances, the very *ousia,* the essence or nature that underlies those appearances, that stands under them, as the Romans will say later on with their Latin word "substance". But the meaning intended by these various terms is clear. It sets the classical philosophy of Socrates, Plato, and Aristotle apart from the Sophists by expressing its openness to an intelligible order of reality beyond the level of the senses, the higher order that the intellect knows. Aristotle is fundamentally at one with Plato.

This underlying reality abides throughout the flux of changes that the senses observe. Accidental modifications come and go, changes in size and quantitative measure, in the qualities of the different kinds of substance. But the *ousia* abides. An apple is an apple when small and green in the spring or large and red in the autumn. It has remained itself. It is the same substance or nature or being or reality.

Aristotle was deeply interested in this abiding being of things. He was without question a philosophical genius. But he was oriented strongly toward the being of the things that the senses observe in this cosmos. The empirical sciences as they are known today, in the times since Copernicus, were not separated from philosophical study in Aristotle's time. But they existed in their rudiments. Aristotle is credited with the founding of biology as a science because of his systematic observation of living things and his structured exposition of this empirical knowledge. He wrote a treatise on meteorology and taught a systematic course on animal life.

This indicates Aristotle's basic orientation. He was turned down toward the things of this earth. Was he a child of his secularized age? For him the *ousia* meant chiefly the forms of bodily things that animate the matter of each one. Beings for him, the ones that engross him, are the material things formed this way, as in a statue, a tree, or a dog, or that way, as in a human being.

His teaching confirmed in Western culture the philosophical anthropology that sees man as an animal specifically different from the beasts. This is because man's animating principle, his "soul", is different in kind from their animating principles. The difference is in that power to know the intelligible truths that give him his understanding of the forms of things, the ideas that make them what they are.

The great achievement of Aristotle lies in the field of education. He organized these bodies of learning into the basic treatises that have formed the program of Western education ever since: the embryonic empirical sciences and the branches of philosophy: metaphysics, philosophical anthropology, and ethics. In addition to these disciplines, which study the realities of the cosmos, Aristotle organized the study of man's mental processes and the procedures that govern the movement of the mind in the discovery and learning of the content of the real disciplines. This is his *Organon,* as he termed it, using the Greek word for "instrument", the Aristotelian discipline studied across all the centuries and vicissitudes of Western mankind as the science of logic. Francis Bacon wrote his *New Organon,* one of the classic treatises early in the Copernican revolution in the empirical sciences, out of this fundamental background, to provide the specific guide for the process and procedures of the empirical sciences, now at last being separated from philosophy.

The major part of Aristotle's work is the body of disciplines that constitute the program of Greek education as reformed in his school, the school of Socrates and Plato. Philosophy as such will be the seventh art, the one that orients all the studies and gives purpose to the program as a whole. The program is the study of wisdom, and its outcome is to be the love of wisdom.

Aristotle rose to the challenge. He drafted the syllabus for the study of being as such, in itself and in its principles. He saw clearly that all the other sciences, in their study of particular aspects of reality, call for that ultimate science that studies reality as such. He wrote a treatise known and studied across the centuries as Aristotle's *Metaphysics.* As the name indicates, it is the science that studies the reality above and beyond the physical. It is devoted to the intelligible order as such, and thus stands full in Plato's tradition.

How successful was Aristotle in drawing up this culminating science, the science of wisdom and virtue? Aristotle was able to see that this science seeks to know the abiding reality that must exist beyond sensory appearance. He went so far as to call this science "theology", the natural human science that studies God, the Supreme Being. The fact is, however, that he seems to have been able only to structure the principles that govern being as such, by which the mind ascends to the intelligible order. This is what moderns call "ontology", the first half of the academic discipline known as metaphysics. The application of these principles to the study of the Supreme Being, his attributes, his relationship to the cosmos and especially to mankind, seems to have been more than even Aristotle could accomplish. If he did actually teach a systematic treatise on natural theology, applying his metaphysical principles, the lecture notes have not survived. What has survived is his intention, and the openness of his ontology to such an ascent, to a study of God and divine things on the level of unaided and natural power of thought.

Central to Aristotle's situation is the fact that he failed to achieve the philosophical doctrine of creation. Interested almost exclusively in the forms of bodily things, he too took the existence of things for granted. He too simply accepted the eternity of matter. He too philosophized basically within the religiosity of the ambient pantheism. A question remains, then, at the end of Aristotle's immense accomplishment. He has structured the sciences and disciplines of human culture. He has projected metaphysics, the science of wisdom and virtue, as their guiding light and capstone. Will he have a disciple, as Plato had Aristotle, and as Socrates had Plato, to build further upon these foundations, reaching at last to God the Father Almighty, Creator of heaven and earth, to him whom the forgotten primitives are recognizing in prayer and worshipping by sacrifice?

Excerpts in Appendix I from the *Physics* and the *Nichomachean Ethics* will help you appreciate the practical and analytical nature of Aristotle's mind.[3]

The Secularized Philosophy of the Hellenistic Age

The ideal situation for an affirmative answer seemed at hand. Aristotle had been the personal teacher of the young Macedonian prince who was to become Alexander the Great, conqueror of the world from Egypt across Mesopotamia into India. The Greek Empire overthrows and replaces the Persian Empire, as it had overthrown and succeeded Babylon. This introduces the Hellenistic age and its cultural unity, when the Greek language, education, and culture were planted triumphantly everywhere. Will the pragmatic materialism of the Sophists dominate this unified world? Or will the reform of the *Paideia* projected by Socrates and his pupils Plato and Aristotle win with Alexander? This is the fateful, deeply philosophical question that broods over classical antiquity for nearly a millennium, until the last philosophical school closes its doors in Athens and the world stands at the threshold of the new Christian era in Western culture. Let us review the essential facts.

The central question concerns the rise of intellectual leadership able to carry onward and upward the edifice for which Socrates, Plato, and Aristotle had placed the foundations, the building of a Parthenon of human culture upon the solid foundations of the intelligible truths and their openness to a natural knowledge of the transcendent Supreme Being of the universe.

After Aristotle many centuries passed before a philosopher of similar stature arose in the person of Plotinus, founder of a system of thought called Neo-

[3] See Excerpts for Part One, Aristotle, pp. 394–95.

Platonism. This was late in the Hellenistic age, in the third century A.D., when the Roman Empire had conquered Greece and replaced Alexander's world empire. In fact, Christian times were already at hand, with the special appeal of Christianity as the solution for the cultural problems that had grown ever deeper as the Hellenistic age proceeded.

Plotinus represents an effort on the part of the ancient pagan religiosity to ward off the Christian upswing by a renewal of the classical Greek philosophy, especially that of Plato. He adopted and systematized that aspect of Plato that expresses the immersion of Greek academic thought in the ancient religious error of pantheism. Thus Plotinus teaches the polytheistic religiosity common to all the cultures that had emerged out of the long millennia of prehistoric time. The essence of Plotinus' thought is a mysticism of self-identification with the World Soul, emanating from the One, the ineffable source of all multiple beings, itself beyond being and knowledge. There is no concept of creation, and no idea of a moral doctrine that expresses the will of the Creator for his creatures. There is nothing to teach the young in the *Paideia* but the vague pantheistic mysticism that leaves each with that pagan concept of freedom: the freedom to be a law unto oneself, for lack of knowledge of a Supreme Being and his stated and specified will for men.

What had happened in the centuries of the Hellenistic age between Aristotle and Plotinus? Numerous schools of philosophy arose, founded by various thinkers famous in their day and studied still in the histories of philosophy. A typical representative is Pyrrho of Elis, founder of Pyrrhonism, a philosophically cultivated skepticism, at about 300 B.C. Education polishes the individual for cultivated earthly life and prepares him for success in the various professions and callings of civil society. But as to the intelligibles of Socrates, Plato, and Aristotle, certainty in such questions is unattainable. Philosophic doubt is the hallmark of the wise man. Suspension of judgment is indicated for all matters beyond sensory observation, with continuing search and research.

Sextus Empiricus develops and confirms this approach, teaching that knowledge derives from experience alone. There is no such thing as a second and higher power of knowing, distinct from the senses and giving human beings an opening to intelligible reality and the Supreme Being. The Cynics are simply a despairing variation on the theme. In later Roman times the Stoics, expressing the unmoved severity of the Romans in their administrative tasks, will be yet another expression of the same outlook. Pilate's famous question to Christ, "What is truth?" reflects the spirit of the Hellenistic age. It is a scornful and cynical rhetorical question, in despair of a positive answer. Cicero, who attempted to bring the best of the Greek philosophical heritage into the Latin language for use in the Roman schools, sympathized with the philosophical ideal of Socrates, Plato, and Aristotle. But as a practical Roman, he knew well that the centuries-old conflict over the *Paideia* had long been won by the Sophists. Lucretius, with his materialistic poem *The Nature of Things,* carried the day.

The result was that philosophy, while sought and cultivated by individuals, was nowhere in the Hellenistic age, in either Athens or Rome, adopted in the schools generally as the seventh of the seven arts. When philosophy was studied and its classic works cultivated, it was done within the rhetorical education in the programs of the professors on the level of higher education, who were called in Latin simply the *Rhetores.*

The outcome, then, was the victory of the approach of the Sophists throughout the Hellenistic age of both Athens and Rome. The death sentence of Socrates had been indeed a portent. Both Plotinus and the various forms and schools of Skepticism end in a generalized secularism: an education that gives verbal polish and competence for success in earthly pursuits. Each is formed in his early schooling to be his own law, since there is no certitude of a law coming from a transcendent Supreme Being standing above and beyond the cosmos. In practice the self is supreme. The ancient and inveterate error of mankind, pantheism and its religiosity, is philosophically confirmed in philosophies that are rationalizations of human self-divinization.[4]

How did this academic discipline, this member of the liberal arts, actually work in the schools? When a given *Rhetor,* contrary to the Sophist system, installed it as the culminating science, it was studied in a pagan mode proper to classical antiquity. It was limited to what moderns call ontology, the study of the concept of being from the viewpoint of the beings in this cosmos. In practice this meant a study of the forms of bodily things in and of this world. Man himself, with his strikingly superior form of being, was the central object of study, together with approaches to human life, happiness, and social welfare proper to the various schools. It was a study of wisdom and an effort to give the oncoming generation a love of wisdom. Classical Philosophy is thus a kind or mode of philosophy, a way of thinking about ultimate reality and hence about the meaning of human existence.

The literature that has survived from the pens and lectures of the classical pagan philosophers exhibits much discussion of being, being as such, being in the world, and the human mode of being. But there are only glimmers of an ascent to the higher reality; when these insights and aspirations occur, they are in the pantheistic direction of Plato and Plotinus, with their concern for the religion of beauty and humanistic cultivation of the self. Against the higher aspiration are the many schools of full-fledged philosophical rationalization of outright materialism, satirical denial of the second and higher kind of knowledge in man, and the despair of Stoicism and Cynicism.

---

[4] See Excerpts for Part One, Epictetus, pp. 396–98.

In other words, Classical Philosophy even at its best remained on the level of a particular kind of ontology. It failed to ascend from the principles of being discerned in the beings of the cosmos to a true natural theology, the study of the Supreme Being in his mode of existence, in his attributes, and in his relationship to the visible cosmos.

Pagan Classical Philosophy, to put this another way, was a kind of philosophy, a way of thinking about ultimate reality, that proceeded within the pantheistic religiosity that had become the generalized religious condition of mankind, whether in the historic cultures now gathered into the vast empires of Greece and Rome or in the agricultural villages and among the tribal hunters of the spaces beyond the civilizations. The new knowledge of prehistory, especially the new insight into its immensely long ages of time, puts philosophy into a new and different light. The contrast is with that other religion of the Hebrews with its transcendent God, to which the contemporary primitives seem to point as the original condition of mankind. Classical Philosophy philosophized within the pantheistic "faith", never breaking free from its confinement of the human spirit within the cosmos.

Was the pagan way of thought and life good for mankind? Did it produce personal happiness? What of social welfare? The institutions of slavery and temple prostitution and the furnaces of the god Moloch for the disposal of unwanted babies indicate the answer. The literature of classical antiquity is not a song of happiness but rather of cultivated stoical despair. The search for the truth never achieved proved not to be in itself sufficient and satisfying for the human spirit.

Paul of Tarsus, a Jew of bilingual education and culture, well versed in the teaching at Jerusalem and the wisdom of Athens, knew the philosophies of classical antiquity from within. "The anger of God", he writes in the first chapter of his Epistle to the Romans, at midpoint in the Hellenistic age,

is being revealed from heaven against all the impiety and depravity of men who keep truth imprisoned in their wickedness. For what can be known about God is perfectly plain to them since God himself has made it plain. Ever since God created the world, his everlasting power and deity—however invisible—have been there for the mind to see in the things he has made. That is why such people are without excuse: they knew God and yet refused to honor him as God or to thank him; instead, they made nonsense out of logic and their empty minds were darkened.

The more they called themselves philosophers, the more stupid they grew, until they exchanged the glory of the immortal God for a worthless imitation, for the image of mortal man, of birds, of quadrupeds and reptiles.

That is why God left them to their filthy enjoyments and the practices with which they dishonor their own bodies, since they have given up divine truth for a lie and have worshipped and served creatures instead of the Creator, who is blessed forever. Amen!

That is why God has abandoned them to degrading passion: why their women have turned from natural intercourse to unnatural practices, and why their menfolk have given up natural intercourse to be consumed with passion for each other, men doing shameless things with men and getting an appropriate reward for their perversion.

In other words, since they refused to see it was rational to acknowledge God, God has left them to their own irrational ideas and to their monstrous behavior. And so they are steeped in all sorts of depravity, rottenness, greed, and malice, and addicted to envy, murder, wrangling, treachery, and spite. Libelers, slanderers, enemies of God, rude, arrogant, and boastful, enterprising in sin, rebellious to parents, without brains, honor, love, or pity. They know what God's verdict is: that those who believe like this deserve to die—and yet they do it, and what is worse, encourage others to do the same (Rom 1:18-32).

This chapter of Paul of Tarsus is a massively comprehensive indictment of human culture four thousand years after its earliest recorded history, and a sufficient indication of the failure of the Classical Philosophy to cope with the human situation. Confining itself to a thinking within the ancient and inveterate error, what could it do but rationalize that strange bent in human nature away from the transcendent God of creation, moral law, and personal judgment? The fact remains that the divine judgment did not go into action so much as the divine mercy, with a plan to purge and clean, to lift up and reorient this humanity in the apostasy of its fall from transcendence. The very condition of mankind ministers to this plan, for it prepares men to give God a hearing.

Classical Philosophy as a Preparation for the Gospel

Christian thinkers from earliest times have recognized that the Hebrew Prophets prepared for the gospel in a direct way. But the Fathers of the Church, most of them converts from paganism who had studied the pagan philosophers in their youth, saw a second and parallel preparation in the heritage of Classical Philosophy.

Since philosophy takes its point of departure from the given in the human scene, such a preparation should be studied as the prerequisite for recognizing the nature of Christian Philosophy as a kind of philosophy in its own right, valid as philosophy and at the same time qualitatively distinct in itself and specifically different from other kinds of philosophy. This includes its difference from the philosophy of Socrates, Plato, and Aristotle, a difference frequently overlooked in the histories of philosophy.

Since the larger perspectives upon the age of mankind have become known and the religious condition of pantheism and idolatrous polytheism better understood, the philosophical preparation for the gospel can be seen in a new and better light. It illuminates the ambiguity of the philosophical experience of mankind.

It is indeed ambiguous, for it is both positive and negative. This preparation had a positive aspect, consisting chiefly in the work of Socrates, Plato, and Aristotle. For they knew that they knew reality. They were not locked up within themselves, thinking that they were knowing the contents of their own consciousness. They had a healthy and wholesome openness to being, to existing reality as such, abiding in and through the variety of substantial forms of things and the changing flux of their accidental variations. Unlike the Sophists and the Skeptics, these classical Greek thinkers recognized that the really real reality is not the appearance of things that the senses know but the underlying *ousia,* or being or essence or nature or substance. Whatever the terminology, they achieved an insight upon which an insight could follow regarding the principles of being, by which existing things exist in the way the senses observe that they do in fact exist.

As has been noted, Socrates, Plato, and Aristotle remained on this intermediate level. They had arisen from materialism to the level of the intelligibles and had laid down the foundation for the study of being as being. Christian thinkers recognized the abiding value of this philosophical achievement. They were able to build upon the foundations, ascending to a true natural theology, which sees the Source of being as such and studies him as a really existing substantial reality who has his own unique mode of existing, personal attributes, intellectual and volitional qualities, and a definite, ascertainable relationship to the cosmos.

All of this lay beyond what the classical Greeks, at their best and in their most lucid moments, were able to achieve. But the fact that they laid the foundations was something positive. It was in its own way a preparation for the gospel, for the gospel requires ears to hear. These ears to hear presuppose this second and higher kind of knowledge, distinct from the senses, which Socrates, Plato, and Aristotle were recognizing and seeking in their various ways to describe and to express. It is a prerequisite for hearing the gospel to recognize a power in human nature to know the principles of being as being, not as things that the senses see but as realities of the intelligible order, which the intellect knows by insight and understanding: the underlying substance or abiding reality of bodily things. And this opens upward, points to an ascent toward a realm of substances, substantial realities that are not bodily things. This releases the human spirit from confinement within the cosmos, breaks the fetters of the ancient and inveterate error of pantheism, opens the way to an entirely different concept of God, and provides the human spirit with ears, as it were, to hear some word from him who is an existing personal reality beyond the cosmos.

Socrates, Plato, and Aristotle, on the largest perspective of universal history, were distinguished by a thirst for this kind of true wisdom and taught that it should be loved, loved sufficiently to be the seventh of the seven arts. Christian thinkers could adopt this position, make it their own, and build upon it. This aspect of pagan Classical Philosophy provided solid footing for many young people in Christian times, which began to open in the second half of the Hellenistic age. They used that footing to come to Christ, hearing the good news that he first announced to mankind from a small and unique province of the Roman Empire called Palestine, with its capital, so difficult to govern, called Jerusalem, the City of Peace. Most of the Fathers of the Church were Greek and Roman converts to Jesus' Church, which had come forth from Jerusalem. They came to his Church by way of this highest type of pagan philosophy. They represent the preparation made visible in their thought, lives, and writings, at the same time as they began at long last to usher in a victory for Socrates over the Sophists, that victory that the pagan schools of philosophy by themselves had not been able to win.

There is a second aspect of the philosophical preparation for the gospel. It is negative in character. It is that inability of philosophy to win the victory over the ancient idolatry rooted in the pantheistic fall from the concept of the transcendent Supreme Being. Classical Philosophy proved unable to achieve the renewal of the *Paideia,* of the classical education and culture, to which it aspired. And it failed to achieve a natural theology or philosophical knowledge of God. Above all, it failed to rise to the doctrine of creation, that central doctrine of all philosophy because it is the doctrine concerning existence as such in its origin, its nature, and its modes.

Even at its best, the pagan philosophy remained immersed in the ancient error of pantheism and ministered to the ambient social practices connected with idolatrous religiosity in all its forms.

The final outcome of the schools of philosophy was skepticism, the doubt and despair about the existence of anything abidingly true, or anything knowable with certitude regarding human destiny and any order of reality beyond the senses and earthly life. Do the gods really exist? The question whether there is one Supreme Being, the heavenly Father, Creator of heaven and earth, was not even asked. The attitude of cultivated paganism was indeed contained in Pilate's scornful question: "What is truth?"

But this negative outcome proved to be likewise a preparation for the gospel in an unexpected way. The philosophies were unable to satisfy the human heart and the human mind. They helped men in the late Hellenistic age to recognize a need for something quite new and different, a teaching that contained and communicated a power of regeneration and renewal. In its very despair of the truth, in its rationalizations for the denial of the intelligibles, pagan philosophy prepared spirits to give another hearing to the teaching that emanated from Jerusalem and was being heard in the marketplaces of the imperial pagan cities.

It is this teaching that introduces the adjective "Christian" as a new modifier for the noun "Philosophy". To it, then, one must turn in order to understand what this kind of philosophy, Christian Philosophy, is going to be.

III

THE REVEALED WISDOM OF THE HEBREW PROPHETS

Since philosophy is the study of the nature of ultimate reality, and hence of human life and destiny, it is fundamentally important to recognize the fact that there are different kinds of philosophy. This point is especially basic in the analysis of the apostasy from God and its contemporary consequences for the human situation in the late twentieth century. It is quite naive to pick and choose among philosophies like a person walking along a smorgasbord or salad bar, especially when many of the kinds laid out are far from personally or socially harmless. One must cultivate discernment of philosophical kinds.

Christian Philosophy as a Specific Kind of Philosophy

Christian Philosophy is a different kind of philosophy from other philosophies. It has its own specific nature. What is it, in itself? Exactly how does it differ? Only verbally? Or more deeply, in a way that bears upon the concept of reality? How does it relate to Classical Philosophy of pagan antiquity? One can ask this question in general or specifically in relationship to Socrates, Plato, and Aristotle. How does Christian Philosophy relate to Modern Philosophy? These are fundamental questions that involve the nature and the continuity of the Western heritage of civilization and culture. This introduces the question of the liberal arts: Is Christian Philosophy one of them? Where does it fit into that conflict between Socrates and the Sophists, between philosophical education and culture versus the rhetorical ideal for the *Paideia*?

The nature of Christian Philosophy, which is the key to these and many similar questions, can be understood only when its origin in the teaching program of the Fathers of the Church is explored. This will make it clear that Christian Philosophy is philosophizing that proceeds within a religious faith, just as Classical Philosophy philosophized within the pantheistic religiosity of mankind's general situation in all the cultures of historic times, which began around 4000 B.C. But it is a very different religious faith from pagan pantheism, with its consequent polytheism, animism, and idolatry. Christian Philosophy is a large phenomenon, therefore, on the panorama of universal history, far larger than any one Christian thinker, however famous and important for his role in its development. This makes it clear that attention must be given to its origin, nature, and development.

49

Otherwise, the nature of the West itself will remain obscure, and the heirs of Western civilization will not know their own roots. Furthermore, the theme of the apostasy from God as a concrete historical event in the recent life of Western civilization can be understood only against this nature and social presence of Christian Philosophy in Western culture. For it is not a phenomenon of China, India, or Islam but of the European West in Christian times.

It is essential, therefore, to look at that new and different religious faith within which Christian Philosophy philosophized.

Abraham, Moses, and the Prophets

Moses is the commanding figure of the Jewish people. He towers above them as their lawgiver in the way grasped so well by Michelangelo in his famous statue. Moses is the spokesman of God who transmitted to the Hebrews the revealed religion that set them apart both in doctrine and in life. The religion of the Hebrews is a prime example of prophetic religion, namely, religious faith and practice that are taught to the people by persons accepted as men of God. Across the long ages of prehistory, many peoples had this teaching approach to religion with shamans and medicine men, quite different from the idea that each person is his own prophet, so to speak, who depends upon personal experience and thought. Prophetic religion is a practical teaching program with a body of doctrine that comes from the words of the prophets, accepted by the people as men enlightened by God in a special way proper to themselves.

Among the Hebrews, prophetic religion reaches its highest level on the human scene. And Moses is the mighty prophet and teacher who organized and consolidated the religious belief and practice of the Hebrews as a people.

Men enlightened by God: What does this special enlightenment mean? How did the Hebrews themselves see their prophets?

To answer these questions, one must reflect upon the various kinds of light. First, there is ordinary sensory light, the daylight of the earthly scene. Organic senses react to this light with perceptions of visible bodily objects. Man and the higher animals know by sensory perception through similar sense organs. The animals do not reflect on the nature of this light. They simply make use of it as given. Man, however, has acquired in recent times an immensely enhanced understanding of the nature and properties of this corporeal light, relating it strikingly to the stuff of the visible cosmos. There always have been schools of philosophy that limit human knowledge to this level of the senses and this kind of light. The Copernican revolution, however, gives pause, for the new empirical knowledge about sensory light points toward a power of understanding in humans that animals do not possess.

Other philosophers, including especially Socrates, Plato, and Aristotle, who, as we have seen, were distinguished by this insight, recognize the existence of an intelligible light, qualitatively distinct from and immeasurably higher than the light of the senses. The human intelligence is a power of knowing distinct from the senses and related to insights and understandings "seen" in this intelligible light. This was at the heart of the issue between Socrates and the Sophists. It is the watershed between humanisms; it divides philosophies into the materialisms, on the one hand, and those open to intelligible reality and its philosophical anthropology, on the other.

Who, then, is a prophet? A prophet is not a philosopher, using the power of human reason illumined by this intelligible light. A prophet is a person singled out to receive and perceive the prophetic light. It is a light, indeed, that illuminates the mind of the prophet, but it is as far above the intelligible light as the intelligible light stands over the sensory.

What is it in itself? The prophetic light is a special participation in the divine light, the fourth kind of light, the one that is identical with the reality of the Supreme Being. It is not the same thing as the divine light. But it participates in it much more directly and reflects its nature much more closely and fully than the other two forms of light, which are open to all human beings simply by the constitution of human nature.

There are then basically these four kinds of light: the sensory, the intelligible, the prophetic, and the divine light itself. The prophet is a person called apart from his fellowman to receive the higher illumination of this third and qualitatively distinct kind of light. Such a person will know many things by virtue of this calling and will be in a position of unique religious leadership before his fellowman. The prophet speaks what he has been divinely taught: he proclaims his knowledge to his people. This builds up revealed religion among them.

Why do the Hebrews accept the teaching of their prophets as truly the very word of God and not as simply words of men elaborated out of the sensory and intelligible forms of light? Chiefly because of two factors that they were able to observe: the prophets frequently did things beyond human power, and often they foretold future events in a strikingly accurate way, which likewise lies beyond human power. It has come to be commonly accepted doctrine in the Hebrew-Christian Tradition, therefore, that the prophetic light is a most special participation in the divine light, which makes possible a higher knowledge of all realities, whether human or divine, spiritual or corporeal. The Hebrews always were distinguished by a reverence for their prophetic word, both in their heritage of oral teaching and in the writings to which the words of the prophets were officially consigned by their governing authorities. The Hebrews always had faith that their prophetic word is divine revelation and that their book, the Bible, is the inspired written record and memory of the great deeds and teachings of God for them as his chosen people. The Hebrews are known throughout their history to the present day as the people of the book.

Moses, then, is the preeminent prophet, so the Hebrews believed and believe, who received revealed truth from God and who organized the life of the people upon it. From their beginning they were the religious people par excellence, whose entire national program for life and conduct, both personal and social, was simply the living of this revealed truth and religion.

Philosophy takes what is given in human experience as its point of departure. The phenomenon of the Hebrews is a fact of human experience and may therefore be made the subject of philosophical inquiry.

The first point in the program by which Moses shaped and formed the Hebrews into a special people of God is its historical dimension. They were to be a people in movement, from the past into the future, indeed toward a particular future graphically foretold.

Regarding the past, Moses held up the figure of Abraham as the patriarch from whom they were descended. Moses taught them the call of Abraham from God to come out from the city of Ur of the Chaldees, out from its inveterate polytheism and idolatry, to the nomadic life of the tent-dwellers in the deserts and steppes. The Hebrews were herdsmen, always in movement with the seasons of the pastures. A remarkable fact discovered by the modern sciences of ethnology and anthropology is that the nomads preserve a much closer resemblance in religion to the absolute primitives and manifest much less of the idolatrous pantheism and polytheism that prevail among the agricultural villagers and the cities of the great historic cultures. In any case, the Hebrews rejected all pantheism, polytheism, and idolatry. Moses taught them the purest kind of monotheism, the *Shema,* which echoes through the ages as the faith of Israel. He said (Dt 6:4–9):

> Listen, Israel: Yahweh our God is the one Yahweh. You shall love Yahweh your God with all your heart, with all your soul, with all your strength. Let these words I urge on you today be written on your heart. You shall repeat them to your children and say them over to them whether at rest in your house or walking abroad, at your lying down or at your rising; you shall fasten them on your hand as a sign and on your forehead as a circlet; you shall write them on the doorposts of your house and on your gates.

Moses and Monotheism

The Hebrew religion unfolds from the teaching and practice of this monotheism. It sets this people apart from the now universal idolatry of all the other branches and peoples of mankind. This God of the Hebrews, whose name, Yahweh, was revealed to Moses, is a Pure Spirit. He is the Almighty. He is all-knowing. Above all, he is the Creator of heaven and earth and of all that the earth contains, all its forms of life, and especially of each person. Men owe the Creator the responses of worship by sacrifice, of obedience to the Creator's law stamped upon their natures, and of personal prayer. Moses' religion provided this teaching about God and contained the arrangements for these creaturely responses to the revelation of God's nature and attributes. And it is all rooted in the meaning of the divine name, Yahweh: I AM. The Hebrew root signifies the supremely existing Being, the personal Reality who is the source of the existence of all other realities.

Moses sealed this revealed religion in a covenant between Yahweh and this people chosen to be the bearer of divine revelation by instituting the Passover sacrifice. By a major religious development, Moses reinstituted the age-old sacrifices of prehistoric and historic peoples, the offering of the firstfruits of the flocks and the fields. He reoriented their meaning into a new sacrifice offered now to God as the Lord of history as well as the Lord of creation. This is the meaning of the offering of the Passover lamb, recalling the memory of the great deeds of Yahweh when he liberated the people from slavery in Egypt and recognizing the special Providence of Almighty God over the historic life of this people, past, present, and to come. He established the priesthood for this religion of sacrificial offering in the family and descendants of Aaron. In due time, under King David and King Solomon, this ritual of sacrifice took place at a great temple, which they built in Jerusalem, the one and only place where these central rites of the Hebrew religion could be offered.

This worship of God the Father Almighty, Creator of heaven and earth, sustained the personal and social life of the Hebrews as a choice of the way of life instead of the way of death followed by the surrounding Gentiles, with their various abominable practices resulting from religious ignorance and worship of false gods. So the Hebrews thought. Always the prophets taught the doctrine of the two ways, echoing and confirming this basic teaching of Moses (Dt 30:15-20):

> See, today I set before you life and prosperity, death and disaster. If you obey the commandments of Yahweh your God . . . he will bless you in the land you are entering to make your own. But if your heart strays, if you refuse to listen, if you let yourself be drawn into worshipping other gods and serving them, I tell you today, you will most certainly perish. . . . Choose life, then, so that you and your descendants may live, in the love of Yahweh your God, obeying his voice, clinging to him, for in this your life consists, and on this depends your long stay in the land that Yahweh swore to your fathers Abraham, Isaac, and Jacob he would give them.

Without question Moses defines apostasy from God in this passage and warns the Hebrews against it. Is it now possible that a kind of philosophy will arise that, from its own analysis of the human situation, will concur with Moses' teaching and recognize that the definition and the warning may well apply to all mankind?

It is remarkable that Moses' teaching program for the Hebrew people not only informed them and kept them conscious of their origin in Abraham as a specific nomadic people but also took them back to absolute human origins in one original first couple. In the Hebrew language Adam means simply "the man", namely, the first newly created human being; and Eve means "the mother of all the living". Moses, speaking as the Hebrews believed, out of the prophetic light, taught the descent of all mankind from one original pair, created by the one and same Yahweh who is the Creator of heaven and earth. The doctrine of creation and the unity of the human race distinguish the teaching program of the Hebrew people. Moses, furthermore, consolidated into the Hebrew consciousness the teaching of original sin with the resulting propagation of a fallen condition of human nature, an aversion to God and a proneness to sin, in each human being. The revealed religion that he gave to the Hebrews as the Covenant or Testament between themselves and God functions in this realistic context of the actual condition of mankind. It is a religion of personal prayer and worship by sacrifice, a worship in which sin offerings play a central role. It is a religion, furthermore, of the most conscious awareness of the relationship of Yahweh to the moral life, specified now by the Ten Commandments, which Moses gave to the Hebrews as coming from God.

An overview of mankind's philosophical experience, taking its departure from the human situation as given by the facts, cannot at this point but note the striking similarity of Moses' religious teaching to the thinking and practice of the absolute primitives. The pointer facts uncovered by the new empirical sciences have been noted as indications that the original religion of mankind is reflected in vestiges still visible among contemporary absolute primitives. Moses' religion appears to be a renewal of that original religion, which earliest mankind practiced before gradual deviation set in, hardened, and became a generalized condition in the long prehistoric ages of mankind. Philosophy today, no longer beginning with the relatively recent Pre-Socratics, still studies human reality as given to the senses, in perceptions now enhanced by the progress of the empirical sciences. The Hebrews, of course, accepted Moses' teaching on human origins not as science or philosophy in Western academic terms but as truly a word of God from a higher order of reality and knowledge. When the time comes to recognize Christian Philosophy as a new kind of philosophy, it will be clear that this teaching of the Hebrews on human origins will have a special interest for it. For it relates directly to the doctrine of creation, for which Christian Philosophy will cultivate a rational openness.

For the moment, one can say that the discoveries of the new empirical sciences pointing toward original monotheism, worship by prayer and sacrifice and obedience to the moral law given by the Creator, are strikingly illuminated by the teaching that distinguishes the new Hebrew people, which arose in historic times, at approximately 2000 B.C. in the call of Abraham, with a sense of mission to all mankind.

The Hermeneutical Function of Philosophy

What is philosophy to make of this? The role of philosophy is hermeneutical when it stands before facts, correspondences, and indications. What is the meaning? How to interpret them? It seems correct to say that the empirical sciences give only indications, not demonstrations in their own order, for original monotheism. Perhaps mankind is not to learn about human origins by way of full and demonstrated knowledge from the empirical sciences. Could it not be that such knowledge is reserved for faith in a word from the heavenly Father, who created heaven, earth, and the first pair of human beings? Philosophy can only ponder and wonder. In any case, children do not learn their own family origins by themselves. After several years totally devoid of memory, they receive instruction about their family tree by listening to and trusting their parents.

There was a further basic fact about the teaching of Moses and the prophets. It concerned the past, but it was even more conscious of the future. It was immersed in historical consciousness, attuned to historical movement and oriented toward climactic future events. In this it was utterly unlike the ambient Greek and Roman pagans, who thought in cyclic terms. The Hebrews from their very beginning as a people were linear and historical in their consciousness. They transcended the astral cycles of the ambient pagan thought and worshipped Yahweh as the Lord of history.

How did this work out in practice? Quite simply in the doctrine of the messianic expectation. Surprisingly enough, Moses and all the prophets taught that their Covenant was provisional, preparatory, and temporary. They taught the Hebrews to expect a prophet like unto Moses who would establish a new and everlasting Covenant. Each Hebrew was to prepare for his coming by faithful practice of the religion established by Moses. Even the sacrifices at Jerusalem's Temple were to be changed by the Messiah, with a different oblation and a different priesthood. "From farthest east to farthest west my name is honored among the nations," writes the prophet Malachi, "and everywhere there is burnt sacrifice, there is offering to my name and a pure offering." The prophets hold up many other things before the Hebrews, who received their teaching as the very word of God: the conversion of the Gentiles from their idolatry, their acceptance of the moral life of the Ten Commandments, and their streaming to Jerusalem in personal prayer to Yahweh, the God of the Hebrews, the God of divine revelation. A most unlikely prospect on human terms, the Hebrews always thought, one that only divine power could bring about, with the mode of accomplishment impossible to imagine in advance. Peoples do not easily give up their ways, especially when rooted in the inveterate error of mankind.

The fact remains that the prophets taught the Hebrew people that their calling in Abraham was for the benefit of all mankind. This is why Moses was careful to relate the Hebrews to absolute origins in the first human pair. The Hebrews are to prepare for "an anointed One", *Messiah* in the Hebrew language, a redeemer who would institute the new and eternal testament sealed by its own ritual of worship by prayer and sacrifice. In his times, their own pure and elevated monotheism with its strict morality was to be extended from them and by them to all the Gentiles. These peoples would turn away from their idols and toward Yahweh, sharing in the knowledge of him that had been revealed to the Hebrews. Thus it was the calling of the Hebrews, their prophets taught, to be "a light to the Gentiles", as Isaiah stressed. This light is nothing else than their pure monotheistic religion, their faith in God the Father Almighty, Creator of heaven and earth, together with the implications for personal and social living. Such a God is a Pure Spirit, transcendent over the cosmos, distinct from it, in no sense reducible to the cosmos, its energies and forces. He is the intelligent Creator who gives his creatures his laws, expects obedience to them, will judge them, and offers everlasting life as the reward for those who choose his way of life. Prayer, thanksgiving, adoration, and social worship by sacrifice: all make good sense when Yahweh is known in his revealed nature and attributes. The light to the Gentiles is nothing else than sharing in this religion of the prophets, light already possessed and practiced by the Hebrew people. The question is how to extend it to the Gentiles, and when Yahweh, the Lord of history, will bring it to pass.

IV

JESUS, THE DIVINE TEACHER

Jesus of Nazareth is an immensely forceful and influential personality in the historic life of mankind and especially in that of Western man. He is the reason why members of Western civilization are so conscious of the Judeo-Christian heritage. Jesus, the Teacher among the Jews at the time when the Roman Empire conquered Palestine and added it to its provinces, has had the primary historical role in the matter. His teaching, both in its content and its process, has reached the group of Gentile peoples dwelling in the geographical area organized and unified into the Roman Empire, who thus possess it as their common social heritage and have it woven into their intellectual and moral fabric. To his teaching, as a result, persons of this culture constantly return when they need to rediscover and renew their roots.

Jesus as a Teacher in Israel

All of this, it is quite clear, results from events in the realm of the *Paideia,* the process of education and the culture that is its social result. Teaching is of the essence. The essential point is the fact that Jesus was a teacher, indeed the most effective and influential one ever to appear.

What exactly was Jesus' program as a teacher? Did he have a content? How does it relate to the teaching of Moses and the prophets? Did he have a method? Did he structure his program? What was his purpose in his teaching? Where does the Greek *Paideia* fit in, with its seven arts and its ongoing debate on the nature and place of philosophy? Did Jesus confine his program to the Jews? The origin of Christian Philosophy is bound up with the answers to such questions, and likewise its nature as a specific kind of philosophy. Hence one must continue this survey of the new revealed religion that arises with Moses and as the Hebrews understood and practiced it with an overview of its modification and completion in Christianity.

Jesus of Nazareth had a standard Jewish upbringing, a meticulously full upbringing, one may say, in the heritage of his ancestors. He was born into the impoverished but still definitely self-aware family, or house, of King David, with its accepted original location at Bethlehem. He learned his family trade of carpentry, which he practiced at Nazareth out of the house of his mother, who was known to be of royal ancestry, a direct descendant of King David. It seems that his mother knew he would not always be a carpenter. Upon entering into the Hebrew man's estate at his bar mitzvah, he clearly indicated to her at the Temple school at Jerusalem, where she found him talking to the teachers of Moses' law, listening to them and asking them questions, that his business in life was to be along this line. Nevertheless, he returned to Nazareth and continued the quiet life of the village carpenter, with his mother as his cook and housekeeper, until he was thirty. His mother had seen to his elementary schooling at the synagogue school at Nazareth, something common to all Jewish children at that time. It is reasonable to suppose that he continued to be active at that synagogue during the eighteen years after the deeply significant incident at the Temple school at Jerusalem following his bar mitzvah. His mother would not have withheld from the men of the synagogue at Nazareth such a recommendation from the central authorities of Jewish higher education. Perhaps, therefore, he was one of the teachers in his own synagogue school at Nazareth. In any case, the day came when he left the carpenter shop, taking his mother with him, and emerged as a publicly recognized rabbi, or teacher, of Moses' Torah in Israel. For three years he taught in the standard pattern of higher education among the Greeks and Hebrews at the time. He went from synagogue to synagogue as a guest lecturer and spoke to large crowds, which gathered in various public places to hear him. Above all, he gathered about himself twelve full-time students, rabbinical candidates, one would say today, who went about with him, participated in his program, assisted with his public appearances, and had the benefit of private instruction and discussion. The closeness of this full-time teacher-learner relationship is matched today only in the advanced seminars of the most rigorous European university traditions for doctoral candidates.

There is no question about the fact that Jesus of Nazareth was a recognized teacher of the word of God as given in the Hebrew revelation and handed on by the teaching. The recognition was completely public, given by his inner circle of disciples, by the crowds who followed him, by his rabbinical opponents, and especially by the representatives of the Jewish government at Jerusalem.

It was central to his sense of mission and calling that he confined his personal program to the Jewish people but prepared his inner circle of students or disciples to reach out to all Gentiles, teaching them by means of the content and process that they learned from him. It was further central and basic, as he explicitly stated and stressed, that he had not come to destroy the prophets but to fulfill them. He intended his teaching to be a comprehensive fulfillment of the Hebrew revelation, with a content and a methodological structure that would minister to the extension of his teaching program to the Gentiles of the world beyond Palestine. He was systematically planning this outreach to the whole world every step of his way.

Jesus as a Prophet in Israel

Jesus saw himself as a prophet in Israel and, as a matter of fact, referred to himself as such. The people generally held him to be a prophet, standing like his own immediate forerunner, the man of God who pointed him out officially to the Jews, John the Baptist, in that line of recognizable men of God, "Moses and the prophets", which the Jews knew so well and which gave them their identity as a people. The inner circle of his disciples, furthermore, saw him as that great final prophet of whom Moses wrote. Thus that specific faith in him that accredited him as the very personification of the messianic expectation began to grow among them. As Philip said to Nathaniel, "We have found him of whom Moses, in the law, and the prophets wrote, Jesus, the son of Joseph of Nazareth" (Jn 1:45).

If Jesus was a prophet, then he taught the prophetic word out of the prophetic light. As noted above, this was essential to the understanding of the calling of a prophet among the Hebrews. At the same time, all the prophets, beginning with Moses, were teachers of the prophetic word to the people. So too Jesus: he too was a herald and a teacher of the prophetic word. It was perfectly natural, therefore, that he should have been a rabbi, or teacher of the Torah, and have grouped about himself not only crowds of followers in a broader sense but also that inner circle of *mathetai,* the New Testament Greek word for full-time students, as the disciples who would learn how to carry his teaching program forth to the Gentile world intact and authentic both in content and methodological structure. He himself, at the end of their training, sent them out on this worldwide mission: hence the Twelve came to be called his "Apostles", from the Greek word for "men who have been sent".

Jesus' Doctrine Regarding God

It would take the present survey beyond its scope even to summarize the teaching of Jesus. Here one can only concentrate on that concept of God the transcendent Creator whom the Hebrews knew and served because of Moses' teaching. Was it the same in Jesus' doctrine? The answer in the documents is a clear and explicit affirmative. Challenged in public on an occasion described in the documents to state his basic and central position, he simply gave Moses' *Shema:* "Jesus said, 'You must love the Lord your God with all your heart, with all your soul, and with all your mind. This is the first and the greatest commandment. The second resembles it: you must love your neighbor as yourself. On these two commandments hang the whole law, and the prophets also'" (Mt 22:37–40). He insisted furthermore on an even more public and formal occasion, when he was giving a comprehensive summary of his teaching to a full assembly of his followers, that it was his calling not to destroy the prophets but to fulfill them.

Jesus was certainly a theist and in no sense a pantheist. He gave his teaching program to the Jews, indeed, but it was deliberately intended for the Gentiles as well, where it would replace the ancient and inveterate error of pantheism. He stood fully and completely in the line of Moses and all the earlier prophets in upholding the original call of Abraham to come out from among the pagans with their idolatry. He was at one with them in his practice of personal prayer, the Ten Commandments, and the Jewish ritual of sacraments and sacrifice. For him, the one he called "My Father" was the heavenly Father, the absolute and almighty Supreme Being, the intelligent, loving, and provident Creator. "Your Father, who sees all that is done in secret, will reward you" (Mt 6:6). "I am telling you not to worry about your life . . . look at the birds in the sky. They do not sow or reap or gather into barns; yet your heavenly Father feeds them" (Mt 6:26).

This has a quite different sound from the teachings in the Gentile philosophical schools at Athens and Rome. It is in the line of the prophets. Jesus' followers looked upon him as speaking from the prophetic light, just as the Jews believed about Moses and the earlier prophets. Jesus' religious teaching about God, however, does indeed contact philosophy, for, as Aristotle taught, philosophy is the natural knowledge of God, the science that either affirms or denies this knowledge and attempts to state the reasons for one or the other. Hence one must single out this theistic dimension of Jesus' teaching in order to sketch the full background for the emergence of Christian Philosophy as a new and distinct kind of philosophy.

Jesus was not much given to arguing and debating on the level of natural reason. He simply presented his teaching as one who sees its truth and states it with outright authority. This too pleased his Jewish hearers, who recognized it as further evidence that he stood in the line of the prophets.

The distinguishing feature of his teaching, the one that has characterized his followers across the intervening Christian centuries to the present day, is the doctrine of the Trinity of Divine Persons in the one unique Godhead of Yahweh. "You must believe me when I say that I am in the Father and the Father is in me" (Jn 14:10). "The Holy Spirit, whom the Father will send in my name, will teach you everything and remind you of all I have said to you" (Jn 14:26).

How did his Jewish followers receive this teaching? They accepted it as a mystery beyond the full understanding of human intelligence, a truth received by faith in a revelation from a higher order coming to the human mind by the prophetic word spoken out of the higher light, the prophetic light. Jesus' followers took his teaching to mean that there is absolutely only one God, on the one hand, and that there are three equal Persons in God, on the other hand, each really distinct from each other: the Father, the Son, and the Holy Spirit. They could not and did not fully understand on the level of human reason how the three Divine

Persons, although really distinct, are only one God. This kind of revealed truth is called a mystery. Thus Jesus' followers came to realize that there is a twofold order of knowledge, distinct not only in origin but also in object. These two orders are distinct in origin because in one knowledge derives from natural reason, while in the other it derives from divine faith, namely, from the acceptance of the prophetic word. They are distinct in object, because in addition to what natural or philosophical reason can attain, the second and higher order of knowledge teaches for human belief a set of mysteries, namely, truths that cannot be known unless God reveals them.

The doctrine of Jesus, therefore, is theistic through and through. It supposes from its beginning to its end the real existence of the transcendent and personal Supreme Being distinct from the cosmos, able to speak through his prophets, whom he calls to this mission, and using their human discourse to communicate the word of God. Jesus' teaching stands fully in this perspective of Moses and the prophets, even more so because of the dimension of fulfillment. The more his followers absorbed this teaching on the three distinct and equally Divine Persons in Yahweh, the more it dawned upon them that Jesus was indeed that mysterious figure whom the earlier prophets had foreseen and had called *Emmanuel*, the Hebrew word meaning "God-with-us".

Where can philosophy possibly fit into this teaching? Jesus' followers will explain that faith in the prophetic word is a knowledge of truths above reason. But this does not mean that they have to disagree with reason, for the God who reveals mysteries through the prophetic light is the same who placed the light of reason in the human mind when he created it. In the pantheistic reduction of the concept of God, none of this makes sense. But if the transcendent and intelligent Person exists above and beyond the cosmos, then the possibilities are quite different. In any case, Jesus is at one with Moses in his teaching on the transcendence of the Supreme Being.

It is significant that Jesus' teaching on the three Persons in the one Godhead of Yahweh took place entirely within the Jewish people. It has nothing in common with the polytheism of the pagan Gentiles. There was a certain predisposition from Moses and the prophets to give a hearing to Jesus' teaching about this newly revealed inner life of Yahweh. A common name for God in Hebrew was *Elohim,* a plural. In Genesis 1:26, "God said, 'Let us make man in our own image.' " Many similar instances are to be found in the Hebrew Scriptures, which prepared the way for Jesus' followers to recognize in them a preparatory hint of their Rabbi's teaching.

Jesus was very practical. He insisted on personal conversion to this God he was revealing in final fashion. He confronted each person with the doctrine of the two ways and expected a personal choice of the way of life. Then he taught his followers how to have confidence in taking it up, by linking the conversion with faith in the triune God of his revelation. In relationship to God the Father he formed his disciples and followers by his word and by his example, in personal prayer. For prayer is the language of creaturehood: prayer is the creature's recognition of dependence upon the Creator in the very order of existence. Prayer presupposes the intelligent, all-powerful personal Supreme Being. Pantheism can and does offer a rationale for magical practices, but pantheists as such do not pray. In relationship to God the Son, Jesus attached his followers to his own Person, giving them an example to imitate and saying to them, "I am the Way, the Truth, and the Life" (Jn 14:6), and, "If you love me you will keep my commandments" (Jn 14:14). These are the Ten Commandments of Moses, fulfilled with his new motive of love for God and neighbor. In relationship to God the Holy Spirit, Jesus taught his followers that he intended to send this third Divine Person to each of them personally as a special gift through the sacraments, which he gave to his Church. Thus he built confidence into the human heart for taking up the rigors of the moral life. He intended to send this Divine Person as the Spirit of truth to support the worldwide teaching program he was projecting, as the Spirit of supernatural life to animate the sacraments of his religion, and as the Spirit of holiness to sustain the practice of prayer and gospel morality in his Church.

Jesus' Apostles and Their Worldwide Mission

Jesus the Teacher was preparing his Jewish disciples for their mission to the Gentiles, itself long foretold by the prophets and expected as an integral part of the Messianic age. In doing so, however, he came into serious conflict and confrontation with many other rabbis and especially with the official Jewish government at Jerusalem. The reason was the set of national customs and traditions that had grown up in the centuries since Moses as a very natural and human effort to secure Abraham's call to come out from the idolatrous Gentiles, to be different, and to guard against any participation in their pagan religious practices. The divine revelation given to the Hebrews through Moses, so Jesus taught, had become encrusted within an intricate set of merely human traditions: regulations, practices, and customs that constituted a simply human and national way of earthly life. This was natural and understandable, indeed, and it had served God's purposes in its time. But the time of the preparation was over. The Messianic age was opening. Its chief feature was to be the outward extension of the revelation as a light to the Gentiles. This would remove the religious barrier between Jew and Gentile by removing from the Gentiles their ancient and inveterate idolatry. The Gentiles would stream to Jerusalem, as Isaiah foresaw it and expressed it poetically, leaving their idols behind, and coming to the knowledge and worship of Yahweh.

The clash with Jewish officialdom, witnessed in all the documents, was direct and fierce. Basically it turned about a fundamental point in Jesus' teaching. There was a central question that recurs constantly in the documents. "Who do men say that I am?" Then, very pointedly he puts this question of his personal identity to his Twelve: " 'But you', he said, 'who do you say I am?' Then Simon Peter spoke up, 'You are the Messiah', he said, 'the Son of the living God' " (Mt 16:16–18). There are many instances in which Jesus of Nazareth is reported as using the divine name, the I AM revealed to Moses, which Jews to the present hesitate to use or to put into print, in reference to himself. Obviously philosophy is involved in this drama, because the name I AM bears upon existence as such and in its source: all of this points forward to Christian Philosophy as a future reality on the philosophical landscape. But to return to the scene. These instances were most arresting to his Jewish hearers. Some gave him a hearing. Others could not believe their ears. "He has blasphemed", they said. But they understood him clearly. Some thought him deserving of death. Others made Peter's confession their own. Indeed, Peter's confession became the touchstone of the following of Christ and of the baptismal faith of the Church into which he organized his followers.

The clash with the official government and structure of the Jewish people, therefore, was very real, and it turned upon the most fundamental issue one can imagine. It led to the arrest of Jesus by night with the help of betrayal, for he was not easy to seize due to his widespread popular support. He was crucified on a Passover festival, died, and was buried.

What the authorities deemed the end of the matter proved to be actually its beginning. Jesus fulfilled Moses and the prophets in final fashion by turning his crucifixion into his own offering of himself in sacrifice to God his Father as a redemption for the sins of all mankind. This sealed by his blood the New Covenant between God and man, which Moses and the prophets had foreseen and for which they had taught the Hebrews to prepare. As Moses refounded the sacrifices of the firstfruits common to all mankind throughout all places and times, so Jesus refounded the Jewish sacrificial worship, soon to end in 70 A.D. when the Romans destroyed the Temple at Jerusalem.

This refounding of the age-old worship by sacrifice, a concept and a ritual practice so difficult for the human sciences to explain and for philosophy to interpret, makes Jesus one of the primary religious teachers and founders of universal history. The Crucifixion came to have a new meaning for his followers, who immediately saw it as the new Sacrifice that brings spiritual redemption or liberation from sin and guilt. Thus the teaching program of Jesus is completed. There is now a new religion established by a New Testament, to be carried out to the Gentile peoples. This fulfills Isaiah, Jeremiah, Malachi, and all the prophets. It is to be carried out by a set of new teaching priests, replacing the Aaronic priesthood of Moses. These priests are Jesus' own twelve specially trained disciples, ordained into his own priesthood by himself at the Last Supper, which was the beginning of his offering. As he ordained them, so they ordained successors as time went on and the program extended beyond Palestine. His followers saw this as the fulfillment of Moses and the prophets, especially the prophet Malachi.

This scene, the gathering of human groups about an altar to worship God by offering a victim in sacrifice to him, is perhaps the most significant as well as the most universal in the panorama of human history. There is the puzzling world-wide fact of the simple offering of the firstfruits of hunting and gathering by the absolute primitives, whether contemporary or at human beginnings. Then untold centuries later there is the figure of the Aaronic priest standing at the altar of the Temple in Jerusalem, with sword held high over the quivering Passover lamb before him. Similar scenes took place everywhere among the Gentiles, in all the historic cultures of mankind.

The scene changes with Jesus, not in the sense of removal but in that of fulfillment, by what the Germans call his *Umstiftung:* his refoundation of Moses' Passover sacrifice, offered now in bread and wine according to the order of that earlier Gentile priest Melchizedek. Jesus and his priests stand at altars, indeed, but now in every place. The sword held high over a visible and tangible lamb has been replaced by the twofold word that Jesus spoke at the Last Supper, a separate consecration of bread and wine, thus symbolizing sacramentally that actual separation of his body and blood during his Crucifixion. Thus he empowered his Church to offer everywhere in space over and over in time, drawing ever more persons into the oblation, the one unique Sacrifice of the New Testament.

Does this central action of mankind's religious life and history involve philosophy? It does indeed, and on two counts. First, sacrifice bears witness to creation, which turns about the concept of existence. Where existence is involved in itself, in its principles and in its source, philosophy cannot but be involved as well. Secondly, Christian Philosophy, when its time comes, will be a kind of philosophical thinking that is open to such questions regarding the existence of things, whether that of substances such as bread and wine, of persons like Jesus and his priests, or of the almighty power of the Creator who gives existence to things.

Thus this fundamental religious fact, Jesus' refoundation of the worship of God by sacrifice, is an important part of the background for the eventual emergence of Christian Philosophy as a mode of philosophizing within this particular religious faith. This background will be chiefly the teaching about the nature, attributes, and historical plan of Yahweh, the God of the Hebrews. But there will be the further matter of this new rite of sacrifice, which replaces in every place out among the Gentiles the animal sacrifices, which had been confined to the one place, the Temple at Jerusalem. This new rite, since it is a sacrifice in bread and wine according to the order of Melchizedek, visibly embraces the entire religious history of mankind back to the absolute primitives. But now it is a life-giving bread and a saving cup. For Jesus gave the supreme challenge for faith in God to his followers. They are challenged to take the revelation of Yahweh seriously in his almighty power, universal presence, and creative domination of the very principles of being by which things or substances such as bread and wine exist: their substantial being or reality and their accidents and appearances. The philosophical question raised by Socrates is involved: Is there a second and higher power in man that knows a reality in things beyond that which the senses perceive? Thus philosophy itself finds itself questioned, and out of the process of this questioning Christian Philosophy will emerge.

In any case, when Jesus, alive after his death, called his disciples together after the Crucifixion, forgave them their cowardice, and briefed them in final fashion for the Gentile mission, he placed in their hands this Sacrifice of the New Testament. It was exactly that *Umstiftung* mentioned above, the refounding of an institution universally visible in human history. From a memorial of the passage of the Hebrews out of bondage in Egypt, it now commemorates and accomplishes passage out of the old pagan way of living into the new way of life, understood as the Christian hope for the resurrection of the body, each redeemed person in his particular body, and life everlasting.

Jesus' disciples received all of this, his teaching given across the three years of intensive, full-time learning, and now the sudden turn of the redeeming Sacrifice and the sealing of the New Testament in the blood of Jesus as the very Lamb of God, as a precious treasure. It is to be handed on by a teaching that guards its purity and integrity. It is a teaching that centers upon him who is offered in this Sacrifice of the New Testament, for as all men everywhere have understood, there is no sacrifice unless the victim that is offered be really present. This concern for the purity and integrity of the teaching is the hallmark of the apostolic succession, which projects Jesus' Church out among the Gentiles and into the future. "O Timothy," Apostle Paul admonishes his own ordained successor, "guard the deposit!" (1 Tim 6:20). This guarding is done by a teaching that hands on faithfully what Jesus gave to his Twelve Apostles by his own teaching.

V

THE TEACHING CHURCH

This concept of a deposit of teaching to be handed on by teaching, by a teaching that guards its purity and integrity, is absolutely basic to original Christianity as it came from Jesus, the founder of Christianity. In this respect it was no different from the Hebrew religion from which it proceeded. It was, rather, the continuation and fulfillment of the same attitude that is fundamental to prophetic religion: "We accept this teaching for what it really is, God's message and not some human thinking", as St. Paul says of the Thessalonians (see 1 Th 2:13). The teaching program of Christianity was quite different from that of the schools of philosophy, and the early Christians were very aware of this fact. It was a teaching that communicated knowledge shining from the prophetic light, in the standard pattern of the Hebrews, to education and culture, to personal and social life.

"A Light to the Gentiles"

Jesus' teaching, then, is on deposit with the Apostles and their ordained successors, called "bishops", from the Greek word meaning the "priestly overseers", of each community that the formative teaching brought into being. It is not something inert, like a piece of gold or silver deposited in a bank vault, but a living teaching given by living teachers to living learners called "catechumens", from "catechesis", the specially chosen Greek word for "oral teaching". And hence the depository of Jesus' teaching came to be known throughout the early Church as the catechumenate. Bishops were in charge wherever Christian communities were established among the Gentile pagans, and they built up their groups of Christians by means of this catechetical teaching program, which they supervised personally as their primary responsibility.

Forty years after Jesus' Crucifixion, in 70 A.D., a devastating event overtook the Jewish nation and religion. The Romans laid siege to Jerusalem, destroyed the Temple, and scattered the Jews among the nations. In the ensuing decades a double set of facts emerges to dominate the landscape of Western mankind. On the one hand, the Jewish priesthood disappears and the animal sacrifices offered at the one place, Jerusalem, cease. On the other hand, spreading from people to people of the Roman Empire, the Catholic priesthood emerges into view offering in every place the new Sacrifice, which had been instituted by Jesus Christ according to the order

67

of Melchizedek in the manner described above. The entire teaching program centers upon this Sacrifice, for the people of each community becomes a unified group by participation in the offering of it.

It is a teaching Church that emerges into ever greater visibility in the first five centuries, as the documents accumulate, and especially as the voluminous writings of the Fathers of the Church, a group of well-educated early priests and bishops, were published. From Jesus' initial mandate, "Going, teach all nations, baptizing them" (see Mt 28:16–20), the apostolic Church is everywhere a teaching Church. It has always and everywhere one and the same doctrine and pattern in its Catechumenate. It teaches the same original profession of the trinitarian faith in Yahweh, the one God of the Hebrews, which the Apostles learned from Jesus, whom this early Church now reveres as the Divine Teacher. It is a practical teaching, which helps the catechumens in their personal conversion to this God of revelation. It is the way of life, a real and vital conversion expressed by prayer, gospel morality, and sacramental living. The elements of this teaching were the same for all comers, whether unlettered slaves, persons polished and cultivated by the seven arts, or the children of converts. These elements contained the precious content of Jesus' deposit. They were carried forward in the standard way of those times long before the invention of printing, by four compact, easily remembered outlines that functioned as syllabi: The twelve Articles of Faith in the Apostles' Creed, the seven sacraments, the Ten Commandments, and the seven Petitions of Jesus' prayer, the Our Father. The people accepted this teaching and its new way of life as a revealed doctrine coming from above the level of the schools of philosophy in the ambient culture of the pagan Roman Empire.

It is difficult from the distance of the late twentieth century to realize the challenge that this teaching Church put to the degenerate pagan culture and personally to the pagan Gentiles immersed in the immoral practices and pansexism of ancient idolatry. Perhaps one can sense the nature of the teaching and the confrontation it entailed from these words of Paul, addressed to a group of his converts from paganism at Thessalonica (see 1 Th 4:1–8):

> Brothers, we urge you and appeal to you in the Lord Jesus to make more and more progress in the kind of life that you are meant to live: the life that God wants, as you learned from us, and as you are already living it. You have not forgotten the instructions we gave you on the authority of the Lord Jesus. What God wants is for you all to be holy. He wants you to keep away from fornication, and each one of you to know how to use the body that belongs to him in a way that is holy and honorable, not giving way to selfish lust like the pagans who do not know God. . . . The Lord always punishes sins . . . , as we told you before and assured you. We have been called by God to be holy, not to be immoral; in other words, anyone who objects is not objecting to a human authority, but to God, who gives you his Holy Spirit.

It would be difficult to put the contrast with the religious condition of the idolatrous Gentiles more starkly. Yet the new religion made progress, even rapidly, and in the face of determined efforts by the imperial Roman government to stamp it out by violence. From the Fathers of the Church through all the Christian teachers down to the times of Thomas Aquinas nearly a thousand years later this conversion of the pagan Gentile peoples was looked upon as a moral miracle, something beyond the condition of human nature, either on the part of the pagans who entered this Church by taking the course of instruction in the Catechumenate or on the part of the persons who carried the Church out of Palestine. For Jesus' original Apostles were not men of higher education. When he called them to that full-time discipleship, they were men of the Jewish working class, mostly fishermen, who had the basic elementary education of the synagogue schools, but no more. Even the Jews recognized this in one of their own early efforts, shortly after the Crucifixion, to stifle the movement at its inception. "They were astonished at the assurance shown by Peter and John", Luke records, "considering they were uneducated laymen" (Acts 4:13). It was a teaching from a different source and on a different plane. Yet it drew up its battle line, as John Chrysostom puts it in the fourth century, before the whole world of the classical pagan culture and launched the conquest of it. Christian teachers explained the remarkable phenomenon by the presence and power of God, which sustained the conversion of the persons gathered about the altars of the Sacrifice of the New Testament. For, to repeat, all the teaching centered here and upon personal participation in the Sacrifice according to the order of Melchizedek, the refounded sacrifice in bread and wine, which summarizes wonderfully the religious life and history of mankind, now a life-giving Bread and a saving Cup.

It is of course beyond the scope of this approach to Christian Philosophy even to summarize this teaching. But there is no need to do so. The contact with philosophy, frequent in the case of persons educated in the schools of philosophy who came to the Catechumenate, took place in the very beginning of the instructions, in the explanation of the First Article of the Apostles' Creed. The contact with philosophy is contained in those words that summarize the Hebrew *Shema* and the Jewish religion: "I believe in God, the Father Almighty, Creator of heaven and earth." It is in the explanatory teaching of this article in the Catechumenate that Christian Philosophy takes its origin and in which its specific nature as philosophy first becomes visible. One must turn, accordingly, to the kind of teaching about God that was given to the Gentiles as the foundation and the first step in that wonderful transformation of the depraved world of pagan culture, steeped in the inveterate error with its permissive idolatry.

The Church Continues Jesus' Teaching Program

There is a wealth of documentation on the way the Church continued Jesus' teaching program. It followed "a beaten track", as Augustine terms it in his treatise *The First Catechetical Instruction.* All comers were prepared for baptism into the Christian way of life by this beaten track, namely, a traditional pattern of teaching that began with the elements proper to children. Every teaching program has an elementary level upon which the secondary and higher levels are built. So too Jesus' program. It was the same for all, whatever their background. Jesus himself had stressed that no one enters except by the way proper to children. One should bear in mind, furthermore, that the Gentiles were simply immersed in the ambient culture of pantheistic religiosity. The ancient error had generated a mentality that infected everyone, whether educated or devoid of education, whether adult or the Christian children growing up in a pagan atmosphere. The Church had to start where the people were: with the loss of the concept of the transcendent God, with the consequent loss of the doctrine of creation and the sense of creaturehood.

Catechesis, then, the ordinary and universal teaching for every pagan upon entering, begins by teaching the doctrine of creation. Everywhere the Gentiles are learning that God created us. We humans are his creatures. He is our Creator.

This is a direct confrontation with the ancient and inveterate error. It establishes the true concept of God forthrightly, without ambiguity, and at the very beginning. The catechumens from the ambient paganism were given a teaching that no school of pagan philosophy had been able to attain, not even those of Socrates, Plato, and Aristotle. Yet the Christian teachers gave it as the beginning of their teaching, easily and as a matter of course. They taught it in one and the same way, in its elements, to everyone who applied for the first catechetical instruction: slaves totally illiterate, the multitudes of uneducated freedmen, the children. Candidates for baptism who had been educated in the liberal arts were the exception, not the rule. Universal education, of course, did not exist at that time.

The mode of the teaching, furthermore, is not a philosophical one. It is a teaching given with authority. It is explained, and the reasonable questions and difficulties of human reason are addressed, but the doctrine itself is not presented as something to achieve by rational procedures and philosophical discussion. The mode is that of the Hebrews, not that of the Greeks. It is the handing on of truths received from the prophetic light. Creation, the Creator, and creaturehood were taught as truths given to mankind from above, through Jesus' fulfillment of Moses and the prophets.

The teaching illuminates and transforms the mentality of the pagan convert. No place is left for pantheism in any form. Hence no place remains for the pagan religiosity. The convert turns away from the idols, the superstitions, the magical practices, the furnaces of Moloch, from all the perversions of religiosity, and turns to Yahweh, the God of the Hebrew revelation fulfilled in Jesus. In the conversion to this God, the convert begins to be a person of prayer in an entirely new way, different from the verbalisms and perfunctory civil recitals of paganism. Prayer is the very language of a creature as such, the very expression of creaturehood. In order to become persons of prayer, the converts had to learn the attributes of the Creator. If they are taught these attributes and qualities of the Supreme Being, so the Christian teachers were convinced, then the attitude of prayerfulness will arise of itself as the natural product of the teaching, and all the other aspects and practices of the conversion to the new new way of life will follow.

The catechetical teaching, then, always, and everywhere, following its beaten track, began with the doctrine of creation. Who made us? God made us. Why did God make you? And the purpose of human existence is stated and explained. How could God make heaven and earth and all things, including you and me? Because he is "the Almighty"—that name for God that the Hebrews commonly used. At this point the teaching immediately opens up and branches out, with highly personalized and animated discussion out of each convert's background. For example, what does one mean by the word "God"? The teaching explained that this means the Supreme Reality, intelligent, distinct from the cosmos, the one and unique all-perfect Being who is the Creator and Lord of heaven and earth. What does "all-perfect" mean? Immediately another branching opens for the teaching. The Christian teachers had their answer ready. It means that every perfection seen in the cosmos, everything in the cosmos that makes it good, attractive, and beautiful, is to be found in the Creator, but far more perfectly, with complete perfection in a way proper to his majesty, greatness, and divinity. Above all, no perfection in him has any defect of any kind, and especially no perfection in him has any limitation. He is the unlimited Reality, "infinite"; if the convert were a Roman speaking Latin: "without limit".

Then the teaching always took up the concept of creation in detail. It means that the Supreme Being gives existence to all other things. He made all other things out of nothing. Where nothing was, he gives existence, calls into existence. In this he is unique, for all making of things by man presupposes a material that is used: wood, cotton, clay, or whatever. Hence human beings cannot imagine the process of creation, for they never see it taking place. But they can understand that it does indeed take place, for otherwise things would still be nothing. It is clear that there is an emphasis on existence in the Christian teaching about God the Creator, an emphasis that will play an essential role in the nature and specificity of the Christian Philosophy yet to come.

Then the teaching explains that this all-perfect personal and intelligent Creator was under no necessity in creating. He made his creatures to be because he wanted them to be. This provides the Christian teachers with the foundation for commenting on the Christian revelation, contained in the writings of those who studied under Jesus, that God is love (see 1 Jn 4:16), and for teaching the doctrine of the redeeming Sacrifice of the Cross. Directly linked is the next logical step, the Lordship of the Supreme Being over his creatures. Because he is a Pure Spirit, because he always was and always will be, because he is everywhere and thus immediately and equally present to each of his creatures, he takes care of them, indeed easily, for his power to do so is unlimited. This is called God's Providence: he provides for his creatures as a father on earth provides for his children. God takes care of his creatures in a way proper to himself, namely, in a way including but also far transcending the food, clothing, and shelter needed for earthly life. As one would expect of an intelligent Creator, he provides special help for his rational creatures: he guides them and teaches them so that they can cooperate with him in achieving the purpose he had in mind when he created them. This is the providential care that rational creatures need most, for to miss this purpose is to go astray and to fail in the very order of existence.

The question always came up in the course of this teaching: Why did God create me? The answer again was forthright, and it was taught with authority: God made me to know him, to love him, and to serve him in this world, so as to be happy with him forever in the world to come.

Again the branching in this oral teaching. The world to come: an immense subject, and one that inspires many more questions. Is this what people mean by heaven? What of our bodies? In heaven will we know each other? This ordinary and universal teaching of the Hebrew-Christian revelation had direct and positive answers to all such questions. The contrast with the tentative groping of the philosophers at best, or with their studied skepticism at worst, is easy to see.

Children at the age of seven received a teaching beyond anything in the schools of philosophy. For example, the children of the converted Gentile peoples are now being taught that God does not have a body, for he is a perfectly Pure Spirit. Thus materialism as a basic outlook on life is precluded from the first dawn of reason. Then the question that agitates so many: How do we find God? This question had a ready answer, which the children learned: God is everywhere. Does this mean that God is where you are? Indeed. Does it mean that God is where your father is, away on business? Indeed. If God then is everywhere, and always everywhere, and is where you are, does he see and know you? Indeed. God knows all things, even our thoughts. To think otherwise would be an obvious failure in our concept of him, imposing a limit upon him. In this way, handing on the heritage of revealed teaching about God, the Christian teachers laid the foundation in the children for a new kind of personal spiritual life based on the sense of responsibility in every human act toward the Supreme Being, our Creator and Judge, who is everywhere, knows everything, and sees everything. This is the beginning of wisdom, the Christian teachers knew, for it begets a holy fear of God, but one immediately tempered by the teaching on God's goodness in creating and especially by the teaching on the redemption. Thus the formation of children was based from the very outset upon extremely fundamental convictions, rocklike foundation stones to stand on permanently throughout their lives.

The ever-present stumbling block for the schools of philosophy, the question and the problem of evil in the world, was not avoided by Christian teachers. The confrontation with sin and evil took place at this same beginning of childhood. If God can do all things, then can he do something evil? No, he cannot, for his goodness is absolutely unlimited, without any shadow of stain. God is absolutely innocent of all evil. How does it happen, then, that one finds evil in the world? It results from sin on the part of creatures. God creates his rational creatures with freedom to choose him in the way of life, rejecting the way of death. But when creatures choose wrongly, committing sins, God tolerates the evil they do and brings good out of it by his wisdom and power.

Thus the catechumen, the adult convert from the ambient paganism, and the children of the converts are confronted with the world of free decision, of merit and demerit. Who merits heaven? Every good person who serves God. What of the wicked, persons who choose the other way, who refuse to serve God? At this point the Christian teachers explain the four last things that the prophetic word reveals to mankind: death, judgment, heaven, and hell. How was hell explained? As a part of personal responsibility to the Creator, as a part of the doctrine of merit. Hell is something merited by the creature. It results from failure in the order of the Creator's purpose in creating human beings. Hence sin produces an eternal suffering of remorse for this failure, which each one could have avoided; coupled with the remorse there is to be some kind of suffering of fire. Mysterious. But the prophetic word, confirmed by Jesus over and over, always confronted men with this matter of the choice between the ways, a choice with everlasting consequences. Thus the Catechumenate taught.

The teaching, it is clear, was an introduction into the moral order. God is infinite justice, along with his infinite goodness and knowledge and power. We live in a moral universe, one constituted by these responsible decisions. The Christian teachers were not in the least afraid to go directly to the heart of the matter regarding human existence, with the children just as with adult converts, because they were doing so in the context of confidence and trust in the goodness of the Supreme Being. The Catechumenate was a school of the love of God based both on the doctrine of creation and on the doctrine of redemption.

The schools of philosophy, even at their best, were unable to achieve this concept of the transcendent God, the Creator and Judge present everywhere to each creature. Christian Philosophy, when it is finally elaborated as a body of teaching on the rational level, will be able to achieve the concept of the metaphysical necessity of the presence of the First Cause to sustain all created existences in being. But even here there will be a striking contrast of philosophy with the prophetic word, which teaches children these truths with both ease and authority: for philosophy achieves such insights only with great labor and after long and arduous study.

The Catechumenate, then, is a teaching of the revealed concept of God, proper to the Hebrews, and fulfilled in Jesus' teaching. It goes forth from Jerusalem and passes to the Gentiles, immersed in the darkness of the ancient error and its idolatries. It is the light of Abraham's blessing for them: it illuminates them and makes them baptized Christian peoples.

The Expansion of Christianity

It would be difficult to overemphasize the relative quickness with which this teaching program spread to all the peoples who had been gathered into the vast administrative unity of the Roman Empire, which had absorbed into itself the earlier empires of Babylon, Persia, and Alexander's Greece. All the peoples, with one striking exception: the fractured and scattered Jews, a few individual converts apart, remained aloof as a people and continued to conduct a shadowy national life. They did this by gathering about their rabbis in their synagogues. The Jewish sacrifices had ceased, of course, but the synagogues continued as focal points of Jewish national identity for prayer, study, and the schooling of the young.

The Christian enterprise of teaching was remarkably extensive, covering the entire empire and even going beyond its boundaries. At the same time it was remarkably unified, for it took great care to add or subtract nothing from the original deposit that Jesus had placed in trust with his Apostles when he taught them and sent them. In this too the Church was fulfilling the principles that had guided the Hebrews in teaching the Torah, which had been given to Moses.

This vast turning of the pagans of the Roman Empire away from their idols and to the God of the Hebrews is one of the most remarkable and visible facts of universal history. The Gentile pagans literally streamed into this Church. The more pagan Rome declared the Christians illicit—*non licet vos esse,* as the imperial decrees stated: it is not allowed to you even to exist—the more the pagans continued to enter the Church. From the court proceedings that condemned the "martyrs", Greek for "witnesses", for this religious Faith, and from the many eyewitness accounts of their firmness under torture and attitude in dying for their religion, it is clear that the pagans became more and more interested in a doctrine that had such results. The point frequently overlooked is that the pagans could not simply flock as such into the Church, with some kind of mass sprinkling, as it were, and a mere formality of nominal registration. Each pagan adult was required to take the regular course of instruction in the standard pattern and content noted above as coming from Jesus to his Apostles. The program included a period of probation and with scrutinies on the manner of life of the candidates and testimonials from their friends who were already Christians. The physical magnitude of this program boggles the modern mind. It dawns that Jesus Christ was indeed a teacher on a scale never hitherto matched. It was simply his program carried on under the supervision of the bishops, who had succeeded Jesus' Twelve Apostles, with the help of the priests, deacons, and cadres of catechetical teachers in every place where the Church was organized. In fact, the principles of this supervision and fidelity to the deposit of faith were an explicit criterion for ordination.

The nature and the magnitude of this Christian program of teaching for initiation into Church membership does not come home to minds of today until its substance is projected onto the panorama of universal history. This substance can be summarized briefly as follows. First and foremost, it taught the pagan Gentiles that God is a Pure Spirit, transcendent, distinct from the cosmos, an intelligent Person. This Supreme Being is the Creator of all things, of heaven and earth, and of every kind of living thing on earth, especially mankind. The Creator is good and kind: he is the heavenly Father. He imprints his law on the natures he creates, and when the created nature is a rational one, this law is the moral law, entailing responsibility on the part of man and a coming judgment on the part of the Divine Creator.

It is obvious that this new teaching is remarkably like the religions of the absolute primitives. Living in the mainstream of culture descending through historic times since about 4000 B.C., the peoples of the Roman Empire had no idea that these primitives existed. The Romans had no contact with them, for they lived in remote margins of the continental land masses utterly beyond the reach of the Romans. Contemporary philosophical reflection and analysis, however, after the Copernican revolution and its discovery of the religion of the contemporary absolute primitives, cannot ignore so striking a correspondence in the facts as given. It is a point that will be considered more amply later.

It is important to recognize the existence of this teaching program, which emerged from Jerusalem and Palestine, its surprising success, and its rather awesome unity, day in and day out across all the centuries of the early Church. It is a very ordinary teaching program, carried on universally.

It was ordinary in another sense, in that it did not proceed on the level and in the mode of the educational system of the pagan Gentiles. The Greek and Roman *Paideia* was a thing apart, reserved for the small elite of the imperial governing class. This new teaching program admitted all men without distinction: men and women; rich and poor; slave and free; Roman, Greek, and barbarian. If an educated Roman wished to enter, he bowed his cultivated head and took the same course of instructions as all the rest, with the same elements of the teaching in the same beaten track: beaten since the Apostles.

Basically, then, it is a teaching that gives the self-revelation of the Hebrew God as a light to the Gentiles. The Hebrews had learned the attributes of Yahweh from their prayer book, the book of Psalms. When the Gentiles entered this universal Church, learning to pray with it and to take part in the offering of its Sacrifice, they found themselves using that same book of Psalms. Every attribute of the Supreme Being, every aspect of the substance of the teaching summarized above, is found in the Psalms over and over, expressed with utmost clarity and great beauty. Yahweh is the transcendent Pure Spirit, the Father Almighty, Creator of heaven and earth. This does away with pantheism at one stroke. The ancient and inveterate error disappears. And not by philosophy, so to speak, for the mode of the teaching is different, unique. This doctrine of God is not taught as a philosophy, a human doctrine elaborated by human intelligence with reasons and arguments. It is taught with authority, taught as the very word of God in his self-revelation, and received as such. This is the mode of prophetic teaching, with a content coming from the prophetic light. It does not use the polished discourse of the educated classes of the Roman Empire. It uses fishermen's language, so to speak, in a way that presupposes that the intellectual pride of the educated will be set aside as one of the basic conditions for entering the Church and enrolling for its Catechumenate. With this, then, the background is sketched against which and out of which Christian Philosophy emerges as a new and different kind of philosophy, yet authentic as philosophy from every point of view. It remains to examine its origin, its nature, and its relationship to the Western cultural tradition.

VI

THE PATRISTIC ORIGIN OF CHRISTIAN PHILOSOPHY

Among the converts to the Catholic Church, mostly persons of the lower classes and even slaves, were nevertheless a significant number of well-educated pagans and even some professional philosophers. The earliest example was the philosopher Justin, known to Christians today as St. Justin Martyr. He was put to death at Rome about 165 A.D. in the great persecutions. The official acts of his trial and condemnation because of professing the Christian Faith have survived. His parents were well-to-do Roman citizens whose family had come as colonists to Flavia Neapolis, the Nablus of today in Palestine, a Roman city built when the legions under Vespasian and Titus were reducing Jerusalem and destroying its majestic Temple. Recognizing talent in their son, Justin's parents gave him the full education into the pagan culture of Greece and Rome. After thorough grounding in the seven arts, Justin traveled widely, frequenting the various schools of philosophy, the Stoics, the Peripatetics, and the Platonists, for philosophy had become his great love. He quickly dropped the Materialists and the Sophists, with their reduction of the human mode to only one kind of knowledge, that of the senses. He describes his quest for a truth beyond the senses, going from teacher to teacher and school to school, never satisfied. "In a troubled state of mind," he writes in his *Dialogue with Trypho* (Chapter 2),

> the thought occurred to me to consult the Platonists, whose reputation was great. Thus it happened that I spent as much time as possible in the company of a wise man who was highly esteemed by the Platonists and who had but recently arrived in our city. Under him I forged ahead in philosophy and day by day I improved. The perception of incorporeal things quite overwhelmed me and the Platonic theory of ideas added wings to my mind, so that in a short time I imagined myself a wise man. So great was my folly that I fully expected immediately to gaze upon God, for this is the goal of Plato's philosophy.

St. Justin Martyr: The First Christian Philosopher

Justin completed his studies with what today would be called the Ph.D. with a major in philosophy. He was now a professional philosopher, entitled to wear the philosopher's stole, a scarf or neckband designed to bear public witness to the calling of the philosopher, as different stoles would witness to the physician or other professional callings. Not being able so quickly to gaze upon God, Justin continued his remarkable quest for that truth that is God, or, rather, who is God. It happened that he fell in with a Jew who introduced him to the Hebrew prophets. He studied them avidly. They led him to Jesus Christ. Justin asked for baptism into the Catholic Church and took the course of instructions in the Catechumenate. After his baptism he went to Rome, where he opened his own philosophical school in the standard pattern of the time; but it was a school dedicated to the teaching and propagation of the Christian Faith on the level of higher studies, teaching about it and defending it in the accepted mode of philosophical studies.

Was Justin still a philosopher? In his own mind there was no doubt or hesitation, for he continued to wear that philosopher's stole, the pallium that denoted the professionally qualified graduate of the schools of philosophy. Justin was not alone in this public profession of philosophy after baptism as an instructed and professed Christian, for Aristides of Athens did the same after becoming a Christian, and Heracles of Alexandria likewise, even after he became a priest and then the bishop of Alexandria. Apparently Justin proceeded quietly at Rome, for he seems to have conducted his school for some years, having at least one other Father of the Church, Tatian, among his students. The inevitable day came, however, when his activities were reported to the Roman police; he was arrested, his school was terminated, and his trial took place.

In a sense Christian Philosophy begins with Justin Martyr. It began whenever an educated pagan turned to God in Christ, and especially when that pagan had been trained in the schools of philosophy as such. Most of the Fathers of the Church were well-educated converts from the pagan education and knew its philosophies well. One need but think of Tertullian, the Roman lawyer, or Cyprian, or Chrysostom, or Ambrose, the imperial administrator who became a priest, then the bishop of Milan who supervised the Catechumenate in which one day Augustine came to enroll in preparation for his own baptism. There was thinking about God within the Catholic Faith whenever the First Article of the Apostles' Creed was taught and explained. Christian Philosophy was in gestation, so to speak, or in its aurora during all the instruction of converts from paganism in these centuries of the early Church and its Catechumenate.

St. Cyprian of Carthage

A direct practical consequence of this teaching of the revealed concept of the transcendent personal God was a full course of catechetical instruction on the conversion to God by taking up the life of the sacraments, the Commandments, and personal prayer. The conversion was no vague and sentimental matter, but a definite program for living that demanded practical knowledge on how to do it, so to speak. From many instances in the patristic literature, beyond the scope of this survey, Cyprian of Carthage offers one typical example, in both his person and his writings, which can stand for them all.

Cyprian, born probably at Carthage around 200 A.D. into a wealthy pagan family of the governing class, received the full standard education as a rhetorician and professional teacher of rhetoric. He became disgusted with the immorality that prevailed in private and public life, with its consequent corruption in government. Among his friends he counted a certain Catholic priest, from whom he learned of Christ's power, which liberated men from this sinfulness and set them as new creatures upon a higher way of life. Cyprian determined to devote himself to the study and practice of the Christian Faith. He became a priest himself and, already a public figure by family position and personal eloquence, was soon, about 248 A.D., elected bishop of Carthage. For ten difficult years he provided the local Church with leadership—difficult because the imperial persecutions of the Catholic Church, now an all-out war of extermination, were at their climax. Cyprian's writings give an insight into Christian leadership in the situation, both encouraging the confessors of the Faith in the face of martyrdom and denouncing those who lapsed when they were arrested and forced under court order to choose between worship of Rome's pagan gods or death by torture. Cyprian's turn came in 258 A.D. He practiced what he had been preaching and was steadfast until death for his faith in Christ.

In his years as a bishop he participated actively in the teaching program in the Catechumenate. His course of instructions *The Lord's Prayer* has survived as a Christian classic, one that illustrates the link between the explanations of the concept of God given in connection with the First Article of the Apostles' Creed and the teaching of prayer as a direct practical application of the concept.

Cyprian takes up this prayer phrase by phrase in the standard methodology of oral teaching, but because of his background he is able to record his work in polished Latin. Explaining the words "Thy Kingdom come", he writes: "Your Kingdom, O God, is in us. And let us bear in mind that there never was a time when God did not reign in his Kingdom. For we cannot ask when something began with him who always was and who never will cease to be." This is a concept of God that Cyprian did not learn from the schools of philosophy in the pagan academies. It is catechetical, not philosophical, handing on the self-revelation of God as the eternal reality, the transcendent Pure Spirit. Cyprian has the cultivated language that he learned as a youth in the pagan *Paideia,* but the content of his teaching comes from a different source, from the teaching program that had come forth from Jerusalem and is being given to the Gentiles. "All who pray", Cyprian continues,

should cultivate a spirit of quiet and proper decorum. When we go to our prayer, let us stop to think that we stand under the eye of God. Hence we must take care to proceed suitably, in a manner pleasing to the divine eyes—and this indeed both in our bodily posture and in our manner of speaking to the Supreme Being. In his teaching our Lord told us to pray in secret and indeed in hidden and remote places and even in our rooms with the door closed. For it is proper to the Catholic Faith that we should recognize the presence of God everywhere, that he hears every word we say and sees everything we do. The fullness of God's majesty is present in every distant and secret place. The Scriptures say, "I am a God who comes close to you and not a God who stands far away. If a man should hide himself in caves, would I not see him there? Do I not fill the very heavens and the earth?" All through the divine Scriptures we are taught that the eye of God is upon all men, both the good and the wicked.

Such was the teaching that was taking place everywhere in the Roman Empire, as the pagans turned from the idols of the ancient polytheism to the God who revealed himself to Moses in the divine name. "Who shall I say sent me? . . . I AM WHO AM. . . . Go, tell the Hebrews that HE WHO IS sent you." One must recall that exegesis explains the Hebrew root of this name as denoting the Source of existence for all existing things. The reason for the coming emphasis upon existence and the One who is its Source, rather than merely upon the forms of things in the cosmos, is clear to see in this kind of catechetical teaching. This will form the background for the emergence of Christian Philosophy, a way of philosophizing that has its attention drawn to existence by reflecting upon the Person who is existence itself, the fountainhead of all other existences. For all other existing realities participate in existence by free gift from this Person in the process called creation.

Christian Philosophy as such, however, has not yet appeared, although it is in its dawn. Before turning to its emergence into formal visibility as such, a glance should be given to Plotinus, founder of Neo-Platonism, the last great pagan school of philosophy, for two reasons. First, he illuminates the contrast between the pagan Classical Philosophy and the new Christian Philosophy as a qualitatively different kind of philosophy. Second, he does so exactly because of the relationship of his thought and its terminology to Augustine, the founder of Christian Philosophy. Hence, although he was encountered briefly above in his proper place among the pagan schools, it is worthwhile to look more closely at him and his teaching before going on to Augustine.

Plotinus: The Failure of Pagan Philosophy

Plotinus was born around 200 A.D. in Upper Egypt of parents able to give him the full education of the classical culture beginning with "the school of grammar" in childhood. He did higher studies in Alexandria, then the intellectual capital of the pagan world. Majoring in philosophy, he took up the love and practice and teaching of wisdom as his life work. In his late thirties he attached himself to a military expedition of the Roman emperor headed for the Far East, as he wished to obtain direct knowledge of the philosophy practiced in Persia and India. The emperor was assassinated in Babylonia, however, and the military venture came to nothing. Plotinus returned to Rome in 245 A.D., where he taught philosophy and directed the consciences and ways of life of many high in the government of the pagan Roman Empire until his death twenty-five years later. It is noteworthy that the fiercest persecutions of Christianity were raging throughout these years. Plotinus saw himself as a philosopher in support of the imperial religion and culture, dedicated to the renewal of the ancient paganism according to his interpretation of the mind and spirit of Plato. In fact, he planned with the Roman government to build a new and perfect city on the *Campagna* outside Rome modeled upon Plato's *Republic,* an enterprise that was never actually accomplished.

Disciples gathered around him, including especially Porphyry, who published his lectures, known today as the *Enneads,* and wrote his biography.

The professional teachers of the Greco-Roman *Paideia* and the specialists in the schools of philosophy had been hammering out for centuries a standard way of teaching basic philosophy, the science of being as being together with the principles and categories of beings as such, as seen in reality, the science of logic on the procedures of human reason in its processes of thinking and learning about reality, and the critical discussion of the other schools in what today would be called the history of philosophy. Thus, in the Fourth Tractate of the Second *Ennead,* Plotinus reports a common agreement on matter as a recipient of Form-Ideas. "Thus far", he says,

> all go the same way. But departure begins with the attempt to establish what this basic Kind is in itself, and how it is a recipient, and of what. To a certain school, body forms exclusively are the Real Beings; existence is limited to bodies; there is one only Matter, the stuff underlying the primal constituents of the universe: existence is nothing but this Matter: everything is some modification of this. . . . The school has even the audacity to foist Matter upon the divine beings so that, finally, God himself becomes a mode of Matter. . . . Another school makes it incorporeal. . . . We are obliged, therefore, at the start, both to establish the existence of this other Kind, and to examine its nature and the mode of its Being. . . . We discover these two — Matter and Idea — by sheer force of our reasoning.

Plotinus, then, is not a crass materialist. He recognizes the existence of the intelligibles and the corresponding intellectual power of knowing, distinct from the senses, which specifies the human mode of being. By his study of the forms and being of things, on the level of the science of being in itself and in its principles, what moderns call ontology, he intended to ascend to the higher order of intelligible reality, just as the Atomists, the Materialists, and the Skeptics did the same study to show the impossibility of such an ascent. There was thus a common academic substrate for philosophical discussion, this commonly taught basic or *Koine* philosophy. It was an eclectic tradition to which all the great philosophers, Aristotle as well as Plato, Zeno the Stoic as well as Sextus Empiricus, had contributed. It was this common philosophical patrimony that the Fathers of the Church had studied as young men, and that Augustine had not only studied but had also taught in his years as a professor of rhetoric in the pagan schools.

But what kind of ascent did Plotinus achieve? He reaches what he calls the "One", an impersonal One, not a *he* and not even an *it* because it is not a thing, not a being. He imagines it to be beyond being, that is, beyond anything that exists. Beings exist because they are emanations, or "outflows", to use Plotinus' constantly recurring word, from this ineffable One, this first principle that has no being. In plain language, fishermen's language, the language that expresses the natural metaphysics of mankind, such a first principle has no reality. If it is beyond being, it does not exist in reality but only as a concept in Plotinus' mind. Thus Plotinus begins with a violation of the principle of contradiction and can build only an artificial mental construct, a speculation in the mode of the Gnostics of his day, who were mixing Christianity with the philosophies and religious mythologies of the pagan culture.

The One accordingly is not a person, not a Supreme Being to whom his creatures are responsible, for in Plotinus there is no doctrine of creation. It is all a speculative and artificial construct made by the imagination asserting a mythical imagery with regard to the cosmos. The beings seen in the cosmos are simply there as a result of this everlasting outflow. One may take them, enjoy them, use them, or not use them. But the question of their existence is not asked. Thus it is a metaphysical system that evades the transcendent Creator and ends by rationalizing the ambient polytheism and idolatry. It is a typically Gnostic type of imaginative speculation, which Augustine will encounter in the form of Manicheanism. Thus both Plotinus' ontology and his attempted ascent from it minister to permissivism and waywardness in human living, to a pantheistic religiosity of beauty, of secular humanism, and of pagan Roman civic virtue. The practical personal outcome, the effect of this final philosophical version of the ancient and inveterate error of mankind, this mixture of Plato's ideas with Oriental mysticism (as the textbooks define it), is the secularization of the inner life of each human personality. Nothing in Plotinus' *Enneads* indicates even a trace of prayer. It makes no sense to pray to the One as Plotinus forms the concept within his own mind, imagining it as a principle somehow beyond being, intelligibility, and human knowledge.

To see correctly the origin and nature of Christian Philosophy, this failure of Plotinus to ascend to the concept of one living God, one unique spiritual substance, one really existing personal Supreme Being distinct in reality and essence from the cosmos, the omnipotent Creator and Lord of heaven and earth, must be noted carefully. It is on this point of the real being and existence of the Creator that

Christian Philosophy diverges from Platonism as a different kind of philosophy, just as it is on this point that Augustine, the founder of Christian Philosophy, separated the substance of his thinking from Neo-Platonism and left it behind.

Plotinus might well have been one of the great Fathers of the Church. But he philosophized within the ancient error of pantheism, taking the religiosity of the ambient pagan culture as his guiding star. His attempt at the philosophical renewal of this culture came to nothing. For over a thousand years, until the times of Giordano Bruno, Descartes, and Spinoza, when Plotinus will have a renaissance in Modern Philosophy, the future was to belong to a different kind of philosophy with its own way of philosophizing, that of Augustine, which followed a quite different *stella rectrix* as its guiding star.

ST. AUGUSTINE, THE FOUNDER OF CHRISTIAN PHILOSOPHY

"Among all the Fathers of the Church," writes Bardenhewer in his *Patrology,* "Augustine is undoubtedly the greatest, the most original, fruitful, and versatile." This voices the common consent of specialists in this discipline, which studies scientifically the early Church Fathers. Augustine's greatness on the landscape of universal history, however, today goes beyond this long-standing recognition of his position among the Fathers of the Church, whom he sums up in his person and in his works. This new visibility results from the discovery of the long prehistory of mankind and the light it throws upon the comparatively recent and brief historical period since about 4000 B.C., with its succession of cultures as the largest units of human life on earth. Augustine occupies a pivotal role in the history of human civilized life in these six thousand years because of the nature of his life and career and because of the cultural impact of his work in education and philosophy. The world-historical position of Augustine bears directly upon the apostasy of mankind from God, which lies at the heart of the drama of the human cultures succeeding each other in historic times. Return must be made to this dimension after the essential facts of his career are summarized.

Augustine was born in 354 A.D. of a Catholic Christian mother and a pagan father, an official in the North African administration of the Roman Empire. Augustine's anguished and prayerful mother saw her son, who was not baptized in infancy, succumb for years to the ambient pagan culture, with its thought patterns and mores. This spiritually devastating victory of the culture resulted from his schooling, as he reports in his *Confessions.* His parents gave him the standard education in the pagan school system, in which he quickly showed great talent and promise for the future. His father, accordingly, continued to support Augustine in the higher studies that prepared for the legal profession, the avenue to advancement in the empire. In the meantime, in his adolescence Augustine fell into the profligate way of living that he describes unforgettably in his *Confessions.*

A Teenager Discovers Philosophy

When Augustine was nineteen, the turning point came in his life: he discovered philosophy, and as a result changed his major, as one says today, from law to education. He determined to become a professional teacher in the schools rather than a lawyer headed for the imperial administration. The reason? Because at his time, in late antiquity, philosophy could be studied and pursued and taken up as one's basic interest in life only within the teaching of rhetoric. By this time the victory of the Sophists over the ideal sought by Socrates, Plato, and Aristotle was everywhere complete. Everywhere rhetoric was the seventh and culminating art. Education for success in practical affairs had become the standard, hence philosophy had no independent place. But it could be cultivated on a personal basis, indeed, in the life and work of a professional *Rhetor,* and its literature could be used in teaching. It was this path that Augustine took up in the momentous decision that he describes in *Confessions* (IV, 7). In the ordinary course of his studies, he recalls, he came upon the *Hortensius,* Cicero's exhortation to philosophy, indeed, to the philosophy of Socrates, Plato, and Aristotle, which recognizes the intelligence and a higher order of intelligible reality beyond the senses that the intelligence is able to know. "This book changed my affections", Augustine writes.

> It turned my prayers to you, Lord, and caused me to have different purposes and desires. All my vain hopes forthwith became worthless to me, and with incredible ardor of heart I desired undying wisdom. I began to rise up, so that I might return to you. . . . I did not use that book to sharpen my tongue, nor did it impress me by its way of speaking but rather by what it spoke. . . . Love of wisdom has the name of philosophy in Greek, and that book set me on fire for it.

Two focal points of Augustine's life and career emerge here. It would be difficult to illustrate better the importance of sound philosophy for adolescents. These focal points will be the study of philosophy as mankind's natural wisdom, on the one hand, and the field of education, on the other. Christian Philosophy will result as a different kind of philosophy, and it will be the seventh art on a new program of academic studies. Thus the ancient cultural heritage of the *Paideia,* structured according to the principles and aspiration of Socrates, Plato, and Aristotle, will emerge in the Christian times after Augustine, visible as the same educational and cultural reality in its natural substance but wonderfully renewed from within, in its mode, as the Christian education of youth and with the historic reality of Christian culture as its social outcome.

From this time in early youth, then, Augustine takes up philosophy, the love and the study of wisdom. He never deviates from it but goes on to develop into one of the authentic philosophical geniuses of mankind.[1] He describes his transfer from law to education, and how, to his mother's further consternation, he took up Manicheanism because it appeared to be the wisdom he was now seeking. But his daily occupation was that of a professional teacher of rhetoric in the pagan school system. In his teaching he offered many courses in philosophy and culti-

[1] A summary of his philosophy can be found in Excerpts for Part One, Augustine, pp. 399–404.

vated out of personal predilection the classic works of the philosophers. He became in this way a true philosopher, well versed in that common heritage of the *Koine* philosophy and its ontology that has been seen above in Plotinus. His personal life and thought continued to evolve and to develop in and through his daily professional activity as a teacher, an activity in which he won great renown and promotion from North Africa to Rome and thence to Milan as a teacher at the pinnacle of his profession in the imperial court itself.

Augustine spent some years with the Manicheans, a typical Gnostic sect that mixed Christian teachings with Oriental mysticism and resulted like Plotinus in a philosophical rationalization of the ancient error: the eternity of matter, the conflict of light and darkness, the avoidance of personal guilt in sin, and a Neo-Platonic support of the religiosity of the pagan culture. Eventually, however, he came to see its defects. He dropped from it to the school of the Academics, vaguely Platonic but actually dedicated to Skepticism. It was in this condition of mind and soul, always personally searching for true wisdom yet still always held prisoner in the immoralities of the pagan life-style, that the famous scene of his conversion to Catholic Christianity, which he describes in *Confessions* (Book VIII) took place: "I thought that the reason I deferred from day to day to reject worldly hopes and to follow you alone", Augustine says to God, "was because there seemed nothing certain by which I could direct my course. But the day had come when I stood stripped naked before myself, and my conscience upbraided me . . . and with most bitter contrition I wept within my heart." At this point a child's voice came to him from a nearby house, chanting and repeating over and over, "Take up and read. Take up and read." "I interpreted this solely as a command given to me by God", Augustine continues.

And I snatched up the volume of the Apostle Paul, opened it, and read in silence the chapter on which my eyes first fell: "Not in rioting and drunkenness, not in chambering and impurities, not in strife and envying; but put you on the Lord Jesus Christ, and make not provision for the flesh and its concupiscences. . . . " Instantly, in truth, at the end of this sentence, as if before a peaceful light streaming into my heart, all the dark shadows of doubt fled away. . . . Thereupon we went in to my mother. We told her the story, and she rejoiced.

This took place in early autumn, 386 A.D. Augustine resigned from his teaching post, the chair of rhetoric at Milan, and retired to a friend's suburban villa, Cassiciacum, to prepare for the course of instructions in the Catechumenate in Lent of 387 and for baptism into the Catholic Church at Easter. During these months he continued teaching a small group of young people who shared his intention and decision in what he called *schola nostra,* "our school", as distinct from *schola illa,* the pagan school system from which he had resigned. At the same time he took advantage of this teaching to begin the new approach in both philosophy and education mentioned above. He even had his lectures to the small group, together with the discussions which he guided, recorded by a stenographer. He then edited these manuscripts into the first published works of his immense future literary output: they are the beginning of the philosophical dialogues of his first years as a Christian convert and layman up to his unexpected ordination to the Catholic priesthood four years after his baptism. These famous *Dialogues of Cassiciacum*, it is clear, form the primary documentation for the origin and nature of Christian Philosophy. This is a good point, therefore, to pause for a brief summary of this documentation and the substance of its philosophical content.

Augustine's Philosophical Dialogues And Doctrine

First, the writings. The *Dialogues of Cassiciacum* reflect the educational application of his new metaphysics, for that was his immediate activity and project: *schola nostra* in contrast with the kind of education in the pagan *schola illa* from which he had just resigned. Then comes a series of works, chiefly against the ancient pantheism cultivated by the Manichean sect of Gnosticism from which he was recently liberated, in which the treatise *On Free Will* is especially noteworthy. Finally, there is the centerpiece among these philosophical works, the book *The True Religion*, deeply personal and thoroughly matured across these years as a Catholic layman. It contains the substance of Christian Philosophy and states the principles of its metaphysics. Augustine's mode of exposition is not that of a modern textbook in philosophy, articulated and rather abstract, more like a skeleton than a living body of doctrine. Philosophy in classical antiquity was much closer to life because it was a part of life: it affected the way people lived. Hence Augustine uses the classical form of the dialogue in these works. This is especially true of *The True Religion*, the dialogue with his long-standing friend Romanianus and all readers like him who are ready to consider joining personally that movement of the conversion of Rome and its classical culture, including the seven arts that form its educational dynamism, to God in Jesus Christ and his teaching Church. It may be said with justice that the other writings of this period in Augustine's life form a cluster about this central one and provide the best commentary upon and enlargement of its various points of basic philosophical doctrine. Thus one has at hand the sources and the mode for pursuing the nature of Christian Philosophy in its seminal works.

Second, the content of Augustine's metaphysics, that central core of philosophy constituted by three fundamentals of doctrine: ontology, the principles of being as such; the ascent to the intelligible order of truth and reality; and the resulting natural knowledge of the existence, nature, and attributes of the Supreme Being. Each of the three can be fleshed out readily from these works of Augustine and summarized briefly as follows.

Ontology is a modern term, also called "general metaphysics" in the textbooks. But the substance is in Augustine, just as it is in Plato, Aristotle, and Plotinus, where being and essence are discussed in relation to the various categories of beings, to the simple and composite substances, and where these realities are related to the logical concepts of human knowledge such as genus, species, and specific differences among things.

The next fundamental of doctrine has been noted frequently in the present study. Can the mind ascend from these principles of being to a higher order of truth and reality that transcends the bodily things seen in this cosmos? It is the watershed question. Augustine credits the school of Plato for teaching him how it is reasonable to give an affirmative answer and thus to leave both materialism and skepticism behind. But he is quick to point out that Plotinus undertakes this ascent in a mistaken way and thus ends in pantheism, the failure and fall of natural reason regarding the concept of the Supreme Being. "He vainly excogitates vast spaces of light exactly like ordinary light", Augustine writes in The True Religion (20, 40); "he does not know that he is still entangled in the lust of the eye, and that he is carrying this world with him in his endeavor to go beyond it. He thinks he has reached another world simply by falsely imagining the bright part of this world infinitely extended." This passage actually contains the departure from the ancient error and the birth of Christian Philosophy as such. It will achieve a stronger and more accurate insight into the nature of the intelligible light and the qualitative difference of man's intellect from the senses. Thus Christian Philosophy fulfills the positive aspirations and principles of Platonism, whereas Neo-Platonism develops not the positive qualities but the defects in Plato's teaching, which caused his failure to reach the transcendent Supreme Being and the doctrine of creation. Hence Augustine's constant stress upon the fact that the philosopher must not use his imagination: it is not the instrument by which the principles of being are known. "Nothing", he writes in The True Religion (3, 3),

> hinders the perception of truth more than a life devoted to lusts and the false images of sensible things. . . . Therefore the mind has to be healed so that it may behold the immutable form of things which remains ever the same. . . . Men do not believe in its existence, though it alone truly and supremely exists . . . , not seen by the eyes or conjured up by any phantasm, but beheld by the mind alone, by the intelligence.

With this the mind arrives at the third fundamental of metaphysical doctrine, the concept of God, the natural knowledge of the Supreme Being achieved by Christian Philosophy. Space does not permit a detailed elaboration of Augustine's teaching. Suffice it to say that the ancient and inveterate error of mankind disappears. In all the various places in these early philosophical works where Augustine discusses the existence, nature, and attributes of the Supreme Being, the transcendence of God is explicitly recognized. God is the all-perfect and change-less reality, truly eternal and truly immortal. All other beings have their existence from him, but their existence is not a part of his existence, as in Plotinus' concept of the outflow from the unknowable One or in the Manicheanist idea that all earthly substances are particles of the Divine Substance as pieces chipped from a stone. The things that God creates, Augustine constantly teaches, are not the same thing as the reality that he himself is. This is already to achieve "the sublime truth", as Aquinas will term it eight centuries later, which is the most fundamental distinguishing mark of Christian Philosophy. It is thus a different kind of philoso-phy from the classical pagan philosophy in any of its forms, even in those of Plato and Aristotle, for it achieves insight and understanding about God as absolutely transcendent and at the same time closer to each of his creatures, as Augustine says, than they are to themselves.

The substance of Christian Philosophy stands completed in Augustine's mind as the intellectual aspect of his conversion from the ancient error of pantheism. It is furthermore rather comprehensively expressed in this attractive set of philosophi-cal writings that came from his pen during his years as a Christian layman. When popular demand, to his surprise, led to his ordination to the priesthood, his new interests and responsibilities resulted in a change in his writings. They become more scriptural and address religious topics rather than philosophical ones. The very language he uses becomes more pastoral. But his Christian Philosophy abides without change. He puts it to work on behalf of his new religious concerns and uses it in his catechetical explanation of Christian doctrine, but without having to change its fundamentals. It is still the seventh of the seven arts: it is taught and learned as such in his program for Christian education outlined later in his *De doctrina Christiana,* a fundamental and culturally programmatic work, which will be discussed in some detail below.

God and the Soul: The Distinctive Character of Augustine's Thought

With this as a summary of the essential structure and metaphysical content of Christian Philosophy, one can reflect upon its most general characteristic and contrast with other kinds of philosophy its concern with the existence of things rather than the forms of bodily things in the visible cosmos. For it is this question-ing of existence that liberates the human mind and spirit from confinement within this cosmos in deafness to a word from beyond.

Looking back from the *Confessions* written ten years later when he was a Catholic bishop, Augustine reviews the emergence of a new kind of fundamental thinking as the intellectual side of his conversion. The emphasis is on the existence of things rather than on the forms of things as in the Classical Philosophy of the pagan past. "Lo, heaven and earth exist", he writes in Book X (4–5), they cry out that they have been created, for they are subject to change and variation. . . . To have what once was not is to change and vary. They also cry out that they did not make themselves: "for this reason do we exist, because we have been made. Therefore, before we came to be, we did not exist in such wise as to be able to make ourselves. . . . " You, therefore, O Lord, who are beautiful, made these things, for they are beautiful; you who are good made them, for they are good; you who are made them, for they are. . . . All these praise you, the Creator of all things. But how do you make them? O God, how have you made heaven and earth? . . . You did not hold in your hand anything out of which to make heaven and earth: whence would you obtain this thing not made by you, out of which you would make a new thing? What exists, for any reason except that you exist?

This emphasis on the existence of things rather than their forms distinguishes Christian Philosophy from the classical pagan philosophies and will be its abiding hallmark as it develops into the future. Christian Philosophy understands and studies being in the meaning it has for the common sense of all men everywhere in the natural good judgments of daily life. Being refers to existing: to be is to exist. Christian Philosophy adopts the common heritage of ontology, which Augustine knows well, having studied it and taught it, and then makes a much less impeded, more rapid and clear-sighted ascent from it to the higher order not only of the intelligible truths but also to the Supreme Being among the beings of the universe. Existence is seen in them as something metaphysically deeper and more fundamental than their various forms. But above all the existences of things are recognized as demanding a source and cause. Full existence, the apex of existing reality, is recognized in the Creator who gives existence to things out of his goodness. Then the process of creation is recognized, analyzed, and studied as the making of things out of nothing, a making of them to be where nothing was before. The eternity of matter disappears where it had been the common philosophical doctrine, from Plato and Aristotle through Plotinus.

Augustine of course uses much of the philosophical terminology of Platonism and Neo-Platonism: it had been for years the daily fare of his thinking and teaching. But the substance of his philosophy after his conversion is utterly unlike that of Neo-Platonism. On fundamentals of ontology the words have his own meaning. For Augustine there can be no source or principle imagined beyond being and intelligibility, from which beings are imagined as outflows or emanations. God is the Supreme Being, One and good, knowable as such, the intelligent Creator. Augustine is philosophizing within God's self-revelation when he gave his name to Moses: "I AM: my name is HE WHO IS", the existing One, for I am the source of existence for everything else that exists. Hence Augustine's ascent from being and its principles to God himself in the higher order of intelligible reality is akin to prayer, a lifting of the mind and heart to the Supreme Being and

Creator, that quality that is visibly absent from the philosophy of Plotinus. For prayer is the very language of the creature: it expresses recognition, praise, dependence, and thanksgiving. Philosophizing that ascends to a level where the Creator can be seen and the fact of creation can be recognized ministers to prayerfulness.

This quality of Augustine's philosophy, which separates it from Neo-Platonism and from the ancient error of pantheism in all its forms, characterized his thinking from its beginning in his philosophical dialogues. One of the earliest, the *Soliloquies,* written at the villa of Cassiciacum before his baptism, is a dialogue on God and the soul between himself as a person inquiring and his reason giving philosophical answers. The new emphasis is clear: philosophy is no longer bent toward the *physis,* the nature of the cosmos with its things in various bodily forms. The center of philosophical interest and study is now explicitly God and the soul, together with the dependence of the soul on God both in the order of existence and in the order of knowing.

Augustine opens the *Soliloquies* with his decision to write down the things that his reason discovers, not to win a host of readers but simply as notes to help a few of his followers. His career as a writer is beginning, and it will gradually build the vast *opera omnia* that he bequeathed to the mind of the West. His reason admonishes him "to pray for health and assistance in order to attain what you desire, and commit this to writing, so that you may be the more heartened by your achievement". Accordingly, Augustine opens with prayer:

> O God, who from nothing hast created this world. . . . O God, who dost not cause evil. . . . O God, the Father of truth, the Father of wisdom, the Father of happiness. . . . O God, intelligible Light, in whom and by whom and through whom all those things that have intelligible light have their intelligible light. O God, whose domain is the whole world unknown to sense. . . . Come to my aid, thou, the one God, the one, eternal, true substance . . . by whose laws the poles revolve, the sun rules the day, and the moon presides over the night. . . . O God, above whom, beyond whom, and without whom nothing exists. . . . Teach me how to come to thee. . . . Grant me increase of faith, of hope, and of charity.

Behold, Augustine continues, "I have prayed to God." His reason replies, "Sum up briefly then, what you prayed for and want to know." "I desire", Augustine answers, "to know God and the soul." Christian Philosophy has its program. Its difference from all the classical philosophies, including especially Platonism and Neo-Platonism, has been made clear to Augustine's first readers, the select group of young students with him in *schola nostra* at Cassiciacum. Augustine speaks of "the noble Plato" and credits the "books of the Platonists" with assisting him to see the intelligible order of reality and thus to break free from Manicheanism, Skepticism, and Neo-Platonism. But he never gives this kind of praise to Plotinus and Porphyry, the Neo-Platonists of the century before his own; in fact, as noted above, the contrary seems to be the case.

This is the concept of God professed by the First Article of the Apostles' Creed, the baptismal faith that Augustine already knows and is preparing to hear explained by the Church in the Catechumenate and to receive from the Church in his baptism. But now Augustine is bringing his philosophically trained powers of natural reason to bear in a conscious effort to know better what he is professing as a convert, namely, God's self-revelation to Moses when he gave his divine name to the Hebrews and that he completed in Jesus of Nazareth. Augustine's philosophical mind sees this God as Truth itself, for God as Truth is the means of establishing a natural philosophical link and contract between God and the human soul. "There is an immutable truth embracing all things that are true," Augustine writes in his philosophical dialogue *On Free Will* (II, 12, 33), "a truth you cannot call yours, or mine, or any man's, but which is present to all and gives itself alike to all who discern the things that are immutably true, as a light that in some miraculous way is both secret and yet open to all." This is Augustine's favorite concept of God. It enables him to fulfill the aspiration of Plato for knowledge of the ideas of intelligible realities of metaphysics, visible already in preparatory fashion in the truths of mathematics. For now Plato's Ideas are located in the mind of God. The creation of things takes place according to them, so that created natures are indeed reflections of the divine ideas. But there is another dimension here, one which Augustine will elaborate comprehensively in his vast work *The City of God*, which separates Christian Philosophy still further from pagan Greek thought, typically unhistorical and cyclic. It is the dimension of linear history. For among the ideas in the mind of God is included his plan to introduce a set of wonderful works into human history. Their temporal sequence unfolds as the salvation history of all mankind. It is this insight, gained by thinking within his Faith, that made Augustine the progenitor of the philosophy of history.

From this position Augustine comes to his basic concept of the human soul, the philosophical anthropology that is the other wing of the Christian Philosophy emerging in these philosophical dialogues. Human nature is created with two chief powers. The first is the intelligence, a power of insight that understands the natures of things and sees the intelligibles because of its illumination through participation in Truth itself. God is, as it were, the sun that shines upon human souls, and thus illuminated they know the intelligibles. This fulfills the aspiration and the thirst of Socrates, Plato, and Aristotle and at the same time transcends them. By reaching HIM WHO IS, the Creator of all other existing realities, Christian Philosophy becomes able to accomplish a higher level of synthesis.

The second chief power of the human soul is free will. Here Augustine reaches the insight that evil is not a substantial reality, not a creature of God, and certainly not the product of a Manichean evil principle, independent and in strife with God. Evil is a defect in created things that results from the wrong use of created free wills. Evil is not a thing, a substance, a created nature. It fastens upon such substances and natures as the result of the action of deficient causes. This philosophical solution for the problem of evil provides the rational basis for perceiving both the goodness and innocence of God the Creator and the reality of sin and guilt among free creatures. Thus the evasion of guilt in pantheism is eliminated and the way is open to a true conversion to the personal transcendent God in sorrow for personal sins.

With this set of insights into God and the soul, Christian Philosophy emerges as a distinct kind of philosophy. At one stroke the ancient and inveterate error of mankind is dispelled in the philosophical order. The transcendence of God is recovered by the very fact that the pantheistic reduction has ceased. And the elevation of man as a particle of the Divine, autonomous, uncreated, and a law unto himself, has been humbled by the vision of man as he is: a creature of God who has from God both his human nature and its proper natural law.

Augustine as an Educator

In his philosophical dialogues Augustine is explicitly conscious of the fact that he is an educator as well as a philosopher. These dialogues came forth not only from his general background as a professional teacher but also from his actual teaching at the villa in those months from early fall 386 A.D. until Easter 387; they were discussions with his students, it has been noted, recorded by a stenographer and then edited by Augustine himself for publication as his first written works. He had a philosophical purpose in mind, it is quite clear: that of philosophizing within the religious Faith in God's self-revelation through Moses and in Jesus. But he also had an educational purpose in mind. "It is the duty of good education", he writes in Soliloquies (I, 13, 23), "to arrive at wisdom by means of a definite order; without order this is a matter of chance hardly to be relied upon." He was concerned in these philosophical dialogues to justify the right order of studies and to see to their culmination in the Christian Philosophy that he is founding. This definite order is simply the heritage of the seven liberal arts of the Greco-Roman Paideia, which the Latins translated by the word doctrina, a rich word denoting the activity, the program, and the content of teaching. But Augustine, concerned now for a content of truth in education by which students will arrive at Truth itself, and thus come to true wisdom, places his Christian Philosophy firmly in the culminating position as the seventh of the seven liberal arts. In him, rightly called the Christian Plato, the centuries-old opposition between Socrates and the Sophists is finally decided in favor of philosophical education. The rhetorical education of the Sophists, which had prevailed across the Hellenistic age and had progressively secularized the classical culture, was fading out with the passing of the ancient and inveterate religious error. The future belonged to the approach to education and culture that Augustine was structuring by his reordering of the studies and by the qualitative character of his philosophy.

All of this was already in his mind when he wrote the philosophical dialogues in his years as a layman after his conversion and baptism. But the future belonged to his new approach because he became a priest and then the bishop of Hippo. This gave him the base for implementing his vision of an order of studies that would know by one and the same program or curriculum both the objects of the earthly sciences and the object who is God, the Father Almighty, the Creator of heaven and earth, the same Supreme Being who reveals himself through the teaching in the Catechumenate and the practice of its revealed religion. For Augustine the seventh art is now the natural science of God, unified with the other six arts that prepare the young people for it. This Christian Philosophy is both the goal of the other six liberal arts and the source of light for their own internal orientation. Hence the entire curriculum of studies leads the minds of the young people to God and provides the natural foundation in education for their practice of the revealed religion that they learned in childhood.

It was Augustine who, in the "Christian times", as he called the Christian era that had begun to become socially visible on the landscape of universal history, saw that provision had to be made for a new kind of social leadership, both for the Church and for civil society. All the peoples in the Roman Empire were now Christian, with the exception of the Jews, and had already in Augustine's day turned largely to the God of revelation in Christ and his Church. It was a quite visible social phenomenon, to which Augustine refers constantly in his writings as a primary fact of life and experience in his day. Leaders are men who have the benefit of education with its cultivation of the powers of expression and persuasion. The new kind of social leadership for which these Christian times are calling must have the power and the polish of the historic seven arts of the Greco-Roman *Paideia*. This is the point at which Augustine comes on the scene. He was a full-fledged professional educator who understood the heritage of Greco-Roman culture from within, and who knew by personal experience what took place, to the person and to society as a whole, as the number of converts increased, gradually dominated, and finally were the only persons left. The complete social triumph of organized institutional Christianity could be projected quite confidently in Augustine's time, when Christians were filled with a surging spirit of victory over the ancient paganism. For a philosopher this meant victory over the ancient and inveterate error of pantheism with its consequent idolatries and secularism. Augustine was more than an educator: he was also a full-fledged philosopher. He was exactly the man for the hour, the one who had the background and the personal talent to found this new thing, Christian Philosophy, as one of the seven arts of the historic *Paideia,* now Christianized, so to speak, for its role in what everyone in Augustine's day sensed as the education and the culture to which the future belonged. With this the immediate specifics of the origin, nature, and development of Christian Philosophy are at hand.

The documentation for this fundamental point in the cultural life of mankind in the short historic period after the immensely long prehistoric ages is contained in Augustine's treatise on Christian education, *De doctrina Christiana,* written when he was a bishop as a set of guidelines for the program of studies at his cathedral school. He was training leaders for the new "Christian times", the *tempora Christiana,* as he called what is known today as the Christian era. *Doctrina* was the Latin word customarily used to translate the Greek *Paideia:* with the adjective "Christian" it means the use of the heritage of the seven arts for the education and enculturation of young Christians, not only for the priesthood and religious life but also for all the callings and professions of civil and political life. Augustine is purging the academic liberal arts of Greece and Rome of their pagan condition, cleansing them of superstition, orienting them toward the transcendent God of revelation, and putting them at the service both of the teaching mission of the Church and of the need of the resulting Christian culture for social leadership.

Book I of *De doctrina Christiana* discusses the purpose of educational and cultural activity in terms of the transcendent God, Creator of mankind for a destiny that likewise transcends this cosmos and its earthly life. Thus the secularization of the earlier pagan condition is healed, and the human spirit is liberated from its pantheistic confinement within the cosmos.

Book II takes up each art, science, and discipline in the program of studies, showing how each is to be taught when the ancient error of the pagan religiosity and its superstitious consequences are left aside and the orienting light of the transcendent Supreme Being is allowed to shine upon the object that each one studies. For the object of each is part of God's creation; each of the first six arts has its own particular openness to God and bears its own witness to him. This is particularly true of the mathematical and physical sciences, which Augustine reaffirms on his program, since it is no longer exclusively a cultivation of polished human discourse. The tradition of the Sophists is left firmly behind. This is confirmed and finalized in the chapters of Book II that take up philosophy as the seventh of the seven liberal arts. Philosophy is now in place, in the place desired by Socrates, Plato, and Aristotle; but it is now itself elevated from within, qualitatively distinct from their philosophy in the way noted above in Augustine's earlier philosophical dialogues. The emergence of Christian Philosophy as a fact and as a specific kind is clear to see when the *De doctrina Christiana* is studied together with those dialogues. Since it is a program of education rightfully called a *Doctrina Christiana,* this academic discipline, which illuminates, unifies, and is the culmination of the entire program, will be Christian Philosophy. The origin, nature, and academic existence of Christian Philosophy are now a fact in the ongoing social and cultural life of Western man.

The keystone in the edifice of the mind Augustine is building is the fact that this philosophy does not limit itself to mere ontological discussions of the principles of being but ascends from them to the Supreme Being in person, whom Augustine calls *Ipsum Esse*, "Existence itself", or *Summa Essentia*, "the Supreme Reality", the One who gives existence to all other realities by creating them as his creatures. This is a philosophical teaching that reaches that one and same Supreme Being who reveals himself through Moses and in Jesus. This self-revelation of God is mediated through the humble and practical program of the Catechumenate, which is now forming all Western men in the baptismal faith and the practice of revealed religion.

Book III of *De doctrina Christiana* takes up the study of the Bible, which in Christian times will largely replace the study of pagan authors. The times are changing: it is the same set of liberal disciplines, indeed, but their character, content, and purpose are illumined by the new light for the Gentiles that has shone forth from Jerusalem. Book IV, finally, discusses the science of rhetoric, now subordinated to both philosophy and revealed religion and put to work in the proclamation and the teaching of the word of God.

A Program for the Coming Christian Culture

In Augustine, "the Christian Plato", Socrates' plan for a philosophical renewal of education and hence of culture has at last won out over the Sophists, with their mere rhetorical and pragmatic approach, aiming and preparing young people simply and solely for success in earthly affairs. This program of the seven liberal arts, which contains the natural knowledge of God by philosophical reason within itself as its animating academic soul, gives the baptized Christian young people an academic education that equips them for leadership among the people at large, baptized Christians themselves who have the instruction of the Catechumenate and its formation of souls for the Christian way of life. Christian Philosophy, which had its dawn across the Patristic age from Justin Martyr, is now fully founded and functioning in the life and work of Augustine, philosopher and educator. It offers intellectual peace to the times ahead in the form of a promising cooperation between the catechetical and the academic orders of teaching. It is this fact about Augustine that gives him his special greatness and his unique position at that axial turning point from the pagan culture of the past to the historic reality of the Christian culture that was to come.

PART TWO

THE ESSENTIAL CONTENT OF
CHRISTIAN PHILOSOPHY

INTRODUCTION

The Setting in the Ongoing Life of the Church

St. Augustine stood at the axial point in the historic life of human culture, which began about 4000 B.C. It was the axial turning point from the pagan religion, philosophy, education, and culture of the past to the Christian culture that was to come, the social product of the Catholic Faith, Christian Philosophy, and the Christian education of youth.

Nor did Augustine simply stand as a witness at that moment of time. It was his providential calling, by his work in the distinct but related fields of philosophy and education, to be perhaps the chief positive factor in this immense sea change in human social and cultural life.

Christian Philosophy in the Schools of Christendom

From the Fathers of the Church and the founding of Christian Philosophy to the great "scholastics", as they are sometimes called, roughly a thousand years went by. In this millennium to the times of St. Thomas Aquinas, Christian Philosophy, as founded by St. Justin Martyr, St. Augustine, and the other Fathers of the Church, was cultivated in the schools of Christendom.

These schools belonged to the academic order of teaching and not directly to the catechetical order of teaching. These academic institutions enculturate young people on the level of higher education. They cultivate the powers that give social leadership. But they function within the Catechumenate, just as the philosophy they teach philosophizes within the Catholic Faith. It suffices, then, to recall that the Gentiles, both the Greeks and the Romans and now the barbarians settling among them, are being illuminated by the teaching that has gone forth from Jerusalem. This is the ongoing life of the Church. It is a light to the Gentiles because the concept of God that it gives them dispels the ancient and inveterate error of paganism, replacing it with the Divine Transcendence. The Gentiles learn that God is *Emmanuel*, GOD WITH US, and that he is present to each person. The Gentiles learn about God out of the prophetic light and come to know the name that he gave to Moses: I AM: the ONE WHO IS. The Gentiles learn that the Almighty Creator has come as the Redeemer from the human proneness to sin through disordered desire for what is seen and touched in the cosmos. This catechetical teaching included mighty things, simple in wording, but transcendent in meaning: for example, "this is my Body" and "I will raise him up on the last day". Furthermore, sacrifice is offered everywhere, that form of worship that is the witness of a creature to his Creator. All of this needs only allusion here, to recall to memory. But the details of this catechetical order of teaching lie beyond this consideration of the new Christian Philosophy, which is philosophizing within this revealed religion. Because it does so, it establishes an academic order that is at peace with teaching given in the catechetical order.

Only when this intellectual peace is properly considered will one be in a position to recognize concretely an apostasy from God, which might take place within this ongoing drama of the cultural succession of human life since 4000 B.C., should such a phenomenon ever take place.

The schools of Christendom are academic institutions that arose everywhere in the Western world after the Fathers of the Church, and after that earlier pagan Rome with its line of emperors and its pagan schools, had come to their end.

St. Benedict and Monte Cassino symbolize the monastic institution that grew mightily after St. Augustine everywhere in the West. It branched into many forms as time went on under many other famous religious leaders such as St. Bernard, St. Francis of Assisi, and St. Dominic. "Pray and work" was their basic principle: agricultural work, which transformed the face of Europe, but primarily intellectual work. The monasteries were scholastic centers with teaching on all levels, with the production of hand-copied books, and with great libraries standing to this day. Eight centuries after St. Augustine the parents of Thomas Aquinas enrolled their young son in the monastery school of Monte Cassino for his elementary and secondary education. Without Augustine's *schola nostra,* would men like Aquinas have been possible? The foundation of St. Thomas' work in Christian Philosophy was the thorough grounding he received in the Christianized *Paideia,* the seven liberal arts taught now in the Christian way.

But it is perhaps the Cathedral of Notre Dame in Paris that symbolizes best this emergence of the schools of Christendom. This is for two reasons. First, the cathedral's great facade captures in stone the entire program for the teaching of revealed religion in the Catechumenate. The second reason is seen in the heroic equestrian statue of Charlemagne, crowned emperor of the converted Roman Empire in Rome in 800 A.D., which marches forward in front of the cathedral as if marking the forward motion of Christian times. Charlemagne, whose favorite book was Augustine's *City of God,* legislated for his vast Holy Roman Empire, which embraced most of the countries of present-day Western Europe, an educational program that fostered an elementary school in every parish and an institution for secondary and higher education in every bishop's see city. Alcuin, Charlemagne's minister of education, writes that a new Athens is arising everywhere in the West in these new academies for the Christian education of youth. The Cathedral School at Paris grew mightily. Four centuries later it had become an international center for the study of all the arts and sciences and of advanced training for all the professions, including the priesthood. It merited a charter from Rome as a *Universitas studiorum*. Thomas Aquinas was one of its professors, together with his friend who is known to us as St. Bonaventure. And it continues today as the University of Paris, known popularly as the Sorbonne. This was the birth of that characteristic institution of Western culture, the university, where the guiding principle was the same one that had operated in the schools of Christendom since Augustine. The arts and sciences lead the mind of youth to God, if the teaching is done in the right way, namely, if philosophy, qualitatively distinct as Christian Philosophy, be kept carefully in its place as the seventh of the seven liberal arts.

In the twelfth century Peter Lombard, a professor before he became the archbishop of Paris, produced his *Book of Sentences* when teaching at the Cathedral School of Paris. This work illustrates the nature and the unity of this vast culturewide educational program and shows its continuity from the Fathers of the Church and St. Augustine in particular. It gathers into a convenient handbook the "sentences", the teachings of the various Fathers of the Church, organized under headings that became titles of lecture courses in the program of studies.

Professors at the University of Paris customarily lectured on this *Book of Sentences* and developed their own teaching as a commentary on it—so St. Bonaventure, and so St. Thomas Aquinas.

The teaching was both theological and philosophical. It reveals the development of Christian Philosophy into a fully elaborated academic discipline, vastly developed since St. Augustine's time but substantially the same in its teaching. This Christian Philosophy ascends from ontology, its doctrine on the concept of being and the principles that belong to being as such. It assumes the characteristic emphasis of Christian Philosophy on the existences of things rather than on their forms. Then it ascends to that remarkably clear intellectual knowledge of the Supreme Being as personal, intelligent, and free in giving existence to all other beings, his creatures. The Supreme Being is transcendent, for he is the Creator. At the same time transcendence is not understood as separation by distance. God is present personally to each of his creatures. "One must know", writes Peter Lombard, as if giving directions to the teachers who will use his book,

that God, who exists in his own way in himself without ever any change, is nevertheless in each created nature of every place and at all time by his presence, his power, and his essence. Furthermore, God dwells in a still more excellent way by grace in the holy angels and in the souls of the just. God is present in the most excellent way of all, finally, in the man Jesus Christ, in whom the fullness of divinity, as St. Paul teaches, dwells in a bodily manner: for in him God dwells not by the grace of adopted sonship, but by the grace of union.

Thus succinctly Peter Lombard summarizes the heart of the concept of God, which has been taught in the schools of Christendom since the Fathers of the Church. St. Thomas Aquinas in the century after Peter Lombard was entirely devoted to the comprehensive rational elucidation of this concept of God.

The Life and Work of St. Thomas Aquinas

The figure of Thomas Aquinas comes upon the scene in this manner. It is eight hundred years after St. Augustine: the time is the middle of the thirteenth century. After his early schooling at Monte Cassino and Naples, Thomas Aquinas joined the new Dominican Order. Soon he is studying under St. Albert the Great at Cologne in Germany, after which he will be assigned to the Dominican House of Studies in Paris, the Dominican college associated with the newly emerging University of Paris.

Soon Thomas Aquinas was appointed to a professorship at the University of Paris, where he produced his commentary on the *Book of Sentences* of Peter Lombard. His teaching and his writing were illuminated by a special philosophical light, which soon made him famous among all of the professors at the university. As his teaching proceeded, and out of his teaching, he wrote his commentaries on the Scriptures and his disputed questions, which came forth from the great philosophical discussions that distinguished the life of the University of Paris at that time. Because of the need of the Church for a teaching that missionaries could take with them in their outreach to Islam and even beyond to the Far East, he wrote his philosophical *Summa contra Gentiles.*

Finally, and above all, he composed his *Summa Theologiae,* written for use in the schools of Christendom for those who are taking up the study of theology. It is this work for which he is chiefly famous.

These works of Thomas Aquinas are immense treatises, perhaps baffling to the student. Embarking upon the study of Thomas Aquinas is much like the approach to the works of St. Augustine: the quantity of the material is simply immense. There is a secret, however, a key, as it were, which unlocks these immense later works that came forth from Aquinas' university teaching. It is a very short philosophical treatise that contains that special philosophical light mentioned above, which illuminates all his works. This treatise has a special significance for the essential content of Christian Philosophy, and hence one must give it some special reflection.

The Treatise On Being and Essence

The time is now 1252 A.D., well into the ninth century after St. Augustine. Thomas Aquinas is twenty-seven years old and has just been assigned to teach in the Dominican House of Studies at Paris as a bachelor of Scripture. His students are his own fellow Dominicans, younger men whom he is teaching. It is here and in this circumstance that he wrote the short masterpiece that is actually his "metaphysics", with both of the parts of metaphysics, "ontology" and "natural theology", compressed lucidly and luminously in its short compass. Why did St. Thomas Aquinas write this short explanation of metaphysics? He tells us himself, for he marked the original manuscript "for my brothers": he wrote it for the younger Dominicans who were his own students.

With this treatise Christian Philosophy emerges into full view, settled in its concepts and polished in its terminology, as the result of the eight centuries of Christianized academic teaching in the schools of Christendom since the times of St. Augustine. In this treatise Thomas Aquinas has no idea of producing a work of creative self-expression, so to speak; his purpose was simply to gather into a helpful synthesis for students that metaphysical teaching that had come across the centuries since the founder of Christian Philosophy, St. Augustine. Thomas Aquinas, of course, had a remarkable lucidity and synthetic power in compressing the discipline of metaphysics, the very core of the content of any philosophy, into this short space. The treatise *On Being and Essence* occupies less than fifty printed pages. It discusses the essential content of Christian Philosophy in six short chapters. One must think of an acorn, which will grow gradually into a mighty oak tree. This treatise *On Being and Essence* is like the acorn; the later works of Thomas Aquinas are the mighty oak tree that grows from it, the original seed and root. It is the same with the mentality of an educated Catholic today: this luminous treatise contains the seed from which the understanding of Christian Philosophy grows, and thus the understanding of the scriptural and theological heritage of the Christian era. Thomas Aquinas gathers these roots coming from the Fathers of the Church and out of the Scriptures into a mighty synthesis, which rests on this solid philosophical foundation.

The philosophical scholar Grabmann says of the treatise *On Being and Essence,* "Thomas Aquinas reduced metaphysics . . . to its simplest expression . . . this treatise is the prologue to his entire scientific activity and all his later writings."

But, one may ask, how does this fit into the life and thinking of the young person today? Here one can do no better than to listen to Cardinal Joseph Pecci, the professor of Christian Philosophy a century ago who was the brother of Pope Leo XIII. Cardinal Pecci helped his brother the Pope greatly in launching the renewal of Christian Philosophy that characterizes the life of the Church in our present day. In his teaching of Christian Philosophy, Cardinal Pecci wrote a companion to *On Being and Essence,* with the purpose of helping young people read St. Thomas "more easily, profitably, and pleasurably". Young people, the cardinal writes, are often tempted to give up the enterprise of entering into their own heritage and making contact with their roots because of the immensity of the writings that face them. Furthermore, when they look into these writings, such as the *Summae* of Thomas Aquinas, they often find them opaque and unintelligible. The philosophy is simply beyond them. What are they to do? Shall they take courses in philosophy in some university in order to read the works of St. Thomas Aquinas? This would be good if one could find the right kind of philosophy. But where does one do this? Furthermore, not many young persons have the time and the situation that permit this kind of specialized philosophical study.

Therefore Cardinal Pecci continues, "I think that St. Thomas' small work entitled *On Being and Essence* offers us a short and easy way to achieve this same purpose.... Why is this? To me it seems that we have here the entire metaphysics that St. Thomas uses in almost every line of his later writings. One finds here in this short treatise a succinct statement of the natural instruments of right reason, according to which a person learns how to explain, to sustain, and to defend the treasure of the divine mysteries, the doctrine revealed by the Eternal Wisdom."

This present study has no other purpose than this same introduction to the works of Thomas Aquinas, and hence to the entire heritage that extends back to the Fathers of the Church, and to the biblical revelation. Our explanations here, therefore, will follow the treatise *On Being and Essence* closely, and the readings in Appendix I will be taken chiefly from it. Thus young people of today can enter into their heritage and contact their roots. If a person were to do systematic and daily reading from the Bible, from St. Augustine, from St. Thomas Aquinas, and from John Henry Newman, that person would soon possess the heritage of sound thought, the natural metaphysics of mankind, which sustains revealed wisdom. In the process, such a person would find that his intellectual ability is deepened and sharpened, and the Christian content learned in catechesis as a child will be filled out and consolidated. Furthermore, one's power of English expression will be greatly enhanced, for the exercise of Christian leadership.

The Philosophical Unity of the Christian Era

A straight line of metaphysical teaching runs for a thousand years, from the early Fathers of the Church to the great scholastics in the time when the university, that characteristic institution of Western and Christian culture, came on the scene. To put it in terms of persons, the teaching runs from Augustine to Aquinas. The terminology varies somewhat, naturally; it is more precise and finished in Thomas Aquinas, for he stands at the end of those many centuries of teaching in the schools of Christendom. But the substance of the metaphysical doctrine is the same: it is that Christian Philosophy that supports the instruction given in the Catechumenate, and that provides a unifying rational foundation for the work of revealed religion in the Christian times. Always it is a metaphysics that is more concerned with the existences of things, the very fact that something exists rather than being nothing, more than their particular bodily forms in the cosmos. And it always is characterized by that powerful ascent of natural reason to the personal Supreme Being himself, who makes the universe intelligible rather than absurd, and who has spoken to mankind in his public revelation.

Throughout this necessarily brief study of the essential content of Christian Philosophy, one should watch for the unity and continuity of the Christian era. This is the natural foundation for explaining the First Article of the Apostles' Creed, "I believe in God, the Father Almighty, Creator of heaven and earth" on every level and situation of catechesis. Furthermore, it is the natural foundation for explaining the Articles of Faith, summarized in the Apostles' Creed, always in the same meaning, the same meaning for men and women today as it had for the Apostles, who learned that meaning from the Lord Jesus himself. Thus this study of philosophical foundations is not a mere abstract academic exercise, speculative and distant from life. Quite the contrary. This study of philosophy, and now its essential and metaphysical content, from the catechetical point of view, reveals a quite different picture. It is close to life, the very life of the Church herself. It is the God of ultimate intelligibility in whom we believe, not some vague divine presence, equally to be appropriated by any and all religions.

One can think of it like a railway: the train moves bulletlike with great speed, securely, constantly into the future, because of the rails and the roadbed. This teaching in higher education is like the rails on which the train of the Catholic Church moves into the future of the Christian era. The deposit of faith is secure and is guarded faithfully when this roadbed is intact. Without it, however, the train will derail and wreck. No one, therefore, should make light of philosophical studies. When they are properly conceived, they are seen to relate directly to the highest concerns of mankind and to that "guarding of the deposit" that St. Paul hands on to his successor Timothy as his weightiest charge (1 Tim 6:20).

PROLOGUE

The Natural Metaphysics of Mankind

St. Thomas Aquinas as a good teacher gives his plan for his treatise *On Being and Essence*,[1] in order to enlist the active participation of his students and to minister to their own independent personal thinking. He does this in his remarkable short prologue to the treatise. He tells us that philosophy and the study of philosophy both begin with "what is meant by the terms *being* and *essence*".

Then he gives a warning. "A small mistake in the beginning is a great one in the end." What does he mean? It is one thing to make a mistake regarding objects seen with the senses: for example, in reality it may be an oak tree, when we mistake it for a hickory or a maple. Thomas Aquinas does not mean this kind of small mistake. He means a mistake, even a slight one, on the principles of being can throw an entire philosophy into a false direction and discolor, falsify, and distort its entire concept of the nature of ultimate reality. The reason is clear: philosophy is a body of doctrine built up by logical progression from its set of first principles of being. And since the concept of ultimate reality that each person forms determines the way he lives, it follows that humanism itself is at stake. Hence, this short prologue opens a large question that has become more urgent since the time of Thomas Aquinas. Let us give it some brief consideration.

What Kind of Humanism?

"The first conceptions of the intellect", St. Thomas writes, "are 'a being' and 'an essence'." This is the heart of the matter regarding the different kinds of philosophy and the nature of Christian Philosophy. Why is this the case? Because one must ask whether this "first conceiving" by the human intelligence is done only after one studies philosophy, or whether it is done from the very first use of human reason in all of its natural human situations. The answer of Christian Philosophy, fulfilling the aspirations of classical pagan philosophy, is that these first conceptions of the human intelligence begin with the dawn of natural reason in the life of each person, and they continue in the daily natural life of each person, whether educated or not, and especially whether one has taken formal courses in philosophy or not.

---

[1] See Excerpts for Part Two, Aquinas, p. 405.

Putting this another way, one must ask whether persons conceive these basic concepts before, or after, an academic education in philosophy?

If only after an education in academic philosophy, then humanism will depend on the various philosophers who have dominated the academic studies. Will the humanism reflect the thinking of Jean-Paul Sartre? Will it reflect a secular humanism? Will it be a humanism according to the thinking of Karl Marx?

Here one does indeed, then, stand before the supreme question of philosophy. In Christian Philosophy, continuing the natural heritage from the classical past, these basic concepts, these first conceptions of the intelligence, arise out of natural human living. Here one must recall the first chapter in Part One of this book, which discussed human rationality and the beginning of human thought. It was noted that the beginning of philosophy is properly among the primitives, rather than among the pre-Socratics. This is fundamentally important. Unless a "humanism" is fully natural, it cannot minister to personal happiness and social welfare on this earth or to the hearing of the gospel, which announces the good news of the promises of Christ.

This great question, therefore, determines what kind of philosophy Christian Philosophy is. It is not a philosophy that is seen and defined in its basic concepts according to whatever mode of philosophy happens to be popular in academic study in given times or places, or that one picks up by osmosis from a cultural environment determined by academic studies of certain philosophical kinds. Thus one does not come to life, or to the understanding of the Catholic Faith, from the philosophical order as such: from Kant, Hegel, Marx, or existentialists of the twentieth century.

These first conceptions of the intelligence, being and essence, are formed by us at a deeper level than academic education and prior to academic philosophical studies. This means that there is really and truly a natural level of philosophy, common to all men, and hence the natural foundation for a common doctrine that has the power of unifying men of various times, places, and cultures and the power of providing a natural foundation for an abiding and constant understanding of the word of God.

The implications of Aquinas' brief statement in the prologue are immense indeed. They bear upon the kind of philosophy that Christian Philosophy is, as distinct from other kinds of philosophy. It is authentic as philosophy but with its own specific quality. It is that philosophy that is rooted in, and that analyzes and develops academically, that natural right reason called common sense or good judgment, as it functions among ordinary persons everywhere in the basic situations of human life on this planet.

Along these lines, then, one can appreciate what Thomas Aquinas means when he says, "A slight initial error eventually grows to vast proportions."

Natural Reason: Foundation and Source of Metaphysics

Human rationality becomes visible at human beginnings. To make a tool, one must judge about things, understanding substances and their purposes and practical uses. This means that men think causally, and always have done so since human life first appeared on this planet. This means that men exercise a power of judgment that is quite distinct from sensory perception.

Men look on things with understanding. Animals look on things with the same kind of eyes—but without understanding. Hence they are called "dumb animals": they cannot name things according to understandings of what they are. This is the beginning of metaphysics: this recognizes a power in men to know the essences and substances of things, as distinct from the appearances that the senses perceive.

All knowledge begins in the senses, but with humans knowledge does not remain on the level of the senses. This gives human life its specific character. There are many forms of life on earth; plant life, animal life. The human form of life is similar to them in some ways, but quite different in other ways, and quite different as a whole. Plants live their kind of life automatically. So do animals, but less automatically: they follow inborn instincts. With human beings, however, life proceeds on the basis of the knowledge of things in their earthly environment, according to their various kinds, so that purposeful use of them for living becomes a human possibility. Furthermore, we have a mode of communication that fits this human way of life. This is deeply significant for philosophy, and we shall return to it.

The foundation and source of metaphysics lies in this human capacity to know things. Human beings, all through human history, indicate that they simply know that they know things and hence can use them in various helpful and practical ways. The truth in knowing is simply assumed, without question, implicitly.

In academic life of recent times in Western civilization, it has become common to think that we do not know things directly, but only our interior mental states and images. This raises the eyebrows of the common man everywhere. A famous philosopher whom we shall meet later in this course, Immanuel Kant, teaches that we do not know things at all. Things in themselves, he maintains, are unknowable. We only think that we know things in themselves. What we actually know, once we adopt his academic point of view in philosophy, is the a priori configuration of our own subjective self. Here again the natural judgment of men from the very origins will do more than raise an eyebrow. Other philosophical currents, in very recent times, deriving chiefly from Kant, teach that there is nothing that changes in the world about us. We only think that there is something that changes. Change takes place all by itself, without a thing there that changes. We experience simply a series of changes. Once again, the common good judgment of practical persons living human life across the ages on this planet will raise the eyebrow. The learned professor who teaches such doctrine will be asked: Do you mean there is nothing there that changes, not a thing that changes? That change is in a vacuum?

In discerning what kind of philosophy Christian Philosophy is, its basic connection with natural reason living ordinary natural life in the way proper to the specific character of human persons is fundamentally important. Men of all times and places have lived out of the knowledge that things change. There is a primacy of the being or thing that changes. Things somehow usually abide through many changes. Sometimes, however, they do not—as when they are burned up in fire, or when they provide nourishment for human beings, changing into the thing, the being, the person who is nourished.

Garrigou-Lagrange, one of the greatest followers of Thomas Aquinas in the present century, writes in the preface to his book *God: Existence and Nature* as follows: "In my book entitled *Common Sense and the Philosophy of Being,* it was shown that common sense or natural reason is a rudimentary philosophy of being, opposed to the philosophy of the phenomenon and to the philosophy of becoming. This demonstration shows that being and the principles implied in the concept of being constitute the formal, primary, and adequate object of common sense." Garrigou-Lagrange goes on to show that "the natural, spontaneous knowledge that we call common sense" is the substrate out of which the Classical Philosophy of Socrates, Plato, and Aristotle grew, and that the Fathers of the Church, headed by St. Augustine, provided with a new home and a higher level of luminosity as Christian Philosophy. "All these are the principles of our natural intelligence", he writes. "They are first manifested in what we call common sense, that is, the natural aptitude of intelligence, before all philosophical culture, to judge things sanely. Common sense, natural reason, seizes these self-evident principles from its notion of intelligible reality. But this natural common sense could not yet give these principles an exact and universal formulation."[2]

Philosophy, then, begins with the experience of human life as it has been lived since man appeared on this planet. This is a human life that proceeds by using unscientific knowledge: men used the power of reason and spoke in human language long before there were any schools, liberal arts, empirical sciences, or philosophy. These were developments that flowed out of the living of human life through the exercise of natural reason. And this exercise of natural reason grasps the concrete sensible things around us by the power of judgment. Men see things with understanding.

In conclusion, then, the prologue of St. Thomas Aquinas indicates the kind of philosophy that Christian Philosophy is: it is that kind of philosophy that

---

[2] *God: Existence and Nature* (St. Louis, Mo.: B. Herder, 1934) pp. 33 and 35. See also Excerpts for Part Two, Maritain, p. 406.

continues the heritage of the classical Greeks and the work of St. Augustine in building philosophy on the first principles of natural reason. Christian Philosophy does not begin with a priori and arbitrary substitutes for the first certitudes of natural reason. It is important to note, furthermore, that Christian Philosophy does not come out of religious faith. It is not some strange and esoteric kind of philosophy "fallen from heaven", as it were, imported from outside the domain of the ordinary exercise of natural reason in daily human life. Philosophy in its Christian form and kind comes out of natural human life on this planet. This human form is basically an animal life, but rational in its specific character. Christian Philosophy founded by St. Augustine and developed into a luminous exposition in St. Thomas Aquinas' treatise *On Being and Essence* is simply human philosophy drawn from human life and the things of daily living, and then made into an intellectual discipline, the seventh of the seven liberal arts.

Christian Philosophy, as summarized and taught by Thomas Aquinas, organizes and polishes *reflectively* the first concepts and the first principles, which are really present in man's *unreflected* rational thought and life. This rational foundation of human life becomes visible and audible in the fundamental structure of all human languages. This must be given a brief consideration.

Language: The Human Mode of Communication

Once again, that beginning of all knowledge and philosophical thought is a matter of common observation, that men possess a mode of communication that fits the natural and specific way of human life just considered. The lower animals communicate with each other by signals and sounds of various kinds. The human mode of communication, while similar generically, is specifically different in that it is not confined to mere emotional states, signals that communicate the presence of "danger", the "all clear" sign, and the like. Human communication expresses the natures and kinds of things in a way that can be handed on to others, and especially to the young. This is the secret of human social life on earth, and its ability to make progress and to develop a heritage that is handed on by teaching done in this human mode of communication.

In Genesis 2:19–20, we read, "Out of the ground the Lord God formed every beast of the field, and every fowl of the air; and he brought them unto the man to see what he would call them; and whatsoever the man would call every living creature, that was to be the name thereof. And the man gave names of all cattle, and to the fowl of the air, and to every beast of the field." This Masoretic text of the book of Genesis indicates with wonderful accuracy the relationship between the Creator who makes things and the man who names them. Thus language is a human convention, but it is a response to things as they are seen to be in reality.

Thus human language has been a distinctive and specific characteristic of human life since the beginning on this planet. The man and woman talk to each other about things: they discuss what they are, what good they are, how they work (according to their various properties and qualities), and what the different quantities and qualities mean for human living. Thus the man and the woman name things and describe their quantities and qualities and activities—in the kitchen, the kinds of food, and the ways of preparation; in the shop, the kinds and materials of things good for this or that, in making and doing things, in the forming of tools; and finally, in the field, what to plant, when to plant, how to plant, and why to plant. The same thing holds true for the domestication of animals. Thus, from beginning to end, human life on earth exhibits this specifically human mode of communication, which relates to the substances of things, their kinds, and their various properties, which relate to practical uses.

Philosophy has always recognized its close relationship to human language. "Linguistic philosophy", popular in recent decades, is not actually a new discovery. Since the ancient Greeks and through Christian times, especially in the works of St. Augustine and St. Thomas Aquinas, this closeness to the human reality as given in sensory perception, in seeing things with understanding, has always been a foundation of philosophical analysis.

Human Culture and Its Transmission

From these considerations it becomes immediately apparent that culture is specific to the human form of being. Man is capable of building a heritage and transmitting it to his children by teaching. Family life, therefore, always has involved the teaching of children. Men have a cultural heritage, which they transmit, as distinct from the biological and instinctual mode of life of the lower animals. Furthermore, this cultural heritage is not confined to the conditions of material life. It is not limited to concerns of the body. It does not concern itself solely with the economic order. This is a very recent idea, a philosophical construct originating in a dislocated and troubled academic life in the recent times of Western civilization. Lifting one's gaze to the wider perspective of mankind as a whole across the planet and back through the ages, it is clear that the cultural heritage always has included the burial of the dead, religious worship, recognition of the Creator, and the transmitting of values in the moral order to the oncoming generation. Philosophy has this human scene to consider as something given.

In the accumulation of the cultural heritage, and the handing on of its practices, the apprenticeships in the practical arts were developed from the earliest times. Thus so many pursuits emerged in developing human life: carpenters, bricklayers, stonecutters and metalworkers, and now more recently electricians and data processors. The very names of families are often rooted in these various practical arts: the Weavers, the Potters, the Carters, the Coopers, the Dyers, and so many other names that denote the practical arts in human life.

It was the glory of the Greeks to develop a different set of arts, the liberal arts, which cultivate knowledge for its own sake. These seven liberal arts, the substance of academic education among the Greeks and the Romans, were given a home in the Catholic Church by the Fathers of the Church and were handed forward chiefly in the form of St. Augustine's plan for the Christianized *Paideia*.

Metaphysics: The Word and the Reality

The word "metaphysics" is the ordinary name for the core discipline or central branch of philosophy. There are at least two reasons why this name came to be attached to this central branch. The first is a rather contingent and historical one. Aristotle, in ancient times, wrote his treatises on physics, the inanimate things of the cosmos, and on the soul, before proceeding to the general science or discipline that studies being as such and the principles of being. In the publishing of his treatises, this more general and fundamental branch of philosophy came after the physics—thus "meta-physics", in Greek. It simply refers to the treatises in philosophy that Aristotle published after the physics. They were located in this position in the scrolls, and then reprinted later on after his books on the physics: "metaphysics".

There is, however, a second reason, which writers always have noticed, namely, that these treatises after the physics study a reality beyond the things that we can touch, weigh, see, and analyze empirically. Thus "meta" indicates an object of study that is higher than that of physics and beyond the perception of the senses. It has a different formal object. It is that philosophical study that has the ability to ascend beyond the order of the senses to the intelligibles, as was noted in St. Augustine's foundational work. Metaphysics, then, is the philosophical discipline that studies reality in itself, above and beyond the physical reality open to the five senses.

Aristotle himself named this branch of philosophy "natural theology"—the *logos* or learned discourse regarding God that is built up by our natural powers of reason. This aspiration toward God by means of one of the seven natural liberal arts was the glory of Greek philosophy in the times of Socrates, Plato, and Aristotle. The idea was established. But it was not until the Fathers of the Church and St. Augustine that the idea was developed fully, so that the ascent to intelligible reality continued until it reached the Supreme Being in person who is the Creator of heaven and earth.

One can see this effort at ascent to intelligible reality in Plato's cave metaphor, but especially in Augustine's ascent to Truth itself, the Almighty Person, Creator of the universe.

Thomas Aquinas customarily calls this central branch of philosophy "the divine science". One must note that this is not the same as theology, the science that studies divine revelation, but that it is a natural science of divine things: God, his existence, and his attributes. Thomas Aquinas and Christian philosophers generally have customarily called this branch of philosophy "first philosophy". Why is metaphysics the first philosophy? Because it discerns the principles of existing realities as such, so that from the viewpoint of building intellectual life, it is the first discipline, the one that studies the source and the principles of all the other sciences.

So much for the word. The reality is that metaphysics is the core discipline of the seventh of the seven liberal arts. In the study of metaphysics one makes contact with the deepest and most fundamental roots of human cultural life. Metaphysics, for Thomas Aquinas, is not a "creative self-expression", but it is the intellectual discipline that has been fostered and cultivated as a part of human rationality from the beginnings of prehistoric life, through prehistoric times, and then intensively, as one of the seven liberal arts, during the times of historic cultural life. From the viewpoint of contacting one's roots as an intelligent person and an educated member of the Western heritage, the study of metaphysics is the most fundamental of all. In conclusion, in the English language, according to the *Oxford Dictionary,* metaphysics means first "the works of Aristotle which were placed after the physics". Then the word comes to have the meaning of that branch of philosophy that studies being and knowledge. Thus metaphysics is the culmination of the love for wisdom, the seeking after wisdom, because it deals with ultimate reality and its causes and principles. In Christian Philosophy the ascent to the intelligible order, as seen best in St. Augustine, reaches not mere abstractions, or the limited pagan concepts of emanations, or the World Soul, but the unique Supreme Being himself, who is the existing One, the source of existence for all other existing realities.

All of these considerations are implied in St. Thomas Aquinas' short prologue to his treatise *On Being and Essence.* Holding firmly in mind, then, that Christian Philosophy is "the natural metaphysics of mankind" in its highest and most polished academic statement, one can turn to consider the short chapters of *On Being and Essence.*

I

THE FIRST CONCEPTS AND THE FIRST PRINCIPLES

This present study of the essential content of Christian Philosophy is conceived as a companion to St. Thomas' treatise *On Being and Essence*. In some circumstances, *On Being and Essence* could be used as a textbook; in other circumstances, simply as companion reading. In any case, there will be a close correlation between this study and St. Thomas' treatise.[1]

In his prologue St. Thomas has told us that "the first conceptions of the intellect are 'a being' and 'an essence'". Here again one must stress that St. Thomas is explicitly conscious of teaching the common heritage in philosophy, and not elaborating some new discovery of his own. Notice the implication in the word "conception". The first concepts are what the intellect first conceives. The first concepts are "being" and "essence". Notice that the intellect first conceives a thing as existing and not a mental picture about that thing. The message from St. Thomas is clear. The intellect does not conceive the configuration of the subjective self, or a priori forms, as Kant will call them. In Christian Philosophy the first concepts are concepts of reality, and not of the mind or subjective knowing self. They are conceptions of the mind upon which the mind can then begin to reflect and use in thinking. But philosophy does not begin with the self: it begins with things in reality. Here again is the importance of care in the small beginnings, lest an error be made that becomes immense later on.

Next, St. Thomas says that we ought to go from the meaning of being to the meaning of essence. He explains why: it is because the concept of being is easier to form than the concept of essence. He will bring us to this later.

Being: The First of the First Concepts

Notice that all knowledge begins with things that the five senses perceive. All human knowledge begins in the senses, with existing things surrounding the knower. Then philosophy studies and analyzes these existing things from the viewpoint of their existence. It asks first why they exist at all, distinct from nothingness; and then it asks why they exist in the various ways that they do.

Cats and dogs and the lower animals generally have sensory perception of the same things that we see in our environment. A human being, however, sees the

[1] See Excerpts for Part Two, Aquinas, p. 405.

things of sense with understanding. This is the supreme challenge of philosophical study: to bring into explicit and open awareness this understanding of what being is.

It is good to approach the concept of being by replacing it with the Anglo-Saxon English word *thing*. Somehow the word *thing* is more earthy, more concrete. The word *being* seems to elude us. The word *thing* then simply means an existing reality in front of us. It is a reality that subsists of itself. It is a thing that is there. It stands out from its environment, distinct from its causes. It can be anything that exists: a notebook, a chair, a desk, a tree, another human being, or whatever.

Thus there are two good Anglo-Saxon words, since English is a mixture of the Germanic and the Latin, the words *thing* and *being*.

One can take a step further in this pursuit of the concept of being by going for a moment to the Latin, which was the mother tongue spoken by St. Thomas Aquinas and in which he wrote *On Being and Essence (De Ente et Essentia).* Customarily, we shall avoid Latin, knowing that we discuss these fundamentals in our own mother tongue, English, but for the moment will consider the Latin for a being or a thing. The Latin word is *Ens*. It simply means an existing reality. In the ablative it is *ente,* hence St. Thomas' title *De Ente.* In Latin whenever the letters *ns* are associated with a word, one knows that the activity of doing something is expressed. Thus, *currens* means someone running; *dicens* means a person saying something; *tacens* means someone being still for the moment; *orans* means the activity of someone who is praying. In other words, this facet of the Latin language conveys immediately the meaning of doing something, exercising an activity.

With the word *ens,* it becomes clear that an activity is being exercised. It is the activity of existing. Thus we come to the word *being.* To feel the impact of its meaning, one must hyphenate it: be-ing. This is because "ing" in English corresponds to *ns* in Latin: the activity, the actual act, of doing something.

With this said, one must reflect that these other various activities—running, talking, being silent, praying—each and all presuppose a higher and previous activity, namely that of existing. Is existing the highest and ultimate act or activity? Yes, indeed, because if one does not exist, one can do none of those other activities, including praying. If one does not exist, one is no-thing: nothing.

Thus existence is seen immediately, by intuition, to correlate with nonexistence. This first concept, resulting from seeing things with understanding, results from the understanding that if a thing exists, it absolutely cannot at the same time be nothing. The first principles are already beginning to emerge by intuition from the first concepts, namely, by insight and understanding.

The Two Meanings of the Word "Being"

There are two ways of using the word "being", as St. Thomas points out. In the first way, it denotes the ten categories of Aristotle. In the second way, it signifies the truth of propositions, expressed by the word "is" (as in "the dog *is* black"). St. Thomas postpones this second use, and we shall meet it in a coming chapter. Obviously it is important for human knowledge, because human knowledge is stated in the form of propositions, and it is basically important that the statements be true. This is especially important for the field of catechetics, because the Articles of Faith are propositions that are true by the truth of divine revelation, not merely our culture's way of symbolizing religious yearnings!

For the time being, however, we ponder the first use of the word "being", meaning things that exist. This is the beginning of all philosophizing: again, it is a beginning by using the five human senses, but philosophy does not remain on their level.

The Concept of Being

The student of philosophy should not, therefore, be deterred by this word "being", as if it were extremely difficult to formulate mentally the insight and understanding that the word denotes. "In this first sense of being," St. Thomas writes, "only that can be called a being that posits something in reality." Note the words: *something in reality.* This is the beginning of healthy realism as a fundamental orientation in philosophy.

This is so fundamentally important that one should listen to St. Thomas in several other places in his writings, for this is a philosophical fundamental in Christian Philosophy. "The first act of the human intellect is to know being, namely, a reality as the first and proper object of the understanding, just as sound is the first and proper object of hearing, and as sight is the first and proper object of our eyes" (*S.T.* I, 5, 2). St. Thomas frequently compares our intellectual insight and understanding of things with our sensory perception of things. The eye of the senses is not the same thing as the inner eye of the mind; they are analogous, however, and eyesight especially helps one to understand what it is to see intellectually, to penetrate below the level of the senses to an understanding of the inner nature of the thing that stands before us in reality. This was a favorite thought of St. Augustine, and it passed from him to all Christian thinking and teaching in the schools of Christendom. Thomas Aquinas receives this heritage from the Fathers of the Church and develops in a marvelous way his teaching on "the inner eye of the mind". He remains always the disciple of St. Augustine.

"By nature", St. Thomas writes in *C.G.* (II, 83), "the human intellect knows being and the immediate principles of beings as such. Out of this knowledge arises the understanding of the first principles, for example, the principle that affirmation and denial cannot coexist, and other similar principles." Notice how he links the first concepts with the first principles. One stands here at the very rock bottom of philosophy, the concept of being as the first concept, from which the first principles of being and reality begin immediately to arise before the insight and understanding of the inner eye of the intellect.

One should not, therefore, think that the concept of being is elusive, or abstract, or difficult. In the study of philosophy one should keep close to what words denote: the important thing is the understanding of the meaning of the words, and here it is quite simple: it denotes the reality about us as existing, simply as existing.

The Categories of Being

This is the proper place to note for a moment the heritage of teaching coming from Aristotle on the categories of being. Aquinas has alluded to the categories as the first meaning of the concept of being. The categories form the content of a short portion of Aristotle's treatise *The Organon.* From Aristotle this treatise on the categories passes to the Fathers of the Church, and in fact St. Augustine made a special study of it. Christian Philosophy received this report on the way things are, the kinds of ways in which things are, from the classical heritage. Augustine passed the understandings about these categories forward to the schools of Christendom, so that it became a commonplace for all young people studying the cycle of the arts. We have here Thomas Aquinas' summary of a standard, widely known point of doctrine coming from Classical into Christian Philosophy.

What then are the categories? The Greek word indicates that they are simply the ways or kinds of existence. They are ways or modes in which things existed. Aristotle analyzed things around him and concluded that there are ten categories, the first called "substance", the second comprising nine kinds of "accidents": i.e., quantity, quality, relation, place, time, position, state, action, passion.

By this he means that any thing that we encounter in the living of our lives has substantial reality. The first category, then, simply denotes beings about us. The other nine categories are attributes or modifications of the various substances. Aristotle taught that one can say every thing is good for some purpose. Some things are intelligent; others are not. Some are human beings; some are brute animals; some are plants; some are rocks. Thus there are various sorts and kinds and classes of substances. Regarding each of these substantial realities, one can affirm nine modalities. One can state that such and such a substance is small, large, long, or short. One can say whether one saw it yesterday, or expects to see it tomorrow. One can say whether it is here nearby, or over there, or far away. In other words, one can affirm all of the other nine categories of being regarding each of their substances: their quality, the qualities they have, the actions they do, the ways they can be modified, the ways they can suffer actions to take place upon them, their relationships to other things, their location in space and time.

It is clear that Aristotle's short treatise on the categories is related to human language, which has parts of speech that communicate these characteristics of realities about us. In his treatise, then, Aristotle's categories reflect the structure of every human language on earth: nouns, things, activities regarding things, active and passive modifications, the adjectives, the adverbs, and all the rest. This is an instance of the way in which Classical Greek Philosophy reflected the exercise of spontaneous natural reason, as we have noted already. These modes or categories in which things exist relate closely to the basic parts of speech and reflect that close relationship between human discourse and philosophical studies, especially when philosophical studies abide faithfully and closely by natural reason.

It is immediately clear that one could perhaps group these categories differently and have a larger or a smaller number. One could simply say that the categories are substance on the one hand, and accidental modifications of substance on the other hand. Philosophers always try to improve Aristotle's list of the categories. Immanuel Kant, for example, reduced them to four. Perhaps the best philosophical comment was given by a philosopher who wrote, "it is easier to criticize Aristotle's list of categories than to draw up a better one".

This simple but very fundamental concept of the categories of being are simply the general modes in which real things exist. In his treatise Thomas Aquinas presupposes all of this, because his brothers for whom he wrote his treatise had studied it all in the cycle of liberal arts. Hence he says simply, "the word being is used with two meanings: the first meaning, that of the ten categories, and the second, the truth of propositions".

Intelligible Reality: "The Intelligibles"

By way of conclusion on this first concept, the concept of being, one should note the implication at the very beginning of philosophy that men have two kinds of knowledge. One is that of the five senses, and the other is a different kind, qualitatively different in kind, the endowment of the person with intelligence. The concept of being is not something an animal sees but something a human being understands. The human being conceives this idea of existing reality. This implies a second and higher kind of knowledge in the human mode of existing. This will run through the entire study of philosophy until we come to full philosophical anthropology and understand philosophically the specific difference of human beings from all other kinds of things, especially the higher animals on this planet.

Epistemology (the philosophy of knowledge) is already coming into view as an integral part of metaphysics. Note that it is not a preliminary to but rather a consequence of metaphysics. Thus the watershed between idealism, which ends by locking the human self up within the self, and realism, that healthy recognition of natural reason that we know existing realities, and indeed as existing. This basic fundamental, this parting of the ways among philosophers, already comes into view. Thus again, the importance of great care in these small and early beginnings, lest an error in them grow to immense proportions.

Essence: The Second of the First Concepts

The second of the basic and first concepts, the one that Thomas Aquinas said we should take up after being, because it is harder, is the essence of a thing. It is that in the thing by which it exists in its own way. It is that by which it is its own kind of thing—a dog, a tree, a book, a human being, or whatever. It is that in the thing by which it is the kind of thing that the mind understands it to be. Notice that we continue to think and to speak of a thing that is and not simply of a configuration of the human mind.

The idea of essence is something common to all existing things. Every reality must have an essence of some kind. It must have a principle by which it is this instead of that, a dog instead of a cat; otherwise, it could not be this particular kind of thing. Hence, at the beginning of his Chapter II, St. Thomas will summarize this first chapter in the words "Essence is that according to which a thing is said to be". It will hardly be possible to find a more simple and clear statement on the essence of a thing. He says in the same place, "The essence is that by reason of which a thing is called a being."

At this point Thomas Aquinas, very helpfully, takes up other names for this same reality, this same principle, this same basic and initial concept or understanding of the mind. "Essence is that by which a thing is placed in its proper genus or kind." Suppose one has a basket of potatoes: Does each one have the essence of a potato? Indeed, for otherwise it could not be the kind of thing that it is. Thus essence is seen to be common to many things, if they are similar in the way they exist. Is there an essence of the human mode of existing? If so, it would be "humanity". Does such an essence exist? Indeed: every human person whom we meet participates in this essence.

Then Thomas Aquinas brings up the word "quiddity", not familiar to us, because it simply transliterates the Latin *quidditas.* It comes from the Latin word *quid,* which asks the question What? Quiddity then tells us what the thing is, and it does so by giving us its definition. Hence we see that definitions state the essence of things. This helps us to obtain a better insight and understanding into this second of the first concepts.

Again, essence is frequently called the form of a thing, namely, the form in which it exists. We ask in biology for the forms of life. There is the cat's form, or the dog's form, or the form of life proper to a tree. The word "form" means the essence in relationship to the activities of the thing.

Again the word "nature": this is the essence considered from the viewpoint of the activities flowing from that being and proper to it. Nature denotes the essence of the thing in relationship to its proper operation. Every being or thing has a set of operations or activities proper to itself.

Regarding all these various basic words of philosophical study, one can summarize by saying that each existing thing, each being, has its own proper essence by which it is its own kind of thing. Thus St. Thomas concludes, "Essence means that through which and in which and by which a thing has its act of existing." Notice again how Thomas Aquinas continues the heritage of Christian Philosophy founded by St. Augustine, with its emphasis upon the act of existing, as distinct from the forms of bodily things visible in the cosmos. This was the great step forward and upward made by Christian Philosophy from the characteristic limitations of the earlier pagan Classical Philosophy.

The Act of Existing

With this we are turning from the first concepts toward the first principles. When the human intelligence sees things with understanding, recognizing existence as necessarily distinct from nothingness, we begin to identify principles by which things are, or exist. In the first principle, it is the essence that determines what kind of thing each thing is. Now we come to the second principle, the principle by which it exists. This is its act of existing in its particular kind or essence.

It may be helpful at this point to ponder for a moment the short Latin word *esse*. It is very common in the works of Thomas Aquinas, and a constant problem for those who translate his works into English. The reason is its simplicity. It is the Latin infinitive meaning "to be". Some treatises in Christian Philosophy translate *esse* quite literally, so that Christian Philosophy is sprinkled with "to be". It is important not to bring St. Thomas into an English that is no longer English. It is better to use "the act of existing", or simply the word "existing". The important thing is to understand the meaning of *esse:* it is the infinitive that always means the activity of doing something. We recall the activities mentioned above in the participle, *ens* and the like. These various activities that things exercise depend on a prior reality, namely, the act of existing. This is the most fundamental activity. Unless a thing exercises this act of existing, it is nothing.

The study of philosophy turns entirely around this fundamental concept and the principles that derive from it. Furthermore, without these simple and fundamental basics of philosophical analysis, one cannot come to a natural knowledge of God established by reason. This foundation is presupposed by revelation and by the catechesis of the First Article of the Apostles' Creed.

Christians do not say, "Who knows if God literally *exists;* what is important is that I attain 'a higher level of consciousness,' or 'interior peace' ". Christians know

God by faith as Supreme Being: an all-powerful Being, the source of all created life, able to save us from the powers of dissolution.

We stand here, then, at the very heart of the Christian Philosophy taught by St. Augustine, St. Thomas Aquinas, and all of their colleagues. It was not their personal philosophy so much as the philosophy of Christian mankind, receiving the heritage of that earlier classical liberal art.

"There are two principles to be considered in a thing," writes St. Thomas Aquinas, "namely, its nature or quiddity or essence, and its act of existing." This is a golden statement, the briefest statement of the Christian Philosophy of Thomas Aquinas. The entire content of Christian Philosophy is actually contained in this statement, as a mighty oak tree is contained in a small acorn. Having arrived at an understanding of these two principles, one develops all the content of metaphysics from its implications, including those for the existence and reality of the Supreme Being.

One can conjure up a picture of this set of philosophical fundamentals in the following way. One can picture any being that exists. Any reality that exists in its own name and right, any of the things about us. Then one can picture principles by which such things exist. One can put on a blackboard, for example, the words "any being". Then one can draw a line down toward the left, marking its "essence". This denotes the principle by which it is the kind of thing that it is. Then one can draw a second line down toward the right parallel to the first, the essence, and write, "The act of existing". This is the principle by which it actually is in reality what it is. It is now beyond the realm of mere possibility and is an actually existing thing. Thus one can conjure up mentally this small diagram to help to consider and to understand the difference between things that exist, and the principles by which they exist in the way that they are seen to do. All of Christian Philosophy, coming from the heritage of the greatest of the Greeks, is contained in this basic insight and understanding.

The Principles of Being

We recall that Thomas Aquinas recommends that we move from the concept of being, as something easier to grasp, to the concept of essence. We human beings are constitutionally created to prefer images. We live among bodily things, and we are bodily things ourselves. Our five senses give us images. Now an existing reality, any being, need not necessarily be one of us bodily things. However, at least for many years of our life, we do not realize this because we never meet anything but bodily things. We live in a world of images and are at home in this world.

When we come to the principles by which things are, even material things, we are leaving the world of images behind. The imagination is not the instrument for philosophical study. We recall this from St. Augustine. The conception of the intellect is not the same as the perception of the senses.

Returning then, to this basic statement: two principles are to be considered in each thing, namely, its nature, quiddity, or essence, and also its act of existing. These are principles of being, by which a reality is the way it is. They cannot be imagined. The imagination must be left behind. This is the challenge of metaphysics, its difficulty, and at the same time its importance. One must remember that we are lovers of images, and this long before the advent of the image industry. As a matter of fact, it is said that we are becoming more and more creatures of the image because of television. We can imagine a gigantic black horse with a flowing mane and beautiful wings, with diamonds for its eyes and golden teeth. But at the same time it is very difficult for us to understand what the two principles of being are.

Another way of putting this is to consider that the principles of being are metaphysical. They are beyond the physical: they are deeper in reality than the physical. The senses perceive the phenomena, the surfaces of reality. A philosopher must rule the imagination out, knowing that he has begun a journey beyond imagery, beyond the physical. Metaphysics! The philosopher, then, continuing St. Augustine's admonition, must simply bracket out the imagination. It cannot help us. It prevents us from philosophical understandings. If we introduce our imagination into our philosophizing, we end up as very poor philosophers. We will end, indeed, by calling philosophy a generalized statement of the findings of the empirical sciences. This is being done widely in our own times, but it is being done because of a departure from Christian Philosophy and a failure to keep it alive among us. Christian Philosophy is not superficial, and it is something quite different from the generalized statement of the findings of empirical sciences.

Turning this matter around to see it perhaps better from a different direction, one can say that the principles of being are in the realm of intelligibility. They are the very beginning of the perception of the intelligibles by the intellect. They belong to the realm of understanding and insight, as distinct from the realm of sensory perception. Again: to see things with understanding.

This is a watershed among philosophers and philosophies. Are these principles of being truly and really real? Are they themselves a part of reality? Or are they simply modes of speech? Do they perhaps simply result from our inward subjective configurations? Again, that admonition to be careful in the beginning about small error, which becomes a great one later. A primary instance is at hand. This error becomes immense very quickly, when we begin to think that these principles of existence are no longer in things. This is the basic mistake, for example, of current existentialism. As a matter of fact, it is a basic mistake in all philosophies that are blind to the Supreme Being. All atheistic modes of philosophizing take their beginning at this point. They cannot or will not understand that there are principles in reality that one cannot perceive with the senses or form an image of by the imagination. But we can understand that they exist in reality. This is to see things with understanding.

Anticipating for the moment, there will arise a modern philosophy, especially in the form of Kantianism, that declares such realities to be unknowable, so that we have left only our inner subjective configurations. The ability to see these principles intellectually, with insight and understanding, must be cultivated. This is the reason for studying the science of metaphysics. Later on, one will obtain an insight upon these principles of being and existence from the viewpoint of him who stands far above our human scene, who makes things to be, giving them their act of existence. At this point in our study one can say that if there is a creating God who makes things to be what they are, then these principles of being are the realities by which he makes them to be. And this will help immensely in coming to a synthetic grasp of metaphysics.

At the present point, the important thing is to recognize the value that this discipline, metaphysics, the culminating discipline among the seven liberal arts, has in itself, with its own proper object of study. Here we have before us this proper object: it is these principles by which things exist. We have moved already beyond the physical. The proper object of this discipline is different from the object of ordinary observation or from the objects of the various empirical sciences.

In our time, science has assisted philosophy. Philosophy studies a different kind of reality, beyond the whole possible order of what microscopes and telescopes reveal, namely, the underlying principles that govern existence as such. The recent sciences assist philosophy because they assist the eye, revealing dimensions and perspectives that go beyond what the five natural senses perceive. This points toward true metaphysical analysis.

In conclusion, then, the philosopher must leave the imagination behind, not expecting to have images of these principles of being. No matter how powerful a microscope might yet be invented, it will never see a principle of being. This is achieved by insight and understanding in a different order from that in which even the most powerful scientific instruments function.

Putting this negatively, one can understand that these principles of being, if denied, will leave us without a sufficient reason for existence. This leads directly to absurdity, to the view that reality is irrational. Thus one ends with contemporary existentialism. The root is the metaphysical refusal of the evidence for these principles of being. One cannot overstress this insight: "What the intellect first conceives is *ens,* the reality of the thing, together with its principles by which it is what it is." Perhaps this can be clarified from another direction by considering the degrees of abstraction.

The Three Degrees of Abstraction

"Abstraction" is a technical word used in practically all systems of philosophy. Phenomenologists talk about bracketing things out in order to consider only what remains. This is a way of talking about abstraction. Abstraction is a power of human thinking by which certain aspects of things are omitted. In Christian Philosophy it means that the material aspects of things are dropped out of consideration. For example, I can consider that a book in my hand weighs so much, just as I can consider different kinds of three-ring notebooks, without considering whether they are made of light plastic or of heavy board with metal rims. The heaviness of the thing can be left out of consideration. This is a form of abstraction.

Abstraction is always a dematerializing of things, or, to put it positively, it is a step toward understanding spiritual reality. The less material a thing is, the more it moves toward the immaterial and the world of the spirit. All knowledge, even the knowledge that lower animals have, is incipiently spiritual. It is not yet actually spiritual, among them, but yet it is oriented toward this higher world of things that exist apart from the concrete conditions of matter. Thus abstraction is a power of the human intellect that spiritualizes, if one will, the object of knowledge.

There are three degrees of abstraction. In the preface of his commentary on Aristotle's *Metaphysics,* St. Thomas Aquinas has a beautifully lucid treatment of these three degrees.

The first degree of abstraction is simply the relinquishing of the individual aspects of sensible objects, so that one studies not this one or that one but simply that kind of thing in general. Take water as an example. In the first degree of abstraction, one leaves aside this pitcher, that pool, a lake, or the Atlantic Ocean of water in order simply to study water in itself, as such. By this study scientists come to learn its properties, just as men using natural reason come to know many of the properties of water and to make use of them. One can see that this first degree of abstraction opens the door to every empirical science: physics, chemistry, biology, and now recently nuclear physics.

The second degree of abstraction permits the mind to prescind from all content of bodily things, in order to consider nothing but their dimensions and their movements. Immediately, the mathematical sciences come into view. This is the reason why Plato insisted that mathematics is the proper and natural preparation for philosophy. He knew that it is a higher level of mental preparation, one that prepares for the third degree of abstraction.

The third level of abstraction is the highest: there is no fourth level. This third and highest degree of abstraction omits all the characteristics of the thing, any thing, and considers only the ultimate reality common to any thing that is or can be, namely, its being or existence together with the principles by which it exists as it does. This produces the science of metaphysics, which is the heart and core of every system of philosophy. Every kind of philosophy has a metaphysical view of ultimate reality, ultimate existence, as its heart and core.

Again let us illustrate this with water. We have been using water throughout our history, sometimes with due admiration and even gratitude. Since the first man and the first woman we have been drinking water. We have been washing ourselves and things that we use in water. We have been using water in countless other ways. It is a simply beautiful substance, one that serves us magnificently. Wondering about water, such a common element on earth, the Pre-Socratics began to speculate that there are four elements: earth, air, fire, and water. They argued much about an order among these four elements. In those early times of the Greek heritage, no one doubted that there are at least these four basic elements. Their question was whether fire is more recent than the other three, or whether perhaps water is the more recent. While this speculation was going on among the handful of Pre-Socratic philosophers, people continued to use water with their natural reason, as always. They continued to know that the water in a bucket is quite different from a jar containing apple juice. As time went on, men learned to make something called wine—again quite different from water. People used it with the recognition that it has its own different substantial nature and character, constituting it to be the reality that it is.

In our own times, scientists have arrived at the precise knowledge that water is really a compound of two atoms of hydrogen with one atom of oxygen: H_2O. Thus science now understands that water cannot be the ultimate element. This discovery, however, remains in the first degree of abstraction. It has no effect whatsoever on the mathematics of liquids: how they behave, how they move, and the like. Even more, it has no effect whatsoever upon the metaphysical knowledge of the principles by which all things are, including therefore this particular thing, water. So too with the substantial reality of bread, or of any other material object or thing studied by scientists. In the twentieth century, nuclear physicists working in their laboratories are in a strange world indeed. It was long thought to the threshold of our day that atoms were the ultimate reality, indivisible, final. Now, in the twentieth century, atoms have been literally split apart. A nuclear physicist now knows well that a bucket of water from the nuclear point of view is almost entirely empty space. The atoms of water, the H_2O, are so constructed that they have a very tiny nucleus, and then immensely far away from that nucleus, relatively speaking, they have particles circulating, something like a planetary system. The distances in this tiny atom of water are proportionately so great that a bucket of water becomes almost nothing from the viewpoint of solid matter.

Is a human being constructed in this same way? Indeed, yes, because a human being is a material body. A physicist, professor of nuclear physics, comes home from his daily work in the classroom and the laboratory and picks up his beautiful little daughter and places her on his knee. He reflects on what a marvelous being she is. Looking into her eyes, listening to her chatter about the events of the day, he stops to think that as a physicist he knows very well that all the matter sitting on his knee could fit inside the head of a pin, from the viewpoint of its "solidity". But the physicist, whether as a normally reacting human being or as a philosophically well-educated person, knows that this creature on his knee is far more than just matter.

So Adam names things. Parents, whether they are nuclear physicists or not, name their little daughters. People call things water, bread, wine, and so on, denoting the essence of things. The study of philosophy, if it is done in the right way, if it is the right kind of philosophy, is like a slow and gradual dawn in the morning, whereby one gradually sees these things and understands them better.

An important catechetical application follows. Through careful philosophical analysis, one can arrive at the intellectual conviction that the order of the empirical sciences is different from that of the mathematical sciences, and that metaphysics again exists in its own order of knowledge. Do people need to study academic philosophy in order to know such things? Not really. People in general, the ordinary people using natural reason, understand these basic truths without studying philosophy. Natural right reason perceives these things without analyzing them and without being able to discuss them in the academic manner. In particular, catechesis teaches people by faith that there is more to reality than what the senses perceive. When people are catechized correctly, prior to any theologizing, prior to the study of philosophy, they know this on religious grounds. And thus people quietly accept the teaching of the Church regarding the Holy Eucharist, because it is based on the insight and understanding that there is indeed more to reality than what the senses perceive.

Potency and Act

"Potency" and "act" are terms used in the heritage of Greek and Christian Philosophy to help understand better the principles of being that we have been studying. As we shall see, potency is a real capacity for a certain type of existence, and an act is what brings that capacity to reality in the order of things. Here one must return to that mental picture, that diagram of an existing being, with the two lines dropping from it, one toward that by which it is its kind of thing, the essence, and the other toward the act of existing. There is a principle of being called "essence", and there is a principle of being called "the act of existing".

Circling around this for deeper understanding, we can recognize that the essence is a potency for existence. The act of existing is the actuality, or act, that activates, so to speak, or makes real, that kind of thing.

This enables the mind to see that the essence is correlated with the act of existence, so that one must recognize that they are really different from each other, even though the one looks toward the other. This is the famous distinction between essence and existence, which recognizes that one is potential and that the other is the actualization of that potentiality. This helps the mind to see that they are really distinct in things that exist. They are principles that are different from each other.

A second point about act and potency is that they are correlative to each other—really distinct from each other but correlative to each other. This is the basic philosophical doctrine in Christian Philosophy regarding the principles of being. They are correlative in the fullest sense in that only this particular act of existing can fulfill this particular potentiality. This is true for any being whatsoever, except one unique Being whom we shall meet a bit later in this metaphysical analysis.

Potency, then, is a real capacity, that is, a capacity that really exists, for a certain type of existence. It is a capacity in reality to receive a particular and definite act of existing. The act of existing is the perfection that brings that capacity to be real in the order of things. Hence we say that both the act and the potency are real, existing in each thing.

What is the case before the thing actually exists? At that level, the thing is a possibility and not an actuality. One cannot understand this properly until we come to that unique Being, God the Creator. But one can begin to see that a possible being is one seen by God in his mind. If it becomes actual, God will be involved somehow. For the present, that must be pigeonholed for further explanation, leaving it in the realm of possibility for the moment.

In his commentary on Aristotle's *Metaphysics,* St. Thomas Aquinas gives an explanation that may be helpful. "The primary simple principles", he writes, "cannot be defined, for in definitions one cannot go back to infinity. Act is such a principle; therefore, it cannot be defined. Yet through its correlation with potency, the proportion of these two things to each other can be seen by the mind, and thus the mind comes to insight and understanding on what actual existence is."

One can take the homely example of an architect, who has in mind a house that he intends to build. That house is in potency. But it can be built and brought into actuality, so that it stands existing on a given street. One can think of numberless similar examples, and by means of them arrive at that insight and understanding of what act and potency are, generic terms for the principles of being that are in existing realities.

The First Principles of Being and Knowledge

So far, following Thomas Aquinas' short exposition of the essential content of Christian Philosophy, we have been speaking of the first concepts, essence, and the act of existing. We have noted that these concepts are actually the source of principles. They put us into contact with the principles by which things are, the principles of being. We are coming now to something slightly different, to consider the first principles of reality from the viewpoint of our understanding of them. First principles seen intellectually by insight and understanding are the most fundamental elements of human knowledge.

The First Self-Evident Understandings

These self-evident principles or understandings, in the literature of philosophy, are called simply "the first principles". Often, however, it is left ambiguous whether they are simply first principles in the mind, or whether they are in reality in the manner that we have been noting. It is fundamental to Christian Philosophy to recognize that these principles are in reality before they are in our minds. We know them with internal knowledge because we see them in reality by intellectual insight and understanding. Why is this? If they did not exist in reality, the reality we see and know could not exist at all, nor could it exist in the way that it does with its kind of essence.

Here we shall list a few of the first principles that we encounter in the heritage of Christian Philosophy, and indeed in the heritage of philosophy generally in the entire cultural heritage of our Western world. These first principles can be studied in Socrates, Plato, and Aristotle. They can be studied in Neo-Platonism. They can be studied in the Fathers of the Church and especially in St. Augustine, the founder of Christian Philosophy, who handed this body of philosophical knowledge forward to the schools of Christendom purified and elevated. These principles can be studied in Boethius, and in many teachers in the schools of Christendom across the centuries to Thomas Aquinas. All the colleagues of Thomas Aquinas in the early days of the Western universities taught these first principles. What we are saying is that these first principles are common property in our human heritage, not a discovery of Thomas Aquinas, not the exclusive property of Christians, and much less mere personal opinions of St. Thomas, St. Augustine, or any other philosopher. They are not the result of creative self-expression, to mention the phrase once more, but they are the result of intellectual insight and understanding into reality. There is a sort of order among the first principles, which philosophers discuss in learned journals. There seems to be general agreement that one principle is more "first" than the rest. It is the one that is really first in reality. Let us therefore begin with it.

1. *The principle of contradiction*

It is appropriate to listen for a moment to Thomas Aquinas (*S.T.* I–II, 94, 2):

> Being is the first thing that the intellect apprehends. This understanding is included in all further intellectual apprehension, and, therefore, it is the first indemonstrable principle, so basic that it cannot be demonstrated by anything prior to itself. This first indemonstrable principle is the impossibility of simultaneously affirming and denying, because in it is the very idea of being and nothing. For example, a table cannot be round and not round in the same respect. It could have a round top and square legs, but not a round and nonround top. All

the rest of philosophical knowledge follows from this principle, as Aristotle teaches in the fourth book of his *Metaphysics*.

Here one sees the principle of contradiction arising by immediate insight and understanding of the intelligence, out of the first concept. It is absolutely basic in philosophy to see this intellectually. Mothers often show their children the small diamond on their wedding ring, allowing the fascinated child to see the diamond flash with a wonderful light, with a display of variously colored lights, as the mother's hand turns. It is as if that diamond had a tiny fire, flashing variously. Philosophy, the study and the analysis of the first principles, is similar. The slightest small turn of these first concepts gives us another principle of being and knowledge. But it is that original concept of being that generates them all. This is what St. Thomas means by saying that being is the formal object of the human intelligence.

This principle can be stated in many ways, and every language on earth can be used to express it. But the meaning is always the same: "Whatever exists, cannot at the same time be nothing." This is an absolute certitude. It is universally and necessarily true. A person of perverse intention can tell you verbally that he does not believe its truth. But the fact is, in his living, he acts as if it were true. With such a person, one can only show that the denial of a first principle introduces absurdity and irrationality. And one can pray for such persons. Sometimes, it gives a strange kind of feeling of freedom in a perverted and negative way to deny the first principles. Sometimes persons prefer their perverted concept of freedom to the truth, even so basic a truth. This is the very definition of Satan, the one who prefers his self-concept of freedom to the truth. This first principle is very basic, and one hardly finds anyone, except those with highly specialized philosophical systems, who would quarrel with it.

With this one can ask what would be the second among such intelligible principles.

2. *The principle of sufficient reason*

The principle of sufficient reason seems something proper to a kindergarten. "Whatever is, is; whatever is not, is not." What do these words mean? It means that whatever exists must have a sufficient reason for existing, either in itself, or outside itself. Only naughty children explain a mess by saying, "I don't know, Mommy, it just happened!" Now one sees that this principle of sufficient reason for existence opens up a variety of situations and questions. Why does this thing exist this way? Or how does it come to happen this way? How does it come to happen at all? Why is it here? What does it exist for?

These questions are the names of four causes, and thus the four causes come into philosophical view. The four kinds of causes arise out of this principle of sufficient reason. Two of these causes are intrinsic to each thing. In philosophical literature, these intrinsic causes are usually called "the material cause" and "the formal cause". We shall consider these causes in the next chapter.

For the present, we can note the external causes. If the act of existing did not exist at some time or other, but came to that being, that thing, at a certain point, then there must be an external cause, external to this thing, in the order of existence. This is called "the efficient cause", and it explains the sufficient reason for the existence of such a thing that once did not exist. The efficient cause is simply what makes the thing to be or to exist. A chisel is one of the efficient causes of the rock becoming a statue.

Finally, the efficient cause would itself lack a sufficient reason for going into action, unless there were another extrinsic cause, the fourth of the four causes, namely, the reason why. This is the purpose. If the efficient cause did not have a purpose in view, an end that is foreseen, it would not merit action. Hence each thing has a purpose, which the efficient causes seek, carry out, achieve, and desire. The purpose of chiseling the rock is to produce the finished statue. Thus directly out of the principle of sufficient reason philosophical insight reaches the four causes. These four causes answer the question Why?—the typical question of the little child. Philosophy, Aristotle taught, begins by wondering why. In Christian Philosophy this wondering concentrates upon the order of existence as such. "When I ask why about something", Thomas Aquinas writes in his commentary on Aristotle's *Physics,* "I am inquiring into its cause. Indeed as little children inquire, but in answering this question we must make use of one or other or all of the four causes."

The principle of sufficient reason, then, answers the question Why? It has four meanings, partly different, partly the same. They are analogous to each other. When one puts these four meanings together, one has the four causes, which give a complete philosophical answer to the reason why each thing exists.

3. The principle of substance

Various philosophers state this principle variously, but the meaning is always the same. It comes to this: that that exists, the thing itself, the subject of existence, is distinct from the various modes, qualifications, attributes, qualities, quantities, and actions that it may have. Putting this very simply, the thing itself is different from its attributes. The attributes tend to be variables. The thing itself usually abides through a wonderful variety of changes in its modes and attributes. One needs but think of the apple blossom changing gradually across the summertime to the apple in the fall. This principle is crucial in the ethics of abortion. Underlying *stages* of growth is the substance of the individual human being of a preciousness size cannot measure.

Returning to that diamond ring, turning the diamond ever so slightly, one sees again the first concept. The principle of substance derives from the principle of identity. What exists as the subject of existence is one and the same underneath all this variety of attributes and accidental qualities, differences in quantity, measurement, and the like. The substance is what stands under these attributes, so to speak, which exist in the order of phenomena, or appearances. The substance stands under them, in the sense that it is a deeper reality known by the power of insight and understanding. Again, the admonition of Psalm 32, "Do not be like the horse and mule who do not have understanding." The human mode of existing entails the seeing of things with understanding.

4. The principle of causality

Philosophical treatises usually discuss the principle of causality separately at some point in the discussion of the first principles. This means the discussion of "efficient causality" separately and by itself, although we know that it is simply one of the four causes.

The important point is to recognize that the principle of causality means in metaphysics a philosophical principle. It is not something that one sees happening, as David Hume was trying to do when playing billiards. It is indeed true that the senses only see a succession of phenomena. But the intellect understands that there is a principle of causality concerned with the change in the existing state of things. The empirical sciences study the appearances. Metaphysics studies the principles in the order of existence as such, not in the order of billiard balls or anything else visible even with the most powerful microscope. The principle of causality means a sufficient reason in the order of existing. Hence, its full correct statement proceeds as follows: "If the sufficient reason for existing, for having the act of existing, is not within the thing itself as one of its intrinsic principles, then it must have an efficient cause external to itself." Why is this? Because otherwise it would still not be in the order of existence. It would be still—nothing. In philosophy, in metaphysics, the discussion proceeds in the order of existing.

5. The principle of finality

This principle, likewise, can be separated for discussion. The principle of finality states that every efficient cause, namely, everything that acts for doing or making something, has a purpose in doing so. One of the chief differences between the mentality of believers and atheists lies here. Atheists often think there is no purpose to anything. All comes by chance. Sometimes the purpose is fulfilled unconsciously, as we see throughout nature. An archer has a conscious purpose, and the arrows fly purposefully. But the arrow in itself has no conscious awareness of the purpose toward which it has been aimed. Another way of stating this is that everything exists for some good, namely, the purpose or end in view. This brings the mind immediately to the next principle.

6. The first principle of practical reason or of the moral order

In the practical order of making and doing things, this is the overruling first principle. One can state it in a practical way as follows: "Good is to be done and evil is to be avoided." Immediately the intellect recognizes the concept of oughtness: what ought to be done, what ought not to be done. This is the moral imperative. It is rooted in the principle of identity and in the principle of contradiction. If something is good, namely, within the purpose, then it is metaphysically good. If not, it is bad. In various times and cultures, granted the miseries of the human condition, people will relate things differently to this fundamental principle. Yet no natural normal human being on earth would ever disagree on this principle: good should be done and evil avoided.

7. The principle of the primacy of being

What does this principle state? It means that being has primacy over becoming, namely, the changes that take place in things. Changes do not exist in themselves apart from the thing or reality that changes. And this thing or reality has the primacy. It is the prior reality. Is this important? Indeed, yes. A small error regarding this primacy changes one's entire concept of ultimate reality. For example, marriage vows depend on affirming an unchanging self to which one will be faithful, underlying diminishments of looks, health, and so on.

Intuition of the First Principles

The word "intuition" brings up contemporary crosscurrents in philosophy. Does the heritage of Christian Philosophy recognize intuition in any form? The answer is in the affirmative. First, intuition functions constantly in the case of our five senses. The intuition of eyesight is simply eyesight.

Is there intellectual intuition? In Christian Philosophy the answer is that men are indeed endowed with intellectual intuition of the first principles. Christian philosophers, in the heritage coming from the Greeks through St. Augustine and St. Thomas, limit intellectual intuition to the first principles. From that point human knowledge grows gradually by building upon these original blocks. Other philosophers in more recent times have represented the idea of the intuition of essences in general, or, as in the case of Bergson, the intuition of the flow of time. Christian Philosophy teaches that a false "angelism" should be avoided. Our human mode entails laborious study in order to accumulate knowledge from the first principles.

The First Principles and Common Sense

Here one recognizes that the first principles explicate and develop the implicit understandings of natural reason among men of all times and places. Philosophical study states these principles and explains them. Then it analyzes the consequences that result from denying them or from carelessness in their use. Finally, philosophical study begins to reason from these first principles and thus to build up a body of philosophical knowledge. With that one takes an additional step in answering that important question, What is Christian Philosophy? What does the noun mean? What does the adjective do to the noun? For the present, we can leave these questions to be answered as this study proceeds. In any case, there is the constant relationship of Christian Philosophy to the natural heritage of human philosophy and to the natural use of right reason in human life.

The Beginning of Reason's Ascent to God

In his first chapter of *On Being and Essence,* Thomas Aquinas does not mention God. Yet the idea of God is at stake in these initial fundamentals. If these first concepts and first principles are correctly seen and stated, one recognizes an opening toward a higher reality. A small error in these beginnings can lead to the immense error of atheism, with its vast consequences for personal and social living. The catechetical application is apparent: one cannot explain the First Article of the Apostles' Creed except by standing on the solid rock of these first concepts and first principles.

II

ESSENCE AS UNDERSTOOD IN BODILY THINGS

The philosophical study of material realities found in this visible cosmos builds logically upon the understandings regarding the first concepts and the first principles achieved so far.

St. Augustine, one recalls from Part One above, urges the philosopher to leave his imagination behind, to bracket it out, as twentieth-century phenomenologists say, because it hinders philosophical study. Philosophy is the analysis of the underlying principles by which things exist in the way they are seen to do. Underlying principles: that is, they "stand under" the phenomena or appearances that the senses perceive. They are understood to exist in reality not because they are seen or imagined but because intellectual insight and understanding know that they must exist in reality. They necessarily must be in the existing thing, else it could not exist, either at all or in the way it does.

So far, then, we have noted the distinction between the empirical or scientific and the philosophical or metaphysical orders of knowledge and analysis. This is fundamentally important. It is basic to bear it in mind when studying bodily things, to use the Germanic component of the English language, or corporeal, material realities, to use the Latin component.

All knowledge begins in the senses. St. Thomas' treatise *On Being and Essence* is governed by this insight. It determines the structure of his treatise. Substance comes before the various accidental modifications of substances. His treatise reflects this aspect of reality. Furthermore, some substances, such as God, are simple, that is, not composed of additional metaphysical principles; other substances, such as a table, are composite: that is, they are composed of additional metaphysical principles. In themselves, he teaches, the simple substances come first, and in themselves are more luminous and knowable. Regarding us, however, the composite substances are more near at hand, closer to us, because they comprise the bodily things and corporeal realities of the cosmos in which we exist and in which our knowledge begins. Therefore, in the order of teaching and learning, St. Thomas Aquinas begins with these composite substances. This is simply an application, in the structure of *On Being and Essence,* that follows upon the fact of common sense and natural right reason, that all human knowledge begins in the senses.

Does all human knowledge end in the senses? This is the great question in philosophy, the watershed between materialistic atheism in philosophy, on the one hand, and openness to a higher order of intelligible reality, on the other. This openness to a higher order characterizes the natural metaphysics of mankind and its academic developments and expressions in both Classical Philosophy and Christian Philosophy.

Experience, Metaphysics, and the Physical Sciences

We live in a cosmos of bodily things. Bodies of all kinds surround us. All of them occupy space and exist in a continuum of time. Human beings are participants; a human being is a bodily thing. Bodily things are extended in space and therefore can be measured. This opens the way to all of the empirical sciences.

The experience of natural reason works with these material realities in practical human living. Let us return to water as our example. We recall that water is always water, when the substance of water is present: this is the principle of identity. The natural experience of water is prior to all scientific analysis. Water is the same substance with the same practical significance for human living, whether it is deemed one of the four elements, or H_2O, or analyzed by a nuclear physicist. It is always this particular thing, this substantial reality, this being. Men in practical living have always recognized its substantial reality, with its truly remarkable and even wonderful qualities for human living. It washes things so well. It is so good to drink. Without it, we thirst to death. Sometimes it is ice; sometimes it is steam. Natural reason perceives these properties and qualities, knowing this substance with understanding regarding its practical services and uses.

Natural reason, as we have seen, recognizes many different substances—bread, water, wine, cloth, wood, stone—each with its own properties, which the human intellect knows and judges in relation to human living. Natural reason judges that these realities are substantially different. They are really different, that is, in extramental reality. The common sense of natural reason judges that a bodily thing or substance is any being or reality made specific by having an exclusive group of properties that belong to it and to nothing else in exactly the same way. The empirical and physical sciences, physics, chemistry, and the others, build upon this natural foundation.

Chemical analysis and analysis of bodily things made by physicists are confined to the first order of abstraction. They elaborate the observations of the unaided senses. They come to know the properties and qualities of bodily things with scientific exactitude. They enhance the practical utility of bodily things for human life. All technology comes from these scientific analyses and observations. It is important to note that metaphysical analysis is different from the analyses carried on by the physical sciences. The very words "metaphysics" and "physics" indicate this difference. Metaphysical analysis concerns the underlying principles by which bodily things simply exist, prior to and more fundamental than the properties and qualities. Everything in philosophy turns about this recognition of the principles by which things exist, constituting philosophy in its own order, in the third degree of abstraction. Unless this is kept in mind, confusions between these various approaches to the understanding and knowledge of reality will necessarily arise, as we shall see.

The Analogy of Being

The first step in the philosophical study of the bodily things that form this cosmos is taken when the mind recognizes that there are indeed different kinds of substances in the world about us, and that some are more perfect and more noble than others. "In any kind of existing reality," writes St. Thomas, "the more noble a thing is, the more simple it is" (C.G. I, 18). This is the first glimmer of the distinction in reality between different kinds and substances of things. It is the beginning of the ascent of the mind to a higher reality.

"Different kinds of things", St. Thomas teaches further, "have different acts of existing; and the more noble a substance is, the more perfect and noble will be its act of existing" (C.G. II, 68).

This is the basic meaning of the philosophical teaching regarding the analogy of being. This simply means that the acts of existing, by which things are in reality, are not all the same. They are similar to each other from the viewpoint of existence as such, but unlike each other from the viewpoint of the various ways in which they exercise the act of existing. This opens up important perspectives for human knowledge of bodily realities, and of realities that do not have bodies: the immaterial substances and realities. It will be of extreme importance in human knowledge of the Supreme Being himself, with whom creatures have existence in common but whose mode of existing is absolutely unique. This is to anticipate, and we shall return later to this principle, the analogy of being, or of the act of existing. The standard textbooks in philosophy elaborate the details regarding the analogy of being.

Matter and Form

With this, one can come to the heart of the matter regarding bodily things. How is essence found in bodily things? Bodily things must have their own proper essence; otherwise, they could not exist at all. The question now is, why do they exist in the way they do, namely, as material realities, or bodily things? Putting this another way, one can ask how bodily things are defined. We recall that the essence gives the whatness, or *quidditas*, of the thing. This is the insight and understanding expressed in human discourse.

St. Thomas answers directly and lucidly. Apart from all qualities and properties that distinguish various material substances, to be a bodily thing it must have an essence that is itself composed of two distinct and correlative principles of being. These are the principles by which it is a bodily thing, existing in space and time, subject to measurement and to the analyses of the physical sciences. Thus he says, "Form and matter are found in composite substances, for example, soul and body in man." St. Thomas uses the human mode of existence characteristically in *On Being and Essence* to illustrate the philosophical principles. Later on, these illustrations will be gathered together to form philosophical anthropology.

It cannot be stressed too much that we have here two more metaphysical principles in the realities that are being analyzed philosophically. In that mental diagram of an existing thing, with the principle of essence and the principle of existence depending on it, existing within it, we now subdivide the essence, so to speak, with two additional principles, one a potency, called "matter", and the other its actuality, called "form". Thus one has this kind or form of material substance, as distinct from that kind. They are different from each other by their different forms of being, but they are all material realities, because these forms are received into this basic potency called "matter".

The central understanding here, and misconception if philosophical fundamentals are not analyzed carefully, is that matter in this case means "first matter". The existing bodily thing is "second matter". Second matter is seen by the senses and analyzed by the physical and empirical sciences. The senses and the physical sciences do not see or know or observe "first matter". It is a metaphysical principle, by definition beyond the physical. First matter, then, and substantial form are additional metaphysical principles within the essence of each and every material reality or bodily thing in the cosmos. Otherwise, they could not exist precisely as bodily things, subject to measurement and having the various qualities and properties that the senses observe. These are metaphysical principles by which the essence of the existing thing is quantified, has dimensions, and exists in a place or space and in a process of unfolding in time. Thus it has an essence that makes it to be this particular bodily thing, here and now. This insight and understanding regarding the nature of material realities arise in the third degree of abstraction, as a result of philosophical or metaphysical analysis. It is quite distinct from chemical analysis or from the analyses of physical science. This is the watershed between philosophy as such, as a distinct discipline among the seven liberal arts, and the empirical sciences.

It may be helpful to follow the argument of Thomas Aquinas in this analysis. Bodily things exist in various kinds, with large numbers that obviously belong to the same kind. This is a fact of experience given directly in human knowledge. Bodily things have an essence, as bodily things, or they could not exist at all. They have an essence by which they are material realities. Their essence limits their act of existing to what is proper to a material, or bodily thing. Thus the essence of a bodily thing is itself composed of two distinct, correlative principles of being, by which each one is this particular bodily thing. Aquinas' analysis proceeds as follows: Could the essence be simply matter alone? Evidently not, he replies, because this "first matter" is mere potency: it is simply the possibility of receiving any kind of form of the different material and bodily things seen in reality. Thus he excludes the crass materialists. Could it be the form alone? Some, the idealists, have said so. But this is an impossible confusion of the three degrees of abstraction and conflicts with the direct observation and natural experience of all men.

To anticipate, it is well to bear in mind that this failure to perceive the metaphysical principles within the essence of bodily things can, and will later on, lead to two reductionist aberrations in philosophy. The first will hold that philosophy is nothing but the generalized statement of the findings of the empirical sciences. This eliminates metaphysical analysis and is in fact already simply materialism. The other aberration is known as symbolic logic or linguistic analysis. It reduces philosophy to the second degree of abstraction, presenting it as a rarefied form of higher mathematics. Thus symbolic logic attempts to reduce philosophy to nothing but the logic of mathematics. When these fundamentals are carefully analyzed, keeping the nature of metaphysical principles in mind, then it is seen that philosophy is concerned with definitions of really existing material realities. It remains rooted in natural reason, in common sense, of which it is an academic development and refinement.

Again to anticipate, since it is helpful to do so, one should bear in mind that this metaphysical analysis regarding the essence of bodily things or material realities will be dismissed later on in the period of Modern Philosophy. It will be dismissed first in the name of mechanism, as if material realities were nothing but the mechanics of their dimensions and movements in space. Thus there is nothing in the universe but eternal matter in perpetual motion, with the consequence that change is an illusion, in that the underlying substance is one and the same. Change is only apparent because bodies are really homogeneous and have only one basic property, extension.

The other way in which this metaphysical analysis is dismissed is called dynamism. This explains material realities as nothing but forces in motion, which operate somehow to create the illusion that different substances exist in the kinds of things about us. It should be borne in mind that these explanations are superficial, remaining on the surface of sensory observations of the senses, either unaided in themselves or with the apparatus of the laboratories. When the metaphysical principles are understood in the way of the philosophical heritage, then the door stands open to harmony with common sense and to a pluralistic view of bodily things existing in their various substantial realities.

Scientists, ordinarily, do not raise the questions of existence. They stop with the properties and activities of the various substantial realities. The philosopher, however, goes on to the third degree of abstraction, asking why these various bodily things exist as they do. The answer is that corporeal substances have essences that are composite, not simple. The essence as found in a bodily thing is itself composed of a new order of potency and act, called customarily by philosophers since the ancient Greeks "first matter" and "substantial form". They are related to each other as a new order of potency and act. It is important to remember that these are principles by which these substances exist and are not substances that exist. They will never be isolated in any test tube or seen by any microscope, however powerful. They are metaphysical principles, known to exist by intellectual insight and understanding, explaining their act of existing as such.

The Principle of Individuation and of Number

Here again one notes the way philosophy arises out of the natural experience and use of natural reason by mankind throughout its life on this planet. Take, for example, a grove of oak trees. They are all composed of the minerals in the soil beneath them. Yet they are so different from that inert soil. They stand upright, beautiful to behold, as living beings. Their kind of thing, their essence, must contain some additional principle, which forms them to be this kind of living thing, the oak tree.

One can ponder the same phemonenon in any human family: the father, the mother, and their children. Again, material realities, bodily things, but with the physical and chemical properties gathered together in some truly marvelous way, so that the material component is formed to be this kind of thing, a human person.

And again, the several individuals, all of whom are equally human beings, constituting this family.

In other words, as philosophers have noted since the Pre-Socratics, there is the challenging phenomenon given in reality and the experience of it, of the one and the many. Philosophers always have tried to reduce the many things in the cosmos to some kind of unity, seeking a unifying principle. Bodily things constitute a special case of the one and the many. How can they be one in kind and at the same time exist in many individuals of that same kind? We have seen already that kind relates to essence: that kind, in this case, relates to the substantial form of each bodily thing. What about the many individuals in each single kind of thing? This relates to the other subprinciple in their essence, namely, first matter. With this we can proceed to discuss briefly the principle of individuation.

First matter, it follows, is the principle of individuation. It is the root and source of the existence of many bodily things of the same kind in numerous individuals.

This individuation of bodily things is expressed by the demonstrative pronoun "this". This pronoun designates a particular bodily thing. It indicates that the principle of individuation is being considered, and its effect is being expressed. Thus human discourse points out this book here, as distinct from that book over there.

It is possible to think about these books without considering the "thisness" of them, the designation as this or that particular thing. Can one, then, think of the essence of books in general, or the essence of trees in general, or the essence of human beings? Is that essence, in such a case, both particular and universal? Quite obviously, it could not be both at one and the same time, in the same respect, for this would violate the principle of contradiction.

Here the mind stands before another watershed in philosophical discourse and understanding. Man can be defined universally, because in such a case the mind includes only the undesignated matter of the bodily thing called a human person, and prescinds from considering the individual characteristics of this person or that person. The definition of man, St. Thomas teaches, does include undesignated matter. Thus matter is of the essence of man. It is the very nature of man to be a bodily thing. But the mind can consider this essence apart from the particular actualization or realization of that essence as this particular human being.

Perhaps one can clarify this with the help of fundamentals from the field of catechetics. A thing is designated as individual when it can be pointed to with the finger. Thus St. John the Baptist is called the greatest of the prophets because he pointed to the Messiah not from afar, as the earlier prophets did, but with his finger, pointing to Jesus of Nazareth: "This is the Lamb of God", he said. This particular human being, who looks so much like his mother, this is the Lamb of God, this is the expected one, the Messiah. Again, later on, this same Jesus of Nazareth, using human discourse, taking a particular substantial reality in his hands, said, "This is my Body." These are fundamentally significant expressions. They show how philosophical fundamentals enter into human discourse, determining basic meaning.

One notes at this point that human knowledge is entering into view, as metaphysical analysis proceeds. A human person as such can be defined, universally, because in doing so the mind considers the essence of human beings, humanity, including matter, indeed, but undesignated. It prescinds from pointing out this or that particular instance or individual in this kind of reality, human beings. "The definition of man", St. Thomas writes, "does include undesignated matter." In other words, flesh and bone belong to the essential nature of men, but not this particular flesh and bone of this individual human being.

Metaphysical analysis opens up perspectives that lead to the mathematical sciences in the second degree of abstraction, and to the empirical sciences in the first degree of abstraction. Since bodily things exist as individuals, they can be counted. The numbering of them becomes a possibility. The count or sum of the units of things can be given, in written or spoken symbols. Thus the count can be communicated. Furthermore, laws of number and proportion can be discovered and seen to pervade all nature. Cosmology is at hand, and the mathematical and natural sciences that provide raw material for the philosophical study of the cosmos. In most recent times, binary numbers, using only zero and one, have become significant in a new way connected with computer science. It should be noted that none of these discoveries and observations in the first and second degrees of abstraction make any changes whatsoever in metaphysical analysis, in the third degree of abstraction, where the principles by which bodily things exist as they do, in kinds and in numbers, are seen to exist necessarily. These principles, substantial form and first matter, must be in any existing reality if it is to be a bodily thing, and able therefore to be seen by the human mind in kinds of things that have many individuals belonging to one and the same kind.

Porphyry's Tree: The Kinds of Bodily Things

The natural and spontaneous use of human reason in human living always has grouped things into different kinds, having different properties and therefore different practical uses, as we have noted. Philosophers, accordingly, have attempted to group the kinds and classes of things comprehensively into treatises explaining their "categories"—thus Aristotle's famous *On the Categories.* In the third century A.D. a Neo-Platonist philosopher, Porphyry, wrote an introduction to the *Categories* of Aristotle. In it he gives a diagram as a teaching device, as it were, of the ascending order in the basic kinds of things that we know and experience in this cosmos.

One can picture in the mind's eye this tree of the kinds of things as Porphyry presents it. At the bottom, standing as the soil in which a tree is rooted, is the most fundamental kind or essence or nature of things: the substance. Rising above it are bodily things; continuing upward, living things; further upward, animal life; on upward, human beings; and then above the human beings, the various individuals of the human kind: Peter, Mary, James, John.

In our times physics, chemistry, geology, and especially biology are devoted to the empirical analysis of these various kinds of things, with their divisions and subdivisions. In classical antiquity, the empirical sciences of observation and the philosophical sciences of metaphysical analysis were not yet differentiated as they are today. Advancing intellectual culture has resulted in this differentiation.

In Porphyry's tree, it should be noted that each kind of thing on the ascending scale is distinguished further by specific differences, which give basic kinds as the tree ascends. For example, above substance it is entirely possible that immaterial substance be distinguished from material substance. Not all existing realities necessarily have to be bodily things. Furthermore, living things are specifically distinct from inorganic or nonanimated things. Animal life is distinct from plant life in that it is sensitive. Finally, human life is distinguished from animal life by its rationality. Thus the kinds of things are divided into species by their specific differences. This is the basic concept of Porphyry's tree. All intellectual culture is constituted by advancing knowledge regarding the kinds of things, their properties, and hence their value for various human endeavors.

In theistic philosophy, this order in the kinds of things is seen as a creative work of God. The book of Psalms is full of the praise of God for the beauty and variety of his creation. It is at the basis of the order in the visible cosmos. Natural reason using common sense recognizes a qualitative difference in these basic kinds of things. The doctrine of the Catholic Church has spoken specifically about man, where it is Christian teaching that the human mode of existing is qualitatively distinct.

The atheistic philosophy sees Porphyry's tree as standing somehow by itself, moving upward by a process that pushes from below, by itself, evolving by itself, as it has been put more recently. Thus these forms of being come to be in their distinctiveness by themselves, as it were, by some process or other.

One of the intensely interesting borderline cases between philosophy and empirical science is the question of life.

III

HUMAN KNOWLEDGE OF THINGS

In his prologue to the treatise *On Being and Essence,* it will be recalled that St. Thomas Aquinas begins by exploring how the first concepts of the intellect, being and essence, are found in different things. This he has done, beginning with bodily things. In his prologue he states that the next step will be to explore how they are related to the logical concepts of genus, species, and difference.

This he does in Chapter III, introducing a major turn in his metaphysical analysis. He now begins to consider human knowledge and to reflect on its interior acts. So far, he has been discussing "beings of reality". Now he turns to "beings of the mind". At his time, young people came to the study of philosophy after having completed the study of the other six liberal arts. Hence Aquinas presupposes the study of the trivium: grammar, rhetoric, and now especially logic. For it is the science of logic that studies "beings of the mind", the so-called logical concepts of entities. Thus St. Thomas can be very succinct in this Chapter III.

It is important to note that the discussion so far has considered the principles by which things exist in the way that they do. These principles are not the same thing as concepts of the human mind, although the contents of the human mind derive from the principles of being, in a particular human way. The ontological order, the principles in realities, must be distinguished carefully from the logical order. St. Thomas explains these fundamental correlations carefully and succinctly in Chapter III. Here we shall simply draw attention to the major principles and implications of his treatment, which bring the special character of Christian Philosophy ever more clearly into view.

Philosophy of Knowledge: Epistemology within Metaphysics

The structure of St. Thomas' treatise *On Being and Essence* is perhaps even more important than its condensed content. In its structure, one sees the philosophy of knowledge emerging out of metaphysics and having its own being within metaphysics. It does not stand independently of metaphysics, and certainly not prior to metaphysics.

This fundamental approach to the study of human knowledge is implicit in the natural metaphysics of mankind, by which practical life has been conducted by all men since the beginning. This approach is, furthermore, more or less explicit in pagan Greek philosophy, especially in that of Socrates, Plato, and Aristotle. For men in practical life, and for the early pagan philosophers, it is recognized that all men know things and make use of them according to that knowledge. This is a healthy attitude toward human knowledge, which was passed forward into the Christian times, especially through the hands of St. Augustine. After him, this approach to epistemology received an ever more lucid and explicit exposition in Christian Philosophy.

On Being and Essence simply supposes and summarizes this immense human heritage in life and thought.

To anticipate, one should bear in mind that a different approach to human knowledge began to appear in the times of Modern Philosophy, which will be studied in Part Three below. In this approach metaphysics will be set aside and replaced by mathematics. As a result, epistemology, as it were, becomes homeless and will try to stand alone. Philosophers will attempt to begin philosophy with epistemology, analyzing the contents of human consciousness. Some of these philosophers will intend and hope to pass from thence to a knowledge of extramental reality, things in themselves, but there will also be philosophers later in the modern period who will resurrect the ancient skepticism, denying that such cognitive contact with reality is possible.

Having made anticipatory note of this coming philosophical situation, one can return to Thomas Aquinas and the philosophy of knowledge in Christian Philosophy, seeing it in the largest perspectives of human life and thought.

Concepts: The First Acts of the Intellect

In Christian Philosophy, as indeed in the entire heritage of philosophy coming from the Greeks, the acts of the intellect are carefully distinguished from the images of the imagination. Concepts are different from percepts. Not all philosophies, of course, recognize this distinction. In fact, it is the basic division between philosophies, the most important criterion for distinguishing the different kinds of philosophies. This will be considered again below in connection with the problem of the universals. For the present, one simply recognizes that the concept is an insight for understanding of the intelligence, which is distinct in nature from the percepts of the senses and the images that result.

Christian Philosophy, like the Classical Philosophy that it carries forward, purified and brightened, is centrally concerned with the small verb "is" and its infinitive "to be". These words express human knowledge bearing upon things. The verb "is" is fundamental not only in the trivium, in grammar and in the rhetoric of human discourse, but in philosophy itself. The reason is that it expresses a personal judgment on a thing in reality as distinct from the subjective self. The verb "is" concerns reality, not states of the subjective self. It is the dynamic verb of the infinitive "to be", expressing the act or activity of existing in reality.

The Latin word for reality derives from *res,* which simply means what the Anglo-Saxon expresses by the word "thing". Thus the title of this chapter: "Human Knowledge of Things". It is intrinsic to human life and to the thinking that grows out of the exercise of natural reason, that human knowledge is a knowledge of things, realities, turning out from the states and conditions of the subjective self to a direct contact with things. In one way or another, this is what is meant by "realism" in the philosophy of knowledge. It is distinct from the "idealism", which makes knowledge begin with subjective states and ends by confining the human spirit within the human self.

The Transcendental Concepts

Among the first acts of the intellect are the concepts that have been studied thus far: being, which is the concept of a thing recognized as existing in extramental reality. The transcendental concepts are understandings that attach to such existing realities, helping the human intellect to understand existing reality better. These truths are called transcendental because they transcend all of the divisions among things seen in Porphyry's tree. They rise above all categories. In addition, then, to the concept of existing, there is the concept of oneness, of unity: each being is its own self, one single being. This concept, oneness, adds to being only a negation of division, and considering the fact of indivision, each thing is a thing, not two things. The next transcendental is "truth", which adds to each existing reality not some additional entity but simply a relationship first to the divine mind, and second, to created minds. It means that existing realities can be known. Then comes the transcendental concept "goodness", where existing realities, beings, are seen as a final cause, in the order of purpose. This is being, or existing reality, as of perfective of another in the manner of an end. This makes it something good, which can be desired. Finally, there is the transcendental concept "the beautiful". It is contained in goodness but adds to goodness a relationship to the knower, who appreciates it from the cognitive point of view. Thus beauty is the good of the intellect.

These concepts transcend the categories of Porphyry's tree, which intends comprehensively to present the different kinds of things seen in this cosmos. Does this mean that the transcendentals transcend, go beyond, this cosmos? This is a question to bear in mind. If there is a reality that is being itself, then it will be immediately just one unique being, it will be truth itself, it will be goodness itself, it will be beauty itself. One can see readily, therefore, that philosophical analysis already is pointing toward the possibility of reality, an existing being, beyond the cosmos.

It is clear that atheistic philosophy will want nothing to do with this orientation beyond the cosmos. This has been dramatically presented to the contemporary world by the intellectual life within Poland. At the Catholic

University of Lublin, since World War II, Christian philosophers have cultivated the transcendentals from this point of view, giving to their young students an insight into the possibility of ascending beyond the cosmos, from these ultimate concepts.

In the schools of atheistic philosophy in the state universities of the same country, philosophy is confined to the "universal concepts", with careful exclusion of these considerations regarding the transcendentals.

This, of course, confines philosophical study to the things that are seen in this cosmos, which is the very definition of the materialist approach.

In Christian Philosophy there is an openness to the transcendentals, and at the same time a concern for the universals. The transcendentals and the universals are not the same thing: they are different kinds of concepts. A wider and more comprehensive philosophy will study both, analyzing them with the tools of human intelligence.

What, then, is a "universal concept"? It is a concept that relates directly to Porphyry's tree. It has been noted above that the basic concepts are those of essence and the act of existing. Putting this in the Anglo-Saxon manner of expression, things exist in various kinds. Each thing is one individual thing, individuated. At the same time, these things exist in kinds, which are like each other. Thus classes and groups of things arise before the mind. How can this be? What is it in things that makes apples to be like apples, all apples being apples? Then there are, beside the apples, the bananas: What makes these individuals to be all the same kind of thing? And so on for all of the different substances, on Porphyry's tree, up to human beings themselves: What is it in each person that constitutes this class or kind of thing called human beings?

It is important to note that this characteristic of human knowledge is a fact. One accepts it as a fact; it is something given in the experience of human life. The challenge is to explain this fact. It should be explained, not explained away or treated as if it did not exist.

This fact bears upon philosophical anthropology, as we shall see. Why is this? Because only human beings discern these kinds and classes and categories of things. A camera does not do so: it only records the individual things as individuals. The same is true of the animals in their mode of knowledge, confined to the sensory apparatus. The senses recognize only individuals. What is this in the human mode of existing that can recognize and discern the kinds of things? This can be postponed for the moment, for it is the beginning and the central consideration of philosophical anthropology.

For the present, then, one can proceed with Thomas Aquinas, philosophizing on the basis of the knowledge at hand from the trivium, those first three liberal arts that study grammar, human discourse, rhetoric, the uses of human discourse, and logic, the processes and procedures within the mind, in its activities with these concepts.

Judgments and the Propositions of Human Discourse

In one of the polished and synthetic insights that abound in *On Being and Essence,* St. Thomas writes, "Predication is something achieved by the intellect in its act of combining and dividing, having for its foundation in reality the unity of those things, one of which is attributed to the other." This mental act of either combining by positive assertion or dividing by a negative assertion is what is meant by judgment. It is fundamental to note that judgment is the connection of the human mind and self, by means of human knowledge, with extramental reality. Judgment is the act of using that dynamic existential verb "is" to affirm that what I know in my mind is true of reality.

To give a few examples: "This is water." Here the mind affirms that a substance before it is known to be in extramental reality the substance of water.

Or take a piece of bread: "This is bread." Again, the mind asserts that the concept in the mind is, in extramental reality, bread.

Or, in the act of dividing or negating: a person may take a piece of metal in hand and say, "This is not wood." In this case, dividing, as St. Thomas says, the concept in the mind is divided from reality, or negated with respect to reality.

Such examples could be multiplied indefinitely from the practical activities of daily life, which take place by exercising such judgments regarding things in the cosmos. This is noted as characteristic of human activity and human life since prehistoric beginnings.

The act of judging, then, affirms the unity of the intellect and reality with respect to the kind of thing that is under consideration. What I conceive in my mind is the valid extramental nature or essence or substance of this thing. This is the heart and the essence of the human knowledge of things. We recall from the prologue of this treatise that "being" is used in two ways: in reference to the essence and act of existing of things in the categories perceived around us; then as the verb that links concepts together, expressing and affirming the existential unity between the intellect and reality. The very "is" is existential, dynamic, the expression of the act of linking the act of existing in such and such a way. Thus it is the synthesis of being and essence, or, in Anglo-Saxon, of things and their kinds.

Immediately metaphysical analysis confronts the mind with the reality of the truth of human knowledge. Truth is in the judgment. Truth, the transcendental concept, shines its light of intelligibility on all human discourse, all use of the universal concepts regarding the kinds of things on Porphyry's tree. All of this St. Thomas states succinctly when he says that the foundation of the judgment, its validity and its justification, is in reality. This means that the two concepts predicated of each other, spoken or asserted of each other, are actually united in reality, in the thing that the intelligence sees with understanding.

From the philosophical point of view, this establishes the nature of human language. It is the expression of judgments through verbal symbols that can communicate with other persons. Human discourse is constituted basically from these judgments, which affirm or deny, in the mind, with respect to what is the case in reality. This is the root principle of all social communication, and of all education, the handing on of knowledge to others.

It should be noted that religious faith for Christians is grounded in judgments, as in the Creed, rather than being only a matter of feeling. Continually using the word "feeling" rather than "thinking", as in "I feel that Christ was more than man", can be a subtle sign of skepticism.

Reasonings: The Progressive Character of Human Knowledge

Christian Philosophy, one must constantly bear in mind, is simply natural human philosophy purged of its pagan condition and elevated to a brighter state of intellectual insight and understanding. It is the same natural metaphysics of mankind, shining more brightly. This character of Christian Philosophy as embodying the philosophical heritage of mankind, and indeed the natural reason of mankind from human beginnings, can be seen exceptionally well at this point. Aristotle, as a member of the school of Plato, summarized the philosophical heritage of the Greeks in treatises that are basic to human education and culture ever since, especially in Western civilization. Central to these treatises of Aristotle is his *Organon*, on the activities of the mind considered as the organ or instrument for the pursuit of knowledge and truth. Early in his conversion to philosophy, St. Augustine made a special study of Aristotle's *Organon*. Eight centuries later, Thomas Aquinas wrote a commentary on Aristotle's *Organon;* the following is quoted from his Introduction.

> There is a twofold operation of the intellect, as the philosopher says in his Book Three, on the soul. One is the understanding of simple objects, that is, the operation by which the intellect apprehends just the essence of a thing alone; the other is the operation of composing and dividing. There is also a third operation, that of reasoning, by which reason proceeds from what is known to the investigation of things that are unknown. The first of these operations is ordered to the second, for there cannot be composition and division unless things have already been apprehended simply. The second, in turn, is ordered to the third, for clearly we must proceed from some known truth to which the intellect assents in order to have certitude about something not yet known. Since logic is called rational science, it must direct its consideration to the things that belong to these three operations of reason that we have mentioned.

This science of reasoning, this rational science, is the meeting point, so to speak, between human knowledge and reality. Metaphysical analysis is concerned with the principles by which things exist in reality. These principles generate human knowledge in the way we are studying at present. This science of logic is one of the seven liberal arts, belonging to the trivium. It is not strictly philosophy itself, but rather a preparatory science for philosophy. Philosophy is the seventh of the seven liberal arts, coming after the trivium. It is the science that analyzes the activities of the human mind as it develops its knowledge of things and their kinds, analyzing the principles by which they exist as they are seen to do. This rational science establishes the order between concepts, judgments, and reasonings. In his treatise, Aristotle gives his famous analysis of the manner in which judgments are linked together by the mind to form syllogisms, chains of reasonings, which proceed from judgments that are known to new judgments that express newly discovered knowledge. All of this is, of course, studied in the treatises on logic and is simply assumed here.

The manner in which the Greek heritage of Socrates, Plato, and Aristotle was passed forward in Western culture by means of Aristotle's treatise the *Organon* illustrates the difference between progress in the empirical sciences and in metaphysics.

The empirical sciences make progress by discovering new facts. When new facts are discovered, frequently theories that had been held to explain facts up to that point are no longer valid. New theories must be constructed to embrace the newly discovered facts. Thus progress in the empirical sciences consists of the discovery of new facts and the elaboration of new theories, which supplant the old theories. Progress is by the substitution of new theories for older ones.

Progress in philosophy is of an entirely different nature, qualitatively distinct. Progress in philosophy does not consist of the discarding of theories as a result of newly discovered empirical facts. Progress in philosophy does not set older knowledge aside but rather penetrates more deeply into it by both personal and social insight and understanding. Progress takes place by a process of concentric deeper understanding, not by substitution. Thus the *Organon* of Aristotle, once seen and elaborated, becomes an abiding heritage, which successive generations can make their own, and in doing so deepen their grasp of it and extend its applications But philosophical progress does not set Aristotle's *Organon* aside. This distinction between progress in the empirical sciences and progress in the philosophical disciplines should be kept in mind, for it will become crucially important in Part Three below, in the times of Modern Philosophy. Since metaphysics concerns existence as distinct from nothingness, its knowledge, once achieved, is abiding. Thus progress takes place by deeper understanding of the same truth once achieved. The same can be said of theology, which should not be viewed as innovative but as deepening.

The Fact of the Universals

Human knowledge contains universal concepts. This is a fact given in human experience and implied by the human mode of language and practical life. It is not a theory; it is a fact. Philosophy begins with facts as given. Somehow, these universal concepts relate to the kinds and categories of things that are observed in the cosmos and studied by the empirical sciences.

So far, metaphysical analysis has reached the principles by which each individual thing exists, in its particular kind or mode. Thus, *de ente et essentia: On Being and Essence:* on things and their kinds. Human knowledge does not remain at the level of mere registration of individual percepts, but proceeds to understand these various kinds with their properties and hence in terms of their purposes and practical utility. Each kind of category of thing is understood to be good for this or for that, or not good for this or for that. Thus the human mode of living proceeds.

These principles of being, it should be recalled, are not physical parts subject to the imagination. They cannot be predicated of things as if they were such parts. Human knowledge proceeds differently, and its process calls for careful analysis— first, as to the fact of the universals; then, as to the ways by which philosophers have attempted to explain the fact.

In considering the universals, one comes to the very heart of human discourse. In Chapter Three of his treatise, St. Thomas writes, "Predication is something accomplished by the intellect's act of combining and dividing." This, as has been noted, is the process of forming judgments in the mind and expressing them in human language.

"This predication", Aquinas continues, "of one thing with regard to another has its foundation in reality, in the very unity of those things, one of which is said of the other." This is the doctrine of metaphysical and epistemological realism. Notice that the principle stated by Thomas Aquinas is valid of every object around us in daily life. Take, for example, this glass pitcher. It exists. I judge that it is a glass pitcher, containing water. The foundation for this judgment is the unity of the glass, forming the kind of thing that the pitcher is in reality. This can be said of a piece of bread, a piece of wood, a stone, or a human person. "It is nature considered in this way", St. Thomas continues, "that we predicate of all individual things." Then he gives the definition of the universal concept: "The nature applies to all the things of that class." Thus, the universal concept applies to all the kinds of things in a given category. So, for example, individual human beings: John, Mary, Joseph, and all the rest have one and the same human nature, because they belong to this category or kind, namely, human beings. Thus nature is a universal concept and is predicated universally in human thought and discourse.

Against the background of this analysis, Thomas Aquinas states his conclusion:

"This nature has a twofold act of existing, one in individual things, the other in the mind." With this, we have come to consider how essence is found in human thought and in human language. The existence of this essence, this nature, this concept in the mind makes human beings cognitive beings. This is the beginning of the philosophy of knowledge. Predication is the assertion of the universal concept about this particular individual thing. This is a human being. This is bread. That is water. Over there is a tree. From this beginning all human knowledge begins to accumulate, and all the branches of the teaching profession, the disciplines of the liberal arts, are gradually constructed.

These universal concepts are predicated in human discourse of all the individuals of each kind or category. They have two fundamentally important qualities, unity and community. They express the one nature that is common to each and all of the individuals in a given category. This has special importance when the universal concept is that of human nature, for then the implications of unity and community touch each of us in a very personal and vital way. This is the philosophical foundation for human community and its common good. All of the liberal disciplines arise from this root, the taproot of all human education. And from the activities of persons thus educated, all human culture flows forth in social life.

The possibility of one, true Faith, desirable for *everyone* to hold, presupposes the unity of human nature. Asians and Indians need Christ as Savior just as much as Frenchmen or Americans. There can also be a universal set of rights and morals.

So much for the fact of the universals. Their basic importance indicates that great care must be exercised in attempting a philosophical explanation for the reason these universals exist on the human scene. Again, that admonition: a small mistake in the beginning of these fundamentals can lead to an immense aberration later on.

The Active Intellect

We turn, then, to the explanation for this fact observed in the human mode of knowing things. Philosophers seek the reason why things exist as they do. Why does this fact of the universal concepts exist? How does it exist? What explanation can be given from the philosophical point of view?

Historically, there have been two extreme explanations, with a moderate one standing between them having the hallmarks of the truth of the matter. This is the great "problem of the universals", which has agitated philosophical discussion across the ages and been recorded in the histories of philosophy.

The first extreme is that of the ancient Sophists, in the time of Socrates, reflecting the thinking of the Atomists and the Materialists. In this way of thinking, the kinds and categories are nothing but names that people assign more or less arbitrarily to groups and classes of things. Hence, "nominalism", from the

Latin word *nomen,* "name". In this thinking there is nothing in reality but the individual things; the kind or category results from the imposition of the common name. Universals are simply verbal matters.

What is to be said? This nominalism is a superficial approach, because it begs the philosophical question: Why are these kinds and categories of things to be found in reality? What is the reason for the various substances that constitute these kinds of things, which human beings judge as serviceable for various purposes and uses? This is the question in the existential order, which is proper to philosophy.

This is the objection to the superficial nominalism that Socrates raised in his discussions with the Sophists. Plato took this criticism of Socrates and developed his explanation of the universals as an extreme position at the opposite pole from the nominalism of the Sophists. He taught that the universals exist as such in reality in an intelligible world of their own beyond sensory perception. Thus the universals exist as such in extramental reality, in the world of the ideas, as well as in the mind with its universal concepts. Then he proceeded to his theory of remembering, saying that human souls saw the world of the universals before birth into the body in this life, so that human knowledge is explained by a process of remembering what was seen in that earlier existence.

Aristotle introduced a correction in Plato's thinking, in the direction of a personal power of knowledge in human beings distinct from that of the senses, by which the nature common to each kind or category is seen intellectually, apart from its material or individuating characteristics.

It was this achievement of the Greek philosophy that was developed in Christian times by St. Augustine and St. Thomas Aquinas. St. Augustine, one will recall, located the ideas in the mind of God and explained human knowledge of them by an illumination of the human cognitive apparatus coming somehow from God.

This brings us to the active intellect, which is Aquinas' term for this cognitive power proper and specific to men. St. Thomas cites St. Augustine on the divine illumination, teaching that rational creatures receive from their Creator, as his special image impressed upon them, a light of insight and understanding regarding the natures of things. "The Light by which our human mind understands", he writes in his treatise *On Spiritual Creatures* (Article 10), "is the active intellect.... Our active intellect illuminates our sensory knowledge as a light given to us by God."

Putting this in other words, the active intellect is an active power or light possessed by the human mind, by which it "abstracts" the intelligible idea or universal concept from its individuated mode of existing in extramental things. Thus it is able to see the things of sensory perception with understanding. It is the eye of the mind, so to speak, analogous to the eye of the bodily senses, but immensely higher, brighter, and more powerful than the sensory eye because it opens upon a higher order of reality, the intelligible order, which is manifested by its reflection in the things seen by the senses. This higher order of reality constitutes the intelligibles, as distinct from sensory percepts.

With this one can recognize that Christian Philosophy has developed natural pagan philosophy in its highest expression, coming gradually from Augustine's illumination to the explanation of human knowledge given by St. Thomas Aquinas. It stands as the true position between the two extremes of Materialist nominalism on the one hand and the Platonic theory of the Ideas on the other hand. This has implications for the concept of human nature and will lead directly to philosophical anthropology, as we shall see below.

The Personalism of Christian Philosophy

At the time of St. Thomas Aquinas, the world of the emerging universities was agitated by a question coming from the Arabian commentators upon the texts of Aristotle. These commentaries were circulating in the schools of Christendom from the Arabs in Spain. The question was this: Is the active intellect separate and distinct in each person, or is there just one and the same active intellect for all human beings? The Arabian commentators taught that there is only one active intellect, operating in human beings as its modes of expression. In other words, this is a pantheistic interpretation of Aristotle, deriving from Plotinus and the Neo-Platonists.

It is the great merit and scientific credit of Thomas Aquinas that he penetrated this misinterpretation and in doing so saved the authenticity of Christian Philosophy as it had been founded by Augustine and developed in the schools of Christendom. One may say that this is the most important intellectual achievement of Thomas Aquinas, one that merits a moment of special consideration. He was so convinced that this pantheistic interpretation of Aristotle falsifies Aristotle himself that he commissioned William of Moerboeke to do a new translation of Aristotle's treatises, especially the *Metaphysics,* directly from the Greek, in accordance with the literal and original meaning of Aristotle's discourse. Aquinas then composed his commentaries on Aristotle from this new and scientifically accurate translation of Aristotle's texts. He thus made a scientific move to circumvent the misinterpretation coming from the Arabians through Spain. On the basis of this accurate knowledge of Aristotle, he proceeded in his own works to develop his teaching of the active intellect as a property and power of each individual human being. This establishes the foundation for Christian personalism, the philosophical foundation for the dignity of each human person. In fact, as he goes on to explain, it is this rationality, with which the human person is endowed, that provides the foundation for human liberty.

For the moment one can simply refer this fundamental forward to philosophical anthropology, which will be taken up after the doctrine of creation has been considered. This philosophy of knowledge receives its full illumination only from the doctrine of creation, when existence is seen as something given to things by the Supreme Being, existence itself, the author and the source of all other existences.

Thus, from him who gives existence to things, it follows that he gives existence in such a way that each created thing can pursue its own proper purposes. For human beings these purposes are rational and free. As a bird's wings are made for flying, as men make knives for cutting, so God the Creator has made men with this light by which they understand the nature of things. This, of course, is to anticipate.

To conclude, then, one can say with Thomas Aquinas that we have now seen what "an essence" means in bodily things, and then how it is related to the concepts of genus, species, and difference, the framework of Porphyry's tree, denoting the different kinds of things. The philosophy of human knowledge has emerged from within metaphysics and abides on its metaphysical foundation. It explains how we know things in their various kinds. It explains why we see things differently than do the lower animals. Human beings see things with understanding. This understanding turns about the very existence of things, and this brings us to consider the metaphysical ascent.

IV

THE METAPHYSICAL ASCENT TO GOD

Everyone knows that there are many philosophers, philosophies, philosophical systems: this has been called by Maritain "the misery of metaphysics". From the catechetical point of view, it is deeply important to recognize this fact about the human condition so as to cultivate discernment among these various kinds of philosophies.

Many of the differences are quite superficial and of lesser importance: modes of expression and varieties of application. At the basic level of fundamental principles and of impact upon human life, however, the differences between philosophies become desperately important. The most basic difference of all is the question whether or not the transcendent Supreme Being whom all men call God actually and really exists. This divides all philosophies into basically two different kinds. At this question of the metaphysical ascent, therefore, the questions whether a higher order of intelligible reality exists, and whether man has a cognitive power to make the ascent and what the steps in such an ascent are, are vitally important for mankind and far from a mere academic exercise.

Some of these philosophies are incompatible with revealed religion and its deposit of faith, and likewise incompatible with natural rights and the dignity of man. All philosophies that deny the metaphysical ascent are thus incompatible.

Metaphysics functions even when it is denied. The denial of the metaphysical ascent is already a metaphysical assertion regarding the nature of ultimate reality. It asserts that ultimate reality is the material cosmos visible with the human senses. Nothing exists beyond this cosmos. This is the very essence of atheistic philosophy.

In generic terms, this approach is called materialism. In Parts Three and Four below, its two chief specific kinds will be studied in the chief persons of their genesis and development, together with the distinctions and exceptions necessary in the cases of personal histories moving from theism toward atheism, or from atheism toward the natural metaphysics of mankind.

There is an additional question that philosophers must face and analyze. It is the proneness in human nature to desire an evasion of God. Frequently, thinkers will desire to rationalize or justify the aversion of one's human face from the face of God present to each person. This is a deep-seated aversion to the Supreme Being, complemented by a conversion to the things of this world, and, concretely, to the human self living among the things of this cosmos, dominating them and enjoying them, as if there were no God who created them, giving them their natures and acts of existing.

A further complication that must be kept in mind is called pantheism. This is a failed and deceptive form of the ascent of the mind to the intelligible order. One will recall the quotation from St. Augustine on those philosophers who take the world along with them in their purported ascent to the intelligible order.

The metaphysics of outright materialism, and the metaphysics of pantheism in all its forms, constitute a block of the human mind with reference to the ascent. This blockage is itself metaphysical. The philosopher must note that such a blockage constitutes a prison for the human mind and spirit, confining men within this visible cosmos, dooming them to death.

The natural metaphysics of mankind is open to the higher order of intelligible reality. This natural openness was structured into an academic discipline by the pagan Greeks, especially Socrates, Plato, and Aristotle. This openness to the ascent was developed further by Christian thinkers from Augustine to Aquinas. Thus Christian Philosophy rests on the metaphysics of ascent from bodily things in the cosmos to intelligible reality, and then on to the existing reality of the intelligent and personal Supreme Being himself.

It is indeed a vast gulf that separates the metaphysics of the ascent from the metaphysics of the materialisms. The perceptive founder of Christian Philosophy put all of this into classic form in his *City of God* (XIV, 28): "What we see, then, is that two societies have issued from two kinds of love. Worldly society has flowered from a selfish love that dared to despise even God, whereas the communion of saints is rooted in a love of God that is ready to trample on self."

It is this living connection with the purpose of existence, each one's human existence, that lends real excitement to the study of metaphysics, when this watershed point is reached, the parting of the ways, between the blockage of the mind and the confinement of the human spirit, and the liberation of the mind and openness of the human spirit to transcendent reality. This ascent is analyzed in Chapter IV of Thomas Aquinas' treatise *On Being and Essence,* perhaps the most compressed and at the same time most luminous short piece of philosophical writing in the annals of the history of philosophy.

The Possibility of Nonmaterial Reality

When one analyzes Chapter IV in St. Thomas' treatise *On Being and Essence,* one recognizes a set of insights and understandings about the nature of objective reality that can be compared to a set of steps by which the mind ascends upward toward the intelligibles and to God. From what does the mind ascend? It ascends from the principles that have been learned in Chapters I, II, and III, when analyzing the principles by which bodily things exist. The ascent is made from the realities perceived by the human senses, from Porphyry's tree of the kinds of bodily substances, natures, or essences. The first step upward beyond this visible cosmos of these bodily substances is to wonder whether substances, natures, or essences could exist without matter? Putting this in other words, can immaterial reality exist? Immaterial reality is simply spiritual reality. The idea of spiritual reality is a thing that is not a bodily substance, composed of first matter and substantial form. It is nothing but that form.

This wonderment, asking this question, is the first step in breaking free intellectually from materialism by recognizing the possibility of nonmaterial reality. St. Thomas makes this step by asking how essence exists in things without bodies. Can a form exist simply by itself, without entering into a composition with first matter? Such a form would be a pure form, a nonbodily, or nonmaterial, reality: in other words, a spiritual being, a pure spirit.

The positive answer to this question began to emerge in the heritage of Western philosophy in the discussions between Socrates and the Sophists. The Sophists, one will recall, confined human life and human thinking to worldly pursuits within this cosmos. Socrates held for the existence of a higher, intelligible reality. Thomas Aquinas summarizes this immense philosophical heritage coming from the classical Greeks through Augustine by considering the universal concepts in the human mind, just as Socrates did with the Sophists. These universal concepts are understandings that are separate from matter. Justice is always and everywhere justice, and likewise goodness, and so also truth. Such concepts of the human mind bear upon really existing reality, which is nonmaterial in nature. Thus, immaterial reality begins to be known. This was Socrates' insight, which Plato and Aristotle developed further. Augustine understood the matter as a divine illumination, giving the eye of the mind a vision of a reality that the bodily senses cannot perceive. In Thomas Aquinas, this is the power of the active intellect, human reason, the capacity and power of human rationality.

Thus the intelligible truths are the first step for the human mind in recognizing the possibility of nonmaterial reality.

The Possibility of Angelic Spirits

Philosophy has a long tradition from the Greeks concerning the "intelligences". St. Thomas uses this term in the present chapter. This philosophical term corresponds to what the Tradition of the Hebrew-Christian revelation calls God's messengers, his angels.

The discussion of Thomas Aquinas turns about the concept of "separated substances", substantial realities that exist in a mode separated from matter. The pure intelligences are such forms. St. Thomas gives the principles in the present treatise and discusses the matter fully in his book *On Spiritual Creatures,* where he gives a scholarly and synthetic summary of all previous thought about the possibility of spiritual substances. Immediately there opens before the philosophic mind another tree, as it were, corresponding to Porphyry's tree of the corporeal substances. This would be a tree, so to speak, exhibiting the various levels of pure spirits, with philosophical analysis of their individuality and the different degrees of perfection found among them. "The first natural philosophers", St. Thomas writes in *On Spiritual Creatures,* "used to think that nothing existed but bodies . . . but later philosophers, transcending corporeal things in a rational way through the intellect, arrived at a knowledge of incorporeal substance." This history of pagan philosophy is in its own way a preparation for revealed religion, in which the presence and activities of angelic spirits are a constantly recurring teaching. Through this discussion, Thomas Aquinas is lucidly aware of the fact that his philosophy is different from the pagan philosophy that entered the Church in the times of the Fathers. Christian Philosophy sees the possibility of angelic spirits with a new lucidity, and for different and better reasons than the pagans knew. All of this can be studied in *On Spiritual Creatures.*

Can philosophical reason move from the possibility of such spiritual beings to their actuality? It can discern a high degree of probability, because of the order and fullness of the universe of beings. But the actual fact will become fully clear only when philosophical reason continues its ascent, arrives at the highest Being, and then disposes itself to listen to the question whether this highest Being has spoken a word to mankind.

The Possibility That God Exists

Looking upward, moving upward intellectually, philosophical reason now stands on the third step that can be discerned in Chapter IV of St. Thomas' treatise. Here the mind looks higher still and begins to discern the source of existence as such, as distinct from the forms of bodily things. Here that fundamental and characteristic difference of Christian Philosophy from the earlier pagan philosophy comes to the fore. Why do things exist, apart from their essences, natures, and forms? The question of existence, as distinct from nothingness, constitutes the nature of this third step, this final upward movement of the intellect. In modern terms, "why should there be something instead of nothing?"

It is noteworthy that St. Thomas continues to discuss the existence of God in terms of possibility. He does so as follows, in Chapter IV. "Every essence or quiddity", he writes, "can be understood without knowing anything about its actual existence. I can know, for instance, what a man or a phoenix is and still be ignorant whether it has actual existence in reality. From this it is clear that existence is distinct from essence or quiddity—unless perhaps there is a reality whose essence is its existence. This reality moreover must be unique and primary."

This recognition of the real distinction between essence and the act of existing in all beings except one is the final step of the intellect in its upward journey. Here the intellect begins to see the fundamental distinction between the Supreme Being and all other realities. The mind is preparing to step up to the recognition of Almighty God.

The Ascent to the Fact That God Exists

This is the fourth step, so to speak, that ultimate movement of the human mind to the level where God himself is seen by the natural power of the intelligence. Here again one can not improve upon the incisive words in St. Thomas' Chapter IV:

> The act of existing cannot be caused by the form or essence of a thing . . . because that thing would then be its own cause, and it would bring itself into existence, which is impossible. It follows that everything whose existence is distinct from its essence must have that existence from another reality. And because everything that exists through another is reduced to that that exists through itself as to its first cause, there must be a reality that is the cause of existing for all other things, because it is pure existence. If this were not so, we would go on to infinity in causes, for everything that is not pure existence has a cause of its being, as has been said. It is evident, then, that an intelligence is form and being, and that it holds its existence from the first Being, which is being in all its purity. And this is the first Cause, or God.

In this remarkable passage, one can recognize that truth that *On Being and Essence* is as the bud that opens into the flower of St. Thomas' full doctrine of the five ways in his *Summa.* For the famous five ways of ascending to the existence of God as a fact and a reality are simply the development of this fundamental insight stated so concisely in the present treatise.

It is worthwhile, accordingly, to glance briefly at the five ways of ascending to God, which St. Thomas discusses in Article 3 of the second question in the first part of the *Summa Theologiae.* These five ways are meditations, as it were, on what one sees in this cosmos of bodily things. They are ways of seeing the cosmos with understanding. This understanding is the ascent through the steps, which culminates in recognizing the Supreme Being in his own unique and particular way of existing. The answer to the question "How is essence found in him?" is the outcome of these processes of meditative and reflective thought. There are, then, five ways, or roads, as it were, leading up to this recognition of God in his real and factual existence. Let us look at them briefly.[1]

1. The first way is the experience of change in this cosmos of bodily things. The principle of contradiction operates immediately. "Of necessity," St. Thomas

[1] See Excerpts for Part Two, Aquinas, p. 411.

writes, "anything in process of change is being changed by something else. . . . Hence one is bound to arrive at some first Cause of change not itself being changed by anything, and this is what everyone understands by God."

2. "The second way is based on the nature of causation . . . if you eliminate a cause you also eliminate its effects, so that you cannot have a last cause, or an intermediate one, unless you had a first. . . . One is therefore forced to suppose some first Cause, to which everyone gives the name 'God'."

3. "The third way is based on what need not be and on what must be, and runs as follows. . . . A thing that need not be, once was not; and if everything need not be, once upon a time there was nothing. But if that were true there would be nothing even now. . . . One is forced, therefore, to suppose something that must be and owes this to no other thing than itself; indeed, it itself is the Cause that other things must be." Notice that Christian Philosophy turns always around the central concept of existence itself, the kinds and acts of existence seen in the world, and the fact that they point to a source of existence beyond themselves.

4. "The fourth way is based on the gradation observed in things. Some things are found to be more good, more true, more noble, and so on, and other things less. But such comparative terms describe varying degrees of approximation to a superlative. . . . There is something therefore that causes in all things their being, their goodness, and whatever other perfection they have. And this we call 'God'."

5. "The fifth way is based on the guidedness of nature. . . . All bodies obey natural laws, even when they lack awareness. . . . Nothing however that lacks awareness tends to a goal, except under the direction of someone with awareness and with understanding; the arrow, for example, requires an archer. Everything in nature, therefore, is directed to its goal by someone with understanding, and this we call 'God'."

In this way, one can see that lapidary synthesis in Chapter IV of *On Being and Essence* opening out, unfolding, in these five different ways by which the mind reaches HIM WHO IS, the necessarily existing Supreme Being. It is important to note that Thomas Aquinas is summarizing and putting into lapidary synthesis the effort to achieve a natural theology that has characterized the Western tradition of thought since Socrates, Plato, and Aristotle.

All-Perfect Existence Subsisting

The time has come to reflect upon the most basic name for God that the natural intelligence of man can achieve. For this one time, one should use St. Thomas' Latin: *Ipsum Esse Subsistens.* It will be recalled that these Latin words came to St. Thomas Aquinas from St. Augustine. For he put Christian Philosophy on this path of recognizing existence in things rather than their forms, and of rising from them to existence itself, the Supreme Being who is the source of existence in all other existing realities. This insight constitutes the nature and the specific character of Christian Philosophy, constituting it in its difference from pagan philosophy even at its highest and best.

This insight into the mode of the divine existence, namely, how essence is found in God, characterizes the present chapter of *On Being and Essence*. The most basic names of God already occur: the first Being, the first Cause, existence itself subsisting. Philosophical thought, in Christian Philosophy, recognizes God as the all-perfect Being, infinitely intelligent and good, unlimited existence—subsisting as a personal reality. It should be noted, furthermore, that Christian Philosophy is in contact with what ordinary men everywhere mean when they use the word "God". St. Thomas stresses this in his five ways, pointing out that they lead up to the recognition of the Supreme Being whom all men have in mind when they use the name "God".

Since it is the acts of existing in things that have provided the way of ascending upward to God, and since the limited character of these acts of existing call for a source beyond themselves, this ascent to the Supreme Being stands ready to recognize him as the Creator or Cause of the acts of existing in all other realities.

The Almighty Creator, Creation, and His Creatures

The doctrine of creation is one of the most central doctrines of Christian Philosophy, again a teaching that distinguishes it from other kinds of philosophy. Why is this? Because the recognition of the Creator, which results from the ascent by the five ways, distinguishes Christian Philosophy from the materialist philosophies, which simply take the existence of things for granted without asking the philosophical question, and distinguishes it from all forms of pantheism, which look upon things in the cosmos as emanations or pieces or parts or modes of a universal divine substance that becomes manifest in the things of the cosmos.

The ascent of the mind in Christian Philosophy sees the limited character, by each one's essence, of each act of existing. Thus it comes to the unlimited existing reality, and sees that this unlimited subsisting existence is the source of the existence of all other realities. This constitutes a view of the universe that is quite distinct from materialism and pantheism. This is theism, which understands creation to be God's goodness giving existence to all other realities. Thus he is the Creator. These other realities, then, are his creatures, depending upon him in the very order of existence itself. This opens immense perspectives upon catechetical teaching and the explanation of the First Article of the Apostles' Creed. The fact that Christian Philosophy thinks within the Faith is visible in the doctrine of creation, perhaps better than at any other point. Christian Philosophy sees the Supreme Being, existence subsisting in unlimited perfection, as the source of existence for all other existing realities. Our religion lays out for us different modes of expressing our dependence in gratitude and praise.

St. Thomas makes a specific point regarding the angels. Are they also creatures of God? His answer is perfectly clear: they are indeed creatures, and depend upon God in the order of existence. For they are pure forms, indeed, separated from matter, but those forms are essences, which limit their acts of existing. They are not parts or pieces of the Supreme Being, or emanations from his substance in the pantheistic sense. They have separate acts of existing, given to them by their Creator, acts of existing received in an essence proper to each created spirit. Implicitly throughout his treatment, St. Thomas implies that if this is true of the angels, then how much more so regarding human beings, who have essences composed of matter and form, in the manner that has been discussed.

The Sublime Truth of God's Transcendence

The ascent of the mind to God has reached him in his uniqueness. His mode of existing, his act of existing, is unique in the whole universe of beings. Why is this so? Because his act of existing is identical with his essence and is not received into an essence limiting it in the slightest way. This distinguishes God's way of existing from the way of each creature, from the highest angel to the least grain of sand. Every creature, by definition, exercises an act of existing given to it by God, which is received into and limited by its particular essence. Thus the nature and purpose of *On Being and Essence* emerges into clear view. In the diagram that shows the principles of being, act of existing, and essence, form and substance, form and first matter, one can draw a line across the top of the diagram, recognizing all beings below it as creatures, and placing above the line that unique Being whose essence is his unlimited and all-perfect act of existing. This philosophical insight, this culmination of natural theology, establishes the foundation for revealed religion. The foundation is "this sublime truth", as St. Thomas terms it, of the divine transcendence. The word "transcendence" merely means that God's mode of existing, his way of exercising the act of existing, is unique to himself, distinct from that of creatures, in whom there is a real distinction of essence and the act of existing, so that their acts of existing are limited to this or that kind of thing that each one is. As St. Thomas points out in Chapter IV, there can be only one such unlimited act of existing. Thus philosophical reason supports the revelation given to the Hebrews and taught by the Christians, that mankind must pause and hear that God is one.

The glory of philosophical reason is to recognize this sublime truth, just as it is the shame of philosophy not to recognize the Creator. Christian Philosophy lays the foundation for revealed religion in this ascent to an intellectual vision of the divine reality and the nature of his act of existing. It recognizes him as the Creator and lays the foundation for doing so with thought and words, indeed, but even more so in the living of created life according to God's plan in creating each created nature or essence. When he gives existence to an existing reality according to this or that nature or essence, then the response of that creature is to live according to that nature. This lays the foundation and sets the stage for catechetical explanation of the First Article of the Apostles' Creed.

V

GOD, THE ANGELS, THE COSMOS, AND MANKIND

This corresponds to St. Thomas' Chapter V in his treatise, his masterful summary of the metaphysical analyses achieved in Chapters I through IV. Chapter V exhibits Thomas Aquinas as a great teacher in action. In the first four chapters, he has been asking, In what way is essence present in all substances? There are four chief ways in which things have essence: God's way, the way of the angels, the way of the bodily things that are seen to form this cosmos, and a quite special way, the human way.

Thus Christian Philosophy presents a magnificently comprehensive view of the universe: God, the transcendent Creator; and the created universe below him, consisting of the angelic spirits, the material cosmos, and mankind as the link between spiritual and bodily beings.

This is the philosophical heritage proper to Christians. These are the roots of authentic Christian intellectual life. Our purpose here is to indicate some of the implications of St. Thomas' chapter, with respect to each of these four major components of the world view illuminated by the metaphysics of Christian Philosophy.

Natural Theology

All of natural theology, the natural science of God achieved by human reason, is contained in God's way of having essence, summarized by Aquinas in these words: "There is a Being, God, whose essence is his very act of existing." Notice that God's act of existing *is* his essence. God does have an essence, but since it is without limit, it follows that "God is not in a genus". In other words, he is absolutely transcendent, above and beyond every other substance, whether the bodily ones of Porphyry's tree or those of the spiritual universe. This is the origin of the concept of the supernatural: God's essence is absolutely transcendent, above and beyond all other natures or essences.

Why can there be only one God? The philosophical reason proceeds as follows: "The first cause . . . is individualized by its unalloyed perfection. . . . God, being purely and simply the act of existing . . . possesses all perfections of all genera of beings." Were another being to possess a perfection that God does not have, then God would not be God. With metaphysical necessity, therefore, Thomas Aquinas teaches that there can be only one God, if God's nature and act of existing are understood correctly. Contrast this sublime vision of God with the deformity consisting in present-day paganism revisited, in the attempt by some to bring other gods and goddesses into the liturgy.

All of natural theology follows from this basic insight. All of the divine attributes follow from God's way of existing. It becomes clear that "it is not necessary that God lack the other perfections or excellences". This removes the idea of a process God. In his unlimited and uniquely ever-present reality, "He possesses these perfections in a more excellent way than all other things, for in him they are one, while in all other things they are diversified. The reason for this is that all these perfections are his according to his simple act of existing." In his two *Summas,* St. Thomas will unfold this understanding of the divine reality in his treatises on natural theology, opening as the flower from this concise statement of principle in *On Being and Essence.*

It cannot be emphasized too much that there are two ways of having essence: God's way, and the way of every creature, every other existing reality, from the highest to the lowest. This establishes the divine transcendence, places the concept of God in the order of truth, and opens the way to the correct concept of creaturehood, that way of having essence that owes existence to the Supreme Being, with the correspondent obligations of dependent gratitude if the creature happens to be a rational one.

Importance of the Concept of God

The relationship between creatures and the Creator, which is the very concept of religion, depends upon accuracy in the concept of God. The metaphysical ascent reaches the insight of the divine transcendence, together with the simultaneous divine immanence. God is utterly transcendent over the whole created order, as we have seen. At the same time, by virtue of creation he is close to each of his creatures whom he brings into being, closer indeed to each one than his creatures are to themselves.

The shadow of the ancient and inveterate error of pantheism hangs over Christian times in a way that needs careful attention. The pagan Greek philosophers, even at their best in Socrates, Plato, and Aristotle, as we have noted, could not rise to the doctrine of creation. The Neo-Platonists, headed by Plotinus, continued this failure of pagan thought. Plotinus reduces the relationship between the higher reality and the lower ones to emanation. Creation is reduced to an eternal and necessary, impersonal, gradually descending emanation. This adulterates the doctrine of creation and disfigures the concept of God. It was this that the founder of Christian Philosophy, St. Augustine, removed so carefully and vigorously from Christian Philosophy. In the time of Thomas Aquinas, however, the works of Aristotle came into the schools of Christendom from the Arabian commentators in Spain and the Near East. These Arabian commentators were imbued with Neo-Platonism. Thus many of the later works of St. Thomas Aquinas will defend vigorously the true concept of God as the transcendent, intelligent, and personal Creator. The doctrine of Christian Philosophy, summarized in Chapter V of St. Thomas' small treatise, is the insight into the personal transcendence of the Creator, close to his creatures but infinitely distinct from them. Seen from the viewpoint of the thirteenth-century intellectual crisis, St. Thomas' work is a rejection of the Neo-Plotinian, pantheistic misinterpretation of Aristotle. It is a restoration and a renewal of that concept of the Supreme Being that St. Augustine placed in the foundations of Christian Philosophy.

The importance of this concept of God, his transcendence simultaneous with his immanence, lays the natural foundation for God's self-revelation in revealed religion. In this self-revelation God comes close to his creatures in mercy and love, in a new way, not metaphysical, unlike the hidden way that metaphysics can only overcome in the arduous ascent that not many can achieve in practice. Christian Philosophy lays the foundation for understanding in more than one way these words of Jesus Christ: no one comes to the Father except through me.

Reason and Faith

Beginning with St. Augustine, Christian Philosophy discussed carefully and at length the relationships between reason and philosophy on the one hand, and faith, sacred theology, and revealed religion on the other. In St. Thomas' teaching, philosophy provides the preambles for religious faith. It does not enter into religious faith as its substance but serves it in the initial stages of the return of the soul to God.

One can see this relationship between reason and faith in the method of St. Thomas in his later works. For example, in his *Summa contra Gentiles* (IV, 1), he explains that there are two orders of knowledge: reason and revelation. Then he explains that Books I to III of this *Summa* take their departure from creatures, ascending by the work of reason to God. Book IV will take its departure from divine revelation, descending from God to the creatures of the created universe. In other words, St. Thomas' method exemplifies the relationship between faith and reason, and can be seen in this structure of the *Summa contra Gentiles*. Furthermore, in the first three books, which are philosophical in nature, the philosophizing proceeds within the Faith, which is its guiding star, so that it will not fall to one side or the other, deviating into errors of various kinds.

This same method can be seen from another point of view in the *Summa Theologiae,* where rational theology is expounded in classic form in the first questions of the *Summa,* which is devoted to sacred doctrine. Thus philosophy is seen as thought functioning visibly within the Faith. Yet it remains natural theology, the work of natural reason ascending to God, and discerning his most basic attributes, out of the principles that are summarized in this Chapter V of *On Being and Essence*.

Thus it is clear that philosophy in a Christian mind is not a "separated subject", that is, separated from God and forming a secular subject. Christian Philosophy was a philosophizing within the Faith of his conversion in the work of the founder, St. Augustine: it continues to be philosophy within the Faith in the work of St. Thomas Aquinas.

Natural Theology and Sacred Theology

Natural theology is the academic discipline that recognizes the ability of the human reason to know the existence and divinity of the Supreme Being. We recall from Part One that the ancient Greeks aspired to this discipline, natural theology, an aspiration that the Fathers of the Church received and developed, especially in the work of St. Augustine.

It is important to distinguish this natural philosophical discipline, natural theology, the second part of the science of metaphysics, from sacred theology. The people of God, in the words of Thomas Aquinas, have "a science of the things that can be concluded from the Articles of Faith" (*On Truth*, 14, 9, ad 3). This is a science that seeks to understand the Articles and mysteries of the Faith more deeply, to perceive their interconnections, and to defend them from error. It does not receive its principles from the human sciences, not even from metaphysics, but takes them immediately from God through the revelation proposed by the Church. Sacred theology, therefore, is a science that stands on a higher level, using the natural arts, sciences, and disciplines as it judges them to be helpful. It itself, however, is the science that teaches divine revelation, elaborating it and developing it in its own order. Sacred theology is called "sacred" because of this fact that it takes its departure from the Articles of Faith and develops its discourse in their light. One must recall that the Articles of Faith summarize divine revelation by the authority of the Church, which gathered them into the basic profession of baptismal faith called the Apostles' Creed. St. Thomas Aquinas is at special pains to show that sacred theology takes its point of departure and the light of its discourse from the Apostles' Creed.

In summary, then, the very existence and nature of natural theology, the result of the metaphysical ascent of the mind to God, manifests the manner in which philosophy relates to faith and revealed religion. The one and same transcendent reality of Almighty God, who is seen and recognized by the metaphysical ascent, is heard speaking his word to his creatures and revealing himself to them by doing so.

There is no need, therefore, "to fall into the mistake of those who assert that God is the universal existence whereby each thing formally exists". Thus St. Thomas removes pantheism, and its derivative, secular humanism, which reduces "God" to the set of ideals that animate human striving.

"Thus God is immanent to and in each of his creatures by reason of his creating causality. And that immanence, just as much as his transcendence, is a property of his being" (Nicholas). Thus St. Augustine can write, "God is closer to me than I am to myself", and can discuss the fact that Almighty God is completely present with his whole being, everywhere and always simultaneously.

The Intelligences, or Angels

Taking the next step in his summary of the metaphysical analysis, St. Thomas asks how essence is found in the intelligences. The intelligences, recognized by pagan philosophy, are called angels in the heritage of revealed religion. The full reason why philosophical thought can be open to their actual existence is now clear. Once the intellect makes the ascent to the Supreme Being, then it can recognize what a hiatus would exist in the universe if there were no beings between bodily things and the Supreme Being. Thus it becomes reasonable to think that there would be an entire order of spiritual beings, personalities, without bodies, constituting an entire segment of the universe between man upward to the Supreme Being himself.

These angelic spirits are in no sense "gods". Their act of existing is not unlimited. "It is limited and restricted to the capacity of the receiving nature", as St. Thomas says, and hence the angels are "unlimited from below and limited from above". In other words, they do not have the composition with first matter, but they do have a limited act of existence, limited by the essence that receives it. There can be, therefore, a multitude of such angelic spirits, intelligent persons, each one distinct from the others by its degree of potency, which receives and limits its act of existing. The higher an intelligence, St. Thomas teaches, the closer it is to the first Being, having more act and less potency. In no case, however, is an angelic spirit anything but a creature, with an act of existing limited by its particular essence. Thus is essence found in these angelic intelligences.

Since the angels are creatures, it follows that they must accept the basic attitudes of the interior life: humility, prayer, and adoration. Each angelic intelligence, looking at self and the other angels, should cry out, who is like unto God? The implication: no one of us is like God. Each angel will have to say that each of us, even the highest of us, is more like a grain of sand at the lowest level of the created universe than any of us is like unto God. It is in the study of the angelic way of having essence that Thomas Aquinas analyzes the nature of intellectual pride and humility. These attitudes of spirit turn about the concept of creaturehood. Creatures in themselves are nothing. They are substantial realities only in their relationship to the Supreme Being, who gives them their acts of existing.

It has been said that the denial of the intelligences, or the angelic spirits, is a teaching that reeks already of atheism. Christian Philosophy, with its openness to and vigor in accomplishing the ascent, stands at the antipodes of the materialistic thinking, which usually begins to manifest itself by the denial of the angels. Christian Philosophy, by virtue of its ascent to the transcendent Supreme Being, has a reasonable and philosophical openness to the teaching of revealed religion regarding the fact, the nature, and the functioning of the angelic spirits in the divine plan for his creation.

Cosmology: The Philosophy of Nature

Turning now to the way in which bodily things have essence, St. Thomas writes, "In substances composed of matter and form . . . the act of existing is limited both from above and from below." What does he mean? He means that they are limited, as the angels are, from their Creator above, who gives them their act of existing, received into a potency, namely, their particular kind of essence or nature as seen on Porphyry's tree. He means furthermore that this same essence or nature is "received in designated matter". This is the limitation, as it were, from below. Thus there are many individuals of these bodily things, multiplied in the same nature, their "species": he refers to Chapter III on the manner in which these essences are related to the logical concepts of the human mind.

Thus the metaphysics of bodily things. The next point to consider, which is implied by *On Being and Essence,* is the question of the place and movement of these bodily things in the visible universe. This exhibits the system of distances between the bodily things that we call space. This brings us to a question of absorbing interest, that of the relationship between the metaphysics of St. Thomas Aquinas and the empirical science of his day.

The Philosophy of Nature

This phrase, "philosophy of", indicates an application of metaphysics to a particular subject matter. Philosophy enters into many combinations with other disciplines and bodies of information, indicated by the word "of": thus, philosophy of man, philosophy of knowledge, philosophy of education, and the like. So here: philosophy of nature, or of the cosmos. This indicates the application of metaphysical principles of understanding to these other bodies of knowledge, in order to understand them better, unify them more vigorously, and support their own fundamental principles and foundations.

Cosmology, the philosophy of nature, always has had an absorbing interest. People marvel at the processes close at hand, wonder at the changing of the days and seasons, and admire the splendor of the sky at night. Does all of this bear witness to the same Supreme Being to whom metaphysics has ascended? If so, how?

Cosmology is the study of the cosmos, the universe as an ordered whole. Cosmology is that branch of philosophy that is applied to man's perception of bodily things in the visible cosmos: it is the *logos,* or philosophical discourse, about the cosmos as seen by us.

The World View of the Ancients

Throughout most of the life of mankind on this planet, the physical cosmos was perceived only by the unaided senses. Empirical science was in a rudimentary stage, confined to the practical arts. This perception of the cosmos by the unaided sense was proper to mankind throughout prehistory and to the threshold of our own day in the twentieth century. This perception of the unaided senses was the same in all places, times, and cultures.

This common world view of earlier mankind perceived a stationary earth, with the sun, the moon, and the stars moving overhead in a beautiful starry canopy arching over the earth. It was imagined that crystal spheres existed in several levels of the heavens, accounting for the movements that the senses perceive. All of these celestial bodies and spheres were thought to be made of an imperishable, heavenly matter, far more perfect than ordinary matter of the earth, not subject to the change and decay of the earthly scene. Within this canopy, bodies were perceived as located in space, the real space of human observation beneath the celestial bodies, a space that means the system of distances between bodily things. Within the canopy, space is found in which bodies are located, in which they move, in which they function, acting according to their natures. The Greek word for nature, one recalls, is *physis,* from which the name of Aristotle's treatise *On Physics,* and from which the current English word "physics". *On Physics* is Aristotle's discussion of the natural observation and the state of empirical science that he knew at his time.

Cosmology in Pagan Philosophy

It is important to recall that pagan philosophy in all its forms, even the most competent ones, those of Plato and Aristotle, did not rise to the doctrine of creation. Hence cosmology in pagan philosophy was the application of a defective metaphysical view of reality. For this reason, pagan philosophy was exposed to those typical cosmological aberrations, the eternity of matter as taught by Aristotle, the World Soul of the Stoics, and the emanations of the Neo-Platonists. The philosophies of the pagan Greeks and Romans did not look out on the cosmos with the kind of understanding that results from the doctrine of creation. Putting this another way, the cosmology of the ancients was an application of that ancient and inveterate error pantheism.

Cosmology in Christian Philosophy

From the study of St. Augustine and St. Thomas Aquinas, it is clear that Christian Philosophy comes before the cosmos with a quite different metaphysical light, one already achieved in the manner just outlined in Thomas Aquinas' treatise. This metaphysics has ascended to the Almighty Creator, and it now sees the cosmos with the understanding that it is God's creature. The entire physical universe depends on him, in the very order of existence.

The mind that has been educated and formed academically in this Christian Philosophy as the seventh of the seven liberal arts comes humbled in spirit after its ascent to the ineffable Creator. It recognizes now with an educated insight that he has appointed an entire order of intelligences or angels above this visible cosmos. Such a mentality, schooled philosophically in this metaphysics, is open to the idea that these intelligences or angels assist the Supreme Being and serve him in conducting the marvelous array of orderly processes and natural laws that govern the visible cosmos.

The great difference in cosmology, then, results from the difference in metaphysics, and specifically the doctrine of creation. The pagan Greeks and Romans did not look out on the cosmos with this understanding. In the metaphysics of Christian Philosophy, the entire physical universe is seen with a different kind of understanding. The fundamental difference in cosmology comes from the sublime metaphysical truth of God's transcendence and almighty power to give existence and order to every other reality. Thus, not only the existence of the bodily things in space but also their movements and their processes are subject to the Supreme Being, who administers the course of things in time, as Augustine puts it.

Thomas Aquinas and the Pagan World View

In St. Thomas' day, seven hundred years ago, the cosmos was seen by the unaided senses as it had been from time immemorial. The empirical sciences were still in that rudimentary stage, virtually confined to the practical arts. Thomas Aquinas too, like all Christian teachers from Augustine to his time, conceived the earth as the motionless center over which the canopy arches, moving with its bodily entities in those crystal spheres, all of them made of that different kind of celestial matter.

This is the context of the philosophical commentaries done by Thomas Aquinas on the treatises of Aristotle. In these commentaries, the intention of St. Thomas is to present the truth contained in Aristotle's work, to refute the false interpretations, especially the Neo-Platonist ones coming by way of the Arabian commentators, and thus to save the perennially valid and useful principles and methods of the original thought of Aristotle.

This general purpose applies in a special way in St. Thomas' commentary on Aristotle's *Physics*. The Christian thinker refuses the pantheistic idea of a World Soul, inhabiting the cosmos, and teaches firmly that the entire visible universe is simply the creation of God. It is radically distinct from him and below him, and at the same time radically dependent upon him at the roots of its being. Radically: namely, at the very root of the essence and act of existing of each bodily thing in the visible universe. St. Thomas' commentary is not designed to change the "science" in Aristotle's *Physics,* but rather to correct the metaphysics. The correction bore upon Aristotle himself, for example, in the doctrine of the eternity of matter, but it bore especially upon the Neo-Platonist interpretations of Aristotle at the hands of his Arabian commentators, impacting the schools of Christendom in Aquinas' lifetime. His commentary, therefore, was an intellectual service both to the Church and to the development of human culture.

Metaphysics Distinct from Empirical Science

It is at this point that the distinction between metaphysics, cosmology, and empirical science takes on fundamental importance. Metaphysics is an independent philosophical science, with its own object of study and its own method proper to itself. It is not the same as cosmology, a branch of philosophy, because cosmology applies philosophy to man's current perception of the empirical universe. Much more is metaphysics distinct from the empirical sciences, which gather and study the observed facts about this physical universe.

Metaphysics, in other words, studies "philosophical facts", which exhibit things simply as existing. Philosophy does not depend upon a store of scientifically established facts. Its interest in facts lies in a distinct order, that of existence as such. To make philosophy depend upon empirically observed facts would result in a pseudophilosophy. Metaphysics is the science of existing: its "facts" turn about the existence of things, the plurality of existing substances, the changes in things, and the like. Metaphysics bears on existence as such, together with the principles by which things exist as they do.

Perhaps this can be illustrated by mentioning the difference between the principles by which things exist, and the system of distances between bodily things that constitute space, and the orientation and centering of the movements of these bodies. These are quite different orders of knowledge and illustrate the difference between metaphysics and cosmology.

It follows that the question whether space, and in St. Thomas' time, the crystal spheres of the canopy, have a center at the earth, or the sun, or elsewhere, or perhaps nowhere is a small question, confined to cosmology. It pales before the sublime metaphysical truth of the divine transcendence. In the light of this metaphysical insight and understanding, all space, however oriented or "centered", is seen as the result of the creation of bodily things by the transcendent and intelligent Supreme Being. Metaphysics knows that God is the center, transcendent, and yet simultaneously immanent and present to every creature, and this entirely apart from questions of cosmological centering of bodily things and their motions.

In his *Compendium of Theology* (No. 98), St. Thomas writes, "I do not go into the question why God arranged the visible universe in the way it appears or why he did not locate bodily things elsewhere. For beyond this present universe there is no space except in our imagination."

With this one may leave the realm of cosmology, carrying this principle and metaphysical insight forward into the times to come after Aquinas. Real space is one thing, and imaginary space is another thing. What lies beyond this real space, wherever centered, and however bounded by the imagined crystal spheres of the overarching canopy — or not so bounded — is another question, one that concerns the empirical sciences of the first six arts and not the seventh of the seven liberal arts with its discipline called metaphysics. With this one can turn to the philosophical principles that govern the position of mankind in the cosmos.

Philosophical Anthropology: The Philosophy of Man

Thomas Aquinas points out a fourth way of having essence, calling it an exception. It is an altogether unique way, and highly interesting. It is the human way. St. Thomas has used it throughout *On Being and Essence* to illustrate the various metaphysical principles by which things exist. Here we need only gather these illustrations together in order to have the metaphysics of man, upon which the philosophy of man rests. St. Thomas elaborates these metaphysical principles in his later works, especially in the two *Summas,* where this unsurpassed philosophical anthropology can be studied in detail.[1]

A Spiritual Form Animating an Animal Body

Bodily things, one recalls from Chapter II, have essences that are composite: composed of first matter and a substantial form. Human beings are obviously bodily things: they have essences composed of these two principles. What then is unique and exceptional? It is the fact that the substantial form is a spiritual reality. Thus the human being is the link between the corporeal realm of being and the

---

[1] See Excerpts for Part Two, Aquinas, p. 413.

spiritual world above. A human being is a marvelous unity between the bodily and the spiritual, a unity that results from the one unique act of existing, by which this essence, so wonderfully composed, exists. From this metaphysical foundation, the entire edifice of the philosophical anthropology proper to Christian Philosophy is built up.

Philosophical reflection recognizes that such a spiritual reality, the animating principle of such a being, could not result from material factors. Hence, Christian Philosophy recognizes that each animating principle of each human being is a direct creation of Almighty God. This is the origin of the human soul.

Since the soul exists in union with first matter, it is individuated in the manner that has been already studied. In the case of the human soul, therefore, because of the body to which it is united, there are many individuals in one and the same human species. Each human being has an individuated act of existing because of its dependence on the body. However, St. Thomas writes, "It is not necessary that the individuation come to an end when the body is removed. Since its act of existing is independent, once it has acquired an individuated act of existing, because it has been made the form of this particular body, that act of existing always remains individuated." This expresses the metaphysical foundation for the immortality of the soul, continuing its life after death, and indeed individuated so as to remain itself, awaiting its own proper body.

The implications of these metaphysical principles for the rights and dignity of each human person are clear to see. From the viewpoint of the body, human beings are readily analyzed into chemical components of indeed very little value: the scientists say that a human being consists of several pails of water, plus two to three handfuls of minerals worth only a dollar or two on the market. It is clear that a materialistic and atheistic philosophy will not value human life highly except out of inconsistency.

But when one turns to the animating principle, the substantial form that is found in this essence, and when one realizes that it is an "intelligence", participating in the nature of the angelic spirits of the order above and beyond the visible cosmos, then an entirely different concept of human dignity and value comes home. Instead of being mostly water with a few chemicals, one realizes now that a human being is mostly the soul, giving the material elements their structure and pattern of being and operation.

These metaphysical principles of humanity give the basis for understanding what it is to be a human person. At the same time, these principles provide the foundation for intellectual humility. The human soul, St. Thomas writes, is "the least of the intelligences". It stands at the lowest level of a spiritual gradation reaching upward beyond the visible cosmos, a gradation that terminates on the human level, which holds the lowest degree among intellectual substances.

The Active Intellect: Philosophy of Human Knowledge

It is clear that human beings perform activities proper to animal life: this is known by direct observation. At the same time, these activities of animal life have a difference in quality that human beings can analyze, different from the activities of the lower animals. This is the mental or rational life proper to mankind. From the analysis of intellectual life, philosophical anthropology concludes that there is a second and higher kind of knowledge in human persons, distinct from knowledge by means of the five senses. It is this higher kind of knowledge, qualitatively distinct, that gives the human mode of existing its specific character and specific difference.

The insight into this human quality characterizes the heritage of Western philosophy from the time of Socrates, as we have seen. St. Augustine developed this insight further, recognizing the human power of intellectual insight and understanding as a divine illumination, resulting from the fact of the creation of each individual soul according to the image and likeness of God. Thomas Aquinas saw his own teaching regarding the active intellect as a development from the position of St. Augustine, itself developing the heritage of the pagan Greek philosophy at its best.

"This is the difference between the active and passive powers of man," Thomas Aquinas writes in one of his later works (On Boethius *On the Trinity,* I, I).

> that the passive powers are unable to embark upon their own operations unless acted upon by their proper type of activators, as we note in the case of the five senses; but active powers can perform their operations without being activated by an external stimulus. Now . . . the active intellect is such an active power of the soul. This agrees with the authority of Scripture, furthermore, which teaches that we human beings are endowed with an intellectual light; Aristotle, too, describes this active intellect by using the term light.

Here St. Thomas cites St. Augustine, who teaches that "it is the very nature of our intellectual power to understand things in a certain incorporeal light, which is *sui generis,* as the eye of the flesh sees things about us in this bodily light. . . . This light," St. Thomas comments on Augustine, "by which our human mind understands, is the active intellect" (*On Spiritual Creatures,* Article 10).

It is this active intellect that illuminates our sensory knowledge, as a light given to us by God our Creator, when he made us to be in this unique way of having essence.

It cannot be stressed too much that one stands here at the metaphysical foundation for personhood. Human beings are persons because they are endowed with this light of the active intellect, which gives them a transcendence over the stimuli and activators in the order of the senses. This is the philosophical watershed between approaches that recognize the dignity and the value of each human person, as distinct from approaches that manipulate and control human beings in various ways, often even by regimes of repression and fear.

The Philosophy of Truth

Every philosophy has its own proper concept of truth, which reveals what kind of philosophy it is. Christian Philosophy has an understanding of truth that flows forth from these metaphysical principles by which the human person exists, and that is expressed in this philosophy of knowledge.

The first point in this concept of truth is ontological truth. As the word indicates, it concerns the truth of the being of things outside the mind. This is the truth of each thing's existence, in its essence and act of existing, which comes to it from the Creator. Ontological truth, therefore, is the relationship of each existing thing to the divine mind: it existed in the divine mind before it was created and given its act of existing. Insofar as each thing reflects the idea of the divine mind in creating, then it has the quality of ontological truth. The very being of each existing thing, in other words, is its ontological truth and is closely linked with creation. It is this ontological truth in things that makes it possible for them to be known by minds other than the divine mind of the Creator. This opens the way to human knowledge and to the next aspect of the concept of truth.

Logical truth is the relationship between this same existing reality, now created and having been given its act of existing, to a human mind that knows it as the object of its judgments. Logical truth means that my mind as a human being knows the reality as it really is in reality. When this is the case, there is conformity between my mind and the reality. I have in my mind the truth about this thing that exists, and as it exists, with its particular act of existing, received into its particular essence.

If the Supreme Being were eliminated from one's thinking, there could be no ontological truth, and logical truth would be defined differently. One would come quickly to the position of atheistic existentialism, which says that "existence goes before essence". And thus a kind of philosophy is born that attempts to determine essences by our human decisions and choices: "Nothing has an essence until existence decides or determines what its essence shall be"—hence no reverence for natural laws based on what God has written into our nature. Abortions, for example, are condoned on the basis not of the *nature* of the human child in the womb but on whether the baby is wanted or not.

Human Judgments and Language

Truth is in the judgment expressed by the word "is". The verb "is" expresses the existential judgment upon the reality, stating the fact that what I have in mind is, in reality, the nature of this existing thing.

Human language is the expression of such judgments through audible symbols, so that we communicate with each other. Human language is basically the communication of such judgments. At this point philosophical anthropology is able to see that human language is unique, incapable of derivation from the mode of communication among the lower animals.

There is an important catechetical application of this philosophy of man and of human knowledge. It is the fact that the validity of the basic judgments of the human mind, expressed in the propositions of human discourse, establishes the foundation for teaching the Articles of Faith. The natural foundation is the objective, universal, and transcendental validity of the first principles of reason and the natural judgments of the mind on things and their various kinds or essential natures. This rational foundation enables the teaching of the word of God to proceed with a set of judgments, expressed in the propositions called the Articles of Faith, which come from the higher order of the Supreme Being. Here again, one can only allude in so large a subject to the fact that grace presupposes nature.

The Philosophy of Human Freedom

Philosophical anthropology, then, recognizes a set of activities among men that cannot be reduced to the activities of the bodily and sensory order. The first of these has been intellectual knowledge. Coupled with it, men are conscious of having dominion over their lives and activities, with a power to choose courses of action. In his work *On Truth* (24, 2), St. Thomas writes that "the root of all human freedom is constituted in human rationality". Explaining why, he says that human beings have an interior domination over the course of their activities, by which they reflect on these activities that flow from the spiritual soul, and know their spiritual nature.

This opens the way to the perception that men become better or worse by reason of the actions that they choose to do. Actions have a moral value inherent in them, which participates in the nature of ontological truth, coming from him who created each nature and essence by giving it its act of existing. Thus the absolute character of the natural law appears out of the metaphysical foundations of philosophical anthropology: it comes from the Supreme Being, who is the Creator of the natures in which and among which men exist, live, and act. When men respect this ontological dimension in activities, their connection with the mind and will of the Creator, they find themselves liberated. Human activities thus become steps on the way to God.

The Philosophy of Education

Because of these spiritual powers of intellect and freedom, human beings participate in their own self-development. Philosophical anthropology concludes with an analysis of the process by which this takes place. In the philosophy of Thomas Aquinas, the intellect and will of each learner are the principal cause of self-betterment, the process called education. The teaching profession, with the apparatus that it uses, is in the realm of ministerial causes: it ministers to the activation of the spiritual powers of the learner. Thus, this philosophy of education stands entirely within the concept of personhood, as a ministry to the dignity and worth of each person.

This introduces another dimension of philosophical analysis, that of the changes in things. There is no more significant change on the earthly and human scene than that which results in the participation of human persons in their own self-betterment and self-creation. These are the changes that result from personal use of these spiritual powers of understanding and free will. And thus one turns to the last chapter of St. Thomas' treatise *On Being and Essence.*

VI

CAUSES OF CHANGES IN THINGS

"Now that we have explained how essence is present in all substances," St. Thomas writes, opening his Chapter VI, "it remains for us to see how essence exists in accidents."

It is fundamental, in metaphysical analysis of the principles by which things exist, to distinguish between the essence (or substance or nature) of things and the accidental modifications of such substances. Since these accidental modifications involve changes, that kaleidoscope of changes that the senses observe in this visible cosmos, the causes of changes in things will come under review.

The Reality of Changes in Things

Change in the appearances or "phenomena" of things is a fact of experience. Some philosophers, including Plato, have attempted to reach the underlying reality or substance of things by declaring that the reports of the senses on these phenomena are illusions. In Christian Philosophy, however, there are a healthy confidence in the sense organs and a recognition that changes in things are real.

The popular illusion in this matter is quite different from the Platonic one. The less people cultivate their intellect, or live by faith, and the more they turn simply to what their senses report, the more change will seem to be at least the basic reality, and then even the only reality. Heraclitus is the philosopher of nothing but change, and his basic metaphysical world view continues in our time as Hegelianism and Marxism. It is fundamentally important, therefore, to achieve an objectively true metaphysical analysis of the changes in things.

Being, Becoming, and the Four Causes

The world view of Christian Philosophy, as we have seen, recognizes both being and becoming. Each has its own reality. So far, we have been studying substances extending from the least material bodies to the Supreme Being himself, transcendent, existence subsisting.

The Four Causes

In Aristotle's metaphysics, an abiding contribution to the philosophical heritage was made in his careful doctrine on the four kinds of causes. Two of these causes are intrinsic, and we have been studying them in the previous chapters. Among bodily things, these intrinsic causes are the principles by which the essence is what it is: a composite of substantial form and first matter. Thus one arrives at material causality, from which quantitative properties and accidents derive, and formal causality, from which the qualitative aspects and accidental features of substantial realities derive.

The other two causes are the efficient cause and the final cause. The efficient cause is that by which something is brought into existence, or into a modified existence: it produces becoming. The final cause is the fourth, extrinsic principle of process, giving the reason why efficient causes go into action, whether consciously, in the case of conscious and intelligent agents, or unconsciously, when the final cause is in the mind of him who administers providentially the process of changes in the cosmos. Take a statue: the material cause is the marble; the formal cause, the shape; the efficient cause, the chisel or other instrument; and the final cause, creating a decorative or beautiful object.

It is clear that the doctrine of causes finds direct application in all forms of teaching, including catechesis. Education cannot just happen but must have its causes. Educational changes in human beings are without doubt among the most important applications of the doctrine of causality.

The First Cause

This is one of the names of the Supreme Being, which metaphysical analysis is able to reach and to express regarding God. He is the unique first cause of all realities that exist outside himself. This is another way of expressing the doctrine of creation. Creation is not a "change" in the ordinary sense observed in the cosmos. The reason is, of course, that it is not a mutation. It is not a change in a preexisting material. It is the production of a substantial reality in its entire being, out of nothing, when God gives an act of existing to a being in its particular essence or kind. No creature can create, but only God. There is only one First Cause. The difficulty of the doctrine of creation comes from the fact that it is not seen by bodily eyes. God is a hidden God, and so is his causality. It establishes a relation of dependence on the part of the creature, by the immediate and free action of the Supreme Being, giving the act of existing, and thus bringing the creature into existence. St. Thomas Aquinas expresses this with classic and lapidary brevity and exactitude in his *Summa Theologiae* (III, 6, 1, ad 1): "Creatures are caused by God, and depend upon him as the principle of their act of existing. And thus, because of the infinity of his power, God is in immediate contact with each being, causing it and preserving it in existence. And it follows that God is immediately in all created things by his essence, his presence, and his power." This is the metaphysical insight into the immanence simultaneous with the transcendence of Almighty God. Metaphysics reaches this insight laboriously by its analysis; the teaching of revealed religion gives the same doctrine on God quietly, simply, and in a manner that even children can receive, as we have noted in connection with the origin of Christian Philosophy in the times of the Fathers.

The Secondary Causes

In the world view of Christian Philosophy, causality is not confined to the Supreme Being. In his greatness and in his goodness, he endows created substances with the power to do things, to make things, and to change the mode in which substances exist. Thus human beings can make and do things with their own efficient causality and have their own final causality in mind, the purpose for which they act. In all exercise of secondary causality, it must be noted, a preexisting material always is necessary for the action of the created cause. Human beings cause changes in things, indeed, but they do not create the existence itself of the things that they cause.

Again to come to education and catechesis: secondary causality need not be confined to modifying the accidental characteristics of external things. Humans exercise a causality upon themselves, the principal causality of learning and of self-formation. Thus in the order of natural education, and in the order of supernatural formation, the intelligent and volitional human person is the cocreator of himself. If the changes are good and to be desired, then the causes must be understood and applied. This is the point where metaphysical analysis contacts human education, in a basic way, and catechetical formation in a doubly basic way.

The Primacy of Substance

Why does St. Thomas take up the discussion of accidents only at the end of *On Being and Essence?* The reason is the primacy of being, out in reality, over the fact of becoming, of changes and accidental modifications in substances, both out in reality.

This means that there is no change without a thing, or substance, that changes. There must be a being before becoming can take place. Putting this another way, there is an abiding reality in and through the change. Apples exist as substances underlying accidents such as greenness or redness. This was the perception that triggered philosophical analysis in the times of the Pre-Socratics; philosophers have circled about this fundamental of reality, deepening their understanding of it, ever since. To be a metaphysician, one must participate in this ever deeper insight and understanding regarding the nature of things. With this one reaches the concept of an accident. Let us use the words of St. Thomas:

> The supervening accident, by its union with its subject, does not cause the act of existing in which the thing subsists, rendering the thing a substantial being. Rather, it causes a certain secondary act of existing, without which the subsistent thing can be understood to exist, as what is first can be understood without what is second. . . . Substance, therefore, which is primary in the genus of being, possessing essence most truly and excellently, must be the cause of accidents, which secondarily and as in a qualified sense share the nature of being.

Thus, the substance is a principle of being distinct from its accidental modifications, even those properties that flow most directly from the principles that compose that substance, as noted in the case of bodily things.

Hence, if one encounters doctrines that changes are simply a succession of appearances, in a vacuum, as it were, with nothing there that changes, one recognizes immediately a metaphysical system that is other than that proper to the heritage of Christian Philosophy. Common sense, expressing the judgment of natural reason, concurs with these words of Aquinas: "That to which an accident is united is in itself a complete being, subsisting in its own act of existing." The appearances of the thing, its accidental qualities, are distinct from its substantial reality and its principles.

The Nature and Kinds of Accidents

An accident is defined in this Christian and human philosophical heritage as an entity that exists not in itself as a subject but in another reality as its subject. In other words, no accident is a subsisting subject; it modifies subsisting subjects in quantitative or qualitative ways. For example, an apple is an apple, substantially, at the time of the blossoming of the tree in the spring and at the time of the apple harvest in the fall. Accidental modifications have indeed taken place, but the substantial reality is that of an apple, never that of a pear, or a plum, much less that of a dog or a cat. Substantial realities are real things.

Accidents are perceived by the senses, for they are the appearances of things, "phenomena", in Greek. Animals likewise see them but simply as if there were nothing else to reality. At the same time, they are metaphysical principles, and can be, indeed ought to be, seen with understanding. For they enable us to understand the substantial reality and to come to know its properties and qualities increasingly better.

It should be noted that accidents are related to their substance as act and potency. The substance must be in potency to receive these additional accidental acts of existing. If the real potency is not present, that substance could never acquire such an accident. Again, taking illustration from men and their development, a child can become an engineer or a surgeon, because the real potency exists in that child's substance from the beginning. A dog or a cat could never become an engineer or a surgeon, for lack of the principle in its substance. In the abortion debate, a crucial point is that a human fetus will never become a cat or dog.

Properties are accidents that flow from the very nature of the substance in a specially direct way. They are not simply the result of external and often adventitious causes, as a dent in a fender. It is the properties, those special accidents, that enable the human mind to understand the substance and to name it for what it is. All of the empirical sciences function in this context, in the first order of abstraction.

As we have noted, intelligence and free will are accidents of the human substantial form, in the sense that they are properties of a spiritual type deriving directly from the spiritual nature of the human substantial form.

The philosopher bears in mind that divine grace is a quality of this particular human person. But it is a wondrous property, the highest of the accidental modifications, in the scale of being. It gives a participation in the very life of God: it heals, renews, and elevates. Thus again, sound metaphysical analysis establishes the natural foundation for the teaching of revealed religion.

The Kinds of Changes

Most of the changes in things are accidental in character, meaning that they are changes or modifications of the substance, the substance itself abiding. There is another kind of change, however, that involves the very substance of the thing. An example is the burning of a log of wood. Accidental changes are superficial modifications of the states or modes of the abiding substance. Substantial changes, such as fire, or nutrition, are profound: they touch the very identity of the substantial being so that the being itself changes into another being. With this reference to nutrition as the most common example of substantial change met by men experiencing life in this cosmos, one stands before the eucharistic Change, which is the most important catechetical application of natural human metaphysical analysis.

Catechetical Significance and Applications

We have mentioned the relationship between faith and reason several times, and have noted that St. Augustine deliberated at length upon this fundamental relationship. It is a constant in Christian Philosophy. Let us therefore at this point draw attention very briefly to a few of the most important applications and points of contact.

The Truth of the Faith

The philosophy of truth, ontological and logical, is constantly at work in the teaching of revealed religion. Why is this true? Because truths are related to substantial realities, which reflect ideas in the Creator's mind.

Applied in revealed religion, this means that the propositions of human discourse that teach the word of God, the prophetic word, on the human scene, are abidingly the same in meaning. Since this is a truth that derives directly from the transcendent Supreme Being, its abiding character is even more present and pronounced than the substantial realities of creatures. Putting this quite plainly, it simply means that the natural foundation is present for teaching the Apostles' Creed in the same meaning to Christians today as it had for the Apostles when they learned it from God Incarnate, their teacher. Thus Christian teachers do not change the meaning of the Articles and the dogmas of divine Faith. Those who do so, or attempt to do so, are victims of the modernist heresy, which will come up for discussion later as the preeminent "philosophical heresy". Christian teachers bear always in mind these words: "Heaven and earth shall pass away, but my words shall not pass away."

Divine Grace

As iron glows in fire, so humans glow, as it were, when God comes close and makes them his adopted sons and daughters. This is the new way, the holy newness, proper to revealed religion. When God thus comes close to his rational creature, a new mode of being, the natural mode purged, renewed, and elevated, comes to exist. As we noted, this is an accidental modification of human nature. Yet it is so profound and so elevated that it gives human nature, as it were, a quasi nature, with its own activities, faith, hope, and charity.

Metanoia: Changes in Human Persons

This is the place to develop the application in revealed religion of the doctrine on the causes of changes in things. The thing in this case is a person, and the change is from aversion to God the Supreme Being to conversion toward him, in the reality of human living and in the fundamental metaphysical sense. These are the changes in human beings from bad to good, and carry out that "daily conversion" that is the Christian way of life.

This *metanoia*, this conversion, is a function of that qualitative change denoted by the phrase "divine grace". The conversion to God is linked with this qualitative change of this person, which sanctifies the person by the divine grace or presence. Grace is a quality of the human person, but wondrous in the scale of being. It is a participation in the very life of God, the beginning of eternal life, and of the beatific vision. Thus metaphysical analysis lays the natural foundation for immense perspectives on human life and destiny.

Satan: A Special Case of Personal Change

Philosophy can have an openness to changes among the angels, but it cannot know whether they exist or what their nature is, unless it cultivates an openness to a word from above through the teaching of revealed religion.

In this teaching of revealed religion, one learns of a change in an angel from natural goodness, beautiful and bright, to aversion to the Supreme Being through pride, so that the angel becomes a devil.

As St. Augustine writes in his treatise *On the True Religion* (13, 26): "Even angels are mutable.... God alone is immutable.... The bad angel loved himself more than God, refused to be subject to God, swelled with pride, came short of supreme being, and fell. He never had supreme existence, for that belongs to God alone." Pondering this teaching, the philosopher recognizes that he stands face to face with the realm of mystery and the problem of evil, resulting from the wrong use of created freedom.

The Transubstantiation

It is proper from the philosophical point of view, when one philosophizes within the Faith as one does in Christian Philosophy, to mention this supreme instance of contact between faith and reason. The transubstantiation is a special kind of change in things that effects the change in persons called the *metanoia,* confirms it, and brings it to its ultimate term in the beatific vision. Sometimes one hears or reads that transubstantiation is a recent invention, a word coined perhaps by Thomas Aquinas. Hence it is good to listen to these words of St. Ambrose, who taught Augustine in his catechumenate and baptized him into the Catholic Church. In his treatise *On the Mysteries,* St. Ambrose writes as follows on this central teaching of revealed religion.

> Perhaps you will say, "I see something else; how is it that you assert that I receive the Body of Christ?"... Let us prove that this is not what nature made, but what the blessing consecrated ... by which nature itself is changed.... For if the blessing of man had such power as to change nature [and here St. Ambrose cites instances from the activities of Moses and Elias], what are we to say of that divine Consecration where the very words of the Lord and Savior operate? For that sacrament that you receive is made what it is by the word of Christ.... You read concerning the making of the whole world: "He spoke and they were made, he commanded and they were created" (Ps 3). Shall not the word of Christ, which

was able to make out of nothing that which was not, be able to change things that already are into what they were not? For it is not less to give a new nature to things than to change them. . . . The Lord Jesus himself proclaims: "This is my Body." Before the blessing of the heavenly words, another nature is spoken of; after the Consecration, the Body is signified . . . and you say, Amen, that is, it is true. Let the heart confess within what the mouth utters; let the soul feel what the voice speaks.

Such are the words that Augustine, the founder of Christian Philosophy, heard from his teacher St. Ambrose. Across all the Christian times, then, this teaching has taken place in the catechumenate of revealed religion. To illustrate the abiding character of this teaching, listen for a moment to No. 25 of the recent *Creed of the People of God,* in the late twentieth century: "Christ cannot be thus present in this sacrament except by the change into his Body of the reality itself of the bread, and the change into his Blood of the reality itself of the wine, leaving unchanged only the properties of the bread and wine that our senses perceive. This mysterious change is very appropriately called by the Church transubstantiation." These are words of the Holy See that make use of the constants of common sense, ordinary human right reason, in judging the differences between the substances of things and their accidental modifications. And with this, one may take leave of the treatise *On Being and Essence,* this compact but comprehensive summary of the content of Christian Philosophy.

GENERAL CONCLUSION

We have studied the founding and development of Christian Philosophy following upon the pagan times of antiquity, incorporating the best of its insights, and developing them further by the exercise of reason in the schools of Christendom. We have noted that Christian Philosophy develops within the Faith. Christian Philosophy is nothing else than the cultivation of ears, so to speak, in the human mind, ears by which it can hear a word from the transcendent reality, that sublime truth, which Christian metaphysics ascends to perceive.

At a certain moment in the establishing of revealed religion, a voice was heard from the transcendent order, like thunder, as follows: "This is my beloved Son, in whom I am well pleased: hear him." This hearing of him is an ability that Christian Philosophy cultivates: it lays the natural foundations for this hearing of him. And what does he say? Many things. But for the philosopher, perhaps nothing more significant than these words, which he spoke and which the philosopher in a special way needs to hear: "Learn of me for I am meek and humble of heart."

Nothing could be more appropriate for the human thinker who has followed the pathway that ascends upward and recognizes the reality of the Supreme Being and the sublime truth of his transcendence.

Taking leave of this summary of the content of Christian Philosophy, one should take along two highly interesting and even fateful questions, fateful because of their possible interaction.

The first question is whether Christian Philosophy will be cultivated in the times after Thomas Aquinas, making progress by its characteristic way. One recalls that progress in metaphysics takes place not by substitution but by ever deeper penetration into and cultivation of truth already perceived. Will the sublime truth of the divine transcendence continue to be cultivated ever more deeply and with increasing application in the times after Aquinas? In his *Summa contra Gentiles* (III, 25), St. Thomas writes: "First philosophy [namely, metaphysics] is entirely directed toward the knowledge of God as the ultimate purpose and end of all things. Hence metaphysics is a divine knowledge, which itself has this same ultimate end or purpose, namely, God. This knowledge of God is likewise the ultimate end or purpose of all human knowledge and activity." This sweeping synthesis contains the natural support of revealed religion, and it contains, furthermore, the principles of human social and cultural activity.

The other question concerns the empirical sciences. It will be recalled that they make their progress by discovery of new facts, which necessitates the replacement of old theories with new ones. Their progress is by substitution, not by deeper penetration. Will the times after Thomas Aquinas introduce developments in the empirical sciences that lead to the discovery of new facts that alter the age-old world view deriving from the use of the unaided senses by mankind from the distant beginnings through the ages of prehistory and across the times of civilized and cultured life since 4000 B.C.?

Bearing these two fundamental questions, distinct but interrelated, in mind, we turn to the origin and development of a different kind of philosophy, quite different from Christian Philosophy, and demanding careful analysis and evaluation.

PART THREE

MODERN PHILOSOPHY:
A CHALLENGING PROBLEM

A New Kind of Metaphysics in Christendom

INTRODUCTION

The Setting in the Ongoing Life of the Church

This is not a study of the history of philosophy as such. It is a study of fundamental philosophical doctrine, done on St. Augustine's catechetical principle of salvation history "from Genesis to the present times of the Church" (*De catechizandis rudibus,* 5). The development of philosophical doctrine does indeed have a historical dimension, which helps in understanding the various metaphysical systems. For philosophy does not exist abstractly in a vacuum apart from human society. Since the effort of Socrates, Plato, and Aristotle, it has aspired to be the seventh of the seven liberal arts, the one therefore that crowns education and inspires human culture. St. Augustine actually fulfilled this aspiration in his book *De doctrina Christiana,* his program for Christian studies. As a result, for a millennium after his life and work, Christian Philosophy was actually taught as this seventh liberal art in the schools of Christendom. We have studied his seminal role in Part One and we explored the essential content of this new Christian Philosophy in Part Two above.

As the seventh and culminating art or discipline on the program of studies, this rational wisdom orients fundamental thinking in all the other arts, sciences, and disciplines of human education and culture. Thus human society and culture take their purpose, human orientation, and humanistic quality from this philosophical formation of the young people, who go forth as leaders in society from their schools, colleges, and universities. One must bear in mind that we are studying the foundational discipline of that Christian culture, which is now the qualitative character of Western civilization. Clearly this is a matter of direct concern for the apostolate of the Catholic Church, which, as we saw in Part One, was involved through the work of the Fathers of the Church in the origin and specific nature of Christian Philosophy.

A Sea Change Comes over Western Civilization

We are standing in the year 1600 A.D., looking ahead into the seventeenth century. Over three centuries have passed by since St. Thomas Aquinas and the rise of the universities in the West. Father Martin Luther, Father Nicholas Copernicus, and Father Giordano Bruno, fellow priests of St. Augustine, St. Bonaventure, and St.

Thomas, yet quite unlike them in fundamental thinking, have come and gone. In the fourteenth century the Black Death wounded society grievously, and especially the Catholic Church, which lost so many priests and religious, her pastoral and teaching personnel.

In the fifteenth century the Italian Renaissance burst upon the scene, deeply ambiguous, for it had simultaneously a pagan side and a religious one. Constantinople, furthermore, fell to Islam: scholarly refugees flooded Italy, bringing with them their Greek language to fuel the avidity of the Italian Renaissance for Ciceronian Latin and classical Greek. Academies of Plato were founded in Florence, Rome, and elsewhere, but soon they were teaching Plotinus and his pantheism rather than Plato. Everywhere there was a growing aversion to Aristotle and what now was called disdainfully "Scholasticism" expressed in its "barbaric" Church Latin. Thus the metaphysics taught so lucidly by Thomas Aquinas fell under eclipse in more than a few youthful minds, even in the Dominican Order. Doubtless this helps to explain the mysterious and unhappy phenomenon of Father Giordano Bruno, O.P.

The Italian Renaissance was more than a cultural rebirth of classical Greece and Rome. It also stimulated mightily that practical inventiveness that long had characterized the Christian West. Inventions led to discovery: for example, the sextant made possible the navigation of Columbus, Magellan, and Henry Hudson. At the end of the fifteenth century the New World was discovered, North and South America were opened as a surprise to Europeans, and the earth was circumnavigated. The Christian West made contact with the rest of mankind, realizing with immense general impact that the earth is a globe and not a flat terrain. The world picture is ready for further changes. The stage is becoming set for the new astronomy of Father Nicholas Copernicus. Galileo and his telescope will soon arrive.

Father Martin Luther, furthermore, has launched fundamental religious disunity into Western Christendom: Protestantism is consolidating rapidly in Northern Europe. At midseventeenth century the Peace of Westphalia will terminate the long and ruinous wars of religion with an ongoing division of Europe into two different religious cultures. As Western Christians begin to approach the rest of mankind in the New World and the Far East, India and China will note with dismay and confusion that Western religion lacks unity and therefore strength and vigor.

These events and developments that historians study had a far-reaching impact upon fundamental thinking and hence upon the teaching of philosophy. Specifically from that philosophical point of view, one must single out two factors in these three centuries since Aquinas for a few words of special consideration, for they are the immediate background of intelligibility for the emergence of Modern Philosophy as a new kind of philosophy different in metaphysics from the Christian

Philosophy of the preceding thousand years. These factors are the Copernican revolution and the decadence of Scholasticism.

The Copernican Revolution

In the literature of modern history, philosophy, and science this phrase has come to denote in a general way the rapid progress of the empirical sciences and the resulting technologies. It began, however, in astronomy, and it continues to mean fundamentally an immense and indeed revolutionary change in mankind's picture of the cosmos.

Some basic questions accordingly face the student of philosophy. Does this drama of change affect only the empirical sciences? In other words, is it to be confined to the first six of the seven liberal arts? Or does it also affect philosophy? If so, how? If not, why not? In particular, is atheism the meaning of this progress in the empirical sciences? Or might that meaning prove to be quite the contrary? Does that progress affect questions of existence as such? Or only how we, with our unaided senses, naturally picture the material cosmos?

The Copernican revolution takes its name from a Polish Catholic priest, Father Nicholas Copernicus, who remained in Rome for a time after completing his studies. The year is 1543. He is writing a letter to the Successor of St. Peter in Rome about the mounting evidence that the geocentric understanding of the cosmos may not be correct. The age-old picture of the visible universe, hitherto common to mankind in all places, cultures, and times, may have to be revised. Copernicus is saying to the Holy See that the possibility of a radically different view of the cosmos has been recognized since antiquity, but so contrary is it to what the senses report that it has never been taken seriously. "I think the time is arriving", Copernicus writes in this letter,

> when we will have to consider it. . . . The earliest suggestion that I have seen that the earth is in motion is a statement by Cicero, *Academica* (II, 123): "The teachers at Syracuse in Greater Greece, as Theophrastus tells us, hold the view that the heavens, the sun, the moon, the stars, and in short all the things on high are stationary and that nothing in the cosmos is in motion except the earth. By revolving and turning around its axis it produces all the same results as would be produced if the earth were stationary and the heavens in motion."

With the knowledge and consent of the Holy See of St. Peter, this Polish priest published his book on the heliocentric universe. The Copernican revolution, a revolution caused by new empirical knowledge, accumulating by progress in the first six of the liberal arts, was under way. There was a burgeoning of evidence associated with the famous name of Galileo. It results from the newly developed technical ability to grind lenses for eyeglasses. A short step took scientists first to telescopes and then to microscopes. Technology is enhancing the power of the human senses to observe facts. Suddenly both the macrocosm and the microcosm are opening to the surprised eyes of mankind, with new vistas, perspectives, and hermeneutical implications.

The geocentric world picture, with its three-storied universe and the beautiful sacred canopy above, collapses like a changed scenario. What about the mental picture of the flat earth? That too is collapsing, during these same decades of the Renaissance, in a series of events linked with the name of Prince Henry the Navigator.

The invention of the sextant is another aspect of progress in the empirical sciences. With the sextant navigation becomes an exact science, uniting mathematics and geography. Suddenly it is possible to sail a ship out of sight of land without getting lost. Prince Henry the Navigator, interested for religious reasons in bypassing the Islamic roadblock on the overland route to the Far East that Marco Polo had used, set up a school of navigation at Lisbon. Young men came from all Europe, including Christopher Columbus from Genoa, to study navigational theory and the practical use of the sextant. Soon Portuguese and Spanish ships were routinely sailing far out of sight of land and returning safely. In 1492 Columbus discovered "the New World", two entire continents hitherto unknown to Western man. Shortly thereafter Magellan circumnavigated the earth, reaching the Far East by sailing around the southern tip of South America. Quickly the word spread: man lives on a globe that turns in space. The fact has been demonstrated empirically. The age-old picture of the three-storied universe is gone.

There was an unforeseen religious consequence. Westerners, whether missionaries such as St. Francis Xavier or traders for spices or ships chartered for power by the royal governments of Europe, sailed forth ever more numerously and frequently to explore every part of the globe. Mankind hitherto had lived and developed in widely separated blocks, like pools of water on a floor, with a minimum of contact. The rest of mankind, headed by China and India, continued in mutual isolation from the West. But now all the other tribes and tongues and cultures began to come under the intensive scrutiny of the Westerners. Information poured back into Europe and was disseminated by writings of every kind. The newly invented printing press played its role. What information? Chiefly about the kaleidoscope of other ways of life on the planet; other religious patterns, traditions, heritages; even other sacred books in the cultures of the Far East that the West by and large had never realized before. These religions and the ways of life they engendered were of the widest variety, with practices across the entire spectrum of conceivable human behavior.

At first there seemed to be no unity in the new information, but only a chaotic mass of data. Gradually, however, men of learning were able to observe some patterns of order in the facts. New sciences were born in the universities of the West, especially ethnology and the science of comparative religion. The

Copernican revolution has moved to a lateral breakthrough across the space of the now-globular planet. There will be consequences for philosophy to ponder. A new world picture of wider space is emerging.

Roughly concomitant with but somewhat later than this opening out of global space, something similar began to take place regarding the perspectives of time. The foreshortened concept of mankind's past in the earlier world view was broken apart. Additional empirical sciences, organized about new data, were added to curricula in the Western universities for the scientific study of the times prior to the invention of writing, prior, that is, to "recorded history". As geography is discovering all the varieties of contemporary man, so the sciences of prehistory are about to reveal a hitherto unknown mankind living in a far more distant past. Again, the older world view crumbles.

Great interest began to arise in the deciphering of geological strata. Expertise was cultivated in discerning the meaning of sequences observed in layers of geological deposits. Suddenly, and the word is not inexact, the concept of a geological development for the planet earth was born. Immediately another segment of the world picture of the ancients disappears, that segment that supposed that the cosmos always has been in its present form and always will be. In summary, it became quite clear that layers of sediment exist and are subject to exact observation that show no sign whatsoever of life. When life does appear, its fossilized vestiges are observed to be above the primary layer. Scientists begin to call this epoch the Mesozoic age, reflected by the secondary layer. In this layer the men of learning catalogued and categorized a wide variety of fossils; seed-bearing plants; and all sorts of animals—reptiles; mammoths; many strange creatures, large and small; and many not so strange. In this geological age, the scientists concluded, life appears. In earlier times, there were no living beings here on the planet.

The research continued with growing intensity. The popularized accounts of the findings multiplied, together with much theorizing. New empirical sciences were added to the roster of the liberal arts: geology, paleontology, and their ever-more-specialized subdivisions. The Copernican revolution in the empirical sciences is gathering momentum. The scientists identify a Tertiary age, because a scientific consensus forms that this time dimension is the meaning of yet another layer that they have identified. Then a Quaternary age, obviously much more recent than the other three, yet shockingly distant in the past when viewed from the natural restrictions of the older world picture. It is dawning upon mankind that these epochs of time were very long indeed. Controversies swirled among the learned when lengths were ventured in thousands or hundreds of thousands of years. The Copernican revolution is indeed in full swing and progress.

In the Quaternary age, it became clear, extensive glaciations took place, which altered drastically the climate and physical appearance of vast areas of the earth's surface. Planet earth experiences the ice ages. At this point in time the scientists identify a special phenomenon: human beings appear in the geological record. Is this scientifically certain? Is the previous absence of humans itself a significant fact? And the sudden presence of humans? Can they be proved to be human? Scientists answer in the affirmative, for they have ways of identifying the human mode of being and existence. This interests philosophy, of course, as the very terms indicate, and we will return to the point.

In any case, an immense breakthrough is taking place regarding mankind's time, extending it into a much more distant past, as the navigation of the oceans is extending Western man's space around that globe that the earth is now known to be.

This Copernican revolution in the empirical sciences is far from over. The next step in its development results from the ever-growing accumulation of facts about those fossil remains of the earliest humans. Scientists gather these facts from various places of the earth, analyze and categorize them, argue and dispute over them, publish articles and books about them, and above all organize programs in higher education about them for students. The science of archaeology is born and appears in university catalogues as a new discipline. The ancients would have said that the liberal arts were proliferating with subdivisions. It is important here to remember that this is progress in the first six of the liberal arts. In and of itself it does not touch philosophy, the seventh liberal art.

How does empirical science establish the humanity of purported human remains? Not entirely by fossilized bones. Other animals have quite similar bones. Are there other signs of rationality? To ask the question is to involve philosophy and to alert the philosophers. There are indeed such signs, uncovered by the spade of archaeological science. If the being that had those bones made tools and used them, then the scientist becomes sure that humanity is present. Again, if the being that walked and worked in those bones practiced religion, then it was human. Has evidence been uncovered? The answer is definitely yes. Those earliest humans practiced the ritual burial of their dead, and they frequented special places, sacred places, one may say, where sacrifices were offered. Again the spade: the stone altars and the bones of the sacrificed animals have been uncovered and identified by the field research of the empirical scientist. This is something quite different from philosophy, even though it may be significant for philosophy.

In any case, the age of mankind upon this planet is a quite different matter than people had assumed prior to the Copernican revolution. This drama of modern man turns next to the development of yet another empirical discipline, the science of prehistory. It studies the newly discovered human time antecedent to written history. Its length? Far longer than ever suspected. Its length makes recorded history seem quite short, almost contemporary: as a fullness of time, one might say. It was a part of that pre-Copernican world view to think that human life as such began at that point about six thousand years ago when writing was invented and recorded history and the age of the civilizations began. The two beginnings were rather naively identified.

In fact, even the beginning of the visible cosmos was placed as a rather sudden event at approximately the same time only about six thousand years ago. Commentators on the sacred books of the Judeo-Christian heritage wrote their footnotes for the Bible, quite naturally, out of this same earlier world picture. Thus a "biblical chronology" became a standard gloss added to the sacred text, presenting a foreshortened "prehistory" from Adam and Eve to the call of Abraham and on to Moses and the Exodus from Egypt. The sacred text itself, however, presenting what the writers of their own time had in mind, has nothing to say about such a chronology of those earlier times. Both the Jewish and the Christian Scriptures say categorically, "A thousand years for God is as one day." Calculation is easy. Ten days will be like ten thousand years; a thousand days, less than three years of human time, will be like a million years. The Scripture is saying that man must be open to a different time scale when the Almighty Creator is concerned.

Apart from the confusions engendered by a biblical chronology resulting from merely human and all-too-human commentaries, the new science of archaeology proceeded to gather evidence for a succession of stages in prehistoric human development. The earliest stage leaves scanty traces in the fossil record, because men in those most primitive beginnings used only tools and instruments made of perishable materials such as wood and bone. No doubt they also used stones in forms found at hand. Scientists do identify tools made of bone by what appear to be the absolute primitives. It was a ray of light upon the prehistoric darkness when shaped and chipped stone tools and weapons were identified and located at a later stage, the Old Stone age, followed by the New Stone age, when man learned how to refine tools and make them more efficient and variously purposive by polishing. Then came the discovery of metals and the ability to melt and smelt and cast and forge them. Thus the Bronze age succeeded the Stone ages, and then came the Iron age, with corresponding advances in human culture and social organization. Mankind grows numerous and social life becomes ever more complex. A definite pattern of succession in prehistoric times is being established empirically. The age of the cities and the civilizations is at hand, only six thousand years ago.

Toward the end of the nineteenth century, scientists began to ask themselves whether some correlation exists between the two new sciences ethnology and archaeology. Do contemporary primitives studied by ethnology correspond in any ascertainable ways to those earliest men, prior even to the Stone ages, who are the object of research in archaeology? The Copernican revolution is a powerful engine, and it is in motion. Scientists of the twentieth century recognize that still another vast sea change is setting in: prehistoric archaeology is moving from a study of scattered and seemingly unrelated early cultures to a study of human culture as such, as a phenomenon of man growing onward and upward toward a fullness of time. Science sees human time and earthly space more and more as a unified picture. A world picture, indeed, but now quite different from that earlier one of the Pre-Socratics studied in Part One above.

Particular scientists pursue this point as a specialization, and the branch called the science of historical ethnology comes to be, again with its lectures, its publications in learned journals, and its offerings on university curricula. The ethnological situation of the newly discovered array of contemporary barbarian tribes and the less-developed primitives, including the "absolute" ones who still live in a purely food-gathering way of life and without stone tools, is projected back by correlation with the eras, epochs, and ages of the archaeological scientists. The research is empirical, indeed, and calls for meticulous, dispassionate concern for the facts.

At the same time, however, there is a factor that comes from philosophy, for philosophy is indeed involved in ways that must be analyzed with care. The hermeneutical question intrudes itself more and more upon contemporary intellectual life. What do these facts mean? How do they involve human destiny? What is this fullness of time, actually, which these recent and short six thousand years seem to be? Hermeneutics is a function of philosophy, not of empirical science. But to bracket it out for the moment, one can say that the confluence of these new empirical sciences reveals a pattern of human cultural growth and development from distant small beginnings in a discernable sequence of stages across long epochs of time. The Copernican revolution is laying mankind bare, so to speak, to contemporary man. Human beginnings can be seen and approximately dated, and the long sequence of prehistoric development is becoming ever better known as the evidence is uncovered and accumulated. This present historic period of mankind, which opened about six thousand years ago, had a preparation that is the indispensable prerequisite for understanding the contemporary historic period of culture as a whole. When the light of the new empirical sciences regarding prehistory is brought to bear upon historic times, the nature, the needs, and the problems of human culture become more intelligible. And the Pre-Socratics themselves become more intelligible, for this prehistoric background goes far to explain why they philosophized as they did.

One thing is certain: that foreshortened view of the human past, an essential feature of the pre-Copernican world picture, as well as the geocentric view of the cosmos, are both gone forever. The scenario is no longer the same. Modern Philosophy rises and develops in this new context.

The student of Modern Philosophy, postmodern in his late-twentieth-century questioning, asks whether the progress in the first six of the liberal arts calls for a different kind of philosophy in the position of the seventh liberal art? Education and therefore the quality of human culture are directly concerned.

What of philosophy, then, in this progressive accumulation of new empirical facts since Copernicus? Is it likewise changed? If so, how? What are the essential steps? The German philosopher Immanuel Kant, we shall see, openly advertised his own thought as "a Copernican revolution in philosophy". It was perhaps just that. But did it follow necessarily, or in any other way, from the Copernican revolution in the empirical sciences?

An even more fundamental claim is made by professed philosophical atheists during the modern period of philosophy. They wish to see atheism as the meaning of the Copernican revolution in the empirical sciences. For them the meaning of science is atheism. The scientific world view, they say, is one and the same thing as atheism. Atheism, they maintain, is the philosophy that the progress of science generates as it goes. Is this true? It seemed so to many thinkers from Copernicus' time through the nineteenth century down to 1914. There were misgivings about that thesis, however, throughout the entire period. And in the twentieth century, since the World Wars and the contemporary developments in the ongoing Copernican revolution? Can atheism continue to ride on the back, so to speak, of the Copernican revolution? For the moment such questions can wait. But the student of Modern Philosophy should bear them in mind.

Before turning to Modern Philosophy as such, however, another fateful aspect of the centuries between Aquinas and Descartes must be considered. It makes intelligible both Descartes personally and the Modern Philosophy that he launched into the "modern" period of history.

The Decadence of Scholasticism

Metaphysics, the central and fundamental discipline of philosophy, suffered a definite decline after St. Thomas Aquinas. The level of teaching that Augustine established as the founder of Christian Philosophy, the teaching about God as *Ipsum Esse,* existence itself, that sublime truth that gives educated and rational insight into the transcendence of the Supreme Being and his distinction from the entire order of created realities as such, was not maintained by the professors of philosophy, most of them Catholic priests, in the universities of Western civilization. We called this a fateful aspect of these three centuries, and rightfully when one considers the fact that this metaphysical eclipse of the Supreme Being is coterminous with all those other developments noted above, not least the Copernican revolution.

This decadence of Scholasticism can be given detailed study in the specialized treatises. Here we shall simply point out the most important names and sketch the immediate intellectual environment of the youthful Descartes when he did his studies in philosophy as a regular part of his course in the liberal arts.

The decadence of "Scholasticism", the rather unfortunate name for the Christian Philosophy taught since Augustine in the schools of Christendom, begins with Duns Scotus (c. 1270–1308) and the Franciscan school when the level of metaphysical teaching about God, reached by St. Bonaventure and St. Thomas Aquinas, was not maintained. Excessively subtle questions begin to mark the teaching, with a growing emphasis on the logical activities of the thinking human subjects instead of the strong ontological orientation that characterizes the metaphysics of Augustine and Aquinas.

One should note carefully that the decline in the quality of metaphysics in the seventh of the seven arts does not mean that these teachers of philosophy were unorthodox in their Catholic religion. It is a small beginning in the area of qualitative excellence on the natural level of academic teaching, and much time will be needed for social and religious consequences to become visible. It is important, however, from the viewpoint of the intelligibility of Modern Philosophy, to recognize these beginnings of decline.

William of Ockham (1280–1347), whose doctrine is commonly called Nominalism, succeeds Duns Scotus as the next major name in this decline, for he held that the classes of things result from names given by human observation and thinking, without foundation in reality. His metaphysics represents a further step toward emphasis on individual things within this cosmos, with a corresponding loss of clarity regarding God and spiritual reality. He is famous for "Ockham's Razor", his principle that entities of the mind are not to be multiplied unnecessarily. This pruned away much subjective questioning and many subtle distinctions, indeed, but in the process it also did away with some basic understandings that are essential to the metaphysical heritage, including that supreme insight into the real distinction of essence and existence in all beings except the unique case of the Supreme Being. Ockham's philosophy is a turn toward individually existing things within this visible cosmos, without the earlier strong insights into the metaphysical principles by which individual things, whether they be material or spiritual substances, exist.

Francis Suarez (1548–1617), a priest of the newly founded Society of Jesus, is the last major figure in the period of the decadence. Note how the dates of these three priests who are influential professors of philosophy mark the period from Aquinas to Descartes.

In Discussion 31 of his erudite *Metaphysical Disputations,* two thick volumes destined to become the standard textbook of metaphysics in colleges of his Order, Suarez takes up the question "whether essence and existence are distinct things". Almost all Thomists, Suarez goes on to say, hold the opinion that existence is a thing really distinct from the essential entity of a creature. Suarez rejects this vigorously: "Existence and essence are not distinguished in the (created) thing itself, even though essence, considered abstractly, be distinguished from actual existence."

The student of Thomistic metaphysics recognizes that Suarez is talking about *things that* exist, whereas Thomas Aquinas is speaking of *principles by which* things exist. A fundamental confusion begins to grow in modern philosophizing: Suarez is saying that a principle by which a thing exists is a thing that exists, something that normally can be seen to exist or imagined to exist. Thus the imagination, proper to bodily things, assumes the role against which Augustine warned in the very founding of Christian Philosophy.

Aquinas, one recalls, cautioned for his part against failure to recognize and avoid small errors in the beginnings of thought. So did St. Ignatius Loyola, founder of the Jesuits: in his original Constitutions of the Society of Jesus, he laid down that teaching should proceed according to St. Thomas Aquinas. Suarez is not teaching the very first principle of Aquinas' metaphysics, that "sublime truth" of the real distinction of essence and existence in every creature, and their real identity in the unique Supreme Being who gives existence to every other existing reality. He is "reifying" the metaphysical principles of being and thus launching a powerful turn of minds to things within this cosmos. In Suarezian metaphysics it will be difficult to avoid a slant toward pantheism.

A straight line leads from Suarez toward Descartes and his disciple Spinoza, for Descartes learned his philosophy at a Jesuit college that was using the *Metaphysical Disputations*. One should be alerted, furthermore, to ponder the extension of that line of intellectual development to Father Teilhard de Chardin, the famous Jesuit priest of the twentieth century. Only thus does one rise to the level of the future program of the Catholic Church for the renewal of Christian Philosophy.

Before taking up the intellectual drama of Modern Philosophy, it may be well to cast a synthetic view over the philosophical experience and endeavor of Western mankind since the Greeks.

Socrates, Plato, and Aristotle rejected the rhetorical education of the Sophists and projected a vast reform designed to replace rhetoric in the position of the seventh liberal art on the program of studies by the philosophical science of wisdom and virtue that they were developing. It was not until the work of their philosophical disciple Augustine of Hippo, however, that this reform of human education actually was accomplished. For a thousand years after Augustine this natural science of wisdom and virtue, known now as Christian Philosophy, was taught in the schools of Western civilization, now a Christian culture in which rational wisdom provided a foundation among educated persons for that revealed concept of God that was taught catechetically to all the children of the now-Christian gentile peoples.

Before the decadence of Scholasticism set in, Emperor Kublai Khan of China appealed to the West to send two hundred scholars to China, persons qualified to introduce these seven liberal arts into his vast land. He recognized the immense cultural significance of these instruments of learning and social progress in the West, and not least because the seventh of the seven arts is precisely this natural science of God, teaching its sublime truth of the identity of essence and existence in God and hence the absolute transcendence of the Supreme Being and Creator of heaven and earth. Who shall fathom the social effects in modern times of the failure of the West to rise to Kublai Khan's appeal? Especially in the light of the coming decadence? And the advent of the coming new and different kind of philosophy in the Christian West?

In the study of Modern Philosophy, finally, one does not pass judgment upon men or analyze the mysterious religious dimension of faith and loss of faith. One simply studies the nature, place, and function of that culminating seventh of the liberal arts, the one that gives orientation and human meaning to all the rest and thus affects the quality of human society and culture. Suppose this seventh art should fall into apostasy from God? Suppose the very idea of philosophy since the Greeks and the Fathers as the science of wisdom and virtue, the natural science of God, should be replaced by something different? This replacement did indeed take place. This replacement is the meaning of Descartes' work in philosophy. It was done, furthermore, at that critical moment when the Copernican revolution burst upon the minds of the Christian West. A drama is about to open, therefore, with important implications for both civil society and religion. Hence there has been a mounting interest in the study of this intellectual phenomenon as the centuries of modern times have proceeded; there is a growing humanistic concern about fundamental thinking, especially among the young, in these contemporary postmodern times of the late twentieth century.

I

DESCARTES: THE FOUNDER OF MODERN PHILOSOPHY

Born in 1596 and living across the first half of the seventeenth century, Descartes gathered into himself all these preparatory currents welling up from the Italian Renaissance and inundating northern Europe. Martin Luther (1483–1546) had launched Protestantism, and Christendom was becoming divided: the Thirty Years' War is at hand in Germany. Descartes will be a soldier in this war. It has been said that his approach in philosophy is the parallel to that of Luther in religion. Rabelais (1492–1533) and Montaigne (1533–92) have spread skepticism in the ancient mode throughout France, discrediting the philosophy traditionally taught in the schools of Christendom. Francis Bacon (1561–1626) has published his *New Organon*, the logic of the empirical sciences that is to replace the old *Organon*, Aristotle's treatise on logic. These proximate and popular works blend with the currents coming from the Renaissance: the disaffection with the old philosophy, as it was felt to be, the enthusiasm for the new scientific vision of the universe, and the desire for a new approach in philosophy, a clear, exact scientific philosophy open to the new science and indeed flowing from it.

Descartes was educated in the context of these currents and aspirations. Born of a family of attorneys and businessmen, his talent was recognized, and he was given the best education at one of the new Jesuit colleges in France. He took the full circle of the liberal arts and read widely in the authors mentioned above. He was full of enthusiasm for mathematics and the sciences, and of alienation from the philosophy, Scholasticism, as the seventh art in its decadent form was now called. He finished his studies quite alienated from the received educational heritage, touched deeply with the reborn skepticism, and determined to strike out on his own.

He enlisted as a volunteer gentleman soldier in a German army assembled by the duke of Bavaria for the Thirty Years' War. He continued his reading, thinking, and conversations on the question of philosophical certitude, deeply affected by Rabelais and Montaigne, always seeing arguments for and against every philosophical position, never able to break through to the truth of the matter. The signs of insufficient early metaphysical grounding are beginning to show.

In 1619 he wintered as a soldier quartered with a family near the Danube in central Germany, studying mathematics and pondering the philosophical questions. This was the turning point of his life, the winter of the famous "dreams of Descartes". His letters reveal how he began to see in his mind's eye an entirely new philosophical science and to formulate "an unbelievably ambitious project". "I was filled with enthusiasm," he writes in a letter of November 10, 1619, "for I discovered the foundations of a wonderful science." He describes a series of dreams in which he reports the impression that "the spirit of truth had opened to him the treasures of all the sciences".

Mustered out three years later, he is back in Paris, frequenting the society of leading churchmen, scientists, and philosophers of the day. Encouraged to pursue his insights, he arranged to live in Holland most of the time, locating near university libraries, developing his "method", and writing his mathematical treatise on the Cartesian coordinates that unify algebra and geometry in the powerful new way of his dream. Meanwhile, he is cultivating a circle of professors in the various disciplines.

From the beginning his thought appeared as something new and different, as one would expect if he is indeed the "founder of Modern Philosophy", the one who launched a different kind of philosophy into the schools of Christendom. He became well known locally even before his works were published, as a result of the teaching his friends and disciples were doing in the universities. Cartesianism, as it was called, came under attack in Protestant Holland as subversive of religion. Descartes was even brought before the city government of Utrecht, but the case was dismissed when influential friends intervened. At least the incident alerts to the fact that a new turn is at hand in philosophy. The sea change that has been setting in is finding the set of works that incorporates its aspirations and states a new program for the seventh of the seven arts.

The publication of Descartes' mathematical and philosophical treatises had an immense effect. Professors of philosophy discussed their positions and adopted them for their classes in "natural philosophy", as mathematical science still was called. Everyone said that a new philosophy had suddenly been born, easily the equal of the great systems that have come down from antiquity. Some felt that it came as a true modern revelation; others resisted it. So it was when he died in 1650.

His *Discourse on Method* is Descartes' basic and abidingly influential treatise. A brief review of his works should begin with this new approach in philosophical method, for it is the key to all his other writings and to his system as a whole. His *Meditations on First Philosophy* and his *Principles of Philosophy* were published later in his life to justify his method and his mathematical approach. At one time he thought of gathering his philosophical writings into one treatise with the comprehensive title *Project for a Universal Science Designed to Elevate Human Nature to Its Highest Perfection,* but discarded the idea as an imprudent infringement on the domain of revealed religion. It indicates, however, the secret redemptive aspirations of Modern Philosophy, which will find full expression after its completion in its chief applications, especially in Marxist Communism and Nietzschean Existentialism.

What is this universal science that Descartes has in mind? One must recall that he was a mathematician of genius, whose works on algebra and geometry are milestones in the history of mathematics. He hit upon the idea of expressing geometrical forms by algebraic equations. Then he worked out the procedure in detail by means of the Cartesian coordinates familiar to every student of high school mathematics. The formula $y = f(x)$ can now be plotted as referring to circles, ellipses, and other forms; solids can be given formulas by adding the third dimension: $y + z = f(x)$. The way is open toward mathematical formulas that express not only the shapes but also the movements of bodies, with their directions and the energies by which they move. Thus Leibniz and Newton will develop the *Calculus.*

All of this is in the eye of Descartes' mind, with its intoxicating vision of a knowledge that has the potential of complete control over the cosmos, its bodies and its forces, by persons who can formulate such equations and use them for practical purposes. Thus Descartes himself is a part of the Copernican revolution in the empirical sciences. The line leads directly from his way of stating geometry in algebraic equations to the infinitesimal calculus of Liebniz and Newton, on to the twentieth-century astronaut who remarked on his way back from the moon that "Newton is in charge out here".

Does this bear upon philosophy? Indeed, because Descartes conceives this "universal science", namely, this tool for understanding and control of bodies in space, as offering a new truth and wisdom for mankind, the true wisdom for human welfare. Putting this another way, he conceives this illuminating mathematico-physical discovery to be first philosophy: he is allowing the metaphysics of Christian Philosophy to be replaced by a different metaphysical system. In briefest terms, mathematics is replacing metaphysics, moving into its place as first philosophy to function as the seventh of the seven liberal arts. This is the philosophical root cause of the great Western sea change that is taking place in the ongoing cultural life of historic mankind.

This fundamental shift in the seventh of the liberal arts will certainly have repercussions upon the view of God and man that young people will acquire in the process of obtaining their education, with its cultivation of their power of reason. It must be borne in mind in the following summary of the Cartesian philosophy, for it opens the way to understanding that an apostasy from God in philosophy is at hand.

The very titles of Descartes' writings indicate the chief headings of his philosophical thought. This summary of their content, of course, is not done for specialists but for generalists, so to speak, interested in the genesis of the apostasy from God and the consequent impasse of the late twentieth century. The same approach will be followed in summarizing the doctrines of the philosophers who develop, complete, and apply this new kind of philosophy, Modern Philosophy, as it is called in the textbooks, in the times from Descartes to the present.

The first and fundamental point in Descartes' philosophical doctrine, then, is the basic approach stated in his *Discourse on Method.* So confident is he that he has truly discovered the powerful new instrument for acquiring knowledge in a certain and trustworthy way beyond skepticism that he begins with universal methodological doubt about all received teaching.[1] Removing it this way, he will teach the use of his new tool in rebuilding the edifice of education and culture. The power of reason will accomplish this, thanks to the discovery of his universal science, namely, mathematical physics functioning in the place of metaphysics as first philosophy. But metaphysics is the central branch of philosophy, the one that teaches the nature of ultimate reality. The question arises immediately: Do this doubt about the received wisdom and this mathematizing of the cosmos include the heritage of revealed religion?

No, Descartes answers; I am a Catholic, I wish to remain one, and I have faith in the teaching of the Church. But I simply bracket all that out: it is in the realm of religious sentiment and emotion, whereas my universal science is in the realm of reason and knowledge. This introduces that cardinal principle of Descartes' method, the separation of religion, faith, and theology, on the one hand, from philosophy and the empirical sciences, on the other.[2] Philosophy suddenly loses its internal relationship to revealed religion and is well on its way toward becoming separated as a secular subject, the step that Descartes' disciple Spinoza will complete.

What is to be said? The least is that Descartes' bracketing is a restriction upon the mind: its view of being and reality is no longer comprehensive and open, as, for example, in Aquinas' *On Being and Essence;* the exercise of reason is limited to the mathematical analysis of bodies moving in space. Regarding God, with Cartesian separation, Descartes departs from the metaphysical ascent of reason to the Supreme Being and discusses God in terms of an intuition called "ontologism". One stands at the first stage of a fall of the human spirit into a position confined within this cosmos. This is the beginning of the philosophical apostasy from God.

Descartes then develops his Rationalism, as it has come to be called, his confidence that revealed religion is indeed not knowledge but only sentiment and feeling, together with his confidence that reason can come to the fullness of knowledge and philosophical wisdom by using his universal science as its tool, as if it were actually mankind's long-awaited true first philosophy. It is at this point that his famous phrase *Cogito, ergo sum,* "I think, therefore I am", enters as his point of departure in philosophizing and as the summary of his philosophy.

Rationalism admits only clear and distinct ideas, Descartes teaches, the ones produced by his method: the first such idea is this *Cogito, ergo sum.* The truth is, however, when seen in the light of the metaphysics of being and existence, that it is not clear but rather ambiguous. It can be interpreted in a benign way, as if merely noting the fact of my existence. Augustine himself took this as his point of

[1] See Excerpts for Part Three, Descartes, p. 417.

[2] Ibid.

departure in Christian Philosophy, that a human being is a thinking self whose consciousness is evidence for the fact of existence. But it can also be interpreted in a revolutionary way, not as the beginning of the philosophical ascent to the Creator who gives this existence but as explaining in a new way why I exist. My existence is conceived as the result of my own autonomous thinking. My thinking establishes me in my existence, and therefore in my truth unto myself, and therefore in my values unto myself. I am, in the order of existence, because I am a thinking being. I think, therefore I am—in and of myself.

Thinkers will come, beginning with Spinoza, who will not set revealed religion safely behind Descartes' brackets. They will develop exactly this revolutionary interpretation of Descartes' method. For one can go on from it in total preoccupation with the human self thinking, asserting values, and exercising the new mathematical tool of control over the cosmos, never breaking out of the capsule to look up to God, let alone actually and effectively accomplishing the ascent to him. Thus a new canopy, so to speak, is being constructed to confine the human spirit within the cosmos, at the very time when the ancient "sacred canopy" of the closed world is being dismantled by the empirical sciences and opened out on the so-called infinite universe.

For the moment, it is sufficient to recognize the central tendency of the *Discourse on Method.* It launches a new and different kind of philosophy, the Modern Philosophy of which Descartes by common consent is the founder. Philosophy is each person's view of ultimate and fundamental reality. Contemporary teachers are well aware of how much this subjectivism permeates the minds of students, blocking consideration of objective truth.

When systematized and structured academically into a "discipline," philosophy is the seventh of the seven arts, the heritage of Western civilization from the Greeks. Christian Philosophy taught a metaphysics of openness to the Supreme Being and even achieved Aquinas' "sublime truth" of his transcendent mode of existing, distinct from and different from the created mode in every other existing reality. This provided a natural foundation for revealed religion that teaches the same basic truth but in the richness, personal qualities, and detail that come from the historic self-revelation of God, which that revealed teaching is. With Descartes' method a new kind of philosophy with a different metaphysics is being inserted into that seventh art. It is absolutely confident, in its rationalism, that the mathematico-physical analysis of cosmic and earthly phenomena suffices for man, constituting the wisdom he needs. But does this not remove the foundation for revealed religion? Is this not already implied by the bracketing? Does it not imply that there is no reality beyond the phenomena, and therefore no teachable word from some Person conceived to exist out there, as it were, beyond the phenomena, beyond the cosmos?

Descartes did not face these questions; he left his system unfinished. Spinoza will complete the system. But one can say that Descartes already is involved in postulatory atheism, in that his method and his principles demand atheism from the logical point of view. They already confine the human spirit within the cosmos. Already the cosmos is nothing but a mechanism. Already it is a question whether mankind knows with the certitude proper to educated persons that God exists, or whether mankind only has feelings in the matter, perhaps due to an earlier philosophical adolescence, so to speak, before intellectual adulthood arrived in the form of this new first philosophy, this universal science.

It is clear that a philosophical apostasy from God is at hand. The postulatory character of Descartes' position will call for development. Modern Philosophy will be this development. It is important to recognize that it is a different kind of philosophy, different in its metaphysics, in its concept of reality, in its point of departure, and therefore in the light it will shed on all the other branches of philosophy, philosophical anthropology, epistemology, especially ethics, and then upon all the other six arts, all the other branches of learning in the curriculum of education on all levels. At the heart of the matter is the loss of interest in the ascent to intelligible reality. Interest in the bodily things of the cosmos takes precedence over that desire to know God and the soul that has been the hallmark of Christian Philosophy since Augustine.

Young people, by virtue of their education, when Cartesianism takes hold in the teaching they receive, will no longer say: I think, yes. Therefore I know the fact of my existence together with its intrinsic limitation. Therefore I begin immediately to recognize that the Author of my existence exists. I begin my own mental ascent; I lift up the eye of my mind toward him, recognizing him as the free giver of my existence to me, acknowledging in him the rule of truth regarding my existence and the rule of law for the actions of my life.

Philosophy studies the cosmos, God, and the soul from the viewpoint of existence by methods proper to itself. In the cultural heritage from the Greeks, each of the seven arts has been considered to have and to use its own proper method. Here again young people will be given a fateful bias in their education: Descartes' method, the one indeed proper to the empirical science of mathematical physics, will appear to be the one and only method that human reason should use in all its endeavors to know reality. This monolithic approach to methodology in the arts and sciences is of the very essence of the dream of Descartes, his universal science. It displaces metaphysics, setting it aside by a fundamental skepticism and replacing it by this same empirical science. It will seem for a long time still to be "philosophy", but the day will come when the powerful philosophical personalities, completing Modern Philosophy, will declare that philosophy is nothing but the generalized statement of the findings of the empirical sciences.

It is fundamentally important, therefore, to recognize this root cause in the sea change that is beginning to overtake education and therefore eventually

Western culture as well, and this at the time of the outreach of Westerners to the rest of mankind. It will become increasingly difficult for educated young people to recognize, for example, that humanistic scholarship has its own valid intellectual methods, which are not the same thing as Descartes' mathematical physics. "Only a very narrow conception of truth", write Professors Wellek and Warren in their *Theory of Literature* (p. 16),

> can exclude the achievement of the humanities from the realm of knowledge. Long before modern scientific development, philosophy, history, jurisprudence, theology, and even philology had worked out valid methods of knowing. Their achievements may have become obscured by the theoretical and practical triumphs of the modern physical sciences; but they are nevertheless real and permanent and can, sometimes with some modifications, easily be resuscitated or renovated. It should simply be recognized that there is this difference between the methods and aims of the natural sciences and the humanities.

Both the Classical Philosophy of Greece and Rome and the Christian Philosophy of the millennium after Augustine had recognized this difference. When the time comes to consider a renewal of Christian Philosophy, return will be made to this basic point in methodology. For the present, however, it is sufficient to note the magnitude of the change that Descartes' new kind of philosophy is introducing.

The *Discourse on Method* contains both the attitude of Descartes in philosophizing, his intellectually proud confidence in human reason when it uses his new tool as an instrument for personal reconstruction of all knowledge and wisdom, and the content of his doctrine. His attitude and his method live on in his followers, but the actual content of his philosophical treatises has long been left behind. It will suffice to be quite brief in summarizing his doctrine on God, the soul, and the cosmos, stressing his attitude in each case and its bearing upon the coming philosophical apostasy from God.

Regarding God, Descartes' ontology does not permit that quick and easy natural ascent of the mind to the intelligible order and then on to the Supreme Being seen as the personal Creator and Lord of the cosmos. The reason is that the metaphysics that understands the principles of being and existence has become obscured by teachers who are using their imaginations in the way that Augustine disapproved. The principles of being and existence are known by the insight and understanding of the intellect as realities, real principles in existing realities, *by which* things are as they are, and not as realities *which* exist as things subject to sensory perception and its imagery.

Descartes learned his ontology, we recall, from the decadent Scholasticism of Suarez, who flatly denied the real distinction of essence and existence in creatures. It is true to say that the youthful Descartes was the prototype of young Christian Westerners, who are deprived of their rightful heritage in metaphysics when receiving their education. They do not study and learn that sublime truth of philosophy that established rationally the absolute transcendence of God; the real distinction in every creature of those two most fundamental principles of being, essence and existence; and their real identity in God. The perfections of his existence therefore exist without limit of any kind. Descartes learned a different kind of metaphysics slanted toward the things in the cosmos and implying a blurring of the transcendence of God. This is of vital interest in any study of the apostasy from God in Modern Philosophy. Descartes had the general preparation symbolized by Giordano Bruno, but Suarez was his proximate preparation, precisely at the fundamental point where Modern Philosophy veers toward pantheism and atheism. High indeed will be the price for departing from the sublime truth that was the central discovery and teaching of Christian Philosophy.

Descartes retains his personal faith in the God of revealed religion, indeed, but in a fideistic manner, bracketed from his reason and its philosophy. "There are very few things that one knows with certainty respecting corporeal objects," Descartes writes in his *Meditations on First Philosophy* (IV),

> and certainly the idea that I possess of the human mind inasmuch as it is a thinking thing, and not extended in length, width, and depth or participating in anything pertaining to body, is incomparably more distinct than is the idea of any corporeal thing. And when I consider that I doubt, that is to say, that I am an incomplete and dependent being, the idea of a Being that is complete and independent, that is, of God, presents itself to my mind with so much distinctness and clearness— and from the fact alone that this idea is found in me, or that I who possess this idea exist, I conclude so certainly that God exists, and that my existence depends entirely upon him in every moment of my life—that I do not think that the human mind is capable of knowing anything with more evidence and certitude.

This passage is worth citing in full, for it actually contains the whole of Descartes' new philosophy. He does not ascend to God from the principles of existence understood in the beings observed by the senses. By a sort of angelism, "being withdrawn from all contact with matter", he thinks to reach the intelligible order and God himself by virtue of his very method of doubting. Descartes is teaching a form of "ontologism", the doctrine that man has an immediate knowledge of God. It is but a short step to the doctrine that the existence of all things in the cosmos is actually the divine existence, the further step into pantheism that Spinoza will take. Their later disciples will make explicit its virtual philosophical atheism.

Perhaps the clearest sign that a new metaphysical view of ultimate reality is operating in Descartes' mind is this ontologistic way of finding the idea of God innate in himself. His skepticism regarding the senses, taken from Galileo and deepened by Montaigne, prevents him from ascending to God from the principles of being recognized by the intellect when seeing the existence of bodily things.

Descartes was philosophically and metaphysically blind to that aspect of the cosmos seen so clearly by St. Paul: "Ever since God created the world his everlasting power and deity—however invisible—have been there for the mind to see in the things he has made" (Rom 1:20). Descartes explicitly eliminates this meaning of the cosmos from human knowledge: "The species of cause termed final", he writes in *Meditations on First Philosophy* (IV), "finds no useful employment in physical or natural things." From this position a new metaphysical view of the cosmos as a mere mechanism is inevitable, and this at the precise moment when progress in the empirical sciences is giving a new physical view of the same cosmos.

In *Meditation* (III), "Of God: that he exists", Descartes asserts the doctrine of ontologism over and over: "I have an idea of God; therefore he must exist." "This idea of a Being supremely perfect", he writes, ". . . is not a fiction of my mind, for it is not in my power to take from or to add anything to it; and consequently the only alternative is that it is innate in me, just as the idea of myself is innate in me." A different kind of philosophy is at hand, replacing the one that ascends to the intelligible order of reality and to God from the principles of being recognized in the bodily things of the cosmos. Descartes is separating God and the soul from the cosmos, and the cosmos becomes a set of bodies devoid of metaphysical purpose: their nature *is* the extension analyzed by mathematical calculation. There is no doubt that Descartes believes in God. But the metaphysics that knows God by the use of reason, cultivated and structured into an academic discipline, has suffered eclipse. The philosophical apostasy is at hand, for Descartes' disciples will simply deny the innate idea of God and assert that it is indeed nothing but a fiction, a mental structure induced by a prephilosophical and prescientific stage of human progress.

Descartes' God is already akin to the God of the Deists. This God exists and perhaps plays an initial role in the cosmos but does not figure in the ongoing movement of bodies in space. Descartes' personal interest lies in the direction of the mathematical analysis of these moving bodies, more in the study of the cosmos than in the ascent of the mind to God. The kinship between Christian Philosophy and prayer disappears in his new philosophy. Hence the spirit of prayer is absent from Descartes' works. They have become secularized, separated from religion: they set the stage for Spinoza.

Descartes brings God in, so to speak, to explain matters that his philosophy cannot cover, but God is no longer abidingly present to his creatures in his essence and his sustaining power. God is more a convenient concept in Descartes' mind than the living Supreme Being, Creator of heaven and earth. Existence is taken for granted, not questioned. Descartes' philosophical orientation is toward the forms of things in the cosmos, in a true basic renaissance of the ancient pagan approach in philosophy among the classical Greeks and Romans. And of course these bodily forms are now seen in their movement and their energies, subject to the control that ability to state their equations gives to human persons. Modern Philosophy participates in the Renaissance of antiquity, indeed, but it is also something more. What is this "something more"? It is an unwarranted philosophical interpretation of the revolutionary progress in the empirical sciences. It begins and ends by reducing philosophy to nothing but the findings of these empirical sciences.

As to the soul, Descartes is chiefly known for his separation of spirit and matter. Mathematics studies matter in motion. But what studies the soul? Descartes simply asserts the soul as a different kind of reality. The soul is the human subject thinking. Thus Modern Philosophy is set upon two separate paths of development, often opposed, the one toward Idealism and the other toward Empiricism, physics, and psychology. This development will preface the completion of Modern Philosophy when it will stand visibly as a different kind of metaphysics, one that will affect education and culture, in the First World of Western civilization, then in the Second and Third Worlds. The sea change in the historic stream of culture will likewise be complete and intelligible in itself, and worldwide in its extent and impact.

Finally, regarding the cosmos, Descartes' attitude far transcends in importance the particular doctrines of his philosophy. His attitude is in the realm of primary interest. The cosmos is at the center, and the tool is his new universal science of applied mathematics. He conceives all bodies to be and function simply in a mechanical way. His followers will apply mechanism even to organisms, including human persons themselves. The legacy of Descartes is mechanistic thinking. It works with bodies moving in the cosmos. But it misses the qualitative dimension of things. Qualities depend ultimately upon God and call for the metaphysics of openness to the transcendent Supreme Being.

Thus Descartes on God, the soul, and the cosmos. Virtually and by implication, a different kind of metaphysics is at hand, a changed concept of ultimate reality. The heritage elaborated by a millennium of teaching in the liberal arts, following upon the work of Augustine as the Christian Plato, is being set aside, or, more accurately, replaced in the education of youthful Westerners. Descartes is not comprehensible without considering two great facts. First, he was not taught his rightful heritage, the metaphysics of Christian Philosophy, when he was in college. Second, the Copernican revolution was affecting him in the very moment of his need for his heritage in metaphysics. The sun continues, so it appears to the senses, to rise and set. Galileo's telescope is showing young men like Descartes that this is an illusion. At the same time, such young men, and Newton will be among them, no longer possess an educated understanding of the divine mode of existing. Hence they will be prone to various intellectual reductions of being to nothing but space and time: this cosmos.

In all of this, Descartes left an unfinished system. His teaching is a blend of the philosophical heritage mixed with his new doctrines, emphasis, and orientation, above all his tendency to move mathematical physics into the position of first philosophy, replacing the heritage of metaphysics. His method became popular in the schools among professors of both science and philosophy. Soon Descartes attracted followers who set about to finish his system by giving it logical coherence. Preeminent among these followers, especially those who will explicate the postulatory atheism of Descartes' philosophizing, is the immensely significant figure of Benedict Spinoza.

II

SPINOZA: THE METAPHYSICIAN OF MODERN ATHEISM

The mysterious figure of Spinoza dominates the stage in the drama of the rise and spread of modern atheism. The reason? Because metaphysics, the view of ultimate reality, was formulated in an atheistic way by Spinoza for moderns, should they choose to follow him. It is the view of reality that studiously omits the transcendent Supreme Being, substituting a pantheistic vision. Hence the abiding and absorbing interest in the study of Spinozism, which is Cartesianiasm carried to its logical completion and the comprehensive fundamental rationalization of the apostasy from God. Nothing brings home the relevance of Spinoza in the late twentieth century more forcefully than the position accorded to him in the Soviet Union. In 1927, for example, 250th anniversary of Spinoza's death was celebrated with elaborate honors to him as "the father of Russian Bolshevism".

Spinoza was born in 1632, spanning the seventeenth century to his death in 1677. He was a youth of eighteen at Descartes' death: he has been under the impact of Descartes' initial popularity in educated circles during his formative years. As an adolescent Spinoza also had come under the influence of Giordano Bruno, whom he always mentions with reverence and from whom apparently he took his monistic concept of substance.

Spinoza's family was devoutly Jewish. His parents gave their son the full religious education offered by their local synagogue in Amsterdam. A rabbi among his teachers has recorded that he was a talented youth, showing a strong philosophical bent, the desire to see things in a unified fashion. He was also constantly in adolescent rebellion against his Jewish religious heritage. First, he gravitated toward a branch of Jewish mysticism that leans to pantheism, the idea that only one substance exists. All things are one in God. An avid reader, he devoured the works of the Italian Renaissance, which were resurrecting Platonism and especially Neo-Platonism, acquiring his compulsive attraction for Plotinus and Giordano Bruno. Spinoza was fascinated by this pantheistic thinking several years before he discovered Descartes at the end of his adolescence. Descartes' works were a decisive illumination for him. He adopted Descartes' method enthusiastically and saw Descartes' doctrines as an unfinished system awaiting completion. This he set out to do. He stands in the founding of Modern Philosophy, therefore, as the interpreter of Descartes who finished his philosophy with a logically unified view of the fundamental reality of this cosmos.

For several years his rabbinical teachers had noted with growing apprehension that this talented young man was on a course of complete intellectual apostasy from the transcendent personal God of the Hebrew revelation, of the *Shema,* and of the Scriptures.

To summarize a wrenching and dramatic experience, in 1656, when Spinoza was twenty-four, the synagogue of Amsterdam passed the sentence of major excommunication against him, placing him outside the Jewish community. Characteristically, Spinoza took it in stride, for he had foreseen the logic of it. He declined a professor's chair offered by a German university in the Rhineland and took up the burgeoning trade of lens grinding instead. Meanwhile, he continued his philosophical studies, accumulating a personal library and a circle of disciples and spreading his influence. Above all, he committed his philosophical thought to a set of writings that have been basic to Modern Philosophy in Western academic life ever since.

Turning to Spinoza's philosophical doctrine, the explicit goal of his thought is the overcoming of the Cartesian dualisms and separations, especially that between the thinking subject, on the one hand, and bodily things, on the other, conceived as two separate kinds of substances. Spinoza accomplishes this with his doctrine of the monism of substance. Descartes had defined substance as any thing that exists in such a way that it needs no other thing for its existing. This is already ambiguous, a decline from the definition of substances taught in Christian Philosophy from Augustine to Aquinas. It applies, strictly speaking, only to God. Descartes hastens to add a correction to his definition, saying that created natures come under it as well, for they need only God's initial action in order to exist as substances, things existing in their own right such as the stones, the trees, and all other bodies in the cosmos.

Spinoza recognizes acutely that Descartes made his correction to avoid pantheism. He himself has no inhibitions in the matter, thanks to his youthful predilection for Plotinus, Giordano Bruno, and the Platonists of the Renaissance. Hence he comes quickly and rigorously to the basic concept in his philosophizing: there is only one Substance, the Perfect Being, which subsists in, of, and by itself. This is the clearest of Descartes' clear and distinct ideas: Substance is a being that needs no other being in order to subsist. Does this idea correspond to reality? Yes, indeed, Spinoza replies: we know this definition of substance by intuition as a *clear* idea. Hence our knowledge of it is infallibly true: we recognize spontaneously in the intuition that this Substance must exist in reality.

This is the birth of Spinozism, the doctrine of the monism of substance. Spinoza is the logically consistent disciple of Descartes. The step he takes completes Descartes and at the same time completes the metaphysics of modern atheism. How so? Because Spinoza, using the traditional word "substance" with a new meaning, forthwith identifies this one infinite divine Substance with Nature, that is, with this visible cosmos. Hence the famous phrase *Deus sive Natura,* which recurs unforgettably in his writings in his careful and precise Latin. The Latin language has two words for "or": *vel,* to state that the two terms are distinct; and *sive,* to state that they are identical. When Spinoza says "God or Nature", therefore, he means that they are one and the same. When he uses the word "God", as he does constantly, he does so deceptively, for he means "Nature". And when he uses the word "Nature" he means what pantheism calls "the Divine".

This confusion between existing *in* itself and existing *of* itself erases the distinction between the Creator and his creatures, who are indeed independently existing substantial realities because they have received from him a participated form of existence. They exist in themselves as distinct substantial realities. But in Spinoza the doctrine of creation disappears. The most basic teaching of the millennial heritage of Christian Philosophy is struck down. The ancient and inveterate error of mankind is reborn: the Renaissance has been completed with the rebirth of the ancient paganism of Plotinus in the classical times of Greece and Rome. The doctrine of the eternity of matter follows as a quick and necessary corollary. And matter is introduced as an element of God: thus the very concept of God suffers a reduction to nothingness. For "God" has become only a word. Pantheism is a disguise for atheism, the final stage in postulatory atheism, the doctrine that calls for explicitly professed atheism and that will evoke the disciples of Spinoza who complete Modern Philosophy with this philosophically systematic profession.

Regarding his "God", Spinoza gives a set of teachings that sound quite harmless to those who read him superficially, without due attention to the metaphysics below the surface. The Substance, he says, is infinite, and cannot be nonbeing in any way. What Spinoza means is that he has gone beyond the closed universe of the ancients to the open universe of the Copernican revolution. This Substance, Spinoza continues, is unique. He means that we have only this one cosmos. This Substance, Spinoza teaches, is the necessarily existing Being, simple, sovereignly independent, and eternal. What he means is the eternity of matter. This "God" has an infinity of attributes, Spinoza concludes, coming back full circle to the human knower, but we know only two of these, thought and extension. Thus he is the complete Cartesian: thinking subjects, extended bodies, and the method of the universal science as the link between them, the instrument of man's control over the cosmos. Mind and matter become simply parallel modes of the universal Substance, which is concretized in these two ways. Thus the cosmos is the Divine, concretized in these two modes, which make it visible and give it its human drive for mastery and control over it. "By body," Spinoza writes, "I understand a mode that expresses in a certain and determinate manner the essence of God insofar as he is considered as the thing extended." The Spinozan metaphysics is indeed the atheistic view of fundamental reality.

Spinoza is called rightly the metaphysician of modern atheism. In his completion of Descartes, the distinctiveness of Modern Philosophy as a different kind of philosophy, metaphysically different from Christian Philosophy, comes into clear view. What Aquinas called "this sublime truth" that sees the transcendence of God and the uniqueness of his mode of existing, distinct from that of every creature, has disappeared from philosophy. The consequences for the remaining six arts, and for the culture that flows from education in them, will follow in the First World with some kind of historical necessity as a great social apostasy from God.

The rest of the characteristic Spinozan doctrines follow directly and logically from this monism of substance and can be summarized readily and briefly. First, there is his doctrine of the modalities. What ordinary people think are separate substances about them—trees and rocks; bread and wine; horses, dogs, and human beings—are actually nothing but modes on the surface, so to speak, of this one unique Substance. Ordinary people are unschooled in Spinoza's philosophy. From this taproot the common sense of natural reason will become more and more separated from an artificial "common sense" taught by an academic order that adopts this new metaphysics and installs it as the seventh and illuminating art in education and culture. Philosophically trained persons will come to have a world view at variance with natural common sense.

The origin, nature, and practical bearing of the apostasy from God cannot be understood if this fundamental of Spinoza's metaphysics is overlooked. As the idea of the transcendent Supreme Being is thus metaphysically obscured, it is quite clear that man himself is ascending into the vacated position, for among all the modes visible on the surface of the Substance, the human mode is the highest. Only the human mode can take control and exercise dominion over the cosmos, because only humans can understand the universal science of mathematical physics and apply it in technology.

As a legacy, we find that many contemporary confused Christians really think of themselves, rather than God, as the center of reality. Religion is but a compartment of human life, not its wellspring.

To proceed with our summary of Spinoza's philosophy, the nonsubstantial modes in which the Divine becomes visible and seeks to express itself constitute the great cosmos in its being and its activity: Nature as nature, and Nature as doing the natural things, as Spinoza writes, using the very terms of Giordano Bruno.

Spinoza resurrects the emanations of Plotinus in the times of the ancient pagan philosophy, replacing the doctrine of creation. The modes of the Substance are simply emanations flowing necessarily from it as water flows from a spring. In philosophical language, efficient causality on the part of a free and intelligent Creator is suppressed, and only formal causality remains. There is no longer an action of the transcendent God to produce things, but only a formal participation in the Divine. Each mode of being, and especially the human mode, to put it plainly, is a piece or particle of the divine Substance, exactly as Plotinus taught in his synthesis of the ancient pantheism. It follows immediately that all reality is extended: whatever exists, exists in some quantity and can be measured by the methods of the universal science. Materialism is at hand, even if not yet explicitly stated, deceptively disguised by the use of the older philosophical terms in this new meaning.

Spinozan metaphysics will pervade subsequent philosophical thought, turning it down from the intelligible order and confining it within the cosmos as monism and process philosophy. Much so-called new-age consciousness today is derived from Spinoza's philosophy.

In the study of the apostasy from God, therefore, it is essential to confront the metaphysics of Spinoza with that of Augustine and Aquinas: his metaphysics of immanence with theirs of the "sublime truth" of the divine transcendence. From the denial of the real distinction of essence and existence in creatures, of created existence as a free gift given by the Creator, and of God's essence as the unlimited and all-perfect fullness of existence, it is but a short step to Spinozism and all the consequent permissivism in education and secularism in culture, for if God is not the *Lord,* but *everything,* then "everything goes".

From this metaphysical position one can turn readily to Spinoza's rejection of revealed religion, for it follows with rigorous logic. In this connection, it should be pointed out that the chapters against revealed religion and miracles in Spinoza's *Theologico-Political Treatise* are frequently omitted in current editions, although excerpts are included here.[1] This deceives the unwary who think Spinozism may serve as an up-to-date form of Christian philosophy.

Spinoza is quite clear and candid in applying his metaphysics of modern atheism. The prophetic light is an impossible concept, he teaches, for there is no higher Being and hence no order of knowledge above human reason. Since the transcendent substantial reality does not exist, there can be no illumination of a prophet to speak a "word of God". For the same reason, any reports of intervention by a higher Being to support the purported prophetic word cannot bear upon reality as it actually happened. Such interventions are ruled out a priori by the necessity of the metaphysics of the Substance, for it operates by the fixed laws of Nature.

Similarly, the idea that certain writings are inspired from on high so that they are the very word of the transcendent God, at the same time that they are words of men, is ruled out in advance by this metaphysics.

Finally, the idea that any synagogue or Church has been mandated by a transcendent personal God to teach divine truth, functioning as the proximate rule of faith for men, is impossible by the same prior philosophical judgment.

If there are any writings that report such miraculous interventions on behalf of prophets and churches, then they must be subjected to a purely rational exegesis

---

[1] See Excerpts for Part Three, Spinoza, pp. 420–423.

and interpretation, that is, philosophical exegesis according to Spinoza's philosophy. So-called revealed religion, as announced by the prophets, was directed at rough and uneducated people, Spinoza writes, who lived long before modern progress in philosophical enlightenment. The prophets had to adapt their discourse to the conditions of those times, hence their use of myths and legendary metaphors. But reason and philosophy have the task of interpreting these Scriptures. Thus the atheistic hermeneutics is placed upon its metaphysical foundation: no personal God exists to speak a revealed word and to arrange that it be announced and taught to mankind. From this initial statement of the atheistic hermeneutics the concept will germinate and find the followers who will enlarge and develop it.

Obviously, a philosophical vacuum is being created at the very heart of the received tradition of education and culture. Will Spinoza offer anything to fill it? He does indeed. It is contained in his concept of an *Ethics,* the name of his famous treatise, done in the geometrical way. He projects the way in which the universal science will provide for human behavior, giving mankind a better and more peaceful future than the older philosophically inadequate approach was able to do.

This brings up for consideration Spinoza's pantheistic religiosity, which lives on as the ideology of secular humanism. Spinoza's followers much later in the development and application of Modern Philosophy will write treatises on philosophical faith contrasted with religious faith. Religious faith is of course a personal acceptance of the prophetic word coming as revelation from the transcendent Supreme Being. Since this is now eliminated, philosophical faith remains to fulfill the human need for guidance in life.

Frequently the roots in Spinoza's metaphysics are no longer recognized. Hence it may be well, in order to identify better the origin and nature of the philosophical apostasy, to cite from Chapter 14 of Spinoza's *Treatise,* "definitions of faith, the Faith, and the foundations of faith, which is once for all separated from philosophy". Spinoza is indeed the disciple who completes Descartes. "We must define faith and its essentials", he writes; "this task I hope to accomplish in the present chapter, and also to separate faith from philosophy, which is the chief aim of the whole treatise."

"Faith is simply those beliefs about God", Spinoza continues, "without which obedience to him cannot exist." And he cites the passages in the New Testament that proclaim that God is love. "Since the value of each man's faith", Spinoza concludes,

is to be judged only by the obedience or obstinacy that it inspires, and not by its truth or falsity . . . , it follows that all dogmas that give rise to controversy among good men are excluded from the Catholic or ecumenical creed. For such dogmas may be good in respect of one man, and bad in respect of another, since they are to be judged solely by the works they inspire. Hence to the Catholic creed belong only those dogmas that are absolutely necessary for obedience to God? . . . Of the rest each man (since he knows himself best) must believe whatever he thinks best adapted to strengthen his love of justice. This principle, I think, removes all possibility of controversy within the Church. I shall now make bold to enumerate the dogmas of the ecumenical creed.

After his list, phrased in general terms, Spinoza continues:

But what God or our model of true living really is, whether he is fire, spirit, light, thought, or something else, is as irrelevant to faith as the question how he comes to be the model of true living; whether it is because he has a just and merciful spirit, or because, being the ground of the existence and activity of everything, he is also the ground of the understanding and the source of our grasp of what is true, just, and good. It does not matter what conclusions an individual has reached on such topics. Nor does it matter whether God is believed to be omnipresent actually or potentially, to govern things freely or by natural necessity, to lay down laws as a ruler or to teach them as eternal truths? . . .

On such topics as these, I say, an individual's views make no difference to his faith? . . . Everyone must adapt these dogmas of faith to his own understanding and interpret them for himself in whatever way he thinks will best enable him to embrace them unreservedly and with complete conviction and thus to obey God with all his heart. For, as I have also observed, just as faith was originally revealed and written in a form adapted to the understanding and beliefs of the prophets and common people of that period, so everyone today must adapt it to his own beliefs, that he may thus embrace it without any mental repugnance or hesitation. For I have shown that faith demands goodness rather than truth, that it is good and a means of salvation only because of the obedience that it inspires, and, consequently, that it is obedience alone that makes a man a believer. . . .

It now remains to show in conclusion that between faith or theology and philosophy there is no connection or relationship, a point that must now be clear to everyone who knows the aims and bases of these two disciplines, which are clearly poles apart. . . . The sole aim of philosophy is truth; the sole aim of faith is obedience and piety, as I have abundantly shown. . . . So far I have been concerned to distinguish philosophy from theology and to show that the latter allows everyone to philosophize in freedom.

With this, Descartes' bracketing has been finalized, and one may say that Modern Philosophy stands completed metaphysically as a different kind of philosophy. It will develop, of course, and the seedling will grow. But always it will conceive of itself as this kind of enlightenment, one that replaces the heritage of revealed religion, as a teaching coming from beyond the cosmos, with its own program for personal redemption and human social welfare. Spinoza's measured and almost solemn conclusion will recur throughout religious thought and religious education in the coming times: "It follows that faith does not demand that dogmas should be true but that they should be pious, that is, such that they will stir up the heart to obey." This is a Spinozan position that will be central in the future religious applications of his metaphysics. It completes the removal of religion from the area of knowledge and therefore from the teaching of a doctrine, for doctrines are about real substantial Being, the Trinity, for example, not about feelings.

It will take time for this view of fundamental reality to work itself out, first in theology, then in religious education, into a fully articulated expression of the pantheistic approach. But, when this full articulation comes in the form of a "new theology" and a "new religious education", it will be imperative to recall its origins in Descartes' bracketing and Spinoza's patheism.

Always the hallmark of Spinoza's presence will be the philosophical reinter-pretation of revealed religion and the philosophical redefinition of the terms, as Spinoza in the passage above has redefined "faith" so that it no longer means the acceptance of the prophetic word taught by the divinely mandated synagogue or Church. And thus the apostasy from the transcendent God will work itself out in religious practice.

Continuing with this summary of Spinoza's doctrine, one may ask whether perhaps he is successful in establishing natural religion, in the form of pantheistic religiosity, to replace revealed religion? This has been the recurring hope of many teachers and preachers throughout the period of Modern Philosophy. But the hope always turns to ashes, for it stumbles on Spinoza's concept of man.

At first sight, his doctrine glorifies man as a mode of the unique immortal divine Substance, the point where the Divine reaches highest expression. There is characteristic ambiguity, however, in all of Spinoza's teaching about the human, for he makes human liberty an illusion. Human beings are modes produced by the mathematico-physical laws that govern every activity of the Substance. Everything operates by the laws of physical necessity. So too the human modes: they simply respond to their environmental stimuli. They do what they must. Freedom then is likewise redefined as doing willingly what one must do in any case. Spinoza's philosophy teaches that this is the way to wisdom and interior peace, much in the line of ancient Stoicism.

Many thinkers in the times after Spinoza will adopt his metaphysical worldview as the tacitly accepted axiom, the substrate for all thinking, and the guide for all research on human behavior. Put plainly, the approach will end in pure permissivism. Young people will no longer be challenged to take up the spiritual combat, striving for the better by means of self-conquest.

Thus Spinoza, the metaphysician of modern atheism, stands at the beginning of a process of fundamental thinking, in the so-called First World, heartland of an erstwhile Christendom, which created an atmosphere of unbelief most harmful to the interior and spiritual life. It arrests the moral struggle and victory that turn individuals into persons. Thus it will minister to social thinking, which sees only masses of individuals and and not human persons. When Spinoza's underlying metaphysical world view is disseminated and applied by subsequent academic thinkers and teachers, the resulting atmosphere will wage war on any idea of an authority higher than man, any idea of a transcendent God, of a personal immortality, and above all of any idea of mortification of a rebellious human self in the present life.

Everything in philosophy turns about the concept of God, either really present or really absent. This pantheistic deception is actually the real absence; already it is atheism present and beginning its work. It is at this fundamental point that the apostasy from God appears, the point at which Modern Philosophy emerges as different in metaphysical kind from the Christian Philosophy of the preceding millennium in the schools of Christendom.[2]

Thus does the metaphysician of atheism proceed, eliminating the very idea of purpose in nature and in things human, because the very possibility of purpose on the part of a transcendent Creator has been eliminated. The very heart of revealed religion has been struck, the very prerequisite for prayer and worship disappears, and only the purest Cartesian fideism with the sternest brackets can still profess the First Article of the Creed. Of course, the basis of a natural law ethics, dependent on purpose and ends, is eliminated.

But the impact upon man in the natural order cannot be evaded. With his rigorous logic Spinoza subverts the eternal concept of truth, the idea that man knows the truth of things when he understands the idea in the mind of God that is reflected in his created nature. For Spinoza there is no such ontological truth. Minds and reality are bound together by the necessary laws of physical reality: coming to know the truth means coming to know the order and connection of things, which science discovers as its laws and mathematics expresses in its equations.

Again, the way is open to human self-assertion. I do what I must. I want what I do. I assert my truth, I create what is true and real for me. I am the author of my existence and my values. The thinkers will come who will articulate all the various practical consequences of the Spinozan metaphysical world view. Thus, from the viewpoint of man, the pantheistic world view introduces a "Copernican revolution" far more fundamental than the questions about the cosmos raised by Copernicus. For when man is no longer the creature of God but only this kind of mode or momentary bubble, as it were, on the surface of the Substance, then he is his own law unto himself.

Man-centrism is the first and immediate corollary of the philosophical rejection of creaturehood. This way of conceiving man as the result of the cosmic environment, an eddy on the ocean of the Substance, is humiliating in one sense and yet strangely exhilarating in another, for it leads to feelings of liberation and self-worship. Natural religion turns to ashes quite quickly in this doctrine, however,

---

[2] In the Excerpts for Part Three, Spinoza, p. 423, there is a passage from the *Ethics* beginning "Nature does nothing . . . " related to this point.

because this world view eliminates prayer at its root. Making the experience of Jesus as "my personal Savior" the litmus test of Christianity could be viewed as a reaction against formless pantheism. The growth of the human person is stunted whenever the man-centric way of thinking and acting is taught, because it tends toward fatalism. It opens the door, furthermore, to the use of force upon individuals on the part of human groups, for the group will have more power to assert what appears to be progressive. Thus militant atheism is already implicit in Spinoza's doctrine and can be expected to emerge as his metaphysical position is developed and applied in social thought.

The apostasy from God can be understood only by putting it into its context, the place and time of the First World since Descartes and Spinoza. This means, from the philosophical point of view, the contrast between Christian Philosophy, which developed within the Faith of revealed religion, and this Modern Philosophy, which declares explicitly that it has become a secular subject.

In revealed religion, which is this contrast and context, one must bear in mind that there is the Sacrifice in the New Testament. Its priesthood no longer wields the sacrificial sword of the earlier oblations of mankind, but instead of that sword, the priests, as the prophet Malachi foresaw, now speak in every place the words of Jesus at the Last Supper. They are spoken over natural substances, bread and wine, separate and distinct substances, sustained in being by their Creator who is really present to them with his essence and his power. For this concept of the Supreme Being is believed from the prophetic word and also taught in the rational philosophy that each such priest has studied. The transcendent Supreme Being is present to this bread and this wine, distinct substantial realities that he created, which this particular priest, ordained in the apostolic succession from that Last Supper, holds in his hands. By the power passed on in that succession, the Victim of the New Testament will be really present by the divine creating power and present under the sacramental symbols of his death through separation of his body and blood on the Cross. Everything in this central act of worship in the revealed religion of the First World stands upon a natural foundation, the philosophical recognition of the Almighty Creator and of the separateness of the substances he creates: human persons, bread, wine. If Spinoza's philosophy should ever enter into these priestly minds as a virus enters a body, then revealed religion in its Catholic form will indeed be thrown into acute crisis. It would be hard to imagine a metaphysical world view more diametrically opposed to the age-old worship by sacrifice than the pantheism of Spinoza. Some contemporary "creative liturgies" reflect just such a shift away from sacrifice to pantheism.

In his *Summa contra Gentiles* (II, 52), Thomas Aquinas teaches that "essence and existence are not the same in created things, for otherwise all things would be only one substance". This is another way of putting that "sublime truth" reached in Christian Philosophy and set aside in Modern Philosophy, the truth of the absolute transcendence of God as an intelligent and free supreme personal reality distinct from the cosmos. For in him essence and existence are one and the same, so that his existence is the unlimited possession of all the perfection found in the universe of things, a universe that only participates in existence but that is not existence itself. In the things of the cosmos, these two metaphysical principles must necessarily be really distinct, else creatures would not be limited to this or that way of existing, and the distinction between them and their unique transcendent Creator could not be maintained.

To identify God with this material cosmos, then, is nothing but the denial of God. Did this atheism result logically from the Copernican revolution? Not at all. When mankind passed from the closed universe, with its three stories and its heavenly canopy of the crystal spheres, to the mathematically infinite universe of the modern sciences, it did not need to conceive this open and "infinite" universe in a finite way, in the way of mathematics. This need was born of a metaphysical fiction, Spinoza's way of turning the cosmos into a mere idol, the renaissance in a new way of the ancient and inveterate error of mankind.

This metaphysics of modern atheism has been stated, however, and it will win its disciples. They will develop it in the times after Spinoza in the two main lines of subjective Idealism and positive Empiricism.

III

THE DEVELOPMENT OF MODERN PHILOSOPHY

The cosmos is pictured now according to the new Copernican world view, no longer closed over by its heavenly canopy but open and infinite, infinite in the mathematical sense of bodies moving in an unbounded space. A particular philosophical reaction to and interpretation of the Copernican revolution has been prepared in the Italian Renaissance and given to the academic order of teaching by the rationalistic attitude and method of Descartes and by the comprehensive metaphysics of Spinoza. This interpretation of the Copernican revolution regarding the orientation and motion of bodily things in space was in no sense necessary. A quite different interpretation was possible on the basis of Christian Philosophy and its sublime metaphysical truth about God. The philosophical key in the matter is the fact that the metaphysics of Christian Philosophy, with its rational openness to the transcendent and intelligent Supreme Being, has been lost in the decadent schools of Christendom and is now being replaced by the new Cartesian method and the new Spinozan metaphysics. Quite literally, mathematical physics, the new instrument for study of the cosmos, is replacing metaphysics as first philosophy, becoming the seventh art that culminates and illuminates all the other arts, the whole of Western academic education. It is correct to say that mathematics replaces metaphysics, for it does not study existence as such together with the principles by which things are understood to exist in the ways they are seen to exist in sensory experience.

Modern philosophy, seen metaphysically, is a retrograde step that continues and completes the renaissance of the ancient pagan culture: it studies the forms of things rather than the existence by which they are, for somehow the things of the cosmos have become the center of interest. A turn from the transcendent God is taking place among educated men, which is one with a turning to the cosmos. This is the apostasy from God. Thus man does indeed again make for himself a manmade idol, the object of his supreme personal interest and desire. This is the very concept of worship.

But humanity has progressed far beyond classical paganism in this idolatry, for now the cosmos as such, in its substances and their energies, has become the domain of a new kind of analysis and control, the dominion promised by Descartes' dream of the new universal science of mathematical physics. It is, furthermore, more than a promise: already in the times of Descartes and Spinoza, applications of the new empirical sciences in the field of technology are beginning to affect the quality and the pace of human social life and culture. With the real and effective presence of authentic metaphysics in the position of the seventh art, this promise of control over nature could have been implemented in the presence of the transcendent and intelligent Supreme Being, as a service to him and in the mode of respect for the laws of his creation.

As it is, however, Western culture has been placed upon a quite different path by the new philosophy founded in Western academic education by Descartes and Spinoza. For now a pseudometaphysical world view begins to be assumed as a self-evidence and to be taught to the young: the dominion of the cosmos will be exercised by minds darkened by the absence of God. If they choose to continue their Jewish or Christian religious heritages, they will bracket them out in Cartesian fashion from their intellectual lives as matters of the heart. But increasingly they will adopt either the Spinozan philosophical reinterpretation or the outright, professed, and militant form of the atheism that will follow with inexorable logic. It will take some considerable time, indeed until well into the twentieth century, until mankind of the First and Second Worlds will have to face new problems in ecology and to ask whether this quite different path in metaphysics has been the right one. For the exercise of the new dominion over the cosmos has taken place apart from God the Creator and Lord of heaven and earth.

Such considerations, however, can be saved for further reflection after the development and then the completion of Modern Philosophy has been sketched.

After Descartes and Spinoza academic life in the West became more and more alienated from the catechetical order of teaching that continued in the general Protestant, Jewish, and Catholic population. This catechetical teaching continued everywhere, imparting the same faith in God, the Father Almighty, Creator of heaven and earth, together with the attributes proper to him as the intelligent and transcendent Supreme Being. This was true in both the Catholic and the Protestant areas into which Western culture had become divided by the well-known series of religious events, which lie beyond either the need or the scope of the present consideration. The reason for this alienation is of course the different concept of God that will increasingly characterize educated people, those who have the privilege of academic studies and the resulting social leadership.

The method and attitude of Descartes and the metaphysics of Spinoza are like a potion, quite different in quality and color, which will proceed to affect the arts, sciences, and disciplines of human culture. This will be the growing cultural effect of the development of Modern Philosophy. This fact should be kept in mind throughout this outline of the two main directions and the chief personalities of the development, lest this new kind of philosophy seem to be a mere academic exercise in the textbooks of philosophy separated from the practical life of Western mankind. The impasse of the late twentieth century is reason enough to suspect the contrary.

The concept of God, then, is at the heart of the matter, that concept that is the ultimate concern of natural reason and its philosophizing. In Spinoza's lifetime the altered philosophical concept of God had already made widespread inroads upon the academic life of Western man. During the night of November 23, 1654, the French mathematician Blaise Pascal was struck by an illuminating insight into what was happening in education and culture. He made his decision and entered this well-known note in his journal: "The God of Abraham, of Isaac, and of Jacob, not the God of the philosophers and learned scholars". What was the meaning of his experience? It was the sudden understanding that a new kind of philosophy was spreading in the intellectual life of Christendom that no longer provided the natural foundation for faith in the God of the self-revelation taught in the catechetical instruction still given to children in the West.[1]

Pascal's insight is one of the first recorded expressions of sensitivity regarding the apostasy from God. This was over twenty years before Spinoza's death, an indication that the changed concept of God, the philosophers' God, was perceptibly present prior to the coming developments in Modern Philosophy.

There was resistance to Spinoza's teaching, indeed, led by Protestants of Holland and Germany, who called it simple atheism taught under the verbal veil of pantheism. But as time went on, Spinoza's metaphysics became the commonly accepted substrate for university teaching and the tacit preconception for philo-sophical applications in psychological, social, and political doctrine. It flows like a subterranean river under both currents of development in Modern Philosophy that followed Descartes and Spinoza.

The study of Modern Philosophy at first sight is a chaos of names, with as many doctrines as personalities. If viewed superficially this ministers to eclecticism, where each to the present day chooses bits and pieces of doctrine from this one and that, standing on a metaphysics of basic skepticism. Each is a law in thought unto himself, so to speak, picking and choosing according to the desires of the self for life-style, or according to the pattern accepted in academia.

The first step in rising above the confusion is to discern the pattern of development after Descartes and Spinoza, the two great founders of Modern Philosophy. The Cartesian separation of matter and spirit launches a double pathway of development, which will lead to the completion of Modern Philosophy in the work of the three powerfully influential thinkers, Kant, Comte, and Hegel. This double pathway is the current of Subjectivism on the one hand and of Empiricism on the other. The first is constituted by thinkers who emphasize the wing of the Cartesian dichotomy that concentrates on the human self thinking. The second is a succession of thinkers who concentrate upon the material bodies extended in space and subject to the powerful new tools of scientific and mathematical

[1] See Excerpts for Part Three, Pascal, p. 424.

analysis. These two currents descending from Descartes and both standing on Spinoza's metaphysics are often in controversy with each other, as Leibniz with Locke. For the Empiricists wish to reduce man and his knowledge to nothing but matter, with its motions and energies, subject therefore to the methods of the physical sciences. The Subjectivists, on the contrary, defend the historic position that man exhibits a second and higher kind of insight and understanding, one that cannot be reduced to mere sense knowledge. Thus this second current of the development will have the appearance of continuing Christian Philosophy, when the defect in its metaphysical concept of God is not taken properly into consideration.

Subjectivism

The current of Subjectivism, as a matter of fact, is far from being a simple continuation of Christian Philosophy. This can be seen best in Leibniz, its most important representative, who lived from 1646 to 1716, and who paid a lengthy personal visit to Spinoza. With Leibniz the preponderance of Germany in Modern Philosophy begins, which will grow toward outright domination in Kant, in Hegel and German Idealism, and in Marx and Nietzsche. Leibniz is Descartes' follower in the fullest sense, even to his greatness in the field of mathematics. Leibniz is credited with Newton as being the simultaneous and independent inventor of the infinitesimal calculus, that powerful new mathematical tool for expressing in equations the motions of bodies in space.

In his philosophizing, Leibniz turns from discourse on the principles of being or existing to discourse on the inner clear and distinct ideas of the human mind. This is far from the metaphysics of Christian Philosophy, for it begets the principle of immanentism, the idea that the activity of human consciousness stands at the root of being and hence of value. Human thinking feels itself independent of an ontological reality as given from the higher Source of existence and indeed conceives of itself as the creator of being and value.

For the purpose of the present study, it suffices to note that Leibniz stresses the human self thinking about the forms of things in the cosmos rather than their existence as such. His ontology, while elaborated in great detail, does not provide the base for the ascent of the mind to HIM WHO IS. This is because he conceives of existence in the way of the decadent Scholasticism, as a mode or attribute of a thing, and not as a metaphysical principle by which essences exist, whether they be essences of bodily things or of higher, purely intelligible realities. Thus Liebniz prepares the way for Kant and the German Idealism that is to come, in which the ideas of human thinking determine all the reality that man can know or needs to know.

The ontology that maintains philosophy as a discussion of the categories of things but fails to recognize and to study the principles of existence that enable the mind to ascend to the Source of all existence was put into the standard textbook of the time by Christian Wolff, Leibniz' disciple, whose texts were used by Immanuel Kant, professor of philosophy at the University of Königsberg, East Prussia. Kant followed this traditional pattern in ontology for some years until he awakened from this dogmatic slumber, as he termed it, when reading the works of David Hume. This set him upon the writing and publishing of his self-styled Copernican revolution in philosophy, the works that belong to the coming completion of Modern Philosophy. Hume represents the culmination of the Empiricist current of development from Descartes, to which one must turn in order to understand what it was that struck Kant with such force.

Empiricism

The current of Empiricism, which shifts the philosophical scene to England, descends from Descartes and Spinoza as a line of development parallel to the Subjectivism of Leibniz. Both lines represent a fall from the transcendent Supreme Being and a downward turn of the educated mind within this visible cosmos where man and his mundane affairs become the primary interest. Subjectivism, often also called Idealism in the textbooks, appears to leave man metaphysically intact with the two qualitatively distinct kinds of knowledge that philosophy has accorded to the human mode of existing and operating, since the pagan Classical Philosophy of Socrates, Plato, and Aristotle and on throughout all the Christian times. But with Empiricism, also called Scientism, or Sensism, or simply Materialism, a radical new departure enters Modern Philosophy, for it denies this second and higher type of human knowledge, reducing it to nothing but the knowledge of the senses made complex by various associations of the images that come into the knowing subject from bodily things and generalized by general names for such groupings.

It would be difficult to exaggerate the revolutionary character of this reduction and its potential impact upon education and culture. Is it a part of the apostasy from God? Indeed so, for the intellect as a specific and higher power of knowing always had been considered in Christian Philosophy as the very image of God in man of which Scripture speaks, according to which the Supreme Being created the human mode of existing, namely, to be a rational animal.

The English disciples of Descartes who launched and then confirmed the development begin with Thomas Hobbes (1588–1679), Bishop Berkeley (1685–1753), and the Deists, mostly Anglican clergymen, who taught the concept of "the Watchmaker God". God started this universe as a mechanism, which then runs by itself. God disappears. The cosmos is a Cartesian machine. There are no substances or substantial forms; only extended things exist. The thinker has only to analyze mathematically how phenomena work. The development from Descartes is the process of including man himself in this mode of analysis. Two names, John Locke and David

Hume, stand out in this development. Between them a French adaptation of this thinking, called the Enlightenment, arises. This summary will concentrate on these three, from the viewpoint of their new doctrine on the human mode of existence.

John Locke (1632–1704), commonly called the founder of British Empiricism, studied brilliantly at Oxford, where the decadent scholasticism of Ockham still was being taught. He discovered Descartes by his own youthful reading, became his enthusiastic disciple, and determined to apply the Cartesian methods to the study of man. This he accomplished in his *Essay Concerning Human Understanding* (1690).

His point of departure in philosophy, since metaphysics no longer is even considered, is the study of the contents of the human mind. Epistemology is moving to the position of first philosophy and is becoming one thing with psychology. The contents of our mind, Locke teaches, consist of simple and complex ideas. The former come from objects about us in space; the latter are made by ourselves, in three ways: by combining these images of things, by relating them to each other, and by separating them one from another. This separation Locke calls abstraction, thus continuing that characteristic of Modern Philosophy that uses older philosophical terms in changed meanings.

In Christian Philosophy the light of the active intellect "abstracts" an insight and understanding of the essence or substance or nature of the reality that is known. For Locke, no such intellectual power exists. We form the idea of a substance by giving a single name to a stable group of sensory qualities that we happen to observe. It is actually a complex idea of our own making, but by inadvertence, Locke says, we begin to look at our concept of a substance as if it were a simple idea. It is as if it were really there, outside the mind in reality. But it is not really so. Unable to imagine, Locke continues, how such simple ideas could subsist by themselves, we accustom ourselves to suppose there is something out there that sustains them, to which therefore men have given the name of substance.

"The idea of 'substance' ", he writes in his *Essay* (II, 23), "is therefore nothing but the idea of I know not what subject which is supposed to be the substratum of the qualities which simple ideas produce in our soul. . . . What we designate by the general term 'substance' is nothing but a subject which we do not know."

It is worthwhile to pause at this famous phrase "nothing but", the signal of the Empiricist reduction that leaves the human reality without the light of the intellect as its own specific higher kind of knowledge. This Empiricist concept of substance, either a stable group of sensory qualities or an unknowable substrate, will dominate Modern Philosophy from this point forward. It is the origin of Kant's distinction of the phenomenon and the noumenon, or thing-in-itself; Comte and Hegel will have no other idea of substantial reality. This approach, furthermore, will dominate the applications that will follow Kant, Comte, and Hegel in both Marxism and Existentialism across the nineteenth and twentieth centuries. What actually is happening is a process of thinking subject to the pervasive influence of Spinoza, the metaphysician of modern atheism: there is only one Substance and it has many modes, the chief of which emerges to view in human consciousness and its mechanism. These modes do not have their own substantial reality, which implies already what Locke will teach.

Locke is explaining this mechanism of the human mind as the central theme of his *Essay Concerning Human Understanding.* He intends to investigate the faculty of human knowledge before proceeding to any idea of reality. There is no trace of the science of metaphysics, with its knowledge of the existence as such of things and its study of the principles by which each act of existing is what it is. Locke places Modern Philosophy, timidly and incipiently, on the path of criticizing human knowledge, and indeed reductively, as the point of departure in philosophizing. His *Essay* was a great success in the academic teaching of philosophy in what were once the schools of Christendom. More and more widely across Europe his *Essay* replaces Aristotle for undergraduate academic courses in philosophy.

The Enlightenment

Nowhere was this triumph of John Locke more complete than in Paris, where *les philosophes* were busy elaborating the further development of Descartes and Spinoza. Much of their work was directed against Leibniz and the German emphasis upon the thinking subject, following the lead of British Empiricism. The scenario shifts in the eighteenth century across the English Channel to Paris, to these French philosophers of the Enlightenment and to the coming French Revolution, two phenomena that historians commonly link as cause and effect. An unforgettable symbol for all this, in its meaning for the apostasy from God and revealed religion, took place in the Cathedral of Notre Dame during the French Revolution, when a young woman was adored on the high altar by the philosophers as the Goddess of Reason.

The Enlightenment is of course an immense object of political and social study. The strictly philosophical aspect, however, may perhaps be summarized quite briefly after drawing attention to the leading personalities and works, a sampling of which illustrates the advancing development of the philosophical apostasy from God. For in the Enlightenment atheism becomes both an open and public personal profession and a program of social action for human welfare. It was conducted by a closely knit group of men of letters, publicists, and social activists, calling themselves "the Philosophers" and standing upon the network of masonic lodges that had sprung up in France since 1715. It will be of interest in later culturewide stages to recall that Lenin always spoke of himself as belonging to these *philosophes* of eighteenth-century France.

Denis Diderot is perhaps the leading name in this review, as Voltaire will be the final and summational one. For Diderot was the editor and publisher of the famed *Encyclopedia,* the instrument for disseminating widely through French education and culture the social applications of Modern Philosophy. It popularizes the mechanical inventions of the dawning industrial age, sprinkling its pages with diagrams that illustrate mechanisms and engines of all sorts. No occasion is lost to teach skepticism regarding revealed religion. Man has become the measure, and his purpose in life is the use of Descartes' universal science for knowledge and control of things and forces in the cosmos.

The *Encyclopedia* is the popularization of Descartes and Spinoza. The atheistic hermeneutics of revealed religion launched by Spinoza is developed systematically by drawing on the resources of Pierre Bayle's *Historical and Critical Dictionary* (1697), teacher of doubt and instigator of a rebellious attitude toward faith in revealed religion, the handbook for all the philosophers of the Enlightenment. Diderot built upon Bayle's work, developing its central but disguised tendency into an explicit profession of atheism. Diderot was a militant atheist for whom "God is that abominable name, the origin of all social troubles", and who looked upon himself as the herald of the Antichrist. He expressed the purpose of his *Encyclopedia,* also the general theme of the Enlightenment, as the cultivation of critical against mythical thinking. His work served to spread an attitude of destructive philosophizing in which the heart of the matter was the final separation of philosophy from religious faith in God. To be a philosopher one had necessarily to be an atheist. Not even a Deist could qualify. Thus the elimination of the science of metaphysics by Descartes and Spinoza, when they created this new kind of philosophy by substituting mathematical physics for it as first philosophy, is bearing visible fruit. The fruit is the emergence of atheistic philosophy as a new and different systematized use of human reason. From the viewpoint of philosophical analysis, one must continually advert to the disappearance of existence as the object of wonder and study, together with the total concentration on the forms, energies, and mechanical working of things in this visible cosmos.

Following Bayle as his mentor, Diderot popularizes the idea of the Good Atheist, removing the social stigma that from time immemorial had attached to the rare individuals who disbelieved in the Supreme Being. The solid consensus of mankind, against the solitary village atheist, was beginning to break down. All of this rested upon Spinoza's metaphysics. Spinoza, in fact, was becoming popular among the personalities of the French Enlightenment, but with a significant development stated by Diderot: *Deus sive Natura sive Materia.* True to the empirical line of development, materialism has arrived.

An anonymous work, *Jordanus Brunus Redivivus,* was circulated widely during the eighteenth century, bearing witness to Spinoza's roots in Giordano Bruno. It places this materialist interpretation upon Spinoza, teaching that matter is self-energizing and self-explanatory. *The essence of matter* is activity and energy. One work after another develops this theme, especially *L'Homme Machine,* man-the-machine, with its Cartesian and Lockian implications for the human mode of existing.

The famed defender of revealed religion, Fénelon, felt called upon to do his *Refutation of the Errors of Spinoza* (1731). But the tide was mounting. The Spinozan mind of the Enlightenment was presented comprehensively by D'Holbach's *System of Nature,* where the subtitle, *The Laws of the Physical and Moral Worlds,* shows the intent to reduce the human, in Locke's way, to nothing but the physical and the measurable.

Jean-Jacques Rousseau must certainly be included by name in any summary of the Enlightenment, for in his *Émile* he wrote the seminal application of Modern Philosophy to the field of education. The Cartesian separation of the humanities from the mathematical and physical sciences is finalized. Revealed religion has nothing to teach, for there was no such thing as original sin. Nature is nothing but goodness, hence the child *Émile* should be allowed simply to grow physically, unfolding from within as a flower from the bud, without the annoying artificialities and distorting hindrances of the traditional arts and sciences of human culture. It is this concept that Immanuel Kant will embrace when he finalizes the metaphysics of Subjectivism. The intention of Rousseau himself is clear: he excludes revealed religion from the education and formation of children.

Voltaire, finally, is that intellectual leader among *les philosophes* who makes this exclusion of revealed religion the comprehensive goal and program that unite the Enlightenment into a moving social and political dynamism. It is this concrete social application of Modern Philosophy that makes the work of Voltaire, himself personally a Deist rather than a declared atheist, a unique expression of the philosophical apostasy from God. "I conclude all my letters", he says, writing in 1762 to a friend, "by saying *Écrasez l'infame.*" All revealed religion is to be crushed out of existence as repulsive and harmful to enlightened mankind. Revealed religion in Voltaire's France, however, meant simply the Catholic Church standing in its traditional social position, operating its catechetical order of teaching, and maintaining its own academic institutions as well, with at least vestiges of the historic metaphysics of openness to the Supreme Being.

Therefore the campaign waged under Voltaire's leadership by these philosophers and men of letters is directed in a concentrated way against Christianity as such, and in particular against the Catholic Church: its institutions, its religious teachings and its philosophy in support of them, its moral principles, its view of the nature and destiny of man, and especially its priesthood and ritual of sacrifice. Voltaire himself, with facile pen and an attractive readable style, made use of all literary forms, especially novels and stage plays, for the dissemination of philosophy, something in which French philosophers have excelled ever since. His favorite project was perhaps his *Philosophical Dictionary,* where all the themes of Descartes, Spinoza, Bayle, and Locke are summarized in a light and superficial but sprightly fashion.

But far and away the most important work of Voltaire, the one that points directly toward the culminating metaphysical systems of Comte, Hegel, and Marx, is his *Philosophy of History.* In this panoramic survey of universal history, written as he says *en philosophe,* he begins with the culture of China and not with the Hebrews. Thus he sets aside the people who are the bearer of divine revelation in the biblical presentation of universal history that has obtained in Western culture since Augustine and the Fathers of the Church. This is a major step in completing both Spinoza's atheistic hermeneutics of the Bible and Descartes' method of universal doubt, which brackets religion away from the purely secular disciplines, philosophy, and the sciences. Religion stands in the realm of feeling and emotion with no knowledge to hand on by teaching.

With Voltaire's philosophy of history, the intellectual background for understanding culture as a secularized domain begins to take shape. Thus the apostasy from God proceeds logically toward its social applications and ramifications. It would be difficult to overemphasize the significance of *Écrasez l'infame,* Voltaire's battle cry for the Enlightenment. But it is a significance rather in the order of a many-sided practical application of Modern Philosophy, one that takes place within France as a model for the later times of culturewide applications in the West. For *les philosophes* actually were not philosophers or even professors of philosophy. They were men of letters and publicists for Modern Philosophy in its Empiricist line of development. To see this philosophical work done in a philosophical manner one must return to David Hume in England, the Scotsman who was equally at home in London and in Paris with these *philosophes,* his personal friends who looked up to him as the thinker who completed their own world view with his final statement of British Empiricism.

David Hume (1711–76) lived a life that spanned both the century of the Enlightenment and the English Channel. Born a landed gentleman of Scotland, he naturally received the full education of a man of letters. In his autobiography he describes his absorbing interest in philosophy and recounts his youthful feeling of a destiny to bring about "a new universe of thought". He spent much time in France, where he sought out lovely places. For several years he was a secretary to the British ambassador in Paris, where he associated closely with the men of the Enlightenment. In fact, he brought Rousseau back to England with him for an extended stay.

As a philosopher Hume actually shows neither originality nor depth. He accepts without question the Rationalistic attitude and the method of Descartes, assuming with him that all knowledge and wisdom will come from mathematical analysis of the corporeal phenomena of the cosmos. Again without question he assumes the metaphysics of Spinoza: nothing exists but the material and visible cosmos. Furthermore, he resurrects without question from pagan Classical Philosophy the Skepticism of Sextus Empiricus, even to the use of his language in attributing the ideas of substance and causality to mere habit and custom.

Thus Hume represents in a sense the final completion of the Renaissance, the rebirth of the ancient pagan philosophy in its restriction of human knowledge to the level of the senses. Finally, encouraged by his French colleagues, he takes the teaching of Locke as his immediate point of departure, developing it to a complete and logically rigorous subjectivism and phenomenalism. With slight variation of terminology, he repeats Locke's doctrine on simple and complex ideas, their threefold mode of association, and explicates his principle of verifiability: to test the validity of an idea one must ask of what sensory impression it is the aftereffect. Nothing else is needed in order to explain human consciousness. There is no active power or light of intelligence in man that pierces through what is given by the senses to concepts that give insight and understanding of the natures of things and the principles by which things exist. The human mind is like Newton's universe in miniature. Images of bodies float about in it; they can be understood by correlations much like those that give knowledge and control of the wider cosmos. Man is thus reduced to a physical object, to be studied in the same scientific and mathematical way as other physical objects.

In his doctrine on substance Hume carries Locke to an explicitness that leaves no doubt that he has banished any abiding substantial reality or "soul" in man. The conscious self is a bundle of perceptions in flux. Each one is observed as it passes, but no abiding reality or self is perceived. Ideas of substances, in general, are nothing but collections of particular ideas united by the imagination, to which human linguistic convention assigns particular or general names. This includes the human soul: what one calls the self, Hume asserts, is nothing but a bundle of perceptions succeeding each other rapidly in perpetual motion and flux. This doctrine will spread in subsequent times from philosophy to psychology, as, for example, in William James and John Dewey, where it will seem to be science rather than philosophy. This reduction sets the stage for a future culturewide philosophical misinterpretation and extrapolation from the scientific aspect of Darwin's findings.

Hume's doctrine on causality has given him his fame. Phenomena, impressions from bodily things in the cosmos, do indeed exhibit a regularity, which mathematicians can state in their equations. $Y = f(x)$ works, so to speak, to express cause and effect. But philosophy, Hume asserts, must look deeper: it must recognize that the causality expressed is actually nothing but a complex idea. It is fabricated by the human subject and is not an extramental reality. One can never know a priori what will eventuate. Experience shows the movement of two billiard balls but never any causal action, any transmission of movement: nothing is observed but the succession of two things moving. Then Hume makes his sweeping extrapolation and generalization: therefore, the principle of causality is nothing but an association of successive impressions. Through habit and custom, those telling words that Sextus Empiricus used long ago, men come to expect that the succession will take place; in reality, however, there is no necessary connection. Once the habit is acquired, one cannot think any other way. Even the physical sciences, Hume dares to teach, have no validity except insofar as they confine themselves to past experience. The prediction of future phenomena is never more than probable. Nothing authorizes a science to formulate universal and necessary laws.

It would be difficult to state more explicitly the inability of human understanding to ascend from the level of experience to establish the existence of a cause that exists and operates in an order of reality above the sensory level. Thus all metaphysics is condemned and removed at one stroke, with its ontology, the principles of existence, and its natural theology, the study of the intelligible truths and the ascent of the mind from them to the Supreme Being, who is the Source of the existence of things. Plainly, human reason cannot prove the existence of God: the ascent of the human mind is blocked. And why? The reason is clear: for Hume, there is no power of insight and understanding in a human being that differs in kind from the bodily senses.

The negation of God is intrinsically linked with this Empiricist reduction of man from the power of intellectual understanding, which had been recognized as his specific qualitative difference and the foundation of humanism as such in education and culture. Hume makes visible in explicitly stated teaching, therefore, the philosophical apostasy from God. With rigorous logic he will apply this doctrine of his *Inquiry Concerning Human Understanding* (1749) to the realm of revealed religion.

This he does in his *Natural History of Religion* (1757) and in *Dialogues on Natural Religion* (1777), his personal favorite. He circulated this latter work in manuscript among friends, who dissuaded him from publishing it in his lifetime lest he upset the established Anglican church. These works contain his philosophy of morality, in which he asks why men act as they do. Morality is not based on reason, he teaches, that is, on matters of fact, but rather upon feelings of various kinds. A moral judgment does not arise until a feeling is excited through the idea of an action. Is it good or evil? You can never answer, Hume asserts, as long as you consider the object. You can never answer until you turn within your own breast and find a sentiment of approval or disapproval. "Here is the matter of fact," he writes, "but 'tis the object of feeling, not of reason. It lies in yourself, not in the object." Vice and virtue, therefore, may be compared to sounds, colors, heat and cold, which, according to modern philosophy, are not qualities in objects but perceptions in the mind.

Hume's doctrine has influenced much rejection of natural law in psychological, legal, and social thinking since his time, logically enough, indeed, when God the Creator of human nature is no longer recognized. Thus skepticism will minister in practice to selfism, with each self free to pick and choose among life-styles. Hume's teaching, of course, opens the door to the possibility of a totalitarian state, like

Hobbes' *Leviathan,* which might seek to control such feelings by programs of systematic conditioning. Again, the philosophical foundations are being laid in the apostasy from God for the Gulag and the Holocaust.

Hume's philosophy of religion is the application of his Empiricism to the question why mankind always has believed in God. Men do so, he answers, because they allow their feelings rather than their reason to evoke their beliefs. Hume fits well into the emerging explicit atheism of the French Enlightenment. His animosity against revealed religion, and especially the very concept and possibility of miraculous interventions by a transcendent, intelligent, and almighty Supreme Being, governs the spirit of these works, which are best understood as a continuation of the atheistic hermeneutics begun by Spinoza.

David Hume, to conclude, develops the finished model for the atheistic use of the human mind. He systematically asserts that human consciousness perceives nothing universal and necessary. A century after his time it will be Edmund Husserl who points out in his *Logical Investigations* (1900) that the assertion evades the evidence offered by both mathematics and the science of logic. But the model exists and spreads widely in Western education and culture, blocking untold numbers of young people from the ascent of reason to the transcendent Supreme Being during the process of their education. The seventh liberal art has been snuffed out like a candle. This is the essence of the philosophical apostasy from God. One can gauge the impact upon Western youth from John Henry Newman's description of his adolescent reading of Hume or by pondering Nietzsche's madman swinging his lantern in Germany, crying out in anguish over the death of God.

Augustine laid the foundations for Christian Philosophy when he specified how reason can ascend from visible and temporal things to invisible and eternal ones. We should not vainly behold the order of the cosmos and the beauty of its measured vital processes but step up from them toward immortal things that abide forever. "The first thing to notice", Augustine continues, "is living nature, which senses all these things. No mass of matter, however great or however bright, is to be held of much account if it is without life. . . . But to judge of bodies belongs not to life that is merely sentiment but to life that has also the power of reasoning." Aquinas, one will recall further, completed the edifice of Christian Philosophy upon this foundation with his doctrine of the intellect as an active power of the human spirit that can perform its operations of insight and understanding without activation by an external stimulus. This power constitutes the natural dignity of men, raises men above programs of conditioning and above education by stimulus and response, grounds the concept of personal freedom, and liberates from confinement within the cosmos by opening the way upward to intelligible reality and to God.

Hume made it clear that Modern Philosophy is indeed a different kind of philosophy, one that blocks the ascent and hence expresses the apostasy of human reason from God. Mysteriously, however, it also suffers the boomerang effect of apostasy from man in his specificity as human, and this a century before Darwin. There is in Hume an impoverishment of man, which in turn improverishes man's education and culture. He himself states this in a rather violent passage:

> When we go through a library, persuaded of the truth of our philosophy, what havoc we will cause there! If we take off the shelf for example a volume of theology or metaphysics, we must ask ourselves: Does it contain reasonings on quantity and number? The answer is, No! Does it then contain experimental reasonings based on questions of fact? No! Away with it, then, and cast it to the flames! For it contains nothing but sophisms and illusions.

There is also a correlated passage: "I am ... affrighted and confounded", he writes in his *Treatise of Human Nature* (VII, 8), "with that forlorn solitude in which I am placed by my philosophy." He was quite accurate. The removal of the intellect as man's specifically human power, the very image of God on his brow, removes likewise the foundation of human communication and therefore also of education, community, and culture.

Immanuel Kant, awakened from his slumber upon reading Hume and aghast at the doctrine, granted the ideological battlefield to the British Empiricist instead of restoring and renewing the human and Christian heritage in metaphysics. Kant will retreat into the rationalized irrationality of his Transcendental or Subjective Idealism. Auguste Comte, son of the French Enlightenment, will welcome Hume with open arms, finalizing his positions in his Positivism. Hegel, finally, will think to transcend and surpass Hume's skepticism with his new Dialectic. Thus we stand at the threshold of the metaphysical completion of both lines of development in Modern Philosophy.

IV

IMMANUEL KANT:
TRANSCENDENTAL, OR SUBJECTIVE, IDEALISM

The textbooks speak of the giant personality of Kant and call him the father of modern Subjectivism and Immanentism. He himself says his work is a Copernican revolution in philosophy. By all accounts Kant is an interesting figure and certainly a basic one in understanding the philosophical roots of the contemporary social apostasy from God.

It would be quite mistaken to imagine that Kant intended a contribution toward atheistic thinking—quite the contrary. Hence his deceptiveness, for he has indeed deceived many in the Jewish and Christian heritages, as if he offered the approach to theism for which the times call. One must proceed with caution, therefore, making note of the particular religious background within which he philosophized.

Immanuel Kant was born at Königsberg, East Prussia, in 1724. His devoutly Protestant family followed a particular sect called Pietism, which had developed within the official Lutheranism of Germany. Kant's mother was especially devoted to it and raised her son in it with lasting effect. In a sense Kant's philosophy is Pietism in philosophical garb.

Lutheranism in North Germany had become a department of the Prussian state, a cold and official branch of the secular government. In the century before Kant's time, a Lutheran pastor, Philip Jakob Spener, launched a program for revitalizing the religious life of his people. His preaching was marked by a constant emphasis on personal experience in religion. Religion, he insisted, is wholly an affair of the heart. Soon he was organizing a movement called "Groups for Piety", which met in small private reunions in homes. At the meetings the Scriptures were read and explained with the aim of warming the piety of the participants. Pietism became a strong presence within the state church, aiming at overcoming its externalism, excessive formalism, and intellectualism by cultivating an inner experience of religion. Faith is an attitude of the heart rather than a doctrine; regeneration and sanctification are facts in the order of experience. Such was the upbringing of Kant in his boyhood, giving him a lasting tendency toward inwardness and the subjective side of life.

Completing his preparatory studies Kant entered the university of his native city as a student of theology, preparing for the Protestant ministry. It is a pattern not uncommon among famous names in Modern Philosophy, for example, Hegel, Feuerbach, and Nietzsche. Like the others, Kant changed his major to the field of philosophy and took up the teaching of philosophy as his professional field. At thirty-one he was appointed to the faculty of philosophy at the University of Königsberg.

The year is 1755. Kant proceeds with the daily routine of university lectures, using and following the standard textbooks in the metaphysics of Descartes and Leibniz, ontology, as it is now called, written by Christian Wolff. He uses the method of Descartes and follows avidly the progress of mathematical physics and the new mechanics of Newton. This is the period of his "dogmatic slumber", from which David Hume's works so suddenly and rudely awakened him. He saw at a glance that the metaphysical system he was teaching stood helpless before the onslaught of Hume's skepticism and reduction of the intelligence to nothing but the associations and combinations of sensory perceptions and images. In such a doctrine, what happens to education and culture? What happens to religion? It was clear to Kant that Hume's philosophy leaves the values of humanism, let alone religion, without foundation. It dawned on him from Hume that there is no metaphysical knowledge, no science of being as such, no way of knowing things in themselves, in their natures and essences. Mankind knows only the appearances of things, not their reality, not what they are in themselves.

In other words, Kant conceded Hume's teaching. He took Hume's reduction of the human intelligence to nothing but sense knowledge for the truth about man. With this as his point of departure, he built his Copernican revolution in philosophy. It was a fateful moment in the stream of human culture, one that will confirm the apostasy from God. For Kant remained a disciple of Descartes, completing his separation between spirit and matter conceived as thinking subjects and bodies extended and moving in space.

Unhappy divisions among Christians had taken place that prevented Kant from recovering his own roots in the Christian era with the metaphysics of its Christian Philosophy. There is nothing in Kant of that heritage of the twofold power of human knowledge, of the distinctiveness of the intellect as a spiritual power of insight and understanding in no way reducible to sense knowledge. The only answer to Hume is contained in the heritage of Classical and Christian Philosophy. But Kant had lost contact with the great teachers of that heritage and had in hand only the decadent ontology that admits nothing but existing things, rather than principles by which things exist. Instead of recovering the heritage of authentic metaphysics, therefore, and restoring it to its central place in philosophical studies, Kant continued and completed the substitution of mathematical physics for meta-physics. For when his system is completed, his students and followers will have no valid knowledge but the mathematical calculations made upon physical phenomena.

From the viewpoint of knowledge, education, and culture, the Cartesian dichotomy is overcome: the thinking subject is revealed to reach nothing but the mechanism of the physical universe. A Christian thinker with Christian intentions is missing an opportunity. His intentions could have been fulfilled had he recovered and applied the heritage of the Christian metaphysics. As it was, his good intentions came to nothing, for his work ministered to the victory of Hume and the project of the Enlightenment toward rigorous professed atheism in education and culture.

There is a deceptiveness in the Kantian philosophy arising from his use of the terminology of the Western philosophical heritage in new meanings, stated by himself out of the short tradition descending from Descartes, especially the separation of mind and matter. The details of Kant's teaching are readily available in the standard textbooks and from his own works. This present summary intends to explain in the language of the natural metaphysics of mankind what Kant meant by his terminology as he worked to complete this Cartesian separation. This will bring the contrast of his system with the heritage of Christian Philosophy into view. Step by step, one must follow the logic of this thinker, for it is indeed logical within the positions of Descartes and Hume, as he builds his systematic exclusion of God from the domain of human knowledge. This exclusion, contrary to Kant's intention, had the effect of promoting the atheistic world view in Western culture; hence his work became a decisive factor in completing the philosophical apostasy from God.

The Critique of Pure Reason

In the years after reading Hume, Kant recast his course of lectures in philosophy and published it in two correlated books, the famed *Critique of Pure Reason* (1781) and the *Critique of Practical Reason* (1788). The titles state his intention: metaphysics is now critical, not dogmatic. This is his Copernican revolution in philosophy. Let us hear Kant describe his intentions and conclusions in the first work.

"I apply the term *transcendental*", he writes in its Introduction, "to all knowledge that is not so much occupied with objects as with the mode of our cognition of these objects, so far as this mode of cognition is possible a priori." First, one must note the new meaning given to the word "transcendental", venerable in the heritage of Western philosophy. The "transcendentals" had always meant the most basic properties of being that belong to being as such, to all beings or realities of whatever kind and category. In other words, they *transcend* the ten categories of Aristotle with a truth that obtains universally. Kant simply redefines this term. It now denotes knowledge that the knowing human subject has of himself, prior to any experience of objects. The mode of human knowledge thus can be known apart from and prior to the exercise of that knowledge in knowing things. This is Kant's initial assertion and point of departure. One will have to return to it, asking what substantiation there is for such preunderstanding, as it has come to be called. It is clear that the human subject is now at the center of the philosophical stage. It is clear further that Kant is preoccupied with human experience of objects and not with the existence of things, together with the principles by which they exist. This is a watershed in metaphysics, for Kant's involution upon the human self precludes the ascent of the mind to the intelligible truths, and among them that sublime truth regarding essence and existence that is the outcome of authentic metaphysical science. In the work of theologians today, influenced by Kant, one can observe a similar shift from the pondering of the mysteries of revelation to the study of interpretation itself: hermeneutics.

What is this mode of cognition that exists and is knowable a priori, prior to experience? One must consider, answers Kant, that knowledge is composed of two elements, its matter and its form. Here again, traditional philosophical terms are used, but are quickly given a new meaning. There is an a posteriori element, Kant explains, which consists of raw material from an outer world of some kind, impressions of all sorts, which strike the sensory apparatus. These are simply phenomena, the Greek word for the appearances of things; in no way do they give knowledge of what things in the outer world are in themselves. Then, Kant continues, there is an a priori element: this is the a priori form of the knowing subject, which shapes and alters this chaotic raw material that comes tumbling in upon the knower. There are several such forms of knowledge, all of them innate and therefore rightly called "transcendental". Men are born with them. Hence they exist prior to any experience: they are the "a priori forms" of knowledge.

One can imagine the students of Professor Kant raising their hands. "Professor Kant, do you know what these various forms are? How do you know that they exist that way in human nature as it is born into this world?" These questions abide and must be considered later. Kant himself simply evades the second question, while going into descriptive detail regarding the first question, as if he were taking the cover off a mechanism or engine to reveal its inner structure and working parts.

There are three sets of these a priori forms, Kant asserts, summarized as follows. First, there are the sensory powers of man, which consist of two innate forms, space and time. "Space", he writes, "is not an empirical concept that has been derived from outer experience. . . . By means of outer sense, a property of our mind, we represent to ourselves objects as outside of us, and all without exception in space." Time, furthermore, is nothing but "the pure form of inner intuition". This launches Kant's Copernican revolution: space and time are nothing but inner configurations of the subjective human self; they are not obtained by observing the relationships and durations of bodies in the world outside the self. The representation of space and time is presupposed for sensation, and it belongs to the human mode of cognition. There is no way to know whether reality itself, things in themselves, exist in space and time.

Kant summarizes this philosophical subjectivism:

What we have meant to say is that all our intuition is nothing but the representation of appearance; that the things that we intuit are not in themselves as they appear to us; and that if the subject, or even only the subjective constitution of the senses in general, be removed, the whole constitution and all the relatives of objects in space and time, nay space and time themselves, would vanish. As appearances, they cannot exist in themselves, but only in us. What objects may be in themselves, and apart from this receptivity of our sensibility, remains completely unknown to us. We know nothing but our mode of perceiving them.

In a sense, Kant proceeds under the tutelage of David Hume, as the recurring "nothing but" of the Empiricist reduction indicates.

What are the implications of such subjectivism? It is well to pause a moment, for one stands here at the taproot of Kant's philosophical doctrine. All the rest will follow logically as corollary and completion. The implications are devastation itself for mankind's use of natural reason throughout all the ages. For Kant's doctrine represents the completion of the apostasy from God from the viewpoint of education. Education will no longer have a discipline that cultivates the use of natural reason in ascending to the intelligible order of truths in general and to the existing reality of the personal and intelligent Supreme Being in particular.

In the realm of psychology, it will become increasingly impossible to distinguish reality from so-called projections. For example, the therapist is to convince the naive mental patient that admiring a particular person for his strength of character is merely "projecting" his subjective need for strength onto an individual who may be as weak as himself. Whether any qualities ever exist intrinsically in anyone becomes unknowable.

Why is subjectivism so ruinous? Consider that mankind universally has recognized the majestic order of the universe, best seen in the starry skies and especially in the sun and moon, which measure time. Kant himself was devoted to the night sky. It must indeed have been a powerfully wrenching influence that came over him from Hume. Metaphysics is the rational procedure that organizes mankind's use of natural reason into the academic discipline familiar in the West since the Greeks, with its two parts: its ontology, which states the principles of being and existence; and its natural theology, which studies the various ways by which the mind ascends from those principles to the Supreme Being. All of this was immensely illuminated in Christian Philosophy, because of its cultivated emphasis on existence rather than forms and hence its rational recognition of the doctrine of creation. It provided academic support among young people acquiring their education for the teaching of revealed religion, which St. Paul summarizes in Romans 1:20: "Ever since God created the world his everlasting power and deity, however invisible, have been there for the mind to see in the things he has made."

This natural judgment and common sense of mankind in use from the beginning of human life on the planet, and this academic discipline of metaphysics, which articulates, develops, and polishes this use of natural reason, are both eliminated by Kant at one stroke. What mankind always has concluded from the natural perception of things in space and time is now asserted to be nothing but the result of subjective configurations and innate structure, a preunderstanding on the part of man, but not a knowledge of reality, the thing-in-itself, to use Kant's phrase. "What objects may be in themselves", he says, "remains completely unknown to us. We know nothing but our mode of perceiving them."

Kant's Copernican revolution in philosophy, occasioned as a response to Hume's atheistic reduction of human knowledge to nothing but the sensory, is in conflict with common sense, the phrase in the English language that means natural reason and the natural metaphysics of mankind. In plain terms, Kant's approach is an artificial construct. If it is adopted in the schools of philosophy in the colleges and universities of the West, an artificial "common sense" will begin to appear among the educated people whom the campus produces, a world apart and quite at variance with the natural metaphysics of mankind. The time will come when Western man will wonder how persons of the once-Christian West could perpetrate, for example, a Holocaust or a Gulag Archipelago. The answer will be obtained when the philosophical apostasy from God is analyzed and understood: such events flow forth from the artificial "common sense" that results from the philosophical apostasy from God.

But to return to Kant's classroom: the professor of philosophy at Königsberg is answering the question with his description of what he asserts to be the working parts of the human mental structure. So much, he says, for the first set of innate forms, which form and shape sensory perceptions into what we think are space and time. Let us go on to the second set, which he calls the four innate forms of the understanding. These are quantity, quality, relation, and modality, he says, reducing Aristotle's ten categories of being to these four headings. In a gesture to Hume, he includes causality in the form of relation.

Clearly, ontology is involved. These are basic components in the traditional teaching on the principles of being. But they are no longer principles understood to exist in things, principles by which things are understood to exist as they are seen to exist. For Kant, they are innate forms of the knowing subject, prior to his particular understandings. Do they give valid knowledge about the way things are, extramentally? Indeed not. These understandings are even more subjective than the forms for space and time, for they represent a further advance of the impressions from outside through the preexisting mental structure that receives them and forms them into the patterns of which human consciousness becomes aware: qualities, causal action, and all the rest. These are subjective, not objective. There is no way of knowing, Kant teaches, whether they are valid regarding things-in-themselves.

Again, the conflict with natural common sense is evident. Mankind always has lived by judgments of natural reason upon the different kinds of things, understanding, naming, and using the different substantial realities according to various purposes of life. Human life is simply the ongoing web of such judgments, expressing understandings and communicating them to the young by apprenticeship, and, in the recent times of literary culture, by education.

Finally, Kant completes his description of subjective structure by explaining that a third set of innate forms of the knowing subject attach to human reason as such. They are three synthetic ideas. The impressions from the outside pass through the sensory apparatus, and hence appear to be spatial and temporal; they then move on through the forms of understanding, and hence seem to manifest causality, qualities of various kinds, and all the modes of being; and now, like a river spreading over its delta, they flow into the cosmological idea, the psychological idea, and the theological idea.

These synthetic concepts or ideas of human reason are nothing but the innate forms of reason. As a result the subjective self thinks the world is an ordered cosmos, thinks that the human self has a unifying and abiding principle of animation called the soul, and thinks that there is a God as the ultimate explanation of it all. But do the orderly cosmos, the soul, and God really exist in extramental reality? Kant's answer, called "agnosticism", is simply that we do not know. Again the fundamental principle of his Copernican revolution in philosophy: "What objects may be in themselves, and apart from this receptivity of our sensibility (or of our other sets of a priori forms) remains completely unknown to us. We know nothing but our mode of perceiving them"—or of understanding them, or of reasoning about them. Clearly, Kant is rejecting the academic discipline of metaphysics, with its principles of being and reality and with its ascent from them to the intelligible order of reality and truth.

This third set of innate forms consummates Kant's philosophical revolution, for it eliminates rational knowledge of God, of the soul, and of the cosmos as witnessing to the Creator. This is an agnosticism that ministers to the atheistic use of the human mind. It states the kind of philosophical thought that will be developed to evade the Creator and to deny explicitly the existence of God. It will complete Spinoza's reduction of all reality to nothing but this visible cosmos. Kant himself, however, did not intend this to be the last word in philosophy. As a disciple of Descartes, he has in mind to bracket religion and the things of God strictly out of the domain of human knowledge, to protect them, as it were, from men like Hume. Such matters will have a domain of their own, where he intends to build them back up upon a new, nonrational, nonmetaphysical foundation. But before taking up his endeavor in that Cartesian direction, it is well to summarize the results of his *Critique of Pure Reason*.

Kant's point of departure is his distinction between the noumenon, the *Ding-An-Sich,* reality in itself, and the phenomenon, the impression that comes in upon the subjective self to be shaped by the three sets of innate or a priori forms. These are preunderstandings that transcend the experience of receiving impressions. They are configurations of the subject, subjective in the self, not objective with respect to the noumenon. What the knower knows, therefore, is his own resulting ideas and not reality as such. Thus Kant's critical metaphysics can be summarized correctly as "transcendental, or subjective, Idealism". Men finish the cognitive process by forming judgments about the natures of substances of various kinds. In them, does the word "is" bear upon reality as such? Are they true of things in themselves? Definitely not. Kant's answer is explicit Subjectivism: they are not founded upon reality, not even the traditional first principles of reason. They are not universally and necessarily true in the objective sense. They are founded not on reality but on the innate forms and structures of the mind. The principle of contradiction, and all other such principles, are laws of human thought, not laws of reality. Furthermore, the concepts linked together by the verb "is", which men hitherto in what he calls the dogmatic way of philosophizing have considered to express extramental existence, now in the critical philosophy do not express reality. They are the result of the subjective forming of the impressions from outside.

Kant's doctrine is a pure phenomenology: our judgments are valid regarding phenomena, and phenomena alone. The equations of mathematical physics that predict and so control phenomena remain intact in Kant's philosophy. But neither our concepts nor our judgments tell us anything about the *Ding-an-Sich,* the noumenon, the nature of reality in itself. Thus human knowledge loses all objectivity. It is relative to the knower, to his innate forms to begin with, and then to the conditioning he receives from the education and culture of his particular time and place.

Thus Kant's Critical Philosophy is actually a refined and modernized form of the ancient Skepticism, which always confined human knowledge to the impressions of the senses. From beginning to end Kant's philosophizing is a systematic and explicit denial of the existence of the intellect as a power of knowing distinct from the sensory apparatus. For him the concept of substance, of a substantial reality abiding amid the flux of phenomena or appearances of things, is "a mere chimera". In fact, he ridicules the idea of "a power of understanding what the things that appear to us may be in themselves".

It is no surprise that Kant rejects the concept of God achieved in the heritage of Christian Philosophy from Augustine to Aquinas. He rejects the very idea of creation as the giving of participated existence to things by the Creator or Source of existence. Logically, therefore, he systematically refuses the very idea of an ascent of the mind from the first principles of being, or ontology, to the Supreme Being known by natural theology.[1] He centers his rejection upon the five ways of Thomas Aquinas, which, as noted above, are designed to show the harmony

---

[1] See Excerpts for Part Three, Kant, p. 428.

between the natural thinking of all men and the cultivated thinking of those who have the privilege of academic education. Kant conducts his rejection by using the standard procedure of skepticism: he gathers the dogmatisms, as he terms them, the teachings of the philosophical heritage, as "theses", against which he pits the "antitheses", the self-contradictions that force suspension of judgment. In Aquinas these are simply the objections that reason solves. But in Kant these "antinomies of pure reason" end with his "Critique of all Theology Based upon Speculative Principles". This is the concluding chapter of the *Critique of Pure Reason* and the animating principle of the work as a whole.

Immanuel Kant understood very well that he had criticized the science of metaphysics, the heart of philosophical knowledge; he had put it out of existence, leaving nothing but the mathematical and physical sciences of phenomena. Again, he is the disciple who completes Descartes and Spinoza in their elimination of metaphysics, as understood and taught in all the classical and Christian times. His Critical Philosophy is actually nothing but, to use the ever-recurring phrase of the Empiricist reduction, the rationalization for the transfer of mathematical physics into the position of first philosophy. It is now firmly and explicitly established in position as the seventh of the seven arts, the one that illuminates all education and therefore culture among Western men. The way is prepared philosophically for "scientism" in all its forms, which will characterize the applications of Modern Philosophy in the contemporary period after Kant, Comte, and Hegel to the present. Kant, furthermore, understood that the values of human culture, not to mention the very idea of revealed religion, are left without rational foundation. He was indeed alarmed at this result of Hume's philosophy, yet he could see no way to cope with it on intellectual grounds.

The Critique of Practical Reason

This introduces Kant's second major work, the *Critique of Practical Reason.* In 1762, when his mind was in ferment from reading David Hume, when he felt he must concede the terrain of knowledge to British Empiricism and at the same time deeply concerned for the values of human and Christian living, an incident reveals the origin and idea of this second *Critique.* Kant's neighbors in Königsberg were accustomed to his familiar emergence from his house, punctually every day, to meet his classes down the street at the university. On one particular day, his door did not open. Later his friendly neighbors accosted him in this fashion: "*Herr Professor,* you had class yesterday, and you didn't come out for it."

"Yes," Kant is said to have explained, "that's true. Yesterday's mail brought Rousseau's *Émile* to me. I began to read it and became so engrossed I did not notice time passing. I remained buried in it until I finished it during the night, entirely forgetting my class. In this book I found the solution to my problem with David

Hume. Rousseau describes the pure, original goodness of human nature. The educated state is something artificial. The values cannot depend on it, and now I see they need not. Man's true self is found in the freshness, spontaneity, and goodness of his natural innocence. This is the source and origin of all that is stable and upright and lasting on the human scene. The foundation for uprightness in living is not in the intellect and its cultivation. The intelligence has its own domain, mathematics and the sciences, as Descartes, Spinoza, and Hume have made clear. That foundation for goodness is the natural human self as given, prior to the intellect and its education. The values rest upon feeling and fervor, on warmth and depth of heart.

"When reading Rousseau's book I saw that there is a categorical imperative in our original nature, deeper than pure reason. This categorical imperative bids us act as if the three master ideas of reason were true—the idea of an ordered universe, the idea of the soul, and the idea of God. This solves a thorny metaphysical problem upon which I am working. This is why I became so engrossed that I didn't notice the passage of time and missed my class. It is something that I think never has happened to me before."

This anecdote from Kant's life summarizes the *Critique of Practical Reason.* The first *Critique,* a deliberate and systematic anti-intellectualism, conceding Hume's skepticism, has demolished the rational foundations for the basic truths of mankind, the essentials for life in earthly society, and the very preambles of any religious faith. Rousseau's *Émile,* the philosophy of education of the French Enlightenment, rejected both the religious doctrine of original sin and the importance of the natural arts and sciences for education and culture. This gave Kant the substitute for metaphysics that he needed. Overlooking the fact that *Émile* is an abstraction, a philosophy of history and human nature constructed by Rousseau's imagination, Kant accepted it as a felt need, so to speak, in the face of Hume's professed and bitterly mordant atheism. Morality and religion can be reestablished on a foundation prior to education and independent of philosophy. It will not rest on principles understood by reason and taught to young people by the seven arts that form their curriculum of studies; rather, it will rest on feeling, fervor, and depth of heart.[2] The dignity of man suffices. The edifice demolished by the *Critique of Pure Reason* can now be rebuilt upon the postulates or social demands of human life in society.

Thus Kant arrives at his "categorical imperative", the absolute commandment of the human will given as a fact in practical human life. It implies law, indeed, but not a law of God; it is the law of each one's being, an innate form in the practical order, again a priori, namely, given prior to any experience. The principles of goodness and morality are not understandings seen by the light of reason but

[2] See Excerpts for Part Three, Kant, p. 430.

consciousness of feeling for beauty and dignity in living, which dwell by nature in each human heart.

This pure innate form of law, with its categorical imperative that begets consciousness of duty, has nothing to do with phenomena. It does not result from anything outside the human self. It is independent of mathematics and physics, indeed of psychology, theology, and any other science. It is the free and autonomous self in action. Autonomy of this human self is the keystone of Kantian ethics. Duty emanates a priori from practical life and its needs as an empirical fact. No principle of reason supports it—the first *Critique* has eliminated such an approach. Nothing is imposed upon the human self from outside. Duty is simply the natural self responding to life as given. To submit to a law from outside would be degrading and incompatible with human dignity. There is to be no subordination to an objective moral order in this metaphysical system of pure subjectivism. Thus the human self gives itself its own law, and this makes it free. Every exercise of the will implies personal freedom, and this free action rebuilds the edifice demolished by the first *Critique*. The categorical imperative, out of which each person freely responds to duty in life, bids each to act as if the three great synthetic ideas of reason were true: the idea that God exists, the idea of the human soul, and the idea that life proceeds in an ordered universe. Occasionally, in life today, one meets a morally minded atheist who tries to be as good as many religious persons are, acting *as if* the metaphysics of goodness were really there in spite of its missing foundation.

Kant is thus the true disciple of Descartes and his bracketing of religion and morality out of the domain of knowledge. The *Critique of Practical Reason* completes this bracketing. Religion and morality are placed in a nonintellectual order and given a frankly declared irrational foundation. Thanks to life, to action, to endeavor, we can contact noumenal reality and, in Kant's basic contradiction, "know" it somehow in a noncognitive way solely from the duty asserted by the innate form.

This "knowledge" of the noumenon and its moral imperatives is not an insight of reason into the truth and goodness of actions and objects that are willed. The truth of the good does not determine duty; it is the duty, felt as an imperative here and now, that determines what good is. Putting this in the context of mankind's historic philosophical enterprise, it is not metaphysics that lays the foundation for ethics and morality, but ethics and morality that establish metaphysics. This is indeed a Copernican revolution in philosophy, which promises to carry over, as always on the human scene, into education and culture, as sincerity of heart becomes more important than objective norms.

What can be said? First, no doubt, one must recognize the naiveté of Kant's position, a naiveté that characterizes all rationalism and especially that of *Émile*. The history of philosophy, by itself alone, offers evidence that there is something more to human nature than this presumed natural goodness. In any case, the

Kantian metaphysics opens the door to fundamental thinking that will apply the apostasy from God in many directions. Never therefore were good religious intentions more disastrously deceived. For Kant's metaphysics replaces God, the Unknowable, with the human self.

Upon this metaphysical foundation philosophers will arise, notably Comte and Hegel, who will complete the metaphysics of declared and professed atheism by asserting an intuitive knowledge of the noumenon that has no place for the transcendent and intelligent Supreme Being. Thus, although he personally intended something else, Kant contributed mightily to the metaphysics of the apostasy from God. Upon his foundation, thinkers will arise who apply this metaphysical position of the categorical imperative in asserting forcibly the good that must be imposed upon mankind. Thus, through Comte and Hegel will come Marx and Lenin, with the twentieth-century Gulag Archipelago, and Nietzsche and Hitler, with the twentieth-century Holocaust. The unforgettable voice of Adolf Hitler, raging over the German radio in the 1930s, storming with subjective conviction, is fully justified on Kantian grounds. His program, as he sees it, is his duty.

Kant, then, had a right to call his two critiques a Copernican revolution in philosophy. It literally overturns the historic process of reason in its project for a science of wisdom and virtue to function as the seventh liberal art, the culmination of human education and the illumination of human culture.

Is Kant's approach in philosophy justified? Is it necessary because of the advances in the empirical sciences? One can only say that the existence of things remains what it always was, unaffected by the motions of bodies in space. The great mistake was the substitution of mathematical physics for metaphysics as first philosophy in the curriculum of Western education. Kant did not rectify this mistake, this rejection of the heritage of both Classical Philosophy and Christian Philosophy; rather, he completed and sealed the mistake, even though he was a Christian with Christian personal intentions.

Philosophical and psychological analysis both reveal that Kant was under no compulsion from the new empirical knowledge. Imaginary space is indeed subjective, but real space is not: Newton is the first to explain this distinction. The theory of the innate forms and their preunderstandings is a construct of Kant's imagination: two centuries of the most intensive kind of psychological research have failed to provide him with empirical and scientific support.

What emerges from Kant is a metaphysics in reverse. It is a philosophical system that locks the person within the human self, precludes any rational ascent to the intelligible order of rational truth, and thus establishes the human self at the center of the universe. This is the metaphysical culmination of the apostasy from God. It completes Spinoza, for it calls for the symbolic interpretation of all revealed religion by a philosophy of religion that replaces the outer, what the Bible calls the wonderful works of God in salvation history, with the inner, the religion of the human heart. It will take many decades after Kant to elaborate the applications of this metaphysics in social, personal, and religious life, but the foundation for proceeding without God, relying solely on the human self, has been laid. Descartes' method and his bracketing have been completed; so has Spinoza's nonpurposive, materialistic, and mechanical *Deus sive Natura,* together with his philosophical reinterpretation of revealed religion.

V

AUGUSTE COMTE: THE SYSTEM OF POSITIVISM

The philosophical scenario changes from the foggy Baltic forests of northeastern Germany, from the small and quite provincial town of Königsberg in Prussia, to Paris, the city of light, for centuries the intellectual capital of Western culture. Two mighty events have taken place, affecting Western civilization like earthquakes. The first was Protestantism, with its epicenter in Germany; the second was the French Revolution, exactly in Paris and by the common consent of historians the outward social expression of the thinking of the Enlightenment. These two events divide modern times since the Renaissance into two halves. Protestantism and religious strife dominate the first half; the emergence and metaphysical consummation of declared philosophical atheism characterize the second. Auguste Comte is the symbolic personality who stands for a host of philosophers and university professors who accomplish this second phase.

Comte was born in 1798 into a devout and practicing Catholic family. As a boy he received the standard instruction and formation in revealed religion that had come forward across Christian times. Noting that they had a talented and promising son, his modestly endowed parents saved and sacrificed to send him to Paris for his higher education.

His family was aghast at what happened: their son lost all faith in God and openly professed his atheism. Thus Auguste Comte illustrates a phenomenon that has occurred countless times since Descartes, Spinoza, Locke, and Hume; the victory of the atheistic use of human reason in young persons who are baptized Christians. In Comte the concrete process of the Western apostasy from God becomes graphically visible. An atmosphere of unbelief in God has been created that engulfs such young people and destroys the interior and spiritual life in them, much as a poison gas destroys the life of a bodily organism. Such young people, full of confidence in natural reason using the Cartesian method, give up any idea of a personal and intelligent God and of a revelation from him having authority over their moral behavior. They rationalize a sense of responsibility in their human actions only to themselves, and not to the Supreme Judge of their earlier catechetical formation. The philosophical apostasy from God fastens upon their personalities in this fashion, and not as something wrong or sinful but as fully justified by the philosophy that imbues their studies and the attitudes of their peers. Any other idea of fundamental reality comes to appear archaic; the common sense and faith of their childhood are replaced by a new common sense that dwells in the academic life and atmosphere of the campus.

Voltaire, Rousseau, and Diderot are the guiding lights of this intellectual life. The French Revolution has secured its social and political triumph. During Comte's boyhood Napoleon is carrying it forcibly by his socially transforming victories over the rest of the heartlands of the Western world. Comte goes up to Paris in these intoxicating times, just as Kant is finishing his career. The bright young Frenchman becomes a professor of philosophy at the University of Paris in the years when Hegel is the dominant professor of philosophy at the University of Berlin. Thus Comte provides a dramatic demonstration of the schism that has opened up in Western culture between the catechetical order of teaching, continuing humbly in the homes and parish schools, and the academic order of higher education in the lands once called Christendom.

The apostasy from God is illustrated with great accuracy in the life and work of Comte, for he removes it from vague generality and concretizes it. He enables the analyst of the apostasy to recognize its philosophical root and its location in that seventh art, which determines the character of education and thus the quality of human culture. Auguste Comte, furthermore, personalizes and dramatizes the sea change that has overtaken higher education in Christendom, bringing into view the vast shift from the theistic metaphysics taught in Augustine's original model for a cathedral school at Hippo, in Peter Lombard's burgeoning cathedral school at Paris in the twelfth century, and in its expansion to include all of the arts, sciences, and professional studies at the University of Paris in the time of Thomas Aquinas, Bonaventure, and Roger Bacon.

With Comte, then, the scene does indeed change. On the surface, furthermore, his works are utterly different from those of Kant, with their opaque and stiffly expressed Subjectivism and their attempt to ground the values upon feeling and sentiment rather than reason. In the works of Comte there is little room for feeling and sentiment. Everything proceeds with Gallic precision and clarity to a fully articulated and openly professed atheism applied militantly to social organization for social welfare. In all his work he aims consciously at completing the philosophy of the Enlightenment, projecting the thought and social program of Diderot, Voltaire, and all the rest. In fact, Comte first rose to fame in Paris as the editor of the works of Voltaire.

Under the surface, however, where the metaphysical substrate of Modern Philosophy stands like its bedrock, Comte and Kant both represent components in the completion of the world view of Spinoza's metaphysics, or, rather, anti-metaphysics. Both Kant and Comte assume as their point of departure that there is no power of reason in man to ascend from what is given to the senses in the cosmos upward to a higher order of truth and reality. Their particular contributions to the metaphysical completion are very different philosophically and quite unlike in their cultural and linguistic modes of expression. Basically, Kant completes the current of development from Descartes and Spinoza on the side of the human subject thinking, while Comte completes the current of empiricism that descends through Locke and Hume to the French Enlightenment.

The young Auguste Comte, then, achieves his higher education with distinction at the University of Paris, absorbing avidly its Cartesian philosophy and its apostate atmosphere. In the process he became the disciple of Saint-Simon, founder of French Socialism, serving as his secretary for six years from age twenty, decisive years for a youthful intellectual. Saint-Simon was engrossed in his project for a "New Christianity", writing his book under that title. Saint-Simon looked upon himself as the new Messiah called to take up the mission of the Church to renew the face of the earth, which the Church itself, he maintained, had palpably failed to accomplish. His influence reaches toward the present through Karl Marx, who learned from both Saint-Simon and Comte in his years at Paris what he will call "scientific socialism". Comte inherited from Saint-Simon much of his basic doctrine; it is no accident that the future communism of Marx and Lenin will appear as one of the variants on Comte's theme.

Comte in the meantime received an appointment as professor of philosophy at the University of Paris. This determined his career and separated him from Saint-Simon, not so much in doctrine as in method. For the Socialist leader wanted revolutionary action now with activist programs for seizing power and thus reforming society without delay. Comte decided that unity of fundamental thinking among men had to come first. The spiritual power of the professors, he taught, is more important than the political power of the state and its civil servants. For if their own minds have not been enlightened, how can the politicians lead people at large and institute a new set of social structures? Comte turns firmly toward the reform of academic higher education, therefore, and maintains a lifelong dream of taking the Catholic Church over as the instrument already at hand. It is waiting to be used among the people, he thought, as the best way to popularize the new approach that illuminated his mind and guided the teaching of his course of lectures at the university.

Thus began that long professorial career of teaching and publishing that lasted until his death in 1857. His intellectual power and influence rose steadily in France, until he came to be the very symbol of the Sorbonne. From his teaching these works came forth: The *Course of Positive Philosophy* in six volumes; his *System of Positive Political Philosophy* in four volumes; his *Treatise on Sociology,* the plan for a scientific reorganization of society to install on earth "the religion of humanity"; and his *Catechism of Positivism,* published in 1852. Throughout his life he worked actively and energetically on behalf of this Positivism through conferences and correspondence. Among others he contacted the Jesuit General in Rome hoping to enlist the Jesuit Order and its educational institutions. Above all, he maintained a flow of letters to and from his principal supporter and disciple, the famous philosopher John Stuart Mill in England.

The titles of his chief works indicate the general tendency of his teaching, with its constant effort to establish a new philosophical religion and hence a new society on the basis of Descartes' method, Spinoza's metaphysics, and the progress of the empirical sciences. Comte's Positivism as a doctrine can be summarized under the following five general considerations.

First, Positivism rests on the Spinozan metaphysics of atheism, accepted at the outset and without question as the correct view of ultimate reality. By this time, however, the union of Christianity with the political order has been eliminated by the French Revolution; hence atheism can discard its pantheistic disguise. Instead of Spinoza's careful "God or Nature", for Comte it is simply "Nature", in an open profession of atheism. Comte continues and completes David Hume in his scorn and ridicule for the very idea of a science of metaphysics and a power in man to ascend from sensory data to a higher intelligible order of truth and reality.

No such reality, or any such intellectual power to know it, exists: Comte develops this thesis of the Spinozan world view systematically and in detail. It is important to note that Positivism does not ask why things exist, or what kind of existence things manifest and enjoy, or what the meaning of their various modes of existence might be. Positivism is a "philosophy", indeed, but a very particular kind of philosophy, a truncated one that systematically and studiously avoids the questions about existence that are the very heart of the historic heritage in philosophical thought.

As Spinoza before him, and as the pantheists, Materialists, and Atomists of pagan philosophy in antiquity, Comte simply accepts existing things as there, as given to the senses, with the constant implication that matter is eternal. Thus, the facts, nothing but the facts, the facts as the senses and scientific observation determine them to be—nothing else exists, and mankind has no other kind of knowledge. Even to ask questions beyond this restricted domain is useless and a waste of time, for they are essentially meaningless.

Facts, as they are called somewhat worshipfully, are thus at the essence of Positivism, as indeed the very name was chosen to indicate. Knowledge of the facts is positive knowledge, and it alone is valid. Metaphysical knowledge by definition is invalid. Hence no science of metaphysics exists. All the knowledge and all the wisdom mankind needs will come forth from the generalized statement and application of this new philosophy, Positivism, which functions in Comte's mind and system as the final realization of Descartes' universal science. Spinoza is called correctly the metaphysician of modern atheism. But the completed statement of this metaphysical system came in the works of Comte after its development in Locke, Hume, and the French Enlightenment. If a philosophy, however, systematically evades the questions of existence, is it really philosophy? Bearing this in mind, one can turn to the further points in this summary of Comte's Positivism.

Second, therefore, one must note that Comte is the disciple who completes Descartes as well as Spinoza. He does this by his monolithic approach to methodology. The physical facts that are given in this metaphysical view of fundamental reality are subject to mathematical analysis and hence control. Patterns of cause and effect in phenomena can be observed and then stated in equations that give control over their recurrence. One must know the facts this way in order to foresee similar factual situations and thus exercise control over them. Comte in his own way is imbued with the dream of Descartes.

The crucial point about Positivism is its universalization of this method of mathematical physics to embrace the biologically living and the human as well as the physics and chemistry of inanimate bodies. Only this one method of knowledge is available, and it suffices. Indeed, it offers the prospect of a beneficent new age for mankind that will usher in an improved and even perfected social condition on earth. Here is an early predecessor of B. F. Skinner's deterministic utopia *Walden Two*.

Here at last the fact that Modern Philosophy is a different kind of philosophy from the preceding Classical Philosophy and Christian Philosophy comes so clearly into view that it cannot be mistaken. In both of those earlier philosophical approaches a definite pluralism in methodology was maintained: each of the seven arts, each science and discipline of human culture, has its own proper, valid, and distinctive method for knowing the real.

In Positivism this pluralism in methods disappears under a relentlessly monolithic approach. The underlying reason? One must recall that metaphysics is now explicitly eliminated and replaced by mathematical physics as first philosophy. This replacement, which Descartes began, stands now completed in Comte's Positivism. Putting this another way, philosophy itself has disappeared, having become the generalized statement of the findings of the empirical sciences. In the first flush of the intoxication, this seems like the rise of scientific philosophy and the promise of Comte's somewhat messianic hope. But upon reflection it is nothing but the natural result of the Spinozan metaphysics and its refusal to ask questions about existence.

Third, and with great logic, comes Comte's famous "law of the three stages of human development". This is his rationalization for his sweeping departure from the metaphysics open to the transcendent Creator, with its pluralism in methods for the various arts, to a rigidly mechanical empiricism that encloses the human spirit within this visible cosmos. But everything proceeds as if the final enlightment, the ultimate wisdom, and the supreme good of mankind are at last available through the ministry of university teaching and in particular through his own system of Positive Philosophy. Comte teaches with all the confidence of Cartesian Rationalism that the human mind must necessarily pass through three stages of development. This is a necessary law, simply asserted by Comte as his fundamental insight into the working as well as the nature of ultimate reality. The remarkable correspondences with the contemporaneous and independent doctrine of Hegel at the University of Berlin will become apparent.

The first stage is the theological one: facts of nature are explained by the intervention of supernatural beings. When lightning strikes the steeple of the local church, the people think God did it in anger and mercy, as if bidding them to turn to him from their sins. Historically this stage is manifested by the age of absolutism in rule by priests and kings, of fetishism and superstitions of all kinds.

The second stage is the metaphysical one, which eliminates the animism of supernatural powers and spirits thought to dwell in natural phenomena and replaces it with abstract concepts of natures and substances immanent in things. These abstract powers inhere in natures, so that the mind, by a priori reasonings, can deduce the effects from them as causes and thus understand the facts that take place, facts such as that bolt of lightning. This stage follows necessarily in historical succession after the theological stage.

In the third stage comes the positive phase of mankind, also in necessary succession from the preceding. Comte is fully certain that his age is witnessing this transition, and indeed that his Positivism is the concrete vehicle in university teaching for bringing it about. In this stage the human mind gives up its previous attempts to know inner essences, substances, or natures of things. It recognizes that such efforts and questions are meaningless. Rather, it simply accepts the facts as given in the cosmos, observes and researches the relationships that may appear among them, analyzes these relationships mathematically, and states the findings in equations that express scientific laws of constancy in behavior. This kind of positive knowledge, the only knowledge man has or needs, enables him to dominate nature and control it for the benefit of humanity. This is Positive Philosophy, or "Positivism", because it sheds past speculative illusions and deals exclusively with empirically verified observations and their mathematically demonstrated linkages. Men now know that electrical charges develop in clouds and on earth and discharge upon such high points as church steeples.

Thus Descartes and Spinoza are brought to completion. Everything in Comte's exposition is logical and coherent, granted that mathematical physics operates in the position of first philosophy, and granted that metaphysics does not exist. If metaphysics, the science of the ascent to the First Cause, disappears, then nothing but secondary causes remain. Again the language of the reduction: it is "now known", and "nothing but".

If, on the other hand, the science that bears upon existence in itself and in its principles illuminates the mental scene, then all three can exist and operate simultaneously: the positive relationships, the substantial natures, and the intelligent and intentional supervision of the almighty First Cause of existence and operation.

In the comprehensive metaphysics of Christian Philosophy, built upon the natural reason of mankind and the pagan schools of the pre-Christian times in the manner that has been noted, this kind of understanding and insight into the nature of things is available to youthful students as a part of their education. But the Comtean Positivism expresses the apostasy of God in one of its philosophically completed forms precisely because of its systematic elimination of this metaphysical heritage and its substitution of the Cartesian universal science.

From the viewpoint of the coming historicism, which will dominate Western intellectual life after Kant, Comte, and Hegel, this law of the three stages completes Voltaire's philosophy of history and needs only the additional dynamism of Hegel's dialectic. Thus Spinoza's metaphysics of atheism is being perfected in its own line by thinkers who develop his static view of *Deus sive Natura* into a dynamic and active focus upon the life of mankind in history. This is, of course, the very focus given in revealed religion in its teaching about the self-revelation of the First Cause and his interventions in his creation out of concern for his creatures. In Comte's vision of human history, a vision in no sense empirically observed in the facts as given, everything depends upon an assertion of the human self that follows logically from the absence of the science of existence as such and its ascent to the intelligible order and the Creator.

The fourth point in summary of Comte's Positivism is his reform of the arts and sciences. The program of higher education must be refashioned by the outright elimination of both theology and of the older kind of philosophy, which entertained the idea of metaphysics as its central branch. It is this approach that occasioned John Henry Newman's *Idea of a University,* in which he analyzes the question whether a university of studies is truly universal if it excludes the discipline that rises to the study of the Supreme Being. It is the same question that Nietzsche's madman will shout, swinging his lantern in the public squares of the German cities.

When theology and metaphysics are eliminated, what happens to the program of studies? A vast transformation will take place in contemporary education as a whole, a process that will occupy the ten to fifteen decades from Comte at midnineteenth century to the present. This process will essentially consist of the spread of two Comtean concepts among all educators, the professors in higher education and the teachers on the elementary and secondary levels as well. First, a new discipline is created by Comte to occupy that controlling and illuminating position as the seventh of the seven arts. This is the science of sociology, which both in name and concept is commonly traced back to Comte as its founder. Secondly, this new discipline will reign over every aspect of intellectual life by means of the monolithic approach mentioned above. For example, in Church life today, note the prevalence of analysis of social structures and statistics over traditional supernatural norms.

Does this mean that sociology in itself is something untrue and evil? Not at all. In itself it is a legitimate development in the general context of the Copernican revolution in the first six of the liberal arts. The untruth and the evil for mankind arise from the transfer of sociology into the position of first philosophy, substituting it for the authentic metaphysics of the human heritage in philosophy.

In the new age of Positivism, Comte teaches, continuing his project for the reorganization of Western education, the empirical sciences must be organized into a curriculum that runs from the most general and abstract to the most concrete and specialized. This places the branches of mathematics at the beginning of student life, then mechanics, physics, astronomy, chemistry, and the rapidly developing new science of biology. The final science is sociology, which replaces both the theology and the metaphysics of the older approaches. Has philosophy then disappeared? When philosophy is understood as the science that studies existence as such, then the answer is indeed affirmative. Comte, of course, redefines the word philosophy: it is now Positive Philosophy, understood as the generalized statement of the findings of all the other empirical sciences, especially in their bearing upon man and his social life. And this is simply sociology. Ethics is included in this new science, and thus are born what will be developed into the behavioral sciences, with their emphasis on surveys and statistical analyses that report what people do, study the influences at work, and ponder upon the management and control of human behavior. Basic to Comte's Positivism is a rejection of introspection as a source of knowledge. Psychology, which includes logic, is itself a part of either sociology or biology. But wherever it is located, it must proceed by observing human behavior, singly and collectively, for only thus can one come to a factual knowledge of man. The behaviorists in the coming application will be standing on Comtean metaphysics.

Sociology, then, is the supreme and perfect science, the one that gives purpose to all the rest and sheds its light upon them. In the area of human interests and endeavor sociology is especially foundational: ethics, economics, political science, philosophy of history, and all similar specializations can be studied correctly only when they are placed on the foundation of this new science. When this is done, then young people will be prepared for social leadership toward "action now" and the reform of society. Their vision will then be cultivated and sharpened regarding actual social conclusions, what is right about them and what is wrong. Man is indeed a special form of biological life, participating generically in the animal ways of life. But human group life has its own set of facts. These must be analyzed under the guidance of Positivism in order to reveal both the social statics and the social dynamics of mankind. Clearly, Comte already has sketched that activist concept of philosophy that Karl Marx will define and implement in his social program.

Comtean Positivism thus has implications for philosophical anthropology. It assumes that the knowledge of man results from the study of man as a physical object. Man is the product of physical and chemical energies and is therefore knowable by the methods of physics and chemistry. Again, Descartes' dream of the universal science is working out into comprehensive completion by absorbing the thinking subject into itself. In the coming times of the applications of the completed metaphysics of Modern Philosophy, this "scientific" approach to man as an object will trigger the existentialist revolt by thinkers who retain in their world view a larger proportion of the Kantian metaphysics. Later on, the effect of Positivism will become visible in *The Two Cultures* of C. P. Snow, the "hard sciences" on the one hand and the humanities on the other. Knowledge is the exclusive domain of those sciences, while the humanities have become the domain of subjective experiences and their forms of self-expression. Thus the humanities will end as the instruments for teaching existentialism to the young.

These outcomes, socially visible in the twentieth century, were of course far in the future when Comte was meeting his philosophy classes at the University of Paris, and few foresaw what would come if his Positivism were to be widely adopted and applied. Little did one anticipate, in the rosy dawn of the new age, that this kind of fundamental thinking can serve to support man's rationalized and philosophically grounded inhumanity to man. Seen from the metaphysical position, however, the lines are already pointing directly forward to the Holocaust and the Gulag. For the philosophical apostasy from God is now explicit and ready to reach out to shape the mentality of the coming generations in their years of educational preparation for social leadership. Comte perfects and completes the militant side of modern atheism, which began to emerge with Diderot and other leaders of the French Enlightenment. This militancy, organized into political and social programs, will be a legacy of Comte for the times ahead.

The fifth and final heading for this summary of Comte's Positivism often comes as a surprise. It is the so-called religion of progress, which was born in the development of Modern Philosophy, especially with Voltaire, Condorcet, and the other activists of the Enlightenment and the French Revolution. True to the original metaphysical inspiration of Spinoza, it assumes that the three Comtean laws must necessarily operate, and then it makes its act of philosophical faith: society must necessarily become better day by day as the new age dawns and develops. Auguste Comte saw his philosophical system as the culmination of this new "religion", which will replace the older religions of the theological and the metaphysical epochs. Nothing exists but the visible cosmos. In it mankind is obviously the dominant form. Hence Mankind must be capitalized, for here one has what is actually the Supreme Being. Here is the object of worship, this ongoing and upward-marching entity on planet earth. All persons, past, present, and future, who contribute in any way to this progress of mankind toward social welfare and personal happiness are comprehended within this great Being, which merits worship and devotion. They can think rightly that their existence is meaningful. They can take an optimistic view of human life. As their education improves under the influence of Positivism and its reordering of the studies, men and women will become more and more altruistic.

Love is the principle, Comte taught, scientific order is the means, and progress is the purpose. This is mankind's religion. Through it the earth becomes the great fetish, the space where philosophy redeems mankind. Again the straight line of development and completion, which runs from Descartes and Spinoza to Comte and his school, becomes visible. This concept of "philosophical faith" and "philosophical redemption" will find fullest application in Nietzschean existentialism, especially in the work of Karl Jaspers, and in Marxist communism. But the basic concepts exist already in Auguste Comte, where the pantheism of Giordano Bruno and Spinoza stands completed.

The Copernican revolution in the empirical sciences is a phenomenon with two aspects that should be carefully distinguished—and yet they are frequently confused. The first is the legitimate and beneficent progress of these sciences in their own order. The second is the new "metaphysics" of Bruno and Spinoza, replacing the heritage of classical and Christian metaphysics. This replacement is based on the notion that the elimination of the geocentric world view, with its canopy of the heavens and a dwelling place for God beyond, calls for an infinite spatial cosmos identified with "God". The *Deus sive Natura* of Spinoza does indeed express the metaphysics of modern atheism. It provides Comte with the tacit foundation for his worship of Mankind as the highest manifestation of existing reality.

It is readily apparent, of course, that the concept of God in Christian Philosophy remains intact whatever the discoveries regarding the motions and the "centers" of bodies in space and time. The crucial question has been the elimination of that academic discipline elaborated since the Greeks and the Fathers, based on the natural metaphysics of mankind and concentrated on the analysis and understanding of existence as such. The crucial question is its substitution by mathematical physics. It is this substitution that is completed in the Positivism of Comte. In a true sense, it completes the Renaissance of pagan antiquity, for it becomes a philosophy that concentrates upon the forms of bodily things in the cosmos rather than upon their acts of existing and the principles by which they are as they are seen to be.

Such is the background of Comte's rather surprising *Catechism of Positivism*, published in 1852. It comes late in his career and in a sense validly synthesizes his thought and reduces it to practice in the new religions' worship of The Great Being, as he writes, becoming visible in Man. Comte projected a set of solemn rites for his new worship of Humanity: a calendar of feast days commemorating the great philosophical personalities, a group of nine social sacraments for initiation into common civil life, for marking its chief moments, and for the burial of the dead. He quite openly represented the priestly character of the professors of the sciences imbued with the method and vision of Positivism and assumed to himself the office of high priest.

It must be said that this religion as programmed by Comte was never widely accepted, although one can find a similar ethos in American ethical culture societies. One temple of Positivism was built in Rio de Janeiro. For the most part, however, his followers accepted his method and adopted his approach in the various sciences and disciplines, simply dismissing religion as a thing of the past for which mankind feels no further need. It is probably under the aegis of Karl Marx in the future that this idea for a philosophical religion will find its real application.

The influence of Comte's system of Positivism upon academic education, however, cannot be overestimated, especially in its impact upon the English-speaking world, where the ground had been prepared well by Locke and Hume. Many personalities arise to disseminate Comte's kind of thinking, often called "scientism", and entire schools are developed under various names and with their own terminology. But the substance is always one and the same, the empiricist reduction of human knowledge to nothing but that of the senses. Everything else in human consciousness is explained as the association of sensory images, the grouping of them, and the giving of names to such groups.

A few names of Comte's chief followers will serve to symbolize the transition of this Positivism, this seventh and controlling art among the educational disciplines, to a broadening influence upon the culture of Western man. Foremost among them is John Stuart Mill (1806–73), Comte's declared disciple in England. An accomplished mathematician, Mill attempted to create a positivist logic based on nothing but generalizations from experience, an effort that Husserl will subject to devastating criticism in his *Logical Investigations* (1900). For Mill only inductive inference is valid, and causality must be understood in Hume's way. Alexander Bain (1818–1903) typifies the positivist approach to psychology as "behavioral science". In the United States, Comte has had a fundamental influence through William James and John Dewey, who are intelligible only in the light of Positivism. Then come Bertrand Russell, Alfred North Whitehead, and the famed Vienna circle of logical positivists, from Mach and Wittgenstein to Reichenbach, Carnap and Ayer. From them other terminologies arise: linguistic analysis, scientific philosophy, philosophy of science, and many others. Always, however, the same basic concept of ultimate reality underlies the terminology, namely, the confinement of man within the cosmos and the reduction of human knowledge to nothing but the sensory. The absence of God and of anything specifically rational in man are one and the same through them all.

One must pay especial attention, however, to the coming impact of Charles Darwin (1809–82), whose theory of evolution among living things in his *Origin of Species* (1859) will seem to provide the apodictic scientific corroboration of this positivistic religion of progress. For Marx' collaborator Engels it represented the final victory of atheism in human philosophy. But it is the British philosopher Herbert Spencer (1820–1904), with his *Synthetic Philosophy* (1860), who symbolizes best the generalized culmination of Comte's influence upon Western education and culture. He pioneered the extension of Darwin's scientific theory of evolution from living things to all reality as such. Thus the concept of progress in Comte's philosophical religion becomes "evolutionism", an extrapolation in which Comte's Positivism seems indeed to be established once and for all by empirical science as the only possible philosophy in the new age of the Copernican revolution. Philosophy is nothing but the generalized statement of the findings of the empirical sciences. Philosophy disappears as the historic discipline with its own proper object, the existence of things, and its own proper method, the use of human reason as a distinct and higher kind of knowledge.

All of this elaborates the intellectual mechanism of the apostasy from God, one that functions so smoothly and with such apparent apodictic truth that the very name of God disappears from the textbooks, the university classes, the conversations, and the lives of the young. It is taken for granted at the outset of all teaching and research that God is not only an unnecessary hypothesis, as Laplace's commentary on the Copernican revolution in astronomy puts it, but an impossible one. All of this transpires, of course, because the true science of metaphysics, at the very heart of the intellectual heritage of Western mankind, has been replaced in a new kind of philosophy by mathematical physics, which studies the forms and motions of bodily things rather than the existence of things as such, whether corporeal or not.

But this cluster of later positivistic stars, so to speak, in remarkable coincidence with Darwin, belongs to the coming times of the applications. The metaphysics for this seemingly apodictic truth of Positivism did not receive its final form in Comte. There is yet another aspect of the metaphysical completion of Modern Philosophy which will seal the cultural victory of Darwin, Spencer, and evolutionism. This was accomplished by Hegel in Germany, to whom therefore one must turn for the completion of the metaphysics of Modern Philosophy and its apostasy from God.

VI

HEGEL: THE DIALECTIC OF THE OUTMODED PAST

With Georg Wilhelm Friedrich Hegel (1770–1831) the philosophical scenario changes mightily once again, from the University of Paris to the University of Berlin, from the mathematicism and mechanism of empiricism to vitalism, life philosophy, intuition, feeling, and the primacy of the experiencing self. These are the decades of Napoleon. His stunning military victories east of the Rhine and below the Alps installed new French Revolution governments across central Europe, awakened German nationalism, and shifted the balance of power in the Germanies from Vienna and Austria to Berlin and Prussia—a shift symbolized by his termination of Charlemagne's historic Holy Roman Empire in 1806. Men felt all this as another mighty sea change in human culture, and nowhere so much as in Germany: *Sturm und Drang,* "Storm and Stress", the age of Romanticism. Goethe (1749–1832), with his Faustian and Spinozan poetry, and Beethoven (1770–1827), with his powerful music, are contemporaneous with Hegel. Such is Hegel's setting.

Telescoping the setting to philosophy, it is the time of German Idealism. What, exactly, is this philosophical phenomenon? In the textbooks on the history of philosophy it is a teaching linked with three famous German philosophers, Fichte (1762–1814), Hegel (1770–1831), and Schelling (1775–1854), in the *Sturm und Drang* period after Napoleon in the first half of the last century. These men are not only philosophers but professors of philosophy: they represent the final triumph of Modern Philosophy in the academic institutions of the West and hence in Western culture. They form a school of philosophy because all are disciples of Immanuel Kant, disciples who are dissatisfied with Kant's declaration that ultimate reality, the *Ding-an-Sich,* is unknowable.

Each of these philosophers, leaders of the intellectual life of emerging Prussian Germany and the University of Berlin, professes to have a knowledge of this reality by his own powerful personal intuition. He proceeds to teach this intuitive grasp of the noumenon to his students and to publish the university lectures that he gives. What do the political authorities at Berlin and the leaders of the established Protestant Evangelical church have to say? The intuition of these Idealists is closely related to the fierce upswing of German nationalism after Napoleon; it seems to be quite Christian, for it uses the terminology of Christianity in a way that moves with the times. Thus the German Idealists in their own setting were actually great national heroes, whose university lectures were intellectual events.

What then is meant by Idealism? It expresses the basic concept that these disciples of Kant take from their master: the a priori forms of the human mind are the determining factor of both knowledge and reality. Thought and being are identical. Being and reality are projections of human subjectivity. Hence, each one can say out of his Kantian formation, my intuition of reality *is* reality: it constitutes reality in its very being. In truth, Idealism is the immense philosophical deceit that simply asserts that phenomena, as I see them, are reality and the whole of reality. In contemporary terminology, this is expressed simply as "it's true for *me*", hence no further discussion.

The presence of Spinoza's metaphysics should be noted. With the German Idealists Spinoza emerges into full view as the seminal metaphysical thinker of Modern Philosophy. For all their verbal Christian dress, their use of Christian terms and concepts, although with changed meanings, these thinkers are Spinozan pantheists who verge upon open atheism and lead directly to atheism in Marx and Nietzsche, their own immediate followers.

Thought and being are indeed identical in God, but not in human beings. In man thought is always an activity of a particular substantial reality, this human person or that one. It provides valid knowledge of substantial realities, ourselves, and others, but our thoughts are not the same thing as those realities. When the intellectual heritage of the metaphysics that is open to the higher and transcendent reality disappears, a metaphysics of man-centrism enters. This process began with Descartes and Spinoza. The German Idealists complete the process by way of Kant's Subjectivism.

Among the Idealists Hegel is preeminent; he deserves to represent them all. In a true sense he completes Spinoza and thus finalizes Modern Philosophy from the metaphysical point of view, a matter that the following summary of the main points of his teaching will endeavor to clarify.

Hegel was born in Stuttgart into a comfortable middle-class family. Noting the talent of their son, his parents gave him the full schooling of the day and sent him after gymnasium to the University of Tübingen, where he enrolled in theology, with Schelling as a schoolmate, intending to study for the Lutheran ministry. Hegel completed the full course in Protestant theology; at the end, however, he did not take up the ministry. In a striking shift of direction he gave up his calling, enrolled in philosophy, and prepared himself for a career as a professor of philosophy. Throughout his theological studies, as a matter of fact, he was already gravitating toward the other field. Now he could study natural science as well as philosophy and follow the deep personal attraction he felt for Spinoza, Rousseau, and Kant. Perhaps the most significant expression of his position and of the orientation of his own life and teaching was his repeated admonition to his students: "If you wish to be a philosopher, you must steep yourself in Spinoza."

Appointments followed to posts at Bern, Frankfurt, and Jena, where he witnessed Napoleon's battle of Jena in 1806, apparently unmoved. He went on to Nürnberg. In 1818 he was appointed to the chair of philosophy at the University of Berlin, the highest position in Prussian academic life. Until his death in 1831 Hegel enjoyed supreme fame and influence in this post, where his philosophical lectures were events of the day in Berlin, and indeed for all Germany. In the meantime his works had been appearing, beginning with the fundamental *Phenomenology of the Spirit* (1807), the *Encyclopedia of the Philosophical Sciences* (1817), and the *Philosophy of Law* (1821). The *Philosophy of History*, perhaps his most famous work and the one that exemplifies best how Hegel saw the working of his dialectic, was published posthumously by his students from lecture notes, together with the deeply significant *Philosophy of Religion.*

The key to Hegel's concept of ultimate or metaphysical reality is without doubt what he calls the *Weltgeist*, the World Spirit, together with its relationship to mankind and world history. For Hegel is the philosopher of the philosophy of history, who transfers this branch of philosophy from the subordinate position it held in Augustine's Christian Philosophy to the position of first philosophy. Thus yet another move is made to fill the void created by the elimination of metaphysics from this central, intellectually controlling and illuminating role as the seventh of the liberal arts.

Another way of putting this is to say that Hegel is the philosopher who announces the advent of historicism in contemporary culture. One might well say that he implements comprehensively what Comte had in mind to do with his three ages, which fulfill Voltaire's philosophy of history. But Voltaire and Comte were pioneers who put the beginnings in place: it is Hegel who completes this historicism, generalizes it philosophically, and sets the stage for its social application by Marx and Nietzsche later in the nineteenth century and throughout the twentieth.

There is no way to understand Hegel's concept of reality except through Spinoza. He assumes from Spinoza without question that there is no reality but this visible cosmos. The heritage of the metaphysics of the ascent from it has disappeared. Coining the terminology that the future Existentialists will exploit, Hegel stresses that reality is not *Das Sein*, the abstract concept of being that prevailed in the pre-Germanic era of Greek philosophy, but rather *Dasein*, what "exists there", concretely, in this visible cosmos.

Then Hegel transcends Kant and transforms Spinoza. As to Kant, Hegel professes to know the noumenon. Our cognitive activity, he teaches, creates both phenomena and noumena. All the real is rational, and all the rational is real. How can this make sense? It does so because the absolute Spirit, which unconsciously animates and energizes the cosmos, needs to exteriorize himself (or itself). This takes place in the consciousness of man, where the Divine pushes into self-expression. Man is the highest expression of The Divine. Hegel, however, is not thinking of individuals but rather of mankind as a whole in human history.

Granted that Spinoza's metaphysical world view is correct, then it appears self-evident that mankind is the highest manifestation or mode of *Deus sive Natura.* Thus, considered qualitatively, there is actually no significant reality but human history. This history is animated and makes progress because it is pushed onward, forward, upward by the World Spirit. Bergson, the direct and conscious disciple of Hegel and especially Schelling, will have something similar in mind with his *Élan vital* in the times of philosophical evolutionism after Darwin and Spencer.

It follows, Hegel teaches, that there is no static reality. All reality is dynamic. Everything moves. John Dewey, who did his doctorate at Johns Hopkins on Hegel, will say in summary, "To exist is to be in process, in change". Thus Hegel is transcending Kant, whom all his students at the University of Berlin knew well. "I shall explain the noumenon to you. It is not unknowable. We can know it by this intuition, this intuitive insight into the progressive character of historic human life on this planet." And at the same time Hegel is transforming Spinoza, who had a rather early and static view of the cosmos. The transformation of Spinoza's metaphysics takes place by means of the dialectic. It explains how the progressive movement takes place that constitutes reality in its very being.

With the dialectic one comes to the central and architectonic principle of Hegel's thinking, the one that governs all his treatises on the branches of philosophy, and especially his philosophy of history. The World Spirit, Hegel tells his classes at the University of Berlin, pushes reality forward by a dialectical process.[1] You must acquire a historical consciousness, for only so can you grasp reality as it really is, as a process of becoming taking place concretely in human history. Reality is not being but becoming, and becoming is simply history. There is no other reality, by definition, by Spinoza's definition. But now we can complete his excessively static metaphysics, Hegel teaches, by understanding the inner dynamism of cosmic reality.

It is important to note that Hegel's dialectic comes forth from his Spinozan concept of ultimate reality, and especially out of its limitation of reality to nothing but this visible cosmos. Existence is *Dasein,* being active in the cosmos, not dead and passive substance or the abstraction called "being", but *Geist:* process, life, Spirit. Truth is the living unity of this moving universal Substance with the subjectivity of individual consciousness. When you see this, Hegel explains to his students, you are on the way to becoming modern philosophers and modern men. You will begin to think in harmony with the way reality is. For the World Spirit works in and through the many individual modes of consciousness, and from them to all the other branches of philosophy, then into all the other sciences and disciplines of education, and thus out into all the forms of culture.

The World Spirit, Hegel states in his sweeping historical way, has had the patience to pass through all the cultural forms of mankind in their long temporal

[1]See Excerpts for Part Three, Hegel, p. 433.

series, shaping by its immense labor the varied content of world history. Hegel stresses the concreteness of it all: any particular person or cultural form exists only in its relations to its historical and cultural environment. One ceases to think of a substance or a thing, for we now realize that reality is nothing but a continually changing process of events—namely, a human history. Thus Hegel builds the basis for his transfer of the philosophy of history to first philosophy, where it functions as if it were the science of metaphysics, now no longer understood and indeed long forgotten.

Hegel is ready now to introduce his students into the mystery of the dialectic. Let me tell you how to think, he suggests; you must learn to think dialectically. To begin with, you must cease distinguishing between logic and metaphysics, as Greek philosophy always did. The dialectic is one and the same in thought and reality, the same law for both. You learn how to think dialectically by observing how history advances. It moves by clashes and conflicts of opposites. This is the law of progress. This law governs all movement forward in time. Progress is the dialectic of the World Spirit in its onward march through time. By making this dialectic one's own, one becomes a modern person who understands the secret of human progress. This is to cross the watershed from the medieval past to the modern age. Echoes of this rhetoric pervade the words of those today who reject Tradition as automatically invalid, since it is part of the past.

Hegel emphasizes that in the past, under the influence of Aristotle and his *Organon,* men had only a static logic, which set up a primary opposition between being and nothingness, supposing that things cannot coexist with their contradictories. But I tell you, Hegel stresses, things *do* coexist with their contradictories.[2] The political and social life of mankind in history exhibits it before your eyes. Did we not say that concrete historical reality is all that the human mind can know, because nothing else exists? The traditional logic of Aristotle is useless for understanding the processes of change that enable history to make progress. Aristotle regards the contradictory as totally excluded: a thing cannot be and not be simultaneously. He conceives this to be necessarily true, always and everywhere. Every A totally excludes every not-A, because for Aristotle this not-A is a mere abstraction, a nothing. But in real life this not-A is actually something positive: it is B, something that exists over against A and in clashing opposition to it.

Thus the contradiction is really a relation between two opposed things, which can be removed by a relational synthesis between them. This removal is motion: it moves from both positions to a new one, a synthesis of A and B. This is the way the real and concrete life of *Dasein* operates. This movement from contradictories in opposition and conflict is the dialectic. It keeps on moving, furthermore, because the synthesis will generate a new thesis position, which will begin to evoke its own opposition, a new antithesis to it, and thus movement takes

[2]See Excerpts for Part Three, Hegel, p. 433.

place to yet another synthesis. This continues without end as the hidden dynamism of progress in history.

The key point in understanding Hegel is of course the substrate of Spinozan metaphysics, which he assumes at the outset and which confines his vision to the social and political affairs of the earthly scene. For on this horizontal human level there are indeed a measure and an appearance of truth in the view that human groups soon generate out of themselves their own opposites or contradictions and fall into conflict with them. Hegel calls any initial human position a "thesis", whether in thought or in some social grouping in human history. The opposing doctrine or social movement that the thesis generates out of itself he calls the "antithesis". The dialectic comes into operation by means of the conflict and tension between these two: it drives men forward, out of whatever historical position in which they find themselves, whether in matters of doctrine or of social practice, to a new "synthesis". This synthesis leaves the original thesis behind as a mere relic in past human history: it is literally dead, outmoded, irrelevant to the newly created times. Hegel's new logic, then, is dialectical: it is dynamic, not static; it is simultaneously the law of both thought and historical reality. One may call it quite correctly the dialectic of the outmoded past, for it makes impossible the very idea of a teaching that hands on to the young a heritage of abiding truths and values.

What can be said about Hegel's dialectic? Perhaps the most basic comment is the fact that it presupposes the Spinozan metaphysics of modern atheism. It works only within the cosmic confines of Spinoza's pantheism, and indeed only within the one aspect of the cosmos called human history on the planet earth. On this horizontal level of human life and conflicts, it has a certain limited truth and application. This provides the rationale for moving the philosophy of history, which is the dialectic in operation, to the position of first philosophy, where it can illuminate and control the understanding of the rest of education and culture.

When Hegelianism is seen as historicism, the philosophical completion of Spinoza, then his thinking comes into view as the completion of the apostasy from God. It presupposes the absence of the metaphysics that is open to the ascent above and beyond this cosmos to the level of the abiding intelligible truths and the changeless Supreme Being. The sublime truth, as Aquinas described it, reached in the metaphysics of Christian Philosophy, has completely disappeared. The dialectic is horizontalism rationalized. But in the vertical dimension of intelligible reality, the logic of the principle of contradiction continues as valid as ever, for it bears upon the question of being and nonbeing. Hegel never asks the questions about existence. He too presupposes the eternity of matter, confining his vision and his philosophy to its successive forms, now understood as the forms of things in history.

With this one can summarize readily the principal components of the Hegelian philosophy, for they are direct applications of this dialectic. It is the architectonic factor in his philosophy, his claim to originality, and the fundamental reason why he has become "the professors' professor" in academic life since his time. He has taught contemporary mankind how to think in a way that eliminates the very idea of an abiding truth, whether in the realm of the natural metaphysics of mankind or in the handing on of a body of revealed truth in revealed religion. This new concept of truth, always at least implicitly looking upon the past with its heritage as something outmoded, is the first and most essential application of the dialectic.

Hegel teaches contemporary man to expect no intellectual peace. Only the search for provisional truth remains in ever-new syntheses, always in the hope that the flux will generate progress. Truth is never something seen and possessed. Always there are the further qualification and the expectation of new perspectives. When truths of a heritage are opposed, the Hegelian mentality will bless the conflict and mutter the hope that something good will emerge from it. Men are taught that it is somehow impossible, in the sense of no longer good, to be a person of any thesis, however venerable a past it may have had. One can be only a person of the antithesis, and if this feels psychologically unsuitable, then there is the wide variety of ways in which one can be a person of the synthesis.

Hegel himself was quite aware of the task and purpose of his dialectic to redefine the concept of truth. He wished to change fixed concepts into fluid ones. No concept or idea has an abiding meaning. There are no such things as eternal truths, expressible in propositions that are valid always and everywhere. Hegel represents a fundamental completion in the metaphysics of Modern Philosophy because he states all philosophical concepts in essentially historical terms, then applies the historicism to all the other branches of philosophy and on to all the other disciplines of education and approaches in the activities of human culture. His dialectic is a way of thinking in which every truth, when opposed, is constrained to leave its position and move on to what is considered a new truth, conceived as a synthesis of the conflict between the thesis and its antithesis. Thus no truth abides. "Truth is the daughter of time", as the motto of Giordano Bruno expressed it, the plaything of this dialectic of the outmoded past. Absolute historicism follows immediately, complete historical and cultural relativism. Thought and being are identical. But being is process and change. Hence truth changes in man and with man, for both are nothing but the product of human history and its succession of cultural developments.

What are the consequences of this philosophical doctrine for the concept of God? It should be noted at the outset that Hegel is not a declared and professed atheist like *les philosophes* of Paris and Auguste Comte. But neither is the atmosphere at Berlin like that of revolutionary France: Protestantism is the established religion. It has the support of a stern political censorship. Furthermore, while specialists debate on the personal religion of Hegel, it seems probable that he was dedicated to a pantheistic religiosity expressed in Christian terminology. Thus his philosophical works seemed quite acceptable to the form of Protestantism that was beginning to take shape in northern Germany. This will be discussed further below in connection with Hegel's *Philosophy of Religion.*

With this said, one can analyze Hegel's concept of God. It is in no sense that sublime truth, as Aquinas called it, about the transcendent Supreme Being seen metaphysically in the heritage of Christian Philosophy. Hegel uses the word "God" constantly, as Spinoza also did, calling him "the Absolute" and "the World Spirit", his favorite names for God. This is deceptive from the viewpoint of revealed religion, however, for Hegel is using these words in the new pantheistic meaning coming from Spinoza's metaphysics. This Absolute is immanent in the cosmos, and now specifically in the human consciousness that makes up the human world of history, with its institutions, social entities and movements, and especially its organization into political states. The Absolute is not prior to this world of men or above it; it is not the creating source whence earthly reality derives, nor is it distinct from it.

Thus the Absolute is not a "substance", meaning an existing and already achieved Being or Reality, but rather a "subject", that is, a process of development in and of and through the earthly human social reality.[3] Thus Hegel's world view and its dialectic stand at the origin of the many process philosophies and concepts of God-as-Process that have arisen since Hegel in the period of the applications of Modern Philosophy. For Hegel the Absolute does not yet really exist, but it will exist at the term of its evolution. It is striving to exist. Before being fully itself, it is the process by which this earthly reality, namely, mankind and human social cultures, develop and become. All of this, of course, is conceived philosophically by Hegel long before it will seem to be a scientifically supported discovery, changing its name from historical development to evolutionism. It is not difficult to recognize a metaphysical correspondence with Comte's law of the three historical stages and the worship of humanity as the great Being. Underneath both forms of completion stands Spinoza's metaphysics of modern atheism.

What of men in this process of the Absolute? Here again the doctrine of Hegel will be significant for the young Karl Marx when he enrolls at the University of Berlin. Particular things, Hegel teaches, and this includes individual persons, are only moments or phases in this developmental process of the Absolute. To consider a thing by itself, separately from this larger process that constitutes it, is to view it abstractly. By a strange inversion, concrete individual things will seem in Hegelianism to be abstractions. The future existentialist revolt will be a response to this aspect of the Hegelian suppression of the human person as much as a reaction to the Positivist approach to man as an object. But the future Marxism will subscribe fully to Hegel's doctrine that a human being becomes a person only

---

[3] See Excerpts for Part Three, Hegel, p. 433.

insofar as he gives up his claim to individual uniqueness as a subject, content to be nothing but an aspect of a larger social whole.

It is becoming clear why the authorities of the Prussian state viewed the professor of philosophy at the University of Berlin with benevolence. In his *Philosophy of Law* (1821) Hegel teaches that the political state is the moving progress of God in the world, to be honored as a reality at once human and divine. "Progress" is the operating word in this concept: it denotes the presence of the dialectic, the dynamic process or mechanism by which political states are constituted as the embodiment of social movement in human history. From the viewpoint of the present study, it is clear that the fundamental metaphysics of pantheism is leading directly to the divinization of the state as the supreme manifestation of the World Spirit moving in historical time. This brings into view the *Philosophy of History*, Hegel's most famous work and the one that exhibits best the practical application of his dialectic.

For Hegel, change and flux are the very essence of reality, and reality is concentrated in the dialectical history of mankind within this present time and cosmos. History is nothing else than the dialectic spread out and made visible in time. It would be a mistake to think that Hegel arrives at his philosophy of history from a study of the documented facts of historical science in the manner of the historians. The philosophy of history results rather from what Hegel calls philosophical insight making application of the dialectic: it is produced from within the subjective self of the thinker who imposes a dialectical interpretation upon the data of history.

It is instructive to survey Hegel's *Philosophy of History* in comparison with Voltaire's earlier work under the same title. It is difficult to avoid the thought that Hegel did his planning with Voltaire before him as a model, so close is his basic outline. Hegel, like Voltaire, begins his narrative of universal history with China. Then he sees a succession in mankind's cultural life that moves from the Far East toward the Near East and then to the West, exactly as in Voltaire. But in Hegel the World Spirit, a concept totally lacking in Voltaire, becomes ever more visibly incarnate in the process.

Anti-Semitism of a strange new intellectual type thus enters the academic institutions of France and Germany. This substitution of China for the Hebrews at the beginning of the historical narrative is a fundamental application of Spinoza's atheistic hermeneutics of revealed religion. Seen in the light of the revealed religion that has been handed on in the heritage of catechetical teaching in the manner already described, this rewriting of human history is a rejection of the very idea that the Hebrews are the bearers to mankind of a revelation from the transcendent Supreme Being. This rejection of the position of the Hebrews in the universal history of mankind represents the secularization of historical understanding and the point at which the emergence of philosophical atheism in Western culture becomes most acute. We shall have to return to the future cultural applications of this fundamental shift in Western intellectual life.

When the World Spirit moves dialectically from the Far East to the West across the centuries of cultural life, the age of the civilizations since 4000 B.C., what exactly does Hegel mean? He is quite explicit: the West is "the German world", the object of the fourth and concluding part of his work. "The German world", he writes,

> took up the Roman culture and religion in their completed form and proceeded to develop them in three periods. . . . The first half of the sixteenth century forms the beginning of the third period. Secularity now appears as gaining a consciousness of its own intrinsic worth—it becomes aware of its having a value of its own in the morality, rectitude, probity, and activity of man. . . . This third period of the German world extends from the Reformation to our own times. . . . Not until this era is the freedom of the Spirit realized.

Thus Hegel, like Voltaire, is a philosopher of secularism. He accomplishes this philosophical result, however, not in opposition to the Christian name but by a consistent redefinition of the meaning of the basic concepts denoted by this name. Thus Hegel becomes the founding father of Liberal Protestantism and Catholic Modernism, a matter to which we must return in connection with his *Philosophy of Religion* and especially when the future applications of Modern Philosophy are considered.

When Hegel presents the German world as the goal of the dialectic of the World Spirit across six thousand years of human culture, he has explicitly in mind the Prussian state of his own day. For him this is the final embodiment of the World Spirit and the final aim of its progression, a concept to which one now must turn in order to understand fully what Hegel has in mind with the application of his dialectic in the *Philosophy of History*. "The principles of the successive phases of Spirit", he writes, "that animate the nations in a necessitated gradation are themselves only steps in the development of the one universal Spirit. . . . This necessarily implies that the present form of Spirit comprehends within it all earlier steps. . . . The life of the ever-present Spirit is a circle of progressive embodiments."

With this concept of the embodiment of the World Spirit in the succession of political entities across time, the student of Hegel stands before his work *The Philosophy of Law*, which may well be called the rationale of the totalitarian state, and which reveals how truly it has been said that Marx can be understood only in the light of Hegel's philosophy but in an application that Hegel himself did not foresee. "The true state", Hegel writes, "is the realization of freedom. The state is the Spirit that lives in the world and there consciously realizes itself. . . . The state is the march of God through the world. . . . The state is the world that the Spirit has made for itself. . . . We must therefore worship the state as the manifestation of the Divine on earth."

"The state", Hegel concludes in this treatise, *The Philosophy of Law,* "is nothing but the organization of the concept of freedom. The determinations of the individual will are given objectivity by the state, and it is through the state alone that they attain truth and realization. The state is the sole condition of the attainment of the particular end and good." It has seemed appropriate to cite this passage by way of exception in the present work, because this redefinition of individual liberty will become one of the key points in Karl Marx' coming application of the Hegelian philosophy. And one should include the famous passage that concludes *The Philosophy of Law: Die Weltgeschichte ist das Weltgericht:* "Out of this dialectic rises the universal Spirit, the unlimited World Spirit, pronouncing its judgment upon the finite nations of the world's history; for the history of the world is the world's court of justice." It was recorded by his students at Berlin that there was something of the prophet's stance about Hegel as he stood at his professor's podium—but of course, one must add, in a quite secularized form.

This leads to the final point in this summary of Hegel, drawn from his treatise *The Philosophy of Religion,* which represents the advent of what Karl Jaspers will call "philosophical faith" upon the contemporary religious scene. In the movement of the World Spirit from the Greco-Roman past to the Germanic world, the Bible has been left behind. Continuing and completing the atheistic hermeneutics of Spinoza, Hegel sees the Bible not as a witness to the historical truth of interventions by a transcendent and personal Supreme Being but as nothing but (again the phrase of philosophical reductionism) a book of symbols that can be understood by modern man only after a process of philosophical reinterpretation.

Thus Hegel subordinates religion to philosophy by the dialectical movement of the World Spirit in space and time. He brings religion inside philosophy, so to speak, seeing philosophy as a superior wisdom that studies, judges, and evaluates religion. In this he is quite logical, for in the Spinozan metaphysics religion cannot derive from an independent and higher order of knowledge. Beginning with the name of God, which occurs in Hegel as freely as in Spinoza, Hegelianism makes use of all the terminology of the Judeo-Christian heritage but with a philosophically redefined and reinterpreted meaning. To give but one example: the "Incarnation", according to Hegel, is nothing but an early mythical expression of the truth of the dialectic, which reveals the progressive incarnation of the absolute Spirit in human history. It is this philosophical reinterpretation of the heritage of revealed religion that led Kierkegaard, Hegel's coming opponent in religious matters, to declare him merely an atheist who disguised his unbelief in the Spinozan mode. In any case, Hegel certainly has a "reinterpreted" or "modern" understanding of the Judeo-Christian religious Tradition, to which we must return when the applications of Modern Philosophy are considered. For Hegel is the philosophical progenitor of Liberal Protestantism, Catholic Modernism, and Reform Judaism.

VII

CONCLUSION: THE METAPHYSICS OF
APOSTASY FROM GOD

A New Personal, Social, and Pastoral Problem in Christendom

The completion of Modern Philosophy was accomplished in the first half of the nineteenth century in the turbulent times after the French Revolution and Napoleon. It was a completion, of course, only from the viewpoint of its metaphysics, its idea of ultimate reality, its fundamental world view. Then the contemporary period opens, from midnineteenth century to the present, devoted to the various applications of this metaphysical world view to all aspects of life and culture. These applications will color variously the personal, political, social, and especially the religious life of Western mankind; always, however, they will rest on the one and same Spinozan metaphysics of modern atheism, expressed and developed in these three bold and far-reaching types of finalization.

These three influential philosophical personalities, Kant, Comte, and Hegel, took the method of Descartes and the pantheism of Spinoza, together with the input from the thinkers in the two lines of development from them, and produced the metaphysical completion of Modern Philosophy. Each has his own system, his characteristic way of bringing Modern Philosophy to its completion. Later thinkers who make the applications naturally will mix them in different ways and proportions. But the thing itself, Modern Philosophy as an entity of the mind, in its metaphysical view of ultimate reality, stands finished and complete in their work. From the viewpoint of metaphysics, there will be no new and creative work but only the socially influenced applications. These will indeed be in a sense the practical test of their truth, as William James, for whom the test was positive, says in his *Pragmatism*. But William James lived and thought in the rosy glow of the nineteenth century and its religion of progress, before the cataclysmic wars, social upheavals, and ecological menace of the present century.

Always the heart of the matter is the bias against the metaphysics of Christian Philosophy. Kant and Comte reject outright the idea of such a philosophical science: they continue and complete the Cartesian substitution of mathematical physics for the science of metaphysics as understood in the Western heritage since Plato, Aristotle, and Augustine. Hegel does not reject the idea of a "metaphysics", but he changes its nature and meaning by his new "dialectic", his new way of understanding ultimate reality as he thinks it really is, as a moving dynamic within this cosmos. In a sense Hegel completes the completion: learn how to think by my dialectic, he tells contemporary mankind, and you will be a modern person. Until now men have thought in a static way, using Aristotle's logic. That is now in the outmoded past. You must think dynamically, by my dialectic, if you wish to be a modern person. It is the temptation to use the mind in the atheistic way.

Do these three influential and representative modern personalities also complete the philosophical apostasy from God that began with Descartes and Spinoza and has been developing since them? Indeed they do. Kant, Comte, and Hegel finish the foundations upon which the applications both in militant professed atheism and in secular humanism will take their stand. In these three seminal metaphysicians of the modern mind, agnosticism and professed atheism are established in Western civilization as the educated person's understanding of existence. There is no personal and transcendent Supreme Being. Matter is eternal. It is simply there for men to shape, form, and enjoy. The cosmos, multitudes of lesser minds will repeat parrotlike, is all that is or ever was or ever will be. Materialism becomes the first principle and point of departure. The question of existence, why things are, apart from what they are or how they are oriented in the cosmos, is never raised. The seventh of the seven liberal arts, Augustine's "science of wisdom and virtue", has faded from the human scene as the age of the civilizations plunges onward into the twentieth century.

The disciples of Kant, Comte, and Hegel will make various applications of atheism in education and culture in the century and a half from their day to the present. Much philosophizing will continue, of course, but it will consist largely of commentary upon Kant, Comte, and Hegel. In the applications these three will be mixed in differing ways, giving various flavors and colorations to philosophical writing. But underneath the surface, and beneath the various personal expressions, there will always be the Spinozan metaphysics of modern atheism as the substrate of the policies and programs of social planning.

What would Augustine say? Plato? The prehistoric primitives? "We have seen all this already", they would say; "it is simply our idolatry over again in an updated form." For when the ascent to the transcendent Supreme Being is blocked, and young students are precluded from making it, then people begin to think that "the Divine" manifests itself in mankind and that progress in the empirical sciences is its "revelation". Progressive mankind becomes the idol.

But is this true in reality? Will it be good for mankind as the twentieth century proceeds? With such questions in mind one can turn to a short review of the chief applications of modern philosophical atheism, a sketch of their threatening personal and social outcomes and especially to the consideration of philosophical anthropology. For what happens to the human person, human dignity, and human personal rights when this metaphysics of apostasy from God is applied to the human mode of existing?

We began the study of Modern Philosophy by recognizing that it contains a challenging problem. Now we can see the fundamental nature of this problem. It is the substitution of a different kind of metaphysics, actually mathematical physics, in the position of the seventh liberal art. This erodes the natural foundation for receiving the deposit of faith as the revelation that comes from the Supreme Being.

This will be the context of the First Vatican Council and the ensuing pastoral program of the Catholic Church for the renewal of Christian Philosophy. This renewal will be the object of study in Part Four, especially from the viewpoint of the philosophy of man. For without the metaphysics that is open to the transcendent Supreme Being, the nature of man suffers a reduction that divests human life of its meaning and purpose.

One should not think that the various applications of this other and different metaphysics, which is actually an option for darkness and for the confinement of the human spirit within this cosmos, will be unattractive for modern man. On the contrary, the new metaphysics will generate deceptions that cannot be discussed, pierced, and solved on a superficial level. Liberty, equality, fraternity, social justice, personal liberty: these are all human and Christian ideals. But they can be sought apart from God, in the context of the new metaphysics. In such a case they turn to ashes and debase man in the process. This is doubly true when the new metaphysics is introduced into the realm of revealed religion, for then the very idea of an abiding deposit of faith is thrown into disarray.

For these and similar reasons, one must face the fact that Modern Philosophy generates a deep-seated challenge both to humanism and to revealed religion. Hence one must hold discussion of the coming applications firmly on the level of the underlying metaphysics, analyzing whether it closes off the ascent of the mind to intelligible reality, or whether it is the metaphysics of the open mind, open to the real existence of substantial reality above and beyond the material mode of existing. Only thus does the call of the Church for the renewal of Christian Philosophy become intelligible.

Regarding these metaphysicians of Modern Philosophy, and their disciples who will make the applications, Marx, Nietzsche, James, Dewey, Sartre, and so many others, Thomas Aquinas makes an important observation in his *Summa Theologiae* (II–II, 172, 6). Truth is related to intellectual pursuits, he writes, as goodness is related to things outside the mind. In those things it is impossible to find any existing reality that is entirely evil, deprived of all good whatsoever. Similarly, it is impossible that any body of knowledge or philosophical system be totally false, without any mixture of truths with its falsehood. Indeed, the intellect is enticed to false fundamental thinking through the appearance given to it by the truths it contains.

What is Aquinas saying? He is providing the principle that explains the superficial attractiveness of the various applications of Modern Philosophy. One must always go below the surface to analyze carefully whether the metaphysics of apostasy from God lies hidden beneath that surface. With this one can turn to Part Four, alerted to the metaphysical reason and the pastoral motive for the renewal of Christian Philosophy in the life of the contemporary Catholic Church.

PART FOUR

THE RENEWAL OF
CHRISTIAN PHILOSOPHY

Man in Contemporary Postmodern Times

INTRODUCTION

The Setting in the Contemporary Life of the Church

The study of philosophy acquires a new dimension of interest and even urgency in present times because of the implications of atheistic metaphysics for the natural values of personal and social living and because of its challenge to revealed religion. On the sands of the metaphysical rejection of God one can hardly build a preparation for the priesthood of the eucharistic Sacrifice, for the religious state of the way of perfection, or for the catechetical teaching of the deposit of faith. Hence the Catholic Church has set in motion a vast worldwide renewal of Christian Philosophy in all her schools as the fundamental prerequisite for all the other contemporary renewals: the liturgical, the catechetical, the spiritual, and all the other aspirations for renewal that characterize Catholic life today. Central to this renewal is the great need for a new and authentic philosophical anthropology, which has arisen in the twentieth century as a result of the self-confident but disastrous applications of atheistic metaphysics to social and personal life during the nineteenth century.

To embrace this setting for the renewal of Christian Philosophy adequately, one must bear in mind the stark contrast between the nineteenth and the twentieth centuries, which became socially visible with World War I and crudely tangible with World War II and the Holocaust. That other era, the modern period, with its "Modern Philosophy" and its "religion of progress", is receding rapidly into the past. The twentieth century is postmodern. The study of philosophy in the context of this renewal may well be placed under the patronage of Edith Stein, whose life, philosophical career, and death summarize its meaning and symbolize its significance. Edith Stein makes it clear that contemporary man, by the very movement of his vaunted historicism, has been carried beyond the scientific and philosophical categories of the modern age, which began in the Renaissance and ended with the outbreak of World War I: scientific, because in the present century the ongoing Copernican revolution in the empirical sciences has entered upon a surprising new revolution within itself, which points toward, and indeed demands, the metaphysics of openness to God; philosophical, because the metaphysics that confines the human spirit within the material cosmos belongs now to the out-moded past. All of this has become socially visible since World War I. But the dawn of this new age was already perceptible in the First Vatican Council to the religious observer with eyes to see.

First, then, one must survey briefly the applications of atheistic metaphysics, for they have brought home to man today his acute need for a more human philosophical anthropology. Then one can proceed to the drama of the renewal of Christian Philosophy, its significance for human values, and its necessity for handing on the deposit of faith in the same meaning that it had for the Apostles.

I

APPLICATIONS OF THE METAPHYSICS
OF MODERN PHILOSOPHY

It is fundamentally important to bear in mind that Modern Philosophy was constituted as a distinct kind of philosophy by its suppression of the science of metaphysics as it had been developed and taught in the intellectual heritage of the West from the Greeks through Augustine and Aquinas. It is equally important to note that metaphysics was taught in this heritage as the seventh of the seven liberal arts: it was the culmination of the enculturation of young Westerners into contact with their own roots and foundations for the values of their humanism. Furthermore, one will recall, the void left in intellectual and educational life by this suppression was filled by the introduction of mathematical physics into the culminating position as the capstone of the educational process. Thus philosophy itself suffered the typical reduction: it became nothing but the generalized statement of the findings of the empirical sciences.

This reduction characterizes all the applications. It constitutes an intellectual aversion to the transcendent Supreme Being and a conversion to this cosmos that is studied and exploited with an unbridled avidity, "liberated", as it were, from any idea of laws placed in natures when made by their Creator. This fundamental metaphysical situation of the modern period, with its Modern Philosophy, recurs in each of the applications. This, and not the details of the various applications, for which an abundant literature exists in each case, is the concern of the present chapter. For it is this metaphysical dimension in each application that evokes the insight that the very personhood of man is being endangered and that places the program for the renewal of Christian Philosophy in its true light.

The Atheistic Interpretation of the Copernican Revolution

Since philosophy is the seventh of the seven liberal arts, it cannot be kept in a vacuum separated from the other six areas of the curriculum, which study mental operations in the trivium and the cosmos in the sciences of the quadrivium. In practice, this means that the philosopher must be aware of the progress of the empirical sciences during modern times. And why is this? It is because philosophy performs the indispensable hermeneutical function with regard to the findings of those sciences. It is the rational light under which the findings are seen and interpreted—interpreted especially from the viewpoint of their meaning for mankind.

It is immediately clear that the interpretive hermeneutical function depends upon the nature of the metaphysical view of ultimate reality that philosophy brings to bear upon these findings of the empirical sciences. The nature of the rational light is determined by that fateful fork in the road that confronts the human mind as it works its way through ontology, the first half of the science of metaphysics. At the fork, one way leads up to the intelligible truths, on further to the intelligible realities, including the immaterial ones, and finally to that sublime truth that recognizes the transcendent Supreme Being as the existing reality who is the source of the acts of existing by which all other realities exist. When the mind takes the other way at the fork, it turns down within the cosmos. It forms its notion of ultimate reality by cosmic imagination. Thus it refuses the ascent to intelligible reality and natural theology: it becomes an inner-cosmic metaphysics that confines the human spirit within the cosmos. It erases the intelligibles from the intellectual horizon of the young generation, as Nietzsche puts it, and imprisons them within this world. This kind of metaphysical light is thus a form of darkness, a darkness visible, a darkness that seems to illumine the cosmic landscape and human life within the cosmos. Out of this negative illumination, professors will proclaim confidently to their students that the cosmos is all that is or ever was or ever will be.

To understand this confinement of the human mind to nothing but the material cosmos, one must analyze the reduction of human knowledge to nothing but cosmic imagination. This dehumanizes the human mode of existing, for it suppresses that second and higher kind of knowledge that the intellectual heritage of the West recognized as the specific difference between man and the lower animals, and indeed as the very image of God upon the brow of human persons.

It is fundamental, then, to analyze the Copernican revolution carefully, for one must face the question whether atheistic metaphysics is a function of the recent progress in the natural sciences. The atheistic way of philosophizing affirms this intrinsic connection. But is this reduction of metaphysics to nothing but a summary of findings made within the material cosmos by the empirical sciences valid from the viewpoint of truth? Is it viable from the viewpoint of the values upon which human personal and social living depend? What are the consequences for philosophical anthropology?

To get at the answer, one must recall that philosophy and empirical science function in different orders. They are separate liberal arts. Science makes progress by accumulating new facts, which frequently call for the substitution of new theories for older ones. A memorable instance was the removal of the geocentric world view, with the theory of the crystal spheres in which the sun and the stars revolved around the earth. Philosophy makes its progress in a quite different way because its core is the discipline of metaphysics, the study of existence as such. It functions and makes progress in a different intellectual order, namely, by deeper insight and understanding of the nature of existence and of the principles by which things exist.

The drama of Western intellectual life in the modern age has resulted from a strange parallelism: the time when the Copernican revolution in the empirical sciences began to gather momentum was the very time when the heritage of metaphysics, the natural philosophical science of God and his attributes, was suppressed in Western education and replaced by mathematical physics.

But how, exactly, did this lead to the idea that "atheism" and "the scientific world view" mean one and the same thing?

In answer, one must turn briefly to Sir Isaac Newton (1642–1727) and the so-called classical physics that he brought to completion. It dominates the nineteenth century and then is set aside in the twentieth century, not by philosophy but by the ongoing progress within empirical science. Newton, like Descartes, illustrates the effect upon young Westerners when they no longer receive their full intellectual heritage, the discipline of metaphysics as the seventh liberal art. All his life Newton maintained a personal fidelity to the God of his early Protestant upbringing, but his educated concept of God can only be called the result of the homemade metaphysics of an autodidact, so to speak. Let us hear his own words.

"The atoms", Newton writes, "are predominantly mathematical, but they are also nothing but smaller elements of sensibly experienced objects." Newton has in mind what scientists have come to call molar matter, matter in bodies that the unaided senses perceive. "All bodies are movable," Newton continues,

> and all are endowed with certain powers that we call the forces of inertia, by which they persevere either in their motion or their rest. And thence we conclude that these smallest particles are likewise extended and hard and impenetrable. All these things being considered, it seems probable to me that God in the beginning formed matter in solid, massy, hard, impenetrable, movable particles incomparably harder than any porous bodies compounded of them.

This opens the way to the "Clockmaker God" of the Deists, who launched the cosmic process, which then proceeds without him, not needing him because the bodies move in space by their own laws. The way is also open to the atheistic metaphysics of Kant, Comte, and Hegel. Thinkers arise who do not share Newton's theological restraint. The ancient Atomism of the Greek Materialists is adopted as the first principle and point of departure in interpreting the findings of the scientists. The atoms, hard and indivisible, are ultimate reality. Nothing else exists. Nothing else is needed. No Creator is needed. Matter is simply eternal. Thus the classical physics of Copernicus, Galileo, and Newton is open to the particular philosophical interpretation given during the nineteenth century by the metaphysics of Kant, Comte, and Hegel. The crystal spheres are gone, indeed, and this earth is no longer the center. Bodies move now in an infinite space, in the mathematician's infinity, meaning indefinitely extended, and governed by the laws of inertia.

Atheistic metaphysics was quick to declare the absentee God of Deism unnecessary and in practice nonexistent. The cosmos is reduced to nothing but a soulless mechanism composed of parts that have no function but motion in space, unrelated to any concept of purpose or human value. An entirely mechanical universe had resulted in this mental construct, despiritualized and dehumanized. Since this view of ultimate reality has now replaced the heritage of the ontology open to natural theology, and functions in the place of the seventh liberal art, it must be anticipated that its world view will shine forth upon the other six arts and through the young people thus educated out into every aspect of personal and social living. For example, if man is but a material mechanism, it is easy to imagine that mechanisms less functional, such as the bodies of unborn children, the handicapped, and the incapacitated elderly, are not worth enough to have any right to life. The human being is viewed only as a body in need of rest in order later to perform its functions in the work force. Therefore, any kind of pleasurable relaxation is positive with no reference to a morality itself based on a personalist ontology.

This view constitutes the metaphysical substrate of the applications under review here, and the general background that makes the contemporary renewal of Christian Philosophy a matter of pastoral necessity.

In this way the idea has been generated that atheism is the meaning of modern science. Everything is predicated on this atomism and the eternity of matter. Young people are recruited for atheistic projects and life-styles on the basis of this truncated view of existence. The more you know what science is, says, and does, so the intellectual solicitation goes, the more you will be an atheist. When the first Soviet cosmonaut returned from space in 1967, his announcement made worldwide headlines: there is no God sitting enthroned in space beyond the earth's atmosphere. This illustrates the disappearance of metaphysics, for it presumes a childish concept of the Supreme Being. It also illustrates the atheistic interpretation of the Copernican revolution. And it introduces the person and work of Karl Marx in his application of the metaphysics of modern philosophy.

Marx and Atheistic Communism

Karl Marx (1818–83) exemplifies forcefully the metaphysical roots of contemporary personal, religious, and social problems. To become a philosopher, we recall Hegel's admonition to his students at the University of Berlin: "You must steep yourself in Spinoza." The young Marx, enrolling there to study Hegelian philosophy, took the lesson to heart. He went on to become the founder of the social system that applies the world view of Spinoza, the metaphysician of modern atheism.

To understand Karl Marx as well as coming religious applications of Modern Philosophy, one must glance at the schism between the Hegelian Right and the Hegelian Left, which divided Hegel's students in the years after his death in 1831. For Hegel had left open an important question: Does religion have any existence apart from man and society? Is religion an aspect of the World Spirit moving progressively in time? Or is religion nothing but an objectivized experience of people in a given epoch? These questions are still with us today, as manifested in the religious relativism that presumes that all religions are equally valid, each being nothing but an expression of a particular culture. In this way, Christians can avoid what Kierkegaard called the "offensive challenge" of the absolute claims of Christ, in order to blend comfortably into the pluralistic mind set of our age.

The young Hegelians who were preparing for the Lutheran ministry proclaimed that religion is indeed an aspect of the World Spirit: religion makes progress in its movement by philosophical reinterpretation. These young men of the Hegelian Right went on to become the leaders of Liberal Protestantism and its characteristic Spinozan hermeneutics of the Bible.

Other young Hegelians, wanting nothing to do with this religiosity, formed the Hegelian Left, under the leadership of Ludwig Feuerbach (1804–72), author of the seminal *Essence of Christianity*. In it Feuerbach reduces religion to nothing but—again the phrase that shows the atheistic metaphysics at work—a projection of man, his feelings, and his experience of life out of a given historical situation. It is important to note Feuerbach's dehumanization of man summarized in his famous phrase "man is what he eats", an untranslatable play on the German words *Man ist was er isst.* This states the coming problematic of the atheistic philosophical anthropology: Is man nothing but matter? Physical energies? Limited to sense knowledge? Is the human soul a myth? Is the intelligence nothing but associations of images? This question, the impact of the atheistic metaphysics upon the human mode of existing, is an integral part of the renewal of Christian Philosophy, and we shall return to it later.

Karl Marx attached himself immediately to the Hegelian Left and made his own Feuerbach's doctrine on God and religion. "What do you affirm when you affirm God?" Feuerbach asks. "My answer: you affirm your own understanding. God is your highest idea and power of thought, . . . the sum of all the affirmations of your understanding." In the old "onto-theology", Feuerbach continues, human qualities were projected out upon an imaginary Supreme Being. This alienated those qualities from their own human selves. Then Feuerbach applies the Hegelian doctrine of alienation. Mankind is the only existing reality. Those alienated qualities must be returned from that imaginary location to their rightful possessors. In the preface of his book he foresees a reproach that he is reducing religion to nothing but illusion. "This would be true", he answers, "if I did not offer a positive part, namely, anthropology. While reducing theology to anthropology, I exalt anthropology into theology."

This is of course a strange theology, an intellectual perversion of the concept, for the *logos* concerning God, the natural science of God, is now totally absent. Feuerbach states repeatedly his thesis that religion is nothing but the projection of man's self-consciousness, in that it reveals his alienated and suffering human spirit. This is Hegel, indeed, and the entire Spinozan metaphysical thrust of Modern Philosophy, but it is also Marxism in germ.

Karl Marx adopted this ideology avidly, together with the atheistic interpretation of the Copernican revolution in the empirical sciences. Then he elaborated his own doctrine. He steeped himself at Berlin in Spinozan cosmic materialism and in the Hegelian Dialectic. Then he transferred to Paris, where he became equally at home in the world of Saint-Simon and Auguste Comte, the world of "scientific socialism". His career as a writer and social organizer began to unfold with a series of works that document and form the mind of atheistic communism. Here a set of points will be given briefly to indicate the logic of his doctrine.

1. The first principle and the light under which Karl Marx develops his teaching is the atheistic metaphysics of Spinoza. This cosmos is all that is. He simply begs the question of existence, the initial and central question of philosophy, for he assumes the eternity of the atoms of matter. On this intellectual substrate Marx accepts Feuerbach's concept of religion as one particular form of Hegel's alienations.

2. Marx then states his own logical corollary: all reality is economic, political, and social, for nothing is real except the life of mankind on earth. Marxism was born on the day when the youthful student of Hegel rejected the *Phenomenology of Spirit* while retaining the Hegelian dialectic. There is no need for a World Spirit moving through the structures and groupings of human history. The subject of historical evolution is simply men doing their work. Not the World Spirit but people working: there is no other reality.

3. Marx then puts the Hegelian dialectic to his own use for his analysis of this phenomenon, people working. The more you study this concrete social reality, Marx teaches, the more you realize that men are suffering from alienation. What they produce by their work is largely taken from them: the product of work becomes alienated from the worker. In fact he is enslaved, for he must sell his labor: he becomes nothing but one of the instruments of production, like the other machines, turning things out for others.

Many books have been written about this analysis of work and alienation that point out its simplistic reduction of the factors of production. Even Marxist authors in the twentieth century will write on the emergence of "the New Class" in Communist societies. In this present kind of philosophical study, however, one needs but note the essentials of Marx' own thinking in order to recognize the philosophical problem, namely, the presence of the modern metaphysics in Marx' mind and the absence of the human heritage in metaphysical thinking. Marxism thus becomes visible as the socially organized form of Modern Philosophy in its apostasy from the Supreme Being and hence in its dehumanization of man.

4. The doctrine of the New Man. At this juncture Marx began his intellectual cooperation with Friedrich Engels (1820–95) to elaborate jointly the concept of scientific socialism, which will produce a new and better human being, altruistic and unselfish. Men can realize their essence only in social life: it alone enables individuals to be what they could be and should want to be. For individuals are nothing apart from the social relationships in which they exist. Alienation results from a wrongly structured society. Capitalism manifests this evil acutely in social structures, but earlier societies were likewise incorrectly structured. Hence society must be changed. When this is done, people will cease their aggressiveness, their acquisitiveness, in a word, their selfishness: the New Man will emerge. The utopian socialisms of the past were ineffective because they were the work of idealists and dreamers. The New Man can come forth only if socialism is scientific, applying the sciences to structure society in a scientific way. This will produce the new human mode of existing. It is clear that Comte and Hegel both flow metaphysically into the thinking of Marx and Engels, and that philosophical anthropology is deeply involved.

5. Dialectical or historical materialism follows logically as the means for achieving this scientific socialism. This immense project for the creation of the New Man, so formidable and even crushing for man to face, is actually taking place in history and society because of the Hegelian dialectic. The project and process are actually under way. This is the meaning of human history. Hegel was correct in his dialectical way of thinking. As modern men, Marx and Engels conclude, we must think dialectically as we face the forces, stresses, and conflicts of social life and action. The onward and upward progressive sweep of the dialectic is producing this newly structured society before the very eyes of modern mankind. Individuals join this victorious progress when they adopt the dialectic as their personal mode of thought and action. Thus the theory of revolution is born. The dialectic operates in the conflicts of opposed groups in the class wars of economic and social life. These are simply forms in which matter energizes. Nothing else exists. Dialectical or historical materialism is the very nature, structure, and functioning of reality. "Philosophers thus far have only interpreted the world in various ways", Marx writes in his *Theses on Feuerbach.* "The task now is to change the world."

6. The theory of the epiphenomena, the next point of Marxist teaching, reveals anew the Spinozan metaphysics, which recognizes nothing but this material cosmos as ultimate reality. The phenomenon is the reality one sees, the reality of human labor producing the various aspects of man's life on earth. Reality is like a freight train loaded with lumber, steel girders, motor cars, refrigerators, and all the other products of the workers. As the train moves ahead in time, its wheels cast off a display of sparks as epiphenomena. They are all the other aspects of social life:

art, literature, philosophies, religions. All are nothing but reflections of economic life. Their character is determined by its character. Change the conditions of economic life, and you will change all those epiphenomena.[1] Religion in particular will vanish as scientific socialism with its scientific world view takes root in a population. In due time dialectical materialism will see to it that religion will be nothing but a memory in the museums.

7. The New Redemption is the final point in this summary of Marxist doctrine. Marxism becomes a strange form of religion in reverse, for Marx sees the proletariat, these oppressed and alienated workers of the world, as the "redeemer class". The dialectic of the class war is destined to cease—mysteriously somehow (and quite illogically)—and all mankind will be redeemed (to borrow and adapt an older word) by the sudden advent of the final and perfected classless society, a paradise upon earth. Such was the message and even prophetic tone of *The Communist Manifesto,* which Marx and Engels published in 1848.

8. The *Diamat:* philosophy becomes political ideology. With this slogan, the *Diamat,* dialectical materialism reaches into the present century as the political ideology organized by Vladimir Lenin (1870–1924), the most important disciple of Karl Marx. Taking seriously Marx' *Theses on Feuerbach,* "The task now is to change the world", Lenin organizes Marx' version of the metaphysics of Modern Philosophy into the driving political ideology of the social revolution. Marxism remained rather bookish theory until Lenin gave it its face and social reality. He did this as the consummate organizer of the Bolshevik Revolution in 1917 during Russia's collapse in World War I. Always considering himself a modern philosopher and dedicated to atheism as the scientific world view, Lenin personifies the movement of the Spinozan metaphysics out from the heartlands of the once-Christian West eastward into Asia. What was Lenin's secret? It was his insight into the practical necessity of a salaried elite of professional revolutionaries in order to bring Marx' philosophical project into social reality. This was the birth of the Communist party, exactly this elite of salaried activists on behalf of scientific socialism. One can be a professor of physics in a Western university, for example, or hold other similar positions and at the same time belong to this additionally salaried elite. This was Lenin's accomplishment. The elite grows mightily in the twentieth century, and its children form the New Class, with its own well-stocked grocery stores and all the rest.

With Lenin, then, Modern Philosophy does indeed become a political and social ideology. It is imposed upon minds by techniques of thought control, raising massively the question of philosophical anthropology. For it is dedicated to a pseudoreligious faith that the progress of science will establish atheism everywhere, simply by virtue of its progress. It assumes that individual men will find happiness

---

[1] See Excerpts for Part Four, Marx, p. 436.

and fulfillment in the process, amalgamating their lives into it as cogs in the new social machinery. This assumption appears quite different in the late twentieth century, however, than it did in late nineteenth century and casts a special light on the renewal of Christian Philosophy. This mechanistic approach to the human mode of existing, furthermore, did not go unchallenged even in Modern Philosophy, for a contrasting application, equally misguided from the viewpoint of philosophical anthropology, rose up against it.

Nietzsche and Heidegger: Existentialism as Individual Redemption

With this famous current of applied Modern Philosophy, it is Kant and Hegel who predominate from the metaphysical point of view, just as it is Comte and Hegel who stand behind Marx and Lenin. Hegel continues to contribute his dialectical thinking, the hallmark of the mind under the influence of Modern Philosophy. This existentialism, furthermore, is likewise a variation on the theme of Spinoza's metaphysics, the reduction of all reality to nothing but what the human type of senses perceive within this cosmos. There is a religiously oriented existentialism full of splendid insights, to be sure. But lacking an authentic ontology, it cannot effectively act to overcome the subjectivist individualism characterizing the mainstream.

Nietzsche stands opposite Marx, symbolic of a host of philosophers since Kant who resist the idea that mechanism is ultimate reality and that man is a mere machine. To the contrary: the human subject experiencing life in time is the ultimate reality, prior to and more fundamental than mathematical science and social structures.

This is a school of philosophical thought that has a special importance for the renewal of Christian Philosophy, for it will prove to contain its major obstacle. The most important names in the existentialist current bring the mind across the times from Kant to the present. Schopenhauer (1788–1860) and Kierkegaard (1813–55) come from Kant to Nietzsche himself (1844–1900). The school continues into the present century with Bergson (1859–1941), with the cluster of German Existentialists centering in Heidegger after World War I, and the derivative cluster of French Existentialists after World War II centering in Sartre.

This existentialism presents its world view in a wide variety of literary forms and with utmost individual self-expression. Can a unifying metaphysical substrate be identified that recurs underneath all the forms, the novels, plays, and poetry? It can indeed. It is the revolt against the reduction of the human mode of existing to nothing but the mechanical interplay of physical forces and energies. Existentialism is characteristically alienated from social structures, and not least from that rigid one of scientific socialism. While it too is born out of the emptiness left in the heritage of the liberal arts by the loss of authentic metaphysics, it continues to use the word "metaphysics", as Bergson in his *Introduction to Metaphysics* and Heidegger in his *Being and Time*. By this word it means its way of going beyond mathematical physics, but in no sense the ascent of the mind to intelligible reality and on to the sublime truth of the transcendent and personal Supreme Being.

Metaphysics, for the Existentialists, means nothing but the human reality as a form of biological life within this cosmos. To exist is to be there in the cosmos, experiencing life in time. This bold generalization, extending human life in time to mean reality as such, characterizes all the Existentialists. When the metaphysics of Christian Philosophy is no longer a part of their education, this vitalism can deceive religious thinkers such as Kierkegaard and the so-called Christian Existentialists generally: thus the Spinozan substrate, the absence of authentic metaphysics, becomes visible. For this entire school takes from Kant the basic doctrine of the primacy of the irrational in human life. This is the vitalism that Nietzsche expresses in his works and hands forward to the Existentialists of the twentieth century. Following the lead of these thinkers, who avoid systematic presentations of doctrine, one may well likewise dispense with a logically ordered set of teachings.

Following Kant, these thinkers agree on this basic position in philosophical anthropology. The human intellect is useful for the pragmatic matters of science and technology in the order of phenomena, but it is not the instrument for knowing the noumenon, reality as such. For this one must turn to direct intuition, a sympathy or empathy for life as lived and experienced. Ultimate reality is biological, not mechanical. Hence man cannot be satisfied by social structures, no matter how scientifically organized. A new metaphysics is needed for the redemption of man, a prelogical and nonrational intuition of the human reality. This will support the value and dignity of man. It will create the values of human existence by self-affirmation and self-assertion. As Sartre proclaimed, man is a being whose existence is prior to his essence: his essence will be what he decides it is to be.[2]

Echoes can be heard among religious people in the tendency to overvalue creativity above conformity to objective realities and norms. "Do your own thing", the slogan of the 1960s, was by no means confined to the "hippie" culture. It permeates all aspects of life in the misguided adulation of individuality above humble obedience. Students are indeed alarmed when it is pointed out to them that if their main yardstick for accomplishment be originality, Hitler would seem to rank higher than the Virgin Mary. Gradually, it is being realized that acceptance of God as Supreme Reality and of moral law as normative may be the only escape from a culture of destruction.

The Existentialists are seldom seen accurately because they are seldom subjected to rigorous metaphysical analysis. Again the context for the renewal of Christian Philosophy comes into view. All Existentialists are well educated in the first six arts, indeed, and especially in the verbal ones, but they lack formation in that

[2] See Excerpts for Part Four, Sartre, p. 437.

seventh of the liberal arts, the metaphysics of the Greeks and the Christians from Augustine to Aquinas. This heritage in philosophy is characteristically absent from their writings. From the metaphysical point of view, they represent various mixtures of Kant, Comte, and Hegel, not indeed in treatises, from which they are alienated, but in works of literary self-expression. Always they are in revolt against the out-there, on behalf of the in-here, the experiencing subject who is *The Rebel* of Camus in metaphysical rebellion.

Schopenhauer and his disciple Nietzsche bring this kaleidoscope of applied Modern Philosophy perhaps best into focus, for it is basically a Kantian and German philosophical phenomenon. A straight line leads from them to Heidegger, the professor of philosophy who will swing the German universities behind Hitler and his Nazis: for this National Socialism in the present century gives social expression to Nietzsche as Lenin did to Marx.

Each distinct kind of philosophy has at its center its own specifically different kind of metaphysics, namely, its view of the nature of ultimate reality. This basic fact about human thinking must be kept in mind when approaching the program for the renewal of Christian Philosophy. It is helpful to ponder more deeply the kind of metaphysics that underlies the myriad forms of existentialism. Ultimate reality, for the Existentialist, is the experience of organismic life in time. If perchance he passes beyond, it will be by a blind leap, not by a metaphysics of natural theology. Each individual human organism experiences fear of life, hopes in life, striving for this or that, often filled with dread, always concerned with the here and now, but always fundamentally without hope: for this organismic life is confined metaphysically within this cosmos. Being is in time: it flickers out into nothingness. Schopenhauer's pessimism hangs like a dark shadow over existentialist philosophizing. What is this being-in-time? Nothing but the practical activities of practical life, because existence itself, as such, is nothing but human existence, time conditioned within the cosmos. In this way, the study of existentialism illuminates the great need of modern man for a philosophical anthropology that liberates because it rests on a metaphysics of openness to intelligible reality beyond this cosmos.

The existentialist world view can only repeat the teaching of the ancient pagan philosophies: enjoy this organismic life for the moment. Project your value judgments into it. Be sincere. Be authentic. Be . . . stoical. The essential point is to note the presence of Spinoza's atheistic metaphysics: there is no reality but the one unique visible substance, *Deus sive Natura.* Spinoza is the metaphysician of modern atheism who stands behind both the Marxist and the existentialist doctrine. For the one, authentic experience of life in time is that of human groups; for atheistic Existentialists, that of human individuals, thrown there somehow.

Nietzsche is central in this application of Modern Philosophy because, thanks to the existentialist literature and to National Socialism, he casts a shadow across the twentieth century easily matching that of Marx. Metaphysics does matter, and professors of philosophy do indeed have their impact upon culture and society.

Born and raised in the home of a Lutheran pastor, Nietzsche reports that he was quite devout as a boy, with aspirations to become a clergyman himself. But, as so frequently in modern education, he encountered the metaphysics of atheism in his student years: Spinoza, Kant, and Schopenhauer removed every vestige of the Supreme Being from his mentality. Theism, he concluded, stifles organismic life and represses nature. Religion depreciates the vital forces and drains the values of their richness and power. Intellectually he moves ever more explicitly into avowed atheism and nihilism that characterize his philosophical writing and his impact upon the twentieth century.

Appointed to a university professorship, Nietzsche soon published his *Birth of Tragedy,* which glorifies Dionysus over Socrates, biological life over intellectual reason. Nietzsche asserts creative self-expression, the will to power, the cult of animal instinct. Dionysus is the Greek god of wine and alcohol. Nietzsche extols him as the model for life because he is truly individual, creative, sincere, authentic. He of course has no future beyond his being-in-time, but he does live his moments authentically, sincerely, and courageously.

This work launched Nietzsche's career and his series of works that elaborate this biological view of ultimate reality. Truth is not something apart from experiencing subjects, out there in systems devised by human reason. Values? *The Happy Life,* one of his later titles, results from the option for atheism. Happiness is applied atheism. Nihilism? For Nietzsche, this means the rejection of all values received from the culture of the past, especially in its Christian form. All structures, especially those of Christendom, are refused with fierce animosity. The option for atheism empties all past values and replaces them with new values to be created by the coming Superman, the blond beast whose *Will to Power,* another of Nietzsche's works, will dominate the future. The Superman thus is again the New Man, who will be generated by the application of the metaphysics of Modern Philosophy. He lives gloriously, *Beyond Good and Evil* (another Nietzschean title). This Superman will produce his own new set of values: self-assertion, power, domination, "survival of the fittest"—namely, the most ruthless. The human animal will step up to a higher level of being and action by means of this application of atheistic metaphysics. Again, therefore, philosophical anthropology moves to the center of the stage in this contemporary time of the applications.

Toward the end of his career, as the twentieth century was dawning, Nietzsche published a strange work entitled *The Antichrist,* in which he sees his way of philosophizing, marked by denial of Christ, rejection of Christendom, and hostility to Rome, as the final elimination of the Christian era from this age of the civilizations. Mankind is now mentally free to build a new and better world, the world of Supermen, out of atheistic intuitions about life in time.

Nietzsche had a gift for expressing philosophical thinking in literary form. In his book *The Happy Life,* he evokes the unforgettable picture of his Madman, a picture that abides to illustrate the impact of the atheistic metaphysics upon the once-Christian West. The Madman leaps forth among the startled citizens, well educated in the first six arts, enjoying the morning sun in any public square of any Western city. Swinging a lantern in broad daylight, the Madman cries out a *kerygma* announcing the death of God. The passage became the talk of Europe. What did Nietzsche mean? Opinions differed. Reviews in learned journals took sides. But superficiality reigned: the passage was dismissed as a Good Friday memory from Nietzsche's boyhood. People did not get the point until well into the coming century, at whose door, Nietzsche foretold, a stranger called nihilism would stand knocking.

Certainly one has here an important part of the content for the renewal of Christian Philosophy. But for the moment Nietzsche's Madman can be left swinging his lantern in the daylight: Heidegger will clarify the meaning later, after the educational application of the modern metaphysics has taken place. Nietzsche expresses the existentialist application of the atheistic world view in the mode of shock treatment. He teaches life without doctrine, *bios* without *logos.* The educated cultivation of reason with judgments bearing upon reality and grounding values for living has fallen by the wayside. Metaphysics, the natural science of God and hence of values that abide, has disappeared. Disappeared from where? From education, the heritage of the seven liberal arts. Nietzsche's Madman introduces the application of Modern Philosophy to education and culture.

James and Dewey: Education for Being in Time

The metaphysics of Modern Philosophy was put into practice in almost all Western educational systems, always in the way that James and Dewey exemplify in America and perhaps have expressed most clearly and applied most fully in the teaching profession.

William James (1842–1910), after brilliant undergraduate studies at Harvard, went to Europe for his graduate degrees. Soon he was at home in England, France, and especially Germany. He studied Kant, Comte, and Hegel, blending them in his personal way but always as a special disciple of Kant. Upon his return to America Harvard granted him a double professorship in psychology and in philosophy. The titles of his works bear eloquent witness to the orientation of his teaching: *The Principles of Psychology* (1890), *Varieties of Religious Experience* (1902), *Pragmatism* (1907), and *The Meaning of Truth* (1909).

William James is strongly anti-intellectualistic and at the same time empiricist and evolutionistic, blending Hegel's historicist dialectic with the new Darwinism. But above all he is a Kantian with a lifelong interest in the concept of truth, the point at which philosophy and education meet. For the concern of philosophy is to define the nature of truth, and the concern of teachers is to communicate it by teaching. In elaborating his doctrine, James put the two *Critiques* of Immanuel Kant into readable English. His rejection of metaphysics and any ascent of the mind to an intelligible order of abiding truth reflects Kant's *Critique of Pure Reason.* He satirizes the five ways of Aquinas and rejects Augustine's concept of the soul as an abiding substantial principle of life and animation in man. What people call the soul is nothing but a flow of conscious states without any substrate, resting on nothing. Again, metaphysics thrusts philosophical anthropology to the center of the stage.

James' Pragmatism, often mistakenly considered an indigenous American philosophy, is actually a rewriting of Kant's *Critique of Practical Reason,* again in his gift for facile English prose. Seen in the light of his Kantian metaphysics, James' Pragmatism is readily understandable as his concept of truth. Truth is what works in practice for you or for me. The truth of an idea depends on its practical value for earthly life. If an idea works for you, succeeds for you, then for you it is true. "Pragmatism" is Kant's practical reason operating in the metaphysical nihilism left by the *Critique of Pure Reason.* True ideas are those that harmonize with other aspects of individual experience. Truth is not the result of intellectual insight, which pierces beyond the flux of experience to see abiding reality and to express its nature in judgments. After Kant, this older idea is no longer tenable. Men now see that truth is what succeeds for you or for me, what works out well in practice for you or for me. True ideas are those an individual can assimilate, validate, and verify empirically because they work in practice. James summarizes his doctrine in a crude but famous expression: truth is the cash value of an idea.

What about God? True to his pragmatic dictums, James considers that God's reality is proven by the success religious belief has in overcoming the melancholy gloom that can arise from fear of a Godless world. While James' bestselling book *Varieties of Religious Experience* has influenced many doubters to look into religion with greater interest, its denial of any metaphysical basis for the reality of God makes it just as much a contribution to pluralistic subjectivism as to religious philosophy.

It is readily apparent that William James' redefinition of the concept of truth is a rather homespun application of the Spinozan metaphysics in its Kantian completion. How will it affect education? It is here that John Dewey (1859–1952) enters the American scene as the declared disciple of William James.

After a good Protestant upbringing in a New England home, Dewey enrolled for doctoral studies at Johns Hopkins University in Baltimore, for the graduate level had recently been added in American colleges. He wrote his dissertation on Hegel. From this point, the idea of education as a dialectical process between an organism and the environment it experiences runs through his long career and his many writings as their fundamental theme.

Appointed to the University of Minnesota, he soon received an invitation from the University of Chicago. In reply, he demanded a double professorship, one in the school of philosophy, the other in the school of education. His demand was granted, launching his career of philosophical influence upon the teachers of America. Always he wore two hats, so to speak, publishing in both fields. *The Impact of Darwin in Philosophy* (1910) reveals his view of ultimate reality, which has been reduced to nothing but organisms adjusting to environments. The metaphysics of Modern Philosophy has replaced the concept of the Supreme Being from his religious upbringing as a boy.

Wearing his other hat, he writes his famous *Democracy and Education* (1917), his handbook for teachers, in which his philosophical atheism is carefully disguised. It is pervasively present, however, for it is tacitly assumed that to exist is to be in process, to be in change. Existence is conceived in the Hegelian mode as a dialectic of organisms living in time, adjusting to environment as they grow. Truth is a set of provisional hypotheses that emerge for each one out of the process. And teaching? Teaching must recognize the new metaphysics of Modern Philosophy, supported now and purportedly verified by the impact of Darwin on philosophy. A teacher is a facilitator who arranges the environment to foster the dialectical process. The idea of a set of disciplines, called historically the liberal arts, which Johnny must learn because they sharpen his intellect, polish his inner eye, and brighten his mind in its grasp of the natures of things, has vanished. Education is becoming something different. Teachers under Dewey's tutelage begin to call it life adjustment. The reason is the fact that in Dewey's philosophy there is no higher order of intelligible reality and no intellectual power in man for ascent to such reality.[3] Thus the apostasy from God in metaphysics results in an apostasy from man's specific nature in philosophical anthropology. This is the meaning of this reduction of man to nothing but the organismic mode of existence.

The heritage of the liberal arts as a set of tools for sharpening the eye of the mind is suffering a metaphysical eclipse, not only in the area of the seventh but also in the first six arts, and even in the very elements and basics that open the door to the study of the liberal disciplines. One can analyze this in the triumph of Dewey's look-say method of teaching reading. Flash cards replace the patient teaching of the reasons why these written symbols mean these spoken words. Because of the shift in philosophical anthropology, the minds of the young are no longer taught to understand what reading is. The outcome can be anticipated. When the intellect as a nonorganismic power of understanding is no longer present in the philosophy of education, illiteracy cannot but be produced by the teachers. Thus it has come about in late twentieth-century America that experts identify the phenomenon of functional illiteracy in the graduates of the schools. They profess to be puzzled as to its cause, however, because they fail to analyze the underlying philosophical nature of the causality.

[3] See Excerpts for Part Four, Dewey, p. 439.

Needless to say, similar results can be found in Catholic education. While gains have been made in the method and equipment for multimedia presentation of catechetical materials, failure to include a systematic study of theological truth, graduated for different levels of learning, has led to widespread religious illiteracy.

Thus the metaphysics of apostasy from God cannot but produce an apostasy from man in that it suppresses the specific difference, the intelligence, that distinguishes the human mode of existing from that of all lower organisms. The cultivation of this specific difference has been the object of educational endeavor throughout the age of the civilizations since 4000 B.C. and in particular throughout the classical and Christian times of the West.

With this the correlation between Nietzsche's nihilism and this new education emerges into view. James' concept of truth and Dewey's application of it to educational content and method represent the elimination of the intelligible order of abiding truths together with the lasting human values for which such truths provide the foundation. What, then, did Nietzsche mean by his Madman swinging his lantern in the cities of the West? What was that proclamation of the Death of God? Some Good Friday memory?

Heidegger, a leading Existentialist and a foremost authority on Nietzsche, in his book *Holzwege,* "Loggers' Roads" (a graphic image of existentialism, for they begin as roads indeed but fade and go nowhere), denies all such superficialities. What Nietzsche means by "God", Heidegger explains, is the set of intelligible truths once held intellectually in Western civilization and taught by its teaching profession to its young people. They did this by the set of tools proper to their profession, the seven liberal arts. This kind of education provided for the coming generation a solid and abiding foundation for the values of this Western and Christian civilization. These intelligible truths, by their very definition, transcend the flux and flow of sensory experiencing, the emotions and the entire order of organismic responses. Heidegger stresses that Nietzsche means the death of the natural metaphysics of mankind in the programs of Western education, begun by the Greeks and developed in the Christian schools after Augustine. This seventh of the seven arts always taught young people that intelligible reality exists, that the intellect can rise to its level, see it with the eye of the mind, and then can look up higher to recognize the personal Supreme Being, source of the existence of all other existing realities.

Heidegger places Nietzsche's meaning firmly and explicitly in the field of education—the kind of education that James and Dewey symbolize and accomplish. Was it not always the function of the teaching profession, Heidegger asks, to sharpen and brighten the eye of the mind for perception of the intelligible truths? Did not all six arts minister to metaphysics? This is what is now dead. The horizon of the higher reality has been wiped away. Men see only the empirical and the sensory. Their minds are imprisoned within this cosmos. Indeed, the teaching profession does not even understand anymore what its function is, let alone know the use of the tools that achieve that purpose. It thinks it does nothing but arrange environment for stimuli and responses.

Nietzsche means that God is dead because of the eclipse that has fallen over the intelligible truths. The natural science of God no longer functions in programs of education. It is getting darker, Nietzsche cries, swinging his lantern. Also colder. God is dead.

A striking literary device, indeed, and one that Heidegger analyzes accurately. It points up this educational application of the new Spinozan metaphysics of Kant, Comte, and Hegel, an application for which every Gentile nation of Western civilization has its James and Dewey. The natural heritage of doctrine, the arts or tools by which teachers sharpen the eyes of youthful minds to perceive nonmaterial intelligible reality, is fading away. Only organismic responses, pragmatic concerns, the irrational factors of the human mode remain. The apostasy from God in metaphysics is begetting a philosophical anthropology that is an apostasy from man: finally man as image of God is reduced to a mechanism to be programmed by the B. F. Skinners. This brings us before yet another fundamental application of the new metaphysics, one that is perhaps even more surprising, for it takes place in the parallel heritages of religious doctrine in the West.

Religious Applications: Modernism and Its "New Hermeneutics"

The very idea of the Christian era of Western civilization contains the concept of a sacred doctrine that hands on a revelation from God by its teaching. This doctrine emanates from Jerusalem. Augustine and the Patristic age of the early Church correlated this distinct spiritual heritage of doctrine with the natural heritage of doctrine, the liberal arts, coming from Athens. This natural heritage functioned within the program of holy teaching, indeed as an intellectual preparation for it, and, thanks especially to metaphysics as the seventh liberal art, at home within it. A comprehensive analysis of the application of the Spinozan metaphysics demands a consideration of its impact upon this spiritual heritage of teaching, which has come to specify the West in the age of the civilizations.

Western culture is characterized and indeed sustained by its three chief traditions of religious teaching, Protestant, Jewish, and Catholic. Each purports to represent a contact with the personal Supreme Being of the universe by certain persons, called prophets because they speak for him, chosen by God to receive his message and to communicate it to their fellowman. It is a message of salvation, both personal and social. As Jesus Christ, whom Christians see as the Prophet who stands at the end of the line of the Hebrew prophets, said to a Gentile, "Salvation comes from the Jews" (Jn 4:22). The Jews are the bearers of this divine revelation and the people of the Book, called the Bible, in which its chief events and teachings were written down over the course of many centuries. This Bible contains revealed religion, which the prophets called the way of life. It provides the abiding instrument for teaching this way of life in a practical and formative manner.

These three religious traditions of the West differ among themselves, of course, and the conflicts sometimes have been sharp indeed. But they agree on the essential point that they have a heritage of divinely revealed doctrine, a divine deposit entrusted to them as a community, which they hand on by their teaching. It is perhaps true to say that the recent impact of the Spinozan metaphysics upon all three alike is ministering to a lessening of these differences and to a growing unity among them. For the Spinozan metaphysics, as noted already in connection with Spinoza himself, dissolves all three traditions, so that a new philosophical religion results within the empty shell of each by means of the new philosophical interpretation or hermeneutics applied to the concepts and doctrines that each one teaches.

One of the most fundamental functions of philosophy on the human scene is the hermeneutical one. For philosophy casts a light upon all the data and activity of the first six arts. The quality of this light depends upon the kind of metaphysics that generates it. In this hermeneutical process, therefore, the fork at the end of ontology is crucially significant. If the mind continues upward into the realm of the intelligible, then the hermeneutical function will be a corresponding theistic illumination. But if the mind chooses the other fork in the mental road, the one that denies natural theology and turns down atheistically within the cosmos, the hermeneutical function will be correspondingly different. The former case may be likened to wearing clear glasses, which permit vision of all existing reality; the latter is like wearing dark glasses, which limit vision to the sensory, screening out intelligible reality. It is this hermeneutical function of the atheistic metaphysics that produces throughout the nineteenth century Liberal Protestantism, Reform Judaism, and Catholic Modernism. This is doubtless the most profound reason for the renewal of Christian Philosophy in the contemporary Catholic Church. For the metaphysics of Modern Philosophy generates a new total heresy that affects comprehensively the Bible, the Apostles' Creed, and the defined dogmas of faith, changing their meaning by a new philosophical interpretation. In this process of subjecting revealed religion to philosophical judgment the Hegelian dialectic is basic, for it declares outmoded the meaning that the revealed teaching has had across the centuries since biblical times.

For this hermeneutics is always a denial of the historicity of the revealed message. Among the Jews there had been no doubt through the centuries that the prophetic contacts with the Supreme Being actually took place as events and teachings cherished in corporate memory. The authority that made them to be the people of Abraham and Moses certified this historicity. So too among the Christians. The writings of the New Testament have been accepted for over seventeen centuries on the authority of the Apostles as a faithful record of what Jesus did and taught. Generations of Christians formed their lives by constant meditation upon these records, and supreme artistic geniuses of the West accumulated an immense heritage of Christian art that depicts these scenes.

When the metaphysics of Modern Philosophy is applied to these three heritages in the teaching of revealed religion, each is affected immediately in substantially the same way. The Bible is "demythologized", as the saying goes, and reduced to nothing but a set of human experiences of life in earlier times. The historical character of the prophetic messages and the authenticity of the interventions by the personal and transcendent Supreme Being, who spoke through his prophets and who acted on behalf of his people, cannot but vanish under the darkened light of the new metaphysics, for it declares that no such Being exists. This is the metaphysical taproot of what is called "the rationalist prejudice" in biblical studies, the a priori declaration that a word of God or a free intervention by God in his creation is impossible. This is the closed mind, devoid metaphysically of any openness toward the transcendent Supreme Being, who becomes a symbol instead of a *living* God.

After seventeen centuries, then, the heritages of revealed religion suddenly face a new kind of philosophical challenge. The personalities who originated it are well known, and the intellectual formation of their minds by the metaphysics of Modern Philosophy is subject to rigorous and extensive documentation. The details are available in the specialized research. The purpose here, always with an eye upon the coming renewal of Christian Philosophy, is to summarize briefly the application of the Spinozan metaphysics, ministered variously by Kant, Comte, and Hegel, in this vast modern intellectual project for the philosophical reinterpretation of revealed religion.

Liberal Protestantism

By all accounts Friedrich Schleiermacher (1768–1834) is the pioneer in this hermeneutical project. During his studies for the Protestant ministry, he was deeply imbued with Spinoza and Kant. Appointed to a professorship in Protestant theology, he proceeded forthwith to build a reinterpreted Christianity upon the two *Critiques* of Kant. Religion is a matter of the heart, not of the mind, a fact of experience by a pious life prior to any religious doctrine. Losing a clear intellectual grasp of the divine transcendence and giving up the received teaching of Protestantism on sin and redemption, Schleiermacher makes religion something independent of all factors outside the experiencing subject, whether articles of faith by authority of the early Church or dogmas of faith by authority of a teaching Church. We have nothing but a few records of religious experiences by persons in the past, which may serve as models for our own religious experiencing proper to our own times and culture. Thus the concept of revelation shifts from a teaching delivered of old to an ongoing process fully in the pattern of the Hegelian dialectic. The philosophical fall from transcendence, resulting from the loss of the metaphysical heritage in the liberal arts, is being introduced into a major tradition of revealed religion. The result will appear outwardly still to be that same religion, but deceptively so, for the substance has been changed within the familiar Christian forms and terminology.

Schleiermacher is furthermore the originator of the introduction of the political categories "conservative" and "liberal" into revealed religion, as the very name "Liberal Protestantism" indicates. For Christianity is now no longer seen as a transcendent doctrine, because there is no transcendent personal Supreme Being to declare his prophetic word to mankind and to see to the teaching of it on the human scene. Thus the new approach is felt to be a liberation from any binding teaching, formulated doctrine, or Church authority in teaching, creeds, or dogmas.

A series of well-known Liberal Protestants succeed Schleiermacher. Here only the chief names can be given as pointers toward further research on this phenomenon of philosophical application. First in the series and seminal for the application of the Spinozan hermeneutics to the New Testament stands David Friedrich Strauss (1808–74), who lost his boyhood Protestant religion in his studies of Kant, Hegel, and Schleiermacher when preparing for the Protestant ministry. Imbued with the philosophical prejudice of the Spinozan metaphysics against the free, sovereign, almighty, and personal God of creation and revelation, Strauss developed his analysis of the New Testament as the faith experience of Christ by an early credulous and myth-making community of believers. This Christ of faith has little in common with the Jesus of history. It was the substance of Strauss' *Life of Christ,* which Ernest Renan brought over into French for Catholic Modernism.

Albrecht Ritschl (1822–89) suffered the same metaphysical eclipse of the personal Supreme Being and of the very concepts of sin and redemption. Called the first theologian to take Immanuel Kant seriously, he adopts a practical and pragmatic approach to religion, teaching that we attain to the Divine in the value judgments of our living. Ontological statements, the study of philosophy, the use of metaphysics in theology, must be replaced by value judgments. One asks about the personal and moral meaning of Christ for persons today, not about persons and natures in Christ.

These seminal applications lead into the present century, for example, with Paul Tillich (1886–1966) for theology, the religious philosopher of ongoing revelation, and with Rudolph Bultmann (1884–1970), the biblical exegete who was a declared Existentialist and disciple of Heidegger. The Bible is a record of experiences in the mythical mode of earlier times, in no way grounding a doctrine that is binding for persons today. As earlier times and cultures conditioned earlier religious experience, so the present times and cultures condition such experience today. Popular Bible-study programs should be carefully examined on this matter.

Reform Judaism

Around the middle of the nineteenth century a group of rabbis met in Germany to dissociate themselves from Orthodox Judaism and to found their own institutions to train young men for the rabbinate and for their own separate synagogues. Spinoza occupies a central position in their thinking, and the Hegelian dialectic is at work in the production of a simplified and rationalized form of Judaism. Externally the historic Jewish religion seems to be present, but deceptively so, for the substance has been changed into a philosophical faith more akin to Liberal Protestantism than to the Orthodox synagogues, with their retention of traditional observances. Many contemporary Jews are now atheists.

Catholic Modernism

Toward the middle of the nineteenth century and following the pioneers of Liberal Protestantism as models, and likewise in Germany, a group of Catholic priests, professors in various universities and teachers of candidates for the priesthood, began to elaborate a similar reinterpretation of the Catholic heritage of teaching. Again as a guide for separate study, the leading names included Fathers George Hermes (1775–1831), Jacob Froschammer (1821–93), and Anton Günther (1783–1863), whose name lives on as "Guentherism" in the histories of philosophy and theology, for Günther is the chief exponent of this opening stage of the new hermeneutics within the Catholic Church.

These priestly teachers began by embracing Descartes' initial doubt, applying it to the deposit of faith in order to approach its truths in a new and modern way. Each represents a personal mixture of Kant, Comte, and Hegel, and each is convinced that the teaching program of the Catholic Church must be renewed, updated, and modernized by adopting Modern Philosophy. Only thus, they became convinced, can the Church communicate successfully with modern man. Their approach introduced novel teachings under the plea that very little in the ordinary teaching of the past has been defined as dogma by the Extraordinary Magisterium. And when such dogmatic definitions did take place, one must recognize that while they were indeed infallibly true, their truth is relative to the state of science and philosophy at the cultural moment when the definition took place. The dogmas of the Church are relative to the level of education and scientific progress at the time. But as culture changes and advances, as science and philosophy make progress, the dogmas must be accordingly reinterpreted. The dogmatic definition was the best one possible at its time, indeed it was infallibly true at the time, but now a better statement is possible and even urgent because of modern progress. Thus for these professors the Hegelian mentality has become the criterion of truth: truth is the daughter of time. It is this basic intellectual position that reveals the loss of the metaphysics that constitutes in a special way the heritage of the Catholic priest. It is this, furthermore, that reveals the presence of the new hermeneutics, which declares that dogmas proposed by the Church can be given a meaning different from the one that the Church has understood and still understands.

These priests in the first stage of this new hermeneutics carefully avoided any reference to the Articles of Faith, confining their project to the dogmas enunciated in the course of the history of the Church. The implications for the Articles are clear, however, and were noted by the Supreme Magisterium time and again.

Is there a common taproot from which the mind of Liberal Protestantism, Reform Judaism, and Catholic Modernism grows? There is indeed. It is the absence of the heritage of metaphysics, the fact that sets the stage for the program in the Catholic Church to renew the heritage of Christian Philosophy. For these intellectual movements begin with Kant, proceed in the mentality of Hegel's dialectic of the outmoded past, and look upon philosophy through the eyes of Comte as nothing but a generalized statement of the findings of the empirical sciences. Fundamental in each project for the reinterpretation of revealed religion is the world view of Immanuel Kant. God is inaccessible to the human intelligence. Objective revelation is impossible; purported instances therefore must be subjected to Spinoza's hermeneutics. Articles and dogmas of faith handed down in synagogues and churches are subjective creations without noumenal validity. Hence religion must be put on a new basis, that of modern man experiencing life in his own time and culture. The concept of a deposit that contains a message of transcendent truth from a personal God delivered of old to the prophets and entrusted to a teaching institution must be replaced by an unfolding of human self-consciousness. The Supreme Magisterium of the Catholic Church early in the project stated formally that "these priests profane their teaching office and adulterate the sacred deposit of the Faith". It is this dimension that led to the First Vatican Council and to the program for the renewal of Christian Philosophy that stems from it.

The Impact of Modern Philosophy on Man

Before turning to Vatican I and the ensuing renewal of metaphysics, a brief consideration should be given to an application of Modern Philosophy that will produce increasingly a human necessity for the heritage of Christian Philosophy. It is the fact that the metaphysical denial of God generates as time goes on a threat to man.

Here again a large subject, one that calls for separate study and research, can only be indicated by a few seminal names as symbols and by the immediate outcomes of the new philosophical anthropology, which call for philosophical renewal.

For this a new philosophy of man is the final application of Modern Philosophy, the one that applies its metaphysical world view to man himself, an application that alters his own perception of his human mode of existing and of knowing and changes his judgment regarding his place and role in the cosmos.

Augustine, the founder of Christian Philosophy, centered the interest of rational thought on God and the human soul, with the cosmos in third place. God is the Creator of the entire cosmos, indeed, but within it he creates each human soul as an altogether special creature qualitatively unique. In this Augustine continues and develops the teaching of the pagan philosophers, who recognized a second kind of knowledge in human persons that makes them to be persons. This is a higher kind of knowledge, qualitatively different from that of the senses. From this difference in mode of operation there follows a qualitative difference in human nature itself. By the bodily senses man participates in the corporeal world of the visible cosmos, but by his intellect and free will he becomes a person who participates in the higher world of the pure spirits.

The Spinozan metaphysics, reducing man to a mode of the unique material substance, opened the way for Locke, Hume, and their associationist school of psychologists to explain away that higher form of knowledge as nothing else than sets of associated sensory images, and not a set of spiritual concepts giving a higher understanding of the natures of things. Hume himself, one recalls, admitted that he was "affrighted" at the implications of this philosophical reduction in the human mode of knowing and existing. With Kant, the soul becomes only an a priori form of the experiencing subject and not an objectively real principle of man's being and operation. William James stated the final outcome lucidly on behalf of this entire school of applied Modern Philosophy: what has been called the "soul" in the past, he teaches, is nothing but the flux and flow of conscious states. Man possess no abiding reality in which these conscious states inhere. There is no abiding self, he concludes, fully in the Kantian metaphysical tradition, which by his time had become a commonplace in Western higher education.

Sigmund Freud (1856–1939) may well be taken, along with William James, as another symbol and exponent of this philosophical reduction of man. He introduced atheistic metaphysics into psychology with extensive impact on modern personal and social life. For Freud, a human being is essentially a complex of chemical and physical energies in which the libido, as he terms the sexual drive, dominates and exercises control. Philosophical anthropology in the Freudian system has adopted the mechanical and empiricist Positivism of Auguste Comte. In the proliferation of psychological studies that characterizes the nineteenth century, the light that interprets the findings, often true and valuable in themselves, is filtered by the colored glass of atheistic metaphysics and its blindness to the possibility that the animating principle in man might be a qualitatively unique and special creation.

As the new philosophical anthropology took root in the laboratories and classrooms of higher education in the West, it became axiomatic that man is reduced to the status of nothing but an ordinary and mere animal, with only the one kind of sensory knowledge proper to animals. The specific difference of man that had distinguished the intellectual life of the West and had guided its education has been thus philosophically suppressed, a suppression that now seems to have scientific support since the publication of Darwin's *Origin of Species* in 1869.

At the same time that the new philosophical anthropology is rising throughout the nineteenth century to dominate Western intellectual life, the ongoing Copernican revolution in the empirical sciences is producing an immense new body of knowledge about the cosmos; its magnitude; and the orientation of nature, and the laws of motion of its bodies. Educated man looks out now upon this cosmos without the light of metaphysics regarding its transcendent Supreme Creator. As he does so, man thinks to himself that he is only a meaningless momentary mode on an insignificant and noncentral planet. Freud's pleasure principle offers no hope, nor does the exploitation of the cosmos that ignores the laws given to the natures by their Creator. Gradually the planet itself, as the prophet Isaiah said long ago (24:5), "is defiled under its inhabitants' feet, for they have transgressed the law, violated the precept, broken the everlasting Covenant". This passage, quoted by Pope Pius IX when opening the First Vatican Council (December 8, 1869) points toward Bertrand Russell, perhaps the most representative British Empiricist of the twentieth century, who in his book *A Free Man's Worship* (1918) voices eloquently the impact of Modern Philosophy upon modern man. "Purposeless (and) void of meaning", he writes,

> is the world which Science presents for our belief. Amid such a world, if anywhere, our ideals henceforward must find a home. That man is the product of causes which had no prevision of the end they were achieving; that his origin, his growth, his hopes and fears, his loves and his beliefs, are but the outcome of accidental collocations of atoms . . . and that the whole temple of Man's achievement must inevitably be buried beneath the debris of a universe in ruins— all these things, if not quite beyond dispute, are yet so nearly certain, that no philosophy which rejects them can hope to stand. Only within the scaffolding of these truths, only on the firm foundation of unyielding despair can the soul's habitation be safely built. . . . Omnipotent matter rolls on its relentless way.

It would be difficult to find a better example of the mind well trained in the first six of the liberal arts, indeed, but completely lacking in the seventh, the heritage of metaphysics and its natural theology. Metaphysics has been replaced by mathematical physics, and this cultural fact will evoke Vatican I and the program for the renewal of Christian Philosophy.

This hopelessness, stated starkly by Russell in the camp of the British Empiricists and harmonizing with the pessimism of the continental Existentialists, Max Scheler's *Stellung des Menschen im Cosmos* and the writings of Sartre and Camus in France, expresses the psychological outcome of this application of atheistic metaphysics to man. No one has put this impact more succinctly than St. Pius X. "An atmosphere of unbelief has been created", he writes in one of his catechetical documents, "that is most harmful to the interior and spiritual life. This atmosphere wages war upon any idea of a higher authority, any idea of God, of revelation, of the life to come, and of mortification in this life."

What creates this atmosphere? Fundamentally it results from the practical effect of the metaphysics of Modern Philosophy upon the human person. Closed to the transcendent personal Supreme Being as it is, it militates against prayer and stifles prayerfulness. Religion itself becomes secularized by the new hermeneutics and begins to participate strangely in this eclipse of God.

This effect of atheistic metaphysics upon man goes far toward explaining the rise of the new hermeneutics in the Western religious traditions. For it induces religious minds to embrace activism within the cosmos and to reorient their endeavors to human life in time. Thus all three of its forms, Liberal Protestantism, Reform Judaism, and Catholic Modernism, participate in this philosophical apostasy from man in his specific humanism, a participation in the reduction of the human mode of existing to nothing but a cog in the social machinery or an organism in the web of stimuli.

With this the renewal of Christian Philosophy can be appreciated in both its human and its religious dimensions. For the applications make clear how erroneous is the use of Modern Philosophy in reaching out to modern man, and how great a disservice to modern man himself the project of the new hermeneutics must necessarily prove to be.

II

THE PASTORAL CONCERN OF THE CHURCH
FOR PHILOSOPHY

This chapter studies the documents of Vatican I from the philosophical point of view and then the ensuing program for the renewal of Christian Philosophy. Here only a summary of these documents and of the leading personalities of the renewal, both positive and negative, will be given. Time and occasion permitting, the documents should be read in their entirety. No summary can do them justice, for they represent a masterful confrontation of the Supreme Magisterium with the rise and spread of philosophical pantheism and atheism in the once-Christian culture of the West, which has been studied in Part Three above.

It is a fact frequently overlooked, and indeed one fears sometimes suppressed, that the new metaphysics studied in Part Three and the various applications noted in Chapter One of this Part Four became the explicitly stated reason why the Catholic Church convened the Ecumenical Council of 1869–70, the First Vatican Council. Since this fact is fundamentally important for the contemporary life of the Church, it may be well to draw special attention to this matter, lest the renewal of the metaphysical heritage be deemed a mere personal option instead of a crucial matter for both contemporary humanism and for the ongoing hermeneutical purity and integrity of the deposit of faith.

In his allocution opening Vatican I on December 8, 1869, Pope Pius IX makes the philosophical dimension perfectly clear. He tells the Council Fathers assembled in St. Peter's Basilica that they are "gathered to pass judgment with us on the contradictions of so-called knowledge", citing 1 Timothy 6:20. Thus philosophical error and the deposit of faith are placed in correlation. Taking up "the warfare against Christ's holy Church", the Pope continues: "Continually before your eyes are disorder and confusion concerning the sound doctrine on which depends the proper ordering of human affairs." Then he points out the pastoral effect, namely, the "rooting out completely from souls of their Christian faith". In fact, he goes so far as to say that, were she not supported by divine power, "the destruction of the Church of God might be feared as certain at this time". "We are thinking", he concludes, "of the wretched condition of great numbers who have been deceived and who are straying from the path of truth and therefore from happiness."

The philosophical background for the calling of the Ecumenical Council becomes even more explicit in the remarkable Introduction to the Dogmatic Constitution *Dei Filius* approved unanimously on April 24, 1870. It notes that the failure of the Protestants to attend, even though urgently invited, and to heed the Council of Trent, resulted in the disintegration of their movement into numerous sects and in the fact that "even the holy Bible itself, which was earlier held to be the sole font and judge of faith, began to be regarded no longer as divine, but to be reckoned among the fabrications of mythology". This clear reference to the new hermeneutics leads Vatican I to discuss the unforeseen rise of the new metaphysics of Modern Philosophy.

> Then was born and spread far and wide the doctrine of rationalism, or naturalism, which in every way opposes the Christian religion as a supernatural institution; and which strives with utmost diligence to exclude from men's minds and moral life Christ, who alone is our Lord and Savior, and then to establish the reign of so-called pure reason or nature. Thus the minds of many abandoned and rejected the Christian religion, denied the true God and his Christ, and at last sank into the abyss of pantheism, materialism, and atheism.

The Introduction to *Dei Filius* then refers to the first or German phase of Catholic Modernism:

> It has unfortunately happened that many, including sons of the Church, have strayed from the path of true piety. Their Catholic sense became enfeebled with the gradual dilution of the truths within them. Misled by diverse and strange teachings (see Heb. 13:9), and erroneously confusing nature and grace, human knowledge, and divine faith, they learn to distort the genuine meaning of the dogmas that Holy Mother Church holds and teaches, and to imperil the integrity and the soundness of the Faith.

It would be difficult to express more explicitly and accurately the pastoral impact of the new hermeneutics born of the infiltration of Modern Philosophy into the minds of "sons of the Church", namely, priests teaching on the level of higher education.

This philosophical background and reason for the convocation of the Ecumenical Council is given detailed analysis in the teaching of the two Dogmatic Constitutions themselves, to which we now turn.

The Constitutions of Vatican I and the Field of Philosophy

The solemn and authoritative decisions of the Supreme Magisterium always concern catechetical teaching and the science of Sacred Theology primarily and directly. In the case of Vatican I, however, because of the metaphysical problems induced by the rise and development of Modern Philosophy, the Dogmatic Constitutions have a definite and altogether unprecedented significance for philosophy, as the considerations above lead one to expect. For they bear upon the

First Article of the Apostles' Creed, the fountainhead of catechesis, upon the revelation given to mankind by the Creator, and upon the teaching and hermeneutics of this revealed word of God. This is especially visible in *Dei Filius*.

The Dogmatic Constitution *Dei Filius* (April 24, 1870)

In its four chapters and their canons this Constitution teaches and solemnly defines the existence and attributes of "God, Creator of all things", and then does the same for the Catholic doctrine on "revelation", "faith", and "faith and reason". Fundamentally important is the fact that "Holy Mother Church holds and teaches that God, the beginning and end of all things, can be known with certitude by the natural light of human reason from created things", with the corresponding canon. This rejects the Spinozan metaphysics of Kant, Comte, and Hegel and reaffirms the metaphysics of Christian Philosophy. From this position of the Supreme Magisterium, the exclusion of Modern Philosophy from the institutions of higher education in the Church and the renewal of Christian Philosophy in them follow with rigorous logic. For Christian Philosophy is the heritage of natural teaching, which develops the rational foundation for the concept of God contained in the biblical revelation and which is summarized in Chapter One of the Constitution. The attributes of God are listed, and his transcendence is affirmed, for "God, Creator and Lord of heaven and earth, . . . is one unique spiritual substance, completely simple and unchangeable, distinct in reality and in essence from the world". This is exactly "the sublime truth", as St. Thomas Aquinas terms it, to which that metaphysics ascends that is the Catholic heritage since Augustine and the Fathers of the Church. The doctrine of creation, furthermore, and the taproot of Christian philosophical anthropology are reaffirmed with utmost clarity: "This one true God produced from nothing both the spiritual and the corporeal creature . . . and afterward the human creature that is common to both, as it were, being constituted of spirit and body."

This first chapter, on "God, Creator of all things", has five correlative canons of supreme philosophical importance for the contemporary Church, for they condemn the characteristic metaphysical positions of Modern Philosophy: its atheism, its materialism, its pantheism, its Plotinian emanationism, and its refusal of the doctrine that Almighty God created out of nothing the entire substance of each reality existing outside of himself.

This teaching of the Ecumenical Council, then, calls for that kind of metaphysics that is open to the transcendent personal and intelligent Supreme Being, the beginning and final end of the universe that he freely creates. It calls, furthermore, for the kind of philosophical anthropology that declares the existence and the validity of human reason to know with certitude God's existence and fundamental attributes. One can say, therefore, that the Catholic Church is rejecting the most fundamental and characteristic position of Modern Philosophy, the suppression of the heritage of metaphysics in the intellectual life of the West and its replacement by mathematical physics. For this substitution focuses the attention of educated persons exclusively upon the cosmos and leads to oblivion and neglect of the transcendent Supreme Being. Vatican I reaffirms the foundation of religion in all the times and cultures of mankind and in the Bible itself, namely, the ability of natural human reason to know God. When this ability is cultivated in the process of education, the academic discipline called metaphysics results as the central branch of philosophy. This reaffirmation points forward to the hope for the academic institutions of Christendom, which will animate the Holy See when launching the coming program of philosophical renewal.

Nothing can replace the study of the actual text of *Dei Filius*. It is sufficient here to draw attention to the lucid teaching in Chapters 2, 3, and 4 on revelation and faith and on the relationship of human reason to each. This body of teaching solves succinctly the problems created by the atheistic hermeneutics and its application to Catholic teaching. Most fundamental of all, perhaps, is the opening sentence of Chapter 4 on "faith and reason": "The constant consensus of the Catholic Church has also held and still holds that there is a twofold order of knowledge, distinct not only in origin but also in object." The operating word here is "knowledge": faith is a form of knowledge, not an experiencing of life in the cosmos or a vague pantheistic trust in "the Divine". Indeed, it is a higher order of knowledge because it responds to divine revelation given on the human scene in human words but out of the prophetic light, a higher light of insight and understanding than the light of human reason. Thus Cartesian rationalism is eliminated at its root. Since both orders of knowledge relate to one and the same God of truth, "faith and reason can never oppose one another". Hence the Church always has promoted the cultivation of the human arts and disciplines, for they not only benefit the earthly life of human persons, but "lead to God . . . , the Lord of knowledge, with the aid of his grace, if they are rightly used". Implicit in this teaching is the fact that this right use of the empirical sciences depends upon the kind of metaphysics that crowns the study of them as the seventh liberal art.

Finally, one must note the solution to the problems of the atheistic hermeneutics and its application in Catholic Modernism. The words "meaning" and "explain" are the operating words in the following passage from Chapter 4:

> For the teaching of faith, which God has revealed, has not been proposed as a philosophical discovery to be perfected by human ingenuity but as a divine deposit handed over to the Spouse of Christ to be guarded faithfully and to be explained infallibly. Hence that meaning of sacred dogmas must perpetually be retained that Holy Mother Church has once declared; nor is that meaning ever to be abandoned under the pretext and name of a more profound comprehension.

Associated with this passage is the corresponding canon, which bears directly upon Günther and Catholic Modernism in its first or German phase: "If anyone should say that with the progress of knowledge it is sometimes possible that dogmas proposed by the Church can be given a meaning different from the one that the Church has understood and still understands, let him be anathema." To grasp the full philosophical significance of this teaching of the Supreme Magisterium one must recall the hermeneutical function of philosophy. If the light under which revealed religion is interpreted is the darkness visible of Kant, Comte, and especially Hegel, then its teaching will be emptied of its original and authentic content, and its words will be explained in terms of novel meanings. Thus once again it is clear that Vatican I is calling for that metaphysics as the basis of hermeneutics that ascends to the transcendent Supreme Being of creation and revelation.

The Dogmatic Constitution *Pastor Aeternus* (July 18, 1870)

At first sight a philosophical dimension will perhaps seem absent from this document. Yet, upon closer consideration, it will emerge as the practical corollary of the four chapters of *Dei Filius* and their contact with philosophy. For Christian Philosophy, by its metaphysical ascent to the transcendent and intelligent Supreme Being, cultivates in the human mind, so to speak, ears to hear the word of their God, should he reveal himself by speaking his word to mankind. The Constitution *Pastor Aeternus* is a basic reaffirmation of the fact of divine revelation against the Spinozan current of Modern Philosophy. It does this concretely by identifying the proximate rule of faith in divine revelation, defining it in terms of the teaching office committed by God himself to Peter and his Successors. Thus "the Roman pontiff alone is the successor of blessed Peter, the chief of the Apostles, and is the true Vicar of Christ, head of the entire Church, and father and teacher of all Christians". One must ponder this document in its full original text. In it the so-called free examination of the word of God is condemned, namely, that done by the philosophical hermeneutics opposed to this "teacher of all Christians". For the transcendent and intelligent Supreme Being, whom the authentic heritage in metaphysics is able to recognize, possesses the almighty power to choose a people to hear his word and to sustain the teaching that explains its meaning. In the document, furthermore, the fact is confirmed that the deposit of divine revelation has been entrusted to Peter and his Successors for this divinely supported infallible teaching and hermeneutical explanation of meaning.

The Dogmatic Constitutions of Vatican I bear primarily, of course, upon the fields of catechetics and theology. But because of the nature of the errors that the Council was convened to address, they have a marked philosophical dimension. It is noteworthy that the *General Catechetical Directory* of Vatican II, discussing catechetical methods for adolescents, states in paragraph 83 that "it is important not to continue at this age the simple and objective kind of instruction that is appropriate for children". What then is to be done? In paragraph 88 the *Directory* calls for "the formation of a religious way of thinking . . . (because) the intellectual building up of the faith of adolescents . . . is an essential for the life of faith". And the *Directory* refers to the Dogmatic Constitution *Dei Filius* of Vatican I. This pastoral and catechetical dimension contained within the documents of Vatican I leads directly to the renewal of Christian Philosophy.

The Program to Renew Christian Philosophy: Aeterni Patris (*August 4, 1879*)

On February 20, 1878, Pope Leo XIII succeeded Pius IX: a quite different personality, humanly speaking, but without the slightest departure from that unity of intellectual life that characterizes the See of Peter. For with *Inscrutabili* (April 21, 1878), his initial and programmatic encyclical "On the Evils affecting Modern Society", he identifies his pontificate with Vatican I and its philosophical dimension. The taproot of the evils is "the widespread subversion of the primary truths on which, as on its foundation, human society is based". The applications of unsound thinking function as a deadly kind of plague, which infects society in its inmost recesses, allowing it no respite and foreboding ever fresh disturbances and final disaster".

Leo XIII returns to this apocalyptic note more than once. Noting the contrast with "those happy times when the Church was revered as a mother by the nations", he sees it as "beyond all question . . . that our epoch is rushing wildly along the straight road to destruction". The reason for this situation is the new kind of philosophy that has arisen in the West: "The very notion of civilization is a fiction of the brain if it rests not on the abiding principles of truth and the unchanging laws of virtue and justice . . . a worthless imitation and a meaningless name." "The spreading of false principles", he concludes, "must sooner or later bring the standing and peace of the state to the very brink of ruin." The root of the evils "lies in philosophy, upon which the foundation of the other sciences in great measure depends", and in the resulting secularized education, which is being organized to impart to the young "such instruction as darkens the mind and corrupts morals". Already the mind of Leo XIII is turning to the remedy for these evils, namely, "a suitable and solid method of education . . . wholly in harmony with the Catholic Faith in its literature and system of training, and chiefly in philosophy". Pope Leo XIII was no pessimist: he recognizes the evils that afflict Western mankind, but he also knows their cause. Hence he can turn to their remedy, which he did in his encyclical *Aeterni Patris* (August 4, 1879).

This is the fundamental document in that renewal in the contemporary Church that is concerned with the nature of philosophy in itself, and with the qualities and the specific kind that that nature assumes when it merits the adjective

"Christian". It calls for the renewal of Christian Philosophy in every Catholic institution of higher education in every part of the world, in all Catholic colleges, universities, novitiates, and seminaries for training candidates for the priesthood. In a later document Leo XIII refers to *Aeterni Patris* as "our letter on the renewal in Catholic schools of the Christian Philosophy in the spirit of St. Thomas Aquinas". Since the other arts and sciences depend upon philosophy for their principles and for soundness of judgment on the meaning and human applications of their findings, as the Pope stresses in several documents, this fundamental renewal holds out the hope for a healing of the modern social evils at their root. In fact, the Holy See harbors a great hope; while the Church does not control the secularized universities now operated by the various nations of the West, the hope is that young Catholics, restored to their philosophical heritage in their own schools, will win their colleagues in secular institutions by the very power and truth of the metaphysics that they represent in dialogue with them. A great hope, indeed: in such a case the evils resulting from the rise and spread of atheistic metaphysics would be healed, and the once-Christian culture of the nations would recover its health.

Aeterni Patris, then, is a major document of the Holy See, one that flows directly from Vatican I as the practical means for realizing its teaching. It too must be read and studied in its unabridged text,[1] for no summary can do it justice. Here only a few points will be given as guides for such study and research.

While the thrust of the renewal when launched a century ago was definitely that hope for a general restoration and renewal of academic education, the encyclical opens with a pastoral reference to the deposit of faith, to which a return will be made in the final chapter below. "According to the warning of the Apostle (Col 2:8)", Leo XIII writes, "the minds of Christ's faithful are apt to be deceived and the integrity of the Faith to be corrupted among men by philosophy." Hence pastors in the Church always are concerned to advance knowledge and science rightly so called, and "especially philosophy, on which a right apprehension of the other sciences in great part depends". Thus the hermeneutical function of philosophy with regard to revealed religion is present at the outset of this renewal. "Looseness of intellectual opinion", the Pope continues, "influences human actions and perverts them." Thus the relationship of the renewal with the evils afflicting society is established. On the other hand, sound philosophy leads to religious faith as its indispensable preamble.

The lucid discussion on atheistic philosophy as a wrong and perverted use of human reason is fundamental in *Aeterni Patris*. It establishes the central fact that Modern Philosophy is a new kind of philosophy with a different metaphysics at its core: it gives the mind a darkened view of ultimate reality and confines the human spirit within this cosmos. The direct purpose of the renewal is the restoration of

---

[1] See Excerpts for Part Four, Leo XIII, p. 444.

open metaphysics to its rightful place in programs of study, so that educated young Catholics can continue to profess the First Article of the Apostles' Creed and to live as persons of prayer. For this will be the outcome of the renewal, the result of the restored cultivation of the natural science of God, with its metaphysics open to God and the soul, to man as the creature of God endowed with personal intelligence as the image of the divine reality.

Another crucial point made by *Aeterni Patris* for research and study is the personality of St. Thomas Aquinas: the kind of philosopher he is and the method he exemplifies. To clarify this point, Leo XIII begins with St. Justin Martyr and stresses St. Augustine. St. Thomas Aquinas comes into view not as a writer who develops his own opinions and views as creative self-expressions in the existentialist mode, but as an authentic philosopher who synthesizes the entire intellectual life of the Christian era as such, placing the rightful heritage of Catholic young people into a pruned and chiseled summary for teaching and learning. Thus Aquinas exemplifies the mode of progress that is proper to philosophy as such, namely, deeper penetration into its abiding metaphysical truth, as distinct from the progress proper to the empirical sciences by accumulating new facts and the substitution of new theories for old. From its inception the renewal of Christian Philosophy is primarily concerned with the recovery and restoration to its position of metaphysics as the culminating discipline in liberal education. For the loss of authentic metaphysics has given to the West "a philosophy not firm and stable and robust like that of old, but tottering and feeble".

A further remarkable point is the anticipation by *Aeterni Patris* of the coming deviated and corrupted "Thomisms", which will constitute a special problem in later stages of the renewal: Christian philosophers must study Aquinas' teaching in his own writings. "Be watchful", this encyclical admonishes, "that the doctrine of Thomas be drawn from his own fountains. . . . Be careful to guard the minds of youth from those . . . rivulets that are said to flow thence, but in reality are gathered from strange and unwholesome streams."

Again, in view of coming vicissitudes, attention should be paid to that central passage in which the Holy See defends the authenticity of Christian Philosophy *as philosophy* among the various kinds of philosophy on the contemporary human scene. "Those who to the study of philosophy", Leo XIII states when analyzing the atheistic mode in philosophy, "unite obedience to the Christian Faith are philosophers indeed; for the splendor of the divine truths, received into the mind, helps the understanding, and not only detracts in no wise from its dignity but adds greatly to its nobility, keenness, and stability."

Furthermore, there is the crucially important recognition that Modern Philosophy is a different kind of philosophy because it teaches, implicitly or explicitly, a different metaphysics. "To the old teaching", Leo XIII points out, a novel system of philosophy has succeeded here and there ... philosophizing without any respect for faith, (indulging) the power of inventing in accordance with one's own pleasure.... And this new pursuit seems to have caught the souls of certain Catholic philosophers, who, throwing aside the patrimony of ancient wisdom, chose rather to build up a new edifice than to strengthen and complete the old by the aid of the new—ill-advisedly, in fact, and not without detriment to the (empirical) sciences.

The entire program of the renewal is contained in these words, which will perhaps become fully intelligible only in the light of vicissitudes many decades later and especially in the philosophical anthropology that will be developed at the Catholic University of Lublin in Poland to counteract false philosophies.

As a matter of fact, these words summarize *Aeterni Patris* as a whole as a recognition that Modern Philosophy is not merely an alternate option among kinds of philosophy, but a poisonous kind because of its metaphysical apostasy from God. This generates, on the one hand, the cultural evils experienced in its applications, and, on the other hand, the spiritual and pastoral need to avoid participation in it. This need can be met only by the renewal of Christian Philosophy that is proper to Augustine's "Christian times" of the age of the civilizations in universal history. Thus the pastoral motives of the Holy See stated in the opening and closing paragraphs of *Aeterni Patris* become fully intelligible and reasonable.

Finally, one should not overlook this fundamental personal feature of St. Thomas Aquinas, which makes him the model for teachers and learners of Christian Philosophy. He was a man of prayer, that personal quality that withers and disappears wherever Modern Philosophy pervades the academic world, creating its "atmosphere of unbelief", as St. Pius X will put it in the passage already noted. "Let us follow the example of the Angelic Doctor", writes Leo XIII in conclusion, "who never gave himself to reading or writing without first begging the blessing of God, who modestly confessed that whatever he knew he had acquired not so much by his own study and labor as by the divine gift."

Leo XIII lived through a long pontificate distinguished by numerous remarkable religious and social documents that live across the twentieth century; *Rerum novarum,* "On the Rights and Duties of Capital and Labor", for example, or "On Freemasonry", "On the Christian Constitution of States", "On Human Liberty", seminal for philosophical anthropology in the present century, and many others. At the end of his long life he published an encyclical that reviewed these documents. Which did he consider the most important? *Aeterni Patris!* And the reason? Because it restores the Western heritage of metaphysics, the core of Christian Philosophy, to its rightful position as the seventh of the seven liberal arts, the culmination of the Christian education of all Catholic young people, whatever the professional calling they take up. This is the reason why *Aeterni Patris* underlies all the social documents of the Leonine corpus.

Worldwide Flowering of the Renewal to World War II

The Church intended that the renewal of Christian Philosophy take place as a visible and tangible matter in all Catholic schools. It was not to be a mere intellectual exercise, or something only verbal, accorded lip service and then forgotten, with the internal structure and content of teaching continuing unchanged. The renewal was to be a practical matter with far-reaching internal effects upon the quality and content of the teaching of philosophy. Catholic higher education was to install the metaphysics of St. Thomas Aquinas at the heart of philosophy and then to follow his method of extending its light to all the branches of philosophy, especially philosophical anthropology, and thence to the hermeneutical illumination of all the other arts, sciences, and disciplines of human culture. Furthermore, this metaphysics was to function in theology according to the method and approach of St. Thomas Aquinas so that all the sacred sciences would likewise participate in this renewal of Catholic intellectual life. All of this called for practical steps in the reorganization of studies.

Leo XIII himself took the lead in these steps, which made the renewal a juridically structured and concretely functioning educational reality throughout the Catholic world. These practical measures enabled Catholic institutions of higher education to function according to the subtitle of *Aeterni Patris,* "On Christian Philosophy according to the Mind of St. Thomas Aquinas to be Renewed in the Catholic schools". It was indeed a remarkable and even magnificent philosophical phenomenon, to which we now turn. It fills the decades up to midtwentieth century and World War II. Only the bare facts regarding the actions of Leo XIII will be given here, with dates that permit the documents themselves to be located and studied.

Shortly after *Aeterni Patris* Leo XIII announced his intention to found the Pontifical Roman Academy of St. Thomas Aquinas (October 15, 1879) and approved its constitutions (May 9, 1895). This institution still functions at Rome over a century later. Then Leo XIII set up a Commission of Cardinals to supervise a new critical edition of the works of St. Thomas Aquinas (January 18, 1880), nearing completion a century later, thanks to the firm finalizing support of Pope John Paul II. On March 7, 1880, Leo XIII recommended the study of St. Thomas to Catholics doing scientific research in all fields and named the Angelic Doctor patron of all Catholic research institutes. This action prepared for his proclamation (August 4, 1880) of St. Thomas Aquinas as patron of all Catholic schools.

Noteworthy is Leo XIII's letter to the Jesuits (December 30, 1892) expressing his concern lest this largest religious order, powerful in the Church, with its colleges, universities, and seminaries, fail to carry out the philosophical renewal forthrightly and comprehensively according to the mind of the Holy See. Leo XIII addressed a similar letter (November 25, 1898) to the Franciscan fathers.

Perhaps the most positive and productive of all the measures taken by Leo XIII to consolidate this philosophical renewal was his letter (December 25, 1880) to Cardinal Descamps in Belgium urging and supporting the founding of an Institute of Thomistic Philosophy at the University of Louvain. It was done forthwith by the Belgian bishops, who placed it under the young Father Mercier. He will become one of the lights of the renewal by his writings and later leadership as the famous Cardinal Mercier.

When he looked back at the end of his long pontificate, Leo XIII had the satisfaction of seeing concrete steps on the part of bishops and religious superiors in every part of the world. He had never ceased to foster and urge the renewal in all his audiences with them, especially the *ad limina* visits of the bishops to him in Rome. The program to implement Vatican I by the regeneration of the intelligence by the renewal of higher education was in full swing. Will the successors of Leo XIII carry it forward and deepen it? Pope St. Pius X will make the answer clear.

Pope St. Pius X and Stress upon Metaphysics

Succeeding Leo XIII on August 4, 1903, the new Pope carried the program forward in every way. He brought to a firm conclusion the initiatives of Leo XIII to quell a certain type of priestly resistance to the renewal in actions, to be noted below in Chapter Four, when this negative phenomenon is reviewed. Here one can turn to his positive action. Both together enabled the renewal program to move on into the present century with remarkable unity among priests and bishops and high morale in every type of Catholic school.

Pope St. Pius X seized every occasion for making the directives of Leo XIII more precise, applying them in practice with a vigor all his own. Shortly after his elevation to the Chair of St. Peter he addressed a letter to the Pontifical Roman Academy of St. Thomas Aquinas (January 23, 1904), confirming the acts of Leo XIII and insisting that fundamental philosophy is the heart and purpose of the renewal. Perhaps his most important contribution is the stress he laid upon metaphysics in his *Doctoris Angelici* (June 29, 1914). "All teachers of philosophy and sacred theology", he writes,

> are warned that if they deviate so much as a step from Aquinas, especially in metaphysics, they expose themselves to grave risk. We now go further and solemnly declare that those who in their interpretations misrepresent . . . the principles and major theses of this philosophy . . . are far astray from the holy Doctor. . . . Teachers of Christian Philosophy and Sacred Theology must bear in mind that they have not been entrusted with the duty of teaching in order to impart to their pupils whatever opinions they please. . . . We hereby order and command that teachers in universities and seminaries enjoying by apostolic indult

the privilege of granting academic degrees and doctorates in philosophy, use the *Summa Theologiae* of St. Thomas as the text of their lectures and comment upon it in the Latin language. And let them take particular care to inspire their pupils with a devotion to it.

In *Aeterni Patris* Leo XIII already was concerned with purity and integrity in teaching the philosophy of St. Thomas. By the time of St. Pius X "interpretations that misrepresent its principles and major theses" already had become visible. Using the name of St. Thomas, certain teachers, especially in influential religious orders, were interlarding their own teaching with a copious array of quotations from St. Thomas taken out of their context. Thus the authority of the Angelic Doctor was made to support a quite different metaphysical substrate, alien and opposed to the metaphysics of the renewal program. Recognizing the ominous threat, St. Pius X set up a commission of experts to identify the major theses of Thomistic philosophy as a guide for teachers. He died a few weeks later, during the outbreak of World War I in August 1914, leaving this project to his successor.

Pope Benedict XIV: The Twenty-Four Theses

The work of this commission was published on March 7, 1915, by Pope Benedict XIV as a set of norms for authenticity in the teaching of Christian Philosophy. This short and lucid work is valuable to this day for discerning metaphysical deviations and for use in answering correctly in classrooms that ever-recurring question: What, exactly, is the philosophy of St. Thomas Aquinas?

Pope Pius XI: The Final Structuring of the Renewal

In the changed times after the wrenching agony of the First World War, the Catholic Church returned to the renewal of Christian Philosophy with new vigor under the leadership of Pope Pius XI (1922–39). His fundamental encyclical *Studiorum Ducem* (June 29, 1923) holds St. Thomas Aquinas up as the leader and guide for Catholic youth in all ecclesiastical studies. The actions of his predecessors for the renewal of Christian Philosophy in all Catholic schools are energetically confirmed. The role of the Thomistic metaphysics in keeping Catholic teaching free of the Modernist heresy is explicitly stated, citing the nature and purpose of *Aeterni Patris* and *Doctoris Angelici*. In particular *Studiorum Ducem* rejects the view that the renewal of Christian Philosophy interferes with research. Philosophy is the seventh liberal art; scientific research belongs to the disciplines of the first six arts. Far from interfering with the physical and mathematical sciences, authentic metaphysics fosters them, stabilizes their first principles, supports their love of truth, provides them with the light of a genuinely human interpretation, and helps them apply their findings for the welfare of mankind.

In a sense the renewal of Christian Philosophy reaches its apex with the Apostolic Constitution *Deus Scientiarum Dominus,* which Pope Pius XI published on May 24, 1931. This is a juridical Constitution that reforms the internal structure of all pontifical universities of the world in order to implement fully the renewal of Christian Philosophy. Noteworthy is the reference to *Dei Filius* of Vatican I, now being implemented juridically, and the roll call of the universities of the West, which, having grown out of the cathedral schools, were chartered and fostered by the Church. The Catholic University of America in Washington and the Catholic University of Lublin in Poland are specifically mentioned, a fact that will become significant in later stages of the renewal. The various schools and faculties are defined, and a detailed *ratio studiorum* is specified. In the school of philosophy the teaching method is to give the Catholic young people "the full and coherent synthesis of philosophy according to the method and the principles of St. Thomas Aquinas; in the light of this teaching, furthermore, the different systems of the other philosophers are to be examined and judged". By the apostolic authority of the Holy See, the document concludes, all other academic laws, practices, and customs, together with any and all privileges granted by the Holy See to physical or moral persons, if at variance with this Constitution, are "abrogated and revoked". These "moral persons", of course, are the various religious Orders with their colleges, universities, novitiates, and seminaries.

Rapid Growth of the Renewal

Within this restructured academic framework the renewal of Christian Philosophy, already flourishing everywhere, could grow by leaps and bounds. Everywhere Catholic students were able to enter into their full intellectual heritage, that circle of studies that culminated in the metaphysics open to the personal Supreme Being and the consequent philosophical anthropology open to human personhood, with all the resulting human rights and human dignity. Not least was the fruitful impact of this Constitution on the novitiates of the religious orders and the seminaries that prepare young men for the Catholic priesthood.

An indication of the widespread success of the renewal is the array of periodicals that were founded as its voice and organ. They stand to the present, many still publishing, in the libraries of the world as a precious mine for researchers on points of philosophical doctrine. A sampling to convey the worldwide impact of the renewal can include the venerable *Revue Thomiste* of France, founded in 1893; the *Revue Scholastique de Philosophie,* the organ of the Institute at Louvain, 1894; the *Archives de Philosophie,* edited by Étienne Gilson at Paris since 1919; the *Gregorianum* of the Jesuits at Rome, 1919; *Die Scholastik* in Germany, 1926; and *The New Scholasticism,* organ of the Catholic University at Washington in the

United States, 1926. This list, suggestive, not exhaustive, exhibits a worldwide philosophical movement without parallel in any of the other philosophical currents descending from Descartes, Spinoza, Kant, Comte, and Hegel.

Eminent scholars arose, furthermore, who began to win recognition in the field of philosophy by their research and publication of books, easily matching anything produced in the atheistic camp. Leaving aside the textbooks designed to introduce Catholic undergraduates to their heritage of Christian Philosophy, for which Cardinal Mercier's work and the famous Stonyhurst Series in England may stand as suggestive symbols, one can select a few names and works that illustrate the kind of scholarly research that the renewal was producing. In Germany there were Ehrle, Otto Willmann, and especially Martin Grabmann, one of the abiding lights of the renewal, whose *History of the Scholastic Method* has been mentioned already. Critical and scientific studies representing every type of philosophical analysis and synthesis began to flow forth before the academic world. One need but mention Sertillanges in France, Gardeil and Garrigou-Lagrange in Rome, Gemelli in northern Italy, and perhaps most symbolic of all, N. del Prado at the University of Fribourg in Switzerland and his treatise *De veritate fundamentali philosophiae christianae* (1911). This abiding classic concerns the fundamental truth of Christian Philosophy, namely, the real distinction of essence and existence in all creatures and their real identity in the Supreme Being, thereby unique and absolutely transcendent in his mode of existing. It is a discussion, therefore, of the very heart of the metaphysics of Augustine and Aquinas, that authentic metaphysical heritage that is the central concern of the renewal.

The persons named above were Catholic priests engaged in philosophical teaching and research on the university level. As time went on, however, more and more Catholic laymen took up the field of philosophy in university teaching, thereby enhancing the presence of the renewal in the world of the university at large in the way that Leo XIII had hoped. Here again two of the most famous professors of philosophy across the twentieth century can stand symbolically for their increasingly numerous younger colleagues. The first is Étienne Gilson, renowned professor of the history of philosophy at the Sorbonne in Paris. His invitation to give the Gifford Lectures for 1931–32 signaled the arrival of the renewal of Christian Philosophy in the world of general scholarship. Gilson's positive research, furthermore, stood on the bedrock of the renewal's metaphysics, as his *Being and Some Philosophers* and *The Unity of Philosophical Experience* testify.[2] The second is Jacques Maritain, a famous convert and professor at the Institut Catholique and a preeminent metaphysical mind, as his *Degrees of Knowledge, Existence and the Existent,* and *A Preface to Metaphysics* bear witness. Maritain's insight of cultivated natural reason regarding the real existence of the transcendent,

[2] See Excerpts for Part Four, Gilson, p. 458.

intelligent, and personal Supreme Being sustained many a young Catholic student across the present century. His prodigious talent in metaphysics, however, was not matched by an equal lucidity in sociopolitical applications; it seems he was never able to elaborate the comprehensive philosophy of history needed for clarifying and mediating such applications.

Germany offers a quite unusual aspect of the renewal of Christian Philosophy that deserves special mention and careful independent study. It revolves around the professional career of Edmund Husserl, the school of Phenomenology that he founded, and especially the disciples who came forth from his teaching. Husserl became famous for his phenomenological method, the philosophical study of reality as given in the appearances of things by an effort to intuit essences as known in those appearances. Thus Husserl's original idea broke free from the Kantian subjectivism, moving out toward knowledge of objective reality. It offered a philosophical approach, therefore, very like that of Christian Philosophy, for it is "intentional" in character, that is, it recognizes the nature of human cognitive powers to reach out to the object, to tend toward objective reality, and to grasp its nature or essence. This was the insight of his important work *Logical Investigations,* published in 1900, which demonstrated exhaustively the failure of empiricism to explain human knowledge as nothing but sensory images and their associations. This was the "first Husserl", who placed his disciples upon the path that leads to discovery of the natural metaphysics of mankind, to the appreciation of Augustine and Aquinas in the natural knowledge of the transcendent Supreme Being, and then on to the intellectual recognition of the preambles of religious faith. Disciples included Peter Wust, with his *Resurrection of Metaphysics;* Dietrich von Hildebrand, with his later career and published works at Fordham University; and above all Edith Stein, Husserl's graduate assistant who did her doctorate under his direction.[3] These and others came to the Catholic Faith and made the renewal of Christian Philosophy their personal endeavor.

Edith Stein in particular became a profound student of Thomistic metaphysics, recognizing its kinship with the ascent of the mind to God in prayer. When she entered the Church, Husserl remarked to friends, "What a beautiful and talented gift the Thomistic renewal is going to receive!" For she was a woman of prayer from her upbringing in a sound Jewish home under a good mother. It was not surprising, therefore, that she became a disciple of Teresa of Avila and entered the Carmelite order where she continued her research and writing on St. Thomas' philosophy and on the way of prayer. But her life was cut short. The Holocaust of the Jewish people, that lurid and horrible *Endlösung* that was the final application of Cartesian rationalism and the Spinozan metaphysics of modern philosophical atheism, was only ten years ahead. She was taken from her convent by the Gestapo

---

[3] See Excerpts for Part Four, Von Hildebrand, pp. 471–76, Stein, p. 477.

because of her Jewish origin and her Catholic profession and hauled in a freight train to Auschwitz, where she was put to death in the gas chambers on August 9, 1942.

Edith Stein, now beatified by the Catholic Church, came forth from "the early Husserl". In 1913 Husserl published a new revised edition of his *Logical Investigations* in which, to the expressed chagrin of his earlier students, he falls back into the Kantian subjectivism of "the later Husserl". Out of this later position Heidegger and his existentialist followers came forth, including Sartre and his confreres in Paris. What had happened to Husserl? The renewal of Christian Philosophy is deeply challenged to research, study, and discussion of the basic error: man does not have an intuition of essences. This is a false angelism. We have an intuition of the first metaphysical principles of reality and of thought, one recalls from Aquinas' treatise *On Being and Essence,* from which we must proceed laboriously in thought, study, and the process of learning under sound and good teaching in order to know the essences, natures, and substances of things. One might say that much of philosophical anthropology turns about this decisive point for human education and culture.

This sketch offers only a few of the personalities and the issues that open avenues for personal study of the burgeoning renewal of Christian Philosophy in the fourth and fifth decades of the twentieth century. These persons and their many colleagues are readily identifiable in the bibliographies and on the shelves of the libraries of the world, not the least of whom is John Paul II himself as a philosopher of the renewal.[4] Taken all in all, the general recognition of the persons and their publications, the periodicals and learned journals devoted to the renewal, speak for themselves. And the increasing flow of young Catholic leaders, in possession of their authentic and full intellectual heritage, with metaphysics firmly restored to the culminating position in their education as Augustine had programmed it early in the Christian era, out into all walks of social life constitutes a unique philosophical phenomenon from Vatican I and *Aeterni Patris* across the first half of the present century.

The Reaction of the Atheistic Philosophers

This phenomenon could not but arouse consternation in the ranks of the atheistic philosophers, who had felt themselves so secure in their position established during the nineteenth century. They began to express their alarm at philosophical congresses and in their publications, perhaps a negative indication of the success of the renewal.

Here again two especially famous professors at the Sorbonne, both professed atheists in philosophy, may stand as symbols, for they bring to a head that great

---

[4] See Excerpts for Part Four, John Paul II, p. 493.

central question: What, actually, is Christian Philosophy? Is it authentic as philosophy? Or does the adjective destroy the noun?

First, then, Professor Léon Brunschvicq, who writes in his Spinozist *Progress of Consciousness in Western Philosophy* (1927), after discussing Gilson, that, since philosophy means pure reason inseparable from the natural sciences and human consciousness, one can only expect from Thomas Aquinas the mere outward appearance of philosophy and the illusion that his is a work of human reason. The illusion of Thomas Aquinas, Professor Brunschvicq maintains, is simply that, while he believed and said he was philosophizing, what he actually did was only a theology in disguise.

The second example is Professor Émile Bréhier in his standard *History of Philosophy* (1928), in which he maintains that Christianity does not stand over against Greek philosophy with a doctrine of its own. The earliest Christians were small unlettered groups, devoid of any teaching program. They expected the imminent return of Jesus and nothing else. In the first five centuries of our era there was no Christian Philosophy original and distinct from the thinking of the pagan philosophers. To summarize, he concludes, there is no such thing as a "Christian Philosophy", a verdict aimed explicitly at his colleague Professor Gilson. The controversy became stormy. Accordingly, the "French Philosophical Society", perhaps the world's most prestigious, determined upon "the notion of Christian Philosophy" as the topic for discussion at its annual meeting on March 21, 1931. Professor Gilson was invited to present the initial paper. The day came. Professors of philosophy from all France sat in rapt silence as four men engaged in flashing and unprecedented intellectual swordplay, Brunschvicq and Bréhier on the one hand, representing the atheistic metaphysics of Modern Philosophy, and Gilson and Maritain on the other, representing the metaphysics of the Thomistic renewal. The transcript stands permanently for the record in the *Bulletin* of the Society (Paris, 1931), and the developed positions are to be found in the publications of the protagonists. In a sense this event marks a high point in the renewal of Christian Philosophy and merits much additional study. Here only a brief summary can be given.

The atheistic philosophers took their position upon that essential thesis of Modern Philosophy since Descartes and Spinoza, that philosophy must be a secular subject held separate from religion. They interpreted this to mean that it must be held separate from any idea of God. Philosophy, to be authentic, must be atheistic. It is not allowed to "philosophize within the Faith", for this is theologizing. Philosophy must deny the existence of a transcendent Supreme Being. It must assert as its first principle and point of departure that the cosmos is all that is. This existence is reduced to nothing but matter, the material things of the bodily senses: atheism and materialism are one and the same thing.

There is an arrogance in this approach conveyed by the authoritarian word "must", a reduction of the scope of human knowledge and even the threat of thought control. These dimensions were not lost upon Gilson and Maritain, as one can read between their lines, but they avoided discussing such psychological conditions of thought and such practical consequences, keeping to the philosophical principles. In fact the day was a courteous one, with Gilson paying frequent personal tribute to Brunschvicq as his former professor.

How then did Gilson and Maritain cope with the allegations?

Gilson took the lead, speaking from the facts researched by the history of philosophy. It is not true to say that the early Christians had no doctrine. One must not overlook St. Luke and St. Paul. Christianity came to fulfill the prophets: the entire doctrinal heritage of Judaism passed on to the Christians, and with it an immense body of rational thought about the Supreme Being and his attributes, thought that takes place prior to revealed religion and independently of it. For God's everlasting power and deity, as St. Paul says echoing the book of Wisdom, are there for the mind to see in the things he has made. The Christians received the academic discipline called "philosophy" from the pagan Greeks and Romans into their own schools and continued to cultivate it as Aristotle's "natural theology", the natural science of God and divine things. The assiduous cultivation of this rational knowledge of the Supreme Being stands for a thousand years, from Justin, Ambrose, and Augustine to Bonaventure and Aquinas, like a mighty mountain range on the landscape of universal history. It is a matter of historical fact that it existed and that it was distinct from theology. It was the heritage of metaphysics, which the Christians did not invent, cultivated in the mode of comprehensive openness to all intelligible reality as such. It is a quibble with words to say that philosophy must be confined to the material things of the sensory cosmos.

Maritain was silent until later in the day. "I want at the outset", he said in his opening words, "to state my full accord with Professor Gilson on the essential point of this debate, the fact of the historic reality of Christian Philosophy." Then he turned to the metaphysical explanation of this fact. "For me," he continued,

> the principle for solving this problem, the significance of the adjective "Christian" with the noun "philosophy", is the classical distinction between nature as such and the various conditions in which natures of things can exist, or, in other words, the distinction between the order of specification and the order of exercise. Thus one can have different kinds of philosophy, always authentically philosophical in nature as a rational discipline but quite different specifically because of the way it exists and is, accomplished in the mind of the human person who philosophizes.... Since philosophy is a form of wisdom, furthermore, the adjective "Christian" can be used properly with this natural discipline called philosophy, one must say against Feuerbach, where it would not be applicable in the same way to mathematics, for example, or to physics. Thomas Aquinas did not have the lofty and even arrogant idea of human reason professed by Descartes or Spinoza, and he certainly did not have the rationalist's idea of reason, but he

did nevertheless regard philosophical wisdom as fully and integrally rational, indeed as the supreme and most perfect work of human reason.

"The denomination *Christian,*" Maritain went on, "when applied to a philosophy, does not relate to its nature or essence *as philosophy:* if it is faithful to that nature, it does not depend upon the Christian Faith, either in the object that it studies, or in the principles and the methods by which it studies that object." Then the recognized philosopher Maritain made a profession with utter frankness before his audience:

> We Christians believe that grace comes from our religion to assist our human natures, so that their natural powers are strengthened and see better their natural objects of study. . . . I think with Professor Gilson, furthermore, that the results are visible in the very history of philosophy. . . .
>
> Thus we see that the expression Christian Philosophy does not designate an essence taken simply by itself, but a complex: an essence in a certain state or condition, . . . that of the human person who is philosophizing.

In this encounter and dialogue, Christian Philosophy was making its point at the highest level of philosophical discourse and discussion. The Christian philosophers, furthermore, were visibly conscious of a certain intellectual superiority as persons standing upon higher ground, able to see farther, open to reality as such, free of that inhibiting imprisonment of the mind within the cosmos, the eclipse contained in that atheistic assertion "the cosmos is all that is". Thus a metaphysical openness stands at the very heart of the renewal of Christian Philosophy, and it was exemplified well in the encounter with the atheistic mentality on that memorable day, March 21, 1931, only a few weeks before the *Deus Scientiarum Dominus* of Pius XI. The dialogue of the two laymen with the leaders of atheistic philosophy in France fulfilled the hope that had animated the Holy See in *Aeterni Patris.* Standing at this point in the present century, victory for the Church Militant over the philosophical atheism that had arisen in Western civilization seemed to be a real possibility.

With this one comes to a set of vicissitudes within the renewal itself that will affect its progress and even relocate it from the academic to the catechetical order of teaching in the later decades of the twentieth century. But before taking up this negative phenomenon, which amounts to a complex betrayal of God and a disservice to contemporary mankind, one should study the humanistic dimension of the renewal. For this will make the disservice intelligible. Putting the matter positively, the renewal of Christian Philosophy was offering contemporary mankind a more human philosophy of man than that resting upon atheistic metaphysics.

III

THE RENEWAL OF NATURAL AND
CHRISTIAN PERSONALISM

For nearly a century after Vatican I, until the midtwentieth century, the renewal of Christian Philosophy in all Catholic colleges, universities, and especially seminaries was a burgeoning worldwide success. In every nation of the Christian West young Catholic priests and religious were formed in their own philosophical heritage as leaders on behalf of the deposit of faith, able to cope with the subtleties of a deviated meaning at the hands of the atheistic hermeneutics. Parallel with them an ever more numerous stream of young lay persons flowed forth from these Catholic institutions of higher education, likewise in possession of their rightful heritage, their own metaphysics and philosophical anthropology, out into every walk of political, social, and professional life.

This success of the philosophical renewal was due in no small measure to the growing presence in the twentieth century of two powerful assisting factors in the cultural life of the West. One was negative, the new threats to the human person due to ongoing applications of atheistic metaphysics. The other was positive, a set of surprising new developments in the continuing Copernican revolution in the empirical sciences. After reviewing each, we shall take this occasion to study the philosophical anthropology that flows from the renewed metaphysics: the specifically human mode of existing and of knowing, and the resulting philosophical foundations of human personhood and liberty. For it is this that so largely explains the victorious march of the renewal in the face of the atheistic way of using the human mind. It gave the contemporary Catholic Church the opportunity to be the Good Samaritan for modern man, healing the wounds inflicted upon the very foundations of natural and Christian humanism and personalism by the atheistic reduction.

The New Twentieth-Century Threats to the Human Person

The impact of Modern Philosophy upon the human person has been noted in Chapter One above. In the present century this impact has been intensified because of the immense political and social changes that have set in since World War I. Modern Philosophy as such came to an end, for its positions were elaborated in earlier times and now began to be perceived as something past. Postmodern times were at hand. The renewal of Christian Philosophy fitted well into the experience of these new times, the twentieth century with its immense world wars and even greater social revolutions. The reason is the advent of ideology, with its mounting repression of the human person.

The Concept of Ideology

One can say that Modern Philosophy did not as philosophy survive World War I. It turned into ideology, something quite different. Ideology means the use of atheistic metaphysics for the construction of social programs and political platforms imposed now by totalitarian systems. These are characterized by techniques of thought control and especially the use of fear, refined forms of the "Reign of Terror" in the French Revolution. A specialized literature on ideology has arisen in the present century, which can be studied to advantage in explaining the success of the renewal of Christian Philosophy at the middle decades of the century. For ideology contrasts with authentic philosophy, the cultivation of true humanism and wisdom on a personal basis. Ideology reduces and represses the individual into a cog in the totalitarian mechanism, while Christian Philosophy offers the foundation for personal freedom, dignity, and rights of individual human beings.

Marxist Communism

Out of World War I the Russian Revolution in 1917 established atheistic metaphysics as its ideology, the thinking of its program for international socialism. From the viewpoint of philosophy, it is a holdover from the earlier period of Modern Philosophy and a consolidation, now worldwide in aspiration, of its nineteenth-century applications. Its repression of the human person and its methods of thought control were reported in the classic work of Solzhenitsyn the *Gulag Archipelago*.

Nietzschean National Socialism

At the opposite pole to all appearances, but similar in its totalitarian methods of control over human persons, was the movement of National Socialism in Germany, called "Nazism" for short. Again atheistic metaphysics, this time in its existentialist form, becomes the ideology for the totalitarian social program and political platform. Professor Martin Heidegger, Germany's foremost Existentialist and disciple of Nietzsche, took the lead in organizing the universities of Germany into the Nazi machinery. Corresponding to the Gulag Archipelago was that frightful genocidal Holocaust under Hitler in World War II, a deliberate plan to exterminate the Jewish people. One cannot forget that one million Jewish children perished in the gas chambers of Auschwitz and other concentration camps. The atheistic attitude toward human beings emerges here into full view: the metaphysical substrate for a philosophical anthropology that supports the value, dignity, and human rights of humans as persons had been lost in the German universities and hence in social leadership and social practice. One cannot forget, furthermore, that as Heidegger proceeded from the second Husserl, the Husserl of relapse into the Kantian subjectivism, so Edith Stein came forth upon the twentieth-century stage as the disciple of the first Husserl, who pointed her toward Thomas Aquinas, metaphysical realism, and openness to the transcendent Supreme Being. She too perished in the gas chambers of Auschwitz.

A World Split Apart

This title of Solzhenitsyn's famous address (1978) at Harvard University indicates well the philosophical character of the twentieth century. Inundated by the applications of the atheistic metaphysics overflowing from the modern period prior to the First World War, this century comes more and more to reflect the personal and social failure of this inner-cosmic metaphysics to provide a foundation for true humanism. In his address to that silent late twentieth-century audience at Harvard, itself so deeply imbued with Marx and Nietzsche, Solzhenitsyn calls it "a disaster, the calamity of an autonomous, irreligious humanistic consciousness". It is worthwhile to hear his own words, which specify the linkage between the present intellectual landscape of planet earth and the rise of philosophical atheism in the West since Giordano Bruno.

"On the way from the Renaissance to our days", Solzhenitsyn states in measured tones born of much suffering in the Gulag Archipelago,

> we have enriched our experience, but we have lost the concept of a Supreme Complete Entity which used to restrain our passions and our irresponsibility. We have placed too much hope in politics and social reform, only to find out that we were being deprived of our most precious possession: our spiritual life. It is trampled by the party mob in the East, by the commercial one in the West. This is the essence of the crisis: the split in the world is less terrifying than the similarity of the disease afflicting its main sections.

This similarity, of course, is the substrate of philosophical atheism, the inner-cosmic metaphysics that reduces the human mode of existing to nothing but an accidental package of matter and energy imprisoned within the cosmos and to liberty condemned, as it says, the "liberty" of the stimulus-response bonds of James and Dewey, the "liberty" of Heidegger's organismic experience of life in time.

This sketch of the philosophical landscape may suffice to indicate what a powerful negative support came to the renewal of Christian Philosophy from the experience of this loss of God. A climate of openness was being created toward its quite different philosophical anthropology, a concept of man based on the meta-physical recognition of spiritual reality, and hence able to offer contemporary man the natural foundation for "our spiritual life".

The Twentieth-Century Copernican Revolution: Science Opens to God

There was, then, this negative support. Was there a corresponding and contemporary positive support for the renewal of the metaphysics of Christian Philosophy in all Catholic colleges, universities, and seminaries? There was, indeed: it came powerfully and unexpectedly from a series of dramatic discoveries by the empirical sciences as the twentieth century proceeded. The ongoing Copernican revolution began to generate a revolution from within the sciences against the atheistic world view. It was nothing less than a new type of openness on the part of the physical sciences for the historic heritage of metaphysics. This could not but strengthen the position of the program for its renewal, which was growing so dramatically in Catholic institutions during the same decades.

In part Three above the beginning of the Copernican revolution in the empirical sciences was studied both in itself and in the ominous fact that the heritage in metaphysics was falling into a decadent state, ready for that fateful substitution by mathematical physics at the hands of Descartes, Spinoza, and their successors. Thus the new findings of the sciences were seen and interpreted without metaphysical understanding, that is, without relationship to the transcendent and intelligent Creator. The Copernican revolution accordingly became a wrenching experience for mankind, because it seemed to eliminate the witness of the visible cosmos to the Supreme Being. By a series of well-known steps, therefore, that strange development took place that was sketched in Chapter One above as "the atheistic interpretation of the Copernican revolution". The idea arose and became entrenched in Western intellectual life that the meaning of science is atheism. In the present century this concept became a slogan of ideology, especially in its Marxist version.

It is this slogan that the twentieth-century revolution within the ongoing Copernican revolution has set aside, hence the dramatic character of these developments in the sciences and their absorbing interest for the renewal of metaphysics. They of course merit a special study far beyond this sketch, which in this space can only draw attention to something that younger scholars are looking into ever more intensively. For there is the ever-present danger that the ideologies will want to suppress this evidence and this emerging meaning of empirical science. The reason is that this unexpected scientific progress has made the agnosticism of Kant and the atheism of Feuerbach, Marx, Nietzsche, James, and Dewey old-fashioned and even naive—more naive even than the naiveté of our pre-Copernican ancestors, who thought, understandably, that the theory of the earth-centered crystal spheres explained best the cosmic panorama that they observed with unaided senses.

"We are living in a unique era", said Pope John Paul II, a former professor in the renewal of Christian Philosophy, addressing in 1985 a group of astrophysicists:

> Within the last few decades we have witnessed more basic advances in our understanding of physical reality than had been made during the entire previous history of our planet. There is strong evidence that this exponential growth of scientific knowledge will continue. . . . These scientific achievements proclaim the dignity of the human being and greatly clarify man's unique role in the universe.

From the Splitting of the Atom to the Contingency of the Cosmos

"Rutherford's discovery of the atomic nucleus in 1911", writes the famous physicist Niels Bohr, "revealed at once the inadequacy of classical mechanical and electromagnetic concepts to explain the inherent stability of the atom."

This epoch-making discovery may be taken as the beginning of these scientific achievements. It opens the revolution within the Copernican revolution because it spells the end of the Lucretian atomism, the concept of ultimate indivisible particles of matter, which had reigned supreme since Giordano Bruno as the basis of the inner-cosmic metaphysics of materialism and atheism. It was a view of ultimate reality that was predicated on the eternity of matter in the form of these atoms, which formed all the realities in the cosmos by the various groupings and motions that the sciences observe and that mathematics analyzes. This discovery of a structure within the atom led step by step to the splitting of the atom, as it is called, and the release of nuclear energy. Obviously, science in the twentieth century has broken new ground. For philosophy this becomes significant as a new witness to the fact that this is an ordered universe, with an order pointing toward an Intelligence far more insistently than the heavenly motions that mankind always has noted with the unaided senses.

To grasp the meaning of such discoveries for the way matter exists, and then for the way the cosmos exists (both philosophical concepts), one must study the interaction in this century between nuclear physics and astronomy, or better, the new science of astrophysics. Here space allows only the mention of Professor Hubble's discovery of the galaxies in expanding motion and the Nobel Prize-winning discovery of what *Time* (October 30, 1978) calls "an echo from creation".

The Contingency of the Cosmos

This "echo" was the identification of radio waves pervading the material cosmos that point back in time to the beginning of this present expanding motion of the galaxies. "The two young scientists, Penzias and Wilson," *Time* magazine reports, "virtually confirmed that the universe began with a bang and, as the Royal

Swedish Academy of Sciences put it, 'has made it possible to obtain information about cosmic processes that took place a very long time ago, at the time of the creation of the universe'."

Let this suffice to indicate the revolutionary change in the scientific world view and as an invitation to further independent study of it from the philosophical point of view. The inner-cosmic metaphysics of the ancient atomism is no longer viable from the scientific point of view. Science itself is becoming open to a different kind of metaphysics, one that is itself open to an order of transcendent nonmaterial reality and indeed to the Supreme Reality, who is intelligent and able to give visible things both their existence and the measure, forms, and purposive order of that existence, to use the terminology of Augustine, the founder of this metaphysics that the Catholic Church is renewing in her schools.

At midcentury the eminent British mathematician and physicist Sir Edmund Whittaker published his *Space and Spirit*, a study of this new openness of the empirical sciences to the metaphysics of St. Thomas Aquinas and its ways of ascending to God. It has become an abiding classic, abundantly consolidated by the most recent achievements of science. Let us conclude with his words. "Recent researches", he writes,

> have led to the conclusion that the universe cannot have existed for an infinite time in the past. . . . There must have been a beginning of the present cosmic order, a creation as we may call it, and we are even in a position to calculate approximately when it happened. . . . At this point we escape from the order of the Newtonian cosmos, and, as in St. Thomas' original proof, the sequence of causes terminates in God. . . . The fact, not known to St. Thomas, that the same mathematical laws are valid over the cosmos . . . leads to the inference that there is only a *single* mind involved in the whole of creation. . . . Just as we recognize that there are other bodies besides our own and these bodies constitute the material universe, so we recognize that there are other minds besides our own, and in particular that there is a mind, akin to our minds, whose operations are revealed in the behavior of non-living matter—the laws of Nature—and this mind is One over the entire universe, whose totality is thus bound into a unity. The proof from order is today more complete, more comprehensive and more majestic than in the form presented in the thirteenth century.

Whittaker's book is indeed a classic summary of the twentieth-century revolution within the Copernican revolution and deserves to be studied in its entirety. But perhaps enough has been presented to show that postmodern times have indeed dawned in the present century: the times of Modern Philosophy and its atheistic metaphysics have been left behind. Science has left that metaphysics in the outmoded past. The success of the renewal of Christian Philosophy across the early and middle decades of this century is due in no small measure to this change in the intellectual climate.

Whittaker's allusion to mind as distinct from matter serves to introduce the study of the philosophical anthropology that is the immediate corollary of the metaphysics of the renewal. For it meets the need of contemporary mankind for a more human philosophy of man.

Toward Renewing Mankind's Philosophy of Man

In the total context of mankind's philosophical experience across the age of the civilizations, which began about 4000 B.C., after the surprisingly long millennia of prehistory, the renewal of Christian Philosophy assumes a new importance when seen from the viewpoint of human personal and social need in the twentieth century. It offers to contemporary mankind the solid philosophical support for recognizing human beings as persons with inalienable rights, dignity, and value. This philosophical recognition of human personhood has been an aspiration of philosophy since the Greeks. The human mode of existing as specifically different from that of the lower animals was seen already by the Greek philosophers, and the insight was developed and deepened when Augustine and the Christian philosophers were able to ascend to the concept of creation, and especially that of man who, as a being with reason, is in the image of God.

In this perspective the philosophical anthropology of St. Thomas Aquinas becomes uniquely valuable and even a dire necessity for contemporary mankind. This is true for two chief reasons. First, he gathered the entire philosophical endeavor to achieve an adequate philosophical expression of human identity into a comprehensive synthesis. The texts of St. Thomas Aquinas are abiding classics in philosophical anthropology and deserve continuing close study. Second, the metaphysical apostasy from the transcendent Creator, which was studied in Part Three above, has had a problem-creating impact, noted in Chapter One, upon the human self-image. The concept of man suffers the characteristic reduction at the hands of atheistic inner-cosmic metaphysics to nothing but a variation of the merely animal mode. Mankind loses the historic specific difference of the human mode, and this long before Darwinism seemed to provide scientific support for the atheistic world view.

The renewal of this more human philosophical anthropology, therefore, places St. Thomas Aquinas in his correct light and justifies the program of the contemporary Catholic Church from a general human point of view. There is a further justification, of course, from the viewpoint of revealed religion and its deposit of faith, which will be studied in Chapter Five below. For the present, however, attention will be drawn to some of the more important texts of St. Thomas Aquinas where his philosophy of man can be pursued. Space here permits only a summary of his doctrine, which these texts elaborate in his sweeping, incisive, and lapidary way.

The Metaphysical Foundation

At this point the metaphysics of St. Thomas, studied in Part Two above, should be reviewed. For his philosophical anthropology is in no sense an exercise in empirical psychology. It is not one of the empirical sciences. It is a philosophical discipline that arises directly out of the metaphysical ascent to the transcendent Supreme Being, who is the source and cause of the existence of all other realities. In these realities, essence and existence are really distinct metaphysical principles of being. This provides the insight into the uniqueness and absolute transcendence of the Supreme Being, for in him these principles are identical: his essence is his act of existing, which accordingly is without limit. It is infinite, to use the Latin root that denotes the same concept: without limit. His act of existing possesses all the positive qualities and perfections observed among his creatures, but without defect and without limit.

The first point that the mind attains regarding human self-identity is the fact of creaturehood. A human being is a creature of this infinite God. St. Thomas' philosophical anthropology recognizes this fact of facts about human life when it sees the substantial form of the human essence, individuated by its union with first matter, as a spirit especially created by the Supreme Being. Each human being, therefore, is an individuated bodily reality, a reality that exists and is alive because it has this specially created animating principle.

Human life, accordingly, is quite special and indeed unique in the whole universe of created reality, visible and invisible, material and spiritual, for mankind is the link between the visible cosmos and the higher order of purely spiritual realities. Man, as it were, is the priest of the cosmos, the being charged with administering the cosmos on behalf of the order and plan from above. In this way philosophy makes contact with the ecological problems of the late twentieth century and points toward the nature of their solutions.

It is supremely important, therefore, to recognize that St. Thomas' philosophy of man is metaphysical in character, and not simply an alternate type of empirical psychology. It depends upon the renewal of metaphysics itself, that authentic metaphysics of the divine transcendence that is stated in the ontology of his *On Being and Essence*.

This does not derogate from the science of empirical psychology, which has been pursued so avidly during the nineteenth and twentieth centuries, from Wundt and his laboratory at Leipzig. To the contrary. The empirical sciences retain their own nature and methodology and make their own contribution to human knowledge. The first six arts do not lose when the mind admits the claims of wisdom, the seventh of the seven liberal arts, which studies existence itself and the principles by which its various modes are able to be as they are actually seen to be in reality. The renewal of metaphysics, and of the philosophy of man that stems from it, does not supplant or inhibit any empirical science or suppress any empirical findings, such as the laws of genetics discovered in late twentieth century. To the contrary: it enables such findings to be interpreted in terms of reality understood comprehensively, rather than in the truncated terms of inner-cosmic metaphysics.

The Thomistic synthesis bridges the gap in the philosophical concept of man between the materialists on the one hand and Plato's extreme intellectualism on the other. He is the disciple of Plato, Aristotle, and Augustine: he draws the truths they saw into a higher reconciliation. The materialists, ancient and modern, hold that the intellect does not differ in kind from sense knowledge. Plato and his disciples have held that the intellect is not only a distinct power from sense but that its activity of thinking cannot make use of bodily organs—hence Plato's theory of the Ideas, and the notion that the soul is related only extrinsically to the body, as a rider to his horse. Aristotle's philosophy articulated a golden mean, the one that Aquinas synthesizes. All knowledge begins in the senses, indeed, but it does not remain within the senses and the cosmos. Reason is the metaphysical fact that the knowing subject is this spiritual creature, the animating soul, which is able to rise from the images of sense to a nonsensory level of insight, where the principles of being and essence are understood to be in things, from which the mind ascends to the intelligible order and to the Creator.

Along these lines, then, one can see the qualitative excellence and the contemporary relevance of St. Thomas' philosophy of man. It emerges from his metaphysics in Chapters IV and V of his *On Being and Essence,* and he elaborates it in many places in his later works. Here particular attention is drawn to his disputed question on the soul (article 1), where the metaphysical foundation of his philosophical anthropology is discussed in ample detail: the human soul is both the animating principle or form of the human bodily reality and at the same time a substantial reality in its own right, able to continue existing individuated when it is separated from its body by death. From this basic metaphysical foundation one can proceed to the philosophical study of human rationality, and then to that of human freedom.

Philosophy of the Human Mode of Knowing

At the end of ontology, one recalls, the mind stands at a fork in the road. Will it take the ascent that leads up to the transcendent Supreme Being? Or will it take the other way, the horizontal way of inner-cosmic metaphysics? This is the fateful decision for philosophical anthropology, for in the ascent the mind recognizes in man two qualitatively distinct kinds of knowledge, whereas in the other way there is only one kind, that of the senses. The renewal of philosophical anthropology as such consists essentially of the rediscovery of the human intellect as a distinct power to know reality, qualitatively different from sense knowledge.

The Intellect as a Spiritual Power of Knowing

It is quite mistaken to believe that this recognition of the intelligence begins by some kind of intuition or Platonic mode apart from the senses. All human knowledge begins in the senses: so too this knowledge regarding the nature of the human intellect. There are certain facts about human knowledge that mankind always has been able to observe and that the empirical psychology of recent times has confirmed. These facts in brief review are the following.

Men know many things in a nonmaterial way, that is, separated from the conditions of space and time. When one knows "possibility", for example, or "cause and effect", or "necessity" as distinct from "contingency", or "judgments" of denial as distinct from those of affirmation, one is already seeing realities that are different from the individual perceptions of the senses. Natural reason always has recognized such dimensions of human knowing and has acted accordingly, as artifacts bear witness, and also the very structure of human language and communication. Man judges and reasons, recognizing the identity of two concepts and then the necessary bonds between sequences of such judgments. They trust these processes and always have used them in life.

Men go beyond the appearances presented by the senses to ask what the things are in their underlying reality. What *is* a plant? What *is* water? What *is* electricity? What *is* a human being? To seek what the things presented by the senses *are* is already to be moving beyond sense knowledge, for it asks the question about existence. It is human to know things in a way that prescinds from the concrete individuals and understands the kinds of things on Porphyry's tree. This is another way of saying that man has a power of knowing that is different from the sensory power to perceive individual bodily things: it is a power to conceive understandings in a universal way. All communication educated by the trivium and all empirical sciences developed in the quadrivium depend on the reality of this second and different power of knowing. Thus man develops his liberal arts, as he prepares to recognize the specific difference in man, the specifically human as such. Materialism is being thus transcended, for sensory reality is being known in a nonmaterial way. The senses know only materially, that is, subject to the individuating characteristics of space and time. Something qualitatively different, nonmaterial, is at hand. This specifically human knowledge is of course linked with sense objects both in its origin and throughout its development.

All of this has been known implicitly throughout human life. But the recent empirical science of psychology has confirmed it in a new way through its intensive research upon human subjects. The natural interpretation of these observations and findings recognizes that there is a specific difference, a qualitative one, one of kind and not simply of degree, between the knowing power of the lower animals and the cognitive ability of the human animal. The lower animals have only one kind of knowledge, that of the bodily senses. The human animal has a second kind of knowledge, the power or light of reason. Hence the philosophical heritage has rightly defined man as a rational animal. By this light of reason, the human mode of knowing is specified: it is a power of insight and understanding that transcends space, time, and all the individuating characteristics of the material order.

The philosophical way is now open to recognize two qualitatively different kinds of knowledge in the human being, irreducible to each other and pointing to the existence in man of a nonmaterial principle or cognitive power by which such spiritual insight and understanding can take place. The philosophical recognition of the special character of the substantial form of man is now possible: the animating principle of the human body, *anima* in Latin and "soul" in English, is a spiritual reality. Man is an embodied spirit, a special creation of God, whom metaphysics as such has recognized as the cause of the really distinct metaphysical principles that constitute all beings other than himself: the act of existence by which each thing is, and the essence, nature, or substance that limits its existence to that of its own particular kind of thing.

"Concerning the act of knowledge by which one actually considers that he has a soul," St. Thomas writes in his *De veritate* (10, 8), "I say that the soul is known through its acts." This brings Aquinas to the basic position in article 9 of the same treatise, where he places philosophical anthropology on the foundation of the concept of truth. Truth is not immediately and primarily in sense knowledge, he writes with a nod to Plato, but the higher kind of knowledge that human judgments about the essential natures of things express. "Truth is in the intellect", he writes,

> as a result of the activity of the intellect, namely, the judgment it makes regarding the essence or nature of the thing it knows. Truth is known by the intelligence when it reflects on this kind of cognitive activity, for it also recognizes its own correlation with reality. This it could not do unless it knew the nature of its mode of knowing, and this in turn could not be known unless it knew at the same time the nature of the intellect as an active principle of knowledge. This nature is recognized as the ability to judge of things according to the way they exist in reality. It follows that the intellect knows the truth about itself by reflecting upon itself.

This reflection upon its acts is something the senses cannot do. Thus it becomes clear that philosophical anthropology takes its point of departure from reflection on the ascent it has made in metaphysics, from ontology to natural theology, rising from the first concepts (things and their kinds, or being and essence) to the intelligible truths and on to the real existence of the unique

Supreme Being, source and cause of the existence of all other existing realities.

With this philosophical recognition of the human intellect as a second cognitive power, qualitatively distinct from the senses, the metaphysical foundation for human personal freedom has been established, that special human quality menaced by the atheistic reductionism of the inner-cosmic metaphysics, and to which the renewal of Christian Philosophy ministers in a special and timely way. Before turning to the study of human freedom, it is well to recall from Part Two above the Thomistic synthesis of Plato, Aristotle, and Augustine. In his treatise *On Spiritual Creatures* (art. 10), St. Thomas cites St. Augustine: "It is the very nature of our intellectual power to understand things in a certain incorporeal light, which is *sui generis,* as the eye of the flesh sees things about us in this bodily light." And Aquinas adds his own comment: "This light by which our human mind understands is the active intellect." This active power with which each human individual is endowed makes each the principal cause of learning and self-development, able to become more and more responsible and discerning with regard to human acts and choices by means of this active power of spiritual insight and understanding. Thus the way is open to a freely exercised domination over the material factors of human existence, and especially over socially organized programs of control over human individuals.

Philosophy of Human Personhood and Freedom

"The root of all human freedom", Thomas Aquinas writes in *De veritate* (24, 2), "is constituted in human rationality." To understand this fundamental principle of humanism, one must study the way Aquinas in the same place contrasts human freedom with the spontaneity of the brute animals. Humans know the natures of things, concerning which they exercise the power of intellectual judgment and not merely their sensory appearances. What is the object of human freedom? It is free choice among the understandings presented by the intellect. Human freedom is not a bodily matter: humans have no liberty, for example, when faced with the law of gravity. Human liberty is in the spiritual realm. Its exercise depends on free will, the power of free choice, which is the endowment of human nature parallel to the rational intelligence.

Transcendence and the Moral Order

To advance a step further in this essential point of philosophical anthropology, one must reflect accurately upon the God that a metaphysics of transcendence affirms. God's existence is not received into a really distinct limiting principle: it is therefore unlimited and in entirely actual possession of all perfections seen in the cosmos, but without defect and without limit. The Supreme Being is thus existence itself, the cause and source of all other existing realities. He is their Creator by giving them the metaphysical principles by which each exercises its act of existing limited by its essence, substance, or nature. The Supreme Being gives each principle: thus his creatures are existing things, each with its own nature. Each nature is its law, reflecting the eternal law, namely, the mind and purpose of the Supreme Being in creating.

Human liberty finds here its most fundamental object. It is able to choose its personal acts in a way that accords with the natural law and the purposes of the various substances that it encounters within the cosmos. Responsibility to the Creator becomes a part of each human act; it grows in human living by the exercise of human freedom.

The Inner-Cosmic Metaphysics

Since Vatican I the Catholic Church has been in dialogue with the atheistic point of view. It has recognized the problems that have been generated for persons and for society as a result of the rise and spread of modern philosophical atheism. One must ask what happens to human personhood and human freedom when minds choose that other fork at the end of the first half of metaphysics, the one that refuses the ascent of natural theology, turns to the inner-cosmic view of ultimate reality, and devotes the remainder of its philosophical enterprise to a "negative natural theology", so to speak, which endeavors to construct a rationale for the older nineteenth-century view, now outmoded, that this material cosmos is all that is. This is indeed a metaphysics of a sort, for it expresses a concept of ultimate reality: it is the inner-cosmic metaphysics of materialism and atheism. Frequently it is disguised with the terminology and religiosity of pantheism. But the view of ultimate reality remains the same: there is no transcendent, intelligent, personal Supreme Being who speaks his word to mankind.

In such a case, what results for philosophical anthropology? A vast change of perspective in personal living must necessarily take place. In the metaphysics of transcendence, life proceeds in fidelity to the Supreme Being, expressed by fidelity to the natural law that he gives each created nature and respect for each substantial reality. At the fork in the ontological road, one chooses God. Philosophy is on the way to becoming a preamble for faith in God, for conversion to him, toward acquiring ears to hear in case there is some word of positive self-revelation from the Supreme Being.

In the inner-cosmic metaphysics an entirely different *metanoia* takes place, a conversion to the human self, for by definition there is no other. Human acts and human life come to be defined in terms of natural religiosity, the expression of the better self, human ideals, and social betterment. All the varieties of secular humanism build their approaches upon this metaphysical substrate. The fact is, however, that the substrate is not solid. It does not support human personal freedom. For it necessarily reduces human knowledge to the sensory order by definition, for it has turned away from the very idea of spiritual reality. Thus the specificity of the human mode of existing and of acting is lost. This is the net result of the efforts to explain the facts about human knowledge, summarized above, by various associations of sensory images. Human liberty, the activity of the spiritual person, becomes more and more like the spontaneity of the lower animals. Human education becomes a matter of stimulus from the cosmic environment and of organismic response. It is but a short step to socially organized programs of control, which induce the stimuli and evoke the desired responses. Thus the Reigns of Terror, the Holocausts, and the Gulags receive their philosophical intelligibility.

Apart from the philosophical anthropology that arises out of the metaphysics of transcendence, that millennial human heritage since the Greeks, which the renewal of Christian Philosophy has been offering to contemporary mankind, the dignity, rights, and personhood of man lack ever more palpably their indispensable philosophical foundation. Once again, then, the very nature of the twentieth century, its need and its suffering from the rise and spread of philosophical atheism in the period of Modern Philosophy, goes far to explain the success of the renewal. Before turning to the more recent vicissitudes of this renewal of Christian Philosophy, however, one should ponder the vigorous rejection of original sin by Modern Philosophy, for perhaps it will help to understand these vicissitudes.

The Proneness to Choose the Inner-Cosmic Metaphysics

When John Henry Newman looked out upon this living, busy world of Western civilization a century ago, in the century of the applications of this metaphysics, he said in his *Apologia* that he saw no reflection of its Creator. "What shall be said to this heart-piercing, reason-bewildering fact? I can only answer, that either there is no Creator, or this living society of men is in a true sense discarded from his presence."

Newman's observation touches philosophical anthropology. For there does undeniably seem to be a proneness in human nature to want that second way in fundamental thinking at the fork in the philosophical road, the one that turns down within the cosmos, choosing a way of thought and life based upon inner-cosmic metaphysics. Modern Philosophy reacted against the doctrine of original sin, which revealed religion had taught to Western mankind. For Modern Philosophy this doctrine is a scandal: Do not all animals grow, mature, and die? Is death not something natural, likewise, for man? Is it not a scandal to call death the wages of sin?

Here the philosophical anthropology that arises from the metaphysics of transcendence makes a simple distinction. Death, although indeed natural to man, can be nevertheless the penalty of sin. Looking at man philosophically as a substantial union of a spiritual and immortal soul with a perishable body, one must say that this union must one day be broken. Death is indeed natural to man, when the material principle of the nature is seen purely in the light of philosophy. At the same time, St. Thomas Aquinas teaches, this substantial form is a spiritual reality, immortal in its own right. When separated from the body it continues to exist, but individuated to the body it had and thus continuing to live in a state less natural to it.

Thus this philosophical anthropology, which shares the metaphysical openness to intelligible reality and the Supreme Being, can hear the teaching of revealed religion regarding the historical condition of mankind. This teaching comes from the prophetic light in which absolute origins are known. The prophetic light sees that death was imposed as the penalty for sin upon the first human pair, who had been given certain gifts contingent upon fidelity to the Gift-giver. The natural sciences of prehistory, even in their recent progress during the Copernican revolution, do not reach back to these absolute origins, indeed, far from it, as we now know from the sciences of prehistory. The Supreme Being, however, was present at these origins. Christian Philosophy is able to ask: Could he not have given his prophets a share in his own higher knowledge of what actually happened?

Thus the scandal of Modern Philosophy at the idea of an original sin, explaining the mysterious proneness toward the inner-cosmic metaphysics, arises itself from the loss of the authentic heritage in metaphysics and its replacement by mathematical physics, studied in Part Three above. This shadow out of the modern period hangs darkly over the twentieth century. Perhaps it helps to understand the negative side of the renewal of Christian Philosophy, a matter that cannot be omitted from consideration, for it too is a philosophical fact of the contemporary life of the Catholic Church.

IV

INTERNAL RESISTANCE TO THE
RENEWAL OF CHRISTIAN PHILOSOPHY

In Chapter One above, on the various nineteenth-century applications of atheistic metaphysics, the religious application was studied under the heading "modernism and its new hermeneutics". It was noted that this phenomenon was a direct cause for the convocation of the First Vatican Council. How did the priests, mostly German, respond to the doctrinal actions of this instance of the Extraordinary Magisterium? With certain exceptions they obeyed the doctrinal judgment of their Church. Peace descended upon the teaching Church. It was not to last, however, for the same program of philosophical relativism in revealed religion, the same because metaphysically identical, was taken up and continued as the nineteenth century ended, this time by a group of priests in Italy, France, and England. As the later twentieth century will experience and demonstrate, the philosophical analysis of this second phase of the program has its own importance from the viewpoint of the renewal of Christian Philosophy.

Catholic Modernism: Second, or European, Phase, 1893–1910

Experience later in the twentieth century has shown that the study of this phenomenon assists priests and catechetical teachers of the Faith greatly, for it helps to link the renewal of Christian Philosophy with the purity and integrity of the deposit of faith. These priests of the second phase who resisted the philosophical renewal were not numerous, but by their positions as teachers on the level of higher education and by their publications they exercised a wide influence and indeed effected a crisis among priests and candidates for the priesthood, especially in France. When their writings are studied from the philosophical point of view, it becomes clear that they did not make their own that metaphysics of transcendence that stands at the center of the renewal. Each one in his own way has allowed his mind to become imbued with Modern Philosophy and its inner-cosmic metaphysics.

Among the leaders one must certainly include Ernest Renan (1823–92). After falling away from his priestly studies, he became a professor of Semitic languages at the University of Paris, where he transferred into facile French the German Liberal Protestantism that was busy applying the atheistic hermeneutics to the New Testament, distorting its witness and reducing Jesus Christ to nothing but an ordinary, mere man. This was the thrust and effect of Renan's famous *Life of Jesus.* Renan's most important connection with this resistance to the renewal of Christian Philosophy, however, was the fact that Father Alfred Loisy (1857–1940) enrolled in his classes and prepared himself according to the mind of Renan as a professor of scriptural exegesis. Loisy became the central figure among the Catholic Modernists of these years. In England Father George Tyrrell, S.J. (1861–1910), and in Italy Father Ernesto Buonaiuti (1881–1946) were leading figures, each surrounded by a small cluster of friends and intellectual disciples. Baron Friedrich von Hügel (1852–1925), a layman born in Italy of an Austrian father and a Scottish mother, played a special role in linking together these priestly personalities of France, Italy, and England. These names will perhaps suffice here, for one leads readily to the others, and the study of them reveals the presence of a closely knit and philosophically like-minded group of priests, all dedicated to the reform of theology on the basis of the metaphysics of Modern Philosophy, rejecting the program of Vatican I and *Aeterni Patris* out of hand. Space here permits only a brief review of Loisy and Tyrrell from the viewpoint of this present study in philosophy.

"Orthodoxy", Loisy writes in his *Memoirs* (Vol. I, pp. 35–36),

> is in a sense the mother of heresy, and one can add that the reciprocal is also true. For orthodoxy is a myth. There is no such thing as a changeless doctrine. A doctrine when contradicted is broken up by the contradiction: either that, or it changes itself so as to evade the contradiction. Thus the orthodoxy of tomorrow will not be the orthodoxy of yesterday. It will be the product of a cross between yesterday's orthodoxy and today's heresy. Orthodoxy is one of those myths upon which traditional Christianity has been founded, and one cannot say that this myth has been beneficial. It is either an illusion or a partisan position in theology, affirming as it does the immutability of a thing that is in itself changeable and that changes indefinitely according to the need and the opportunity of the times. From the moment that a religion affects to teach a changeless doctrine, it goes against the law of nature and of humanity because life is a movement. Thus one can say that orthodoxy provokes heresy. For it is not possible that human thought should immobilize itself in one set of ideas, because experience is in control of them and human reflection modifies them ceaselessly.

The Hegelian dialectic is quite clearly operating in Loisy's mind. This passage should be compared with the Spinozan metaphysics in its Hegelian version, summarized in Part Three above. By Loisy's time the metaphysics of Modern Philosophy had become entrenched in higher education and came to minds by a sort of cultural osmosis. Loisy cannot maintain the positions of Vatican I regarding the dogmas that protect the original and abiding meaning of the Articles of Faith and Morals. He must necessarily subject both the dogmas and the articles to historical relativism. It is but a short step from Loisy's position to the theory of "ongoing revelation" later in the present century, and to its application as "the experience approach in religious education". Truth in Loisy's view has indeed become the daughter of time, Giordano Bruno's motto. There is a palpable absence of the metaphysics of transcendence and a recognizable presence of the Spinozan metaphysics. It comes as no surprise, therefore, to learn that Loisy ended his life in complete apostasy from the personal God of his youth as an atheistic disciple of Kant, Comte, and Hegel. One can recognize that the study of these leaders of Catholic Modernism can benefit the renewal of Christian Philosophy by revealing its link with the abiding apostolic character of the deposit of faith.

Loisy, it is clear, approached the Scriptures without the metaphysical foundation for recognizing them as letters from the personal and intelligent Supreme Being, sent out of fatherly love, for mankind. These are the words of Pope Leo XIII in the encyclical on the Bible *Providentissimus Deus* (November 18, 1893), which was published in direct answer to the "purely rational exegesis" that Loisy was teaching in Paris. For Loisy one takes nothing to the study of Scripture but "faith" and "science". The fact is, however, that this apparent rejection of metaphysics is actually the introduction of the Comtean view of philosophy as the generalized statement of the empirical sciences. From beginning to end the life and career of Father Alfred Loisy supports the need in the Church for the renewal of Christian Philosophy: without it the Spinozan metaphysics and the atheistic hermeneutics cannot but produce his approach.

Pope Leo XIII was quite aware of the inroads of Modern Philosophy into the seminaries, which train young men for the Catholic priesthood. One should perhaps hear his words in *Depuis le jour* (September 18, 1899) addressed to those responsible for training priests and catechists. "In the presence of the combined efforts of unbelief and heresy to achieve the ruin of the Catholic Faith", he writes,

> it would be a real crime if the clergy were to remain hesitant and inactive. In the midst of such a flood of errors, the clergy must not fail its mission, which is to defend Catholic doctrine under attack and Catholic morality travestied. The clergy must hold itself up as a barrier to the errors invading us ... and unmask them, warning their Catholic people.... A superficial learning and a common type of knowledge will not suffice to accomplish this mission. Solid studies are necessary, deep studies, continual studies. In a word, we must have that kind of knowledge of our doctrine that can combat the subtlety and singular astuteness of our modern opponents.

Throughout this encyclical the Pope of *Aeterni Patris* is warning against the effects of Kant, Comte, and Hegel upon future teachers of the deposit of faith. Without the renewal of Christian Philosophy and its metaphysics of transcendence, priestly minds like that of Loisy cannot but arise.

Father George Tyrrell illustrates the experiential approach to revelation. "Former heresies", he writes in the Introduction of his *Christianity at the Crossroads*

(1909), "questioned this or that dogma. Modernism criticizes the very idea of dogma . . . and revelation. What is common to all Roman Catholic Modernists is the belief in a possible reconciliation of their Catholicism with the results of historical criticism. . . . This reconciliation practically consists in a rereading or reinterpretation of their Catholicism. Plainly this implies philosophizing." It would be difficult to state more clearly the need for the renewal of Christian Philosophy and its metaphysics as the hermeneutical light under which the heritage of revealed religion is seen and interpreted. For Tyrrell is using Modern Philosophy for this interpretation and cannot but fall into the project of the atheistic hermeneutics. Toward the end of the present century "the new hermeneutics" will be offered as a discovery of the times after Vatican II; it cannot be understood, however, apart from its metaphysical identity with the historical relativism of the first two phases of Catholic Modernism.

Perhaps this will suffice to indicate the philosophical basis upon which this second phase of Catholic Modernism rested. It is an exercise in the same philosophical hermeneutics of the German priests of midnineteenth century, whose work evoked the *Dei Filius* of Vatican I. It is a reinterpretation of the Catholic religion that sets the entire Apostles' Creed aside at one stroke, so that "its Articles of Faith do not have the same meaning for Christians today as they had for Christians of the early Church". When one recalls that the Apostles learned this meaning from Jesus their Teacher, which they in turn taught to the early Church, it is readily apparent that this philosophical hermeneutics "reduces Jesus Christ to the state of an ordinary and mere man".

These two quotations come from Pope St. Pius X (1903–14), who, succeeding Pope Leo XIII, inherited the problem from him, the problem for the deposit of faith and morals caused by these priests who were resisting the renewal of Christian Philosophy and rejecting it in their teaching. Associates of this holy Pope have recorded that he suffered intensely because of the action he knew he had to take, repeating over and over: I can understand those earlier priests in Germany, but how can one understand this now that the Council has spoken in *Dei Filius?*

St. Pius X published three documents on this Catholic Modernism that have a lasting importance and merit careful study throughout the remainder of the twentieth century. The first was *Lamentabili* (July 3, 1907), his listing of the chief errors in the writings of these priests of the resistance. The second was the encyclical *Pascendi* (September 8, 1907), doubtless one of the most philosophical documents ever published by the Supreme Magisterium. It is a comprehensive analysis of the philosophical foundations of this heresy of historical relativism. With wonderful accuracy it strikes to taproot the idea of "ongoing revelation", ongoing in the natural experience of mankind in and through historical and cultural progress. Third, in an attempt to guard the deposit of faith and to protect the people of God, he published *Sacrorum anestitum* (September 1, 1910), the well-known oath against the Modernist philosophical hermeneutics that professors of the sacred sciences were to take, resigning their teaching posts if they were unable to give its terms a manly subscription. It is worthy of note that Pope St. Pius X, in his *Doctoris Angelici* (June 29, 1914), shortly before his death, reaffirmed the program for the renewal of Christian Philosophy and took a further step toward linking it with the purity and integrity of the deposit of faith and morals. "To depart from the metaphysics of St. Thomas Aquinas", he writes, "is never without danger for teachers of the Faith."

After the publication in 1910 of the oath for professors of the sacred sciences, this second phase of Catholic Modernism came to an end. It seemed, in fact, to have disappeared forever from the life of the teaching Church. It is in this context that the worldwide success of the renewal of Christian Philosophy took place that has been noted above. After some decades, however, it became apparent that further vicissitudes in the renewal were to come.

Schism within the Renewal

This word "schism" introduces a new turn of events in the program for the renewal of Christian Philosophy. The beginning is small indeed, but from it immense consequences were to grow. In order to understand the life of the Church in the second half of the twentieth century, the essential facts must be gathered.

The general context of this schism is the very success in the renewal during the first three decades of the present century, which saw Catholic young people, renewed in their metaphysical heritage and its natural openness to the transcendent Supreme Being, building a dike in society, as it were, against the applications of the atheistic and inner-cosmic view of ultimate reality. This evoked that envious response by the atheistic thinkers symbolized and summarized when Gilson and Maritain met Brunschvicg and Bréhier in direct encounter at the 1931 meeting of the French Philosophical Society.

The Juvisy Conference

The Thomistic Society of France, perhaps the most important organization of professors of the renewal, meeting at Juvisy on September 11, 1933, took up the idea of Christian Philosophy as its topic. Maritain could not attend because of sickness, but Gilson was present among an assembly composed chiefly of priests, famous names of the renewal. Gilson in fact became the focal point of the discussion as the day went on. Speaker succeeded speaker, taking up the relationships between reason and faith and analyzing the historical problem of Christian Philosophy. It became clear that the assemblage was divided on the nature of Christian Philosophy. Is it actually and really a specific kind of philosophy in its own right, different from other kinds, especially the atheistic kind? Is there really a historic reality of Christian Philosophy, as Gilson maintains in one scholarly work after another? Or is this philosophizing actually a religious exercise and not authentic philosophy at all?

At last the chairman called for silence. "Are all the philosophers present here today", he demanded, calling a vote, "united on this point, namely, that Christian Philosophy is an authentic kind of philosophy in its own right?"

It was a standing vote. A large segment, all of them priests, did not stand. This was the opening of a fissure, a true schism in the ranks of those holding teaching positions in the renewal of Christian Philosophy. This segment, Gilson noted with consternation, was joining the position of Bréhier and Brunschvicq at the 1931 meeting. Philosophy, to be authentic as philosophy, must be secular in mode. It cannot bear the adjective "Christian", for it introduces an alien factor.

At the time, this fissure among Christian thinkers, most of them priests, passed unnoticed. It was like a small opening in a dike. But the opening has been made, in a public meeting. It will ripen and mature in ways that must be noted in the later decades of the century. Christian thinkers had been in an embattled position since Descartes' separation of philosophy from religion, leaving it for Spinoza to develop as a purely secular subject. From this origin atheistic thinking came forth and spread in Western education and culture in the way that has been studied in Part Three. The renewal of Christian Philosophy counters this development, for it renews the metaphysics of philosophical openness to the transcendent, intelligent, and personal Supreme Being who is able, as the prophet Amos says, to declare his thoughts to man. Hence it is a philosophy that is able to philosophize toward the Faith as its preamble and within the Faith—precisely because of its metaphysical openness and its resulting ears to hear.

In the bloodless battles of the mind, it is one thing to know the enemy, what he is thinking and where he is located, so to speak, intellectually. It is quite another thing to face suddenly a second front, an attack from the flanks and the rear by thinkers in one's own camp. It cannot but create consternation, much like the effect of infiltration and betrayal.

This watershed meeting at Juvisy had this kind of impact on Gilson, which is given detailed description in his *Christianity and Philosophy* (1939), where he reports extensively on that memorable experience and indeed names names. Gilson was astonished at the turn of events, hardly able to believe his ears when he heard "that stupendous objection that the expression 'Christian Philosophy' has no formally exact meaning". He found it utterly at variance with *Aeterni Patris* and knew profoundly that the program for renewing Christian Philosophy in Catholic institutions was being placed in jeopardy. On the basis of such principles it could not, Gilson foresaw accurately, but lose its upward swing and fall into disarray.

The Juvisy conference, then, seems to document the beginning of a schism in the ranks of the professors of Christian Philosophy. A disaffection for the metaphysics of St. Thomas Aquinas begins to grow. Historical and cultural relativism begin to fasten upon Catholic minds—not generally as yet, of course, but upon more and more Catholic teachers of philosophy. When a mind becomes convinced that there is no "Christian Philosophy", a void is created that demands a substitute. The notion grows that Catholic thinkers should adopt one of the world's philosophies proper to the present moment of time and cultural progress. Would the Church not communicate better? Would her religious gospel not obtain a better hearing and be more successful in the world of today?

The door began to open to the substitution of other philosophical approaches. The renewal of Christian Philosophy according to the mind of St. Thomas Aquinas begins to falter. The problem, however, is the fact that the mind of Aquinas is precisely that metaphysics of openness to the transcendent Supreme Being that had been developed since the Greeks and the Fathers of the Church. The substituted approaches introduce into Catholic philosophical teaching the various components of that other metaphysics descending from the modern period as such, the inner-cosmic metaphysics of Kant, Comte, and Hegel. Hence one had to fear that there would be repercussions for the preambles of the Catholic Faith, as well as a faltering of the benefits for Western civilization.

The Encyclical *Humani generis*

The Holy See, constantly and consistently concerned for this renewal of philosophy, well informed as always took note of these developments with apprehension. In the years after the Juvisy Conference, World War II broke upon the European scene with wrenching effects. It brought devastation, intellectual devastation as well, especially upon France. As existentialism was popular in defeated Germany under Heidegger after World War I, so Sartre's translation of that existentialism into French became popular at the time of World War II. More and more Catholic minds gave way to its metaphysical solicitation. Corporate teaching bodies leaned in its direction, as one can see in the warning allocutions of Pope Pius XII to the first General Chapters of the Jesuits and the Dominicans after the war.

It is in this context that the second major philosophical encyclical, *Humani generis,* was published in 1950, a landmark in the renewal of Christian Philosophy on the level of *Aeterni Patris* and *Pascendi*. It merits careful analysis. Here space permits only a sample to show the steadfast fidelity of the Holy See in this matter of the renewal. "Despising our philosophy," Pope Pius XII writes,

they [the professors who make the substitutions] extol others, ancient or modern, implying that any kind of philosophy can, with a few additions or corrections, be harmonized with Catholic dogma. But this is absolutely false, especially in respect to immanentism or idealism, or to materialism, whether historic or dialectic, or to existentialism, whether atheistic or the type that denies the validity of metaphysical reasoning.

This passage from paragraph 33 gives an insight into the growth of the fissure in the dike since the Juvisy Conference.

The renewal of Christian Philosophy, of course, had not come to an end. It continued everywhere in Christendom. But the earlier unity among its teachers was beginning to crumble. Confusing crosscurrents had their impact upon the students as the years to Vatican II (1962–65) went by.

The Supreme Magisterium, however, remained firmly in position, as Pope John XXIII bears witness. In his *Grata recordatio* (Sept. 26, 1959), he is characteristically forthright: "One should remember that there are today widespread philosophical positions and attitudes that are absolutely irreconcilable with Christian faith. We will continue with serenity, exactness, and firmness to stress the irreconcilable nature of these concepts." During his preparations for Vatican II, the same Pope John XXIII in an allocution (September 18, 1960) stressed the intrinsic relationship between his hopes for the Council and the program for renewing Christian Philosophy. "But if all these things we desire so ardently are to come about," he says, "the first thing necessary is to study the works of St. Thomas Aquinas carefully. And so we are very interested in seeing a steady growth in the number of people who find enlightenment and learning in the works of the Angelic Doctor."

For the Pope of Vatican II, it is clear that the program in fundamental philosophy is not a relic of the past, as historical relativism sees it, but one of the living and vital instruments for renewing the Church and for healing the social problems of modern culture. Nor did Pope John XXIII's Council change this position. It is the first Ecumenical Council to name St. Thomas Aquinas in its documents as the Common Doctor, the one who gathered best into a teachable synthesis the metaphysics of openness to the transcendent Supreme Being. The Council in its documents is indeed faithful to both the renewal and the intention of Pope John XXIII. There is, however, still another vicissitude yet to come in the renewal of Christian Philosophy, called "the Spirit of Vatican II". It calls for careful analysis.

Catholic Modernism: Third, or Worldwide, Phase, 1967–

The true and real Vatican II is contained in the official documents that express its teaching. What then is this "Spirit of Vatican II"? Confining one's view to the matter at hand, it is a philosophical interpretation of the meaning of Vatican II, an interpretation so widely disseminated by the media that a public opinion is created in its favor, even within the Church. The crucial point, therefore, is the nature of the philosophy, exercising the hermeneutical function proper to philosophy, that produces this interpretation. It is a philosophy quite different from that of St. Thomas. It has a different metaphysics, the world view of historical and cultural relativism. It is clear, consequently, that the aftermath of Vatican II will be a turbulent time, first for the renewal of Christian Philosophy in itself, and then for both the academic and the catechetical orders of Catholic teaching, each of which depends upon this heritage in metaphysics as its natural foundation. Grace, the theologians say, supposes nature.

In the analysis of this burgeoning postconciliar phenomenon, Christian Philosophy can well take the Holy See itself as its point of departure.

Always alert to danger for the deposit of faith and morals, the Apostolic See, noting the first indications of a serious doctrinal upset in the aftermath of the Second Vatican Council, published on February 22, 1967, a call for a worldwide "Year of Faith" to begin on June 29, 1967, the feast of St. Peter and St. Paul. "While man's religious sense today is in a decline," the document states, "depriving the Faith of its natural foundation, new opinions in exegesis and theology, often borrowed from bold but blind secular philosophies, have in places found a way into the realm of Catholic teaching." This official recognition is the reason why 1967 is given above as the opening date for the third, or worldwide, phase of Catholic Modernism. It concerns the program for the renewal of Christian Philosophy very directly, as the reference to the introduction of "secular philosophies" into Catholic teaching indicates. The matter merits careful study on a scale beyond the present summary, which can only indicate some of the areas that need ongoing research. After Vatican II the Catholic Church experienced in her members much loss of faith, cessation of religious practice, and doctrinal confusion, even on the level of the catechesis of children. This phenomenon, addressed in a growing volume of literature, can be understood best from the viewpoint of disobedience and disloyalty toward the renewal program on the part of professors assigned to it as teachers on the level of academic higher education. The taproot appears to be a many-sided substitution of some philosophical approach other than that of St. Augustine and St. Thomas Aquinas in the teaching of philosophy.

Substitution for Authentic Christian Philosophy

Under this heading one must gather the various substitutions of an inauthentic Thomism as if it were valid as "Christian Philosophy". Here one must recall the effort of the Holy See to preserve authenticity by the "Twenty-Four Theses" mentioned in Chapter Two above. Despite these norms, the renewal experiences an ongoing effort to substitute a false Thomism with a net result in each case that dims or distorts the metaphysics of transcendence in the minds of students. One must be aware of the effort to make St. Thomas into a "modern philosopher" born out of due time, as if he subscribed to the Cartesian separation of philosophy from revealed religion, making it a secular subject. Then there is the massive problem of "transcendental Thomism", the effort to amalgamate St. Thomas' philosophy with Kant's "transcendental or subjective idealism".

These efforts led the way to still more harmful substitutions, the outright replacement of Christian Philosophy by some form of the Modern Philosophy studied in Part Three above. Here historical relativism operates explicitly in the thinking: St. Thomas is praised for the timely work he did with Aristotle in the thirteenth century but is declared inappropriate for the needs and problems of today.

In the years immediately after Vatican II, however, existentialism, with or without the adjective "Christian", became the common substitution for the Christian Philosophy of St. Thomas Aquinas. The use of "Christian" existentialism was especially deceptive, for it led directly to the resurgence of nineteenth-century "fideism"—faith without reason, as "rationalism" is reason without faith. That a different kind of metaphysics or view of ultimate reality is entailed by this substitution has been indicated sufficiently in Chapter One above in connection with Nietzsche and Heidegger. As the years after Vatican II went by, Marxism itself became another of these substitutions, as the documents of the Holy See on "liberation theology" in the late twentieth century make clear.

The result of these various substitutions was a growing disarray and confusion among Catholic students. Parents noted with anguish that colleges and universities long recognized as leaders in the renewal of Christian Philosophy began to graduate young Catholics who were no longer in possession of their intellectual heritage. The renewal of the Thomistic metaphysics was faltering. Catholics again with surprise and consternation began to observe the same philosophical substitution in the priests and religious. "He has his philosophy," priests were heard to say, referring to the Successor of St. Peter and the authority standing behind the renewal, "and I have mine." The priest who feared at Juvisy in 1933 that the adjective "Christian" destroys the noun "philosophy" ripens into the priest of the 1960s who rubs his hands with glee before an audience of several hundred future nurses at a large Catholic university. "You have been taught", he said, "that Thomas Aquinas is the great bulwark of natural law. Tonight we shall free you from this notion, setting him aside as irrelevant for us today." Toward the end of the twentieth century a priest recognized that Aquinas was significant in his day, together with Wilhelm Schmidt in the first half of the present century. "But now we have the hermeneutics."

Such instances are easily multiplied, and a documentation on the sudden rebirth of historical relativism can be readily accumulated. As Cornelio Fabro points out in his *Introduction to Thomism,* following Leo XIII, Modernism results when Modern Philosophy is used instead of Christian Philosophy in training candidates for the priesthood. The reason is the fundamental substitution of the inner-cosmic metaphysics for the metaphysics of transcendence. Every philosophy results in its specific kind from its way of conceiving the ultimate reality that is its object of study and the act by which the person philosophizing grasps that object. Characteristic of all these substitutions, and the eclectic smorgasbords of opinions that proliferate from them, is the reduction of existence to the organismic experiencing of life in time. Furthermore, the specific activity by which this object is grasped is not the intellect, conceived as a nonmaterial power of insight and understanding. It is some kind of immediate apprehension, an empathy for things, an awareness, an intuition in Bergson's sense. If there is a metaphysics, then, it is a new kind, an intuitive metaphysics in which human existence, within the cosmos, is concretely experienced as such.

To put this another way, the metaphysical positions of Kant, Comte, and Hegel, variously combined, live on in these approaches, which are offered to the young as a better idea of Christian Philosophy. They cannot but turn to ashes, however, because they imply a lack of openness to the transcendent Supreme Being. It follows that these substituted philosophical approaches will lack openness to the human animating principle or soul as a spiritual reality or substance distinct from the matter it forms when giving humans their bodily existence. Truth, furthermore, suffers a characteristic relocation from the judgments of the mind bearing upon the nature of things to organismic sensory apprehension. To put it briefly, the substitutions are not the authentic Christian Philosophy of the renewal. They represent metaphysically the same introduction of Modern Philosophy and its inner-cosmic metaphysics into the thought and life of the Church that constituted the first phase of historical relativism or "Modernism" prior to Vatican I and the second phase under Leo XIII and St. Pius X up to the year 1910.

In any case, when the centenary of *Aeterni Patris* was celebrated at Rome in 1979, it had become abundantly clear that the academic renewal of authentic Christian Philosophy was coming to an end with the strange suddenness of a building in collapse. There were of course still institutions of Catholic higher education that were maintaining the program, and there were numbers of loyal individual professors. But the phenomenon as a whole was by now a general fact of common observation. In the academic order of teaching a far-reaching change was becoming consolidated, the beginnings of which the Holy See had identified as early as 1967: "New opinions in exegesis and theology, often borrowed from bold but blind secular philosophies", had become the rule of the day.

Perhaps one documentary witness will suffice for the many. It comes from Dr. Thomas Sheehan, professor of philosophy at Loyola University in Chicago, who published his "Revolution in the Church" in *The New York Review* (June 14, 1984). "The dismantling of traditional Roman Catholic theology by Catholics themselves", he writes,

is by now a *fait accompli*. . . . The emergence of a radically new Catholic theology
. . . has altered the intellectual topography. . . . This kind of whittling away at
belief in the divinity of Jesus is scarcely new. [He cites Ritschl and Harnack.] But
the surprising thing today is that the scholars who are advancing the reevaluation
of Jesus are neither atheists who attack the Church from without nor Liberal
Protestants of the 19th Century. Rather, these scholars are Roman Catholic
exegetes and theologians, most of them priests.

Professor Sheehan could have cited the *Pascendi* of St. Pius X, who noted the heart
of the matter that results from resistance to the renewal of Christian Philosophy:
"They reduce Jesus Christ to the status of an ordinary and mere man."

There is, then, a third phase of Catholic Modernism. It has been celebrating
its triumph everywhere in Catholic academic institutions during the decades after
Vatican II. This triumph is fundamentally a victory over the program to renew
Christian Philosophy. During this period, more and more young Catholics have
been searching for their intellectual heritage and roots, often at a loss to know
where to find authenticity in Catholic intellectual life and its studies. It is remarkable to note, however, the vigorous alacrity with which they take up the authentic
metaphysics of openness to God when they find it.

Problems, then, do indeed exist for the renewal, both in the teaching of
philosophy and in the area of Sacred Theology, which gives up its authenticity as a
form of ministry of the word of God and suffers a reduction to nothing but
philosophy of religion, full in the mode of the secular campus.

Is there a parallel problem, one may ask, in the catechetical order of teaching?
There is indeed, and it too offers an even greater challenge to younger scholars.
Here the renewal of Christian Philosophy correlates with the divine deposit of
faith itself and the manner of guarding its purity, integrity, and pastoral effectiveness
when it is handed on by catechetical teaching. For the inner-cosmic metaphysics,
bold in its own way and blind to the transcendent God who is able to communicate his word through his teaching Church, suppresses the Church's official
catechisms, which are the chief instruments for this teaching. Hence the words of
Cardinal Joseph Ratzinger in his now-famous catechetical discourse of 1983 in
France: "The suppression of the catechism has been a primary and serious mistake,
together with the declaration that the very idea of the catechism is outmoded."
Since the catechism is the Church's own explanation of the Apostles' Creed
according to the meaning explained, developed, and protected by the dogmas
across the centuries, it is readily apparent that it is the deposit of faith that actually
is being suppressed.

Thus the opening paragraphs of both *Aeterni Patris* and *Pascendi,* which relate
Christian Philosophy to the purity and integrity of the deposit of faith, assume a
new timeliness for young Catholics of late twentieth century. Without the hermeneutics of the articles and dogmas provided by the metaphysics of transcendence,

the outcome stated by another theologian, Charles Journet, becomes the generalized condition of a deceptive religious education that deepens religious ignorance instead of dispelling it. "The Christian terms are maintained," he writes,

> but only to be reinterpreted. The words creation, incarnation, redemption, real presence, transubstantiation, justification, mystical body, and so on, take on new meanings. We have only to recall what has become of the Apostles' Creed from the Hegelian or simply the Modernist point of view. All the words are there, like an empty husk carried about by the winds of history and ideologies at their pleasure.

The internal resistance to the renewal of Christian Philosophy is a fact. It is useless and even counterproductive to pretend that it has not existed for over a century and especially to pretend that it is not at present celebrating a triumph. The study of this resistance and its substitutions, however, can be a personal grace: it can lead to the discovery of a new focus for the renewal as it enters the second century. This new focus is the very deposit of faith itself, seen in the hermeneutical light that preserves for Christians today the same meaning that it had when the Apostles learned it from Jesus their Teacher. It remains in a final chapter to study the renewal of Christian Philosophy in this its most vital hermeneutical function.

V

CHRISTIAN PHILOSOPHY AND
THE DEPOSIT OF FAITH

Philosophy in itself is "the science of wisdom and virtue", as Augustine defines it: it teaches metaphysics as its basic and central branch, then applies this metaphysical light in a cluster of consequent branches—philosophical anthropology, cosmology, philosophy of law, philosophy of education, and many others. This is the first function of philosophy, the direct teaching of its own wisdom. The second is the hermeneutical function of philosophy, something different in nature. Hermeneutics is constituted by the shining of the philosophical light from this seventh liberal art upon the first six, illuminating their endeavors with humanistic orientation and purpose and providing fundamental understanding of their findings and interpretation of their various kinds of didactic statements. This is the hermeneutical function. It has been manifest throughout the philosophical experience of Western culture since the conflict between Socrates and the Sophists.

By means of this hermeneutical function of philosophy persons are able to see the cosmos with an understanding that will be quite different from its interpretation when metaphysics has been replaced by mathematical physics in the manner studied in Part Three. This hermeneutical function plays an even more decisive role in the trivium, the liberal disciplines that teach the human sciences, especially history. The texts of recorded history are statements that report what actually happened in the past. How are these formulated propositions to be understood? Since mankind exists in an unfolding history, this hermeneutical question is fundamentally important. The answer depends upon philosophy.

This importance is doubly true with regard to revealed religion, because it too is historical in nature. It teaches salvation history. It explains and develops the meaning of a set of propositions or sentences that express the truth about the great events in this historic self-revelation of the Supreme Being to mankind.

Epistemology, one of the branches of philosophy that results most immediately from metaphysical analysis, places truth in the judgment of the human mind. The judgment links concepts by the dynamic existential verb "is": the mind sees, knows, judges that "this" is true of "that"—in reality. History, perhaps the most fundamental of the liberal disciplines of the trivium, is made up of such judgments recorded in times past, which have been handed forward as knowledge of what actually took place in reality.

Revealed religion, then, is historical in nature because it teaches salvation history. Salvation history is constituted by interventions of the Supreme Being in the life of mankind, events that constitute a gradual self-disclosure on the part of the same intelligent Creator who is recognized by the natural theology of metaphysics, together with his plan for mankind. Thus this same Creator is presented by revealed religion as the Lord of human history. How are these teachings to be received? How understood? How interpreted? Since interpretation of texts is a major part of the hermeneutical function of philosophy, the kind of philosophical light used becomes intellectually critical in importance.

"It is supremely important in this respect", writes Pope Paul VI in the Introduction to *The Creed of the People of God* (1968), "to recall that, beyond what is observable, analyzed by the work of the sciences, the intellect that God has given us reaches *that which is,* and not merely the subjective expression of the structures and development of consciousness." This sets aside the Kantian agnosticism: it is the briefest possible summary of the metaphysics of Christian Philosophy.

"And on the other hand," the Pope continues lucidly, "it is important to remember that the task of interpretation—of hermeneutics—is to try to understand and extricate, while respecting the word expressed, the sense conveyed by a text, and not to recreate this sense in some fashion, in accordance with arbitrary hypotheses." This summarizes the idea of hermeneutics and indicates its two different kinds. One kind will result from the transcendent metaphysics of *that which is;* the other kind will give the text a new and different meaning, read into it from historically and culturally conditioned subjective structures or mental categories of human consciousness. This arbitrary reading will be the logical result of the inner-cosmic metaphysics.

This hermeneutical function of philosophy is a large subject both in itself and in its application to revealed religion, and which could well occupy a separate course of study with full references to the sources, both Catholic and Modernist. Space here permits only a summary, which may serve as a guide toward further research, reading, and study. This summary will be given under three headings of doctrine: first, the object of the hermeneutical reading in itself, namely, the divine deposit of faith and morals; second, "the new hermeneutics", as it calls itself with increasing insistence since 1835; and third, "the Eternal Hermeneutics", rightly so called, as one can see from the documents of the Supreme Magisterium throughout the same period.

St. Thérèse, the Catechism, and the Deposit of Faith

The divine deposit of faith and morals, then, the content of revealed religion considered in its first and original elements, must be given a brief analysis. For it is that unique object of interpretation that gives the program for the renewal of

Christian Philosophy its current and abiding significance, quite apart from the vicissitudes sketched above that the program has been suffering in the academic order of teaching philosophy as such. The reason is the fact that the deposit is the primary concern of catechesis, which is a different order of teaching.

St. Thérèse of Lisieux exemplifies well this contact of philosophy with this quite different kind of teaching, which hands on the deposit of faith. She never spent a day of her life in an academic classroom of philosophy. In her childhood years she was instructed, chiefly by her older sisters, in the truths of the French national catechism and given formative help in making these truths her way of life. Her saintly mother died when Thérèse was four, but her likewise saintly father supervised the family catechesis. In particular he had the habit of taking his youngest daughter on a daily walk toward the dinner hour, always centering upon a visit to the Blessed Sacrament in some church or chapel of Lisieux. In her early adolescent years Thérèse taught this same French Small Catechism to children of her parish and neighborhood. Entering the Carmel in Lisieux at fifteen, she lived her short life of nine more years on the basis of the truths of this catechism and its way of life. She did not do philosophical studies. At the same time she relates very directly to the great philosophical issues of the twentieth century, especially that of the hermeneutical problem.

This hermeneutical dimension of St. Thérèse of Lisieux becomes clear when the kind of teaching contained in the French national catechism is examined. Like all printed "small catechisms", it states and contains the elements of Christian doctrine. They are derived from *The Roman Catechism* for pastors, which is itself the official printed version of the oral teaching that the Church had been doing since Jesus sent his twelve Apostles forth to teach all nations. These elements of doctrine are stated in the form of propositions expressing judgments of the mind. At various points in this study of Christian Philosophy the nature of truth has been analyzed. It resides not in the isolated percepts and concepts of things, but in the judgments that unite apprehensions by means of the existential verb "is", which affirms and expresses the unity of two concepts, the subject and the predicate, in the nature of things. Thérèse was instructed in a systematic array of such truths. They deserve a brief summary, for they form this deposit that is under philosophical consideration.

She was instructed, then, that God is our Father in heaven. He is the Almighty. God made all things in heaven and on earth. He made man as well. God is our Creator. Jesus Christ is God's only Son. Jesus is true God and true man. He was conceived by the Holy Spirit. Such truths are presented, stated, and handed on as facts. He was born of the Virgin Mary. He died under Pontius Pilate. He died for our sins. On the third day he rose from the dead. The Holy Spirit is the Third Person of the Divine Trinity. He gives a share in God's life through the sacraments. The Holy Eucharist is the central sacrament, for in it Jesus is really present with us: "This is my Body."

Philosophical analysis clarifies the fact that these Articles of Faith, which catechesis explains and hands on by its teaching, are propositions that express judgments. They exist in the general mode of human language and communication. So too the triple response to these credal truths: Thérèse learned from the catechism the elements of formative teaching in sacramental living, relating to the presence and activity of the Holy Spirit, gospel morality, relating to the love and following of Jesus, and personal prayer, relating to God the Father Almighty. These elements of formation are again a set of judgments, doctrines that bear upon the nature of things.

By receiving this teaching into mind and will and soul, the child is in contact with reality and not merely with some human thinking giving subjective expressions of mental structures formed by merely human culture. There are judgments in which the existential verb "is" operates to the fullest. Thus these teachings communicate truth about reality. From beginning to end, furthermore, the child so taught receives these truths on the authority of the Supreme Being of the universe. The very idea and meaning of this teaching is the understanding that God revealed these truths to mankind.

Thérèse of Lisieux received this instruction and formation in exactly the same meaning that characterized the early Church. The teachers of those times emphasized the bearing of these judgments upon extramental reality by using the word "really": God is *really* our Creator; Jesus is *really* true God and true man; he was *really* born of the Virgin Mary; he *really* died for our sins; he *really* rose from the dead; he is *really* present in the Sacrament of the Altar. The documents of the early Church that preserve this emphasis have been handed down and exist today. St. Paul summarized all of this when writing to his Thessalonian converts: "As soon as you heard the message that we brought you as God's message, you accepted it for what it really is, God's message and not some human thinking; and it is still a living power among you who believe it" (1 Th 2:13). The most fundamental reason for this fact that the deposit of faith is "a living power" to elevate and transform human living from the way of death to the way of life is the Real Presence of the Redeemer in the Holy Eucharist. The deposit of faith works the redemption of man by virtue of this Real Presence. Hence this is a Christocentric teaching. Thérèse of Lisieux received the fullness of this meaning of the deposit and could well have become known as St. Thérèse of the Holy Eucharist rather than the Little Flower of Jesus.

There has been much agonizing in the recent literature on divine revelation, whether it can be communicated by the human words of a human process of teaching. It seems to arise from the philosophies that have been substituted for Christian Philosophy by followers of Loisy and Tyrrell in the resistance outlined above. In the heritage of catechetical teaching since the Apostles this never has been a problem. The deposit of faith is a revealed doctrine to be guarded by a faithful teaching. It is neither a purely abstract intellectual doctrine nor a form of orthopraxis or pragmatism. It is a *doctrina sana,* the healing and life-giving doctrine, as Augustine terms it in the concluding words of his *De doctrina Christiana;* it is a *doctrina sacra,* in the words of Aquinas in the opening question of his *Summa,* where he teaches that it is simultaneously speculative and practical. It is a doctrine of the truth that bears on the living of life.

In all of this it is clear that the very heart of revealed religion is at stake in the question whether the Apostles' Creed has the same meaning for Christians today as it had for the Apostles, the same both in itself and in the triple formative response to it. For Thérèse of Lisieux it did indeed have that one same meaning, expressed by the word "really": it is a set of teachings on what is the case in reality. Without this meaning, Thérèse of Lisieux could not have become "the greatest saint of modern times", as St. Pius said of her when he examined the documentation on her life. But this abiding meaning depends for its natural foundation upon the further question of the metaphysical light that shines upon the propositions of human discourse, which express and hand on this deposit. Do they express reality, known on the authority of God revealing? One can answer affirmatively if the mind recognizes the transcendent and intelligent Supreme Being, one who "can declare his thoughts to man". It becomes quite impossible, however, in the framework of inner-cosmic metaphysics, for then it is believed that no such transcendent Person exists. In such a case the propositions that constitute the deposit as a content that is taught necessarily will be understood in a different way. One could say that this is the most basic reason why St. Thérèse of Lisieux is a new omen for the twentieth century, whom Almighty God has raised up for aid and counsel in this matter of the hermeneutics of revealed religion.

Clearly this least "philosophical" of the saints brings the present century face to face with the hermeneutical reason for the renewal of Christian Philosophy. For it is ultimately the meaning of the deposit that has prompted the renewal across the decades from Vatican I to Pope John Paul II in late twentieth century. "The hundred years of the encyclical *Aeterni Patris* have not passed in vain," he said, concluding the centenary (September 13, 1980), "nor has that celebrated document of pontifical teaching gone out of date." "A correct or honest philosophy", he continued on the same occasion, "raises man to God, as revelation brings God closer to man. For St. Augustine, 'the true philosopher is the person who loves God' (*City of God* VIII, 1). St. Thomas in echoing him says the same thing in other words: 'Almost the entire purpose of philosophy is directed toward the knowledge of God' (*C.G.* I, 4)." In his address to the student body of the Angelicum in Rome (November 17, 1979),[1] Pope John Paul II makes his own the exhortation of Leo XIII in *Aeterni Patris* that we follow the example of the Angelic Doctor: "That is

---

[1] See Excerpts for Part Four, John Paul II, pp. 493–94.

what I also repeat. . . . The philosophy of St. Thomas deserves to be attentively studied and accepted with conviction by the youth of our day by reason of its spirit of openness and of universalism, characteristics that are hard to find in many trends of contemporary thought."

With this reaffirmation of the renewal of Christian Philosophy one can turn to a brief consideration of "the new hermeneutics" in itself, in the metaphysics that it presupposes as a replacement for that of Augustine, Aquinas, and the contemporary Successors of St. Peter and in its result for the catechetical teaching of the deposit of faith.

The New Hermeneutics

The meaning of the divine revelation entrusted to the Apostles as a precious deposit and handed on by the Teaching Church that Jesus founded upon them has been subjected to a persistent effort at philosophical reinterpretation. This "new hermeneutics" began as a part of the set of applications of the metaphysics of Modern Philosophy noted in Chapter One above. Vatican I, it will be recalled, was convened primarily to define the truth regarding this philosophical heresy. The renewal of Christian Philosophy was simply the program to implement this Ecumenical Council. The resistance to this renewal of a transcendent metaphysics has turned around the continuation of the hermeneutical effort throughout the present century from Fathers Loisy and Tyrrell to their contemporary late twentieth-century disciples. It remains to summarize the nature of this new hermeneutics as a function of inner-cosmic metaphysics as an introduction to further reading and research, for this negative phenomenon serves in its way to illuminate the nature and purpose of the renewal of Christian Philosophy.

What, exactly, is this new hermeneutics? The Church herself in *Mysterium Ecclesiae* (June 24, 1973) defines it as "dogmatic relativism". This expresses the nature of "Modernism" as the philosophical heresy *par excellence,* the ultimate and total heresy, because it sets the entire Creed aside at one stroke. It does this by changing the original meaning of all the Articles of Faith and Morals and all the dogmas that have explained, developed, and defended this meaning across the centuries. It is perhaps Father Alfred Loisy who best exemplifies and expresses this relativism when he writes in his *Autour d'un petit livre* (1903, p. 192): "Truth, insofar as it is a human good, is no more changeless than man himself. Truth evolves with him, in him, and by him. This does not prevent it from being the truth for man, for it can be such only on this condition." Giordano Bruno's motto, "Truth is the daughter of time", and Hegel's dialectic provide the philosophical background for Loisy's relativism. He is applying the metaphysics of Modern Philosophy to revealed religion and its deposit of divine faith. The implication of Loisy's doctrine is atheistic, for his denial of a truth that abides in the historical and cultural flux is already a denial of the transcendent and changeless Supreme Being. Thus Loisy's thinking stands revealed as a function of that other fork in the road of metaphysics that refuses the ascent of natural theology and turns aside to follow the path of inner-cosmic metaphysics.

Thus the renewal of Christian Philosophy correlates directly with the responsibility of the Teaching Church to "guard the deposit" (1 Tim 6:20). This correlation can be studied further in the documents of the Supreme Magisterium noted throughout this Part Four: *Dei Filius* of Vatican I (1870); the first paragraph of *Aeterni Patris* (1879); likewise the opening words of *Pascendi* (1908); explicitly in *Humani generis* (1950); and *ex professo* in *Mysterium Ecclesiae* (1973). Perhaps the best summary of this correlation is contained in the *Testem benevolentiae* (January 22, 1899) of Leo XIII to the bishops of the United States. "The new opinions", he writes, referring to minds that become imbued with the metaphysics of relativism,

> show some indulgence to modern popular theories . . . not only with regard to the rule of life, but also to the doctrines in which the *deposit of faith* is contained. For they contend that it is opportune . . . to pass over certain heads of doctrines or so to soften them that they may not have the same meaning that the Church has invariably held. . . . Few words are needed to show how reprehensible is the plan thus concerned, if we but consider the character and origin of the doctrine that the Church hands down to us.

And the Pope cites *Dei Filius* of Vatican I.

The larger background of this recent new hermeneutics is the atheistic hermeneutics of Spinoza, noted in Part Three above. "The strategy of contemporary atheism", writes De Lubac,

> is not a direct attack on God's existence or on the Christian mysteries. It is a question rather of understanding and explaining them. A hermeneutics is proposed that strives to go beneath the primary sense (which alone exists for the simple believer in God's existence or the divinity of Christ), in order to disclose a second meaning that is more true, and that finally turns out to be the only true meaning. And this second meaning is purely human. The attributes of God are not necessarily denied, but as Feuerbach said, they are transferred to their true owner. The death and Resurrection of Christ become sublime symbols of what is most profound in man. Since historic processes must be gradual, unbelievers grant that belief in the primary sense of these mysteries was a necessary stage in the development of human consciousness. But today, it is proclaimed, times have changed. Just as the New Testament revealed the hidden meaning of the Old Testament, but by discarding it as old and as belonging to the dead past, so contemporary humanism does with its understanding of Christian theism. It believes that it understands it, does it justice, and raises it up into a second life within itself that is more true and is indeed the only truth. But by that very fact it relegates Christian theism in its first sense to the cemetery of myths. . . . Today such is

the usual claim of atheism, the general form of its strategy, whether it be triumphant, despairing, or placid; whether it inclines to collectivism or to anarchy; whether it derives from metaphysical renunciation or from earthly ambition; or whether in its totalitarian imperialism, it speaks in the name of sociology or psychoanalysis.

This summarizes well the general strategy, as De Lubac puts it. To bring the new hermeneutics into sharper focus, one must analyze the way this strategy becomes tactical with regard to that sampling of the propositions that St. Thérèse received into her mind, will, and heart as the very word of God. We believe God, the new hermeneutics teaches, not propositions. "Once revelation is rightly understood as a divine action," writes Father Avery Dulles, S.J., in his *Survival of Dogma* (1971, p. 182), "it is obvious that there can be no absolute equation between the word of God and the words of men." Hence his idea of the "survival" (p. 173): "I suggest that we focus our attention on the historical relativity of all doctrinal statements." This is given simply as an example of the many writings of the new hermeneutics that reject revelation as "propositions", while deceptively proposing the existentialist concept of revelation as "encounter" with Someone.

It is here, perhaps, that the renewal of Christian Philosophy becomes a particular necessity from the pastoral point of view. For it is spiritually dangerous to desire such an "encounter with Someone" apart from the formulated doctrine of the teaching program that the Apostles received from Jesus, their Divine Teacher, and handed on by the propositions of the deposit. In the authentic catechesis that hands on the doctrine of divine revelation, formulated into propositions by the authority of the Teaching Church, there is indeed an encounter with Someone, none other than Jesus really present in the Holy Eucharist. He is known and recognized by divine faith in this word of the Teaching Church. But who is encountered in the other approach, which uses the language of religiosity and even of mysticism but apart from humble acceptance of the Church's ministry of the word? Might it not prove to be an encounter with the Prince of this World, one mediated by the experiencing of one's fallen self? These may seem to be perspectives quite distant from philosophy. At the same time they have philosophical roots, and they illuminate the ongoing need for the transcendent metaphysics from the viewpoint of the deposit of faith.

Returning to the propositions that St. Thérèse learned in her childhood from the French Small Catechism, and indeed in the same meaning that they had for the early Christians, one recognizes that the new hermeneutics places a new and different value on the nexus between the concepts that the judgments affirm and the propositions express. For St. Thérèse and the twentieth century, and for the disciples of the Apostles in the early Church, they express what "really" is the case: "You are the Messiah"; "You are the Son of the Living God"; "This is my Body." The existential verb "is" expresses what "really" is the truth, the fact that such teachings of revealed religion express what is true in reality. The new hermeneutics removes such understandings and replaces them with quite different explanations, which subject them to historical and cultural relativism in the general pattern described by De Lubac. The present point is to draw attention to the hidden substrate of the inner-cosmic metaphysics. From this one can turn to the quite different hermeneutical light that shines upon the revealed deposit from the transcendent metaphysics of Christian Philosophy.

The Eternal Hermeneutics

"I tell you solemnly, till heaven and earth disappear, not one dot, not one little stroke, shall disappear from the law until its purpose is achieved" (Mt 5:18). "Heaven and earth will pass away, but my words will never pass away" (Lk 21:33).

These words of Jesus of Nazareth, who did his teaching out of the prophetic light, represent the highest point of contact with the rational light that philosophy cultivates as the seventh of the seven liberal arts. This is the point at which philosophy ministers to the abiding meaning of the deposit of faith and morals: it provides the light by which the propositions are understood that express judgments known by the prophetic light.

St. Irenaeus, bishop and martyr at Lyons in the second century, who learned the deposit of faith as a youth in the parish catechetical school of Bishop Polycarp at Smyrna, just as Polycarp had learned the same deposit in the catechetical school conducted by John the Apostle at Ephesus, has left a passage in his treatise *Against the Heresies* (I, 10) that expresses the idea of the abiding and indeed eternal hermeneutics, namely, the philosophical and linguistic foundation for the unity of the Faith in the whole world and throughout all time. "The Church," he writes,

> having received this Faith [he has just given the substance of the Apostles' Creed], although scattered throughout the whole world, yet, as if occupying but one house, carefully preserves it. She believes these points of doctrine just as if she had but one soul and one and the same heart, and proclaims and teaches them and hands them down with perfect harmony, as if she possessed only one mouth. For, although the languages of the world are dissimilar, yet the import of the Tradition is one and the same. . . . Nor will any one of the rulers in the churches, however highly gifted he may be in point of eloquence, teach doctrines different from these, for no one is greater than the Master. Nor, on the other hand, will he who is deficient in power of expression inflict injury on the Tradition. For the Faith being ever one and the same, neither does one who is able at great length to discourse regarding it, make any addition to it, nor does one, who can say but little, diminish it.

The early Church, as St. Irenaeus bears witness, distinguished the import or meaning of the Tradition, namely, the deposit that Jesus the Teacher entrusted to the Apostles and their successors, from the human words by which it is taught and explained. This is the key point in piercing the deceptions of the new hermeneutics. For it opens the way to a natural and human foundation, amid all changing languages, times, and cultures, for a meaning that abides one and the same through them all. This foundation is the natural metaphysics of mankind, which is at home in Christian Philosophy. All human languages reflect this natural metaphysics in their structures. Thus Christian Philosophy provides the basis for what is rightly called the Eternal Hermeneutics. On this basis of the rational light functioning in and through all the languages of mankind, the divine deposit is taught, explained, and interpreted always and everywhere in the same import or meaning. Thus, as St. Irenaeus says, "the Faith is ever one and the same". The Apostles' Creed has the same meaning for St. Thérèse of Lisieux and all Catholics of the entire twentieth century, for whom she has been raised up as aid and counsel, as it had for the Apostles who learned it from Jesus. This turns aside the thrust of the new hermeneutics, solves the pantheistic problems of the inner-cosmic metaphysics, and opens the way to a pastorally fruitful contact with all the peoples and regional cultures of the contemporary world because it is faithful in nature. Thus the most fundamental reason, pastoral and catechetical rather than academic, for the renewal of Christian Philosophy comes into view for the times after Vatican II.

The heart of this ministry of Christian Philosophy to the divine deposit is a corollary of both the metaphysics of openness to the personal Supreme Being and the philosophical anthropology that provides ears to hear his word. It does so by means of its philosophy of truth: truth is located in the judgments of the intellect, not in the apprehensions of sensory experience. In these judgments the intellect knows truths, many beyond its natural power, such as those handed on in catechesis: "In the One God there are three equal Divine Persons"; "Jesus of Nazareth is true God and true man"; "This is my Body." All these catechetical propositions are taught as "really" true in ontological reality, not because the nexus, the truth of the verb "is" asserting the identity of the concepts in reality outside the mind, is seen by natural human powers, but because God has revealed that truth. The truth is accepted from the authorized Teaching Church and thus on the authority of God revealing. Christian Philosophy ministers to the sameness of the meaning, first, by its metaphysical openness to the possibility, and second, by its explanation of the human mode of being and knowledge.

Thus the word of God does indeed reach individuals in the words of human discourse because Jesus' meaning abides, the same then and now. St. Thérèse of Lisieux, and other Catholic children like her, receive the truths of the catechism, expressed in the French language, on the authority of God revealing. In doing so, like persons of all times and cultures, St. Thérèse joins the Thessalonians who received the same teaching from St. Paul: "You accepted it for what it really is, God's message, and not some human thinking" (1 Th 2:13).

This natural philosophical foundation standing beneath the catechetical discourse of the Teaching Church has been under consideration implicitly throughout the present study, which has seen Christian Philosophy as the continuation of the natural philosophizing of the Greeks. Greek philosophy itself, furthermore, was a development of the natural metaphysics of mankind reflected in the structure of all human languages. For further study of this fundamental matter, there are certain classic works of Christian Philosophy, written by disciples of St. Thomas early in the renewal to expose the fallacy of the new hermeneutics of Fathers Loisy and Tyrrell, that are continuing resources in the late twentieth century. They are *Le donné révélé* by Father Ambrose Gardeil, O.P., and *Le sens commun* by Father Reginald Garrigou-Lagrange, O.P. Both are more significant than ever in the decades after Vatican II. They may suffice here as symbols of the resources of Christian Philosophy to support the *Mysterium Ecclesiae* (June 24, 1973) and *Mysterium fidei* (September 3, 1965) of the Supreme Magisterium in the ongoing confusion generated by the new hermeneutics. The human component for the Eternal Hermeneutics is stated succinctly in *Mysterium fidei* in words that provide a fitting conclusion for this study of the highest ministry of the seventh liberal art. *Mysterium fidei* cites St. Augustine, who says that we Christians, unlike the pagan philosophers, "must speak according to a fixed norm, lest the lack of restraint in our speech result in some impious opinion even about the things signified by the words themselves". "The Church, therefore", *Mysterium fidei* continues,

> with the long labor of centuries and not without the help of the Holy Spirit, has established a rule of language and confirmed it with the authority of the Councils. This rule . . . must be religiously preserved, and let no one presume to change it at his own pleasure or under the pretext of new science. . . . It cannot be tolerated that any individual should on his own authority modify the formulas that were used by the Council of Trent to express belief in the Eucharistic Mystery. For these formulas, like the others that the Church uses to propose the dogmas of faith, express concepts that are not tied to a certain form of human culture, or to a specific phase of human culture, or to one or the other theological school. No, these formulas present that part of reality that necessary and universal experience permits the human mind to grasp and to manifest with apt and exact terms taken either from common or scholarly language. For this reason, these formulas are adapted to men of all times and all places.

The study of Christian Philosophy, in itself and in its contemporary renewal, finds in these words both the summary of its content and its justification from the viewpoint of the pastoral care of souls. They set aside the new hermeneutics and assert the Eternal Hermeneutics, namely, the understanding of the Apostles' Creed by Christians of today in the same meaning that it had for the Apostles.

GENERAL CONCLUSION

The concluding chapter above, "Christian Philosophy and the Deposit of Faith", may seem a strange outcome for the study of philosophy. Yet this should not be the case when the philosophical experience of mankind is considered as a whole. One must recall that significant day in 1931 when Gilson and Maritain met Bréhier and Brunschvicg in philosophical encounter. One must recall, furthermore, that fork in the road within metaphysics that that encounter exemplified.

At the fork, the mind must decide whether it will continue up the ascent of the mountain of being in openness to nonmaterial reality until it recognizes the existence of the transcendent, personal, and intelligent Supreme Being—or whether it will take the other way, which remains within the material cosmos to continue its philosophical ministry to the ancient and inveterate religious error of mankind: pantheism and atheism in their various forms. Either it will be open metaphysically to natural theology, or closed metaphysically, asserting that nothing is but this cosmos. And this will be a particular kind of philosophy, one that imprisons man within the cosmos.

In transcendent metaphysics, the mind will philosophize authentically, because of its metaphysical openness to all reality. This openness will make it a different kind of philosophy, quite different from the atheistic use of the mind. Furthermore, it can readily philosophize "within the Faith", as Maritain puts it in the subtitle of his *Science and Wisdom,* written shortly after that famous encounter. For it is that kind of philosophy that first sees the existence of the intelligent First Cause of all other acts of existing and then consequently is able to hear in case he speaks his word to mankind.

The pagan Greek philosophers thirsted for wisdom and wanted to find and love it: hence their noble word "philosophy", for this seventh of the liberal arts. The Christian thinkers, led by Justin Martyr and Augustine, built and developed this liberal discipline further, elaborating upon the Greek foundations a true natural theology, the natural science of God. "Philosophy is the science of wisdom and virtue", writes Augustine. "The true philosopher is a person who loves God." With this openness to God, the deposit of faith and morals, the content of St. Thérèse's Small Catechism, comes into view. For this philosophical openness develops readily into the preambles of faith, the Faith that, making Peter's profession, recognizes Jesus of Nazareth as Wisdom Incarnate.

APPENDIX I

EXCERPTS

Introduction

The following short excerpts concerning Socrates and Augustine will help you to form a vivid picture of the nature of philosophy and its relationship to faith. In this short selection from the dialogue The Apology *Socrates explains to his accusers why he philosophizes and also draws his fellow Athenians into questioning the opinions and patterns of their times (fifth century* B.C.*).*

Socrates

THE APOLOGY

Men of Athens, I honor and love you; but I shall obey God rather than you, and while I have life and strength I shall never cease from the practice and teaching of philosophy, exhorting any one whom I meet after my manner, and convincing him, saying: O my friend, why do you, who are a citizen of the great and mighty and wise city of Athens, care so much about laying up the greatest amount of money and honor and reputation, and so little about wisdom and truth and the greatest improvement of the soul which you never regard or heed at all? Are you not ashamed of this?

And if the person with whom I am arguing, says: Yes, but I do care; I do not depart or let him go at once; I interrogate and examine and cross-examine him, and if I think that he has no virtue, but only says that he has, I reproach him with undervaluing the greater, and overvaluing the less.

And this I should say to everyone whom I meet, young and old, citizen and alien, but especially to the citizens, inasmuch as they are my brethren. . . .

For I do nothing but go about persuading you all, old and young alike, not to take thought for your persons or your properties, but first and chiefly to care about the greatest improvement of the soul. . . .

For if you kill me you will not easily find another like me, who, if I may use such a ludicrous figure of speech, am a sort of gadfly, given to the state by the God; and the state is like a great and noble steed who is tardy in his motions owing to his very size, and requires to be stirred into life.

> — From *The Works of Plato,* translated by Jowett (N.Y.: Tudor Publishing, 1937).

Augustine

The excerpt from Augustine's Confessions *(fourth century* A.D.*) shows how Augustine's previous false materialistic philosophy was an obstacle to faith and how his study of Platonic philosophy, in spite of its errors, nonetheless gave him glimmerings of the realities that form the substance of the Catholic Faith. His intellectual adherence to the truths of the faith made him eager to overcome the moral obstacles that stood in his way, difficulties by no means unfamiliar in our own times.*

CONFESSIONS

Now my evil sinful youth was over and I had come on into young manhood; but the older in years, the baser was my vanity, in that I could not conceive any other kind of substance than what these eyes are accustomed to see. . . . I could not but think of you (God) as some corporeal substance, occupying all space, whether infused in the world, or else diffused through infinite space beyond the world. . . . Whatever I tried to see as not in space seemed to me to be nothing, absolutely nothing, not even a void: for if a body were taken out of its place and the place remained without any body, whether of earth or water or air or sky, it would still be an empty place, a space-occupying nothingness. . . .

My mind was in search of such images as the forms my eye was accustomed to see; and I did not realize that the mental act by which I formed these images, was not itself a bodily image: yet it could not have formed them, unless it were something and something great. . . .

. . . You brought in my way by means of a certain man . . . some books of the Platonists translated from Greek into Latin. In them I found, though not in the very words, yet the thing itself and proved by all sorts of reasons: that [Note: passages in italics are from the Scripture] *in the beginning was the Word and the Word was with God and the Word was God: the same was in the beginning with God; all things were made by him and without him was made nothing that was made; in him was life and the life was the light of men, and the light shines in the darkness and the darkness did not comprehend it.* And I found in those same writings that the soul of man, though *it gives testimony of the light, yet is not itself the light,* but the Word, God himself, is *the true light which enlightens every man that comes into this world; and that he was in the world and the world was made by him, and the world knew him not.* But I did not read in those books that *he came unto his own, and his own received him not, but to as many as received him he gave power to be made the sons of God, to them that believed in his name.*

Again I found in them that the Word, God, was *born not of flesh nor of blood, nor of the will of man nor of the will of the flesh, but of God;* but I did not find that *the Word became flesh.*

I found it stated, differently and in a variety of ways, that the Son *being in the form of the Father thought it not robbery to be equal with God,* because by nature he was God. But these books did not tell me that *he emptied himself, taking the form of a servant, being made in the likeness of men, and in habit found as a man;* or that *he humbled himself becoming obedient unto death, even to the death of the cross; for which cause God also hath exalted him from the dead and given him a name which is above all names, that in the name of Jesus every knee should bow of those that are in heaven, on earth, and under the earth; and that every tongue should confess that the Lord Jesus is in the glory of God the Father.* . . .

. . . I did not read that *in due time he died for the ungodly, and that thou didst not spare thy only-begotten Son but delivered him up for us all.* For *thou hast hid these things from the wise and hast revealed them to little ones,* that *those who labor and are burdened should come to him and he should refresh them, because he is meek and humble of heart;* and *the meek he directs in judgement, and the gentle he teaches his ways, beholding our lowness and our trouble and forgiving all our sins.* . . .

. . . Being admonished by all this to return to myself, I entered into my own depths, with you as guide; and I was able to do it because you were my helper. I entered and with the eye of my soul, such as it was, I saw your unchangeable Light shining over that same eye of my soul, over my mind. It was not the light of everyday that the eye of flesh can see, nor some greater light of the same order, such as might be if the brightness of our daily light should be seen shining with a more intense brightness and filling all things with its greatness. Your Light was not that, but other, altogether other than all such lights. Nor was it above my mind as oil above the water it floats on, nor as the sky is above the earth; it was above because it made me, and I was below because made by it. He who knows the truth knows the Light, and he that knows the Light knows eternity. Love knows it. O eternal truth and true love and beloved eternity; thou art my God, I sigh to thee by day and by night. . . .

To you, then, evil utterly is not—and not only to you but to your whole creation likewise, evil is not: because there is nothing over and above your creation that could break in or derange the order that you imposed upon it. But in certain of its parts there are some things which we call evil because they do not harmonize with other things. . . . I realized that while certain higher things are better than lower things, yet all things together are better than the higher alone. . . .

And I marvelled to find that at last I loved you and not some phantom instead of you; yet I did not stably enjoy my God, but was ravished to you by your beauty, yet soon was torn away from you again by my own weight, and fell again with torment to lower things. Carnal habit was that weight. Yet the memory of you remained with me and I knew without doubt that it was you to whom I should cleave, though I was not yet such as could cleave to you. . . .

I set about finding a way to gain the strength that was necessary for enjoying you. And I could not find it until I embraced the *Mediator between God and man, the man Christ Jesus, who is over all things, God blessed forever,* who was calling unto me and saying: *I am the Way, the Truth, and the Life;* and who brought into union with our nature that Good which I lacked the strength to take: for *the Word was made flesh* that your wisdom, by which you created all things, might give suck to our soul's infancy. But I was not yet lowly enough to hold the lowly Jesus as my God. . . . He built for himself here below a lowly house of our clay, that by it he might bring down from themselves and bring up to himself those who were to be made subject, healing the swollenness of their pride and fostering their love . . . to the end that weary at last they might cast themselves down upon his humanity and rise again in its rising.

When my most searching scrutiny had drawn up all my vileness from the secret depths of my soul and heaped it in my heart's sight, a mighty storm arose in me, bringing a mighty rain of tears.... "How long, how long shall I go on saying tomorrow and again tomorrow? Why not now, why not have an end to my uncleanness this very hour?" . . .

And suddenly I heard a voice from some nearby house . . . repeating again and again, "Take and read; take and read." I ceased weeping and immediately began to search my mind most carefully as to whether children were accustomed to chant these words in any kind of game, and I could not remember that I had ever heard any such thing. Damming back the flood of my tears I arose, interpreting the incident as quite certainly a divine command to open my book of Scripture and read the passage at which I should open. . . . I snatched it up, opened it and in silence read the passage upon which my eyes first fell: *Not in rioting and drunkenness, not in chambering and impurities, not in contention and envy, but put ye on the Lord Jesus Christ and make not provision for the flesh in its concupiscences* (Rom 13:13).

I had no wish to read further, and no need. For in that instant, with the very ending of the sentence, it was as though a light of utter confidence shone in all my heart, and all the darkness of uncertainty vanished away.

— From *Confessions,* From books VII and VIII.

Part One

Plato

The first excerpts given will be from the dialogues of Plato, translated by Benjamin Jowett in the Great Books of the Western World Series (vol. 7).

THE MYTH OF THE CAVE

Let me show in a figure how far our nature is enlightened or unenlightened: —Behold! human beings living in an underground den, which has a mouth open towards the light and reaching all along the den; here they have been from their childhood, and have their legs and necks chained so that they can not move, and can only see before them, being prevented by the chains from turning round their heads. Above and behind them a fire is blazing at a distance, and between the fire and the prisoners there is a raised way; and you will see, if you look, a low wall built along the way, like the screen which marionette players have in front of them, over which they show the puppets. . . .

. . . And do you see . . . men passing along the wall carrying all sorts of vessels, and statues and figures of animals made of wood and stone and various materials, which appear over the wall? Some of them are talking, others silent.

You have shown me a strange image, and they are strange prisoners.

Like ourselves, I replied; and they see only their own shadows, or the shadows of one another, which the fire throws on the opposite wall of the cave?

True, he said; how could they see anything but the shadows if they were never allowed to move their heads?

And of the objects which are being carried in like manner they would only see the shadows?

Yes, he said.

And if they were able to converse with one another, would they not suppose that they were naming what was actually before them?

Very true.

And suppose further that the prison had an echo which came from the other side, would they not be sure to fancy when one of the passers-by spoke that the voice which they heard came from the passing shadow?

No question, he replied.

To them, I said, the truth would be literally nothing but the shadows of the images. . . .

And now look again, and see what will naturally follow if the prisoners are released and disabused of their error. At first, when any of them is liberated and compelled to stand up and turn his neck round and walk and look towards the light, he will suffer sharp pains; the glare will distress him and he will be unable to see the realities of which in his former state he had seen the shadows; and then conceive some one saying to him, that what he was before was an illusion, but that now, when he is approaching nearer to being and his eye is turned towards more real existence, he has a clearer vision, what will be his reply? And you may further imagine that his instructor is pointing to the objects as they pass and requiring him to name them, — will he not be perplexed? Will he not fancy that the shadows which he formerly saw are truer than the objects which are now shown to him?

Far truer.

And if he is compelled to look straight at the light will he not have a pain in his eyes which will make him turn away to take refuge in the objects of vision which he can see, and which he will conceive to be in reality clearer than the things which are now being shown to him? . . .

And suppose once more, that he is reluctantly dragged up a steep and rugged ascent, and held fast until he is forced into the presence of the sun himself, is he not likely to be pained and irritated? When he approaches the light his eyes will be dazzled, and he will not be able to see anything at all of what are now called realities.

Not all in a moment, he said.

He will require to grow accustomed to the sight of the upper world. . . . Last of all he will be able to see the sun, and not mere reflections of him in the water, . . . and he will contemplate him as he is (the sun). . . .

He will argue that (the sun) in a certain way (is) the cause of all things. . . .

And when he remembered his old habitation, and the wisdom of the den and his fellow-prisoners, do you not suppose that he would felicitate himself on the change, and pity them? . . .

And if they were in the habit of conferring honors among themselves on those who were quickest to observe the passing shadows and to remark which of them went before, and which followed after, and which were together; and who were therefore best able to draw conclusions as to the future, do you think he would care for such honors and glories, or envy the possessors of them? . . .

. . . Yes, he said, I think that he would rather suffer anything than entertain these false notions and live in this miserable manner.

Imagine once more, I said, such a one coming suddenly out of the sun to be replaced in his old situation; would he not be certain to have his eyes full of darkness? . . .

And if there were a contest, and he had to compete in measuring the shadows with the prisoners who had never moved out of the den, while his sight was still weak, and before his eyes had become steady . . . would he not be ridiculous? Men would say of him that up he went and down he came without his eyes; and that it was better not even to think of ascending; and if any one tried to loose another and lead him up to the light, let them only catch the offender, and they would put him to death.

. . . This entire allegory, I said, you may now append, dear Glacon, to the previous argument; the prison-house is the world of sight, the light of the fire is the sun, and you will not misapprehend me if you interpret the journey upwards to be the ascent of the soul into the intellectual world . . . my opinion is that in the world of knowledge the idea of good appears last of all, and is seen only with an effort; and when seen, is also inferred to be the universal author of all things beautiful and right, parent of light and the lord of light in this visible world, and the immediate source of reason and truth in the intellectual; and that this is the power upon which he who would act rationally either in public or private life must have his eye fixed . . . moreover, I said, you must not wonder that those who attain to this beatific vision are unwilling to descend to human affairs; for their souls are ever hastening into the upper world where they desire to dwell; which desire of theirs is very natural, if our allegory may be trusted.

— From the *Republic* (Book VII), the Myth of the Cave.

Concerning the immortality of the soul:

PHAEDO

(Socrates):

Do we believe . . . that there is such a thing as death?

To be sure, replied Simmias.

And is this anything but the separation of soul and body? And being dead is the attainment of this separation when the soul exists in herself, and is parted from the body and the body is parted from the soul—that is death?

Exactly: that and nothing else, he replied.

And what do you say of another question, my friend, about which I should like to have your opinion, and the answer to which will probably throw light on our present inquiry: Do you think that the philosopher ought to care about the pleasures—if they are to be called pleasures—of eating and drinking?

Certainly not, answered Simmias.

And what do you say of the pleasures of love—should he care about them?

By no means.

And will he think much of the other ways of indulging the body, for example, the acquisition of costly raiment, or sandals or other adornments of the body? Instead of caring about them, does he not rather despise anything more than nature needs? What do you say?

I should say that the true philosopher would despise them.

Would you not say that he is entirely concerned with the soul and not with the body? He would like, as far as he can, to be quit of the body and turn to the soul.

That is true.

In matters of this sort philosophers, above all other men, may be observed in every sort of way to dissever the soul from the body.

That is true.

Whereas, Simmias, the rest of the world are of opinion that a life which has no bodily pleasures and no part in them is not worth having; but that he who thinks nothing of bodily pleasures is almost as though he were dead.

That is quite true.

What again shall we say of the actual acquirement of knowledge?—is the body, if invited to share in the inquiry, a hinderer or a helper? I mean to say, have sight and hearing any truth in them? Are they not, as the poets are always telling us, inaccurate witnesses? and yet, if even they are inaccurate and indistinct, what is to be said of the other senses? — for you will allow that they are the best of them?

Certainly, he replied.

Then when does the soul attain truth? — for in attempting to consider anything in company with the body she is obviously deceived.

Yes, that is true.

Then must not existence be revealed to her in thought, if at all?

Yes.

And thought is best when the mind is gathered into herself and none of these things trouble her — neither sounds nor sights nor pain nor any pleasure, — when she has as little as possible to do with the body, and has no bodily sense or feeling, but is aspiring after being?

That is true.

And in this the philosopher dishonors the body; his soul runs away from the body and desires to be alone and by herself?

That is true.

Well, but there is another thing, Simmias: Is there or is there not an absolute justice?

Assuredly there is.

And an absolute beauty and absolute good?

Of course.

But did you ever behold any of them with your eyes?

Certainly not.

Or did you ever reach them with any other bodily sense? (and I speak not of these alone, but of absolute greatness, and health, and strength, and of the essence or true nature of everything). Has the reality of them ever been perceived by you through the bodily organs? or rather, is not the nearest approach to the knowledge of their several natures made by him who so orders his intellectual vision as to have the most exact conception of the essence of that which he considers?

Certainly.

And he attains to the knowledge of them in their highest purity who goes to each of them with the mind alone, not allowing when in the act of thought the intrusion or introduction of sight or any other sense in the company of reason, but with the very light of the mind in her clearness penetrates into the very light of truth in each; he has got rid, as far as he can, of eyes and ears and of the whole body, which he conceives of only as a disturbing element, hindering the soul from the acquisition of knowledge when in company with her — is not this the sort of man who, if ever man did, is likely to attain the knowledge of existence?

There is admirable truth in that, Socrates, replied Simmias.

And when they consider all this, must not true philosophers make a reflection, of which they will speak to one another in such words as these: We have found, they will say, a path of speculation which seems to bring us and the argument to the conclusion, that while we are in the body, and while the soul is mingled with this mass of evil, our desire will not be satisfied, and our desire is of the truth. For the body is a source of endless trouble to us by reason of the mere requirement of food; and also is liable to diseases which overtake and impede us in the search after truth: and by filling us as full of loves, and lusts, and fears, and fancies, and idols, and every sort of folly, prevents our ever having, as people say, so much as a thought. For whence come wars, and fightings, and factions? whence but from the body and the lusts of the body? For wars are occasioned by the love of money, and money has to be acquired for the sake and in the service of the body; and in consequence of all these things the time which ought to be given to philosophy is lost. Moreover, if there is time and an inclination towards philosophy, yet the body introduces a turmoil and confusion and fear into the course of speculation, and hinders us from seeing the truth; and all experience shows that if we would have pure knowledge of anything we must be quit of the body, and the soul in herself must behold all things in themselves: then, I suppose, that we shall attain that which we desire, and of which we say that we are lovers, and that is wisdom; not while we live, but after death, as the argument shows; for if while in company with the body, the soul can not have pure knowledge, one of two things seems to follow—either knowledge is not to be attained at all, or, if at all, after death. For then, and not till then, the soul will be in herself alone and without the body. In this present life, I reckon that we make the nearest approach to knowledge when we have the least possible concern or interest in the body, and are not saturated with the bodily nature, but remain pure until the hour when God himself is pleased to release us. And then the foolishness of the body will be cleared away and we shall be pure and hold converse with other pure souls, and know of ourselves the clear light everywhere; and this is surely the light of truth. For no impure thing is allowed to approach the pure. These are the sort of words, Simmias, which the true lovers of wisdom can not help saying to one another, and thinking. You will agree with me in that?

Certainly, Socrates.

But if this is true, O my friend, then there is great hope that, going whither I go, I shall there be satisfied with that which has been the chief concern of you and me in our past lives. And now that the hour of departure is appointed to me, this is the hope with which I depart, and not I only, but every man who believes that he has his mind purified.

— From *Phaedo.*

Aristotle

Readers are referred to Introduction to Aristotle, *ed. Richard McKeon, translated by R. P. Hardie and R. K. Gaye (New York: Random House, 1965) or* The Oxford Translation of Aristotle, *edited by W. D. Ross (London: Oxford University Press, 1925–30)*

Here we will include a summary of some of the most often studied passages from Aristotle.

THE FOUR CAUSES

Aristotle was very interested in categorizing the determinants that explain the why of the coming into being of substances. In the Physics, *Book II, 3, he writes about these causes:*

the material cause: that "out of which a thing comes to be and which persists", such as the metal of which a statue might be made.

the formal cause: the "form or the archetype . . . the essence", such as the shape of the statue, that it is a statue of a man, for instance.

the efficient cause: "the primary source of the change or coming to rest", such as the chisel or hammer which is applied to the metal to make a statue.

the final cause: "the end or 'that for the sake of which' a thing is done . . . " such as the decoration of a building by means of the statue.

> — From *Introduction to Aristotle,* ed. R. McKeon (New York: Random House, 1965).

THE NICHOMACHEAN ETHICS

In the Nichomachean Ethics, *book I, chapter 7 and book II, chapters 4–8, Aristotle explains how ethics is related to the end of man and how to achieve virtue through rational deliberation in the avoidance of extremes:*

Just as in medicine the good is that for the sake of which something is done: i.e., the health of the patient, so it is important to look to see why humans act in terms of the final purpose.

Aristotle maintains that happiness is the purpose for which everything else is done. Intermediary ends—such as honor, pleasure, reason, and even virtue,—are chosen partly for themselves but "we choose them also for the sake of happiness, judging that by means of them we shall be happy. Happiness, on the other hand, no one chooses for the sake of these, nor, in general, for anything other than itself."

For acts to be virtuous three conditions must be satisfied: (1) we must have knowledge;

(2) we must choose the act for its own sake, and (3) the action must proceed from a "firm and unchangeable character".

Actions, then, are called just and temperate when they are such as the just or the temperate man would do; but it is not the man who does these that is just and temperate, but the man who also does them as just and temperate men do them. It is well said, then, that it is by doing just acts that the just man is produced, and by doing temperate acts the temperate man; without doing these no one would have even a prospect of becoming good.

But most people do not do these, but take refuge in theory and think they are being philosophers and will become good in this way, behaving somewhat like patients who listen attentively to their doctors, but do none of the things they are ordered to do. As the latter will not be made well in body by such a course of treatment, the former will not be made well in soul by such a course of philosophy.

Just as a man may be too fat or too thin; exercise too much or too little; so, Aristotle reasons, virtue which is the highest art, should be concerned with aiming at the intermediate between extremes concerning passions and actions. What is best is to feel an emotion "at the right times, with reference to the right objects, toward the right people, with the right motive, and in the right way . . . " Excess of emotion is a defect and can fall on either side; for example, giving away money senselessly is an excess of liberality, and to never give is miserly. The mean is proper generosity.

Here are some more examples of means between extremes described in the Nichomachean Ethics:

extreme	mean	extreme
fearfulness	courage	over-confidence
undue humility	proper pride	empty vanity
passivity	good temper	irascibility
boorishness	wit	buffoonery
surliness	friendliness	flattery

Epictetus

OF THE THINGS WHICH ARE, AND THE THINGS
WHICH ARE NOT IN OUR OWN POWER

Of other faculties, you will find no one that contemplates, and consequently approves or disapproves itself. How far does the proper sphere of grammar extend? As far as the judging of language. Of music? As far as the judging of melody. Does either of them contemplate itself, then? By no means.

Thus, for instance, when you are to write to your friend, grammar will tell you what to write; but whether you are to write to your friend at all, or no, grammar will not tell you. Thus music, with regard to tunes; but whether it be proper or improper, at any particular time, to sing or play, music will not tell you.

What will tell, then?

That which contemplates both itself and all other things.

And what is that?

The Reasoning Faculty; for that alone is found to consider both itself, its powers, its value, and likewise all the rest. For what is it else that says, gold is beautiful; for the gold itself does not speak? Evidently that faculty, which judges of the appearances of things. What else distinguishes music, grammar, the other faculties, proves their uses, and shows their proper occasions?

Nothing but this.

As it was fit then, this most excellent and superior faculty alone, a right use of the appearances of things, the gods have placed in our own power; but all other matters, they have not placed in our power. What, was it because they would not? I rather think, that if they could, they had granted us these too; but they certainly could not. For, placed upon earth, and confined to such a body, and to such companions, how was it possible that, in these respects, we should not be hindered by things without us?

But what says Zeus? "O Epictetus, if it were possible, I had made this little body and property of thine free, and not liable to hindrance. But now do not mistake: it is not thy own, but only a finer mixture of clay. Since, then, I could not give thee this, I have given thee a certain portion of myself; this faculty of exerting the powers of pursuit and avoidance, of desire and aversion, and, in a word, the use of the appearances of things. Taking care of this point, and making what is thy own to consist in this, thou wilt never be restrained, never be hindered; thou wilt not groan, wilt not complain, wilt not flatter any one. How, then! Do all these advantages seem small to thee? Heaven forbid! Let them suffice thee then, and thank the gods."

But now, when it is in our power to take care of one thing, and to apply to one, we choose rather to take care of many, and to encumber ourselves with many; body, property, brother, friend, child, and slave; and, by this multiplicity of encumbrances, we are burdened and weighed down. Thus, when the weather doth not happen to be fair for sailing, we sit in distress and gaze out perpetually. Which way is the wind? —North.—What do we want of that? When will the west blow?—When it pleases, friend, or when Aeolus pleases; for Zeus has not made you dispenser of the winds, but Aeolus.

What then is to be done?

To make the best of what is in our power, and take the rest as it occurs.

And how does it occur?

As it pleases God.

What, then, must I be the only one to lose my head?

Why, would you have all the world, then, lose their heads for your consolation? Why are not you willing to stretch out your neck, like Lateranus,[1] when he was commanded by Nero to be beheaded? For, shrinking a little after receiving a weak blow, he stretched it out again. And before this, when Epaphroditus,[2] the freedman of Nero, interrogated him about the conspiracy: "If I have a mind to say anything," replied he, "I will tell it to your master."

What resource have we then upon such occasions? Why, what else but to distinguish between what is *ours,* and what not *ours;* what is right, and what is wrong. I must die, and must I die groaning too?—Be fettered. Must I be lamenting too?—Exiled. And what hinders me, then, but that I may go smiling, and cheerful, and serene?—"Betray a secret."—I will not betray it; for this is in my own power.—"Then I will fetter you."—What do you say, man? Fetter me? You will fetter my leg; but not Zeus himself can get the better of my free will. "I will throw you into prison: I will behead that paltry body of yours." Did I ever tell you, that I alone had a head not liable to be cut off?—These things ought philosophers to study; these ought they daily to write, these to exercise themselves.

Thraseas[3] used to say, "I had rather be killed today, than banished to-morrow." But how did Rufus[4] answer him? "If you prefer it as a heavier misfortune, how foolish a preference! If as a lighter, who has put it in your power? Why do not you study to be contented with what is allotted you?"

. . . This it is to have studied what ought to be studied; to have placed our desires and aversions above tyranny and above chance. I must die: if instantly, I will die instantly; if in a short time, I will dine first; and when the hour comes, then I will die. How? As becomes one who restores what is not his own.

---

[1] Plautius Lateranus, a Consul elect, was put to death by the command of Nero, for being privy to the conspiracy of Piso. His execution was so sudden, that he was not permitted to take leave of his wife and children; but was hurried into a place appropriated to the punishment of slaves, and there killed by the hand of the tribune Statius. He suffered in obstinate silence, and without making any reproach to Statius, who was concerned in the same plot for which he himself was punished. Tacitus, Ann. xv. c. 60.—C.

[2] Epaphroditus was the master of requests and freedman of Nero, and the master of Epictetus. He assisted Nero in killing himself; for which he was condemned to death by Domitian. Suetonius in Vitâ Neronis, c. 49; Domit. c. 14.—C.

[3] Thrascas Paetus, a Stoic philosopher, put to death by Nero. He was husband of Arria, so well known by that beautiful epigram in Martial. The expression of Tacitus concerning him is remarkable: "After the murder of so many excellent persons, Nero at last formed a desire of cutting off virtue itself, by the execution of Thraseas Paetus and Bareas Soranus." Ann. xvi. c. 21.—C.

[4] Rufus was a Tuscan, of the equestrian order, and a Stoic philosopher. When Vespasian banished the other philosophers, Rufus was alone excepted.—C.

IN WHAT MANNER, UPON EVERY OCCASION, TO PRESERVE
OUR CHARACTER

To a reasonable creature, that alone is insupportable which is unreasonable; but everything reasonable may be supported. Stripes are not naturally insupportable. —"How so?"—See how the Spartans bear whipping, after they have learned that it is a reasonable thing. Hanging is not insupportable; for, as soon as a man has taken it into his head that it is reasonable, he goes and hangs himself. In short we shall find by observation, that no creature is oppressed so much by anything, as by what is unreasonable; nor, on the other hand, attracted to anything so strongly, as to what is reasonable.

But it happens that different things are reasonable and unreasonable, as well as good and bad, advantageous and disadvantageous, to different persons. On this account, chiefly, we stand in need of a liberal education, to teach us to adapt the preconceptions of reasonable and unreasonable to particular cases, conformably to nature. But to judge of reasonable and unreasonable, we make use not only of a due estimation of things without us, but of what relates to each person's particular character. Thus, it is reasonable for one man to submit to a menial office, who considers this only, that if he does not submit to it, he shall be whipt, and lose his dinner, but that if he does, he has nothing hard or disagreeable to suffer; whereas to another it appears insupportable, not only to submit to such an office himself, but to respect any one else who does. If you ask me, then, whether you shall do this menial office or not, I will tell you, it is a more valuable thing to get a dinner, than not; and a greater disgrace to be whipt, than not to be whipt;—so that, if you measure yourself by these things, go and do your office.

"Ay, but this is not suitable to my character."

It is you who are to consider that, not I; for it is you who know yourself, what value you set upon yourself, and at what rate you sell yourself; for different people sell themselves at different prices.

> — From *The Discourses of Epictetus,* translated by Elizabeth Carter and Thomas Wentworth Higginson (Boston: Little, Brown, and Company, 1965).

Augustine

These excerpts are from St. Augustine on his discovery of the metaphysics of Christian Philosophy during his conversion.

ON THE TRUE RELIGION

The way of the good and blessed life is to be found entirely in the true religion, wherein one God is worshipped and acknowledged with purest piety to be the beginning of all existing things, originating, perfecting and containing the universe.

> — From *On the True Religion,* I (I). Translated by
> J.H.S. Burleigh (Chicago: Regnery, 1959).

A corporeal object has some concord between its parts, otherwise it could not exist at all. . . . It was made by God, due to its having form. Without that, it would be nothing. Therefore, God is the Creator of matter . . . , he who is the uncreated and most perfect form. Matter participates in something belonging to the ideal world, otherwise it would not be matter. To ask, therefore, who created matter is to ask for him who is supreme in the ideal world. For every idea comes from him. Who is he, then, save the One God, the one Truth, the one salvation of all, the first and highest essence from which all that exists derives existence as such? . . . For all existence as such is good.

> — From *On the True Religion,* II (21).

Why do bodily things become defective? Because they are mutable. Why are they mutable? Because they have not supreme existence. And why so? Because they are inferior to him who made them. Who made them? He who supremely is, *qui summe est.* Who is he? God, the immutable Trinity. . . . Why did he make them? In order that they might exist. Existence is such a good, and supreme existence is the chief good. . . . From what did he make them? Out of nothing. Whatever is, must have some form, and though it be but a minimal good, it will be good, and will be of God. . . . Every good thing is either God, or derived from God. Therefore, even the lowest form is of God. And the same may be said of species. We rightly praise alike that which has form and that which has species. That out of which God created all things had neither form nor species, and was simply nothing.

> — From *On the True Religion,* 18 (35).

Speaking of a famous pagan philosopher, Augustine writes:

When he thinks, he believes he understands, being deluded by shadowy phantasms. If he does not hold fast to the whole discipline of Divine Providence, but imagines he does, and tries to resist the flesh, he merely reaches the images of visible things. He vainly excogitates vast spaces of light exactly like ordinary light which he sees has fixed limits here, and promises himself a future habitation there. He does not know that he is still entangled in the lust of the eye, and that he is carrying this world with him in his endeavor to go beyond it. He thinks he has reached another world simply by imagining the bright part of this world infinitely extended.

— From *On the True Religion,* 20 (40).

We must not have any doubt that the unchangeable substance which is above the rational mind is God. The primal life and primal essence is where the primal wisdom is. This is unchangeable Truth which is the law of all the arts and the art of the omnipotent Artificer. In perceiving that it cannot judge by itself the form and movement of bodies, the soul ought at the same time to realize that its nature excels the nature of what it judges, but also that it is excelled by the nature according to which it judges and concerning which it cannot judge.

— From *On the True Religion,* 31 (57).

This is truth, the Word that was in the beginning, the divine Word that was with God.... This truth is Unity ... and manifests unity as it is in reality. Hence it is rightly called Unity's Word and Light. Other things may be said to be like Unity insofar as they have being, and so far they are also true.... Things are true insofar as they have being, and have being insofar as they resemble the source of all unity, that is, the form of all things that have being.

— From *On the True Religion,* 36 (66).

Augustine exhorts his students from his metaphysical positions:

Make for the place where the light of reason is kindled. You reach it by seeking, not in space, but by a disposition of mind, so that the inward man may agree with the indwelling Truth.... Do not go abroad. Return within yourself. But remember, in doing so that you must also transcend yourself even as a reasoning soul.

— From *On the True Religion,* 39 (72).

SUMMARY OF IDEAS

In the case of the philosophy of St. Augustine, it seems important to have a brief summary of his ideas to complement the brief quotations in the chapter.

Let us begin with Augustine's ideas about truth. First of all, in the Confessions, *Augustine mentions how despairing it made him when he began to think that the skeptics were correct, that there was no truth to seek.*

In one of his earliest works after his conversion, Contra Academicos *(Against the Academics), Augustine shows that skepticism was totally false. It is logical that he would* concentrate on the proof of the existence of truth right after his conversion because he had found the Truth—an objective reality outside his own mind commanding complete obedience. In our own times it is clear that skepticism erodes not only belief in natural truth but also in supernatural truth for people come to think that nothing is more than a matter of opinion, subjective opinion, so nothing commands complete assent or commitment.

The first argument Augustine advances against the views of the skeptical academicians of his time is very simple, although devastating. Here is how it runs:

The skeptic advances the following proposition:

"There is no truth."

But, if this statement *itself* be *true* then there is at least one truth—that statement. And so the proposition is false. If the statement itself is *false,* then the theory is refuted.

Here is another refutation of skepticism, more practical and less theoretical:

An individual cannot call him/herself a philosopher unless there is something to find out, otherwise all inquiry is foolish. But every philosopher does seek as if there were a truth. Therefore a skeptical philosophy claiming there is no truth is a contradiction.

Furthermore, all human action depends upon at least a certain degree of conviction of truth. (To give an example, I cannot walk down the street if I don't think that probably the street is solid, not a vapor.) Skepticism carried through in life would make life impossible.

In terms of contemporary skepticism, expressed most often in the assertion "X is true for me, but maybe not for you", one could reply by means of the same arguments, especially the last.

From the positive side, Augustine thought that all truth comes from God in the form of illumination.

In many passages scattered throughout his writings, but especially in the Soliloquies, *Augustine marvels at the fact that our human, finite, changeable minds are capable of understanding unchangeable, fixed, truths—eternal truths. How is this possible? If we are such frail creatures, how can we grasp such sublime truth? His answer seems to be that we can do so only if the eternal God enlightens us. At the moment of contact with a given reality, our minds are illumined by a Light that is from God. God is the intelligible light by a participation in which all things reveal their natures. Just as the things of the sense are seen through the light of the sun, so our minds see truth by means of participation in the light of God.*

Augustine's foremost proof for the existence of God is based on his illumination theory of truth.

If there is truth, then there is God.

There is truth (for skepticism can be refuted). Therefore, there is God.

— From *On the Free Will*.

The key issue is the first premise. Why does it follow that if there is truth, there is God? Because our mutable minds could not create truth. Therefore if we discover an immutable, unchanging Truth, we are already in contact with the eternal unchanging realm of truth which is the Divine. If our minds themselves had truth in them intrinsically, then the mind would be absolute and would not need to grow and attain truth.

In coming into the realm of truth, the mind becomes able to know God, for truth has the same attributes as God—eternal, immutable, necessary—could not be otherwise.

If we both see that what you say is true, and we both see that what I say is true, where, I ask, do we see this? Neither I in thee, nor thou in me, but both of us in the truth itself above our minds.

— From *Confessions*, XII, 25.

Augustine shows that God exists not only in relationship to truth but also by means of the contemplation of creatures. Many passages in Augustine's works recognize that he thought that the things in the world show forth God. On the positive side they are reflections, images, traces of God by virtue of their goodness, their order, their measure, and stability. On the negative side they cry out "we have not made ourselves", by their weak changeableness. One can see the influence of this concept on the third way of St. Thomas in terms of the creatures being possible entities rather than necessary ones.

Probably the most famous way to God described by Augustine, however, is the argument from longing. "Restless are our hearts until they find their rest in thee." In the Confessions (Book I, 1) the longing for happiness in mankind is depicted with poignant intensity. From whence comes the universal yearning for total happiness in a world that cannot provide it? Where do we wretched creatures who in no way on earth attain to pure happiness, who always want more, who are never satisfied, who never say "enough" —Where could we even get the notion of total happiness? And without such a concept how would we judge our present content to be so inadequate? Sure, the informal argument would run, only God himself could give us the longing for what he alone can fulfill.

The moral philosophy of St. Augustine stresses happiness, virtue, and love.

Having experimented before his conversion with most forms of sensuality, Augustine was sure that the senses were not the path to true happiness. Instead they lead to satiation and disgust. If you are unsure, try eating seven portions of your favorite delicacy and see if your joy increases sevenfold!

Now the Stoic solution to the disillusioning effects of sensuality was called apathy— roughly, detachment. In some Catholics one can find a Christian version of the same idea. Especially at the beginning of a deeper commitment to Christ, a Catholic might think that the road to virtue is the turning away from all passionate emotions into a kind of quiet and rather grim asceticism.

By contrast healthy spirituality, following the lead of Augustine, teaches that the way to virtue is the ordering of loves so that our emotions correspond to the true value of the object. For example, the sentimental adoration someone might shower on a pet in the form of tidbits should instead be transformed into ardent love for human beings with an appropriate tender affection for animals. Note that the spoiled pet dies earlier from overfeeding, whereas the pet loved truly is given what is good for its own functioning.

For Augustine virtue comes from the right ordering of loves. Absolute love should be given only to an absolute object, God. Far from being the deepest love, idol worship of a human being is a distortion, for it wants to give the beloved only what the world can give rather than being concerned for the eternal welfare of the loved one. Contrast "I love you so much that I don't care if we both go to hell as long as I can have you in sin" with "I will readily sacrifice being with you if that is for our eternal good, for the most complete happiness for us will be in eternity".

The way in which virtues become transformed by love can be seen in Augustine's treatise on the cardinal virtues of the Greeks and Romans to be found in De Moribus Ecclesiae:

Temperance is love keeping itself whole and incorrupt for God.

Fortitude is love easily bearing all things for God's sake.

Justice is love serving God only, and for that reason rightly ruling in other matters subject to man.

Prudence is love well discriminating between what helps and what impedes us to God.

For example, the temperate person does not let go of self-control out of disordered love for inferior goods, as in gluttony, licentiousness, or curiosity. A person of fortitude does not complain or curse fate because of loving confidence in God's Providence. A just person does not trample over the rights of others because he is trying not to serve self-interest but God and his Kingdom. A prudent individual takes time to ponder what is really for the best rather than jumping forward impetuously out of eagerness to satisfy his own will.

Virtue leads to happiness, primarily in the next world. Following the Gospels Augustine insists on the importance of reward and punishment. On earth our hearts are *restless, and they find their rest only in God (*Confessions, *Book I, 1). In eternity this will be the fullness; on earth our greatest happiness is our hope based on the saving acts of Christ on the Cross. In heaven "we shall rest and we shall see, we shall see and we shall love, we shall love and we shall praise". So ends the* City of God.

Part Two

Thomas Aquinas

As Aristotle says in his treatise *On the Heavens* (I, 5; A 271), a small error in the beginning (of philosophy) becomes a great one at the end. Now the intellect begins its concepts about reality with those of a being and its essence, as Avicenna writes in his *Metaphysics* I, 6. Hence, lest ignorance of their meaning introduce such an error, their difficulty must be resolved by discussing, first, what is the meaning of "being" and of "essence"; secondly, how they are realized in various things; and, thirdly, how they relate to the topics discussed in the science of Logic, namely genus, species and the specific difference.

> — From the Preface of *Being and Essence*. This excerpt translated by E. Kevane from *De ente et essentia* (Rome: Gregorian University Press, 1933).

Jacques Maritain

PHILOSOPHY AND COMMON SENSE

Before we know things with a scientific or perfect knowledge by reflecting upon them and by their causes, we know them imperfectly (*unscientific knowledge,* the knowledge of everyday life). We must remember that we are obliged not only to begin with this unscientific knowledge of everyday life; we must be content with it to the end, improving it more or less by study and reading, in that enormous number of cases where science in the strict sense is unattainable.

For, so far as the knowledge of secondary causes is concerned, no man can possibly attain, with the perfection required of the genuine scientist, universal knowledge; in other words, he cannot specialise in all branches of science, a contradiction in terms. He is fortunate, indeed, if he can make himself master of a single science. For all the others he must be satisfied with a knowledge which, however enriched and improved it may be in the case of what is known as a cultivated man, that is to say, a man well acquainted with the scientific knowledge of other people, is always inferior to science in the strict sense. But in the domain of first causes, the science of all things is within a man's grasp, for it is precisely the distinguishing character of the science called philosophy to know all things by their first causes,[1] and it is to the philosopher or the sage, the wise man, that we have the right to apply Leonardo da Vinci's aphorism: *facile cosa è farsi universale;* it is easy for a man to make himself universal.

Ordinary knowledge consists for the most part of mere opinions or beliefs, more or less well founded. But it implies a solid kernel of genuine *certainties* in which the philosopher recognises in the first place data of the senses (for example, that *bodies possess length, breadth, and height*), secondly, self-evident axioms (for example, *the whole is greater than the part, every event has a cause,* etc.), and thirdly, consequences immediately deducible from these axioms (proximate conclusions). These certainties which arise spontaneously in the mind when we first come to the use of reason are thus the work of nature in us, and may therefore be called an endowment of nature[2] as proceeding from the natural perception, consent, instinct, or natural sense of the intellect. Since their source is human nature itself, they will be found in all men alike; in other words, they are common to all men. They may therefore be said to belong to the common perception, consent, or instinct, or to the *common sense* of mankind.

The great truths without which man's moral life is impossible—for example, knowledge of God's existence, the freedom of the will, etc.—belong to this domain of common sense, as consequences immediately deducible (proximate conclusions) from primary data apprehended by observation and first principles apprehended by the

---

[1] It is therefore obvious what a stupendous delusion is involved in the positivist view of philosophy. Were philosophy merely the co-ordination or systematisation of the sciences, its attainment would presuppose a perfect mastery of all the sciences, that is to say, specialisation in every science, which amounts to saying that philosophy is beyond the reach of man.

[2] Kleutgen, *La philosophie scolastique,* i, p. 439.

intellect. All men, unless spoiled by a faulty education or by some intellectual vice, possess a natural certainty of these truths. But those whose understanding has never been cultivated are not able to give any account or at least any satisfactory account of their convictions; that is to say, they cannot explain why they possess them.

These certainties of common sense, conclusions of an implicit reasoning, are as well founded as the certainties of science. But their possessor has no knowledge, or an imperfect knowledge, of the grounds on which he bases them. They are therefore imperfect not in their value as truth but in the *mode* or condition under which they exist in the mind.

Of the self-evident truths (*the whole is greater than the part, every event has a cause,* etc.), which are the object of what is termed *the understanding of principles,* and whose certainty is superior to that of any conclusion of science, common sense possesses a knowledge whose mode is equally imperfect, because it is confused and implicit.

Common sense therefore may be regarded as the natural and primitive judgment of human reason, infallible, but imperfect in its mode.

The wholly spontaneous character of common sense, and its inability to give an account of its convictions, have led certain philosophers to regard it as a special faculty purely instinctive and unrelated to the intellect (the Scottish school, end of eighteenth and beginning of nineteenth century; Reid, Dugald Stewart, and in France, Jouffroy), or as a sentiment distinct from and superior to reason (the intuitive or sentimentalist school; for instance, Rousseau, Jacobi, and in our own time Bergson). But in that case it would necessarily be blind, for we possess no other light than that of the intellect or reason. The light of common sense is fundamentally the same light as that of science, that is to say, the natural light of the intellect. But in common sense this light does not return upon itself by critical reflection, and is not perfected by what we shall learn to know as a *scientific habit (habitus).*

We must now define the relations which obtain between philosophy and common sense.

Philosophy cannot, as the Scottish school maintained, be founded on the authority of common sense understood simply as the *common consent* or universal witness of mankind, or as an instinct which in fact compels our assent. For it is in fact founded on evidence, not on authority of any kind.

But if by common sense we understand only *the immediate apprehension of self-evident first principles,* which is one of its constituents, we may say with truth that it is the source of the whole of philosophy. For the premisses of philosophy are indeed the evident axioms which in virtue of its natural constitution implant in the mind its primary certainties.

It is important to be quite clear that, if philosophy finds its premises already enunciated by common sense, it accepts them not because they are enunciated by common sense, or on the authority of common sense understood as the universal consent or common instinct of mankind, but entirely and solely on the authority of the *evidence.*

Finally, if we take into account the entire body of truths (premises and conclusions) known by common sense with certainty but in an imperfect mode, we must conclude that philosophy is superior to common sense, as the perfect stage of anything (in this case the scientific stage of knowledge) is superior to the imperfect or rudimentary stage of the same thing (in this case the pre-scientific stage of the same knowledge, which is yet true and certain at both stages).

If in common sense we consider not the conclusions which it reaches but the premises alone, it is still inferior to philosophy in respect of its *mode* of knowledge, but superior alike to philosophy and to all the sciences in respect of its *object* and of the *light* in which it knows. For, as we have said above, philosophy and all the sciences are ultimately founded on the natural evidence of first principles (to which philosophy returns—in criticism—to study them scientifically, whereas the other sciences are content to accept them from nature).

Philosophy studies scientifically the three categories of truths to which common sense bears instructive witness: (i) the truths of fact which represent the evidence of the senses; (ii) the self-evident first principles of the understanding, in as much as it clears up their meaning by critical reflection and defends them rationally; (iii) the consequences immediately deducible (proximate conclusions) from these first principles, inasmuch as it provides a rational proof of them. And, further, where common sense yields to the mere opinions of popular belief, philosophy continues to extend indefinitely the domain of scientific certainty. Thus philosophy *justifies* and continues common sense, as, for instance, the art of poetry justifies and continues the natural rhythms of language.

It is also the province of philosophy to decide what are the genuine certainties affirmed by common sense, and what is their true significance; a function which common sense is incapable of performing, for the very reason that it does not understand, or does not understand clearly, the grounds of its knowledge. In this sense philosophy *controls* common sense, as, for example, the art of poetry controls the natural rhythms of language.

Nevertheless, common sense has the right and duty to reject any philosophic teaching which denies a truth of which it possesses natural certainty, as the inferior has the right and duty to oppose a superior who acts in a manner evidently unjust. For as soon as a truth becomes known to us, by whatever channel, it is a sin not to accept it. Common sense may therefore *accidentally judge* philosophy.

It is related of Diogenes that when Zeno the Eleatic was arguing in his presence against the possibility of motion, his sole reply was to get up and walk. Similarly, when Descartes taught that motion is relative or "reciprocal," so that it makes no difference whether you say the moving object is moving towards the goal or the goal towards the moving object, the English philosopher Henry More retorted that when a man runs towards a goal panting and tiring himself,[3] he has no doubt which of the two, the moving object or the goal, is in motion.

These protests of common sense based on the evidence of the senses were perfectly justified. It must, however, be added that they were insufficient—not indeed to confute the respective theses of Zeno and Descartes but to confute them as errors in philosophy. That would have demanded a philosophic refutation of the arguments adduced by these philosophers, and explanations showing why and at what point they went wrong.

It must be observed that though in itself and in order to establish its demonstra-

[3] Letter of March 5, 1849.

tions philosophy does not depend upon the authority of common sense, understood as the universal consent or common instinct of mankind, nevertheless it is dependent upon it in a certain sense (*materially,* or in respect of the subject), in its origin as a human activity and in its development in the mind of philosophers. From this point of view philosophy may be compared to a building, and the great pre-scientific conclusions of common sense (the existence of God, the freedom of the will, etc.) to the scaffolding which nature has erected beforehand. Once the edifice has been completed it supports itself on its rock-bed, the natural self-evidence of its first principles, and has no need of scaffolding. But without the scaffolding it could not have been built.

It is now evident how unreasonable that philosophy is, which prided itself on its scientific knowledge of things, despises common sense *a priori* and on principle, and cuts itself off from its natural convictions. Descartes (who in other respects and in his very conception of science concedes too much to common sense) began this divorce, on the one hand, by admitting as the only certain truths those scientifically established, thus denying the intrinsic value of the convictions of common sense, and on the other hand, by professing as part of his system several doctrines incompatible with those convictions. His disciple Malebranche, and above all the *critical* philosophers of the Kantian school, as also certain *modernist* philosophers, have carried this tendency to its extreme, until for some of these philosophers it is sufficient that a proposition should be acceptable to common sense for it to be questioned or denied by science, which would be contaminated by the "credulity" of the common herd, unless it taught the contrary of what mankind at large believes to be true.

Yet the greater the natural strength of a man's intelligence, the stronger should be his grasp of these natural certainties. He therefore who professes to condemn common sense shows not the strength but the weakness of his understanding.

It is now obvious that in its attitude to common sense, as in its solution of the majority of the great philosophic problems, Thomism keeps the golden mean between two opposing errors like a mountain summit between two valleys.

Philosophy of Aristotle and St. Thomas

The convictions of common sense are valid, and science is untrue to itself if it rejects them. But the basis of philosophy is the natural witness of the intellect, not the authority of common sense.

Scottish School	*Rationalist, Critical, and Modernist Schools*
Not only are the convictions of common sense valid, but the authority of common sense imposing itself as a blind instinct on the mind is the foundation on which philosophy should be based.	Not only is the authority of common sense incapable of furnishing the basis of philosophy, but the convictions of common sense are destitute of any speculative value.

From all that has been said it is evident what an important part the certainties of common sense play as an introduction to philosophy. Those who are beginning the study of philosophy and about to acquaint themselves with the most recent problems, and even perhaps the most misleading systems, ought to repose an absolute trust in the convictions of common sense of which they find their minds already possessed, for they will help them to rise to a higher and more perfect knowledge, conclusions scientifically established.

Conclusion IV. —Philosophy is not based upon the authority of common sense understood as the universal consent or common instinct of mankind; it is nevertheless derived from common sense considered as the understanding of self-evident first principles.

It is superior to common sense as the perfect or "scientific" stage of knowledge is superior to the imperfect or ordinary stage of the same knowledge. Nevertheless philosophy may be accidentally judged by common sense.

For the purposes of this present outline we need only add that philosophy is not constructed *a priori* on the basis of some particular fact selected by the philosopher (Descartes's *cogito*), or principle arbitrarily laid down by him (Spinoza's *substance,* Fichte's *pure ego,* Schelling's *absolute,* Hegel's *idea*) whose consequences he ingeniously develops. Its formal principles are the first principles apprehended in the concept of being, whose cogency consists wholly in their evidence for the intellect,[4] and on the other hand its matter is experience, and its facts[5] the simplest and most obvious facts—the starting-point from which it rises to the causes and grounds which constitute the ultimate explanation. Not a whimsy spun out of his own brain, but the entire universe with its enormous multitude and variety of data must be the philosopher's teacher.

And he must always bear in mind that, if philosophy enables the human intellect to apprehend with absolute certainty the highest and most profound realities of the natural order, it cannot therefore claim to exhaust those realities by making them known to the utmost extent of their intelligibility. From this point of view science does not destroy the *mystery* of things, that in them which is still unknown and unfathomed, but on the contrary recognises and delimits it;[6] even what it knows it never knows completely. The wise man knows all things, inasmuch as he knows them in their ultimate causes, but he does not know, is infinitely removed from knowing, everything about everything. Ignorance, however, is not the same as error. It is sufficient for the philosopher that he knows with certainty what it is his province to know and what it is of the first importance for us to know. Indeed, it is better not to know things which divert the mind from the highest knowledge, as Tacitus remarks: *nescure quaedam, magna pars sapientiae.*

— From *Introduction to Philosophy* (London: Sheed and Ward, 1934), Chap. 8, pp. 100–107.

---

[4] This is what the *Positivists* fail to see.

[5] This is what the *pure intellectualists*—from Parmenides to Hegel—who construct their metaphysics wholly *a priori,* have failed to grasp.

[6] Aristotle (*Metaph.,* i, 2) remarks that the occasional cause of philosophy is *tò Uaymázein, admiratio,* by which he means wonder mingled with dread, in other words *awe,* a wonder which knowledge tends to remove. But we must be careful to understand his meaning of the wonder which does not understand, not of the admiration, indeed the awe, born of understanding. The wise man is astonished at nothing because he knows the ultimate causes of all things, but he admires far more than the ignorant man. *Cf. De Part. Anim.,* i, 5, 645 a 16.

Thomas Aquinas

ON THE ASCENT OF THE MIND TO GOD

Every essence (or "quiddity") can be conceived without any knowledge whether it actually exists. I can, for example, understand what a man is or a phoenix and nevertheless not know whether they exist in extramental reality. It is evident, therefore, that existence is distinct from essence (or "quiddity"), unless there happen to be some reality whose essence (or "quiddity") is its very existence itself. Such a reality could only be the one Supreme Being. . . . If this reality is posited which is simply existence as such, so that its very existence subsists as Existence Itself, then it follows that this Existence does not receive the addition of any specific difference, for then it would not be simply existence, but existence in combination with some (limiting) form. Much less, furthermore, does this subsisting Existence receive the addition of matter, for then it would not be subsisting Existence but only a material being. It remains, as a consequence, that such a Reality, which is its existence, can be only one and unique. It also follows necessarily that in every existing thing other than this Reality, the particular act of existing and the nature (or essence or form) are really distinct. . . .

"Whatever belongs to any reality either is caused by intrinsic principles that constitute its nature, as for example the power of laughter in humans, or is given to it by some principle extrinsic to itself, as light in the atmosphere from the influence of the sun. The existence of that reality, however, cannot be caused by its internal principle of essence (or form), I mean as its efficient cause, for then that reality would be the cause of itself: it would place itself in existence, which is impossible. It follows necessarily, therefore, that every reality of that kind, whose existence is distinct from its essence, must receive that existence from some other being which is external to itself. Now in such a case the mind comes to the reality which exists of itself as the first cause of existence. A Reality must therefore necessarily exist which is the cause of existing in all other things, and this because such a Reality is simply existence as such. Otherwise, one would go back into an infinity of causes, since every reality, if it is not this existence as such, must have a cause external to itself for its act of existing, as already noted.

> — From *Being and Essence,* chap. V, "On the Ascent of the Mind to God". This excerpt translated by E. Kevane from *De ente et essentia* (Rome: Gregorian University Press, 1933).

THE FIVE WAYS

The existence of God can be proved in five ways.

The first and more manifest way is the argument from motion. It is certain, and evident to our senses, that in this world some things are in motion. Now whatever is in motion is put in motion by another, for nothing can be in motion unless it is in potency to that towards which it is in motion. But a thing moves in so far as it is in act. For motion is nothing else than the reduction of something from potency to act. But nothing can be reduced from potency to act except by something in a state of act. Thus that which is actually hot, as fire, makes wood, which is potentially hot, to be actually hot, and thereby moves and changes it. Now it is not possible that the same thing should be at once in act and potency in the same respect, but only in different respects. For what is actually hot cannot simultaneously be potentially hot, though it is simultaneously potentially cold. It is therefore impossible that in the same respect and in the same way a thing should be both mover and moved, that is, that it should move itself. Therefore, whatever is moved must be moved by another. If that by which it is moved be itself moved, then this also must be moved by another, and that by another again. But this cannot go on to infinity, because then there would be no first mover, and, consequently, no other mover, seeing that subsequent movers move only because as they are moved by the first mover, just as the staff moves only because it is moved by the hand. Therefore it is necessary to arrive at a first mover which is moved by no other. And this everyone understands to be God.

The second way is from the notion of efficient cause. In the world of sense we find there is an order of efficient causes. There is no case known (nor indeed, is it possible) in which a thing is found to be the efficient cause of itself, because in that case it would be prior to itself, which is impossible. Now in efficient causes it is not possible to go on to infinity, because in all efficient causes following in order, the first is the cause of the intermediate cause, and the intermediate is the cause of the ultimate cause, whether the intermediate cause be several, or one only. Now to take away the cause is to take away the effect. Therefore, if there be no first cause among efficient causes, there will be no ultimate, nor any intermediate cause. But if in efficient causes it is possible to go on to infinity, there will be no first efficient cause, neither will there be an ultimate effect, nor any intermediate efficient causes, all of which is plainly false. Therefore it is necessary to admit a first efficient cause, to which everyone gives the name of God.

The third way is taken from possibility and necessity, and runs thus. We find in nature things that are possible to be and not to be, since they are found to be generated, and to be corrupted, and consequently they are possible to be and not to be. But it is impossible for these always to exist, for that which is possible not to be at some time is not. Therefore, if everything is possible not to be, then at one time there could have been nothing in existence. Now if this were true, even now there would be nothing in existence, because that which does not exist only begins to exist by something already existing. Therefore, if at one time nothing was in existence, it would have been impossible for anything to have begun to exist; and thus even now nothing would be in existence—which is clearly false. Therefore, not all beings are merely possible, but there must exist something the existence of which is necessary. But every necessary thing either has its necessity caused by another, or not. Now it is impossible to go on to infinity in necessary things which have their necessity caused by another, as has been already proved in regard to efficient causes. Therefore we must admit the existence of some being having of itself its own necessity, and not receiving it from another, but rather causing in others their necessity. This all men speak of as God.

The fourth way is taken from the gradation to be found in things. Among beings there are some more and some less good, true, noble, and the like. But "more" and "less" are predicated of different things, according as they resemble in their different ways something which is the maximum, as a thing is said to be hotter according as it more nearly resembles that which is hottest. There is then, something which is truest, something best, something noblest, and, consequently, something which is most being; for those things that are greatest in truth are greatest in being, as it is written in the *Metaphysics.* Now the maximum in any genus is the cause of all in that genus; as fire, which is the maximum of heat, is the cause of all hot things as is said in the same book. Therefore there must also be something which is to all beings the cause of their being, goodness, and every other perfection. And this we call God.

The fifth way is taken from the governance of things. We see that things which lack knowledge, such as natural bodies, act for an end, and this is evident from their acting always, or nearly always, in the same way, so as to obtain the best result. Hence it is plain that they achieve their end not by chance, but by design. Now whatever lacks knowledge cannot move towards an end, unless it be directed by some being endowed with knowledge and intelligence, as the arrow is directed by the archer. Therefore some intelligent being exists by whom all natural things are ordered to their end; and this being we call God.

> — From *Summa Theologiae,* I, 2, 3 (Great Books Edition), vol 19, pp. 10–11.

ON GOD'S WAY OF HAVING ESSENCE

"From the discussion so far, it has become clear how essence is found in the various kinds of things. There is (to summarize) a threefold way of having essence among the various substances ... [namely, the way of God, the way of the pure spirits, and the way of the bodily things].

"There is, first, the substantial Reality called God, whose essence is his very existence itself.... When we say that God is simply existence itself, furthermore, we need not fall into the error of those who have said that God is that universal concept of being by which each thing is formally what it is.

"God's existence has such a character or quality that nothing can be added to it. It is this very purity which makes God's existence distinct from all other existing realities....

"Likewise, although God is simply existence as such, it does not follow that he is deficient in any of the qualities and perfections of other beings; in fact he possesses all such perfections ..., but in a way which transcends their mode in all those other things. This is because in him they are his one unique reality, while in other beings they are found diversified in the different kinds of things. All these perfections belong to him according to the simplicity of his act of existing. For example, one can think of a person who possesses one special quality which accomplishes all the activities of all other qualities or properties: so it is in the case of God, for he possesses all perfections by virtue of his act of existing as Existence Itself."

> — From *Being and Essence,* chap. IV. This excerpt translated by E. Kevane from *De ente et essentia* (Rome: Gregorian University Press, 1933).

SUMMA THEOLOGICA

I answer that, It must necessarily be allowed that the principle of intellectual operation which we call the soul is a principle both incorporeal and subsistent. For it is clear that by means of the intellect man can know the natures of all corporeal things. Now whatever knows certain things cannot have any of them in its own nature because that which is in it naturally would impede the knowledge of anything else. Thus we observe that a sick man's tongue being vitiated by a feverish and bitter humour, cannot perceive anything sweet, and everything seems bitter to it. Therefore, if the intellectual principle contained the nature of any body it would be unable to know all bodies. Now every body has some determinate nature. Therefore it is impossible for the intellectual principle to be a body. It is likewise impossible for it to understand by means of a bodily organ, since the determinate nature of that bodily organ would prevent the knowledge of all bodies; as when a certain determinate colour is not only in the pupil of the eye, but also in a glass vase, the liquid in the vase seems to be of that same colour.

Therefore the intellectual principle which we call the mind or the intellect has an operation *per se* apart from the body. Now only that which subsists can have an operation *per se.* For nothing can operate except a being in act; hence a thing operates according as it is. For this reason we do not say that heat imparts heat, but that what is hot gives heat. We must conclude, therefore, that the human soul, which is called the intellect or the mind, is something incorporeal and subsistent.

ARTICLE 6. *Whether the Human Soul Is Incorruptible?*

We proceed thus to the Sixth Article: It would seem that the human soul is corruptible.

Objection 1. For those things that have a like beginning and process seem to have a like end. But the beginning, by generation, of men is like that of animals, for they are made from the earth. And the process of life is alike in both; because *all things breathe alike, and man hath nothing more than the beast,* as it is written (Eccles 3:19). Therefore, as the same text concludes, *the death of man and beast is one, and the condition of both is equal.* But the souls of brute animals are corruptible. Therefore, also the human soul is corruptible.

Obj. 2. Further, whatever is out of nothing can return to nothingness, because the end should correspond to the beginning. But as it is written (Wis 2:2), *We are born of nothing;* which is true not only of the body, but also of the soul. Therefore, as is concluded in the same passage, *After this we shall be as if we had not been,* even as to our soul.

Obj. 3. Further, nothing is without its proper operation. But the operation proper to the soul, which is to understand through a phantasm, cannot be without the body. For the soul understands nothing without a phantasm, and "there is no phantasm without the body" as the Philosopher says. Therefore the soul cannot survive the dissolution of the body.

On the contrary, Dionysius says (*Div. Nom.* iv) that human souls owe to Divine goodness that they are "intellectual, and that they have an incorruptible substantial life."

I answer that, We must assert that the human soul which we call the intellectual principle is incorruptible. For a thing may be corrupted in two ways—*per se,* and accidentally. Now it is impossible for anything subsistent to be generated or corrupted accidentally, that is, by the generation or corruption of something else. For generation and corruption belong to a thing, just as being belongs to it, which is acquired by generation and lost by corruption. Therefore, whatever has being *per se* cannot be generated or corrupted except *per se,* while things which do not subsist, such as accidents and material forms, acquire being or lose it through the generation or corruption of composite things. Now it was shown above (AA. 2, 3) that the souls of brutes are not self-subsistent, whereas the human soul is; so that the souls of brutes are corrupted when their bodies are corrupted, while the human soul could not be corrupted unless it were corrupted *per se.* This, indeed, is impossible, not only as regards the human soul, but also as regards any subsistent thing that is a form alone. For it is clear that what belongs to a thing by virtue of itself is inseparable from it; but to be belongs to a form, which is an act, by virtue of itself. Therefore matter acquires actual being as it acquires the form, while it is corrupted so far as the form is separated from it. But it is impossible for a form to be separated from itself, and therefore it is impossible for a subsistent form to cease to exist.

Granted even that the soul is composed of matter and form, as some pretend, we should nevertheless have to maintain that it is incorruptible. For corruption is found only where there is contrariety; for generation and corruption are from contraries and into contraries. Therefore the heavenly bodies, since they have no matter subject to contrariety, are incorruptible. Now there can be no contrariety in the intellectual soul, for it receives according to the manner of its being, and those things which it receives are without contrariety; for the notions even of contraries are not themselves contrary, since contraries belong to the same knowledge. Therefore it is impossible for the intellectual soul to be corruptible.

Moreover we may take a sign of this from the fact that everything naturally desires being after its own manner. Now, in things that have knowledge, desire ensues upon knowledge. The senses indeed do not know being, except under the conditions of *here* and *now,* whereas the intellect apprehends being absolutely, and for all time, so that everything that has an intellect naturally desires always to be. But a natural desire cannot be in vain. Therefore every intellectual substance is incorruptible.

Reply Obj. 1. Solomon reasons thus in the person of the foolish, as expressed in the words of Wisd. 2. Therefore the saying that man and animals have a like beginning in generation is true of the body, for all animals alike are made of earth. But it is not true of the soul. For the souls of brutes are produced by some power of the body, whereas the human soul is produced by God. To signify this, it is written as to other animals: *Let the earth bring forth the living soul* (Gen 1:24) while of man it is written (ibid. 2:7) that *He breathed into his face the breath of life.* And so in the last chapter of Ecclesiastes (12:7) it is concluded: (*Before*) *the dust return into its earth from whence it was; and the spirit return to God Who gave it.* Again the process of life is alike as to the body, concerning which it is written (Eccles 3:19): *All things breathe alike,* and (Wis 2:2), *The breath in our nostrils is smoke.* But the process is not alike of the soul; for man is intelligent, whereas animals are not. Hence it is false to say: *Man has nothing more than beasts.* Thus death comes to both alike as to the body, but not as to the soul.

Reply Obj. 2. As a thing can be created not by reason of a passive potency, but only by reason of the active power of the Creator, Who can produce something out of nothing, so that when we say that a thing can be reduced to nothing, we do not imply in the creature a potency to non-being, but in the Creator the power of ceasing to sustain being. But a thing is said to be corruptible because there is in it a potency to non-being.

Reply Obj. 3. To understand through a phantasm is the proper operation of the soul by virtue of its union with the body. After separation from the body it will have another mode of understanding, similar to other substances separated from bodies, as will appear later on (Q. 89, A. 1).

— From the *Summa Theologiae* I, 75, 2 and 6.

Part Three

René Descartes

MEDITATIONS

It is now some years since I detected how many were the false beliefs that I had from my earliest youth admitted as true, and how doubtful was everything I had since constructed on this basis; and from that time I was convinced that I must once for all seriously undertake to rid myself of all the opinions which I had formerly accepted, and commence to build anew from the foundation. . . .

All that up to the present time I have accepted as most true and certain I have learned either from the senses or through the senses; but it is sometimes proved to me that these senses are deceptive, and it is wiser not to trust entirely to any thing by which we have once been deceived.

But it may be that although the senses sometimes deceive us concerning things which are hardly perceptible, or very far away, there are yet many others to be met with as to which we cannot reasonably have any doubt, although we recognise them by their means. For example, there is the fact that I am here, seated by the fire, attired in a dressing gown, having this paper in my hands and other similar matters. . . .

At the same time I must remember that I am a man, and that consequently I am in the habit of sleeping, and in my dreams representing to myself the same things or sometimes even less probable things, than do those who are insane in their waking moments. How often has it happened to me that in the night I dreamt that I found myself in this particular place, that I was dressed and seated near the fire, whilst in reality I was lying undressed in bed! . . .

Now let us assume that we are asleep and that all these particulars, e.g., that we open our eyes, shake our head, extend our hands, and so on, are but false delusions; and let us reflect that possibly neither our hands nor our whole body are such as they appear to us to be. . . .

Nevertheless I have long had fixed in my mind the belief that an all-powerful God existed by whom I have been created such as I am. But how do I know that he has not brought it to pass that there is no earth, no heaven, no extended body, no magnitude, no place, and that nevertheless [I possess the perceptions of all these things and that] they seem to me to exist just exactly as I now see them? And, besides, as I sometimes imagine that others deceive themselves in the things which they think they know best, how do I know that I am not deceived every time that I add two and three, or count the sides of a square, or judge of things yet simpler, if anything simpler can be imagined? But possibly God has not desired that I should be thus deceived, for he is said to be supremely good. If, however, it is contrary to his goodness to have made me such that I constantly deceive myself, it would also appear to be contrary to his goodness to permit me to be sometimes deceived, and nevertheless I cannot doubt that he does permit this. . . .

But at the end I feel constrained to confess that there is nothing in all that I formerly believed to be true, of which I cannot in some measure doubt, and that not merely through want of thought or through levity, but for reasons which are very powerful and maturely considered. . . .

. . . But how can I know there is not something different from those things that I have just considered, of which one cannot have the slightest doubt? Is there not some God, or some other being by whatever name we call it, who puts these reflections into my mind? That is not necessary, for is it not possible that I am capable of producing them myself? I myself, am I not at least something? But I have already denied that I had senses and body. Yet I hesitate, for what follows from that? Am I so dependent on body and senses that I cannot exist without these? But I was persuaded that there was nothing in all the world, that there was no heaven, no earth, that there were no minds, nor any bodies: was I not then likewise persuaded that I did not exist? Not at all; of a surety I myself did exist since I persuaded myself of something [or merely because I thought of something]. But there is some deceiver or other, very powerful and very cunning, who ever employs his ingenuity in deceiving me. Then without doubt I exist also if he deceives me, and let him deceive me as much as he will, he can never cause me to be nothing so long as I think that I am something. So that after having reflected well and carefully examined all things, we must come to the definite conclusion that this proposition: I am, I exist, is necessarily true each time that I pronounce it, or that I mentally conceive it. . . .

I do not now admit anything which is not necessarily true: to speak accurately I am not more than a thing which thinks, that is to say a mind or a soul, or an understanding, or a reason, which are terms whose significance was formerly unknown to me. I am, however, a real thing and really exist; but what thing? I have answered: a thing which thinks. . . .

. . . Now as to what concerns ideas, if we consider them only in themselves and do not relate them to anything else beyond themselves, they cannot properly speaking be false; for whether I imagine a goat or a chimera, it is not less true that I imagine the one than the other. We must not fear likewise that falsity can enter into will and into affections, for although I may desire evil things, or even things that never existed, it is not the less true that I desire them. Thus there remains no more than the judgments which we make, in which I must take the greatest care not to deceive myself. But the principal error and the commonest which we may meet with in them, consists in my judging that the ideas which are in me are similar or conformable to the things which are outside me; for without doubt if I considered the ideas only as certain modes of my thoughts, without trying to relate them to anything beyond, they could scarcely give me material for error.

But among these ideas, some appear to me to be innate, some adventitious, and others to be formed [or invented] by myself; for, as I have the power of understanding what is called a thing, or a truth, or a thought, it appears to me that I hold this power from no other source than my own nature. But if I now hear some sound, if I see the sun, or feel heat, I have hitherto judged that these sensations proceeded from certain things that exist outside of me; and finally it appears to me that sirens, hippogryphs, and the like, are formed out of my own mind. But again I may possibly persuade myself that all these ideas are of the nature of those which I term adventitious, or else that they are all innate, or all fictitious: for I have not yet clearly discovered their true origin.

And my principal task in this place is to consider, in respect to those ideas which appear to me to proceed from certain objects that are outside me, what are the reasons which cause me to think them similar to these objects. It seems indeed in the first place that I am taught this lesson by nature; and, secondly, I experience in myself that these ideas do not depend on my will nor therefore on myself—for they often present themselves to my mind in spite of my will. Just now, for instance, whether I will or whether I do not will, I feel heat, and thus I persuade myself that this feeling, or at least this idea of heat, is produced in me by something which is different from me, i.e., by the heat of the fire near which I sit. And nothing seems to me more obvious than to judge that this object imprints its likeness rather than anything else upon me.

> — From the *Meditations,* pp. 75–79, 83. Taken from vol. 31 of *The Great Books,* translated by Elizabeth S. Haldane and G. R. T. Ross.

DISCOURSE ON METHOD

I honoured our Theology and aspired as much as anyone to reach to heaven, but having learned to regard it as a most highly assured fact that the road is not less open to the most ignorant than to the most learned, and that the revealed truths which conduct thither are quite above our intelligence, I should not have dared to submit them to the feebleness of my reasonings; and I thought that, in order to undertake to examine them and succeed in so doing, it was necessary to have some extraordinary assistance from above and to be more than a mere man.

I shall not say anything about Philosophy, but that, seeing that it has been cultivated for many centuries by the best minds that have ever lived, and that nevertheless no single thing is to be found in it which is not subject of dispute, and in consequence which is not dubious, I had not enough presumption to hope to fare better there than other men had done. And also, considering how many conflicting opinions there may be regarding the self-same matter, all supported by learned people, while there can never be more than one which is true, I esteemed as well-nigh false all that only went as far as being probable.

> — From the *Discourse on Method,* p. 43. Taken from vol. 31 of the Great Books; translated by Elizabeth S. Haldane and G. R. T. Ross.

Benedict de Spinoza

OF MIRACLES

As men are accustomed to call Divine the knowledge which transcends human understanding, so also do they style Divine, or the work of God, anything of which the cause is not generally known: for the masses think that the power and providence of God are most clearly displayed by events that are extraordinary and contrary to the conception they have formed of nature, especially if such events bring them any profit or convenience: they think that the clearest possible proof of God's existence is afforded when nature, as they suppose, breaks her accustomed order, and consequently they believe that those who explain or endeavour to understand phenomena or miracles through their natural causes are doing away with God and his providence. They suppose, forsooth, that God is inactive so long as nature works in her accustomed order, and vice versa, that the power of nature and natural causes are idle so long as God is acting: thus they imagine two powers distinct one from the other, the power of God and the power of nature, though the latter is in a sense determined by God, or (as most people believe now) created by him. What they mean by either, and what they understand by God and nature they do not know, except that they imagine the power of God to be like that of some royal potentate, and nature's power to consist in force and energy.

The masses then style unusual phenomena "miracles," and partly from piety, partly for the sake of opposing the students of science, prefer to remain in ignorance of natural causes, and only to hear of those things which they know least, and consequently admire most. In fact, the common people can only adore God, and refer all things to his power by removing natural causes, and conceiving things happening out of their due course, and only admires the power of God when the power of nature is conceived of as in subjection to it.

This idea seems to have taken its rise among the early Jews who saw the Gentiles round them worshipping visible gods such as the sun, the moon, the earth, water, air, etc., and in order to inspire the conviction that such divinities were weak and inconstant, or changeable, told how they themselves were under the sway of an invisible God, and narrated their miracles, trying further to show that the God whom they worshipped arranged the whole of nature for their sole benefit: this idea was so pleasing to humanity that men go on to this day imagining miracles, so that they may believe themselves God's favourites, and the final cause for which God created and directs all things.

What pretension will not people in their folly advance! They have no single sound idea concerning either God or nature, they confound God's decrees with human decrees, they conceive nature as so limited that they believe man to be its chief part! I have spent enough space in setting forth these common ideas and prejudices concerning nature and miracles, but in order to afford a regular demonstration I will show—

I. That nature cannot be contravened, but that she preserves a fixed and immutable order, and at the same time I will explain what is meant by a miracle.

II. That God's nature and existence, and consequently his providence cannot be known from miracles, but that they can all be much better perceived from the fixed and immutable order of nature.

III. That by the decrees and volitions, and consequently the providence of God, Scripture (as I will prove by Scriptural examples) means nothing but nature's order following necessarily from her eternal laws.

IV. Lastly, I will treat of the method of interpreting Scriptural miracles, and the chief points to be noted concerning the narratives of them.

Such are the principal subjects which will be discussed in this chapter, and which will serve, I think, not a little to further the object of this treatise.

Our first point is easily proved from what we showed in Chap. IV. about Divine law—namely, that all that God wishes or determines involves eternal necessity and truth, for we demonstrated that God's understanding is identical with his will, and that it is the same thing to say that God wills a thing, as to say that he understands it; hence, as it follows necessarily from the Divine nature and perfection that God understands a thing as it is, it follows no less necessarily that he wills it as it is. Now, as nothing is necessarily true save only by Divine decree, it is plain that the universal laws of nature are decrees of God following from the necessity and perfection of the Divine nature. Hence, any event happening in nature which contravened nature's universal laws, would necessarily also contravene the Divine decree, nature, and understanding; or if anyone asserted that God acts in contravention to the laws of nature, he, *ipso facto,* would be compelled to assert that God acted against his own nature—an evident absurdity. One might easily show from the same premises that the power and efficiency of nature are in themselves the Divine power and efficiency, and that the Divine power is the very essence of God, but this I gladly pass over for the present.

Nothing, then, comes to pass in nature[1] in contravention to her universal laws, nay, everything agrees with them and follows from them, for whatsoever comes to pass, comes to pass by the will and eternal decree of God; that is, as we have just pointed out, whatever comes to pass, comes to pass according to laws and rules which involve eternal necessity and truth; nature, therefore, always observes laws and rules which involve eternal necessity and truth, although they may not all be known to us, and therefore she keeps a fixed and immutable order. Nor is there any sound reason for limiting the power and efficacy of nature, and asserting that her laws are fit for certain purposes, but not for all; for as the efficacy and power of nature, are the very efficacy and power of God, and as the laws and rules of nature are the decrees of God, it is in every way to be believed that the power of nature is infinite, and that her laws are broad enough to embrace everything conceived by the Divine intellect; the only alternative is to assert that God has created nature so weak, and has ordained for her laws so barren, that he is repeatedly compelled to come afresh to her aid if he wishes that she should be preserved, and that things should happen as he desires: a conclusion, in my opinion, very far removed from reason. Further, as nothing happens in nature which does not follow from her laws, and as her laws embrace everything conceived by

---

[1] N.B. I do not mean here by "nature," merely matter and its modifications, but infinite other things besides matter.

the Divine intellect, and lastly, as nature preserves a fixed and immutable order; it most clearly follows that miracles are only intelligible as in relation to human opinions, and merely mean events of which the natural cause cannot be explained by a reference to any ordinary occurrence, either by us, or at any rate, by the writer and narrator of the miracle.

We may, in fact, say that a miracle is an event of which the causes cannot be explained by the natural reason through a reference to ascertained workings of nature; but since miracles were wrought according to the understanding of the masses, who are wholly ignorant of the workings of nature, it is certain that the ancients took for a miracle whatever they could not explain by the method adopted by the unlearned in such cases, namely, an appeal to the memory, a recalling of something similar, which is ordinarily regarded without wonder; for most people think they sufficiently understand a thing when they have ceased to wonder at it. The ancients, then, and indeed most men up to the present day, had no other criterion for a miracle; hence we cannot doubt that many things are narrated in Scripture as miracles of which the causes could easily be explained by reference to ascertained workings of nature. We have hinted as much in Chap. II., in speaking of the sun standing still in the time of Joshua, and going backwards in the time of Ahaz; but we shall soon have more to say on the subject when we come to treat of the interpretation of miracles later on in this chapter.

It is now time to pass on to the second point, and show that we cannot gain an understanding of God's essence, existence, or providence by means of miracles, but that these truths are much better perceived through the fixed and immutable order of nature.

I thus proceed with the demonstration. As God's existence is not self-evident, it must necessarily be inferred from what is so firmly and incontrovertibly true, that no power can be postulated or conceived sufficient to impugn them. They might certainly so to appear to us when we infer from them God's existence, if we wish to place our conclusion beyond the reach of doubt; for if we could conceive that such ideas could be impugned by any power whatsoever, we should doubt of their truth, we should doubt of our conclusion, namely, of God's existence, and should never be able to be certain of anything. Further, we know that nothing either agrees with or is contrary to nature, unless it agrees with what is contrary to these primary ideas; wherefore if we would conceive that anything could be done in nature by any power whatsoever which would be contrary to the laws of nature, it would also be contrary to our primary ideas, and we should have either to reject it as absurd, or else to cast doubt (as just shown) on our primary ideas, and consequently on the existence of God, and on everything however perceived. Therefore miracles, in the sense of events contrary to the laws of nature, so far from demonstrating to us the existence of God, would, on the contrary, lead us to doubt it, where, otherwise, we might have been absolutely certain of it, as knowing that nature follows a fixed and immutable order.

Let us take miracle as meaning that which cannot be explained through natural causes. This may be interpreted in two senses: either as that which has natural causes, but cannot be examined by the human intellect; or as that which has no cause save God and God's will. But as all things which come to pass through natural causes, come to pass also solely through the will and power of God, it comes to this, that a miracle, whether it has natural causes or not, is a result which cannot be explained by its cause, that is a phenomenon which surpasses human understanding; but from such a phenomenon, and certainly from a result surpassing our understanding, we can gain no knowledge. For whatsoever we understand clearly and distinctly should be plain to us either in itself or by means of something else clearly and distinctly understood.

> — From "Of Miracles", *Theologico-Political Treatise,* chap. 6, pp. 81–85. From *The Chief Works of Benedict de Spinoza,* translated from the Latin and with an Introduction by R. H. M. Elwes, 1883. Reprinted by Dover Publications, Inc., New York, 1951.

ETHICS

Nature does nothing for the sake of an end, for that eternal and infinite Being whom we call God or Nature acts by the same necessity by which he exists. . . . The reason or cause, therefore, why God or Nature acts and the reason why he exists are one and the same. Since, therefore, he exists for no end, he acts for no end; and since he has no principle or end of existence, he has no principle or end of action. A final cause, as it is called, is nothing, therefore, but human desire . . . [as when] a man, because he imagined the advantages of a domestic life, desired to build a house. . . . Considered as a final cause, this is merely this particular desire, which is really an efficient cause.

> — From "Ethics", *Theologico-Political Treatise,* Preface to chap. 4. From *The Chief Works of Benedict de Spinoza,* translated from the Latin and with an Introduction by R. H. M. Elwes, 1883. Reprinted by Dover Publications, Inc., New York, 1951.

Blaise Pascal

PENSÉES

No. 347:

Man is but a reed, the most feeble thing in nature; but he is a thinking reed. The entire universe need not arm itself to crush him. A vapour, a drop of water suffices to kill him. But, if the universe were to crush him, man would still be more noble than that which killed him, because he knows that he dies and the advantage which the universe has over him; the universe knows nothing of this. All our dignity consists, then, in thought. By it we must elevate ourselves, and not by space and time which we cannot fill.

No. 72:

For in fact what is man in nature? A Nothing in comparison with the Infinite, an All in comparison with the Nothing, a mean between nothing and everything. Since he is infinitely removed from comprehending the extremes, the end of things and their beginning are hopelessly hidden from him in an impenetrable secret; he is equally incapable of seeing the Nothing from which he was made, and the Infinite in which he is swallowed up.

What will he do then, but perceive the appearance of the middle of things, in an eternal despair of knowing either their beginning or their end. . . .

We sail within a vast sphere, ever drifting in uncertainty, driven from end to end. When we think to attach ourselves to any point and to fasten to it, it wavers and leaves us; and if we follow it, it eludes our grasp, slips past us, and vanishes for ever. Nothing stays for us. This is our natural condition, and yet most contrary to our inclination; we burn with desire to find solid ground and an ultimate sure foundation whereon to build a tower reaching to the Infinite. But our whole groundwork cracks, and the earth opens to abysses.

No. 81:

It is natural for the mind to believe, and for the will to love; so that, for want of true objects, they must attach themselves to false.

No. 194:

Let them at least learn what is the religion they attack, before attacking it. If this religion (the Catholic one) boasted of having a clear view of God, and of possessing it open and unveiled, it would be attacking it to say that we see nothing in the world which shows it with this clearness. But since, on the contrary, it says that men are in darkness and estranged from God, that he has hidden himself from their knowledge ... that he will only be perceived by those who seek him with all their heart. ...

In order to attack it, they should have protested that they had made every effort to seek him everywhere, and even in that which the Church proposes for their instruction, but without satisfaction. If they talked in this manner, they would in truth be attacking one of her pretensions. ... They (doubters) believe they have made great efforts for their instruction, when they have spent a few hours in reading some book of Scripture, and have questioned some priest on the truths of the faith. ...

I can have only compassion for those who sincerely bewail their doubt, who regard it as the greatest of misfortunes, and who, sparing no effort to escape it, make of this inquiry their principal and most serious occupation.

But as for those who pass their life without thinking of this ultimate end of life, ... this carelessness in a matter which concerns themselves, their eternity, their all, moves me more to anger than pity; it astonishes and shocks me; it is to me monstrous. I do not say this out of the pious zeal of a spiritual devotion. I expect, on the contrary, that we ought to have this feeling from principles of human interest and self-love ...

... How can it happen that the following argument occurs to a reasonable man? "I know not who put me into the world, nor what the world is, nor what I myself am. I am in terrible ignorance of everything. I know not why my body is, nor my senses, nor my soul. ... I see those frightful spaces of the universe which surround me, and I find myself tied to one corner of this vast expanse, without knowing why I am put in this place rather than in another, nor why the short time which is given me to live is assigned to me at this point rather than at another of the whole eternity which was before me or which shall come after me. ... All I know is that I must soon die, but what I know least is this very death which I cannot escape. ... Such is my state, full of weakness and uncertainty. And from all this I conclude that I ought to spend all the days of my life without caring to inquire into what must happen to me. Perhaps I might find some solution to my doubts but I will not take the trouble, nor take a step to seek it; and after treating with scorn those who are concerned with this care, I will go without foresight and without fear to try the great event, and let myself be led carelessly to death, uncertain of the eternity of my future state. ... "

Do they (the scoffers) profess to have delighted us by telling us that they hold our soul to be only a little wind and smoke, especially by telling us this in a haughty and self-satisfied tone of voice? Is this a thing to say gaily? Is it not, on the contrary, a thing to say sadly, as the saddest thing in the world? ...

Let them recognize that there are two kinds of people one can call reasonable; those who serve God with all their hearts because they know him, and those who seek him with all their heart because they do not know him.

No. 233:

Let us then examine this point, and say, "God is, or he is not." But to which side shall we incline? Reason can decide nothing here. ... A game is being played at the extremity of this infinite distance where heads or tails will turn up. What will you wager? ... "The

true course is not to wager at all" (you say). Yes; but you must wager. It is not optional.
You are embarked. Which will you choose then? Let us see. Since you must choose, let
us see which interests you least. You have two things to lose, the true and the good; and
two things to stake, your reason and your will, your knowledge and your happiness;
and your nature has two things to shun, error and misery. Your reason is no more
shocked in choosing one rather than the other, since you must of necessity choose. This
is one point settled. But your happiness? Let us weigh the gain and the loss in wagering
that God is. Let us estimate these two chances. If you gain, you gain all; if you lose, you
lose nothing. Wager then, without hesitation that he is. . . .

There is an eternity of life and happiness. And this being so, if there were an
infinity of chances, of which one only would be for you, you would still be right in
wagering one to win two and you would act stupidly, being obliged to play, by
refusing to take one life against three at a game in which out of an infinity of chances
there is one for you, if there were an infinity of an infinitely happy life to gain. But
there is here an infinity of an infinitely happy life to gain, . . . against a finite number of
chances of loss, and what you stake is finite. . . . Now what harm will befall you in
taking this side? You will be faithful, honest, humble, grateful, generous, a sincere
friend, truthful. Certainly you will not have those poisonous pleasures, glory and
luxury; but will you not have others? I will tell you that you will thereby gain in this
life, and that, at each step you take on this road, you will see so great certainty of gain,
so much nothingness in what you risk, that you will at last recognize that you have
wagered for something certain and infinite, for which you have given nothing.

No. 251:

Other religions, as the pagan, are more popular, for they consist in externals. But they
are not for educated people. A purely intellectual religion would be more suited to the
learned, but it would be of no use to the common people. The Christian religion alone
is adapted to all, being composed of externals and internals. It raises the common
people to the internal, and humbles the proud to the external; it is not perfect without
the two, for the people must understand the spirit of the letter, and the learned must
submit their spirit to the letter.

No. 277:

The heart has its reasons, which reason does not know. We feel it in a thousand things. I
say that the heart naturally loves the Universal Being, and also itself naturally, according as it gives itself to them; and it hardens itself against one or the other at its will. You
have rejected the one, and kept the other. Is it by reason that you love yourself?

No. 278:

It is the heart which experiences God, and not the reason. This, then, is faith: God felt
by the heart, not by the reason.

No. 278:

We know truth, not only by the reason, but also by the heart, and it is in this last way that we know first principles; and reason, which has no part in it, tries in vain to impugn them. The sceptics, who have only this for their object, labour to no purpose. We know that we do not dream, and however impossible it is for us to prove it by reason, this inability demonstrates only the weakness of our reason, but not, as they affirm, the uncertainty of all our knowledge. For the knowledge of first principles, as space, time, motion, number, is as sure as any of those which we get from reasoning. And reason must trust these intuitions of the heart, and must base on them every argument. (We have intuitive knowledge of the tri-dimensional nature of space, and of the infinity of number, . . . principles are intuited, propositions are inferred, all with certainty, though in different ways.) And it is as useless and absurd for reason to demand from the heart proofs of her first principles, before admitting them, as it would be for the heart to demand from reason an intuition of all demonstrated propositions before accepting them.

No. 425:

All men seek happiness. This is without exception. Whatever different means they employ, they all tend to this end. The cause of some going to war, and of others avoiding it, is the same desire in both, attended with different views. The will never takes the least step but to this object. This is the motive of every action of every man, even of those who hang themselves. And yet after such a great number of years, no one without faith has reached the point to which all continually look.

All complain, princes and subjects, noblemen and commoners, old and young, strong and weak, learned and ignorant, healthy and sick, of all countries, all times, all ages, and all conditions. A trial so long, so continuous, and so uniform, should certainly convince us of our inability to reach the good by our own efforts. But example teaches us little. No resemblance is ever so perfect that there is not some slight difference; and hence we expect that our hope will not be deceived on this occasion as before. And thus, while the present never satisfies us, experience dupes us, and from misfortune to misfortune leads us to death, their eternal crown.

What is it then that this desire and this inability proclaim to us, but that there was once in man a true happiness of which he in vain tries to fill from all his surroundings, seeking from things absent the help he does not obtain in things present? But these are all inadequate, because the infinite abyss can only be filled by an infinite and immutable object, that is to say, only by God himself.

> — From *Pensées*. Reprinted with permission of E. P. Dutton from the translation by W. F. Trotter (New York: E. P. Dutton, 1958).

Immanuel Kant

ON CONTINGENCY AND NECESSITY

These remarks will have made it evident to the reader that the ideal of the Supreme Being, far from being an enouncement of the existence of a being in itself necessary, is nothing more than a *regulative principle* of reason, requiring us to regard all connection existing between phenomena as if it had its origin from an all-sufficient necessary cause, and basing upon this the rule of a systematic and necessary unity in the explanation of phenomena. We cannot, at the same time, avoid regarding, by a transcendental *subreptio,* this formal principle as constitutive, and hypostatizing this unity. Precisely similar is the case with our notion of space. Space is the primal condition of all forms, which are properly just so many different limitations of it; and thus, although it is merely a principle of sensibility, we cannot help regarding it as an absolutely necessary and self-subsistent thing—as an object given *a priori* in itself. In the same way, it is quite natural that, as the systematic unity of nature cannot be established as a principle for the empirical employment of reason, unless it is based upon the idea of an *ens realissimum,* as the supreme cause, we should regard this idea as a real object, and this object, in its character of supreme condition, as absolutely necessary, and that in this way a *regulative* should be transformed into a *constitutive* principle. This interchange becomes evident when I regard this supreme being, which, relatively to the world, was absolutely (unconditionally) necessary, as a thing *per se.* In this case, I find it impossible to represent this necessity in or by any conception, and it exists merely in my own mind, as the formal condition of thought, but not as a material and hypostatic condition of existence.

ON PROOFS FROM CAUSALITY OR DESIGN

The world around us opens before our view so magnificent a spectacle of order, variety, beauty, and conformity to ends, that whether we pursue our observations into the infinity of space in the one direction, or into its illimitable division in the other, whether we regard the world in its greatest or its least manifestations—even after we have attained to the highest summit of knowledge which our weak minds can reach, we find that language in the presence of wonders so inconceivable has lost its force, and number its power to reckon, nay, even thought fails to conceive adequately, and our conception of the whole dissolves into an astonishment without power of expression— all the more eloquent that it is dumb. Everywhere around us we observe a chain of causes and effects, of means and ends, of death and birth; and, as nothing has entered of itself into the condition in which we find it, we are constantly referred to some other thing, which itself suggests the same inquiry regarding its cause, and thus the universe must sink into the abyss of nothingness, unless we admit that, besides this infinite chain of contingencies, there exists something that is primal and self-subsistent—something which, as the cause of this phenomenal world, secures its continuance and preservation.

This highest cause—what magnitude shall we attribute to it? Of the content of the world we are ignorant; still less can we estimate its magnitude by comparison with the sphere of the possible. But this supreme cause being a necessity of the human mind, what is there to prevent us from attributing to it such a degree of perfection as to place it above the sphere of *all that* is possible? This we can easily do, although only by the aid of the faint outline of an abstract conception, by representing this being to ourselves as containing in itself, as an individual substance, all possible perfection. . . .

We infer, from the order and design visible in the universe, as a disposition of a thoroughly contingent character, the existence of a cause *proportionate thereto.* The conception of this cause must contain certain *determinate* qualities, and it must therefore be regarded as the conception of a being which possesses all power, wisdom, and so on, in one word, all perfection — the conception, that is, of an all-sufficient being. For the predicates of *very great,* astonishing, or immeasurable power and excellence, give us no determinate conception of the thing, nor do they inform us what the thing may be in itself. They merely indicate the relation existing between the magnitude of the object and the observer, who compares it with himself and with his own power of comprehension, and are mere expressions of praise and reverence, by which the object is either magnified, or the observing subject depreciated in relation to the object. Where we have to do with the magnitude (of the perfection) of a thing, we can discover no determinate conception, except that which comprehends all possible perfection or completeness, and it is only the total (*omnitudo*) of reality which is completely determined in and through its conception alone.

Now it cannot be expected that any one will be bold enough to declare that he has a perfect insight into the relation which the magnitude of the world he contemplates bears (in its extent as well as in its content) to omnipotence, into that of the order and design in the world to the highest wisdom, and that of the unity of the world to the absolute unity of a Supreme Being. Physico-theology is therefore incapable of presenting a determinate conception of a supreme cause of the world, and is therefore insufficient as a principle of theology — a theology which is itself to be the basis of religion.

The attainment of absolute totality is completely impossible on the path of empiricism. And yet this is the path pursued in the physico-theological argument. . . .

When from the existence of the universe and the things in it the existence of a cause of the universe is inferred, reason is proceeding not in the *natural,* but in the *speculative* method. For the principle of the former enounces, not that things themselves or substances, but only that which *happens* or their *states* — as empirically contingent, have a cause: the assertion that the existence of substance itself is contingent is not justified by experience, it is the assertion of a reason employing its principles in a speculative manner. If, again, I infer from the form of the universe, from the way in which all things are connected and act and react upon each other, the existence of a cause entirely distinct from the universe — this would again be a judgement of purely speculative reason; because the object in this case — the cause — can never be an object of possible experience. In both these cases the principle of causality, which is valid only in the field of experience — useless and even meaningless beyond this region, would be diverted from its proper destination. . . .

It is now perfectly evident that transcendental questions admit only of transcendental answers — those presented *a priori* by pure conceptions without the least empirical admixture. But the question in the present case is evidently synthetical—it aims at the extension of our cognition beyond the bounds of experience—it requires an assurance respecting the existence of a being corresponding with the idea in our minds, to which no experience can ever be adequate. Now it has been abundantly proved that all *a priori* synthetical cognition is possible only as the expression of the formal conditions of a possible experience; and that the validity of all principles depends upon their immanence in the field of experience, that is, their relation to objects of empirical cognition or phenomena. Thus all transcendental procedure in reference to speculative theology is without result.

> — From *Critique of Pure Reason*, pp. 186, 187, 189, 191, 192. Taken from vol. 42 of The Great Books, 1952, translated by J. M. D. Meiklejohn.

THE METAPHYSICS OF MORALS

Nothing can possibly be conceived in the world, or even out of it, which can be called good without qualification, except a Good Will. Intelligence, wit, judgment, and the other talents of the mind, however they may be named, or courage, resolution, perseverance, as qualities of temperament, are undoubtedly good and desirable in many respects; but these gifts of nature may also become extremely bad and mischievous if the will which is to make us of them, and which, therefore, constitutes what is called character, is not good. It is the same with the gifts of fortune. Power, riches, honour, even health, and the general well-being and contentment with one's condition which is called happiness, inspire pride, and often presumption, if there is not a good will to correct the influence of these on the mind, and with this also to rectify the whole principle of acting, and adapt it to its end. The sight of a being who is not adorned with a single feature of a pure and good will, enjoying unbroken prosperity can never give pleasure to an impartial rational spectator. Thus a good will appears to constitute the indispensable condition even of being worthy of happiness. . . .

. . . Moderation in the affections and passions, self-control and calm deliberation are not only good in many respects, but even seem to constitute part of the intrinsic worth of the person; but they are far from deserving to be called good without qualification, although they have been so unconditionally praised by the ancients. For without the principles of a good will, they may become extremely bad, and the coolness of a villain not only makes him far more dangerous, but also directly makes him more abominable in our eyes than he would have been without it.

A good will is good not because of what it performs or effects, not by its aptness for the attainment of some proposed end, but simply by virtue of the volition, that is, it is good in itself, and considered by itself is to be esteemed much higher than all that can be brought about by it . . . if with its greatest efforts it should yet achieve nothing, and there should remain only the good will (not, to be sure, a mere wish, but the summoning of all means in our power), then, like a jewel, it would still shine by its own light, as a thing which has its whole value in itself. Its usefulness or fruitlessness can neither add to nor take away anything from this value.

. . . Duty is the necessity of acting from respect for the law. . . . Thus the moral worth of an action does not lie in the effect expected from it. . . .

. . . But what sort of law can that be, the conception of which must determine the will, even without paying any regard to the effect expected from it, in order that this will may be called good absolutely and without qualification? . . . *I am never to act otherwise than so that I could also will that my maxim should become a universal law. . . .* The common reason of men in its practical judgments perfectly coincides with this, and always has in view the principle here suggested. Let the question be, for example: May I when in distress make a promise with the intention not to keep it? I readily distinguish here between the two significations which the question may have: Whether it is prudent, or whether it is right, to make a false promise. The former may undoubtedly often be the case. I see clearly indeed that it is not enough to extricate myself from a present difficulty by means of this subterfuge, but it must be well considered whether there may not hereafter spring from this lie much greater inconvenience than that from which I now free myself, and as, with all my supposed cunning, the consequences cannot be so easily foreseen but that credit once lost may be much more injurious to me than any mischief which I seek to avoid at present, it should be considered whether it would not be more prudent to act herein according to a universal maxim, and to make it a habit to promise nothing except with the intention of keeping it. But it is soon clear to me that such a maxim will still be only based on the fear of consequences. Now it is a wholly different thing to be truthful from duty, and to be so from apprehension of injurious consequences . . . to deviate from the principle of duty is beyond all doubt wicked; but to be unfaithful to my maxim of prudence may often be very advantageous to me, . . . The shortest way, however, and an unerring one, to discover the answer to this question whether a lying promise is consistent with duty, is to ask myself, Should I be content that my maxim (to extricate myself from difficulty by a false promise) should hold good as a universal law, for myself as well? Hence there arises a natural dialectic, i.e., a disposition to argue against these strict laws of duty and to question their validity, or at least their purity and strictness; and, if possible, to make them more accordant with our wishes and inclinations, that is to say, to corrupt them at their very source, and entirely to destroy their worth—a thing which even common practical reason cannot ultimately call good.

. . . Without being an enemy of virtue, a cool observer, one that does not mistake the wish for good, however lively, for its reality, may sometimes doubt whether true virtue is actually found anywhere in the world, and this especially as years increase and the judgment is partly made wiser by experience, and partly also more acute in observation. This being so, nothing can secure us from falling away altogether from our ideas of duty, or maintain in the soul a well-grounded respect for its law, but the clear conviction that although there should never have been actions which really sprang from such pure sources, yet whether this or that takes place is not at all the question; but that reason of itself, independent of all experience, ordains what ought to take place, that accordingly actions of which perhaps the world has hitherto never given an example, the feasibility even of which might be very much doubted by one who founds everything on experience, are nevertheless inflexibly commanded by reason; that, e.g. even though there might never yet have been a sincere friend, yet not a whit the less is pure sincerity in friendship required of every man, because, prior to all experience, this duty is involved as duty in the idea of a reason determining the will by a priori principles.[1]

(A man) finds in himself a talent which with the help of some culture might make him a useful man in many respects.[2]

But he finds himself in comfortable circumstances, and prefers to indulge in pleasure rather than to take pains in enlarging and improving his happy natural capacities. He asks, however, whether his maxim of neglect of his natural gifts, besides agreeing with his inclination to indulgence, agrees also with what is called duty . . . but he cannot possibly will that this should be a universal law of nature, or be implanted in us as such by a natural instinct. For, as a rational being, he necessarily wills that his faculties be developed, since they serve him, and have been given him, for all sorts of possible purposes.

(Another person) who is in prosperity, while he sees that others have to contend with great wretchedness and that he could help them, thinks: What concern is it of mine? Let everyone be as happy as heaven pleases, or as he can make himself; I will take nothing from him nor even envy him, only I do not wish to contribute anything to his welfare or to his assistance in distress! Now no doubt if such a mode of thinking were a universal law, the human race might very well subsist, and doubtless even better than in a state in which every one talks of sympathy and good-will, or even takes care occasionally to put it into practice, but on the other side, also cheats when he can, betrays the rights of men, or otherwise violates them. But although it is possible that a universal law of nature might exist in accordance with that maxim, it is impossible to will that such a principle should have the universal validity of a law of nature. For a will which resolved this would contradict itself, inasmuch as many cases might occur in which one would have need of the love and sympathy of others, and in which, by such a law of nature, sprung from his own will, he would deprive himself of all hope of the aid he desires.

> — From *The Metaphysics of Morals,* pp. 256ff. Taken from vol. 42
> of The Great Books, 1952, translated by Thomas K. Abbott.

---

[1] By a priori principles Kant meant principles applicable to all friendships by definition, not ideas of friendship formed only by induction from our experience of friendships.—ED.

[2] Later on in Kant's treatise he gives some other examples of how the categorical imperative can be applied. Two of these are quite relevant to contemporary dilemmas and so are included here.—ED.

Georg Wilhelm Friedrich Hegel

ON THE DIALECTIC

The concept's moving principle, which alike engenders and dissolves the particulariza-tions of the universal, I call "dialectic," though I do not mean that dialectic which takes an object, proposition, etc., given to feeling or, in general, to immediate consciousness, and explains it away, confuses it, pursues it this way and that, and has as its sole task the deduction of the contrary of that with which it starts—a negative type of dialectic commonly appearing even in Plato. Dialectic of this kind may regard as its final result either the contrary of the idea with which it begins, or, if it is as incisive as the scepticism of the ancients, the contradictory of this idea, or again, it may be feeble enough to be content with an "approximation" to the truth, a modern half-measure. The loftier dialectic of the concept consists not simply in producing the determination as a contrary and a restriction, but in producing and seizing upon the positive content and outcome of the determination, because it is this which makes it solely a develop-ment and an immanent progress. Moreover, this dialectic is not an activity of subjective thinking applied to some matter externally, but is rather the matter's very soul putting forth its branches and fruit organically. This development of the Idea is the proper activity of its rationality.

> — From *The Philosophy of Right*, p. 19. Taken from vol. 46 of The Great Books, 1952, translated and with notes by T. M. Knox.

THE PHILOSOPHY OF RIGHT

Further, world history is not the verdict of mere might, i.e., the abstract and non-rational inevitability of a blind destiny. On the contrary, since mind is implicitly and actually reason, and reason is explicit to itself in mind as knowledge, world history is the necessary development, out of the concept of mind's freedom alone, of the moments of reason and so of the self-consciousness and freedom of mind. This develop-ment is the interpretation and actualization of the universal mind.

The history of mind is its own act. Mind is only what it does, and its act is to make itself the object of its own consciousness. In history its act is to gain consciousness of itself as mind, to apprehend itself in its interpretation of itself to itself. This apprehen-sion is its being and its principle, and the completion of apprehension at one stage is at the same time the rejection of that stage and its transition to a higher . . .

In the course of this work of the world mind, states, nations, and individuals arise animated by their particular determinate principle which has its interpretation and actuality in their constitutions and in the whole range of their life and condition. While their consciousness is limited to these and they are absorbed in their mundane interests, they are all the time the unconscious tools and organs of the world mind at work within them. The shapes which they take pass away, while the absolute mind prepares and works out its transition to its next higher stage.

Justice and virtue, wrongdoing, power and vice, talents and their achievements, passions strong and weak, guilt and innocence, grandeur in individual and national life, autonomy, fortune and misfortune of states and individuals, all these have their specific significance and worth in the field of known actuality; therein they are judged and therein they have their partial, though only partial justification. World-history, however, is above the point of view from which these things matter. Each of its stages is the presence of a necessary moment in the Idea of the world mind, and that moment attains its absolute right in that stage. The nation whose life embodies this moment secures its good fortune and fame, and its deeds are brought to fruition.

History is mind clothing itself with the form of events or the immediate actuality of nature. The stages of its development are therefore presented as immediate natural principles. These, because they are natural, are a plurality external to one another, and they are present therefore in such a way that each of them is assigned to one nation in the external form of its geographical and anthropological conditions.

The nation to which is ascribed a moment of the Idea in the form of a natural principle is entrusted with giving complete effect to it in the advance of the self-developing self-consciousness of the world mind. This nation is dominant in world history during this one epoch, and it is only once that it can make its hour strike. In contrast with this its absolute right of being the vehicle of this present stage in the world mind's development, the minds of the other nations are without rights, and they, along with those whose hour has struck already, count no longer in world history.

The history of a single world-historical nation contains (a) the development of its principle from its latent embryonic stage until it blossoms into the self-conscious freedom of ethical life and presses in upon world history; and (b) the period of its decline and fall, since it is its decline and fall that signalizes the emergence in it of a higher principle as the pure negative of its own. When this happens, mind passes over into the new principle and so marks out another nation for world-historical significance. After this period, the declining nation has lost the interest of the absolute; it may indeed absorb the higher principle positively and begin building its life on it, but the principle is only like an adopted child, not like a relative to whom its ties are immanently vital and vigorous. Perhaps it loses its autonomy, or it may still exist, or drag out its existence, as a particular state or a group of states and involve itself without rhyme or reason in manifold enterprises at home and battles abroad.

> — From *The Philosophy of Right*, pp. 110–11. Taken from vol. 46 of
> The Great Books, 1952, translated and with notes by T. M.
> Knox.

ON TRUTH AS PROCESS

The more the ordinary mind takes the opposition between true and false to be fixed, the more is it accustomed to expect either agreement or contradiction with a given philosophical system, and only to see reason for the one or the other in any explanatory statement concerning such a system. It does not conceive the diversity of philosophical systems as the progressive evolution of truth; rather, it sees only contradiction in that variety. The bud disappears when the blossom breaks through, and we might say that the former is refuted by the latter; in the same way when the fruit comes, the blossom may be explained to be a false form of the plant's existence, for the fruit appears as its true nature in place of the blossom. These stages are not merely differentiated; they supplant one another as being incompatible with one another. But the ceaseless activity of their own inherent nature makes them at the same time moments of an organic unity, where they not merely do not contradict one another, but where one is as necessary as the other; and this equal necessity of all moments constitutes alone and thereby the life of the whole. But contradiction as between philosophical systems is not wont to be conceived in this way; on the other hand, the mind perceiving the contradiction does not commonly know how to relieve it or keep it free from its onesidedness, and to recognize in what seems conflicting and inherently antagonistic the presence of mutually necessary moments.

ON THE CONCEPT OF GOD

The truth is the whole. The whole, however, is merely the essential nature reaching its completeness through the process of its own development. Of the Absolute it must be said that it is essentially a result, that only at the end is it what it is in very truth; and just in that consists its nature, which is to be actual, subject, or self-becoming, self-development . . .

. . . The Absolute as Spirit (*Geist*)—the grandest conception of all, and one which is due to modern times and its religion. Spirit is alone Reality. It is the inner being of the world, that which essentially is, and is *per se;* it assumes objective, determinate form, and enters into relations with itself—it is externality (otherness), and exists for self; yet, in this determination, and in its otherness, it is still one with itself—it is self-contained and self-complete, in itself and for itself at once. This self-containedness, however, is first something known by us. . . .

So far as its spiritual content is produced by its own activity, it is only *we* [the thinkers] who know spirit to be for itself, to be objective to itself; but in so far as spirit knows itself to be for itself, then this self-production, the pure notion, is the sphere and element in which its objectification takes effect, and where it gets its existential form. In this way it is in its existence aware of itself as an object in which its own self is reflected. Mind, which, when thus developed, knows itself to be mind, is science. Science is its realization, and the kingdom it sets up for itself in its own native element.

— From *The Phenomenology of Mind,* 2nd ed. Translated by T. R. Baillie (New York: Humanities Press, 1931).

Part Four

Karl Marx

This excerpt from The Communist Manifesto, *by Karl Marx and Friedrich Engels, originally published in 1848, provides a succinct example of the atheism and Hegelianism intrinsically bound to Marxist thought.*

THE COMMUNIST MANIFESTO

The charges against Communism made from a religious, a philosophical, and, generally, from an ideological standpoint, are not deserving of serious examination.

Does it require deep intuition to comprehend that man's ideas, views and conceptions, in one word, man's consciousness, changes with every change in the conditions of his material existence, in his social relations and in his social life?

What else does the history of ideas prove, than that intellectual production changes its character in proportion as material production is changed? The ruling ideas of each age have ever been the ideas of its ruling class.

When people speak of ideas that revolutionise society, they do but express the fact, that within the old society, the elements of a new one have been created, and that the dissolution of the old ideas keeps even pace with the dissolution of the old conditions of existence.

When the ancient world was in its last throes, the ancient religions were overcome by Christianity. When Christian ideas succumbed in the 18th century to rationalist ideas, feudal society fought its death battle with the then revolutionary bourgeoisie. The ideas of religious liberty and freedom of conscience merely gave expression to the sway of free competition within the domain of knowledge.

"Undoubtedly," it will be said, "religious, moral, philosophical and juridical ideas have been modified in the course of historical development. But religion, morality, philosophy, political science, and law, constantly survived this change."

"There are, besides, eternal truths, such as Freedom, Justice, etc., that are common to all states of society. But Communism abolishes eternal truths, it abolishes all religion, and all morality, instead of constituting them on a new basis; it therefore acts in contradiction to all past historical experience."

What does this accusation reduce itself to? The history of all past society has consisted in the development of class antagonisms, antagonisms that assumed different forms at different epochs.

But whatever form they may have taken, one fact is common to all past ages, *viz.,* the exploitation of one part of society by the other. No wonder, then, that the social consciousness of past ages, despite all the multiplicity and variety it displays, moves within certain common forms, or general ideas, which cannot completely vanish except with the total disappearance of class antagonisms.

> — From *The Communist Manifesto.* Taken from *The Marx-Engels Reader,* 2nd ed. Edited by Robert C. Tucker (New York: W. W. Norton & Company, Inc., 1978), p. 489.

Jean-Paul Sartre

This excerpt from an article published in 1944 *outlines the basic tenets of Sartre's existentialism.*

A MORE PRECISE CHARACTERIZATION OF EXISTENTIALISM

In philosophical terminology, every object has an essence and an existence. An essence is an intelligible and unchanging unity of properties; an existence is a certain actual presence in the world. Many people think that the essence comes first and then the existence: that peas, for example, grow and become round in conformity with the idea of peas, and that gherkins are gherkins because they participate in the essence of gherkins. This idea originated in religious thought: it is a fact that the man who wants to build a house has to know exactly what kind of object he's going to create—essence precedes existence—and for all those who believe that God created men, he must have done so by referring to his idea of them. But even those who have no religious faith have maintained this traditional view that the object never exists except in conformity with its essence; and everyone in the eighteenth century thought that all men had a common essence called *human nature*. Existentialism, on the contrary, maintains that in man—and in man alone—existence precedes essence.

This simply means that man first *is*, and only subsequently is this or that. In a word, man must create his own essence: it is in throwing himself into the world, suffering there, struggling there, that he gradually defines himself. And the definition always remains open ended: we cannot say what *this* man is before he dies, or what mankind is before it has disappeared. It is absurd in this light to ask whether existentialism is Fascist, conservative, Communist, or democratic. At this level of generality existentialism is nothing but a certain way of envisaging human questions by refusing to grant man an eternally established nature. It used to be, in Kierkegaard's thought, on a par with religious faith. Today, French existentialism tends to be accompanied by a declaration of atheism, but this is not absolutely necessary. All I can say—without wanting to insist too much on the similarities—is that it isn't too far from the conception of man found in Marx. For is it not a fact that Marx would accept *this motto of ours for man: make, and in making make yourself, and be nothing but what you have made of yourself?*

Since existentialism defines man by action, it is evident that this philosophy is not a quietism. In fact, man cannot help acting; his thoughts are projects and commitments, his feelings are undertakings, he is nothing other than his life, and his life is the unity of his behavior. "But what about anguish?" you'll say. Well, this rather solemn word refers to a very simple everyday reality If man *is* not but *makes himself*, and if in making himself he makes himself responsible for the whole species—if there is no value or morality given a priori, so that we must in every instance decide alone and without any basis or guidelines, yet *for everyone*—how could we possibly help feeling anguished when we have to act? Each of our acts puts the world's meaning and man's place in the universe in question. With each of them, whether we want to or not, we constitute a universal scale of values. And you want us not to be seized with fear in the face of such a total responsibility? Ponge, in a very beautiful piece of writing, said that man is the future of man. That future is not yet created, not yet decided upon. We are the ones who will make it; each of our gestures will help fashion it. It would take a lot of pharisaism to avoid an anguished awareness of the formidable mission given to each of us. But you people, in order to refute us more convincingly, you people have deliberately confused anguish and neurasthenia, making who knows what pathological terror out of this virile uneasiness existentialism speaks of. Since I have to dot my *i*'s, I'll say then that *anguish, far from being an obstacle to action, is the very condition for it, and is identical with the sense of that crushing responsibility of all before all which is the source of both our torment and our grandeur.*

> — From "A More Precise Characterization of Existentialism", *The Writings of Jean-Paul Sartre,* vol. 2. Edited by Michel Contat and Michel Rybalka. Translated by Richard McCleary (Evanston, Ill.: Northwestern University Press, 1974), pp. 157–58.

John Dewey

The following selection illustrates Dewey's optimism about the pragmatic approach to life and his rejection of philosophical absolutes. The passage may also give us a vivid picture of a type of teaching that would surely confuse and undermine a Catholic university student's faith had he no grounding in classical or perennial Christian Philosophy.

PHILOSOPHY'S SEARCH FOR THE IMMUTABLE

In this chapter we are especially concerned with the effect of the ideal of certainty as something superior to belief upon the conception of the nature and function of philosophy. Greek thinkers saw clearly—and logically—that experience cannot furnish us, as respects cognition of existence, with anything more than contingent probability. Experience cannot deliver to us necessary truths; truths completely demonstrated by reason. Its conclusions are particular, not universal. Not being "exact" they come short of "science". Thus there arose the distinction between rational truths or, in modern terminology, truths relating to the relation of ideas, and "truths" about matters of existence, empirically ascertained. Thus not merely the arts of practice, industrial and social, were stamped matters of belief rather than of knowledge, but also all those sciences which are matters of inductive inference from observation.

One might indulge in the reflection that they are none the worse for all that, especially since the natural sciences have developed a technique for achieving a high degree of probability and for measuring, within assignable limits, the amount of probability which attaches in particular cases to conclusions. But historically the matter is not so simple as to permit of this retort. For empirical or observational sciences were placed in invidious contrast to rational sciences which dealt with eternal and universal objects and which therefore were possessed of necessary truth. Consequently all observational sciences as far as their material could not be subsumed under forms and principles supplied by rational science shared in the depreciatory view held about practical affairs. They are relatively low, secular and profane compared with the perfect realities of rational science.

And here is a justification for going back to something as remote in time as Greek philosophy. The whole classic tradition down to our day has continued to hold a slighting view of experience as such, and to hold up as the proper goal and ideal of true knowledge realities which even if they are located in empirical things cannot be known by experimental methods. The logical consequence for philosophy itself is evident. Upon the side of method, it has been compelled to claim for itself the possession of a method issuing from reason itself, and having the warrant of reason, independently of experience. As long as the view obtained that nature itself is truly known by the same rational method, the consequences—at least those which were evident—were not serious. There was no break between philosophy and genuine science—or what was conceived to be such. In fact, there was not even a distinction; there were simply various branches of philosophy, metaphysical, logical, natural, moral, etc., in a descending scale of demonstrative certainty. Since, according to the theory, the subject-matter of the lower sciences was inherently of a different character from that of true knowledge, there was no ground for rational dissatisfaction with the lower degree of knowledge called belief. Inferior knowledge or belief corresponded to the inferior state of subject-matter.

The scientific revolution of the seventeenth century effected a great modification. Science itself through the aid of mathematics carried the scheme of demonstrative knowledge over to natural objects. The "laws" of the natural world had that fixed character which in the older scheme had belonged only to rational and ideal forms. A mathematical science of nature couched in mechanistic terms claimed to be the only sound natural philosophy. Hence the older philosophies lost alliance with natural knowledge and the support that had been given to philosophy by them. Philosophy in maintaining its claim to be a superior form of knowledge was compelled to take an invidious and so to say malicious attitude toward the conclusions of natural science. The framework of the old tradition had in the meantime become embedded in Christian theology, and through religious teaching was made a part of the inherited culture of those innocent of any technical philosophy. Consequently, the rivalry between philosophy and the new science, with respect to the claim to know reality, was converted in effect into a rivalry between the spiritual values guaranteed by the older philosophic tradition and the conclusions of natural knowledge. The more science advanced the more it seemed to encroach upon the special province of the territory over which philosophy had claimed jurisdiction. Thus philosophy in its classic form became a species of apologetic justification for belief in an ultimate reality in which the values which should regulate life and control conduct are securely enstated.

There are undoubted disadvantages in the historic manner of approach to the problem which has been followed. It may readily be thought either that the Greek formulation which has been emphasized has no especial pertinency with respect to modern thought and especially to contemporary philosophy; or that no philosophical statement is of any great importance for the mass of non-philosophic persons. Those interested in philosophy may object that the criticisms passed are directed if not at a man of straw at least to positions that have long since lost their actuality. Those not friendly to any form of philosophy may inquire what import they have for any except professed philosophers.

The first type of objection will be dealt with somewhat *in extenso* in the succeeding chapter, in which I shall try to show how modern philosophies, in spite of their great diversity, have been concerned with problems of adjustment of the conclusions of modern science to the chief religious and moral tradition of the western world; together with the way in which these problems are connected with retention of the conception of the relation of knowledge to reality formulated in Greek thought. At the point in the discussion now reached, it suffices to point out that, in spite of great changes in detail, the notion of a separation between knowledge and action, theory and practice, has been perpetuated, and that the beliefs connected with action are taken to be uncertain and inferior in value compared with those inherently connected with objects of knowledge, so that the former are securely established only as they derived from the latter. Not the specific content of Greek thought is pertinent to present problems, but its insistence that security is measured by certainty of knowledge, while the latter is measured by adhesion to fixed and immutable objects, which therefore are independent of what men do in practical activity.

The other objection is of a different sort. It comes from those who feel that not merely Greek philosophy but philosophy in any form is remote from all significant human concern. It is willing to admit or rather assert that it is presumptuous for philosophy to lay claim to knowledge of a higher order than that given by natural science, but it also holds that this is no great matter in any case except for professional philosophers.

There would be force in this latter objection were it not that those who make it hold for the most part the same philosophy of certainty and its proper object that is held by philosophers, save in an inchoate form. They are not interested in the notion that philosophic thought is a special means of attaining this object and the certainty it affords, but they are far from holding, either explicitly or implicitly, that the arts of intelligently directed action are the means by which security of values is to be attained. With respect to certain ends and goods they accept this idea. But in thinking of these ends and values as material, as related to health, wealth, control of conditions for the sake of an inferior order of consequences, they retain the same division between a higher reality and a lower that is formulated in classic philosophy. They may be innocent of the vocabulary that speaks of reason, necessary truth, the universal, things in themselves and appearances. But they incline to believe that there is some other road than that of action, directed by knowledge, to achieve ultimate security of higher ideals and purposes. They think of practical action as necessary for practical utilities, but they mark off practical utilities from spiritual and ideal values. Philosophy did not originate the underlying division. It only gave intellectual formulation and justification to ideas that were operative in men's minds generally. And the elements of these ideas are as active in present culture as they ever were in the past. Indeed, through the diffusion of religious doctrines, the idea that ultimate values are a matter of special revelation and are to be embodied in life by special means radically different from the arts of action that deal with lower and lesser ends has been accentuated in the popular mind.

Here is the point which is of general human import instead of concern merely to professional philosophers. What about the security of values, of the things which are admirable, honourable, to be approved of and striven for? It is probably in consequence of the derogatory view held of practice that the question of the secure place of values in human experience is so seldom raised in connection with the problem of the relation of knowledge and practice. But upon any view concerning the status of action, the scope of the latter cannot be restricted to self-seeking acts, nor to those of a prudential aspect, nor in general to things of expediency and what are often termed "utilitarian" affairs. The maintenance and diffusion of intellectual values, of moral excellencies, the aesthetically admirable, as well as the maintenance of order and decorum in human relations are dependent upon what men do.

Whether because of the emphasis of traditional religion upon salvation of the personal soul or for some other reason, there is a tendency to restrict the ultimate scope of morals to the reflex effect of conduct on one's self. Even utilitarianism, with all its seeming independence of traditional theology and its emphasis upon the general good as the criterion for judging conduct, insisted in its hedonistic psychology upon private pleasure as the motive for action. The idea that the stable and expanding institution of all things that make life worth while throughout all human relationships is the real object of *all* intelligent conduct is depressed from view by the current conception of morals as a special kind of action chiefly concerned with either the virtues or the enjoyments of individuals in their personal capacities. In changed form, we still retain the notion of a division of activity into two kinds having very different worths. The result is the depreciated meaning that has come to be attached to the very meaning of the "practical" and the useful. Instead of being extended to cover all forms of action by means of which all the values of life are extended and rendered more secure, including the diffusion of the fine arts and the cultivation of taste, the processes of education and all activities which are concerned with rendering human relationships more significant and worthy, the meaning of "practical" is limited to matters of ease, comfort, riches, bodily security and police order, possibly health, etc., things which in their isolation from other goods can only lay claim to restricted and narrow value. In consequence, these subjects are handed over to technical sciences and arts; they are no concern of "higher" interests which feel that no matter what happens to inferior goods in the vicissitudes of natural existence, the highest values are immutable characters of the ultimately real.

Our depreciatory attitude toward "practice" would be modified if we habitually thought of it in its most liberal sense, and if we surrendered our customary dualism between two separate kinds of value, one intrinsically higher and one inherently lower. We should regard practice as the only means (other than accident) by which whatever is judged to be honourable, admirable, approvable can be kept in concrete experienceable existence. In this connection the entire import of "morals" would be transformed. How much of the tendency to ignore permanent objective consequences in differences made in natural and social relations; and how much of the emphasis upon personal and internal motives and dispositions irrespective of what they objectively produce and sustain, are products of the habitual depreciation of the worth of action in comparison with forms of mental processes, of thought and sentiment, which make no objective difference in things themselves?

It would be possible to argue (and, I think, with much justice) that failure to make action central in the search for such security as is humanly possible is a survival of the impotency of man in those stages of civilization when he had few means of regulating and utilizing the conditions upon which the occurrence of consequences depend. As long as man was unable by means of the arts of practice to direct the course of events, it was natural for him to seek an emotional substitute; in the absence of actual certainty in the midst of a precarious and hazardous world, men cultivated all sorts of things that would give them the *feeling* of certainty. And it is possible that, when not carried to an illusory point, the cultivation of the feeling gave man courage and confidence and enabled him to carry the burdens of life more successfully. But one could hardly seriously contend that this fact, if it be such, is one upon which to found a reasoned philosophy.

It is to the conception of philosophy that we come back. No mode of action can, as we have insisted, give anything approaching absolute certitude; it provides insurance but no assurance. Doing is always subject to peril, to the danger of frustration. When men began to reflect philosophically it seemed to them altogether too risky to leave the place of values at the mercy of acts the results of which are never sure. This precariousness might hold as far as empirical existence, existence in the sensible and phenomenal world, is concerned; but this very uncertainty seemed to render it the more needful that ideal goods should be shown to have, by means of knowledge of the most assured type, an indefeasible and inexpugnable position in the realm of the ultimately real. So at least we may imagine men to have reasoned. And to-day many persons find a peculiar consolation in the face of the unstable and dubious presence of values in actual experience by projecting a perfect form of good into a realm of essence, if not into a heaven beyond the earthly skies, wherein their authority, if not their existence, is wholly unshakeable.

Instead of asking how far this process is of that compensatory kind with which recent psychology has made us familiar, we are inquiring into the effect upon philosophy. It will not be denied, I suppose, that the chief aim of those philosophies which I have called classical has been to show that the realities which are the objects of the highest and most necessary knowledge are also endowed with the values which correspond to our best aspirations, admirations and approvals. That, one may say, is the very heart of all traditional philosophic idealisms. There is a pathos, having its own nobility, in philosophies which think it their proper office to give an intellectual or cognitive certification to the ontological reality of the highest values. It is difficult for men to see desire and choice set earnestly upon the good and yet being frustrated, without their imagining a realm in which the good has come completely to its own, and is identified with a Reality in which resides all ultimate power. The failure and frustration of actual life is then attributed to the fact that this world is finite and phenomenal, sensible rather than real, or to the weakness of our finite apprehension, which cannot see that the discrepancy between existence and value is merely seeming, and that a fuller vision would behold partial evil an element in complete good. Thus the office of philosophy is to project by dialectic, resting supposedly upon self-evident premises, a realm in which the object of completest cognitive certitude is also one with the object of the heart's best aspiration. The fusion of the good and the true with unity and plenitude of Being thus becomes the goal of classic philosophy.

— From "Philosophy's Search for the Immutable", *The Quest for Certainty* (London: Allen & Unwin, 1930), pp. 28–36.

Leo XIII

AETERNI PATRIS

The only-begotten Son of the Eternal Father, who came on earth to bring salvation and the light of divine wisdom to men, conferred a great and wonderful blessing on the world when, about to ascend again into heaven, he commanded the apostles to go and teach all nations,[1] and left the Church which he had founded to be the common and supreme teacher of the peoples. For men, whom the truth had set free, were to be preserved by the truth; nor would the fruits of heavenly doctrines, by which salvation comes to men, have long remained had not the Lord Christ appointed an unfailing authority for the instruction of the faithful. And the Church built upon the promises of its own divine Author, whose charity it imitated, so faithfully followed out his commands that its constant aim and chief wish was this: to teach true religion and contend forever against errors. To this end assuredly have tended the incessant labors of individual bishops; to this end also the published laws and decrees of Councils, and especially the constant watchfulness of the Roman Pontiffs, to whom, as successors of the blessed Peter in the primacy of the apostles, belongs the right and office of teaching and confirming their brethren in the faith. Since, then, according to the warning of the Apostle, the minds of Christ's faithful are apt to be deceived and the integrity of the faith to be corrupted among men *by philosophy and vain deceit,*[2] the supreme pastors of the Church have always thought it their duty to advance, by every means in their power, science truly so called, and at the same time to provide with special care that all studies should accord with the Catholic faith, especially philosophy, on which a right apprehension of the other sciences in great part depends. Indeed, venerable brethren, on this very subject among others, we briefly admonished you in our first encyclical letter; but now, both by reason of the gravity of the subject and the condition of the time, we are again compelled to speak to you on the mode of taking up the study of philosophy which shall respond most fitly to the true faith, and at the same time be most consonant with the dignity of human knowledge.

Whoso turns his attention to the bitter strifes of these days and seeks a reason for the troubles that vex public and private life must come to the conclusion that a fruitful cause of the evils which now afflict, as well as of those which threaten us, lies in this: that false conclusions concerning divine and human things, which originated in the schools of philosophy, have crept into all the orders of the state, and have been accepted by the common consent of the masses. For since it is in the very nature of man to follow the guide of reason in his actions, if his intellect sins at all his will soon follows; and thus it happens that looseness of intellectual opinion influences human actions and perverts them. Whereas, on the other hand, if men be of sound mind and take their stand on true and solid principles, there will result a vast amount of benefits for the public and

[1] Matthew 28:19.
[2] Colossians 2:8.

private good. We do not, indeed, attribute such force and authority to philosophy as to esteem it equal to the task of combating and rooting out all errors; for, when the Christian religion was first constituted, it came upon earth to restore it to its primeval dignity by the admirable light of faith, diffused not by persuasive words of human wisdom, but in the manifestation of spirit and of power;[3] so also at the present time we look above all things to the powerful help of Almighty God to bring back to a right understanding the minds of men and dispel the darkness of error. But the natural helps with which the grace of the divine wisdom, strongly and sweetly disposing all things, has supplied the human race are neither to be despised nor neglected, chief among which is evidently the right use of philosophy. For not in vain did God set the light of reason in the human mind; and so far is the super-added light of faith from extinguishing or lessening the power of the intelligence that it completes it rather, and by adding to its strength renders it capable of greater things.

Therefore divine Providence itself requires that in calling back the peoples to the paths of faith and salvation, advantage should be taken of human science also—an approved and wise practice which history testifies was observed by the most illustrious Fathers of the Church. They, indeed, were wont neither to belittle nor undervalue the part that reason had to play, as is summed up by the great Augustine when he attributes to this science "that by which the most wholesome faith is begotten, . . . is nourished, defended, and made strong."[4]

In the first place, philosophy, if rightly made use of by the wise, in a certain way tends to smooth and fortify the road to true faith, and to prepare the souls of its disciples for the fit reception of revelation; for which reason it is well called by ancient writers sometimes a stepping-stone to the Christian faith,[5] sometimes the prelude and help of Christianity,[6] sometimes the Gospel teacher.[7] And assuredly the God of all goodness, in all that pertains to divine things, has not only manifested by the light of faith those truths which human intelligence could not attain of itself, but others also not altogether unattainable by reason, that by the help of divine authority they may be made known to all at once and without any admixture of error. Hence it is that certain truths which were either divinely proposed for belief, or were bound by the closest chains to the doctrine of faith, were discovered by pagan sages with nothing but their natural reason to guide them, were demonstrated and proved by becoming arguments. *For,* as the Apostle says, *the invisible things of him, from the creation of the world, are clearly seen, being understood by the things that are made: his eternal power also and divinity;*[8] and the Gentiles who have not the law show, nevertheless, the work of the law written in their hearts.[9] But it is most fitting to turn these truths, which have been discovered by the pagan sages even, to the use and purposes of revealed doctrine, in order to show that

---

[3] 1 Corinthians 2:4.
[4] *De Trin.,* xiv, I, 3 (PL 42, 1037).
[5] Clem. Alex., *Strom.,* I, 16; VII, 3 (PG 8, 795; 9, 426).
[6] Origen, *Epistola ad Gregorium* (PG 11, 87–91).
[7] Clem. Alex., *Strom.,* I, 5 (PG 8, 718–19).
[8] Romans 1:20.
[9] *Ibid.,* 2:14, 15.

both human wisdom and the very testimony of our adversaries serve to support the Christian faith—a method which is not of recent introduction, but of established use, and has often been adopted by the holy Fathers of the Church. For instance, those venerable men, the witnesses and guardians of religious traditions, recognize a certain form and figure of this in the action of the Hebrews, who, when about to depart out of Egypt, were commanded to take with them the gold and silver vessels and precious robes of the Egyptians, that by a change of use the things might be dedicated to the service of the true God which had formerly been the instruments of ignoble and superstitious rites. Gregory of Neocaesarea[10] praises Origen expressly because, with singular dexterity, as one snatches weapons from the enemy, he turned to the defense of Christian wisdom and to the destruction of superstition many arguments drawn from the writings of the pagans. And both Gregory of Nazianzus[11] and Gregory of Nyssa[12] praise and commend a like mode of disputation in Basil the Great; while Jerome especially commends it in Quadratus, a disciple of the apostles, in Aristides, Justin, Irenaeus, and very many others.[13] Augustine says: "Do we not see Cyprian, that mildest of doctors and most blessed of martyrs, going out of Egypt laden with gold and silver and vestments? And Lactantius also and Victorinus, Optatus and Hilary? And, not to speak of the living, how many Greeks have done likewise?"[14] But if natural reason first sowed this rich field of doctrine before it was rendered fruitful by the power of Christ, it must assuredly become more prolific after the grace of the Savior has renewed and added to the native faculties of the human mind. And who does not see that a plain and easy road is opened up to faith by such a method of philosophic study?

But the advantage to be derived from such a school of philosophy is not to be confined within these limits. The foolishness of those men is gravely reproved in the words of divine wisdom who by these good things that are seen could not understand him that is, neither by attending to the works could have acknowledged who was the workman.[15] In the first place, then, this great and noble fruit is gathered from human reason, that it demonstrates that God *is; for by the greatness of the beauty, and of the creature, the Creator of them may be seen so as to be known thereby.*[16] Again, it shows God to excel in the height of all perfections, in infinite wisdom before which nothing lies hidden, and in absolute justice which no depraved affection could possibly shake; and that God, therefore, is not only true but truth itself, which can neither deceive nor be deceived. Whence it clearly follows that human reason finds the fullest faith and authority united in the word of God. In like manner reason declares that the doctrine of the Gospel has even from its very beginning been made manifest by certain wonderful signs, the established proofs, as it were, of unshaken truth; and that all, therefore, who set faith in

[10] *Orat. paneg. ad Origen,* 14 (PG 10, 1094).
[11] *Carm.* i, Iamb. 3.
[12] *Vita Moysis* (PG 44, 359).
[13] *Epist. ad Magnum,* 4 (PL 22, 667).
[14] *De Doctr. Christ.,* I, ii, 40 (PL 34, 63).
[15] Wisdom 13:1.
[16] Ibid., 13:5.

the Gospel do not believe rashly as though following cunningly devised fables,[17] but, by a most reasonable consent, subject their intelligence and judgment to an authority which is divine. And of no less importance is it that reason most clearly sets forth that the Church instituted by Christ (as laid down in the Vatican Synod), on account of its wonderful spread, its marvelous sanctity, and its inexhaustible fecundity in all places, as well as of its Catholic unity and unshaken stability, is in itself a great and perpetual motive of belief and an irrefragable testimony of its own divine mission.[18]

Its solid foundations having been thus laid, a perpetual and varied service is further required of philosophy, in order that sacred theology may receive and assume the nature, form, and genius of a true science. For in this, the most noble of studies, it is of the greatest necessity to bind together, as it were, in one body the many and various parts of the heavenly doctrines, that, each being allotted to its own proper place and derived from its own proper principles, the whole may join together in a complete union; in order, in fine, that all and each part may be strengthened by its own and the others' invincible arguments. Nor is that more accurate or fuller knowledge of the things that are believed, and somewhat more lucid understanding, as far as it can go, of the very mysteries of faith which Augustine and the other Fathers commended and strove to reach, and which the Vatican Synod itself[19] declared to be most fruitful, to be passed over in silence or belittled. Those will certainly more fully and more easily attain that knowledge and understanding who to integrity of life and love of faith join a mind rounded and finished by philosophic studies, as the same Vatican Synod teaches that the knowledge of such sacred dogmas ought to be sought as well from analogy of the things that are naturally known as from the connection of those mysteries one with another and with the final end of man.[20]

Lastly, the duty of religiously defending the truths divinely delivered, and of resisting those who dare oppose them, pertains to philosophic pursuits. Wherefore it is the glory of philosophy to be esteemed as the bulwark of faith and the strong defense of religion. As Clement of Alexandria testifies, the doctrine of the Savior is indeed perfect in itself and wants naught, since it is the power and wisdom of God. And the assistance of Greek philosophy makes not the truth more powerful; but in as much as it weakens the contrary arguments of the sophists and repels the veiled attacks against the truth, it has been fitly called the hedge and fence of the vine.[21] For as the enemies of the Catholic name, when about to attack religion, are in the habit of borrowing their weapons from the arguments of philosophers, so the defenders of sacred science draw many arguments from the store of philosophy which may serve to uphold revealed dogmas. Nor is the triumph of the Christian faith a small one in using human reason to repel powerfully and speedily the attacks of its adversaries by the hostile arms which human reason itself supplied. Which species of religious strife St. Jerome, writing to Magnus, notices as having been adopted by the Apostle of the Gentiles himself: Paul,

[17] 2 Peter 1:16.
[18] *Const. Dogm. de Fid. Cath.*, c. 3.
[19] *Const. cit.*, c. 4.
[20] *Loc. cit.*
[21] *Strom.*, I, 20 (PG 8, 818).

the leader of the Christian army skillfully turns even a chance inscription into an argument for the faith; for he had learned from the true David to wrest the sword from the hands of the enemy and to cut off the head of the boastful Goliath with his own weapon.[22] Moreover, the Church herself not only urges, but even commands, Christian teachers to seek help from philosophy. For the fifth Council of the Lateran, after it had decided that "every assertion contrary to the truth of revealed faith is altogether false, for the reason that it contradicts, however slightly, the truth,"[23] advises teachers of philosophy to pay close attention to the exposition of fallacious arguments; since, as Augustine testifies, "if reason is turned against the authority of sacred Scripture, no matter how specious it may seem it errs in the likeness of truth; for true it cannot be."[24]

But in order that philosophy may be found equal to the gathering of those precious fruits which we have indicated, it behooves it above all things never to turn aside from that path which the Fathers have entered upon from a venerable antiquity, and which the Vatican Council solemnly and authoritatively approved. As it is evident that very many truths of the supernatural order which are far beyond the reach of the keenest intellect must be accepted, human reason, conscious of its own infirmity, dare not pretend to what is beyond it, nor deny those truths, nor measure them by its own standard, nor interpret them at will; but receive them rather with a full and humble faith, and esteem it the highest honor to be allowed to wait upon heavenly doctrines like a handmaid and attendant, and by God's goodness attain to them in any way whatsoever. But in the case of such doctrines as the human intelligence may perceive, it is equally just that philosophy should make use of its own method, principles, and arguments—not indeed in such fashion as to seem rashly to withdraw from the divine authority. But since it is established that those things which become known by revelation have the force of certain truth, and that those things which war against faith war equally against right reason, the Catholic philosopher will know that he violates at once faith and the laws of reason if he accepts any conclusion which he understands to be opposed to revealed doctrine.

We know that there are some who, in their overestimate of the human faculties, maintain that as soon as man's intellect becomes subject to divine authority it falls from its native dignity, and, hampered by the yoke of this species of slavery, is much retarded and hindered in its progress towards the supreme truth and excellence. Such an idea is most false and deceptive, and its final result is to induce foolish and ungrateful men willfully to repudiate the most sublime truths, and reject the divine gift of faith, from which the fountains of all good things flow out upon civil society. For the human mind, being confined within certain limits, and those narrow enough, is exposed to many errors and is ignorant of many things; whereas the Christian faith, reposing on the authority of God, is the unfailing mistress of truth, whom whoso follows he will be neither immeshed in the snares of error nor tossed hither and thither on the waves of fluctuating opinion. Those, therefore, who to the study of philosophy unite obedience to the Christian faith are philosophers indeed; for the splendor of the divine truths,

---

[22] *Epist. ad Magnum,* 2 (PL 22, 666).
[23] Bulla *Apostolici regiminis.*
[24] *Epist.* 143 *(al. 7), ad Marcelin.,* 7 (PL 33, 589).

received into the mind, helps the understanding, and not only detracts in nowise from its dignity, but adds greatly to its nobility, keenness, and stability. For surely that is a worthy and most useful exercise of reason when men give their minds to disproving those things which are repugnant to faith and proving the things which conform to faith. In the first case they cut the ground from under the feet of error and expose the viciousness of the arguments on which error rests; while in the second case they make themselves masters of weighty reasons for the sound demonstration of truth and the satisfactory instruction of any reasonable person. Whoever denies that such study and practice tend to add to the resources and expand the faculties of the mind must necessarily and absurdly hold that the mind gains nothing from discriminating between the true and the false. Justly, therefore, does the Vatican Council commemorate in these words the great benefits which faith has conferred upon reason: *Faith frees and saves reason from error, and endows it with manifold knowledge.* [25] A wise man, therefore, would not accuse faith and look upon it as opposed to reason and natural truths, but would rather offer heartfelt thanks to God, and sincerely rejoice that in the density of ignorance and in the flood-tide of error, holy faith, like a friendly star, shines down upon his path and points out to him the fair gate of truth beyond all danger of wandering.

If, venerable brethren, you open the history of philosophy, you will find all we have just said proved by experience. The philosophers of old who lacked the gift of faith, yet were esteemed so wise, fell into many appalling errors. You know how often among some truths they taught false and incongruous things; what vague and doubtful opinions they held concerning the nature of the Divinity, the first origin of things, the government of the world, the divine knowledge of the future, the cause and principle of evil, the ultimate end of man, eternal beatitude, concerning virtue and vice, and other matters, a true and certain knowledge of which is most necessary to the human race; while, on the other hand, the early Fathers and Doctors of the Church, who well understood that, according to the divine plan, the restorer of human science is Christ, who is the power and the wisdom of God, [26] *and in whom are hidden all the treasures of wisdom and knowledge,* [27] took up and investigated the books of the ancient philosophers, and compared their teachings with the doctrines of revelation, and, carefully sifting them, they cherished what was true and wise in them and amended or rejected all else. For as the all-seeing God against the cruelty of tyrants raised up mighty martyrs to the defense of the Church, men prodigal of their great lives, in like manner to false philosophers and heretics he opposed men of great wisdom, to defend, even by the aid of human reason, the treasure of revealed truths. Thus from the very first ages of the Church, Catholic doctrine has encountered a multitude of most bitter adversaries, who, deriding the Christian dogmas and institutions, maintained that there were many gods, that the material world never had a beginning or cause, and that the course of events was one of blind and fatal necessity, not regulated by the will of divine Providence.

But the learned men whom we call apologists speedily encountered these teachers of foolish doctrine, and, under the guidance of faith, found arguments in human

[25] *Const. Dogm. de Fid. Cath.,* c. 4.
[26] 1 Corinthians 1:24.
[27] Colossians 2:3.

wisdom also to prove that one God, who stands pre-eminent in every kind of perfection, is to be worshiped; that all things were created from nothing by his omnipotent power; that by his wisdom they flourish and serve each their own special purposes. Among these St. Justin Martyr claims the chief place. After having tried the most celebrated academies of the Greeks, he saw clearly, as he himself confesses, that he could only draw truths in their fullness from the doctrines of revelation. These he embraced with all the ardor of his soul, purged of calumny, courageously and fully defended before the Roman emperors, and reconciled with them not a few of the sayings of the Greek philosophers.

Quadratus also and Aristides, Hermias and Athenagoras, stood nobly forth in that time. Nor did Irenaeus, the invincible martyr and bishop of Lyons, win less glory in the same cause when, forcibly refuting the perverse opinions of the Orientals, the work of the Gnostics, scattered broadcast over the territories of the Roman Empire, he explained (according to Jerome) the origin of each heresy and in what philosophic source it took its rise.[28] But who knows not the disputations of Clement of Alexandria, which the same Jerome thus honorably commemorates: "What is there in them that is not learned, and what that is not of the very heart of philosophy?"[29] He himself, indeed, with marvelous versatility treated of many things of the greatest utility for preparing a history of philosophy, for the exercise of the dialectic art, and for showing the agreement between reason and faith. After him came Origen, who graced the chair of the school of Alexandria, and was most learned in the teachings of the Greeks and Orientals. He published many volumes, involving great labor, which were wonderfully adapted to explain the divine writings and illustrate the sacred dogmas; which, though, as they now stand, not altogether free from error, contain nevertheless a wealth of knowledge tending to the growth and advance of natural truths. Tertullian opposes heretics with the authority of the sacred writings; with the philosophers he changes his fence and disputes philosophically; but so learnedly and accurately did he confute them that he made bold to say, "Neither in science nor in schooling are we equals, as you imagine."[30] Arnobius, also, in his works against the pagans, and Lactantius in the divine *Institutions* especially, with equal eloquence and strength strenuously strive to move men to accept the dogmas and precepts of Catholic wisdom, not by philosophic juggling, after the fashion of the academics, but vanquishing them partly by their own arms, and partly by arguments drawn from the mutual contentions of the philosophers.[31] But the writings on the human soul, the divine attributes, and other questions of mighty moment which the great Athanasius and Chrysostom, the prince of orators, have left behind them are, by common consent, so supremely excellent that it seems scarcely anything could be added to their subtlety and fullness. And, not to cover too wide a range, we add to the number of the great men of whom mention has been made the names of Basil the Great and of the two Gregories, who, on going forth from Athens, that home of all learning, thoroughly equipped with all the harness of

[28] *Epist. ad Magnum,* 4 (PL 22, 667).
[29] Loc. cit.
[30] *Apologet.* 46 (PL 1, 573).
[31] *Inst.* vii, 7 (PL 6, 759).

philosophy, turned the wealth of knowledge which each had gathered up in a course of zealous study to the work of refuting heretics and preparing Christians.

But Augustine would seem to have wrested the palm from all. Of a most powerful genius and thoroughly saturated with sacred and profane learning, with the loftiest faith and with equal knowledge, he combated most vigorously all the errors of his age. What height of philosophy did he not reach? What region of it did he not diligently explore, either in expounding the loftiest mysteries of the faith to the faithful, or defending them against the fell onslaught of adversaries, or again when, in demolishing the fables of the academics or the Manichaeans, he laid the safe foundations and sure structure of human science, or followed up the reason, origin, and causes of the evils that afflict man? How subtly he reasoned on the angels, the soul, the human mind, the will and free choice, on religion and the life of the blessed, on time and eternity, and even on the very nature of changeable bodies! Afterwards, in the East, John Damascene, treading in the footsteps of Basil and of Gregory Nazianzen, and in the West Boethius and Anselm, following the doctrines of Augustine, added largely to the patrimony of philosophy.

Later on the doctors of the middle ages, who are called scholastics, addressed themselves to a great work—that of diligently collecting and sifting and storing up, as it were, in one place, for the use and convenience of posterity, the rich and fertile harvests of Christian learning scattered abroad in the voluminous works of the Holy Fathers. And with regard, venerable brethren, to the origin, drift, and excellence of this scholastic learning, it may be well here to speak more fully in the words of one of the wisest of our predecessors, Sixtus V: "By the divine favor of him who alone gives the spirit of science, and wisdom, and understanding, and who through all ages, as there may be need, enriches his Church with new blessings and strengthens it with new safeguards, there was founded by our fathers, men of eminent wisdom, the scholastic theology, which two glorious doctors in particular, the angelic St. Thomas and the seraphic St. Bonaventure, illustrious teachers of this faculty, . . . with surpassing genius, by unwearied diligence, and at the cost of long labors and vigils, set in order and beautified, and, when skillfully arranged and clearly explained in a variety of ways, handed down to posterity.

"And, indeed, the knowledge and use of so salutary a science, which flows from the fertilizing founts of the sacred writings, the Sovereign Pontiffs, the Holy Fathers and the councils, must always be of the greatest assistance to the Church, whether with the view of really and soundly understanding and interpreting the Scriptures, or more safely and to better purpose reading and explaining the Fathers, or for exposing and refuting the various errors and heresies; and in these late days, when those dangerous times described by the Apostle are already upon us, when the blasphemers, the proud, and the seducers go from bad to worse, erring themselves and causing others to err, there is surely a very great need of confirming the dogmas of the Catholic faith and confuting heresies."

Although these words seem to bear reference solely to scholastic theology, nevertheless they may plainly be accepted as equally true of philosophy and its praises. For the noble endowments which make the scholastic theology so formidable to the enemies of truth—to wit, as the same Pontiff adds, "that ready and close coherence of cause and effect, that order and array as of a disciplined army in battle, those clear definitions and distinctions, that strength of argument and those keen discussions, by which light is distinguished from darkness, the true from the false, expose and strip naked, as it were, the falsehoods of heretics wrapped around by a cloud of subterfuges and fallacies"[32]—those noble and admirable endowments, we say, are only to be found in a right use of that philosophy which the scholastic teachers have been accustomed carefully and prudently to make use of even in theological disputations. Moreover, since it is the proper and special office of the scholastic theologians to bind together by the fastest chain human and divine science, surely the theology in which they excelled would not have gained such honor and commendation among men if they had made use of a lame and imperfect or vain philosophy.

Among the scholastic doctors, the chief and master of all towers Thomas Aquinas, who, as Cajetan observes, because "he most venerated the ancient doctors of the Church, in a certain way seems to have inherited the intellect of all."[33] The doctrines of those illustrious men, like the scattered members of a body, Thomas collected together and cemented, distributed in wonderful order, and so increased with important additions that he is rightly esteemed the special bulwark and glory of the Catholic faith. With his spirit at once humble and swift, his memory ready and tenacious, his life spotless throughout, a lover of truth for its own sake, richly endowed with human and divine science, like the sun he heated the world with the ardor of his virtues and filled it with the splendor of his teaching. Philosophy has no part which he did not touch finely at once and thoroughly; on the laws of reasoning, on God and incorporeal substances, on man and other sensible things, on human actions and their principles, he reasoned in such a manner that in him there is wanting neither a full array of questions, nor an apt disposal of the various parts, nor the best method of proceeding, nor soundness of principles or strength of argument, nor clearness and elegance of style, nor a facility for explaining what is abstruse.

Moreover, the Angelic Doctor pushed his philosophic conclusions into the reasons and principles of the things which are most comprehensive and contain in their bosom, so to say, the seeds of almost infinite truths, to be unfolded in good time by later masters and with a goodly yield. And as he also used this philosophic method in the refutation of error, he won this title to distinction for himself: that single-handed he victoriously combated the errors of former times, and supplied invincible arms to put those to rout which might in after-times spring up. Again, clearly distinguishing, as is fitting, reason from faith, while happily associating the one with the other, he both preserved the rights and had regard for the dignity of each; so much so, indeed, that reason, borne on the wings of Thomas to its human height, can scarcely rise higher, while faith could scarcely expect more or stronger aids from reason than those which she has already obtained through Thomas.

For these reasons learned men, in former ages especially, of the highest repute in theology and philosophy, after mastering with infinite pains the immortal works of Thomas, gave themselves up not so much to be instructed in his angelic wisdom as to be

[32] Bulla *Triumphantis* an. 1588.
[33] *In 2m. 2ae.,* q. 148, a. 4; Leonine ed. Vol. X, n. 6, p. 174.

nourished upon it. It is known that nearly all the founders and framers of laws of the religious orders commanded their associates to study and religiously adhere to the teachings of St. Thomas, fearful lest any of them should swerve even in the slightest degree from the footsteps of so great a man. To say nothing of the family of St. Dominic, which rightly claims this great teacher for its own glory, the statutes of the Benedictines, the Carmelites, the Augustinians, the Society of Jesus, and many others, all testify that they are bound by this law.

And here how pleasantly one's thoughts fly back to those celebrated schools and academies which flourished of old in Europe, to Paris, Salamanca, Alcala, to Douay, Toulouse, and Louvain, to Padua and Bologna, to Naples and Coimbra, and to many another! All know how the fame of these seats of learning grew with their years, and that their judgment, often asked in matters of grave moment, held great weight everywhere. And we know how in those great homes of human wisdom, as in his own kingdom, Thomas reigned supreme; and that the minds of all, of teachers as well as of taught, rested in wonderful harmony under the shield and authority of the Angelic Doctor.

But, furthermore, our predecessors in the Roman pontificate have celebrated the wisdom of Thomas Aquinas by exceptional tributes of praise and the most ample testimonials. Clement VI in the Bull *In Ordine,* Nicholas V in his Brief to the Friars of the Order of Preachers, 1451, Benedict XIII in the Bull *Pretiosus,* and others bear witness that the universal Church borrows luster from his admirable teaching; while St. Pius V declares in the Bull *Mirabilis* that heresies, confounded and convicted by the same teaching, were dissipated, and the whole world daily freed from fatal errors; others, such as Clement XII in the Bull *Verbo Dei,* affirm that most fruitful blessings have spread abroad from his writings over the whole Church, and that he is worthy of the honor which is bestowed on the greatest doctors of the Church, on Gregory and Ambrose, Augustine and Jerome; while others have not hesitated to propose St. Thomas for the exemplar and master of the academies and great lyceums, whom they may follow with unfaltering feet. On which point the words of Blessed Urban V to the Academy of Toulouse are worthy to recall: "It is our will, which we hereby enjoin upon you, that you follow the teaching of Blessed Thomas as the true and Catholic doctrine, and that you labor with all your force to profit by the same."[34] Innocent XII in the Letter in the form of a Brief addressed on February 6, 1694, to the University of Louvain, followed the example of Urban in the case of the University of Louvain, and Benedict XIV in the Letter in the form of a Brief addressed on August 26, 1752, to the Dionysian College of Granada; while to these judgments of great Pontiffs on Thomas Aquinas comes the crowning testimony of Innocent VI: "His teaching above that of others, the canons alone excepted, enjoys such an elegance of phraseology, a method of statement, a truth of proposition, that those who hold to it are never found swerving from the path of truth, and he who dare assail it will always be suspected of error."[35]

The ecumenical councils also, where blossoms the flower of all earthly wisdom, have always been careful to hold Thomas Aquinas in singular honor. In the councils of Lyons, Vienne, Florence, and the Vatican one might almost say that Thomas took part

[34] *Const.* a. dat. die Aug. 3, 1368 ad Concell. Univ. Tolo.
[35] *Serm. de S. Thoma.*

and presided over the deliberations and decrees of the Fathers, contending against the errors of the Greeks, of heretics and rationalists, with invincible force and with the happiest results. But the chief and special glory of Thomas, one which he has shared with none of the Catholic doctors, is that the Fathers of Trent made it part of the order of the conclave to lay upon the altar, together with the code of Sacred Scripture and the decrees of the Supreme Pontiffs, the *Summa* of Thomas Aquinas, whence to seek counsel, reason, and inspiration.

A last triumph was reserved for this incomparable man—namely, to compel the homage, praise, and admiration of even the very enemies of the Catholic name. For it has come to light that there were not lacking among the leaders of heretical sects some who openly declared that, if the teaching of Thomas Aquinas were only taken away, they could easily battle with all Catholic teachers, gain the victory, and abolish the Church.[36] A vain hope indeed, but no vain testimony.

Therefore, venerable brethren, as often as we contemplate the good, the force, and the singular advantages to be derived from this system of philosophy which our Fathers so dearly loved, we think it hazardous that its special honor should not always and everywhere remain, especially when it is established that daily experience, and the judgment of the greatest men, and, to crown all, the voice of the Church, have favored the scholastic philosophy. Moreover, to the old teaching a novel system of philosophy has succeeded here and there, in which we fail to perceive those desirable and wholesome fruits which the Church and civil society itself would prefer. For it pleased the struggling innovators of the sixteenth century to philosophize without any respect for faith, the power of inventing in accordance with his own pleasure and bent being asked and given in turn by each one. Hence it was natural that systems of philosophy multiplied beyond measure, and conclusions differing and clashing one with another arose even about those matters which are the most important in human knowledge. From a mass of conclusions men often come to wavering and doubt; and who knows not how easily the mind slips from doubt to error? But as men are apt to follow the lead given them, this new pursuit seems to have caught the souls of certain Catholic philosophers, who, throwing aside the patrimony of ancient wisdom, chose rather to build up a new edifice than to strengthen and complete the old by the aid of the new—ill advisedly, in sooth, and not without detriment to the sciences. For a multiform system of this kind, which depends on the authority and choice of any professor, has a foundation open to change, and consequently gives us a philosophy not firm and stable and robust like that of old, but tottering and feeble. And if perchance it sometimes finds itself scarcely equal to sustain the shock of its foes, it should recognize that the cause and the blame lie in itself. In saying this we have no intention of discountenancing the learned and able men who bring their industry and erudition, and, what is more, the wealth of new discoveries, to the service of philosophy; for, of course, we understand that this tends to the development of learning. But one should be very careful lest all or his chief labor be exhausted in these pursuits and in mere erudition. And the same thing is true of sacred theology, which, indeed, may be assisted and illustrated by all kinds of erudition, though it is absolutely necessary to approach it

[36] Bucer.

in the grave manner of the scholastics, in order that, the forces of revelation and reason being united in it, it may continue to be "the invincible bulwark of the faith."[37]

With wise forethought, therefore, not a few of the advocates of philosophical studies, when turning their minds recently to the practical reform of philosophy, aimed and aim at restoring the renowned teaching of Thomas Aquinas and winning it back to its ancient beauty.

We have learned with great joy that many members of your order, venerable brethren, have taken this plan to heart; and while we earnestly commend their efforts, we exhort them to hold fast to their purpose, and remind each and all of you that our first and most cherished idea is that you should all furnish a generous and copious supply to studious youth of those crystal rills of wisdom flowing in a never-ending and fertilizing stream from the fountainhead of the Angelic Doctor.

Many are the reasons why we are so desirous of this. In the first place, then, since in the tempest that is on us the Christian faith is being constantly assailed by the machinations and craft of a certain false wisdom, all youths, but especially those who are the growing hope of the Church, should be nourished on the strong and robust food of doctrine, that so, mighty in strength and armed at all points, they may become habituated to advance the cause of religion with force and judgment, *being ready always,* according to the apostolic counsel, *to satisfy every one that asks you a reason of that hope which is in you,*[38] and that they may be able to exhort in sound doctrine and to convince the gainsayers.[39] Many of those who, with minds alienated from the faith, hate Catholic institutions, claim reason as their sole mistress and guide. Now, we think that, apart from the supernatural help of God, nothing is better calculated to heal those minds and to bring them into favor with the Catholic faith than the solid doctrine of the Fathers and the scholastics, who so clearly and forcibly demonstrate the firm foundations of the faith, its divine origin, its certain truth, the arguments that sustain it, the benefits it has conferred on the human race, and its perfect accord with reason, in a manner to satisfy completely minds open to persuasion, however unwilling and repugnant.

Domestic and civil society even, which, as all see, is exposed to great danger from this plague of perverse opinions, would certainly enjoy a far more peaceful and secure existence if a more wholesome doctrine were taught in the academies and schools—one more in conformity with the teaching of the Church, such as is contained in the works of Thomas Aquinas.

For the teachings of Thomas on the true meaning of liberty, which at this time is running into license, on the divine origin of all authority, on laws and their force, on the paternal and just rule of princes, on obedience to the higher powers, on mutual charity one towards another—on all of these and kindred subjects have very great and invincible force to overturn those principles of the new order which are well known to be dangerous to the peaceful order of things and to public safety. In short, all studies ought to find hope of advancement and promise of assistance in this restoration of philosophic discipline which we have proposed. The arts were wont to draw from

[37] Sixtus V. Bulla *Triumphantis.*
[38] 1 Pet 3:15.
[39] Titus 1:9.

philosophy, as from a wise mistress, sound judgment and right method, and from it also
their spirit as from the common fount of life. When philosophy stood stainless in honor
and wise in judgment, then, as facts and constant experience showed, the liberal arts
flourished as never before or since; but, neglected and almost blotted out, they lay
prone since philosophy began to lean to error and join hands with folly. Nor will the
physical sciences, which are now in such great repute, and by the renown of so many
inventions draw such universal admiration to themselves, suffer detriment but find very
great assistance in the re-establishment of the ancient philosophy. For the investigation
of facts and the contemplation of nature is not alone sufficient for their profitable
exercise and advance; but when facts have been established it is necessary to rise and
apply ourselves to the study of the nature of corporeal things, to inquire into the laws
which govern them and the principles whence their order and varied unity and mutual
attraction in diversity arise. To such investigations it is wonderful what force and light
and aid the scholastic philosophy, if judiciously taught, would bring.

     And here it is well to note that our philosophy can only by the grossest injustice
be accused of being opposed to the advance and development of natural science. For
when the scholastics, following the opinion of the holy Fathers, always held in
anthropology that the human intelligence is led to the knowledge of things without
body and matter only by things sensible, they readily understood that nothing was of
greater use to the philosopher than diligently to search into the mysteries of nature and
to be devoted with assiduous patience to the study of physical things. And this they
confirmed by their own example; for St. Thomas, Blessed Albertus Magnus, and other
leaders of the scholastics were never so wholly rapt in the study of philosophy as not to
give large attention to the knowledge of natural things; and, indeed, the number of
their sayings and writings on these subjects, which recent professors approve of and
admit to harmonize with truth, is by no means small. Moreover, in this very age many
illustrious professors of the physical sciences openly testify that between certain and
accepted conclusions of modern physics and the philosophic principles of the schools
there is no conflict worthy of the name.

     While, therefore, we hold that every word of wisdom, every useful thing by
whomsoever discovered or planned, ought to be received with a willing and grateful
mind, we exhort you, venerable brethren, in all earnestness to restore the golden
wisdom of St. Thomas, and to spread it far and wide for the defense and beauty of the
Catholic faith, for the good of society, and for the advantage of all the sciences. The
wisdom of St. Thomas, we say; for if anything is taken up with too great subtlety by
the scholastic doctors, or too carelessly stated—if there be anything that ill agrees with
the discoveries of a later age, or, in a word, improbable in whatever way, it does not
enter our mind to propose that for imitation to our age. Let carefully selected teachers
endeavor to implant the doctrine of Thomas Aquinas in the minds of the students, and
set forth clearly his solidity and excellence over others. Let the academies already
founded or to be founded by you illustrate and defend this doctrine, and use it for the
refutation of prevailing errors. But, lest the false for the true, or the corrupt for the pure
be drunk in, be watchful that the doctrine of Thomas be drawn from his own
fountains, or at least from those rivulets which, derived from the very fount, have thus

far flowed, according to the established agreement of learned men, pure and clear; be careful to guard the minds of youth from those which are said to flow thence, but in reality are gathered from strange and unwholesome streams.

But well do we know that vain will be our efforts unless, venerable brethren, he helps our common cause who, in the words of divine Scripture, is called the God of all knowledge;[40] by which we are also admonished that *every best gift and every perfect gift is from above, coming down from the Father of lights;*[41] and again: *If any of you want wisdom, let him ask of God, who gives to all men abundantly, and upbraids not; and it shall be given him.*[42]

Therefore in this also let us follow the example of the Angelic Doctor, who never gave himself to reading or writing without first begging the blessing of God; who modestly confessed that whatever he knew he had aquired not so much by his own study and labor as by the divine gift. And therefore let us all, in humble and united prayer, beseech God to send forth the spirit of knowledge and of understanding to the children of the Church, and open their senses for the understanding of wisdom. And that we may receive fuller fruits of the divine goodness, offer up to God the most efficacious patronage of the Blessed Virgin Mary, who is called the seat of wisdom; having at the same time as advocates St. Joseph, the most chaste spouse of the Virgin, and Peter and Paul, the chiefs of the apostles, whose truth renewed the earth, which had fallen under the impure blight of error, filling it with the light of heavenly wisdom.

In fine, relying on the divine assistance and confiding in your pastoral zeal, we bestow on all of you, venerable brethren, on all the clergy and the flocks committed to your charge, the apostolic benediction as a pledge of heavenly gifts and a token of our special esteem.

> — *Aeterni Patris,* Aug. 4, 1879. Printed by Daughters of St. Paul, Boston. This translation originally published in *The Catholic World* in 1879.

[40] 1 Kings 2:3.
[41] James 1:17.
[42] James 1:5.

Étienne Gilson

This excerpt from Gilson's book God and Philosophy *consists of the whole chapter entitled "God and Contemporary Thought".*

GOD AND CONTEMPORARY THOUGHT

The present-day position of the problem of God is wholly dominated by the thought of Immanuel Kant and of Auguste Comte. Their doctrines are about as widely different as two philosophical doctrines can possibly be. Yet the Criticism of Kant and the Positivism of Comte have this in common, that in both doctrines the notion of knowledge is reduced to that of scientific knowledge, and the notion of scientific knowledge itself to the type of intelligibility provided by the physics of Newton. The verb "to know" then means to express observable relations between given facts in terms of mathematical relations.[1] Now, however we look at it, no given fact answers to our notion of God. Since God is not an object of empirical knowledge, we have no concept of him. Consequently God is no object of knowledge, and what we call natural theology is just idle talking.

If we compare it with the Kantian revolution, the Cartesian revolution hardly deserved such a name. From Thomas Aquinas to Descartes the distance is assuredly a long one. Yet, although extremely far from each other, they are on comparable lines of thought. Between Kant and them, the line has been broken. Coming after the Greeks, the Christian philosophers had asked themselves the question: How obtain from Greek metaphysics an answer to the problems raised by the Christian God? After centuries of patient work, one of them had at last found the answer, and that is why we find Thomas Aquinas constantly using the language of Aristotle in order to say Christian things. Coming after the Christian philosophers, Descartes, Leibniz, Malebranche, and Spinoza found themselves confronted with this new problem: How find a metaphysical justification for the world of seventeenth-century science? As scientists, Descartes and Leibniz had no metaphysics of their own. Just as Augustine and Thomas Aquinas had had to borrow their technique from the Greeks, Descartes and Leibniz had to borrow their technique from the Christian philosophers who had preceded them. Hence the vast number of scholastic expressions which we meet in the works of Descartes, Leibniz, Spinoza, and even Locke. All of them freely use the language of the Schoolmen in order to express nonscholastic views of a nonscholastic world. Yet all of them appear to us as seeking in a more or less traditional metaphysics the ultimate justification of the mechanical world of modern science. In short, and this is true of Newton himself, the

---

[1] For a general introduction to the criticism of metaphysics by Kant and Comte, see É. Gilson, *The Unity of Philosophical Experience* (New York: Scribner, 1937), Part III, pp. 228–95.

supreme principle of the intelligibility of nature remains, for all of them, the Author of Nature, that is, God.[2]

With the Criticism of Kant and the Positivism of Comte, things become entirely different. Since God is not an object apprehended in the a priori forms of sensibility, space and time, he cannot be related to anything else by the category of causality. Hence, Kant concludes, God may well be a pure idea of reason, that is, a general principle of unification of our cognitions; he is not an object of cognition. Or we may have to posit his existence as required by the exigencies of practical reason; the existence of God then becomes a postulate, it is still not a cognition. In his own way, which was a much more radical one, Comte at once reached identically the same conclusion. Science, Comte says, has no use for the notion of cause. Scientists never ask themselves *why* things happen, but *how* they happen. Now as soon as you substitute the positivist's notion of relation for the metaphysical notion of cause, you at once lose all right to wonder *why* things are, and why they are what they are. To dismiss all such questions as irrelevant to the order of positive knowledge is, at the same time, to cut the very root of all speculation concerning the nature and existence of God.

It had taken Christian thinkers thirteen centuries to achieve a perfectly consistent philosophy of the universe of Christianity. It has taken modern scientists about two centuries to achieve a perfectly consistent philosophy of the mechanical universe of modern science. This is a fact which it is very important for us to realize, because it clearly shows where the pure philosophical positions are actually to be found.

If what we are after is a rational interpretation of the world of science given as an ultimate fact, either the Criticism of Kant himself or some edition of his Criticism revised to suit the demands of today's science should provide us with a satisfactory answer to our question. We might nevertheless prefer the Positivism of Comte, or some revised edition of it. A large number among our own contemporaries actually subscribe to one or the other of these two possible attitudes. The Neo-Criticism has been represented by such men as Paulsen and Vaihinger in Germany, by Renouvier in France; and it has found what will perhaps remain its purest formulation in the works of our own contemporary, Professor Leon Brunschvicg. As to Positivism, it has found important supporters in England, John Stuart Mill and Herbert Spencer, for instance; in France, Émile Littré, Émile Durkheim, and the whole French sociological school; and it has recently been revived, under a new form, by the Neo-Positivism of the Vienna school. Whatever their many differences, all these schools have at least this in common, that their ambition does not extend beyond achieving a rational interpretation of the world of science given as an irreducible and ultimate fact.

But if we do not think that science is adequate to rational knowledge,[3] if we hold that other than scientifically answerable problems can still be rationally posed concerning the universe, then there is no use for us to stop at the eighteenth-century

[2] For a contemporary discussion of the scientific notion of cause, see Émile Meyerson, *Identité et réalité* (2d ed., Paris: Alcan, 1912), p. 42. *De l'explication dans les sciences* (Paris: Alcan, 1921), I, 57; *Essais* (Paris: J. Vrin, 1936), pp. 28–58.

[3] A critical discussion of this unduly restricted notion of rational knowledge is to be found in J. Maritain, *The Degrees of Knowledge* (New York: Scribner, 1938); and also in W. R. Thompson, F.R.S., *Science and Common Sense, an Aristotelian Excursion* (New York: Longmans, Green, 1937), pp. 47–50.

Author of Nature. Why should we content ourselves with the ghost of God when we can have God? But there is no reason either why we should waste our time in weighing the respective merits of the gods of Spinoza, of Leibniz, or of Descartes. We now know what these gods are: mere by-products born of the philosophical decomposition of the Christian living God. Today our only choice is not Kant or Descartes; it is rather Kant or Thomas Aquinas. All the other positions are but halfway houses on the roads which lead either to absolute religious agnosticism or to the natural theology of Christian metaphysics.[4]

Philosophical halfway houses have always been pretty crowded, but never more than they are in our own times, especially in the field of natural theology. This fact is not a wholly inexplicable one. What makes it difficult for us to go back to Thomas Aquinas is Kant. Modern men are held spellbound by science, in some cases because they know it, but in an incomparably larger number of cases because they know that, to those who know science, the problem of God does not appear susceptible of a scientific formulation. But what makes it difficult for us to go as far as Kant is, if not Thomas Aquinas himself, at least the whole order of facts which provides a basis for his own natural theology. Quite apart from any philosophical demonstration of the existence of God, there is such a thing as a spontaneous natural theology. A quasi-instinctive tendency, observable in most men, seems to invite them to wonder from time to time if, after all, there is not such an unseen being as the one we call God. The current objection that such a feeling is but a survival in us of primitive myths, or of our own early religious education, is not a very strong one. Primitive myths do not account for the human belief in the existence of the Divinity; obviously, it is the reverse which is true. Early religious education is no sufficient explanation for the questions which sometimes arise in the minds of men concerning the reality or unreality of God. Some among us have received a decidedly antireligious education; others have had no religious education at all; and there are even quite a few who, having once received a religious education, fail to find in its memory any incentive to think too seriously of God.[5] The natural invitations to apply his mind to the problem come to man from quite different sources. These are the very selfsame sources which once gave rise not only to Greek mythology but to all mythologies. God spontaneously offers himself to most of us, more as a confusedly felt presence than as an answer to any problem, when we find ourselves confronted with the vastness of the ocean, the still purity of mountains, or the mysterious life of a midsummer starry sky. Far from being social in essence, these fleeting temptations to think of God usually visit us in our moments of solitude. But there is no more solitary solitude than that of a man in deep sorrow or confronted with the tragic perspective of his own impending end. "One dies alone," Pascal says. That is perhaps the reason why so many men finally meet God waiting for them on the threshold of death.

What do such feelings prove? Absolutely nothing. They are not proofs but facts,

<hr />

[4] Cf. the philosophical manifesto of Rudolf Eucken, *Thomas von Aquino und Kant, ein Kampf zweier Welten* (Berlin: Reuther and Richard, 1901).

[5] Knowing the temptations to which historians sometimes succumb, I deem it safer to specify that there is nothing autobiographical in this last remark.

the very facts which give philosophers occasion to ask themselves precise questions concerning the possible existence of God. Just as such personal experiences precede any attempt to prove that there is a God, they survive our failures to prove it. Pascal did not make much of the so-called proofs of God's existence. To him, it was incomprehensible that God should exist, and it was incomprehensible that God should not exist; then he would simply wager that God exist—a safe betting indeed, since there was much to gain and nothing to lose. Thus to bet is not to know, especially in a case when, if we lose, we cannot even hope to know it. Yet Pascal was still willing to bet on what he could not know. Similarly, after proving in his *Critique of Pure Reason* that the existence of God could not be demonstrated, Kant still insisted on keeping God as at least a unifying idea in the order of speculative reason and as postulate in the moral order of practical reason. It may even appear to be true that, out of its own nature, the human mind is equally unable both to prove the existence of any God and "to escape its deep-seated instinct to personify its intellectual conceptions."[6] Whether we make it the result of spontaneous judgment of reason, with Thomas Aquinas; or an innate idea, with Descartes; or an intellectual intuition, with Malebranche; or an idea born of the unifying power of human reason, with Kant; or a phantasm of human imagination, with Thomas Henry Huxley, this common notion of God is there as a practically universal fact whose speculative value may well be disputed, but whose existence cannot be denied. The only problem is for us to determine the truth value of this notion.

At first sight, the shortest way to test it seems to judge it from the point of view of scientific knowledge. But the shortest way might not be the safest one. This method rests upon the assumption that nothing can be rationally known unless it be scientifically known, which is far from being an evident proposition. The names of Kant and of Comte have very little importance, if any, in the history of modern science; Descartes and Leibniz, two of the creators of modern science, have also been great metaphysicians. The simple truth may be that while human reason remains one and the same in dealing with different orders of problems, it nevertheless must approach these various orders of problems in as many different ways. Whatever our final answer to the problem of God may be, we all agree that God is not an empirically observable fact. Mystical experience itself is both unspeakable and intransmissible; hence, it cannot become an objective experience. If, speaking in the order of pure natural knowledge, the proposition "God exists" makes any sense at all, it must be for its rational value as a philosophical answer to a metaphysical question.

When a man falls to wondering whether there is such a being as God, he is not conscious of raising a scientific problem, or hoping to give it a scientific solution. Scientific problems are all related to the knowledge of *what* given things actually are. An ideal scientific explanation of the world would be an exhaustive rational explanation of *what* the world actually is; but *why* nature exists is not a scientific problem, because its answer is not susceptible of empirical verification. The notion of God, on the contrary, always appears to us in history as an answer to some existential problem, that is, as the *why* of a certain existence. The Greek gods were constantly invoked in

[6] Thomas Henry Huxley, *The Evolution of Theology: An Anthropological Study,* as quoted in Julian Huxley, *Essays in Popular Science* (London: Pelican Books, 1937), p. 123.

order to account for various "happenings" in the history of men as well as in that of things. A religious interpretation of nature never worries about what things are—that is a problem for scientists—but it is very much concerned with the questions why things happen to be precisely what they are, and why they happen to be at all. The Jewish-Christian God to whom we are introduced by the Bible is there at once posited as the ultimate explanation for the very existence of man, for the present condition of man upon earth, for all the successive events that make up the history of the Jewish people as well as for these momentous events: the Incarnation of Christ and the Redemption of man by Grace. Whatever their ultimate value, these are existential answers to existential questions. As such, they cannot possibly be transposed into terms of science, but only into terms of an existential metaphysics. Hence these two immediate consequences: that natural theology is in bondage not to the method of positive science but to the method of metaphysics, and that it can correctly ask its own problems only in the frame of an existential metaphysics.

Of these two conclusions, the first one is doomed to remain very unpopular. To tell the whole truth, it sounds perfectly absurd to say, and ridiculous to maintain, that the highest metaphysical problems in no way depend upon the answers given by science to its own questions. The most common view of this matter is best expressed by these words of a modern astronomer: "Before the philosophers have a right to speak, science ought first to be asked to tell all she can as to ascertain facts and provisional hypotheses. Then, and then only, may discussion legitimately pass into the realms of philosophy."[7] This, I quite agree, looks much more sensible than what I myself have said. But when people behave as if what I have said were false, what does happen? In 1696, John Toland decided to discuss religious problems by a method borrowed from natural philosophy. The result was his book, which I have already mentioned: *Christianity Not Mysterious*. Now, if Christianity is not mysterious, what is? In 1930, in his Rede Lecture delivered before the University of Cambridge, Sir James Jeans decided to deal with philosophical problems in the light of contemporary science. The upshot was his most popular book: *The Mysterious Universe*. Now, if the universe of science is mysterious, what is not? We do not need science to tell us that the universe is indeed mysterious. Men have known that since the very beginning of the human race. The true and proper function of science is, on the contrary, to make as much of the universe as possible grow less and less mysterious to us. Science does it, and she does it magnificently. Any sixteen-year-old boy, in any one of our schools, knows more today about the physical

---

[7] Sir James Jeans, *The Mysterious Universe* (London: Pelican Books, 1937), Foreword, p. vii. The relation of philosophy to science is curiously misunderstood by some scientists. It is true that "few in this age would willingly base their lives on a philosophy which to the man of science is demonstrably false". But it does not follow that "science thus takes the place of the foundation on which the structure of our lives must be built if we wish that structure to be stable". Arthur H. Compton, *The Religion of a Scientist* (New York: The Jewish Theological Seminary of America, 1938), p. 5. First of all, science itself is not stable. Secondly, from the fact that no set of propositions can be held as true if it contradicts another set of propositions that are demonstrably true, it does not follow that this second set of propositions must provide the foundation whereupon to establish our lives. It is quite possible, for instance, that the philosophical propositions whereupon we must establish our lives are quite independent of all conceivable sets of scientific propositions.

structure of the world than Thomas Aquinas, Aristotle, or Plato ever did. He can give rational explanations of phenomena which once appeared to the greatest minds as puzzling mysteries. The universe of science *qua* science exactly consists of that part of the total universe from which, owing to human reason, mysteries have been removed.

How is it, then, that a scientist can feel well founded in calling this universe a "mysterious universe"? Is it because the very progress of science brings him face to face with phenomena that are more and more difficult to observe and whose laws are more and more difficult to formulate? But the unknown is not necessarily a mystery; and science naturally proceeds upon the assumption that it is not, because it is at least knowable, even though we do not yet know it. The true reason why this universe appears to some scientists as mysterious is that, mistaking existential, that is, metaphysical, questions for scientific ones, they ask science to answer them. Naturally, they get no answers. Then they are puzzled, and they say that the universe is mysterious.

The scientific cosmogony of Sir James Jeans himself exhibits an instructive collection of such perplexities. His starting point is the actual existence of innumerable stars "wandering about space" at such enormous distances from one another "that it is an event of almost unimaginable rarity for a star to come anywhere near to another star." Yet, we must "believe" that "some two thousand million years ago, this rare event took place, and that a second star, wandering blindly through space," happened to come so near the sun that it raised a huge tidal wave on its surface. This mountainous wave finally exploded, and its fragments, still "circulating around their parent sun . . . are the planets, great and small, of which our earth is one." These ejected fragments of the sun gradually cooled; "in course of time, we know not how, when, or why, one of these cooling fragments gave birth to life." Hence, the emergence of a stream of life which has culminated in man. In a universe where empty space is deadly cold and most of the matter deadly hot, the emergence of life was highly improbable. Nevertheless, "into such a universe we have stumbled, if not exactly by mistake, at least as the result of what may properly be described as an accident." Such is, Sir James Jeans concludes, "the surprising manner in which, so far as science can at present inform us, we came into being."[8]

That all this is very mysterious everybody will agree, but the question then arises: Is this science? Even if we take them, as their author evidently does, for so many "provisional hypotheses," can we consider such hypotheses as being, in any sense of the word, scientific? Is it scientific to explain the existence of man by a series of accidents, each of which is more improbable than the other one? The truth of the case simply is that on the problem of the existence of man modern astronomy has strictly nothing to say. And the same conclusion holds good if, to modern astronomy, we add modern physics. When, after describing the physical world of Einstein, Heisenberg, Dirac, Lemaître, and Louis de Broglie, he at last takes a dive into what, this time at least, he knows to be "the deep waters" of metaphysics, what conclusion does Sir James Jeans ultimately reach? That although many scientists prefer the notion of a "cyclic universe, the more orthodox scientific view" is that this universe owes its present form to a "creation" and that "its creation must have been an act of thought."[9] Granted. But

[8] Sir James Jeans, op. cit., chap. i, pp. 11–22.
[9] Ibid., chap. v, p. 182.

what have these answers to do with Einstein, Heisenberg, and the justly famous galaxy of modern physicists? The two doctrines of a "cyclical universe" and of a supreme Thought were formulated by pre-Socratic philosophers who knew nothing of what Einstein would say twenty-six centuries after them. "Modern scientific theory," Jeans adds, "compels us to think of the creator as working outside time and space, which are part of his creation, just as the artist is outside his canvas."[10] Why should modern theory compel us to say what has already been said, not only by Saint Augustine, whom our scientist quotes, but by any and every one of countless Christian theologians who knew no other world than that of Ptolemy? Clearly enough, the philosophical answer of Sir James Jeans to the problem of the world order has absolutely nothing to do with modern science. And no wonder, since it has absolutely nothing to do with any scientific knowledge at all.

If we consider it more closely, the initial question asked by Jeans had taken him at once not only into deep waters but, scientifically speaking, out of soundings. To ask the question why, out of an infinity of possible combinations of physicochemical elements, there has arisen the living and thinking being we call man is to seek the cause why such a complex of physical energies as man actually is, or exists. In other words, it is to inquire into the possible causes for the *existence* of living and thinking organisms upon earth. The hypothesis that living substances may tomorrow be produced by biochemists in their laboratories is irrelevant to the question. If a chemist ever succeeds in turning out living cells, or some elementary sorts of organisms, nothing will be easier for him than to say why such organisms exist. His answer will be: I made them. Our own question is not at all: Are living and thinking beings made up of nothing else than physical elements? It rather is: Supposing they ultimately consist of nothing else, how can we account for the *existence* of the very order of molecules which produces what we call life, and thought?

Scientifically speaking, such problems do not make sense. If there were no living and thinking beings, there would be no science. Hence there would be no questions. Even the scientific universe of inorganic matter is a structural universe; as to the world of organic matter, it everywhere exhibits coördination, adaptation, functions. When asked why there are such organized beings, scientists answer: Chance. Now anybody may fluke a brilliant stroke at billiards; but when a billiard player makes a run of a hundred, to say that he fluked it is to offer a rather weak explanation. Some scientists know this so well that they substitute for the notion of chance the notion of mechanical laws, which is its very reverse. But when they come to explaining how these mechanical laws have given rise to living organized beings, they are driven back to chance as to the last reason it is possible to quote. "The powers operating in the cosmos," Julian Huxley says, "are, though unitary, yet subdivisible; and, though subdivisible, yet related. There are the vast powers of inorganic nature, neutral or hostile to man. Yet they gave birth to evolving life, whose development, though blind and fortuitous, has tended in the same general direction as our own conscious desires and ideals, and so gives us an external sanction for our directional activities. This again gave birth to human

---

[10] Ibid., chap. v, p. 188.

mind, which, in the race, is changing the course of evolution by acceleration,"[11] and so on, ad infinitum. In other words, the only scientific reasons why our billiard player makes a run of a hundred are that he cannot play billiards and that all the chances are against it.

If scientists, speaking as scientists, have no intelligible answer to this problem, why are some of them so keen on talking nonsense about it? The reason is simple, and this time we can be sure that chance has nothing to do with their obstinacy. They prefer to say anything rather than to ascribe existence to God on the ground that a purpose exists in the universe. Now there is some justification for their attitude. Just as science can play havoc with metaphysics, metaphysics can play havoc with science. Coming before science in the past, it has often done so to the point of preventing its rise and of blocking its development. For centuries final causes have been mistaken for scientific explanations by so many generations of philosophers that today many scientists still consider the fear of final causes as the beginning of scientific wisdom. Science is thus making metaphysics suffer for its centuries-long meddling in matters of physics and biology.

In both cases, however, the real victim of this epistemological strife is one and the same: the human mind. Nobody denies that living organisms appear as though they had been designed, or intended, to fulfill the various functions related to life. Everybody agrees that this appearance may be but an illusion. We would be bound to hold it for an illusion if science could account for the rise of life by its usual explanations of mechanical type, where nothing more is involved than the relations of observable phenomena according to the geometrical properties of space and the physical laws of motion. What is most remarkable, on the contrary, is that many scientists obstinately maintain the illusory character of this appearance though they freely acknowledge their failure to imagine any scientific explanation for the organic constitution of living beings. As soon as modern physics had reached the structural problems raised by molecular physics, it found itself confronted with such difficulties. Yet scientists much preferred to introduce into physics the nonmechanical notions of discontinuity and indeterminacy rather than resort to anything like design. On a much larger scale, we have seen Julian Huxley boldly account for the existence of organized bodies by those very properties of matter which, according to himself, make it infinitely improbable that such bodies should ever exist. Why should those eminently rational beings, the scientists, deliberately prefer to the simple notions of design, or purposiveness, in nature, the arbitrary notions of blind force, chance, emergence, sudden variation, and similar ones? Simply because they much prefer a complete absence of intelligibility to the presence of a nonscientific intelligibility.

We seem to be here reaching at last the very core of this epistemological problem. Unintelligible as they are, these arbitrary notions are at least homogeneous with a chain of mechanical interpretations. Posited at the beginning of such a chain, or inserted in it where they are needed, they provide the scientist with the very existences which he needs in order to have something to know. Their very irrationality is expressive of the

---

[11] Julian Huxley, "Rationalism and the Idea of God", in *Essays of a Biologist*, chap. vi (London: Pelican Books, 1939), p. 176. This "scientific" cosmogony strangely resembles the *Theogony* of Hesiod, where everything is successively begotten from original Chaos.

invincible resistance opposed by existence to any type of scientific explanation.[12] By accepting design, or purposiveness, as a possible principle of explanation, a scientist would introduce into his system of laws a ring wholly heterogeneous with the rest of the chain. He would intertwine the metaphysical causes for the existence of organisms with the physical causes which he must assign to both their structure and their functioning. Still worse, he might feel tempted to mistake the existential causes of living organisms for their efficient and physical causes, thus coming back to the good old times when fishes had fins because they had been made to swim. Now it may well be true that fishes have been made to swim, but when we know it we know just as much about fishes as we know about airplanes when we know that they are made to fly. If they had not been made to fly, there would be no airplanes, since to be flying-machines is their very definition; but it takes us at least two sciences, aerodynamics and mechanics, in order to know how they do fly. A final cause has posited an existence whose science alone can posit the laws.

This heterogeneity of these two orders was strikingly expressed by Francis Bacon, when he said, speaking of final causes, that "in physics, they are impertinent, and as remoras to the ship, that hinder the sciences from holding their course of improvement."[13] Their scientific sterility is particularly complete in a world like that of modern science, where essences have been reduced to mere phenomena, themselves reduced to the order of that which can be observed. Modern scientists live, or they pretend to live, in a world of mere appearances, where that which appears is the appearance of nothing. Yet the fact that final causes are scientifically sterile does not entail their disqualification as metaphysical causes, and to reject metaphysical answers to a problem just because they are not scientific is deliberately to maim the knowing power of the human mind. If the only intelligible way to explain the existence of organized bodies is to admit that there is design, purposiveness, at their origin, then let us admit it, if not as scientists, at least as metaphysicians. And since the notions of design and of purpose are for us inseparable from the notion of thought, to posit the existence of a thought as cause of the purposiveness of organized bodies is also to posit an end of all ends, or an ultimate end, that is, God.

It goes without saying that this is the very consequence which the adversaries of final causes intend to deny. "Purpose," Julian Huxley says, "is a psychological term; and to ascribe purpose to a process merely because its results are somewhat similar to those of a true purposeful process is completely unjustified, and a mere projection of our own ideas into the economy of nature."[14] This is most certainly what we do, but why should we not do so? We do not need to *project* our own ideas into the economy of

---

[12] The marked antipathy of modern science toward the notion of efficient cause is intimately related to the nonexistential character of scientific explanations. It is of the essence of an efficient cause that it makes something be, or exist. Since the relation of effect to cause is an existential and a nonanalytical one, it appears to the scientific mind as a sort of scandal which must be eliminated.

[13] Francis Bacon, *The Dignity and Advancement of Learning,* Bk. III, chap. iv, ed. J. E. Creighton (New York: The Colonial Press, 1900), p. 97. Cf. p. 98: "These final causes, however, are not false, or unworthy of inquiry in metaphysics, but their excursion into the limits of physical causes has made a great devastation in that province."

[14] Julian Huxley, op. cit., chap. vi, p. 173.

nature; they belong there in their own right. Our own ideas are in the economy of nature because we ourselves are in it. Any and every one of the things which a man does intelligently is done with a purpose and to a certain end which is the final cause why he does it. Whatever a worker, an engineer, an industrialist, a writer, or an artist makes is but the actualization, by intelligently selected means, of a certain end. There is no known example of a self-made machine spontaneously arising in virtue of the mechanical laws of matter. Through man, who is part and parcel of nature, purposiveness most certainly is part and parcel of nature. In what sense then is it arbitrary, knowing from within that where there is organization there always is a purpose, to conclude that there is a purpose wherever there is organization? I fully understand a scientist who turns down such an inference as wholly nonscientific. I also understand a scientist who tells me that, as a scientist, he has no business to draw any inference as to the possible cause why organized bodies actually exist. But I wholly fail to see in what sense my inference, if I choose to draw it, is "a common fallacy."

Why should there be a fallacy in inferring that there is purpose in the universe on the ground of biological progress? Because, Julian Huxley answers, this "can be shown to be as natural and inevitable a product of the struggle for existence as is adaptation, and to be no more mysterious than, for instance, the increase in effectiveness both of armour-piercing projectile and armour-plate during the last century."[15] Does Julian Huxley suggest that steel plates have spontaneously grown thicker as shells were growing heavier during the last century? In other words, does he maintain that purposiveness is as wholly absent from human industry as it is from the rest of the world? Or does he perhaps maintain that the rest of the world is as full of purposiveness as human industry obviously is? In the name of science he maintains both, namely, that adaptations in organisms are no more mysterious where there is no purposiveness to account for them, than is adaptation in human industry where purposiveness everywhere accounts for it. That adaptations due to a purpose*less* struggle for life are no more mysterious than adaptations due to a purpose*ful* struggle — whether this proposition is "a common fallacy," I do not know, but it certainly seems to be a fallacy. It is the fallacy of a scientist who, because he does not know how to ask metaphysical problems, obstinately refuses their correct metaphysical answers. In the *Inferno* of the world of knowledge, there is a special punishment for this sort of sin; it is the relapse into mythology. Better known as a distinguished zoologist, Julian Huxley must also be credited with having added the god Struggle to the already large family of the Olympians.[16]

A world which has lost the Christian God cannot but resemble a world which had not yet found him. Just like the world of Thales and of Plato, our own modern world is "full of gods." There are blind Evolution, clearsighted Orthogenesis, benevolent Progress, and others which it is more advisable not to mention by name. Why unnecessarily hurt the feelings of men who, today, render them a cult? It is however important for us to realize that mankind is doomed to live more and more under the spell of a new scientific, social, and political mythology, unless we resolutely exorcise

---

[15] Ibid., p. 172.

[16] On the philosophical difficulties entailed by this notion of evolution, see W. R. Thompson, *Science and Common Sense*, pp. 216–232.

these befuddled notions whose influence on modern life is becoming appalling. Millions of men are starving and bleeding to death because two or three of these pseudoscientific or pseudosocial deified abstractions are now at war. For when gods fight among themselves, men have to die. Could we not make an effort to realize that evolution is to be largely what we will make it to be? That Progress is not an automatically self-achieving law but something to be patiently achieved by the will of men? That Equality is not an actually given fact but an ideal to be progressively approached by means of justice? That Democracy is not the leading goddess of some societies but a magnificent promise to be fulfilled by all through their obstinate will for friendship, if they are strong enough to make it last for generations after generations?

I think we could, but a good deal of clear thinking should come first, and this is where, in spite of its proverbial helplessness, philosophy might be of some help. The trouble with so many of our contemporaries is not that they are agnostics but rather that they are misguided theologians. Real agnostics are exceedingly rare, and they harm nobody but themselves. Just as they have no God, these have no gods. Much more common, unfortunately, are those pseudo-agnostics who, because they combine scientific knowledge and social generosity with a complete lack of philosophical culture, substitute dangerous mythologies for the natural theology which they do not even understand.

The problem of final causes is perhaps the problem most commonly discussed by these modern agnostics. As such, it particularly recommended itself to our attention. It is nevertheless only one among the many aspects of the highest of all metaphysical problems, that of Being. Beyond the question: Why are there organized beings? lies this deeper one, which I am asking in Leibniz's own terms: Why is there something rather than nothing? Here again, I fully understand a scientist who refuses to ask it. He is welcome to tell me that the question does not make sense. Scientifically speaking, it does not.[17] Metaphysically speaking, however, it it does. Science can account for many things in the world; it may some day account for all that which the world of phenomena actually is. But why anything at all is, or exists, science knows not, precisely because it cannot even ask the question.

[17] The hostility exhibited by a wholly mathematized science toward the irreducible act of existence is what lies behind its opposition, so well marked by H. Bergson, to duration itself. Malebranche considered the existence of matter as indemonstrable; hence his conclusion that the annihilation of the material world by God would in no way affect our scientific knowledge of it. Sir Arthur Eddington would certainly not subscribe to Malebranche's metaphysics; but his own approach to the problem of existence is an epistemological one, namely, this particular body of knowledge which we call modern physics; hence the analogous consequence that, from such a point of view, "the question of attributing a mysterious property called *existence* to the physical universe never arises". *The Philosophy of Physical Science* (Cambridge: University Press, 1939), chap. x, pp. 156–7. As a substitute for the "metaphysical concept of *real existence*", Sir Arthur offers a "structural concept of existence", which he defines in pp. 162–6. In point of fact, there is a metaphysical concept of *being,* which is not "hazy" (p. 162), but analogical; as to actual existence, it is not an object of concept, but of judgment. To substitute "structural existence" for "real existence" is to be headed for the conclusion that "independent existence" is, for a given element, "its existence as a contributor to the structure", whereas its nonexistence is "a hole occurring in, or added to, the structure" (p. 165). In other words, the *independent* existence, or nonexistence, of an element is strictly dependent upon its whole. To exist is "to be a-contributor-to". Yet, in order to be a contributor to some whole, a thing has first to be; and to define the death of a man by the hole it creates in his family is to take a rather detached view of what appears to the dying man himself as an intensely individuated event.

To this supreme question, the only conceivable answer is that each and every particular existential energy, each and every particular existing thing, depends for its existence upon a pure Act of existence.[18] In order to be the ultimate answer to all existential problems, this supreme cause has to be absolute existence.[19] Being absolute, such a cause is self-sufficient; if it creates, its creative act must be free. Since it creates not only being but order, it must be something which at least eminently contains the only principle of order known to us in experience, namely, thought. Now an absolute, self-subsisting, and knowing cause is not an it but a he. In short, the first cause is the One in whom the cause of both nature and history coincide, a philosophical God who can also be the God of a religion.[20]

To go one step further would be to match the mistake of some agnostics with a similar one. The failure of too many metaphysicians to distinguish between philosophy and religion has proved no less harmful to natural theology than have the encroachments of pseudometaphysical science. Metaphysics posits God as a pure Act of existence, but it does not provide us with any concept of his essence. We know that he is; we do

[18] Sir Arthur Eddington complains that philosophers do nothing to make clear to "laymen" what the word "existence" means. *The Philosophy of Physical Science,* chap. x, pp. 154–7. As an example of its ambiguity, Sir Arthur quotes the judgment: There is an overdraft at the bank. Is an "overdraft at a bank" something that exists? The answer is: Yes, and no. The verbal form "is" has two distinct meanings, according as it designates: (1) the actual existence of a thing; (2) the composition of a predicate with a subject in a judgment. What exists at the bank, in sense number one, is a draft; but it is true, in sense number two, that "this draft is an overdraft". To say that "a draft is an overdraft", is by no means to say that an "overdraft" actually is, or exists.

[19] Some scientists, who still realize the value of the argument on the basis of design, would say that they do not feel "the need of a Creator to start the Universe". A. H. Compton, *The Religion of a Scientist,* p. 11. In other words, they do not realize that these two problems are identically the same. Design appears to them as a fact whose *existence* calls for an explanation. Why then should not the protons, electrons, neutrons, and photons be considered as facts whose *existence* also calls for some explanation? In what sense is the existence of these elements less mysterious than that of their composite? What prevents many scientists from going as far as to ask this second question is that, this time, they cannot fail to perceive the nonscientific character of the problem. Yet the nature of the two problems is the same. If the cause for the *existence* of organisms lies outside the nature of their physicochemical elements, it transcends the physical order; hence it is transphysical, that is, metaphysical, in its own right. In other words, if there is nothing in the elements to account for design, the presence of design in a chaos of elements entails just as necessarily a *creation* as the very existence of the elements.

[20] Dr. A. H. Compton is an interesting instance of those many scientists who do not seem to be aware of crossing any border lines when they pass from science to philosophy and from philosophy to religion. To them the "hypothesis God" is just one more of those "working hypotheses" which a scientist provisionally accepts as true in spite of the fact that none of them can be proved. Hence the consequence that "faith in God may be a thoroughly scientific attitude, even though we may be unable to establish the correctness of our belief". *The Religion of a Scientist,* p. 13. This is a regrettable confusion of language. It is true the principle of the conservation of energy and the notion of evolution are hypotheses; but they are *scientific* hypotheses because, according as we accept or reject them, our scientific interpretation of observable facts is bound to become different. The existence or nonexistence of God, on the contrary, is a proposition whose negation or affirmation determines no change whatever in the structure of our scientific explanation of the world and is wholly independent of the contents of science as such. Supposing, for instance, there be design in the world, the existence of God cannot be posited as a *scientific* explanation for the presence of design in the world; it is a *metaphysical* one; consequently, God has not to be posited as a *scientific probability* but as a *metaphysical necessity.*

not comprehend him. Simple-minded metaphysicians have unwillingly led agnostics to believe that the God of natural theology was the "watchmaker" of Voltaire, or the "carpenter" of cheap apologetics. First of all, no watch has ever been made by any watchmaker; "watchmakers" as such simply do not exist; watches are made by men who know how to make watches. Similarly, to posit God as the supreme cause of that which is, is to know that he is he who can create, because he is "he who is"; but this tells us still less concerning what absolute existence can be than any piece of carpentry tells us about the man who made it. Being men, we can affirm God only on anthropomorphic grounds, but this does not oblige us to posit him as an anthropomorphic God. As Saint Thomas Aquinas says:

> The verb *to be* is used in two different ways: in a first one, it signifies the act of existing (*actu essendi*); in the second one it signifies the composition of those propositions which the soul invents by joining a predicate with a subject. Taking *to be* in the first way, we cannot know the "to be" of God (*esse Dei*), no more than we know his essence. We know it in the second way only. For, indeed, we know that the proposition we are forming about God, when we say: God is, is a true proposition, and we know this from his effects.[21]

If such be the God of natural theology, true metaphysics does not culminate in a concept, be it that of Thought, of Good, of One, or of Substance. It does not even culminate in an essence, be it that of Being itself. Its last word is not *ens*, but *esse*; not *being*, but *is*. The ultimate effort of true metaphysics is to posit an Act by an act, that is, to posit by an act of judging the supreme Act of existing whose very essence, because it is to be, passes human understanding. Where a man's metaphysics comes to an end, his religion begins. But the only path which can lead him to the point where the true religion begins must of necessity lead him beyond the contemplation of essences, up to the very mystery of existence. This path is not very hard to find, but few are those who dare to follow it to the end. Seduced as they are by the intelligible beauty of science, many men lose all taste for metaphysics and religion. A few others, absorbed in the contemplation of some supreme cause, become aware that metaphysics and religion should ultimately meet, but they cannot tell how or where; hence they separate religion from philosophy, or else they renounce religion for philosophy, if they do not, like Pascal, renounce philosophy for religion. Why should not we keep truth, and keep it whole? It can be done. But only those can do it who realize that he who is the God of the philosophers is HE WHO IS, the God of Abraham, of Isaac, and of Jacob.

— From *God and Philosophy* (New Haven and London: Yale University Press, 1941), pp. 109–44.

---

[21] Saint Thomas Aquinas, *Summa theologiae,* I, 3, 4, ad 2ᵐ.

Dietrich Von Hildebrand

RELATIVISM

Ethical relativism is widespread. It is, unfortunately, the ruling moral philosophy of our age. The term "value" is generally employed now as something merely subjective. In speaking of values, one usually takes it for granted that there is general admission of their relative and subjective nature. . . .

The first type of ethical relativism is no more than a subdivision of general relativism or skepticism. As soon as someone denies that we are able to have any objectively valid knowledge, as soon as he argues that there exists no objective truth, he necessarily also denies the existence of any objective value. . . . The unconscious motive for general relativism is very often the desire to do away with an absolute ethical norm. At least deep unconscious resistance against the objectivity of truth frequently has its source in a type of pride which revolts primarily against objective values.

General relativism or skepticism, however, has been overwhelmingly refuted many times, beginning with Plato's *Gorgias* through St. Augustine's *Contra Academicos* (and most especially in his famous *Si fallor, sum* — "if I am mistaken, I am"),[1] through all the many classical *reductiones ad absurdum,* and last but not least in Edmund Husserl's *Logische Untersuchungen.*[2]

Whatever the formulation of the thesis denying the possibility of any objective knowledge or of attaining any objective truth, it is inevitably self-contradictory because in one and the same breath it denies that which it necessarily implies. In claiming to make an objectively true statement by declaring that we are unable to attain any objective truth, this position clearly contradicts itself. Or in other words, it claims to attain an objective truth in the statement that we can never attain an objective truth. . . .

The first well-known argument for ethical relativism (as opposed to general skepticism) appeals to the diversity of moral judgments which can be found in different peoples, cultural realms, and historical epochs. What is considered as morally good or morally evil, this view contends, differs according to peoples and historical ages. A Mohammedan considers polygamy morally justifiable. It does not occur to him to have any pangs of conscience in this respect. With an entirely good conscience he has different wives simultaneously. To a Christian this would seem immoral and impure. Of such diversity in judgments on what is morally good and what is evil, innumerable examples can be offered. Moreover this diversity of opinion concerning the moral color of something is to be found not only in comparing different peoples and epochs, but also in looking at the same epoch and even at the same individual at different times of his life.

Now this first argument for the relativity of moral values is based on an invalid syllogism. From the diversity of many moral judgments; from the fact that certain people hold a thing to be morally evil while other people believe the same thing to be

[1] *De Trinitate,* SV, 12–21; also *De Civitate Dei,* XI, 26.
[2] Edmund Husserl, "Critique of Specific Relativism" (Halle: M. Niemeyer, 1900), Pt. I, chap. 7, §36, pp. 116ff.

morally correct, it is inferred that moral values are relative, that there exists no moral good and evil, and that the entire moral question is tantamount to a superstition or a mere illusion.

In truth, a difference of opinion in no way proves that the object to which the opinion refers does not exist; or that it is in reality a mere semblance, changing for each individual or at least for different peoples. The fact that the Ptolemaic system was for centuries considered correct but is now superseded by our present scientific opinion is no justification for denying that the stars exist or even that our present opinion has only a relative validity.

There exist a great many fields in which can be found a diversity of opinion, among different peoples and in different epochs, and also among philosophers. Does this then confute the existence of objective truth? Not at all. The truth of a proposition does not depend upon how many people agree to it, but solely upon whether or not it is in conformity with reality.

Even if all men shared a certain opinion, it could still be wrong, and the fact that very few grasp a truth does not therefore alter or lessen its objective validity. Even the evidence of a truth is not equivalent to the fact that every man grasps and accepts it immediately. In like manner, it is erroneous to conclude that there exists no objective moral norm, that moral good and evil are in reality illusions or fictions or that at least their pretention to objective validity is an illusion, only because we find many different opinions concerning what is considered to be morally good and evil.

What matters is to see that in all these diversities the notion of an objective value, of a moral good and evil is always presupposed, even if there exist contradictory positions concerning the moral goodness of a certain attitude or action. And just as the meaning of objective truth is not touched by the fact that two persons hold opposite positions and each one claims his proposition to be true, so too the notion of moral good and evil, of something objectively valid which calls for obedience and appeals to our conscience, is always untouched, even if one man says that polygamy is evil and another that polygamy is morally permissible.

The distinction between something merely subjectively satisfying and advantageous for an egotistic interest on the one hand, and the morally good on the other hand, is always in some way implied.

... On the other hand, the fact that there have existed many more conflicting opinions concerning moral values, for instance, the moral character of polygamy or of blood revenge, than concerning colors or the size of corporeal things, can easily be understood as soon as we realize the moral requirements for a sound and integral value perception.

Without any doubt the perception of moral values differs in many respects from knowledge in any other field.... Reverence, a sincere thirst for truth, intellectual patience, and a spiritual subtlety are required in varying degrees for every adequate knowledge of any kind. But in the case of the moral value-perception much more is required: not only another degree of reverence or of opening our mind to the voice of being, a higher degree of "conspiring" with the object, but also a *readiness of our will* to conform to the call of values, whatever it may be. The influence of the environment, of the milieu, of the traditions of the community, in short the entire interpersonal atmosphere in which man grows up and lives, has a much greater influence on this type of knowledge than on any other. . . . The entire atmosphere is so saturated with this moral pattern that the conscious and unconscious influence on the individual is a tremendous one.

And this influence may cripple the capacity for value-perception. Thus it is not difficult to see how errors in this field are more widespread, expressing themselves in conflicting value-judgements in different tribes, peoples, cultural realms, and epochs. . . .

. . . How, moreover, will the moral relativists explain the fact that we often find great moral personalities piercing through the screen laid over morality by the customs and convictions of the environment and discovering parts at least of the true world of values? How do they account for the moral views of Socrates, of Zoroaster, and many others?

Once we have grasped the roots of moral value blindness, it will no longer be astonishing that there exist such diversities of value-judgments; rather we shall be astonished at how many agreements nevertheless exist among all tribes, epochs, and individuals. We must now cautiously examine the origins of this diversity in moral judgments.

In many cases the fact that one tribe in a certain historical age considered as morally evil the same thing which another tribe considered as morally good is due to a difference of opinion or belief concerning the *nature* of a thing, and not its value. If for a tribe certain animals are considered sacred (as, for example, the Egyptians considered the ox Apis to be holy), then to kill this animal assumes the character of something sacrilegious; whereas for one who is aware of the true nature of this animal, to kill it is not at all sacrilegious. . . . A sacrilegious action is in both cases considered to be morally evil. Thus there is no diversity concerning the disvalue of a sacrilegious action, but only concerning the fact as to whether something is believed to be sacred or not. . . .

Moral value is, as we saw before, such an ultimate datum that in order to grasp [it] in spite of all theoretical denials, a person constantly presupposes [it in] . . . his lived contact with reality.

[Ethical relativists] were full of indignation about Hitler's atrocities and racism, notwithstanding the fact that according to their theory there could be no basis for any indignation. Even if, in order to be consistent with their theories, they should deny that they were indignant, nevertheless at the first occasion in which for a moment they forgot their theory, they would be sincerely indignant. . . .

. . . Sometimes we find that those who are in rage against the notion of any objective norm and any objective value nevertheless strive against them in the name of "freedom," or "democracy"; and thereby they fully admit the character of the value of freedom or democracy. They do not speak of freedom as if it were something merely agreeable or as if they wanted it for personal reasons, but they speak of it as an "ideal" which itself implies the notion of value and even of morally relevant value. The entire ethos of those who fight against any objective norm belies the content of their theory. The pathos with which they condemn the attitude of the "dogmatists" is weighted with the pretention of fighting for the nobler cause. Whatever may be the point in which they tacitly admit an objective value and even a moral significance, whatever may be the "ideal" which they presuppose unawares, somewhere the notion of value and even of moral value must inevitably enter. Would they not look with contempt on a colleague who, eager to prove a theory, paid people for giving false testimony, or lied about the results of his experiments? Would they not blame a medical charlatan who foists fake medicines and cures on his unfortunate patients?

— From *Ethics* (Chicago: Franciscan Herald Press, 1953), pp. 106–16.

DUE RELATION

We have already examined the meaningful and deep relation between the value response and its object. . . .

An adequate response ought to be given to every value. . . . Indifference toward a value, an inadequate response, but still more a contrary response, constitute an objective disharmony. . . . We are aware of this disharmony when we hear a judgment about a work of art or a man of genius which does not do justice to the value involved; or still more when we observe somebody responding contemptuously to a personality deserving of veneration or responding with bored indifference to a great work of art.

It is because of this disharmony that we try to persuade other people to change their attitudes when we witness their wrong approach. . . . We try to persuade them, not because we want to impose our opinion on them, but because we have a clear consciousness of the objective interest involved in a true appreciation and adequate response to the value. . . . We ought not remain indifferent to and untouched by the value of an object, and more evidently as the value ranks higher. If someone remains untouched in witnessing a noble moral attitude, e.g., a heroic sacrifice, we clearly grasp the disharmony. Such a sight *ought* to affect the soul: that the soul should be touched is due the value. The liturgy is pervaded by the awareness that we ought to be affected by Christ's infinite love and moved to tears by the divine sacrifice of the God-Man on the Cross, as, for instance, in the (liturgy) of Good Friday. . . . Praise is due to God because he is God, because of his infinite goodness and sanctity. . . .

In every true value response an awareness of this ultimate due relation is implied. Whether it is an act of veneration, of love, of admiration, of esteem, or of enthusiasm, it is always accomplished in the knowledge that the response does not derive from our arbitrary mood, or from the appeal which the object has for us, but that this response is due the object. From this consciousness stems the note of humility and of objectivity which is proper to every value response.

. . . Saying that an adequate response is due every object possessing a value clearly differs from saying that the object *needs* a response.

This becomes especially clear if we think of the supreme value response, the one directed to God: adoring love and adoring praise. They are due God, but it would be nonsensical to say that God needs them.

— From *Ethics,* pp. 244–54.

MORAL CONSCIOUSNESS

There exists a difference between morally conscious and morally unconscious persons. In saying morally unconscious persons, we do not think of evil people who, being a prey of concupiscence or pride, are indifferent or even hostile toward values in general and toward moral values in particular. We are not thinking of the man who knows only one category of importance, the subjectively satisfying, who never asks or cares whether something is important-in-itself, and *a fortiori* never bothers about whether something is morally relevant or not. We are thinking of the type who lives in an indisputed solidarity with himself, and takes it for granted that one need only follow the trend of one's own nature. He may be goodhearted and grasp many values; he may be disposed to respond to them . . . but . . . he has not taken a conscious definitive position toward the basic moral problem. In him there is not this fundamental decision to tread the paths of rightness, to abstain from moral evil, to remain in harmony with moral goodness.

. . . [He may have a] naive general direction toward moral goodness . . . [but] what is considered to be immoral is more or less arbitrary. His natural disposition determines the frame of what is considered morally evil. . . .

Secondly, sometimes we find in morally unconscious persons a general intention to remain in conformity with the implicit ideal of the community or society in which they live. There are many people in whom exists an intention to be a decent man or a respectable man, or to behave like a gentleman. They shrink from seeing themselves as disrespectable, so that it does not matter much whether they want to stand the test before their self-esteem or before the esteem of other people. This general direction may be a powerful deterrent against criminal acts. . . . Yet this preoccupation of the loyal bourgeois to be decent clearly differs from the superactual will to be good of the morally conscious man. First, the conventional taint and, above all, the element of pride which is present in this attitude forbid us to speak of a real value response. . . .

The first type of morally *conscious* man is exemplified in the great figure of Socrates. Here we find a general basic will to be in harmony with the world of moral values, an always present general concern for the moral question, and the resulting attitude of approaching every situation and every value of concrete goods in the light of their possible moral significance. . . .

The second type of morally conscious man . . . is the man who wants above all to obey God and never to offend him, to walk in the paths of the Lord. Here the general will to be morally good assumes a still more definite character, since it is the outspoken response to God, the infinite goodness itself. (Caring for the needs of others becomes part of the desire to live for the goodness the Lord embodies.)

In the third type, for instance the saint, it is in the imitation of Christ that the will to be morally good reaches its highest and most sublime expression. Complete loving abandonment to Christ, one great preoccupation to act in the Spirit of Christ, to avoid anything which cannot stand the test of Christ, to follow him in everything—this lives in every value response to a morally relevant good and is thematic in every morally relevant situation which calls for a response in one way or another. Whether it is the health or the life of our neighbor which is at stake, or the rights of a man, or his moral integrity, whether it is the protection of an innocent person, the response is never made to this value exclusively, but always to Christ as well. . . . We find Christ and his voice in this good, in the suffering neighbor, in the morally endangered man, . . .

The justice and veracity of the saints are filled with a new splendour, a completely new depth and inner freedom. They exhale a new fragrance, they are transfigured by the *lumen Christi.*

— From *Ethics,* pp. 265–75.

Edith Stein

ON THE NATURE OF WOMAN

The vocation of man and woman is not quite the same in the original order, the order of fallen nature and the order of redemption. Originally they were both required to preserve their own similarity to God, their dominion over the earth and the preservation of the race. The superiority of man that seems implied in the fact that he was created first is not yet explained in detail. After their fall their relationship is changed from a pure communion of love to one of governing and subordination tainted by lust. The hard struggle for existence has been assigned primarily to man, the labour of birth to woman. But there is a promise of redemption, because woman is to fight evil, and the male sex will be exalted in the Son of Man who is to come. The Redemption will restore the original order. The superiority of man is revealed in the fact that the Saviour came into the world as man. The feminine sex is honoured in that he was born of a human mother. A woman becomes the gate through which God entered into the human race. Adam was the human type that pointed to the future divine-human king of creation, hence in the kingdom of God every man is to reproduce Christ, and in the community of marriage the loving care of Christ for the Church. The woman, being freely and lovingly subject to her husband, is to honour the image of Christ in him and to be herself the image of the Mother of God; and this also means being herself an image of Christ.

If we attempt to describe the nature of man and woman on the basis of natural knowledge, we shall receive a vivid interpretation of what the Word of God has suggested to us. On the other hand, this latter will be a guide by which to interpret the evidence of life. We shall find in it again the traces of the original order of creation, of the fall and of the redemption.

Man's body and mind are equipped for fight and conquest, in accordance with his original vocation to subject the world and be its king and master. Thus there is a threefold urge in him: he wants to subdue it by knowledge and thus to make it his own, but also to possess it with all the enjoyments it offers, and lastly to make it his own creation by forming it. It is due to the limitation of human nature, which it shares with every created thing, but even more to the deterioration of all his powers in the state of original sin, that man is unable to achieve in equal measure all that is implied in his dominion over the earth. If the desire for knowledge is strong in him and he uses all his energy to satisfy it, he will to a great extent be forced to renounce the possession and enjoyment of the good things of life as well as creative work. If he pursues riches and pleasure, he will hardly achieve pure (i.e., devoid of personal interests) knowledge and creative work. But if he is wholly intent on making a small world of his own creation, whether as a farmer, an artist or a politician etc., pure knowledge and the enjoyment of the good things of life will have to take the second place. And in each of these spheres the single achievement will be the more perfect, the more restricted the field of activity. Thus just the desire to produce as perfect a work as possible will lead to onesidedness and cause the other talents to atrophy.

Yet, for fallen nature the onesided effort can also easily become a perverted effort. Knowledge will not reverently stop at the barriers imposed on it, but will try to break them by violence. Moreover, knowledge itself may bar its own way to what is not on principle inaccessible to it, by refusing to bow to the law of things; instead it seeks to possess them arbitrarily, or lets its judgement be clouded by desires and lusts. The perversion of man's dominion has similar results with regard to the good things of the earth. Instead of reverently and joyfully preserving and developing created things, he greedily exploits them even unto destruction, or senselessly piles them up without being able to use them properly and to enjoy what he has acquired. Related to this is the perversion of creative work that violently distorts and destroys natural things and invents and creates grotesque caricatures.

This change of kingship into brutal tyranny shows itself also in man's relation to woman. According to the original order she was given him as a companion and helpmate. Hence she is equipped in the same way as he in order to assist him in dominating the earth: she, too, is capable of knowledge, enjoyment and creative work. But normally in her these gifts are less intense; thus, on the other hand, she is less in danger of being completely immersed in one of them to the detriment of the others. This indicates a form of co-operation in which the woman could develop her gifts by the side of man in their common tasks, while he would be preserved from becoming inordinately onesided by the more harmonious development of her gifts. But in the state of punishment after the fall this companionship was changed into a state of domination which is often brutally enforced. The natural gifts of a woman and their best possible development are irrelevant, and she is exploited as a means to an end in the service of a work or for the satisfaction of a man's desire. So it may easily come about that the tyrant becomes the slave of lust, and thus the slave of the slave who is to satisfy it.

The perversion of the relations between man and woman is connected with that of the attitude towards posterity. Procreation was originally meant to be the task of both. Since, owing to their differences, both depend on completing each other, this dependence is even more emphasized in their relationship to their children. On the one hand the undeveloped nature of the child makes it necessary to nurse and protect it and to guide its growth. Owing to the close physical relationship between mother and child and woman's special capacity for sharing and devoting herself to another's life, she will have the principal part in its education, which will also be helped by her stronger instinct for the harmonious development of human talents. On the other hand, the demands of motherhood make it imperative that man should protect and care for mother and child. Moreover, because he is more energetic and gifted for outstanding achievements, he has also a duty to instruct. And finally, because he is king of all creation, he has also to care for the noblest of all earthly creatures. Moreover, we have to consider also that not only man and woman have been created to complement each other, but also the generations that follow one another. For each subsequent generation is called to achieve something new of its own, and it is one of the essential tasks of education to observe reverently the new things that want to grow in the young generation. Thus fatherhood appears to be an original vocation of man, given to him beside his particular calling. The vocation of the father may be abused in many ways. On the one hand he may shun his duties, in the lowest form by abusing sexual intercourse for the mere satisfaction of his instincts, without giving any thought to his descendants, perhaps even at their cost. On a higher level he may indeed shoulder his material responsibilities, but neglect his share in their education. On the other hand there is the danger that a father will perform his duties brutally, restricting the mother's responsibilities to the merely physical sphere and depriving her of her higher tasks, while he himself violently represses all the legitimate aspirations of the new generation.

All weaknesses in man's nature that cause him to miss his original vocation are rooted in the perversion of his relation to God. He can only fulfil his principal task of being the image of God, if he seeks to develop his powers in humble submission to his guidance. He must seek knowledge in the form and within the limits sanctioned by God; he must enjoy God's creatures reverently and gratefully for his glory; he must do creative work in order to complete creation in the way God has assigned to man's free action. This would mean truly to be a finite image of the divine wisdom, goodness and power. If man says to God "I will not serve", his relation to all other creatures will be perverted. We have the exact parallel in the nature of woman. According to the original order her place is by the side of man to subdue the earth and bring up posterity. But her body and soul are less suited for fight and conquest, but rather for nursing, protecting and preserving. Of the threefold attitude to the world that consists in knowing, enjoying and creatively shaping, the second is usually best suited to her. She seems more capable than man of reverently enjoying creatures. (We would remark in passing that reverent enjoyment presupposes a specific knowledge of the good things that are enjoyed, which is different from rational knowledge, but is a peculiar spiritual function that is evidently a particular feminine gift.) This is evidently connected with her function of preserving and fostering posterity. It is a sense of the importance of the organic whole, of specific values and of individuals. This renders her sensitive and clear sighted for whatever wants to grow and develop and requires individual understanding. This sense of what is organic benefits not only her posterity but all other creatures, especially the opposite sex; it makes her an understanding companion and help in the enterprises of another. Hence, according to the original order of nature, man and woman evidently complement each other in this way: man's vocation is primarily to govern; his fatherhood is not subordinated to or co-ordinated with this, but included in it; whereas woman is primarily called to be a mother, her share in the government of the world being in some way implied in that.

Just as a woman's knowledge, enjoyment and action do not differ in principle from those of a man, the same forms of perversion appear in both. They are rooted in the desire to gain possession of things by violence and thus to spoil or even destroy them. The three functions just mentioned differ in importance and in the place they occupy in the whole personality and life of man and woman, hence the fall has brought about also different perversions in them. It has already been mentioned that women become one-sided and stunted in their personality less easily than men. On the other hand, the kind of onesidedness to which they are exposed is particularly dangerous. Since women are less gifted for abstract thought and creative action than for the possession and enjoyment of good things, there is the danger that they may become completely absorbed in these. If now the reverent joy in things is perverted into greed, a woman will on the one hand anxiously collect and preserve useless things, on the other sink into a life of sloth and self-indulgence. This in its turn will tend to corrupt her relationship with man. If their free companionship is threatened by his tendency to brutal despotism, she will become even more his slave by surrendering herself to her own instincts. On the other hand, her anxiety to preserve her property may also lead to a domineering attitude towards man. Her relation to her children shows similar characteristics. If a woman leads a merely sensual life she will seek to escape the duties of motherhood as much as the man those of fatherhood, unless she is preserved from this by an instinctive desire for children and an equally instinctive attachment. If a woman anxiously seeks to retain her children as if they were her property, she will try in every way to tie them to herself (also by curtailing as far as possible the rights of their father), and thus prevent their free development. By refusing to serve her husband, her children and all creatures in loving reverence, and so to further their natural development for God's honour and their natural happiness, she will prevent development and destroy happiness.

Again the root of the evil is the perversion of her relation to God. In the fall woman rebelled against God and exalted herself above man by corrupting him, therefore she was punished by being subjected to him. Because the sin to which she tempted him was very probably one of sensuality, woman is exposed more than man to the danger of succumbing entirely to a merely sensual life. And whenever this happens, she becomes once more the temptress, whereas she has expressly been commanded to fight against evil.

We have thus indicated how nature, and hence the original vocation of man and woman, can be realized: this is possible only if both once more become children of God. The redemptive work of Christ assures our adoption if we ourselves do what is in our power. The Israelites of the Old Covenant did what they were asked to do by faithfully following the Law and awaiting the Messias. For women this meant that they were humbly to be subject to men, to preserve their purity and to discipline their sensuality more strictly than men. They were to long for children in order to see in them God's salvation, and to bring them up faithfully in the fear of the Lord. Man, on the other hand, had to carry out the prescribed services of prayer and sacrifice, he had to obey the moral and social commandments, look after the well-being of his family and honour his wife as the mother of his children.

In the New Covenant man takes part in the work of redemption by the most intimate personal union with Christ; he clings to him by faith, because he is the way of salvation who has revealed the truth and offered the means to attain beatitude; by hope which confidently expects the life promised by him; and by love which seeks to approach him. This love will try to know him ever more clearly; it will contemplate his life and meditate his words and want to be united to him most intimately in the holy Eucharist. It will share his mystical life by following the Church's Year and its liturgy. This way of salvation is the same for both sexes; it redeems both, as well as their mutual relationship.

Redemption did not restore fallen nature to its original purity by one stroke.

Christ has placed salvation into the soil of mankind like a seed that must grow with the inner and outer growth of the Church and in every individual soul. Being "on the way" like pilgrims bound for the heavenly Jerusalem, we experience in ourselves the fight of corrupt nature with the germ of grace that wants to grow in us and strives and is able to expel whatever is unhealthy. All around us we see the fruits of original sin in its most frightening forms, especially in the relationship of the sexes. Every trace of their high vocation seems to be lost in a life of unfettered licentiousness; the sexes are fighting each other for their rights, deaf to the voice of nature and of God. Yet we also see that things can be different where grace is efficacious. In Christian marriage man sees his task of being the head of his small community in his duty to ensure as well as he can their material well-being and progress; he will contribute his share so that each member may become the best that nature and grace can make it. This means that he will at times have to come forward and give a lead, at others to remain in the background, or again to intervene and oppose. If inclinations and talents stir spontaneously in his wife and children, he will allow them to develop and give them all the help he can. If he has to do with weaker natures and gifts, if he notices a lack in courage and self-confidence, he will try to bring out the hidden talents. It is one of his duties to develop the intellectual and spiritual side in his wife, and not to let her be immersed in a mere life of the instincts. He may do this by permitting her to share in his own work, or by encouraging obvious tendencies to independent activity. If he takes both possibilities away from her, seeking to confine her to a circle that is too narrow for her gifts, or even only to a life of the instincts, he will have a large share in the consequences that will result from this. He will be responsible for the fact that her higher life will atrophy, for pathological disturbances and her tendency to become too strongly attached to her husband and children, which will be a burden to them, and, moreover, for the dreariness of her life once she is left to face it alone. The same holds good for her relation to her children. On the other hand it belongs to his duties as master of the house to look after the order and harmony of family life. It is part of this duty to exhort each member not only to look after the development of his own personality, but according to his position in the household, to practise consideration to others and the self-denial that his duties entail. And, finally, his concern for the well-ordered natural life of the individuals and the family should not lead him to neglect their supernatural life. A man is meant to imitate Christ as the Head of the Church in his own small circle. Therefore he should regard it as his highest duty to set them an example in following Christ and to further, to the best of his ability, the life of grace that is stirring in them. This he will achieve the better the more closely he himself is united to the Lord.

The domestic burden which these demands place on a man in addition to his professional duties outside his home would be too heavy for him if he were not assisted by the companion who is called to shoulder more than half of it. She wants not only to develop her own personality without hindrance, but desires the same for those around her. Thus her husband will find in her his best adviser not merely for the guidance of herself and their children, but also for his own life. Indeed, he will often be best able to fulfil his duties in this respect if he lets her do things in her own way and submits to her leadership. Care for the order and beauty of the whole household is also among the natural feminine duties, since all need a harmonious atmosphere for their proper development. The feminine nature is particularly receptive to what is morally good and loathes everything that is mean and vulgar. It is thus protected against the danger of temptation and of being submerged in a wholly sensual life; this is in harmony with the mysterious prophecy of a victorious fight of the woman against the serpent, which was fulfilled by the victory which the queen of all women had won on behalf of all mankind.

Closely connected with this is the feminine receptivity to divine things. A woman desires to be personally united to the Lord and to be wholly filled and guided by his love. In a rightly ordered family life, therefore, the moral and religious education will mostly be the task of the woman. If her life is completely anchored in the life of Jesus, this will be her best protection against the danger of losing the right measure in her love for her family and her surroundings; she will not cut the ground from under her feet, on which she has to stand to be a support for others. Independent objective interests of her own would in the natural sphere counterbalance this dangerous tendency to lose herself in another's life; but these alone would lead to the opposite danger of her being unfaithful to her feminine vocation. Only if she entrusts herself wholly to the guidance of the Lord will she be sure to be led safely between Scylla and Charybdis. For whatever is given to him is not lost, but will be preserved, purified, elevated and given the right measure.

These last suggestions lead to the question of a non-domestic profession and to the relationship of man and woman in the professional life. In view of the events of the last decades we may regard as closed that period of history which assigned to women only domestic duties, and to men the struggle of existence outside the home. Today it is not too difficult for us to see how this development could actually come about. The scientific and technical achievements which progressively replaced human labour by the work of the machine relieved women of many burdens, so that they desired to use the energies that had been released in other spheres. In the transition period much energy has been unreasonably wasted in useless trifles, and much valuable human talent has thus been frittered away. The efforts to bring about the necessary changes could not be successful without grave crises of development. On the one hand these were caused by the partisan passion of both pioneers of feminism and its opponents, either side fighting with arguments that lacked objectivity. On the other hand the crises were due to the inertia of the masses which will always cling to ancestral habits without examining their credentials. Eventually the (German) revolution (1918) brought about a sudden reversal also in this sphere, and the economic depression forced even those to take up a job who had until then given no thought to a professional training. Thus the present state is not the result of a normal development, hence not a suitable point of departure for considerations of principle.

In connexion with our former discussions we shall first have to ask whether women's professional activities outside the home are opposed to the orders of nature and grace as such. I think the answer is No. It seems to me that the original order provided for a common activity of man and woman in all spheres, though the parts would have been assigned slightly differently. The fact that the original order was changed after the fall does not mean that it was completely abolished, just as the human nature had not become wholly depraved, but preserved its original powers, though they were weakened and liable to error. All man's powers exist also in the feminine nature, even though they normally appear differently apportioned. This is surely a sign that they would be used in an occupation suited to them. It is only reasonable and in accordance with nature to transcend the circle of domestic duties where this is too narrow to allow of a full development of one's gifts. The limit beyond which we may not go, however, seems to me to be reached if the professional activities endanger the domestic life, that is the educational community of parents and children. Even in the case of man I think the divine order is violated if his professional work absorbs him to such a degree that he is completely cut off from his family life. This will be even more so in the case of a woman. Therefore we must consider as unhealthy a state of affairs in which married women are normally forced to take up work outside the home which makes it impossible for them to attend to their domestic duties. In a time when the average woman would marry and be wholly absorbed by her household duties it could be considered normal that she should be restricted to the domestic sphere.

Owing to the fall the destiny of woman has changed. First, her powers were largely restricted by the difficulties of providing even for the most primitive needs of life. In this respect the technical developments have brought a change for the better. Secondly, she was subjected to man, the scope and kind of her activities were made dependent on his will; but this was not necessarily in accordance with reason, because his intelligence and will are not infallible. Moreover, the harmony between the sexes being disturbed by the fall and both male and female natures corrupted, the subjection necessarily became the occasion for a struggle to be given opportunities for action.

The redemptive order restored the original state of things. The more it is realized in human beings, the more harmoniously will the sexes work together also in regulating their professional life. Moreover, the redemptive order brings about a fundamental change in the position of women by setting up the ideal of virginity. This breaks with the Old Testament principle that a woman can work out her salvation only by bringing forth children. Indeed, even in the Old Dispensation this principle has been set aside in the case of certain individuals called to extraordinary deeds for the people of God, such as Deborah and Judith. Now this is made into a normal way, so that women may consecrate themselves to God alone and engage in manifold activities in his service. The same St. Paul in whose writings we have sometimes found such strong evidence of Old Testament views has also said quite clearly (1 Cor 6) that in his opinion it is good for men and women to marry, but that it is better for both to remain unmarried; and he has frequently praised the achievement of women in the first Christian Churches.

Before passing on to examine the vocation of men and women to the service of God, we would consider whether, according to the order of nature, professions should be distributed between the sexes in such a way that some would be reserved to men, others to women (and still others might be open to both). In my view this question, too, has to be answered in the negative. For there are strong individual differences, so that some women closely approach the masculine, and some men the feminine type. Hence every "masculine" profession may also be very satisfactorily filled by certain women, and every "feminine" one by certain men. Therefore I do not think legal barriers should be erected in this matter, but adequate education and vocational guidance should aim at a suitable choice of profession and eliminate undesirable elements by insisting on the necessary qualifications. For the average man and woman a division between the professions will come about quite normally, since evidently, owing to their natural differences, they will be suited for different kinds of work. Physical strength, predominantly abstract reasoning or independent creative work will be required in the "masculine" professions, that is in heavy manual work, industry, agriculture; in the exact sciences such as mathematics, physics and technology; further in mechanical offices and administrative work, and in certain—not in all—branches of art. A sphere for genuinely feminine work exists wherever sensibility, intuition and adaptability are needed, and where the whole human being needs attention, whether it has to be nursed or educated or helped in any other way, perhaps by understanding it and assisting it to express itself. This means that a woman will find congenial work in the teaching and the medical professions, in all kinds of social work, in those branches of scholarship whose object is man and his activities, and in the arts that represent men; but also in business, in national and communal administration insofar as these have to deal mainly with people.

In times of extreme economic stress like our own[1] a natural distribution of men and women among the professions will not be feasible, since everyone has to seize whatever chance of employment there is, whether it be suited to his specific and individual talents or not. At present it is almost the rule that people have jobs that are not congenial; it is almost a particular 'stroke of luck' if it is otherwise. In such cases no more can be done than to make the best of the existing situation. On the one hand we have to satisfy the professional demands made on us, on the other we shall try not to let our own nature starve by denying its needs, but to make it as profitable as possible in the circle in which we are placed. For a woman this may mean, for example, that she will show herself sympathetic and helpful to her colleagues in a mechanical job; for a man that he will bring his inventive abilities to bear on the organization of his work. This, it is true, demands a high measure of personal maturity and a good will that is ready to adapt itself to any situation and to give its best in it. Such an attitude can hardly be achieved unless we regard the circumstances of our life as given by God and the work as his service, in which we are to develop the gifts he has bestowed on us in his honour. This is true of every profession, not only of the one styled 'consecrated to God', though it is there of course especially evident. . . .

To belong to God and to serve Him in the free surrender of love is not the vocation of a few chosen ones, but of every Christian. Every one of us, whether consecrated or not, whether man or woman, is called to follow Christ. The further he progresses in this way, the more Christlike he will become. Now Christ embodies the ideal of human perfection, in him there are no defects, the advantages of the male and female natures are united in him, the weaknesses abolished. Therefore his faithful disciples will also be increasingly elevated above the limitations of their nature: in saintly men we see tender gentleness and a truly motherly care for the souls entrusted to

---

[1] This was written in the early thirties, shortly before the advent of Hitler, when unemployment in Germany had reached catastrophic dimensions.—ED.

them, in women manly courage, firmness and decision. Thus if we follow Christ we shall be led to fulfil our original human vocation. We shall mirror God in us, the Master of Creation, by protecting and preserving all creatures in our care, the Father, by generating and forming children for his Kingdom in spiritual fatherhood and motherhood. But this transcending of natural barriers is the highest effect of grace; it can never be achieved by carrying on a self-willed struggle against nature and denying its barriers, but only by humble subjection to the divine order.

THE ETHOS OF WOMEN'S PROFESSIONS

Is it possible to speak of a special profession of women or even of a multiplicity of professions? Radical feminist leaders, especially in the beginning of the movement, have denied the first question and claimed all professions for their sex. Their opponents will not admit the second; they recognize only one vocation, the "natural" one. The subject requires a discussion of both points of view. We must first ask whether there is a natural vocation of woman, and what is the psychological attitude it requires.

Only pugnacious passion could blind a person to such an extent to make her deny the palpable fact that the body and soul of woman have been formed for a particular purpose. The clear, unshakable word of Scripture says what daily experience has taught from the beginning of the world: woman is destined to be the companion of man and the mother of men. For this her body is equipped, and her psychological make-up, too, conforms to it. It is again a fact of experience that a psychological peculiarity exists; it also follows from St. Thomas' principle that the soul is the form of the body. Where the bodies are so fundamentally different, there must also be a different type of soul, despite the common human nature. We would outline this typically feminine psychological attitude only quite briefly, since it is really quite familiar to all of us.

Woman tends towards the living and personal; she wants the whole. To cherish, to keep and protect, this is her natural, her authentically maternal desire. The dead thing, the "object", interests her in the first place insofar as it serves the living and the personal rather than for its own sake. This is connected with another feature: every kind of abstraction is foreign to her nature. The living and personal which is the object of her care, is a concrete whole and must be cared for and encouraged as a whole, not one part at the expense of the others, not the mind at the expense of the body or *vice versa,* neither one faculty of the soul at the expense of the others. This she tolerates neither in herself nor in others. And to this practical attitude corresponds her theoretical endowment: her natural way of knowledge is not so much notional and analytical, but envisaging and sensing the concrete. This natural equipment enables a woman to nurse and bring up her own children; but this fundamental attitude is not confined to them; it is also her way of meeting her husband and all those who come near her.

This maternal character is matched by her gift of companionship. To share in another's life, to take part in all that concerns him, in the greatest as well as in the smallest things, in joy and in sorrow, but also in his work and problems, this is her special gift and her happiness. Man is absorbed in "his cause" and expects others to be interested in, and ready to serve it. He normally finds it difficult to enter into the personalities and interests of others. But this is natural to woman, and she is able sympathetically to penetrate into spheres which are in themselves foreign to her, and for which she would never care if a personal interest did not attract her to them. This gift is closely connected with her maternal vocation. If a person takes a lively interest in another, the latter's capacities and performance will be increased. It is a truly maternal function even, and especially, needed by mature people; it will be given also to one's own children the more they grow up, replacing the lower functions.

Participation in the life of her husband requires submission and obedience, as they are enjoined by the Word of God. It is man's nature to serve his cause directly, whereas woman serves it for his sake, and so it is fit that she should do so under his guidance. It is true, the duty of obedience extends beyond this also to the direct domain of woman, to the household and the education of the children; but this is due perhaps not so much to the feminine peculiarity as to the "natural vocation" of man as the head and protector of woman. The natural feminine inclination to obedience and service corresponds to this natural vocation. This presentation of the natural feminine character did not at first include an evaluation. It is immediately evident that, developed in its purity, it has a great vital value. But for this, as well as for its ethical value which has to be considered apart, it is essential that the feminine nature should be developed in its purity. Now this is by no means normal, we may even say that it will be so only in quite particular circumstances. For the feminine nature is as much stained by original sin as human nature in general, and thus hindered in its pure development. Unless its evil tendencies are opposed, they will lead to typical perversions. The personal tendency is usually unwholesomely exaggerated; on the one hand woman is inclined to be extravagantly concerned with her own person and to expect the same interest from others; this expresses itself in vanity, desire for praise and recognition and an unrestrained urge for self-expression and communication. On the other hand we shall find an unmeasured interest in others which shows itself as curiosity, gossip, and an indiscreet longing to penetrate into the intimate lives of other people. The tendency towards wholeness easily leads her to frittering away her energy, it makes her disinclined to discipline her individual talents properly and leads to superficial nibbling in all directions. In her attitude to others it shows itself in a possessiveness far exceeding what is required by her maternal functions. Thus the sympathetic companion becomes the interfering busybody that cannot tolerate silent growth and thus does not foster development, but hinders it. Thus joyful service has been replaced by lust for governing. Only too many unhappy marriages have been caused by this aberration, by which many mothers have also estranged their grown-up or even their growing children.

If, by way of contrast, we would paint the picture of the purely developed feminine nature, of the wife and mother as her natural destiny would have her be, we shall look to the immaculate Virgin. Her life is centered in her Son. She waits for him to be born in blissful expectancy, she protects His childhood, she follows him in his ways, whether closely or from a distance, according to his wishes. She holds his dead body in her arms and carries out his last will. But all this she does not according to her own liking. She is the handmaid of the Lord, who fulfills the task to which God has called her. Therefore she does not treat her Child as her property: she has received him from the hand of God, and she places him again back into his hand, offering him in the temple and accompanying him to his death on the Cross.

If we consider the Mother of God as a wife we shall be struck by her silent, limitless trust that counts on the same limitless confidence, and faithfully shares the other's sorrow. In everything she is subject to God's will that has given her her husband as her human protector and visible head.

In the image of the Mother of God we see the fundamental attitude of soul that corresponds to the natural vocation of woman. She is obedient to her husband, trusts him and takes part in his life, furthering his objective tasks as well as the development of his personality. She faithfully nurses and cherishes her Child, developing his God-given talents. She treats both with selfless devotion, silently retiring into the background when she is not needed. All this is based on the conception of marriage and mother-hood as a vocation that comes from God, and must therefore be fulfilled for God's sake and under His guidance. How is it possible for a woman to reach such moral heights in mind as well as in deed, seeing that in her fallen nature such powerful instincts oppose this end and urge her on to other ways? A good natural remedy for all typically feminine weaknesses is thorough objective work. This demands in itself the repression of exaggerated personal interests; besides, it combats superficiality not only in one's own sphere of work, but provokes a general aversion against this failing. It requires submission to objective laws, hence it is a good training in obedience. But it must not lead to the sacrifice of the pure and praiseworthy personal attitude and to onesided specialization and enslavement by one's particular subject, which is the typical perver-sion of the masculine nature. This natural remedy is very effective, as is shown by the maturity and harmony of many women of high intellectual culture, and of others who have been trained in the discipline of strenuous professional work through the circum-stances of their life. In this we have a parallel to the picture of the perfect gentleman which Newman once outlined in his *Idea of a University,* involving a culture of the personality which might easily be mistaken for sanctity. But in both cases this is only a matter of similarity. If a nature has been disciplined merely through education it will preserve its cultivated exterior only up to a point; if it is subjected to too strong a pressure it will break the barriers. Only the power of grace can transform the fallen nature not only from outside, but completely deracinate and re-form it from within. We shall discuss later how this happens in the case of the feminine nature.

We now approach the second main question: are there women's professions other than the natural one? Only prejudiced blindness could deny that women are capable of filling other professions than that of wife and mother. The experience of the last decades, and really the experience of all times has proved this. We may well say that in case of need every normal, healthy woman can do a job. And, conversely, there is no profession that could not be practised by a woman. If fatherless children have to be provided with a breadwinner, if orphaned brothers and sisters or old parents have to be supported, a woman ready to make sacrifices can achieve the most astonishing things. But individual gifts and inclinations, too, may lead to the most varied activities. Indeed, no woman is only "woman"; every one has her individual gifts just as well as a man, and so is capable of professional work of one sort or another, whether it be artistic, scholarly, technical or any other. Theoretically this individual talent may extend to any sphere, even to those somewhat outside women's scope. In such a case we would not speak of a "feminine profession". For this term can only apply to professions whose work depends on the special feminine gifts, that is all those concerned with nursing, education, social work and sympathetic understanding. Such are the professions of the doctor and the nurse, of the teacher and the governess, of the domestic servant as well as the whole range of those devoted to modern social work. In the sphere of scholarship those sciences that are concerned with the concrete and the personal will be most suited to women, as also anything that tends to assist others, such as translating and editing, and perhaps the sympathetic guidance of the work of others.

It is evident that all this sort of work needs basically the same psychological attitude as that of the wife and mother; but it extends to a wider sphere and mostly to a changing circle of people, hence it is largely detached from the vital blood relationship and elevated to a more spiritual sphere. But for this reason it also lacks the force of the natural instincts latent in the community of life, and needs a greater capacity for sacrifice.

Over and above this, however, we may say that also professions whose strictly objective requirements do not suit the feminine nature and could rather be considered as specifically masculine, may yet be practised in a genuinely feminine way. We are thinking of work in a factory, in a business office, in national or municipal administration, in legislation, in a chemical laboratory or in a mathematical institute. All this needs concentration on things devoid of life, or is concerned with abstract thought. Yet in the great majority of cases the work will involve being together with others at least in the same room, often also in division of labour. And with this we have at once an opportunity for developing all the feminine virtues. One may even say that precisely here, where everyone is in danger of becoming a piece of the machine, the development of the specifically feminine can become a beneficial counter-influence. In the soul of a man who knows that help and sympathy are awaiting him at his place of work, much will be kept alive or aroused that would otherwise be dwarfed. This is one way of feminine individuality forming professional life in a mode different from the average man's.

Another way is also possible. Every abstract thing is ultimately part of a concrete. All that is dead ultimately serves the living. Therefore every abstract activity ultimately serves a living whole. If we are capable of obtaining and preserving this view of the whole, it will remain with us however dull and abstract our work, which will then become tolerable and in many cases be performed much better and more adequately than if preoccupation with the parts made us forget the whole. When working out laws and decrees a man might perhaps aim at the most perfect legal form, with little regard to concrete situations; whereas a woman who remains faithful to her nature even in parliament or in the administrative services, will keep the concrete end in view and adapt the means accordingly.

Thus it might be a blessing for the whole social life whether private or public, if women penetrated increasingly into the most different professional spheres, especially if they preserve the specifically feminine ethos. Here again the Mother of God should be our example. Mary at the wedding of Cana: her quietly observing eyes see everything and discover where something is missing. And before anyone notices anything, before there is any embarrassment, she has already remedied the situation. She finds ways and means, she gives the necessary directions, everything quietly and without attracting attention. Let this be the example of woman in the professional life. Wherever she is placed, let her do her work quietly and efficiently, without demanding attention or recognition. And at the same time she should keep a vigilant eye on the situation, sensing where there is something lacking, where somebody needs her help, and rectifying things as far as possible without being noticed. Then, like a good angel, she will always spread blessing.

We have now surveyed the sphere of feminine activities in the domestic as well as in public life, indeed, a rich and fertile field. Yet this does not exhaust her capacities. Today as at all times since the foundation of Christ's Church the Lord has called his chosen ones from their families and professions to his own service. Can the religious vocation be regarded as a specially feminine one? Both men and women receive this call, which is supernatural. For it comes from above and asks a person to rise above the natural earthly sphere. And thus it looks as if here the natural differences might carry no weight. Yet there is the theological principle that grace does not destroy, but that it perfects nature. Thus we may expect that in the religious vocation, too, the feminine nature will not be eliminated, but will be integrated and made fruitful in a special way. Beyond this it is possible that, like the natural professions, the religious life, too, may make special demands that appeal to the feminine nature in a special way. The religious vocation implies the complete surrender of the whole human being and of its whole life to the service of God. Religious are bound to use all the means suited to promote this end, such as renunciation of property, of vital human ties and of their own will. This may be achieved in many forms, that is to say the Lord may call His own to serve him in many different ways. They may silently contemplate the divine truth or solemnly celebrate the liturgy; they may spread the faith by the apostolate, or devote themselves to works of mercy. Thus the religious body consists of many different members. If we examine the various activities of religious, and how they are apportioned to the sexes, we shall find that they are differently related to them according to their differences. We may safely consider contemplation and liturgical prayer as transcending the difference of sex, since they are truly angelic activities. The spreading of the faith, since it is included in the priestly vocation to teach, is predominantly the task of men, though women, too, are active in this sphere, especially in the teaching Orders. Works of charity, on the other hand, and the sacrificial life of atoning satisfaction, appeal quite definitely to the feminine nature. In the older Orders which have men's and women's branches, the work is normally divided in such a way that the men are engaged in the outside activities such as preaching and giving missions, whereas the women devote themselves to the silent apostolate of prayer and sacrifice, although the education of the young was added to their tasks at an early age. The active women's Congregations of modern times are generally engaged in thoroughly feminine activities in the fields of education and charitable work. Thus today, when the majority of feminine communities devote themselves to external activities, the work of the religious Sisters is materially scarcely different from that of the women "in the world". The only difference is the "formal" one, that in the religious life all is done under obedience and for the love of God.

We would now examine how this formal element of the religious life is related to the nature of woman. The motive, principle and end of the religious life is complete surrender to God in self-forgetting love. The religious puts an end, as it were, to his own life, in order to make room for the life of God. The more completely this is realized, the richer will be the divine life that fills the soul. Now the divine life is an overflowing love that needs nothing for itself, but gives itself freely, mercifully condescending to every needy creature. It is a love that heals the sick and restores to life what is dead, that protects and fosters, nourishes, teaches and forms. It mourns with the mourning and rejoices with the joyful; it makes itself the servant of every being, so that it may become what the Father has destined it to be; in one word: it is the love of the divine Heart.

It is the deepest desire of a woman's heart to surrender itself lovingly to another, to be wholly his and to possess him wholly. This is at the root of her tendency towards the personal and the whole, which seems to us the specifically feminine characteristic. Where this total surrender is made to a human being, it is a perverted self-surrender that enslaves her, and implies at the same time an unjustified demand which no human being can fulfil. Only God can receive the complete surrender of a person, and in such a way that she will not lose, but gain her soul. And only God can give himself to a human being in such a way that he will fulfil its whole being while losing nothing of his own. Hence the total surrender which is the principle of the religious life, is at the same time the only possible adequate fulfilment of woman's desire.

Now the divine love that enters the heart which is surrendered to God is a merciful love that would serve, awaken and foster life. It completely corresponds to what we have affirmed to be the professional ethos demanded of woman.

What practical consequence follows from this? It certainly does not follow that all women who would fulfil their vocation should become nuns. But it does follow that the fallen and perverted feminine nature can be restored to its purity and led to the heights of the vocational ethos such as the pure feminine nature represents, only if it is totally surrendered to God. Whether she lives as a mother in her home, in the limelight of public life or behind the silent walls of a convent, she must everywhere be a "handmaid of the Lord", as the Mother of God had been in all the circumstances of her life, whether she was living as a virgin in the sacred precincts of the Temple, silently kept house at Bethlehem and Nazareth, or guided the apostles and the first Christian community after the death of her Son. If every woman were an image of the Mother of God, a spouse of Christ and an apostle of the divine Heart, she would fulfil her feminine vocation no matter in what circumstances she lived and what her external activities might be.

If I were to end here, the demands I have outlined, which are so frighteningly different from the average life of the present-day women, might seem the dreams of a starry-eyed idealist. I must therefore add a few words on how they can be carried out in practice. We will therefore calmly face the contrast between the average life of modern women and our demands. Many of the best are almost crushed by the double burden of professional and family duties; they are always busy, worn out, nervy and irritable. Where are they to find the interior calm and serenity in order to be a support and guide for others? In consequence there are daily little frictions with husband and children despite real mutual love and recognition of the other's merits, hence unpleasantness in the home and the loosening of family ties. In addition, there are the many superficial and unstable women who want only amusement in order to fill the interior void, who marry and are divorced, and leave their children either to themselves or to servants no more conscientious than the mothers. If they have to take a job they regard it only as a means to earn their living and to get as much enjoyment out of life as possible. In their case one can talk neither of vocation nor of ethos. They are like dry leaves blown by the wind. The breaking up of the family and the decline of morals is essentially connected with this group and can only be stemmed if we succeed in diminishing its number through suitable educational methods. Finally we would consider the by no means negligible number of those who take up a profession that corresponds to their talents and inclination. Nevertheless, many of them will discover after their first enthusiasm is spent that their expectations have not been fulfilled, and will be longing for something else. This may often be due to the fact that they were trying to do their work "just like a man". They have not sought—or perhaps not found—the means to make their feminine characteristics fruitful in their professional work. Then the nature that has been denied and repressed will assert itself.

If we look behind the walls of convents we shall find that even there the average nun does not realize the ideal in its fullness. It is true, at all times there have been religious who did not take in the full meaning of their vows, or who were ready for the complete sacrifice in the first enthusiasm of youth, but could not keep it up. They will usually be a torment to themselves and a burden to their community. Add to this the difficulties produced by modern circumstances: there is, for example, the twofold burden of the nun who has to keep up to the standard of the contemporary demands made on a nurse, a teacher or a social worker, while at the same time fulfilling the obligations of her religious life. Only too often she will lose the right attitude under this twofold strain, in the same way as the wife and mother who has a job.

Yet, despite this sad picture of the average, true heroines may still be met in all spheres of life, working real miracles of love and achievement in their families and professions, as well as in the cloister. We all know them from the records of the Church, but also from our own experience; there are the mothers who radiate warmth and light in their homes, who bring up nine children of their own, showering blessings on them for their own lives as well as for coming generations, and who still have a large heart for the needs of others. There are the teachers and office staff who support a whole family out of their salary, do domestic chores before and after their professional work, and still have time and money for all sorts of Church and charitable activities. There are the nuns who spend their nights praying for souls in danger, and take up voluntary penances for sinners. Where do they all find the strength to perform tasks which one might often think impossible for nature, and yet preserve that unalterable peace and serenity despite the most exacting nervous and emotional strains?

Only by the power of grace can nature be purged from its dross, restored to its purity and made ready to receive the divine life. And this life itself is the fountain from which spring the works of love. If we want to preserve it, we must nourish it constantly from the source whence it flows unceasingly, that is from the holy Sacraments, above all from the Sacrament of Love. A woman's life for which the divine love is to be its inner form, will have to be a eucharistic life. To forget oneself, to be delivered from all one's own desires and pretensions, to open one's heart to all the pressing needs of others—this is possible only through the daily intimacy with our Lord in the tabernacle. If we visit the eucharistic God and take counsel with him in all our affairs, if we let ourselves be purified by the sanctifying power that flows from the altar of sacrifice, if we offer ourselves to the Lord in this sacrifice and receive him into our inmost souls in Holy Communion, then we cannot but be drawn ever more deeply into the current of this divine life; we shall grow into the mystical Body of Christ, and our heart will be transformed into the likeness of the divine Heart.

Something else is closely connected with this. If we have entrusted all the cares of our earthly life to the divine Heart, our own heart will have been freed from them, and our soul will be ready to share in the divine life. We shall walk by the side of the Redeemer in the same way that he walked when he was on earth, and in which he still continues in his mystical life. With the eyes of faith we shall penetrate even into the secret life within the Godhead. Moreover, this participation in the divine life has a liberating power; it lightens the weight of our earthly concerns and gives us even in this temporal life a glimpse of eternity, a reflexion of the life of the blessed, by which we walk in the light. How we can thus walk, as it were hand in hand with God, he has shown us himself through the liturgy of the Church. Therefore the life of a truly Catholic woman will be guided by the liturgy. If we pray with the Church in spirit and in truth, our whole life will be formed by this prayer.

Summing up we would say: every profession that satisfies the feminine soul and is capable of being formed by it is a genuine feminine profession. The inmost formative principle of the feminine soul is the love that springs from the divine Heart. A woman will live by this principle if she closely joins herself to the divine Heart in a eucharistic and liturgical life.

> — From *Writings of Edith Stein*. Selected, translated and with an
> Introduction by Hilda Graef (London: Peter Owen, Ltd., 1956),
> pp. 110–25, 161–73.

John Paul II

The following address was given in 1979 *at the Angelicum to an International Congress of St. Thomas Aquinas, to commemorate the hundredth anniversary of the publication of Pope Leo XIII's encyclical Aeterni Patris.*

PERENNIAL PHILOSOPHY OF ST. THOMAS FOR THE YOUTH OF OUR TIMES

Esteemed professors and very dear students!

1. It is with a feeling of deep joy that I find myself once more, after no short space of time, in this hall. It is well known to me because I entered it so many times as a student in the years of my youth when I also came from far away to the Pontifical Athenaeum "Angelicum" to deepen my knowledge of the teaching of the Common Doctor, St. Thomas of Aquin.

Since then the Athenaeum has grown significantly. It has been raised to the rank of a Pontifical University by my venerated Predecessor, Pope John XXIII; it has been enriched by two new Institutes: to the already existing Faculties of Theology, Canon Law and Philosophy there have been added those of Social Sciences and the Institute *Mater Ecclesiae* which has the aim of preparing future "Teachers of the Religious Sciences." I take note with pleasure of these signs of vitality in the old stock which shows that fresh streams of sap flow through it. Thanks to these it can satisfy, through its new scientific institutions, the cultural needs as they gradually show themselves.

The joy of today's encounter is notably increased by the presence of a select group of learned exponents of Thomistic thought who have come here from many places to celebrate the first centenary of the Encyclical *Aeterni Patris*, published on the fourth of August, 1879, by the great Pontiff, Leo XIII. This gathering, promoted by the "International Society of Saint Thomas of Aquin," links up ideally with that held recently near Cordoba in Argentina, on the initiative of the Catholic Argentinian Association of Philosophy, in order to commemorate the same event by inviting leading representatives of present-day Christian thought to exchange views on the theme: "The Philosophy of the Christian Today." This present meeting, more directly concerned with the figure and the work of St. Thomas, while doing honor to this celebrated Roman center of Thomistic studies where one can say that Aquinas lives "as in his own home," is an act of recognition due to the immortal Pontiff who played so great a part in reviving interest in the philosophical and theological work of the Angelic Doctor.

2. I would like, therefore, to extend my respectful and cordial greeting to those who have organized this meeting: in the first place to you, Reverend Father Vincent de Couesnongle, Master of the Dominican Order and President of the "International Society of St. Thomas of Aquin"; with you I greet also the Rector of this Pontifical University, Reverend Father Joseph Salguero, the distinguished members of the Academic Staff, and all those speakers, noted for their competence in Thomistic studies,

who have honored this meeting with their presence and enlivened its sessions by sharing their store of knowledge.

I would also like to offer my affectionate greetings to you, students of this University, who give yourselves, with eager generosity, to the study of philosophy and theology as well as of the other useful auxiliary sciences, taking as your guide St. Thomas to whose thought you are introduced by the enlightened and earnest efforts of your professors. The youthful enthusiasm with which you approach Aquinas with the questions which your sensitivity towards the problems of the modern world suggest to you, and the impression of luminous clarity which you gain from the answers which he gives to you in his own clear, calm and sober way, afford the most convincing proof of the inspired wisdom which moved Pope Leo XIII to promulgate the encyclical whose centenary we are celebrating this year.

3. It cannot be doubted that the chief aim which the great Pontiff had in mind in taking that step of historic importance was to take up again and to develop the teaching of the First Vatican Council on the relations between faith and reason. As Bishop of Perugia he had played a most active role in that Council. In the Dogmatic Constitution *Dei Filius,* in fact, the Conciliar Fathers had given special attention to this theme of burning actuality. When treating of "faith and reason" they were united in opposing those philosophical and theological trends which had been infected by the then rampant rationalism. Taking their stand on Divine Revelation, as passed on and faithfully interpreted by preceding ecumenical councils, as clarified and defended by the Holy Fathers and Doctors of both East and West, they had declared that faith and reason, far from being opposed, could and should meet in a friendly way (cf. *Ench. Symb.* DS: 3015–3020; 3041–3043).

The persistent and violent attacks of those who were hostile to the Catholic Faith and to right reason induced Leo XIII to reaffirm and to develop the teaching of Vatican I in his encyclical. Here, having recalled the gradual and ever growing contribution made by the leading lights of the Church, both in the East and in the West, to the defense and progress of philosophical and theological thought, the Pope turns to what St. Thomas did by way of deep penetration and of synthesis. In words which should be quoted in their flowing classical Latin, he has no hesitation in pointing to the Angelic Doctor as the one who carried rational research into what faith makes known towards results which have proved to be of lasting value: "Thomas gathered their doctrines together — they had long lain dispersed like the scattered limbs of a body — and knitted them into one whole. He disposed them in marvelous order and increased them to such an extent that he is rightly and deservedly considered the preeminent guardian and glory of the Catholic Church. . . . Again, beginning by establishing, as is only right, the distinction between reason and faith, while still linking each to the other in a bond of friendly harmony, he maintained the legitimate rights of both, and preserved their respective dignities in such a way that human reason soared to the loftiest heights on the wings of Thomas and can scarcely rise any higher, while faith can expect no further or more reliable assistance than such as it has already received from Thomas" (*Leonis XIII, Acta,* vol. I, pp. 274–275; English translation, J. F. Scanlan, in: *St. Thomas Aquinas, Angel of the Schools,* by J. Maritain, London, 1933, Appendix I, pp. 204–206).

4. Statements as weighty as these call to commitment. To us, heeding them a century later, they above all offer practical or pedagogical guidance; for, in so speaking, Leo XIII wanted to set before teachers and students of philosophy and theology the highest ideal of a Christian dedicated to research.

Well then, what are the qualities which won for Aquinas such titles as: "Doctor of the Church," and "Angelic Doctor," awarded him by St. Pius V; "Heavenly Patron of the Highest Studies," conferred by Leo XIII in the Apostolic Letter *Cum hoc sit* of August 4, 1880, that is, on the first anniversary of the encyclical we are celebrating (cf. *Leonis XIII, Acta,* vol. II, pp. 108–113)?

The first quality is without doubt his complete submission of mind and heart to divine revelation, one which he renewed on his deathbed, in the Abbey of Fossanova, on the seventh of March, 1274. How beneficial it would be for the Church of God if also today all Catholic philosophers and theologians followed the wonderful example of the *"Doctor communis Ecclesiae!"* Aquinas treated the Holy Fathers and Doctors with the same reverence, insofar as they bear common witness to the revealed Word, so much so that Cardinal Cajetan did not hesitate to write—and his words are quoted in the encyclical: "St. Thomas, because he had the utmost reverence for the Doctors of antiquity, seems to have inherited in a way the intellect of all" (*In Sum. Theol.* II–II, q. 148, a. 4 c; *Leonis XIII, Acta,* vol. I, p. 273; Scanlan, loc. cit., p. 204).

The second quality, one which has to do with his excellence as a teacher, is that *he had a great respect for the visible world because it is the work, and hence also the imprint and image, of God the Creator.* Those, therefore, who sought to accuse St. Thomas of naturalism and empiricism were mistaken. "The Angelic Doctor," we read in the encyclical, "considered philosophical conclusions in the reasons and principles of things, which, as they are infinite in extent, so also contain the seeds of almost infinite truths for succeeding masters to cultivate in the appropriate season and bring forth an abundant harvest of truth" (*Leonis XIII, Acta,* vol. I, p. 273; Scanlan, p. 205).

Lastly, the third quality which moved Leo XIII to offer Aquinas to professors and students as a model of "the highest studies" is his sincere, total and life-long acceptance of the teaching office of the Church, to whose judgment he submitted all his works both during his life and at the point of death. Who does not recall the moving profession of faith which he wished to make in that cell at Fossanova as he knelt before the Blessed Eucharist before receiving it as his Viaticum of eternal life! "The works of the Angelic Doctor," writes Leo XIII once more, "contain the doctrine which is most in conformity with what the Church teaches" (*ibid.,* p. 280). His writings make it clear that this reverential assent was not confined only to the solemn and infallible teaching of the Councils and of the Supreme Pontiffs. An attitude, as truly edifying as this, deserves to be imitated by all who wish to be guided by the Dogmatic Constitution *Lumen gentium* (no. 25).

5. These three qualities mark the entire speculative effort of St. Thomas and make sure that its results are orthodox. It is for this reason that Pope Leo XIII, wishing to treat "of the method of teaching philosophical studies in such a way as shall most fitly correspond with the blessing of faith and be consonant with the respect due to the human sciences themselves" (*Leonis XIII Acta,* vol. I, p. 256; Scanlan, p. 190), looked principally to St. Thomas as "leader and master of all the Doctors of the Schools" (*ibid.,* p. 272).

The immortal Pontiff recalled that the method, the principles and the teaching of Aquinas had, down the centuries, been especially favored not only by learned men but by the supreme teaching authority of the Church (cf. encycl. *Aeterni Patris,* loc. cit., pp. 274–277). If today also, he insisted, philosophical and theological reflection is not to rest on an "unstable foundation" which would make it "wavering and superficial" (*ibid.,* p. 278), it will have to draw inspiration from the "golden wisdom" of St. Thomas in order to draw from it the light and vigor it needs to enter deeply into the meaning of what is revealed and to further the due progress of scientific endeavor (cf. *ibid.,* p. 282).

Now that a hundred years of the history of thought have passed we are able to appreciate how balanced and wise these appraisals were. With good reason, therefore, the Supreme Pontiffs who succeeded Leo XIII, and the Code of Canon Law itself (cf. can. 1366, par. 2) have repeated them and made them their own. The Second Vatican Council also, as we know, recommends the study and the teaching of the perennial philosophical heritage, of which the thought of the Angelic Doctor forms a notable part. (In this connection I would like to recall that Paul VI wanted an invitation to attend the Council to be sent to Jacques Maritain, one of the best known interpreters of Thomistic thought, intending also in this way to signify his high regard for the Master of the Thirteenth Century and for a way of "doing philosophy" that is in keeping with the "signs of the times.") The Decree on priestly formation (*Optatam totius*), before it speaks of the need for teaching to take account of modern trends in philosophy, especially of "those which are most influential in the homeland of the candidates," requires that "philosophical subjects should be taught in such a way as to lead the students gradually to a solid and consistent knowledge of man, the world and God. The students should rely on that philosophical patrimony which is forever valid" (no. 15; *Vatican Council II,* ed. A. Flannery, O.P., Dublin, 1975, p. 718). In the Declaration on Christian Education (*Gravissimum educationis*) we read: "By a careful attention to the current problems of these changing times and to the research being undertaken, the convergence of faith and reason in the one truth may be seen more clearly. This method follows the tradition of the Doctors of the Church and especially St. Thomas Aquinas" (no. 10; Flannery, p. 735). The words of the Council are clear: the Fathers saw that it is fundamental for the adequate formation of the clergy and of Christian youth that it preserve a close link with the cultural heritage of the past, and in particular with the thought of St. Thomas; and that this, in the long run, is a necessary condition for the longed-for renewal of the Church.

There is no need for me to reaffirm here my intention to carry out fully what the Council has laid down, since I made this quite clear already in the homily which I delivered on October 17, 1978, shortly after my election to the Chair of Peter (cf. *AAS,* 70, 1978, pp. 921–923) and several times afterwards.

6. I am very pleased, then, to find myself this evening among you, who fill the halls of the Pontifical University of St. Thomas, drawn by his philosophical and theological teaching, just as great numbers of students from various nations surrounded the chair of the Dominican friar in the thirteenth century when he taught in the universities of Paris or of Naples or in the "Studium Curiae," or in the House of Studies of the Priory of Santa Sabina in Rome.

The philosophy of St. Thomas deserves to be attentively studied and accepted with conviction by the youth of our day by reason of its spirit of openness *and of universalism, characteristics which are hard to find in many trends of contemporary thought.* What is meant is an *openness* to the whole of reality in all its parts and dimensions, without either reducing reality or confining thought to particular forms or aspects (and without turning singular aspects into absolutes), as intelligence demands in the name of objective and integral truth about what is real. Such *openness* is also a significant and distinctive mark of the Christian faith, whose specific countermark is its catholicity. *The basis and source of this openness lie in the fact that the philosophy of St. Thomas is a philosophy of being, that is, of the "act of existing" (actus essendi)[1] whose transcendental value paves the most direct way to rise to the knowledge of subsisting Being and pure Act, namely to God.* On account of this we can even call this philosophy: the philosophy of the proclamation of being, a chant in praise of what exists.

It is from this proclamation of being that the philosophy of St. Thomas derives its ability to grasp and to "affirm" all that shows itself to the human intellect (what is given by experience, in the widest sense) as a determinate existing being in all the inexhaustible richness of its content; that it derives its ability, in particular, to grasp and to "affirm" that "being" which is able to know itself, to be filled with wonder in itself, and above all to decide for itself and to fashion its own unrepeatable history.... St. Thomas is thinking of this "being" and of its dignity when he speaks of man as that which is "the most perfect thing in the whole of nature" (*perfectissimum in tota natura: S. Th.* I, q. 29, a. 3), a "person," requiring that it must be given exceptional and specific attention. This says all that is essential with regard to the dignity of the human being, even though much more still remains to be investigated in this field, one where the contribution of modern trends of philosophy can be helpful.

It is also from this affirmation of being that the philosophy of St. Thomas draws its power to justify itself from the methodological point of view, as a branch of knowledge that cannot be reduced to any other science whatever, and as one that transcends them all by establishing itself as independent of them and at the same time as bringing them to completion in regard to their true nature.

Moreover, it is by reason of this affirmation of being that the philosophy of St. Thomas is able to, and indeed must, go beyond all that presents itself directly in knowledge as an existing thing (given through experience) in order to reach "that

---

[1] (*Translator's note*). No literal English rendering could convey the meaning which this technical Latin expression—or its equivalent *esse ut actus*—had for Saint Thomas, and presumably retains for Pope John Paul. It does not refer to the mere fact of existing, of "being there," especially if this is taken in a spatial or temporal sense. The meaning of the Latin *esse* is not properly expressed by the infinitive "to be," for this may refer only to the function of the copula in a proposition. Nor is the abstract term "existence" adequate, for we are dealing with the most concrete of all realities. "Actual existing," or "actual be-ing", come closer to the meaning intended; but to avoid the connotation either of "existence" or of "being" which can be taken in a substantive sense, it might be advisable to coin the active and concrete word "is-ing". What St. Thomas has in mind is the most actual of all actualities, the most perfect of all perfections, the inmost principle and source of all the actuality, perfection, reality, and indeed also of the know-ability of anything that is. It is *esse* in this metaphysical sense which makes anything be, and be real; it is the immediate source of the reality and perfection of all things. This may help the reader to appreciate the Pope's insistence on this insight, so central in the thought of St. Thomas, and the implications which he draws from it in nos. 6 and 7 of his discourse.—TRANS.

which subsists as sheer Existing" (*ipsum Esse subsistens*) and also creative Love; for it is this which provides the ultimate (and therefore necessary) explanation of the fact that "it is preferable to be than not to be" (*potius est esse quam non esse*) and, in particular, of the fact that we exist. "This existing itself," Aquinas tells us, "is the most common effect of all, prior and more intimate than any other effect; that is why such an effect is due to a power that, of itself, belongs to God alone" (*Ipsum enim esse est communissimus effectus, primus et intimior omnibus aliis effectibus; et ideo soli Deo competit secundum virtutem propriam talis effectus: QQ. DD. De Potentia,* q. 3, a. 7, c).

St. Thomas puts philosophy moving along lines set by this intuition, showing at the same time that only in this way does the intellect feel at ease (as it were "at home") and that, therefore, it can never abandon this way without abandoning itself.

By maintaining that the proper object of metaphysics is reality "in so far as it is being" (sub ratione entis) *St. Thomas pointed to that analogy which accompanies being as such, finding there the justification of the method for forming propositions dealing with the whole of reality and with the Absolute itself.* In so far as methodology is concerned it would be hard to exaggerate the importance of this discovery for philosophical research, as indeed also for human knowledge in general.

There is no need to stress the debt owed to this philosophy by theology itself, since it is nothing other than "faith seeking understanding" (*Fides quaerens intellectum*) or the "understanding of faith" (*intellectus fidei*). Not even theology, then, can abandon the philosophy of St. Thomas.

7. Is it to be feared that by favoring the philosophy of St. Thomas one will undermine the right to exist that is enjoyed by different cultures or hinder the progress of human thought? Such a fear would clearly be groundless because the methodological principle invoked above implies that whatever is real has its source in the "act of existing" (*actus essendi*);[2] and because the perennial philosophy, by reason of that principle, can claim in advance, so to speak, all that is true in regard to reality. *By the same token, every understanding of reality—which does in fact correspond to reality—has every right to be accepted by the "philosophy of being," no matter who is to be credited with such progress in understanding or to what philosophical school that person belongs.* Hence, the other trends in philosophy, if regarded from this point of view, can and indeed should be treated as natural allies of the philosophy of St. Thomas, and as *partners* worthy of attention and respect in the dialogue that is carried on in the presence of reality. This is needed if truth is to be more than partial or onesided. That is why the advice given by Saint Thomas to his followers in his "Letter on how to study" where he said: "look rather to what was said than to who it was that said it" (*Ne respicias a quo sed quod dicitur*), is so much in keeping with the spirit of his philosophy. That is also why I am so pleased that the program of studies in the Faculty of Philosophy in this university offers, besides the theoretical courses dealing with the thought of Aristotle and of St. Thomas, other courses such as: Science and Philosophy, Philosophical Anthropology, Physics and Philosophy, History of Modern Philosophy, the Phenomenological Movement, as required by the recent Apostolic Constitution *Sapientia Christiana* for Universities and Ecclesiastical Faculties (*AAS* 71, 1979, pp. 495–496).

[2] Ibid.

8. *There is still one more reason why the philosophy of St. Thomas has enduring value: its prevailing characteristic is that it is always in search of the truth.* In his commentary on Aristotle, his favorite philosopher, he writes: "Philosophy is not studied in order to find out what people may have thought but in order to discover what is true" (*De Coelo et Mundo,* I, lect. 22; ed. R. Spiazzi, no. 228: "*Studium philosophiae non est ad hoc quod sciatur quid homines senserint, sed qualiter se habeat veritas*). The reason why the philosophy of St. Thomas is pre-eminent is to be found in its realism and its objectivity: it is a philosophy "of what is, not of what appears," (*de l'etre et non du paraitre*). What makes the philosophy of the Angelic Doctor so wonderfully apt to be the "handmaid of faith" (*ancilla fidei*) is that it has gained possession of truths of the natural order, which have their origin in God the Creator, just as truths of the divine order have their source in God as revealing.

This does not lessen the value of philosophy or unduly restrict its field of research; on the contrary, it allows it to develop in ways that human reason alone could not have discovered. Hence the Supreme Pontiff Pius XI of holy memory, issuing the Encyclical *Studiorum ducem* on the occasion of the sixth centenary of the canonization of St. Thomas, did not hesitate to declare: "In honoring St. Thomas something greater is involved than the reputation of St. Thomas, and that is the authority of the teaching Church" (*In Thoma honorando maius quiddam quam Thomae ipsius existimatio vertitur, id est Ecclesiae docentis auctoritas; AAS* 15; 1923, p. 324; English trans. Scanlan. *loc. cit.,* p. 238).

9. St. Thomas, because his "reason was enlightened by faith" (Vatican Council I, Dogmatic Constitution *Dei Filius,* ch. 4: *DS.* 3016), was in fact able to throw light also on problems concerning the Incarnate Word, "Savior of all men" (Prologue to Part III of the *Summa Theologiae*). These are the problems to which I referred in my first Encyclical *Redemptor hominis,* in which I spoke about Christ as "Redeemer of man and of the world, center of the universe and of history . . . , the chief way for the Church" for our return "to the Father's house" (nos. 1, 8, 13). This is a theme of the highest importance for the life of the Church and for Christian science. Is not Christology perhaps the basis and the first condition for working out a more complete anthropology such as is required by the needs of our day? *We must not forget that, in fact, it is Christ alone who "reveals man fully to himself"* (cf. Pastoral Constitution *Gaudium et spes,* no. 22).

St. Thomas has, moreover, shed the light of reason, purified and elevated by faith, on problems concerning man: *on his nature as created to the image and likeness of God, on his personality as worthy of respect from the first moment of his conception, on his supernatural destiny as found in the beatific vision of God, One and Three.* On this point we are indebted to St. Thomas for a precise and ever valid definition of that which constitutes man's essential greatness: "he has charge of himself" (*ipse est sibi providens;* cf. *Contra Gentiles,* III, 81).

Man is master of himself. He can make provision for himself and form projects towards fulfilling his destiny. This fact, however, taken by itself, does not settle the question of man's greatness, nor does it guarantee that he will be able, by himself, to reach the full perfection of personality. *The only decisive factor here is that man should let himself be guided, in his actions, by the truth; and truth is not made by man; he can only discover it in the nature that is given to him along with existence.* It is God who, as Creator, calls reality into being and, as Revealer, shows it forth ever more fully in Jesus Christ and in his Church. The Second Vatican Council, when it speaks of this self-providence of man "insofar as it involves knowing what is true" (*sub ratione veri*) as a "kingly ministry" (*munus regale*), goes to the heart of this intuition.

This is the teaching which I set out to call to mind and bring up to date in the Encyclical *Redemptor hominis,* by drawing attention to man as "the primary and fundamental way for the Church" (no. 14).

10. I must add one last word at the end of these reflections which, of necessity, have to be brief. It concerns the thought with which Leo XIII ends his *Aeterni Patris.* "Let us follow the example of the Angelic Doctor" (*Leonis XIII, Acta, loc. cit.,* p. 283) is what he advises. That is what I also repeat this evening. This advice is indeed fully justified by the witness which he gave by his manner of living and which gave force to what he said as a teacher. He had indeed the technical mastery befitting a teacher, but, prior to this, his manner of teaching was that of a saint who lives the Gospel fully, of one for whom love is everything: love of God, the primal source of all truth; love of one's neighbor, God's masterpiece; love of all created things, for these also are precious caskets full of the treasures which God has poured into them.

If we look for the driving force behind his commitment to a life of study, the secret urge which led him to consecrate himself through a total dedication, we find it in his own words: "All things issue from charity as from a principle, and all things are ordered towards charity as to an end" (*A caritate omnia procedunt sicut a principio et in caritatem omnia ordinantur sicut in finem: In John,* XV, 2). And in fact the huge intellectual effort of this master of thought was stimulated, sustained and given direction by a heart full of the love of God and of his neighbor. "The knowledge of what is true is given by the fervor of love" (*Per ardorem caritatis datur cognitio veritatis: ibid.,* V, 6). These words could be taken as his motto. They allow us to perceive, behind the thinker able to rise to the loftiest heights of speculation, the mystic accustomed to going straight to the very fountain of all truth to find the answer to the deepest questionings of the human spirit. Did not he himself tell us that he never wrote anything nor gave class unless he had first had recourse to prayer?

One who approaches St. Thomas cannot set aside this witness which comes from his life; he must rather follow courageously the path traced out by him and bind himself to follow his example if he would wish to taste the most secret and savory fruits of his teaching. This is the burden of the prayer which the liturgy places on our lips on his feastday: "O God, since it was by your gift that St. Thomas became so great a saint and theologian, give us the grace to understand his teaching and follow his way of life."

This is also what we ask from the Lord this evening, as we entrust our prayer to the intercession of "Master Thomas" himself, a master who was deeply human because he was deeply Christian, and precisely because he was so deeply Christian was so deeply human.

> — From *The Whole Truth about Man: John Paul II to University Faculties and Students.* Edited and with an Introduction by James V. Schall, S. J. (Boston: St. Paul Editions, 1981), pp. 209–27.

APPENDIX II

QUESTIONS FOR DISCUSSION

Introduction

1. Why study philosophy?

2. Why is the study of philosophy important for Christians?

3. In a few brief sentences, what are some basic ideas about the meaning of life you believe to constitute wisdom?

4. What are some examples of how atheism permeates contemporary culture?

5. Do you think that most Christians bear witness against the errors of their societies with the courage of Socrates? If not, what has made us so weak?

6. Augustine talked to God in prayer about his philosophical problems. What place does the search for meaning have in your own prayer life?

Part One

1. What can we learn from anthropology and archaeology about the philosophy of life of primitives?

2. How was the world view of the peoples after the primitive period but before the Christian era different from the Christian world view?

3. What are some truths and some shortcomings of Plato's philosophy?

4. What contemporary currents of idealistic self-realization share the defects of the classical world view?

5. Compare Plato's myth of the Cave with John 1. How does the symbol of the light correspond and how differ in Plato and John? Can you relate the imagery of John to the role of the Pope in the teaching office of the Church? Are the reactions of some Christians to these teachings similar to the way the cave-dwellers respond to the ideas of the philosophy in Plato's myth of the Cave?

6. Can you devise an analogy about the search for wisdom in our day similar to Plato's myth for his day?

7. How does belief in such higher truths as Plato affirmed in the *Phaedo* elevate us above mundane concerns of survival?

8. Which basic ideas of Aristotle are part of the Christian world view, and which ones are not?

9. Summarize the ideas in the excerpt from Aristotle's *Ethics*.

10. Pick out a virtue of your own and figure out what would be the two extremes of which your virtue is a mean. Then think of what your own greatest defect is and see what virtue would be the mean for which you should aim.

11. As you can see from the excerpt from the Stoic philosopher Epictetus, the Stoics believed that reason is enough to help us to overcome the difficulties of life. Compare this view with the Christian idea of the origin of virtue and peace. Can you think of times in your own life when you have tried reason alone to bring about peace of mind? If so, compare these times to periods of reliance on grace.

12. Reread St. Paul's indictment of the culture of his day in Romans 1 and relate it to our day, with its own apostasy from the principles of Christian wisdom.

13. How does prophetic light differ from other kinds of light?

14. What is the contribution of the prophetic Tradition to the wisdom of Christian philosophy?

15. How does the contemporary emphasis, in some circles, on Jesus as friend put into the background Jesus as Divine Teacher?

16. Summarize the teachings of Jesus.

17. Read through the Gospels, making note of the content of the teachings of Jesus.

18. What does the sacrifice of Christ on the Cross signify for philosophy?

19. What influence might belief in the literal truth of the events in the life of Christ, as opposed to seeing them only as symbols, have on the foundations of a Christian life view?

20. Describe the teaching program of the early Church regarding God's transcendence and creation, the problem of evil, and the nature of the moral order. What methods of the early Church might be of importance in teaching today?

21. Describe the relationship between faith and reason in the teachings of the Church Fathers.

22. Summarize Augustine's philosophy.

23. Why does Augustine's stress on existence make such a difference in the beginnings of Christian Philosophy?

24. How did Augustine bring together philosophy and pastoral catechetics, and what relevance does this have for contemporary Catholic education?

25. As a spiritual meditation, take each theme in this chapter, such as the transcendence of God, creation, God as person rather than idea, the problem of evil, the moral order, the restlessness of the soul, or the ordering of loves, and ponder what they mean for your own life and how you have grown in appreciation of the depths of these aspects of Christian truth.

Part Two

Introduction

1. Are we now in a period of intellectual peace between the academic and catechetical orders? If not, what are the key differences in the starting points and main concepts of each order?

2. Trace your own Catholic intellectual history in terms of doubts caused by differences between concepts learned in catechetics and those in the culture around you.

3. Why it is important in Catholic teaching to have a clear *philosophical* grasp of God's nature? How does that idea differ from the notion of God to be found in movements such as transcendental meditation?

Prologue

1. Why is it necessary to begin philosophy with natural reason?

2. How is the human way of communicating and building up a culture reflected in a philosophy based on natural reason?

3. What is metaphysics in the context of Christian Philosophy?

4. Outline the excerpt from Maritain and pick out lines that puzzle or inspire you.

5. What role does common sense play in the way of viewing life of people who have influenced you in the past? Do you think of common sense as an opposite to spirituality, or as a complement? Can you give examples of false spiritualities that seem to depart from reality?

Chapter I

1. Why is it important that truth be related to being, that is, to the way *things* really are, rather than truth being merely a "truth for me" or a way of symbolizing the mores of our culture?

2. What is the first act of the intellect?

3. What is essence? What is substance? What is form? What is the *nature* of a thing?

4. Why are the first principles of metaphysics crucial for the understanding of the First Article of the Creed?

5. What are the principles of being?

6. What is the nature of abstraction? What are the three degrees of abstraction? Illustrate with examples.

7. What is an instance of a key truth of the Faith that depends on knowing that there is more to reality than what the senses perceive?

8. Are human beings more inclined by nature to use the imagination or pure understanding? If pure understanding is hard for us to use, why is it important to make the effort? In reference to your own reflective processes, give some examples of images that are of great importance to you in your natural life and your religious experience, and then think of some more abstract ideas that are foundational for you.

9. What are potency and act, and how are they related to essence and existence? Give an example.

10. What are the seven first principles of reality from the viewpoint of our understanding of them? Give an example to illustrate each principle.

11. Express in your own words why prolife arguments rest on an underlying abiding human substance.

Chapter II

1. Why does every bodily thing need to be composed of matter and form?

2. The Catholic religion takes individuality very seriously. God does not become man in general, but this man: Jesus whom John the Baptist pointed to with his finger. Give other examples of how the principle of individuation as designated matter figures in Catholic experience.

3. Because of the doctrine of creation, we see physical nature as coming from God and as a gift to us. Find and write down some passages from Scripture that reflect joy in God's creation. Describe the way you meet God in your wonder at natural beauty.

Chapter III

1. What is a concept?

2. What is realism in philosophy?

3. What is a transcendental concept or idea? List some of these concepts and give examples from your experience of them, especially your most striking ones.

4. How do the transcendental concepts open us to a realm beyond the natural?

5. What is a universal concept? Give examples.

6. What is a judgment? Give examples.

7. Show how progress in theology, with respect to a particular doctrine, can be deepening rather than innovative.

8. How is having a universal concept of humanity related to ethics and religion?

9. What is the active intellect? How does it resolve the problem of universals?

Chapter IV

1. What is at stake in asking whether the mind can ascend to the knowledge of nonmaterial reality?

2. Summarize Thomas' five ways of ascending to God.

3. Try to put these five ways into your own words. Which of them seem to you to be most convincing? Try them out on others and see what reaction you observe. If questions arise, discuss them in class.

4. Contrast the attitude toward "the Divine" of people who think of God more as a force or presence than as a personal Creator with the Catholic attitude of loving worship.

Chapter V

1. Why can there be only one God?

2. In what way does the Incarnation fulfill the doctrine of God's closeness to his creatures as conceptualized philosophically?

3. How are faith and reason related in the work of St. Thomas Aquinas? Are faith and reason more separate for most Catholics in our times? If so, what do you think has caused this rift?

4. What does it mean to say God is immanent, yet not one with creatures in the sense of pantheism?

5. In what ways have you experienced God as being closer to you than your own self? Could a Catholic say that one's own soul is divine, as do some Eastern mystics?

6. In what ways are angels like and unlike humans? Like and unlike God?

7. What relationship ought to obtain between metaphysics and the empirical sciences of the day, according to the writers of this text?

8. Outline Thomas' philosophical anthropology.

9. How does human freedom spring from rationality? Give examples.

10. In what way is education based on philosophical anthropology? If possible, think of some systems of education, such as that of Montessori or Skinner, and see what philosophy of human nature underlies each of them.

11. Outline the argument for the immortality of the soul given in the excerpt from the *Summa*. Explain the way it is based on principles already given for study in this book.

Chapter VI

1. Define each of the four causes, using a few examples as illustrations.

2. Describe the four causes in relation to the educative process.

3. What is the difference between a primary and a secondary cause? How does the way God causes differ from all other causes?

4. What is an accident? Give some examples.

5. Outline the applications of the metaphysics of change to Catholic truth. Describe some of your own experiences of these changes.

Part Three

1. What evidence have you seen of the effects of the Copernican Revolution on thinking about the nature of reality as a whole among people of our times?

2. Descartes made doubt a basic methodological category. What role does doubt play in the contemporary mind? In the approach to Catholic doctrine? Have you gone through a period of doubt in the past? Now, in the present? What, if anything, overcame this doubt?

3. Many generations of Catholics came in touch with the transcendent through the medium of soaring Gothic arches, Gregorian chant, solemn High Masses. Do you think that most young Catholics today think of God as Perfect Transcendent Being, or more as a vague spiritual presence? If the latter, how have modern philosophical concepts caused this shift?

4. How has the conclusion of Spinoza that man is the center of reality influenced the way people today view religion in terms of the weight given to God in their lives, morals, the arts?

5. In new theologies and spiritualities, do you find rejection of dogma in favor of pure "process" as heralded by Spinoza? Give examples. Do you think that doctrine and religious experience are opposites, or that they can be integrated with each other?

6. How have modern psychological explanations for behavior undermined the idea of the individual as a free person who can struggle meaningfully between good and evil?

7. In evaluating phases of your own life or that of others, do you see the loss of faith in a transcendent personal God leading to feelings of false liberation and self-worship?

8. In what ways is our present culture more greatly influenced by empirical philosophy than by Christian Philosophy?

9. How do trends in general textbooks and in catechetical writings manifest a spectrum of ideas about human nature with reference to admitting that there is original sin or asserting that humans should just grow naturally without restraint?

10. Dostoevski wrote in *Crime and Punishment* that "without God all things are possible", including the justification of the most heinous crimes. Many modern

philosophers, however, thought that there could be morality without a metaphysical foundation in God. Evaluate both sides of this dilemma.

11. How does "pluralism" in education follow from considering religion, as Kant did, to be an affair of the heart, rather than allowing for an objective foundation for devotion in the truths of revelation? Can evangelization be justified if there is no objectivity concerning religious belief?

12. The direction Comte had received as a boy in Catholic teaching was reversed by his university education. In what ways do present-day youth experience the same "enlightenment"? What forces in today's Catholic world could reverse this tendency to apostasy?

13. In our times how have various "isms" tried to use Christianity as a fulcrum and power base for forwarding their own goals?

14. For Catholics, is the criterion for embracing an idea that it is new, as Hegelian dialectic would suggest? If not, what is the criterion for truth?

15. The Jewish roots of Christian thought were foundational for Catholic catechesis in the past. How has the shift to seeing Christianity as part of the study of world religions been influenced by Hegel's philosophy of history? Distinguish false and true ecumenism with reference to the concept of revelation from the Old to New Testament as opposed to seeing all religions as being part of human process.

16. Modern Philosophy presents itself to many as the inevitable result of the Copernican scientific revolution. Reread Part Three and summarize the ways indicated by which new scientific insights might have been integrated with a sound Christian metaphysics.

Part Four

1. In what ways does the contemporary idea of the nature and destiny of man reflect the inroads of modern metaphysical atheism?

2. How are attitudes toward the value of the unborn child and the incapacitated elderly related to an atheistic metaphysics?

3. The post–Vatican II catechetics, while positive in its emphasis on God's love, has been critiqued as overly this-worldly in its approaches. Comment with regard to the overall scope of specific catechetical series and also with respect to specific ideas or omissions.

4. Does contemporary science prove that there is no absolute Being outside the material cosmos?

5. Many think that Marxism was a good philosophy later corrupted by political leaders. Indicate what you conclude to be valid or invalid in the philosophy of Marx and in its consequences.

6. How has existentialist individualism influenced the contemporary mind in its abandonment of objective reality and objective norms?

7. Pragmatism is often considered the North American contribution to philosophy. How have its characteristic ideas tended to deemphasize objective standards for truth and morality?

8. What is modernism? How did it first arise?

9. What concept of the person emerges from the philosophies of James, Freud, and Russell?

10. Many Christians think that faith is enough, with no need for philosophy. What was the basis, then, for launching the renewal of Christian Philosophy in Vatican I and *Aeterni Patris*?

11. How do papal and conciliar documents of the twentieth century reaffirm the renewal of Christian Philosophy?

12. In what way can contemporary science open a way to God?

13. Outline the philosophy of man as expressed in the writings of St. Thomas concerning human nature, human thought, and human freedom. Contrast this with the philosophical anthropology of atheism.

14. What elements of twentieth-century modernism have you observed in your Catholic education?

15. What signs do you see of a return to principles of true Christian Philosophy in our times: in society, in Catholic education (catechetics, university, seminary)?

BIBLIOGRAPHY

General

We offer this bibliography to students as suggestive, not comprehensive, and as a supplement to the names in the excerpts. It is impossible for reasons of space to include all the meritorious authors in this century of the renewal of Christian Philosophy. We refer our readers to the excellent bibliographies in the publications of these authors and to the counsel of those who make use of this book in their teaching. — R. C. and E. K.

Philosophical works of St. Thomas:

Contra Gentes; commentaries on Aristotle; *On Spiritual Creatures; On the Soul; De veritate; De potentia; Summa Theologiae* (Part I, the questions on God and man).

For specialized research:

Bergamo, P. de. *In Opera S. Thomae Aquinatis Index, seu Tabula Aurea* (Rome: Editiones Paulinae, 1960) (photostatic edition of the earlier classic). For a comprehensive listing of contemporary writings about St. Thomas Aquinas and Christian Philosophy or its contemporary renewal in Catholic higher education, see the volumes of annual bibliography published under the editorship of Father Vansteenkiste, O.P., at the Angelicum in Rome. These volumes list books and articles published worldwide.

Summaries of Thomistic philosophy

James F. Anderson, R. Garrigou-Lagrange, Étienne Gilson, Paul Grenet, Jacques Maritain, E. L. Mascall, Joseph Pieper, Henri Renard, William A. Wallace, and others.

For an introduction to the writings of St. Thomas

M. D. Chenu, O.P. *Toward Understanding St. Thomas* (Chicago: Regnery, 1964).

Particular authors:

Boyer, Charles. *Cursus Philosophiae.* 2 vols. (1935).
Brugger and Baker. *Philosophical Dictionary* (1972).
Cotter, A. C. *The ABC of Scholastic Philosophy* (1946).

De Torre, J. *Christian Philosophy* (1980).

Gardeil, A. *Introduction to the Philosophy of St. Thomas Aquinas.* 4 vols. (1958).

Garrigou-Lagrange, R. *God: His Existence and Nature.* 2 vols. (1939).

——. *The One God* (1943) (important Introduction, pp. 1–39).

Gilson, É. *Being and Some Philosophers* (1952).

——. *Elements of Christian Philosophy* (1960).

——. *God and Philosophy* (1959).

——. *The Unity of Philosophical Experience* (1940).

Hildebrand, D. Von. *What Is Philosophy?* (1973).

Leo XIII, Pope. *Aeterni Patris* (Aug. 4, 1879).

Maritain, J. *Approaches to God.*

——. *Existence and the Existent* (1948).

——. *An Introduction to Philosophy* (1930).

Paul VI, Pope. *Lumen Ecclesiae* (Nov. 20, 1974).

Raeymaeker, L. *Introduction to Philosophy* (1948).

Tresmontant, C. *Christian Metaphysics* (1965).

Wallace, William. *The Elements of Philosophy* (1977).

Part One

Augustine, St. *The Philosophical Dialogues.* These are his works as a layman, prior to his ordination to the priesthood. English translations are available in the standard patristic collections, such as *Ancient Christian Writers, The Fathers of the Church, Library of Christian Classics,* and the *Post-Nicene Fathers.*

Cornford, F. M. *From Religion to Philosophy: A Study in the Origins of Western Speculation* (1957). Important for its recognition that the Greeks philosophized within their pantheistic religion.

Gilson, É. *The Christian Philosophy of St. Augustine* (1960).

John Paul II, Pope. *Augustinum Hipponensem* (Aug. 28, 1986). Apostolic Letter for the sixteenth centenary of his conversion.

McKeon, R. *The Basic Works of Aristotle* (1941).

Plato. *The Collected Dialogues* (edited by Hamilton and Cairns) (1961).

Portalié, E. *A Guide to the Thought of St. Augustine* (1960).

Part Two

For lives of St. Thomas Aquinas

Chesterton, Maritain, Spiazzi, Walz, Weisheipl, and others.

Adler, Mortimer. *St. Thomas and the Gentiles* (1938).

Anderson, J. *An Introduction to the Metaphysics of St. Thomas* (1953).

Aquinas, Thomas, St. *On Being and Essence,* and other works according to time, need, and interest.

Garrigou-Lagrange, R. *Reality* (1950).

Gilson, É. *The Spirit of Medieval Philosophy* (1940).

Grenet, P. *Thomism: An Introduction* (1960).

Knowles, D. *The Evolution of Medieval Thought* (1962).

Maritain, J. *A Preface to Metaphysics* (1978).

Paul VI, Pope. *Lumen Ecclesiae* (Nov. 20, 1974).

Pieper, J. *Guide to Thomas Aquinas* (1962).

Raeymaeker, L. *The Philosophy of Being: A Synthesis of Metaphysics* (1954).

Part Three

Burtt, E. A. *The Metaphysical Foundations of Modern Science* (1954).

Cassirer, Ernst. *The Philosophy of the Enlightenment* (1951).

Collins, James. *God in Modern Philosophy* (1975).

De Lubac, Henri. *The Drama of Atheist Humanism* (1955).

De Torre, J. *The Humanism of Modern Philosophy* (1988).

Fabro, Cornelio. *God in Exile: Introduction to Modern Atheism* (1975).

Gilson and Langan. *Modern Philosophy: Descartes to Kant* (1963).

Kevane, E. *The Lord of History* (1980).

Kuhn, T. S. *The Copernican Revolution* (1959).

Lovejoy, A. O. *The Great Chain of Being* (1964).

Löwith, K. *From Hegel to Nietzsche: The Revolution in Nineteenth-Century Thought* (1967).

Neill, Thomas P. *Makers of the Modern Mind* (1949).

Simon, Yves. *The Great Dialogue of Nature and Space* (1970).

Smith, Wolfgang. *Cosmos and Transcendence* (1984).

Part Four

Alexander, D. *Beyond Science* (1972).

Berdyaev, N. *The End of Our Time* (1933).

Besancon, A. *The Rise of the Gulag: Intellectual Origins of Leninism* (1981).

Borne, E. *Atheism* (1961).

Broderick, J., ed. *Vatican I and Its Documents* (1971).

Copleston, F. *Contemporary Philosophy: Studies in Logical Positivism and Existentialism* (1965).

Dawson, C. *Religion and the Modern State* (1935).

Gilson, É. *Christianity and Philosophy* (1939).

———. *Thomist Realism and the Critique of Knowledge* (1986).

Heisenberg, Werner. *Physics and Philosophy: The Revolution in Modern Science* (1958).

Hildebrand, D. Von. *In Defense of Purity* (1934).

———. *The New Tower of Babel* (1953).

———. *Trojan Horse in the City of God* (1967). Important appendix on Teilhard de Chardin.

Hildebrand, D. Von, and A. Von Hildebrand. *Morality and Situation Ethics* (1966).

John Paul II, Pope. *Two Lectures on St. Thomas Aquinas* (1985). Published by Maritain Institute, Niagara University.

Krapiec, M. *I–Man: An Outline of Philosophical Anthropology* (1985).

LeMaître, Georges. *The Primeval Atom: An Essay on Cosmogony* (1950).

Leo XIII, Pope. *Aeterni Patris* (Aug. 4, 1879).

———. *Depuis le Jour* (Sept. 8, 1899).

———. *Providentissimus Deus* (Nov. 18, 1893).

Lescoe, F. J. *Existentialism: With or without God* (1980).

———. *Philosophy Serving Contemporary Needs of the Church* (1979).

Lilge, F. *The Abuse of Learning: The Failure of the German University* (1948).

McInerny, Ralph. *The Perennial Philosophy* (1977).

Maritain, J. *Bergsonian Philosophy and Thomism* (1968).

———. *The Degrees of Knowledge* (1959).

Paul VI, Pope. *Lumen Ecclesiae* (Nov. 20, 1974).

Pius X, Pope St. *Lamentabili* (July 3, 1907)

———. *Pascendi* (Sept. 8, 1907).

——. *Socrorum Antitistitum* (Sept. 1, 1910).

Pius XIII, Pope. *Humani Generis* (Aug. 12, 1950).

Reinhardt, K. *The Existentialist Revolt* (1964).

Schrödinger, Erwin. *Science and Humanism: Physics in Our Time* (1951).

Whittaker, E. *Space and Spirit: Theories of the Universe and the Arguments for the Existence of God* (1948).

Wojtyla, K. (Pope John Paul II.) *The Acting Person* (1979).

——. *Love and Responsibility.*

Woznicki, A. *A Christian Humanism: Karol Wojtyla's Existential Personalism* (1980).

ACKNOWLEDGEMENTS

The authors and Ignatius Press are grateful to the following authors and publishers for their permission to reprint excerpts from these works:

PART ONE

Socrates, "The Apology", in *The Works of Plato*, New York: Tudor Publishing, © 1937.

Augustine, *Confessions,* Books VII and VIII. Reprinted with permission of Sheed & Ward, 115 E. Armour Blvd., Kansas City, Mo.

Plato, "The Myth of the Cave", from *The Republic,* Book VII, in *The Dialogues of Plato,* translated by Benjamin Jowett. Reprinted by permission of Oxford University Press, Oxford, England.

Plato, from *Phaedo,* in *Dialogues of Plato,* translated by Benjamin Jowett. Reprinted by permission of Oxford University Press, Oxford, England.

Aristotle, "The Four Causes", from *Introduction to Aristotle, Physics,* Book II, published by Random House, New York.

Epictetus, "Of the Things Which Are, and the Things Which Are Not in Our Power" and "In What Manner, upon Every Occasion, to Preserve Our Character", in *The Discourses of Epictetus,* translated by Elizabeth Carter and Thomas Wentworth Higgenson. Used with permission of Little, Brown and Company, Boston, © 1965.

Augustine, *On the True Religion,* published in Chicago, by Regnery, © 1959, I (I); II (21); 18 (35); 20 (40); 31 (57); 36 (66); 39 (72).

PART TWO

Maritain, Chapter 8 "Philosophy and Common Sense", in *Introduction to Philosophy,* published in London in 1934. Reprinted with permission of Sheed & Ward, 115 E. Armour Blvd., Kansas City, Mo.

Aquinas, "The Five Ways", in *Summa Theologica,* published by Benziger Brothers, 1, 2, 3. Reprinted with permission of Benziger Publishing Company, Mission Hills, Ca.

Aquinas, the *Summa Theologica,* published by Benziger Brothers, I, 75, 2 and 6. Reprinted with permission of Benziger Publishing Company, Mission Hills, Ca.

PART THREE

Descartes, *Meditations,* published in The Great Books of The Western World, vol. 31., pp. 75–79, 83. Reprinted with permission of Encyclopedia Brittanica, Inc.

Descartes, "Discourse on Method", published in The Great Books of the Western World, vol. 31, p. 43. Reprinted by permission of Encyclopedia Brittanica, Inc.

Spinoza, "Of Miracles", in *Theologico-Political Treatise,* from *The Chief Works of Benedict Spinoza,* published in New York, reprinted by Dover Publications, Inc., © 1951, chapter 6, pp. 81–85. Used with permission.

Spinoza, "Ethics", in *Theologico-Political Treatise,* from *The Chief Works of Benedict Spinoza,* published in New York, reprinted by Dover Publications, Inc., © 1951, preface to chapter 4. Used with permission.

Pascal, from *Pensées,* published in New York by E. P. Dutton, Everyman's Library, © 1958. Reprinted with permission of J. M. Dent & Sons, Ltd., London.

Kant, "On Contingency and Necessity", and "On Proofs from Causality or Design", in *Critique of Pure Reason,* published in Great Books of the Western World, vol. 42, © 1952, pp. 186, 187, 189, 191, 192. Reprinted by permission from Encyclopedia Brittanica, Inc.

Kant, from *The Metaphysics of Morals,* published in the Great Books of the Western World, vol. 42, © 1952, pp. 256 ff. Reprinted by permission from Encyclopedia Brittanica, Inc.

Hegel, "On the Dialectic", and "The Philosophy of Right", in *The Philosophy of Right,* published in England by Oxford University Press, © 1942, vol. 46, pp. 19 and 110–11. Reprinted with permission.

Hegel, "On Truth as Process", and "On the Concept of God", in *The Phenomenology of Mind,* 2nd ed., published in New York, by Humanities Press, 1931.

PART FOUR

Marx, "The Communist Manifesto", in *The Marx-Engels Reader*, 2nd ed., published in New York, excerpted with permission of W. W. Norton & Co., Inc., © 1978, p. 489.

Sartre, "A More Precise Characterization of Existentialism", in *The Writings of Jean-Paul Sartre*, vol. 2, published in Illinois, by Northwestern University Press, © 1974, pp. 157–58. Used with permission.

Dewey, "Philosophy's Search for the Immutable", published in New York, reprinted by permission of The Putnam Publishing Group from *The Quest for Certainty* by John Dewey. Copyright 1929 by John Dewey. Renewed in 1957 by Frederic A. Dewey, pp. 28–36.

Gilson, "God and Contemporary Thought", in *God and Philosophy*, published in New Haven and London, by Yale University Press, © 1941, pp. 109–44.

Von Hildebrand, "Relativism", "Due Relation", and "Moral Consciousness", in *Ethics*, published in Chicago, by Franciscan Herald Press, © 1953, pp. 106–16; 244–54; and 265–75. Reprinted with permission of Alice von Hildebrand.

Stein, "On the Nature of Woman", "The Ethos of Women's Professions", in *The Writings of Edith Stein*, translated by Hilda Graef, published in London, by Peter Owen, Ltd., © 1956, pp. 110–25, 161–73. Reprinted by permission.

John Paul II, "Perennial Philosophy of St. Thomas for the Youth of Our Times", in *The Whole Truth about Man: John Paul II to University Faculties and Students*, edited by James V. Schall, published in Boston, by St. Paul Editions, © 1981, pp. 209–27.

INDEX

Aaron, 53
Aboriginal Inhabitants of the Andaman Island, The (Man), 19–20
Abraham, 52, 54, 60
abstraction, three levels of, 126–29
Academica (Cicero), 199
Academics, 87
accidents, 185, 187–89
act, 129–30
active intellect, 156–57, 180–81
Acts, 69
Adam, 54
adolescents, catechetical methods for, 323–24
Aeterni Patris (Leo XIII), 324–27, 328, 330, 337, 356, 360, 361, 365, 366, 373, 375
Against the Heresies (John), 377
agnosticism, 253
Albert the Great, Saint, 104
Alcuin, 102–3
Alexander the Great, 41, 42
alienation, 297, 298, 299
Ambrose, Saint, 78, 191–92
Andamanese Islanders, 19–20, 22
angelic spirits, 161–62, 166, 173–74
angelism, 216
anthropology, theology as, 297
Antichrist (Nietzsche), 304
anti-Semitism, 281–82
Apologia (Newman), 352
Apostles' Creed, 68, 69, 78, 79, 93, 107, 358, 373–79
    First Article of, 123, 320–21, 326
archaeology, 202–4
Archives de Philosophie, 331
Aristides of Athens, 78
Aristotle, 38–41

Aquinas on, 127, 130, 132, 133, 152, 157, 177, 364
    Arabian commentary on, 157, 170–71
    Augustine and, 89
    on categories, 118, 120–21, 144, 156, 252
    on causality, 132–33, 186
    educational system of, 40
    golden mean of, 347
    Italian Renaissance and, 198
    James on, 306
    metaphysics of, 115, 116, 127, 130, 132
    Organon of, 40, 120, 152–53, 209, 277
    physics of, 115, 133, 175, 177
    on reality, 46
    Sophism vs., 207
Articles of Faith, 119, 372
astrophysics, 343
atheism:
    Descartes and, 214
    of French Enlightenment, 240, 245, 269
    German Idealism and, 274
    materialism vs., 335
    pantheism vs., 223, 229
    political order and, 264
    primitive cultures and, 23–24
    science and, 23–24, 205, 293–96
    Spinozan metaphysics and, 222–31, 286
    undergraduate study of, 239
Atomists, 81, 264, 295, 343
Augustine, Saint:
    on catechetical instruction, 70
    Christian culture and, 101, 115, 326, 327
    creation doctrine and, 170
    on deposit of faith, 373
    education of, 78, 82, 191

527

II